Studies in Latin American Ethnohistory & Archaeology

Joyce Marcus
General Editor

Volume I — *A Fuego y Sangre: Early Zapotec Imperialism in the Cuicatlán Cañada, Oaxaca*, by Elsa Redmond, Memoirs of the Museum of Anthropology, University of Michigan, No. 16. 1983.

Volume II — *Irrigation and the Cuicatec Ecosystem: A Study of Agriculture and Civilization in North Central Oaxaca*, by Joseph W. Hopkins, Memoirs of the Museum of Anthropology, University of Michigan, No. 17. 1984.

Volume III — *Aztec City-States*, by Mary G. Hodge, Memoirs of the Museum of Anthropology, University of Michigan, No. 18. 1984.

Volume IV — *Conflicts over Coca Fields in Sixteenth-Century Peru*, by María Rostworowski de Diez Canseco, Memoirs of the Museum of Anthropology, University of Michigan, No. 21. 1988.

Volume V — *Tribal and Chiefly Warfare in South America*, by Elsa Redmond, Memoirs of the Museum of Anthropology, University of Michigan, No. 28. 1994.

Volume VI — *Imperial Transformations in Sixteenth-Century Yucay, Peru*, transcribed and edited by R. Alan Covey and Donato Amado González, Memoirs of the Museum of Anthropology, University of Michigan, No. 44. 2008.

Volume VII — *Domestic Life in Prehispanic Capitals: A Study of Specialization, Hierarchy, and Ethnicity*, edited by Linda R. Manzanilla and Claude Chapdelaine, Memoirs of the Museum of Anthropology, University of Michigan, No. 46. 2009.

Volume VIII — *Yuthu: Community and Ritual in an Early Andean Village*, by Allison R. Davis, Memoirs of the Museum of Anthropology, University of Michigan, No. 50. 2011.

Volume IX — *Advances in Titicaca Basin Archaeology–III*, edited by Alexei Vranich, Elizabeth A. Klarich, and Charles Stanish, Memoirs of the Museum of Anthropology, University of Michigan, No. 51. 2012.

Volume X — *Regional Archaeology in the Inca Heartland: The Hanan Cuzco Surveys*, edited by R. Alan Covey, Memoirs of the Museum of Anthropology, University of Michigan, No. 55. 2014.

Volume XI — *The Northern Titicaca Basin Survey: Huancané-Putina*, by Charles Stanish, Cecilia Chávez Justo, Karl LaFavre, and Aimée Plourde, Memoirs of the Museum of Anthropology, University of Michigan, No. 56. 2014.

Memoirs of the Museum of Anthropology, University of Michigan
Number 56

Studies in Latin American Ethnohistory & Archaeology
Joyce Marcus, General Editor
Volume XI

The Northern Titicaca Basin Survey

Huancané-Putina

Charles Stanish
Cecilia Chávez Justo
Karl LaFavre
Aimée Plourde

Ann Arbor, Michigan
2014

©2014 by the Regents of the University of Michigan
The Museum of Anthropology
All rights reserved

Printed in the United States of America
ISBN 978-0-915703-84-5

Cover design by Katherine Clahassey

The Museum currently publishes two monograph series: Anthropological Papers and Memoirs. For permissions, questions, or catalogs, contact Museum publications at 1109 Geddes Avenue, Ann Arbor, Michigan 48109-1079; umma-pubs@umich.edu; www.lsa.umich.edu/ummaa/

Library of Congress Cataloging-in-Publication Data

Stanish, Charles, 1956-
  The northern Titicaca basin survey : Huancané-Putina / Charles Stanish, Cecilia Chávez Justo, Karl LaFavre, Aimée Plourde.
    pages cm. -- (Memoirs of the Museum of Anthropology, University of Michigan ; number 56) (Studies in Latin American ethnohistory & archaeology ; volume XI)
  Includes bibliographical references.
  ISBN 978-0-915703-84-5 (alk. paper)
  1. Indians of South America--Titicaca Lake Region (Peru and Bolivia)--Antiquities. 2. Titicaca, Lake, Region (Peru and Bolivia)--Antiquities. 3. Excavations (Archaeology)--Titicaca Lake Region (Peru and Bolivia) I. Title.
  F3319.1.T57S74 2014
  985'.3600909--dc23
                    2014025195

The paper used in this publication meets the requirements of the ANSI Standard Z39.48-1984 (Permanence of Paper).

Contents

List of Figures	*vi*
List of Tables	*xiv*
Preface, *by C. Stanish*	*xv*

1 Introduction to the Huancané-Putina Survey — *1*

    The Northern Titicaca Basin Landscape — *1*
    Previous Research and Archaeological Context — *17*
    Survey Area and Research Design — *19*

2 Analysis of Ceramics from the Middle and Lower Río Huancané Subdrainage, Department of Puno, Perú — *23*
by Cecilia Chávez Justo

    Results — *24*
    Discussion — *30*
    Summary of the Periods — *32*
    Paste Analysis — *34*
    Description of Wares — *48*

3 Site Descriptions — *173*

4 Huancané-Putina Settlement Patterns: Interpretations and Discussion — *261*

    The Archaic Period — *261*
    Formative I — *264*
    Formative II — *264*
    Formative III — *268*
    Huaña I — *268*
    Huaña II and Tiwanaku I — *268*
    Tiwanaku II — *268*
    Altiplano I — *274*
    Altiplano II — *274*
    Altiplano III — *274*
    Inca I — *274*
    Inca II — *278*
    Inca III — *278*
    Discussion — *278*

Appendix A: Ceramic Materials from the Huancané-Putina Survey — *283*
Appendix B: Lithic Materials from the Huancané-Putina Survey — *391*
References Cited — *403*

Figures

front cover: View of the southern side of the survey area

1.1. South America and the locations of Tawantinsuyu and Lake Titicaca, *2*
1.2. Tawantinsuyu in relation to physical geography and present nations and cities, *2*
1.3. The Inca geography of their empire, showing the four suyus, *3*
1.4. The circum-Titicaca Basin and the location of the study area, *4*
1.5. A landscape within the middle section of the survey area, *4*
1.6. The Putina River, within the northern part of the survey area, *5*
1.7. Vicuña in the survey area, *5*
1.8. Señoríos in the northern Titicaca Basin, *5*
1.9. The physiographic features of the Titicaca Basin and surrounding regions, *6*
1.10. A cultivated section of the survey area near the mouth of the Huancané River, *7*
1.11. A rich area of the survey zone, *7*
1.12. A view of the southern end of the survey area, *8*
1.13. Sections of the northern Titicaca Basin showing extensive flooding, *8*
1.14. A house during the extensive flooding, *9*
1.15. The extensive terraced hillsides near Caya-Caya in the survey region, *10*
1.16. A terraced hill near Arapa, *11*
1.17. A woman preparing oca near Saman, *11*
1.18. A view of numerous cochas in pampa, *12*
1.19. A cultivated cocha in the pampa near Marcacamarca, *12*
1.20. A cocha in the dry season, *13*
1.21. Camelids in the northern Titicaca Basin, *13*
1.22. A prehistoric canal in the survey area near Huancanéwichinka, *14*
1.23. A set of reeds with its owner near Arapa, *14*
1.24. A set of harvested reeds near Chucuito, *15*
1.25. A set of relict raised fields in southern part of survey region, *16*
1.26. A view of the Rámis River, *16*
1.27. Google Map view of the survey area, *20*
1.28. Map of the survey limits, showing the sites in the region, *21*

2.1. Ceramic color key, *35*
2.2. Firing color key, *36*
2.3. Surface treatment key, *37*
2.4. Paste description key, *37*
2.5. Rim shape typology—tazones, *49*
2.6. Rim shape typology—bowls, types A and B, *50*
2.7. Rim shape typology—bowls types C, D, and E, *51*
2.8. Rim shape typology—plates, *52*
2.9. Rim shape typology—cup, *52*
2.10. Rim shape typology—ollas, *53*
2.11. Formative I tazón types A1–A3, *54*
2.12. Formative I tazón types A4 and A5, *54*
2.13. Formative I tazón types B1–B4, *55*
2.14. Formative I tazón types B5–B8, *56*
2.15. Formative I bowl types A1–A3, *57*
2.16. Formative I bowl types A4, A6, A7, and A9, *58*
2.17. Formative I bowl types B1–B3, *59*
2.18. Formative I bowl types B4–B6, *60*
2.19. Formative I bowl types D1, D3, and E1, *61*
2.20. Formative I jar types A, B1, and B2, *62*

2.21. Formative I jar types C1–C3, *63*
2.22. Formative I pitcher types A1–A3, *64*
2.23. Formative I pitcher types B1 and B2, *65*
2.24. Formative I olla types A1–A3, *65*
2.25. Formative I olla types B2, D1, and D2, *66*
2.26. Formative I olla types E1–E3, *67*
2.27. Formative II tazón types A1, A4, and A5, *69*
2.28. Formative II tazón types B1, B2, and B4–B6, *70*
2.29. Formative II bowl types A1, A2, A4, A5, A7, and A8, *71*
2.30. Formative II bowl types B1–B4, *72*
2.31. Formative II bowl types D1 and D3, *73*
2.32. Formative II bowl types E1–E3, *73*
2.33. Formative II jar types A, B1, and B2, *74*
2.34. Formative II jar types C1–C3, *74*
2.35. Formative II pitcher types A2, A3, and B2, *75*
2.36. Formative II olla types A1–A3, *76*
2.37. Formative II olla types D1–D4, *77*
2.38. Formative II olla types E1–E3, *78*
2.39. Formative III tazón types A1 and A3, *79*
2.40. Formative III tazón types A4 and A5, *80*
2.41. Formative III tazón types B2–B4, *81*
2.42. Formative III tazón types B5–B8, *82*
2.43. Formative III bowl types A1–A3, A5–A7, and A9, *83*
2.44. Formative III bowl types B1, B2, and B4, *84*
2.45. Formative III bowl types D1, D3, and E3, *84*
2.46. Formative III jar types A, B1, B2, C1, and C2, *85*
2.47. Formative III pitcher types A1–A3 and B2, *86*
2.48. Formative III olla types A1–A3, B1, and B2, *87*
2.49. Formative III olla types D1–D4, *88*
2.50. Formative III olla types E1–E3, *89*
2.51. Huaña I tazón types A1 and A3–A5, *91*
2.52. Huaña I tazón types B1, B3–B5, B7, and B8, *92*
2.53. Huaña I bowl types A1 and A4, *93*
2.54. Huaña I bowl types A5 and B1, *93*
2.55. Huaña I bowl types B3 and B4, *94*
2.56. Huaña I jar types A, B1, B2, and C1–C3, *95*
2.57. Huaña I pitcher types A1–A3, B1, and B2, *96*
2.58. Huaña I olla types A1–A3, B1, and B2, *97*
2.59. Huaña I olla types D1, E1, and E2, *98*
2.60. Huaña II tazón types B3 and B4, *99*
2.61. Huaña II bowl types A4, A7, B1, B5, and D2, *100*
2.62. Huaña II jar type B1, *101*
2.63. Huaña II pitcher types B1 and B2 and vaso type A1, *101*
2.64. Tiwanaku I tazón types A1 and A2, *102*
2.65. Tiwanaku I bowl types A1, A4, A5, and B1, *103*
2.66. Tiwanaku I jar type A and glass types A1 and A2, *104*
2.67. Tiwanaku II tazón types A1 and A2 and jar type B2, *105*
2.68. Tiwanaku II glass types A1 and A2, *106*
2.69. Tiwanaku II bottle type A, *106*
2.70. Altiplano I tazón types A1, A2, and A4, *106*
2.71. Altiplano I tazón types B1–B5 and B7, *108*
2.72. Altiplano I bowl types A1–A4, *109*
2.73. Altiplano I bowl types A5, A7, and A9, *110*
2.74. Altiplano I bowl types B1–B3, *111*
2.75. Altiplano I bowl types B4–B6, *112*
2.76. Altiplano I bowl types C1, C2, D2, E2, and E3, *113*
2.77. Altiplano I plate type D1 and glass type, *114*
2.78. Altiplano I jar types A, B1, and B2, *114*

2.79. Altiplano I jar types C1–C3, *115*
2.80. Altiplano I pitchers types A3, B1, and B2, *115*
2.81. Altiplano I olla types A2, B2, D1, and D3, *116*
2.82. Altiplano II tazón types A1–A5, *118*
2.83. Altiplano II tazón types B1, B3, B6, B7, and C, *119*
2.84. Altiplano II bowl types A1–A3, *120*
2.85. Altiplano II bowl types A4 and A5, *121*
2.86. Altiplano II bowl types A6, A7, and A9, *122*
2.87. Altiplano II bowl types B1–B3, *123*
2.88. Altiplano II bowl types B5, B6, C1, and C2, *124*
2.89. Altiplano II bowl types D1–D3, E1, and E3, *125*
2.90. Altiplano II plate types D1 and D2, *126*
2.91. Altiplano II cup and jar type A, *126*
2.92. Altiplano II jar types B1, B2, and C1–C3, *127*
2.93. Altiplano II pitcher types A1–A3, *128*
2.94. Altiplano II pitcher types B1 and B2, *128*
2.95. Altiplano II olla types A2, A3, B1, and B2, *129*
2.96. Altiplano II olla types C, D1, and D2, *130*
2.97. Altiplano II glass types A1 and A2, *130*
2.98. Altiplano III tazón types A1–A3, *132*
2.99. Altiplano III tazón types A4, A5, B1, and B3, *133*
2.100. Altiplano III tazón types B6, B8, and C, *134*
2.101. Altiplano III bowl types A1–A3, *135*
2.102. Altiplano III bowl types A4–A7 and A9, *136*
2.103. Altiplano III bowl types B1–B3, *137*
2.104. Altiplano III bowl types B4–B6, *138*
2.105. Altiplano III bowl types C1, C2, D1, and D2, *139*
2.106. Altiplano III bowl types E1–E3, *140*
2.107. Altiplano III plate type A1, cup type, and jar type A, *141*
2.108. Altiplano III jar types B1 and B2, *142*
2.109. Altiplano III jar types C2 and C3, *142*
2.110. Altiplano III pitcher types A3, B1, and B2, *143*
2.111. Altiplano III olla types A2, A3, and B2, *144*
2.112. Inca I tazón types A1–A4, *146*
2.113. Inca I tazón types B1, B5, and B6, *147*
2.114. Inca I bowl types A1–A5, *148*
2.115. Inca I bowl types A6, A7, and A9, *149*
2.116. Inca I bowl types B1–B3, *150*
2.117. Inca I bowl types B4–B6, *151*
2.118. Inca I bowl types C1, C2, and D1–D3, *152*
2.119. Inca I bowl types E1–E3, *153*
2.120. Inca I plate types A1, C, and D1, *154*
2.121. Inca I jar types A, B1, and B2, *155*
2.122. Inca I jar types C1–C3, *155*
2.123. Inca I pitcher types B1 and B2 and olla type B2, *156*
2.124. Inca I glass type A1, *156*
2.125. Inca II tazón types A1–A3, *157*
2.126. Inca II tazón types B1, B3, B4, and B8, *158*
2.127. Inca II bowl types A1–A5, *159*
2.128. Inca II bowl types B1–B3 and B5, *160*
2.129. Inca II bowl types C1 and C2, *161*
2.130. Inca II plate types A2 and C, *162*
2.131. Inca II jar types A, B1, B2, and C3, *163*
2.132. Inca II pitcher types B1 and B2, *164*
2.133. Inca II olla types A2 and B2 and bottle type A2, *164*
2.134. Inca III tazón types A1–A4, *166*
2.135. Inca III tazón types B1 and B7, *167*
2.136. Inca III bowl types A1–A3, *167*

2.137. Inca III bowl types A4–A7, *168*
2.138. Inca III bowl types B1–B4 and B6, *169*
2.139. Inca III bowl types C1, C2, and D1–D3, *170*
2.140. Inca III bowl types E1–E3 and plate type A1, *171*
2.141. Inca III jar types A1, B1, and B2, and pitcher types B1 and B2, *172*

3.1. View of the lower part of the survey area from above Hu-008, *183*
3.2. Huancahuichinka, site Hu-003, *183*
3.3. Monolith found by farmers in the sunken court at Hu-003, *184*
3.4. Relationship of site Hu-003 and sunken court, *184*
3.5. Pukara of Hu-008, *185*
3.6. A circular chulpa on the pukara of Hu-008, *185*
3.7. The site of Hu-011 on a natural mound at the base of a hill, *186*
3.8. A view of the location of Hu-014 from the south, *187*
3.9. An uncarved monolith on the site of Hu-014, *187*
3.10. A view of the location of Hu-015, *189*
3.11. The site of Hu-016 just south of Huatasani, *189*
3.12. The modern town of Putina, *189*
3.13. A view of Putina from a distance, *190*
3.14. A closer view of Putina and Hu-030, *191*
3.15. An exposed section in a construction cut in the mound at Putina, *191*
3.16. An uncarved monolith in Putina, *192*
3.17. Small, looted tomb on Hu-032, *192*
3.18. The site area of Hu-052, *194*
3.19. Site locations of Hu-057, Hu-058, and Hu-059, *194*
3.20. A close-up of the site area of Hu-058, *194*
3.21. A close-up of the site area of Hu-059, *195*
3.22. The site of Hu-067, *196*
3.23. Site location of Hu-068, *196*
3.24. Hu-068 from the base of the hill, *197*
3.25. The high mesa sites of Hu-077 and Hu-078, *198*
3.26. A close-up of structures on the site area of Hu-078, *199*
3.27. A view of the site area of Hu-081, *199*
3.28. Standing, uncarved monolith at Hu-109, *203*
3.29. Site area of Hu-112 with circular structure remains, *204*
3.30. Site area of Hu-113, *204*
3.31. Sunken court on Hu-172, *207*
3.32. Wall of sunken court on Hu-172, *207*
3.33. Site area of Hu-175, *208*
3.34. Site area of Hu-204, *208*
3.35. Hu-205 from a distance, *209*
3.36. Sites Hu-205, Hu-526, Hu-527, Hu-532, and Hu-533, *209*
3.37. Site area of Hu-204 and Hu-205, *210*
3.38. Site of Hu-205, *210*
3.39. Cut stone on the site of Hu-205, *211*
3.40. Site locations of Hu-219 and Hu-222, *212*
3.41. Site of Hu-219 showing collapsed chulpa, *213*
3.42. Uncarved sandstone monolith on Hu-220, *213*
3.43. Site of Hu-225, *214*
3.44. Modern apacheta on Hu-226, *215*
3.45. Circular structure on Hu-226, *215*
3.46. Site area of Hu-227, *216*
3.47. Circular structure on Hu-229, *216*
3.48. Circular structure on Hu-230, *217*
3.49. Site area of Hu-240, *218*
3.50. Circular structures on Hu-243, *218*
3.51. Defensive wall on Hu-243, *219*
3.52. Site location of Hu-247 and Hu-248, *220*

3.53. Site location of Hu-247, *220*
3.54. Prehispanic road above Hu-249, *221*
3.55. Pampa mound of Hu-253, *223*
3.56. Chulpa at Hu-257, *223*
3.57. Large chulpa at Hu-264, *224*
3.58. Close-up of large limestone slab at Hu-264, *224*
3.59. Sunken court at Hu-276, *225*
3.60. Site area of Hu-284, *227*
3.61. Carved limestone block on Hu-284, *227*
3.62. Uncarved sandstone monolith on Hu-291, *227*
3.63. Site area of Hu-298, *229*
3.64. Site area of Hu-298, Hu-299, and Hu-300, *229*
3.65. Relationship between Hu-315, Hu-316, Hu-318, Hu-322, and Hu-323, *230*
3.66. Site area of Hu-316, *230*
3.67. View of mid-Huancané Valley, *231*
3.68. Distance view of Hu-316, *231*
3.69. Location of sunken court on Hu-316, *232*
3.70. View of sunken court on Hu-316, *232*
3.71. View of monolith in sunken court on Hu-316, *233*
3.72. Close-up view of notch on the monolith, *233*
3.73. Cut limestone block on Hu-316, *233*
3.74. Cut limestone block on Hu-316, *233*
3.75. Survey region in the Machacamarca area, *235*
3.76. Chulpa on Hu-323, *235*
3.77. Intact bowl found on slab cist tomb on Hu-340, *236*
3.78. Chulpa on Hu-360, *237*
3.79. View showing Hu-365, Hu-366, Hu-378, Hu-379, and Hu-380, *239*
3.80. View showing Hu-377, Hu-378, and Hu-381, *239*
3.81. View showing Hu-378, Hu-379, Hu-381, Hu-382, and Hu-383, *240*
3.82. View showing site area of Hu-381 and Hu-382, *240*
3.83. Sunken court structure on Hu-381, *241*
3.84. View showing Hu-385, Hu-390, Hu-397, Hu-503, and Hu-504, *241*
3.85. Sketch map showing structures of Hu-385, *242*
3.86. View of lower valley from Hu-406, *244*
3.87. Site area of Hu-411, *244*
3.88. Site area of Hu-411 and Hu-412 in relation to Hu-413 and Hu-436, *244*
3.89. Site area of Hu-414, *245*
3.90. Site area of Hu-415 and Hu-416, *245*
3.91. Site area of Hu-416, *246*
3.92. Site area of Hu-431, Hu-432, and Hu-433, *247*
3.93. Site area of Hu-430, Hu-431, Hu-432, and Hu-435, *247*
3.94. Slab cist on Hu-436, *247*
3.95. Site area around Hu-505, *249*
3.96. Site area around Hu-482 and Hu-496, *251*
3.97. Site area around Hu-506, *251*
3.98. Site area of Hu-483–Hu-487, Hu-497, and Hu-498, *252*
3.99. Mid-valley view, *252*
3.100. Chulpa on Hu-508, *255*
3.101. View of sites Hu-514 and Hu-515, *256*
3.102. Tomb on Hu-514, *256*
3.103. View of sites Hu-515, Hu-516, Hu-520, and Hu-521, *256*
3.104. View of site Hu-517, *257*
3.105. View of site Hu-518, *257*
3.106. Limestone monolith on Hu-521, *257*
3.107. Chulpa on Hu-522, *258*
3.108. Chulpa on Hu-526, *258*
3.109. Chulpa on Hu-531, *258*
3.110. Topographical location of Hu-532, *259*

3.111. Close-up of sunken court area in Hu-532, *259*
3.112. Chulpa on Hu-532, *260*
3.113. Chulpa on Hu-532, *260*
3.114. Site area of Hu-536, *260*

4.1. The Huancané-Putina survey area, *262*
4.2. A bofedal in the Putina area, *263*
4.3. A very large cocha near the village of Kakachi, *263*
4.4. The Cala Cala region looking west from the river, *265*
4.5. The Huatasani area, *265*
4.6. The Formative I ware distribution, *266*
4.7. The Formative II ware distribution, *267*
4.8. The Formative III ware distribution, *269*
4.9. The Huaña I ware distribution, *270*
4.10. The Huaña II ware distribution, *271*
4.11. The Tiwanaku I ware distribution, *272*
4.12. The Tiwanaku II ware distribution, *273*
4.13. The Altiplano I ware distribution, *275*
4.14. The Altiplano II ware distribution, *276*
4.15. The Altiplano III ware distribution, *277*
4.16. The Inca I ware distribution, *279*
4.17. The Inca II ware distribution, *280*
4.18. The Inca III ware distribution, *281*

Appendixes

A1. Ceramic fragments from Hu-004 and Hu-008, *284*
A2. Ceramic fragments from Hu-014 and Hu-015, *284*
A3. Ceramic fragments from Hu-015, *285*
A4. Ceramic fragments from Hu-015 and Hu-016, *285*
A5. Ceramic fragments from Hu-015, *286*
A6. Ceramic fragments from Hu-015, *286*
A7. Ceramic fragments from Hu-016 and Hu-030, *287*
A8. Ceramic fragments from Hu-154 and Hu-173, *288*
A9. Ceramic fragments from Hu-173, Hu-205, and Hu-209, *288*
A10. Ceramic fragments from Hu-219, Hu-251, and Hu-316, *289*
A11. Whole vessel from Hu-340, *289*
A12. Ceramic fragments from Hu-344 and Hu-348, *290*
A13. Ceramic fragments from Hu-348, Hu-382, Hu-385, and Hu-406, *290*
A14. Ceramic fragments from Hu-406, Hu-414, and Hu-424, *291*
A15. Ceramic fragments from Hu-432, Hu-500, Hu-506, and Hu-508, *291*
A16. Ceramic fragment drawings from Hu-008, *292*
A17. Ceramic fragment drawings from Hu-010, *293*
A18. Ceramic fragment drawings from Hu-014, *294*
A19. Ceramic fragment drawings from Hu-014, *295*
A20. Ceramic fragment drawings from Hu-015, *296*
A21. Ceramic fragment drawings from Hu-015, *297*
A22. Ceramic fragment drawings from Hu-016, *298*
A23. Ceramic fragment drawings from Hu-053, Hu-055, Hu-058, and Hu-068, *299*
A24. Ceramic fragment drawings from Hu-069, Hu-074, Hu-077, and Hu-078, *300*
A25. Ceramic fragment drawings from Hu-094 and Hu-095, *301*
A26. Ceramic fragment drawings from Hu-078 and Hu-081, *302*
A27. Ceramic fragment drawings from Hu-099, Hu-109, Hu-118, and Hu-119, *303*
A28. Ceramic fragment drawings from Hu-126, *304*
A29. Ceramic fragment drawings from Hu-156, Hu-160, and Hu-161, *304*
A30. Ceramic fragment drawings from Hu-162, Hu-166–HU-169, and Hu-172, *305*

A31.	Ceramic fragment drawings from Hu-173, *305*
A32.	Ceramic fragment drawings from Hu-174, *306*
A33.	Ceramic fragment drawings from Hu-176, *307*
A34.	Ceramic fragment drawings from Hu-200 and Hu-201, *307*
A35.	Ceramic fragment drawings from Hu-202, *308*
A36.	Ceramic fragment drawings from Hu-204 and Hu-205, *308*
A37.	Ceramic fragment drawings from Hu-205, *309*
A38.	Ceramic fragment drawings from Hu-205, *310*
A39.	Ceramic fragment drawings from Hu-205, *311*
A40.	Ceramic fragment drawings from Hu-205, *312*
A41.	Ceramic fragment drawings from Hu-205, *313*
A42.	Ceramic fragment drawings from Hu-205, *314*
A43.	Ceramic fragment drawings from Hu-205, *315*
A44.	Ceramic fragment drawings from Hu-208, *316*
A45.	Ceramic fragment drawings from Hu-209 and Hu-210, *316*
A46.	Ceramic fragment drawings from Hu-211 and Hu-212, *317*
A47.	Ceramic fragment drawings from Hu-215, *317*
A48.	Ceramic fragment drawings from Hu-216, *318*
A49.	Ceramic fragment drawings from Hu-219, *318*
A50.	Ceramic fragment drawings from Hu-219, *319*
A51.	Ceramic fragment drawings from Hu-219, *319*
A52.	Ceramic fragment drawings from Hu-222, *320*
A53.	Ceramic fragment drawings from Hu-224 and Hu-226, *320*
A54.	Ceramic fragment drawings from Hu-226 and Hu-227, *321*
A55.	Ceramic fragment drawings from Hu-232, Hu-233, and Hu-234, *322*
A56.	Ceramic fragment drawings from Hu-235, Hu-237, and Hu-238, *322*
A57.	Ceramic fragment drawings from Hu-239, *323*
A58.	Ceramic fragment drawings from Hu-243 and Hu-246, *324*
A59.	Ceramic fragment drawings from Hu-246, *325*
A60.	Ceramic fragment drawings from Hu-246, *326*
A61.	Ceramic fragment drawings from Hu-246, *327*
A62.	Ceramic fragment drawings from Hu-247, *327*
A63.	Ceramic fragment drawings from Hu-248, *328*
A64.	Ceramic fragment drawings from Hu-249, *328*
A65.	Ceramic fragment drawings from Hu-251 and Hu-252, *329*
A66.	Ceramic fragment drawings from Hu-253, Hu-254, and Hu-255, *329*
A67.	Ceramic fragment drawings from Hu-255, *330*
A68.	Ceramic fragment drawings from Hu-255, *330*
A69.	Ceramic fragment drawings from Hu-256, Hu-258, and Hu-260, *331*
A70.	Ceramic fragment drawings from Hu-261–Hu-263 and Hu-267, *331*
A71.	Ceramic fragment drawings from Hu-269, Hu-270, and Hu-273, *332*
A72.	Ceramic fragment drawings from Hu-274, Hu-275, and Hu-276, *333*
A73.	Ceramic fragment drawings from Hu-276, *334*
A74.	Ceramic fragment drawings from Hu-276, *335*
A75.	Ceramic fragment drawings from Hu-276, *336*
A76.	Ceramic fragment drawings from Hu-276, *337*
A77.	Ceramic fragment drawings from Hu-278 and Hu-279, *338*
A78.	Ceramic fragment drawings from Hu-280, *339*
A79.	Ceramic fragment drawings from Hu-280, *340*
A80.	Ceramic fragment drawings from Hu-280, *340*
A81.	Ceramic fragment drawings from Hu-280, *341*
A82.	Ceramic fragment drawings from Hu-280, *342*
A83.	Ceramic fragment drawings from Hu-280, *342*
A84.	Ceramic fragment drawings from Hu-281, *343*
A85.	Ceramic fragment drawings from Hu-281, Hu-285, and Hu-286, *344*
A86.	Ceramic fragment drawings from Hu-298, *345*

A87.	Ceramic fragment drawings from Hu-300, *346*
A88.	Ceramic fragment drawings from Hu-304 and Hu-306, *347*
A89.	Ceramic fragment drawings from Hu-309 and Hu-310, *348*
A90.	Ceramic fragment drawings from Hu-310, *349*
A91.	Ceramic fragment drawings from Hu-310, *350*
A92.	Ceramic fragment drawings from Hu-310, *350*
A93.	Ceramic fragment drawings from Hu-312, Hu-313, and Hu-315, *351*
A94.	Ceramic fragment drawings from Hu-316, *352*
A95.	Ceramic fragment drawings from Hu-316, *353*
A96.	Ceramic fragment drawings from Hu-317 and Hu-318, *354*
A97.	Ceramic fragment drawings from Hu-320 and Hu-321, *355*
A98.	Ceramic fragment drawings from Hu-324, *356*
A99.	Ceramic fragment drawings from Hu-325, *357*
A100.	Ceramic fragment drawings from Hu-333, Hu-336, and Hu-337, *358*
A101.	Ceramic fragment drawings from Hu-337, *359*
A102.	Ceramic fragment drawings from Hu-340 and Hu-341, *360*
A103.	Ceramic fragment drawings from Hu-343, *361*
A104.	Ceramic fragment drawings from Hu-346 and Hu-348, *362*
A105.	Ceramic fragment drawings from Hu-348, *363*
A106.	Ceramic fragment drawings from Hu-348 and Hu-353, *363*
A107.	Ceramic fragment drawings from Hu-355, *364*
A108.	Ceramic fragment drawings from Hu-358, Hu-369, and Hu-374, *365*
A109.	Ceramic fragment drawings from Hu-376 and Hu-378, *366*
A110.	Ceramic fragment drawings from Hu-382, *366*
A111.	Ceramic fragment drawings from Hu-382, *367*
A112.	Ceramic fragment drawings from Hu-388 and Hu-390, *368*
A113.	Ceramic fragment drawings from Hu-406, *369*
A114.	Ceramic fragment drawings from Hu-410, Hu-411, and Hu-412, *370*
A115.	Ceramic fragment drawings from Hu-412 and Hu-414, *371*
A116.	Ceramic fragment drawings from Hu-414, Hu-415, and Hu-416, *372*
A117.	Ceramic fragment drawings from Hu-416 and Hu-418, *373*
A118.	Ceramic fragment drawings from Hu-508, *374*
A119.	Ceramic fragment drawings from Hu-521, *375*
A120.	Ceramic fragment drawings from Hu-537, *376*
A121.	Ceramic fragment drawings from Hu-537, *377*
A122.	Ceramic fragment drawings from Hu-537, *378*
A123.	Ceramic fragment drawings from Hu-537, *379*
B1.	Bifaces from various sites in the survey area, *394*
B2.	Bifaces from various sites in the survey area, *395*
B3.	Bifaces from various sites in the survey area, *396*
B4.	Bifaces from various sites in the survey area, *397*
B5.	Bifaces from various sites in the survey area, *398*
B6.	Bifaces from various sites in the survey area, *399*
B7.	Bifaces from various sites in the survey area, *400*
B8.	Bifaces from various sites in the survey area, *401*
B9.	Bifaces from various sites in the survey area, *402*

Tables

2.1. Criteria and levels of analysis, *25*
2.2. Groups and their variants, *25*
2.3. Quantities of pastes by group and period, *25*
2.4. Relationship between groups, pastes, and colors, *25*
2.5. Relationship between groups, wares, and period, *26*
2.6. Open vessels by period, ware, and type, *27*
2.7. Relationship between types, wares, and period, *29*
2.8. Suggested absolute dates for types and ware, *31*

3.1. Sites with a habitation component in the Huancané-Putina survey, *174*
3.2. Cemetery-only sites in the Huancané-Putina survey, *180*
3.3. All Archaic sites recorded in the survey, *201*

Appendixes

A1. Metrics of illustrated ceramic data, *380*

B1. Metrics of illustrated lithic data, *392*

Preface
by C. Stanish

The Northern Titicaca Basin archaeological research program began in 1998. Over several years, various members of Programa Collasuyu conducted reconnaissance in the region from Juliaca to Moho, with the intent to develop a research design for future research. We continued our reconnaissance in 1999, registering almost 75 significant sites. We narrowed our focus the following year to the area between the western side of Lake Arapa to the town of Huancané to the lakeshore, and up the Huancané River to the town of Putina. We conducted an intensive, full-coverage regional survey during the 2000 to 2003 seasons, ultimately covering about 1000 km^2 and locating some 1300 sites that spanned the full known time range of settlement in the Titicaca Basin. Members of Programa Collasuyu have conducted excavations in sites discovered in the region from 2004 until the present time. This initial volume covers the eastern section of the survey only, known as the Huancané-Putina section. Future volumes will cover the rest of the survey known as Arapa-Taraco.

This book has been a long time in preparation, largely due to the serious problems with the ceramic chronology that we encountered in the northern Titicaca Basin as we tried to make sense of the surface diagnostics on the sites. Previous work in the south by James Mathews, Juan Albarracin-Jordan, Carlos Lemuz, and others, plus work by our own team in the Juli-Pomata region, indicated that there was a fairly clear transition between most of the major periods, even if these periods were uncomfortably long. The work of Christine Hastorf and Matt Bandy on the southern Taraco Peninsula (there are two Taracos in the Titicaca Basin), for instance, discovered Early through Late Chiripa, followed by a Tiwanaku sequence that had some clear temporal markers in the ceramic data. Sonia Alconini and John Janusek, among others, refined the Tiwanaku sequence and were able to discover fairly distinct periods based upon iconography and form. The same was true in the Juli-Pomata region where a clearly defined chronological sequence was evident in the settlements (Stanish et al. 1997). These interpretations were confirmed by excavations at many sites in the southern Titicaca region.

The situation in the north is quite different. Here, the early Qaluyu type did not disappear with the appearance of Pukara styles. Rather, we see substantial overlap of as much as 200–300 years when both styles were manufactured, an empirical pattern confirmed by Abigail Levine in her dissertation in 2012 and reconfirmed by subsequent excavations in and around Taraco. Effectively, a type-variety system worked in the south but it did not work in the north. We had to come up with an alternative. Thanks to the extremely dedicated work of Cecilia Chávez Justo (Chapter 2), who analyzed over 30,000 diagnostics, we have an attribute analysis that allows us to break down clusters that generally correspond to chronological periods. Chávez's work is based upon a long and painstaking analysis that combines surface diagnostics with excavation data, many with good ^{14}C associations. Her group called "Formative I," for instance, is consistent with the earlier "Qaluyu" style. Likewise, Formative III is consistent with the traditional Pukara pottery style. Formative II, on the other hand, contains elements of both traditional styles. All of this is explained in great detail in Chávez's work (Chapter 2).

The survey and excavations have taught us much about the northern Titicaca Basin, and we modestly suggest that it improves our understanding of the entire region. The work reported on here and in earlier publications advances our understanding of sunken courts, sociopolitical dynamics between Pukara and other polities, regional settlement patterns, evidence of conflict as early as the Formative I, and so forth. Sites with our earliest Formative I pottery are clearly found on walled sites or pucaras, a pattern also documented by Elizabeth Arkush (2005, 2008) in her extensive work to the northwest. Our work indicates that conflict and cooperation were ever present in the Formative periods, with several centers of political power including Pucara itself, Taraco, Balsas Pata near Ayaviri, Cancha Cancha Asiruni near Azángaro, and Arapa that competed for regional dominance over several centuries.

In short, the data suggest that there was a highly competitive environment in which political centers conquered and were conquered by each other in the Late Formative period. At Taraco, our excavation data indicate beyond little doubt that another group attacked the settlement around AD 150 (Stanish and Levine 2011). It is no coincidence that this event corresponds to the rise of Pucara as a regional power and the cessation of Qaluyu pottery manufacture. It is likely that Qaluyu pottery was a style associated with either Taraco or other political centers that were reduced by Pucara raiders, immediately prior to the apogee of the Pucara polity.

The nature of the Tiwanaku settlement in the study area is different from that in the south as well. Near the capital of Tiwanaku, there is a clear sense that Tiwanaku expanded around AD 650 and co-opted existing cultures. In the north, in contrast, we have a time period (Huaña II/Tiwanaku I) in which there appears to be two discrete settlement types. One type is a Tiwanaku-affiliated settlement system located along the roads, rivers, and lake edge. A second one is local and coexisted with, but did not interact in any significant manner with, the Tiwanaku enclaves. Later (Tiwanaku II in the Chávez system), the Tiwanaku state continued to control the roads and enclaves, but there is greater evidence for a much more intensive Tiwanaku-local interaction for a brief time of perhaps 150–200 years.

The Altiplano or Late Intermediate period in the region is similar to that in the west and south, but considerably more intense. Pucaras dominate the landscape with hundreds of very small, non-fortified Altiplano period settlements on the pampas, clustering around these refuges.

The Inca occupation is likewise quite substantial in this region. Our survey located the source of a major type of pottery that Marion Tschopik called "Sillustani." The kaolin pastes that she felt were from the northwest in fact were manufactured in considerable quantity near the town of Huatasani on the Putina River, between Huancané and the town of Putina in the north. Inca sites dominate the landscape, integrated with the massive Inca regional center at Hatuncolla to the west of the study area.

There are many people that I wish to thank for their support, intellectual input, guidance, and friendship during our many years working in the northern Titicaca Basin. I want to first acknowledge the great work of my UCLA students who are not co-authors of this monograph: Elizabeth Arkush, Abigail Levine, Carol Schultze, Colleen Zori, Alana Johnson, and Amanda Cohen. Their dedication and outstanding publications have helped us better interpret the data presented here. I thank my colleagues Mark Aldenderfer, Sarah Abraham, Christina Moya, Matt Bandy, Brian Bauer, Lisa Cipolla, Javier Chalcha, Larry Coben, Nathan Craig, Christopher Donnan, Kirk Frye, Cynthia Klink, Edmundo de la Vega, Luis Flores Blanco, Chela Fattorini, Elizabeth Klarich, Rolando Paredes, Henry Tantaleán, Adán Umire, Erv Taylor, Garine Babian, Ryan Williams, Donna Nash, Lee H. Steadman, Jose Núñez, Alexei Vranich, Sandy Enriquez, and all the members of Programa Collasuyu.

Funding was provided by the National Science Foundation, the Cotsen Endowments, Executive Vice Chancellor (UCLA) Scott Waugh, Charles Steinmetz, Deborah Arnold, Harris Bass, the Director's Council of the Cotsen Institute, the Friends of Archaeology at the Cotsen Institute, and Mr. Lloyd Cotsen.

As always, I acknowledge the friendship and input of Joyce Marcus and Michael Moseley. I thank all the reviewers of this manuscript. Jill Rheinheimer of the Museum of Anthropology Publications deserves a hearty thank you for her usual outstanding work. All errors are the responsibilities of the authors and editors.

1 | Introduction to the Huancané-Putina Survey

*And in ancient times the entire region of the
Collas was densely populated with great towns.*

[Cieza de León 1553: XCIX]

When the first Europeans began their explorations and conquest of the vast South American continent in the early sixteenth century, they encountered one of the greatest pre-industrial states in all of human history. The Inca Empire was by far the largest and geographically longest expansive state in Andean history, ranking as one of the great pre-industrial empires in world history. Tawantinsuyu, or "Land of the Four Quarters" as the empire was then known, covered an area that stretched from modern Ecuador to central Chile, some 1.5 million square kilometers (Figs. 1.1, 1.2).[1] Its four imperial *suyus*, or quarters, included the vast and populous northwestern Chinchaysuyu, desert lands in the southwestern Contisuyu, the sparsely populated eastern forests called Antisuyu, and—by many accounts the "jewel in the crown" of the Inca Empire—Collasuyu to the south (Fig. 1.3).

Indeed, the Collasuyu quarter was the "jewel" of the empire. It was vast and rich, and it represented the first major conquest of the empire outside its core territory. In many respects, the heart of Collasuyu—the Titicaca Basin—had a deeper and richer cultural history than the Cuzco area itself. The great state of Tiwanaku rose to prominence in the Titicaca Basin in the middle of the first millennium AD, building a capital city of more than 4 km² housing some 40,000 or more people. The rulers of Tawantinsuyu explicitly sought to associate themselves and their royal lineages with Tiwanaku through pilgrimages, marriage alliances, and mythopoetic propaganda. Even earlier in the Titicaca Basin, the Chiripa and Pucara peoples developed complex societies that were part of the great network of Early Horizon interaction systems that we are just beginning to piece together.

The Northern Titicaca Basin Landscape

The large region of the Collas . . . is the greatest country, in my view, of all of Peru and it is the most populous. . . . It is a flat land, and there are many areas where rivers flow with good water, and in these plains there are beautiful, spacious meadows that always have lots of pasture, at times very verdant. . . . The days and the nights are almost the same, and in this country it is colder than any other part of Peru outside of the high and snow-capped mountains. . . . And it is certain that if the Collao was located in a lower valley like Jauja or Choquiabo where maize could grow it would be the best and richest part of these Indies. [Cieza de León 1553: XCIX]

---

1. Tawantinsuyu is translated by Mannheim (1991:18) as "the parts that in their fourness make up a whole."

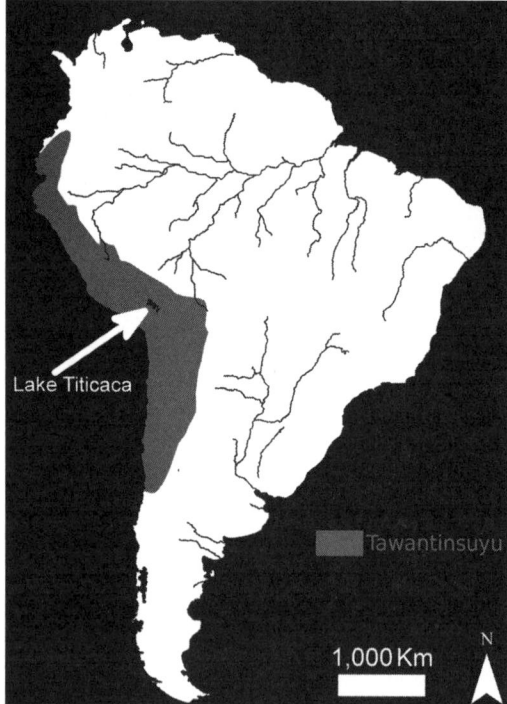

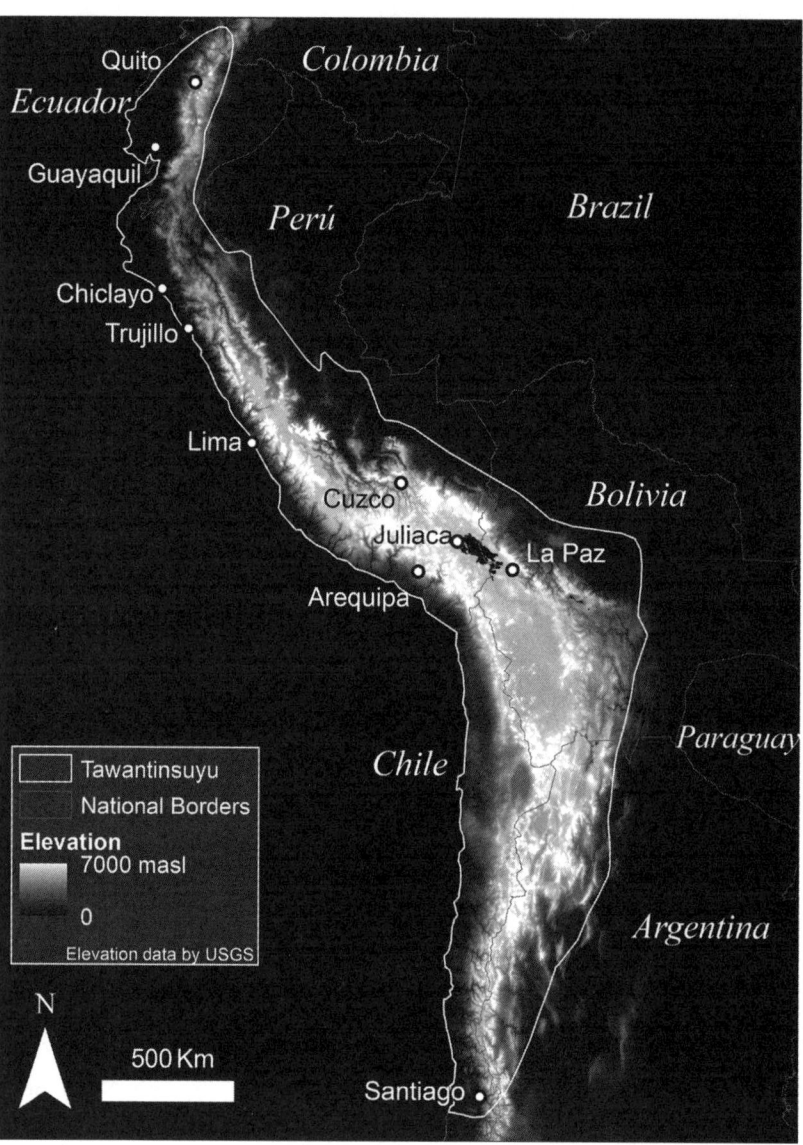

(*above*) Figure 1.1. South America and the locations of Tawantinsuyu (after D'Altroy 2002) and Lake Titicaca.

(*right*) Figure 1.2. Tawantinsuyu in relation to physical geography and present nations and cities.

Geography

This monograph reports on archaeological research in the northern Titicaca Basin (Figs. 1.4–1.7). As a cultural area, the northern Titicaca Basin extends from roughly the Puno area in the west to Moho in the east, and north to Ayaviri. This would correspond to the Colla polity, a late prehistoric group distinct from the Lupaqa (Lupaca) to the south in the western and southwestern Titicaca region (Fig. 1.8). The Collas were a loose confederation of Aymara speakers who extended their influence over a large area of the south central Andes. The term "Colla" is ambiguous. It refers to the specific group of Aymara speakers in the northwest part of the Titicaca region—but also to the entire largely Aymara-speaking territory in the south central Andes. The famous chronicler Cieza de León (1553: XCIX) states that the land of the Collas started near Ayaviri and extended to Caracollo in the far south: "The Collas begin in Ayaviri and go to Caracollo." Cieza in the same chapter tells us that the Canas and Canchis were related to the people of Ayaviri, with the Collas—presumably the Aymara speakers—located near Ayaviri and to the south. This observation conforms well to archaeological and ethnolinguistic information and provides a reasonable characterization of the northern Titicaca Basin.

The Titicaca region is a huge geological basin that sits between two mountain ranges: the Cordillera Real to the east, and the Cordillera Blanca to the west (Fig. 1.9). Between these two ranges is a body of water approximately 8500 km^2 in size. Within the large lake there are a number of islands, some of which are quite substantial in size, including Amantaní, Taquile, and the Island of the Sun (Stanish and Chávez 2012; Stanish 2012c). The lowest part of the region is the surface of the lake itself at 3810 meters above sea level (masl).

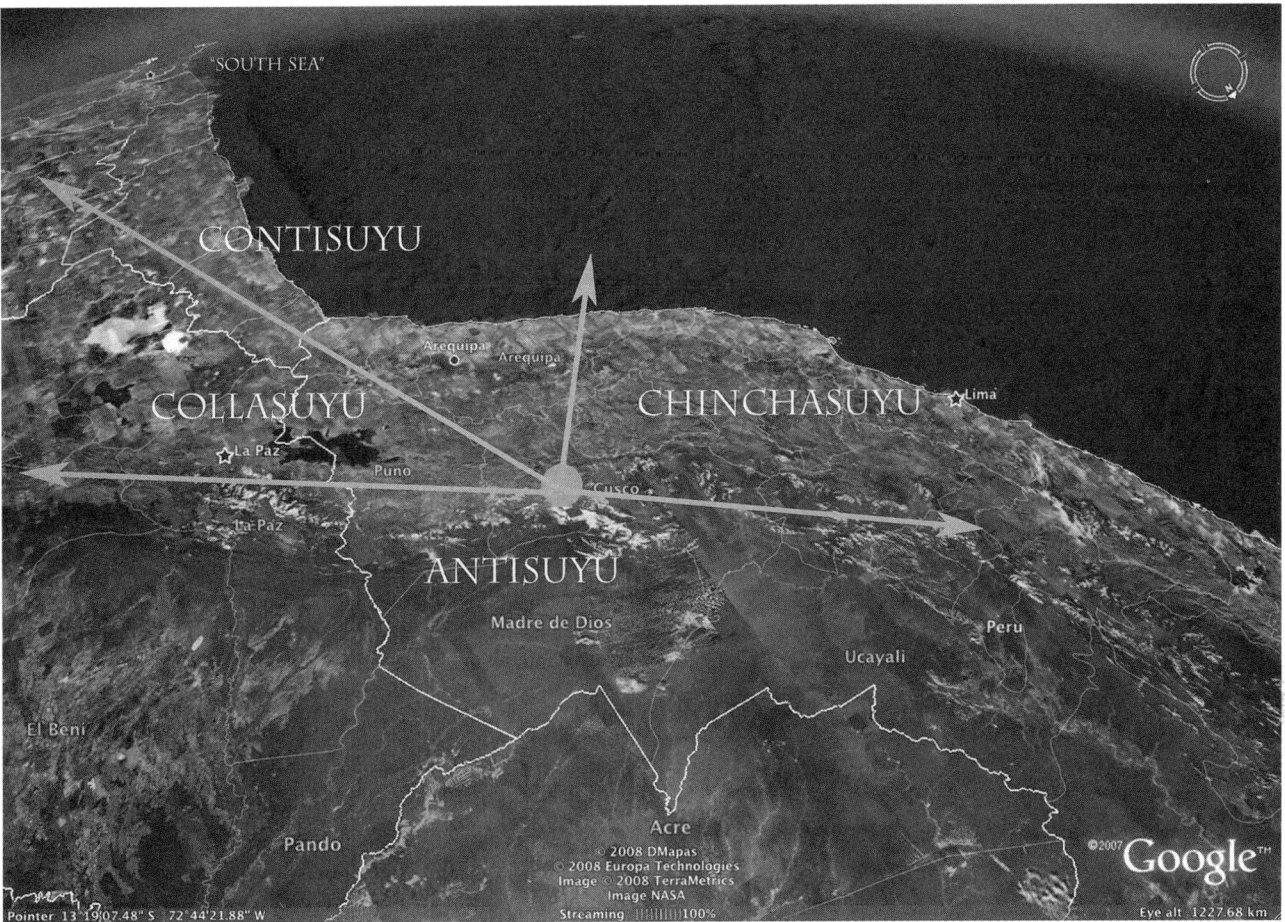

Figure 1.3. The Inca geography of their empire, showing the four suyus.

Climate

Cieza's description (given above) of the Titicaca Basin, known then as the Collao, remains perhaps the best description of the area by an outsider. His words capture the contradiction felt by western observers of a seemingly bleak and harsh landscape with the existence of great cities, towns, and productive villages. This contradiction runs through many descriptions of the Collao by visitors up to the present day, and constitutes one of the key characteristics of this landscape that has intrigued scholars for centuries.

The harsh winter landscape of the Titicaca Basin indeed strikes many as a difficult place to make a living. Yet, behind the seemingly bleak winter landscape is a rich and productive area of lakes, rivers, fertile soils, expansive grassland pampas, rich hillsides, minerals, clays, and countless other resources. This thriving area was the home to some of the earliest complex societies in the highland Andes, a center of cultural development spanning more than three millennia prior to European contact.

The northern Titicaca Basin is actually classified as an intertropical climatic zone, based upon its latitude and high solar radiation inputs (Dejoux and Iltis 1991:11). Mitigating these "tropical" qualities, of course, are the high altitude and associated montane qualities such as low ambient temperatures and low humidity. Dejoux and Iltis note that the area is best understood as "alpine" with substantial rainfall in some areas. While mean annual precipitation in the Titicaca Basin can be as low as 500 mm/year in the south, mean annual precipitation in the northern Basin can be as high as 1500 mm/year (Roche et al. 1992:87). There are areas in the northwest corner of the Titicaca region near Pucara and the Cabanillas, Lampa, Arapa, and Coata drainages that have consistently high rainfall from November through

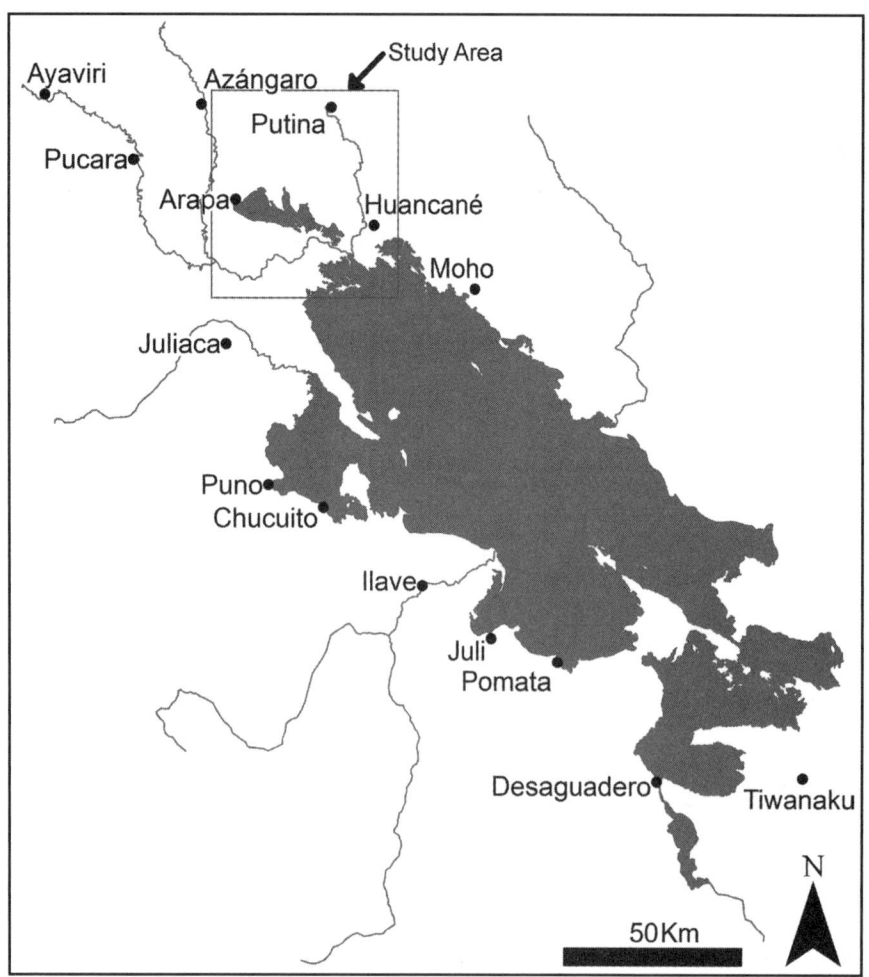

Figure 1.4.
The circum-Titicaca Basin and the location of the study area.

Figure 1.5.
A landscape within the middle section of the survey area north of Huancané and south of the town of Huatasani.

Figure 1.6. The Putina River, within the northern part of the survey area.

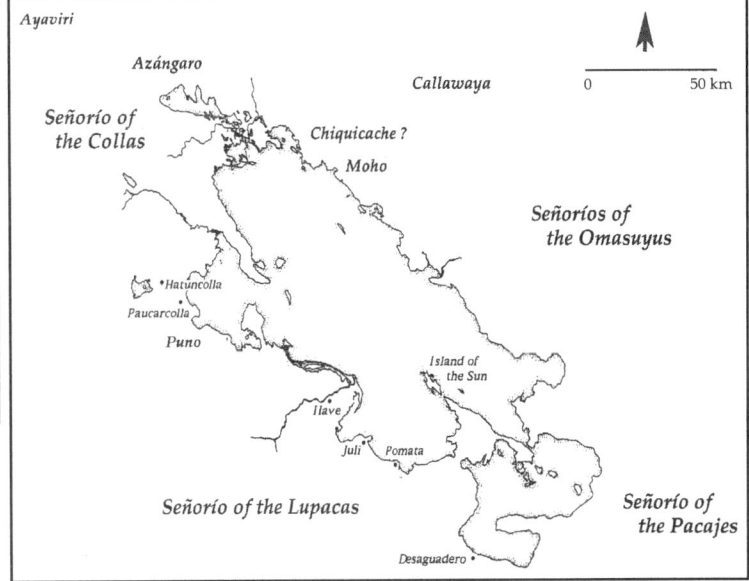

(*above*) Figure 1.7. Vicuña in the survey area (photograph by Adán Umire).

(*right*) Figure 1.8. Señoríos in the northern Titicaca Basin.

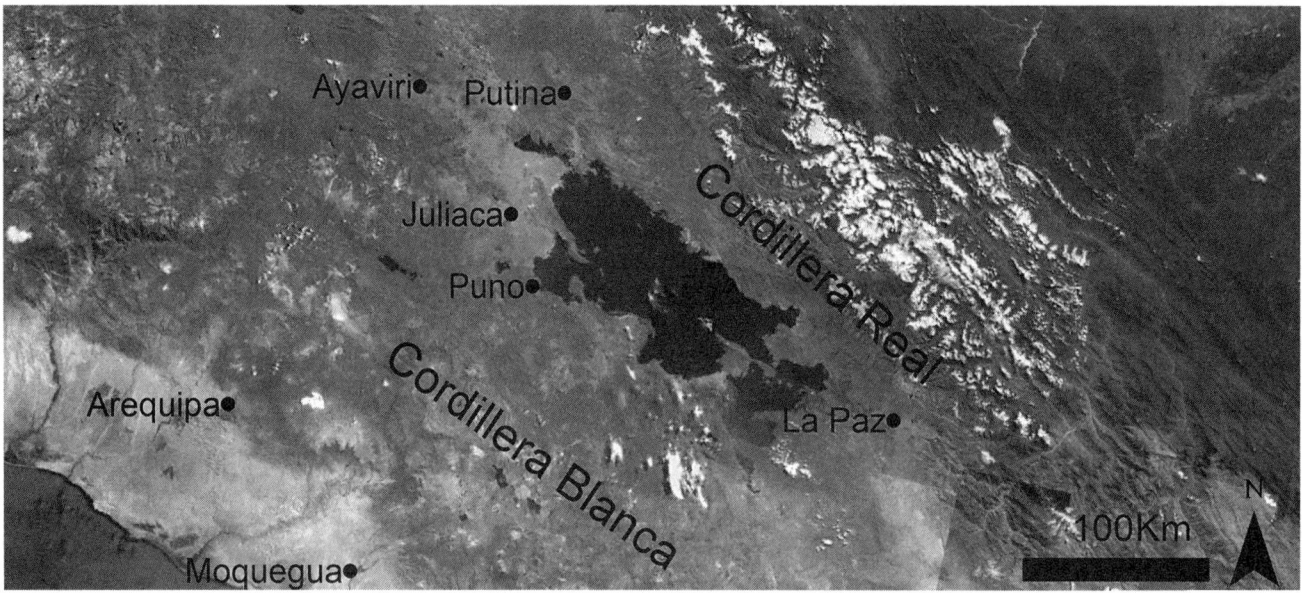

Figure 1.9. The physiographic features of the Titicaca Basin and surrounding regions (satellite imagery by USGS/CNES/Google).

March. As a result, these are extremely productive zones (Figs. 1.10, 1.11). In the periodic "El Niño" or "La Niña" years, rainfall can reach monsoonal levels in the summer and at times the lake floods large areas of human settlement (Figs. 1.12–1.14).

The driest months are June through September, with some months virtually rainless. According to Roche et al. (1992:86), median annual temperatures vary between 7° and 10° C. The lake itself has a mediating effect on the cold, and median temperatures are often higher than 8° C at the lake edge, a temperature higher than expected if the mass of water were not present (Boulange and Aquize 1981). As a general rule, temperatures are warmer near the lake and become progressively colder away from the water. This, of course, is not only a function of the water mass but also a function of elevation.

Paleoecology

The climate of the Titicaca Basin has not been stable. Even in the twentieth century, the lake level has fluctuated more than 6 m (Roche et al. 1992:84). One of the principal reasons for such fluctuations is the lake's relatively large drainage area. While the lake itself is approximately 8500 km² in size, the entire surface area of the drainage that feeds the lake is almost 50,000 km² (Roche et al. 1992:84). Therefore, small fluctuations in rainfall and other hydrological patterns in this vast area can have a substantial effect on the lake level.

There are a number of paleoecological reconstructions of the Titicaca Basin climate, lake levels, and vegetation using a number of distinct data sets. Unfortunately, the methodologies of these studies are not directly comparable to each other, and there are some discrepancies among these reconstructions. The work of Thompson et al. (1988) provides a series of wet and dry periods in the first and early second millennia AD. Abbot et al. (1997:169; 2003) identify four dry periods (900–800 BC, 400–200 BC, AD 1–300, AD 1100–1500), as indicated by low lake levels.

According to existing data, Lake Titicaca did not reach modern levels until sometime between AD 1 and 1000. A potential problem with these data is that the ORSTOM–UMSA (French Institute of Scientific Research for Development in Cooperation–Universidad Mayor de San Andrés) relied almost exclusively on cores from the southern Little Lake (Huiñamarca). As a result, there are some difficulties in extrapolating these data to the large lake and to the region as a whole.

There are some time periods in which the paleoclimate reconstructions are generally quite consistent. One of these is the Little Ice Age (LIA). The existence of an appreciably colder period during the sixteenth through nineteenth centuries is accepted by most paleoecologists (Thompson and Mosely-Thompson 1987:105–7; Thompson et al. 1988:763) and carries important implications for modeling the later prehistory of the Titicaca region. Thompson and Mosely-Thompson (1987:105) suggest that the onset of this period began around AD 1490 but that "[t]he high and typically more extreme values ... did not begin until the 1520's." They argue that precipitation increased at the onset of the LIA around 1490 but that the colder temperatures did not begin until the 1520s. Both the beginning and end of the LIA was very abrupt, as indicated by

Figure 1.10. A cultivated section of the survey area near the mouth of the Huancané River.

Figure 1.11. A rich area of the survey zone between Luriata Mountain and the town of Huancané. The area is a low pampa that periodically floods in the rainy season. Note the extensive reed beds and the quinoa.

Figure 1.12. A view of the southern end of the survey area on the northern edge of Lake Titicaca. This photograph was taken in 2003 during extensive floods.

Figure 1.13. Sections of the northern Titicaca Basin between Taraco and Huancané showing the extensive flooding during 2003.

Figure 1.14. A house on a low hill between Taraco and Huancané during the extensive flooding in 2003.

distinct and dramatic increases in the climate indices in the cores. The end of the LIA is placed at 1880 when the climate began to warm again (Thompson and Mosely-Thompson 1987:107). According to this reconstruction, the early sixteenth century would have been warmer than today, and beginning in the first third of the 1500s, temperatures would have become progressively cooler until the nineteenth century.

Some historical data also indicate that the sixteenth century was warmer than the climate we see today. The Toledo *Tasa*, compiled in the mid-1570s, lists several northern Titicaca Basin towns as providing maize as tribute to the Spanish administration (Cook 1975). The climate would have needed to be warmer than it is today for maize cultivation in this region, given the scale suggested by the historical data. Archaeological evidence is still sparse, but Bermann (1994:185) discovered maize kernels in Tiwanaku (circa AD 600) contexts. While these could have been imported, their discovery in non-elite domestic contexts raises the possibility of maize cultivation at the site.

In general terms, the northern Titicaca region had a climatic history of long and gradual shifts between wet and dry, cold and warm. Perhaps the most significant observation is that the time at which people began to settle in villages, around 4000 years ago, correlates with a general amelioration of the climate (warmer and wetter). However, this general trend was punctuated with periods of drought and cold as well. Work reported by Baker et al. (2009) also demonstrates that there was considerable fluctuation within an overall general increased precipitation trend in the last 7000 years. They note that:

> Our quantitative reconstruction of this trend suggests a ~12% increase in precipitation (from ~560 to 650 mm a^{-1}), coincident with the 6% increase in summer insolation at this latitude over the same period. The increase in precipitation was neither unidirectional nor gradual. Instead, every 240 years on average, precipitation increased or decreased by at least ~8% for periods lasting on average 100 years. The largest of these events had ~15% positive or negative departures from the long-term mean precipitation. [Baker et al. 2009:319]

These data are significant for archaeological interpretation. We must keep in mind that there were major periods of rainfall shifts that almost certainly affected settlement choices and land use over time.

Agriculture and Pastures

Most Titicaca Basin specialists follow the typology of landscapes proposed by the geographer Pulgar Vidal (1946) who divides the Titicaca Basin into two broad agricultural and ecological regions called *suni* and *puna*. The suni is the lower region located between 3800 and 4000 masl. The higher and drier puna lies between 4000 and 4800 masl. The suni represents the general limit of plant agriculture while the puna is a grazing zone for the extensive camelid herds owned by many Titicaca Basin peoples.

The suni includes the lakeshore area plus the zone a few kilometers away from the lake. This zone is generally found up to 4000 masl, but can go higher depending upon the local characteristics. This area is characterized by extensive areas of grassland among ridges and mountains. The suni is the richest area, where most modern and prehispanic settlement is located. It is heavily terraced on the hillsides (Figs. 1.15, 1.16). A large variety of agricultural products grow in the suni, including many varieties of tubers, legumes, and chenopods (Pulgar Vidal 1946:95–98). The major agricultural product of the region is the tuber, which can be grown up to the snowline (Pulgar Vidal 1946:111). Optimal yields occur in the warmer suni zones and sometimes in the lower puna. A huge variety of tubers grows in the region even today (Fig. 1.17).

Pampa lands often have *cochas*, particularly in the northwest side of the lake. Cochas (or *qocha*) are small, periodically water-filled depressions that dot the pampa landscape (Flores Ochoa and Paz Flores 1983). They are human-made wells dug into the lower areas of the basin to tap the groundwater and capture rainfall. Cochas are more abundant in the north than in the area of the Titicaca Basin as a whole (Figs. 1.18–1.20). Binford and Kolata (1996:49) note that they are used both for agriculture and as sources of water for pasturing animals. Cochas are extremely productive areas. They are very important for agriculture today, and archaeological survey indicates that they were important settlement determinants in the past (Albarracin-Jordan and Mathews 1990). We come to the same conclusion here—cochas are very important areas for settlement, an observation reinforced by work in the nearby Azángaro area (Craig et al. 2011).

Today, it is common for large canals to be constructed into the pampas to provide water for pasturage and agricultural fields (Figs. 1.21–1.24). Numerous extinct canals can be seen throughout the lake edge of the Titicaca Basin in the pampas. These former raised canals or aqueducts were fed by springs that

Figure 1.15. The extensive terraced hillsides near Caya-Caya in the survey region.

Figure 1.16. A terraced hill near Arapa. The terraces were used as house platforms for a Formative period village, and were later converted to agricultural terraces.

Figure 1.17. A woman preparing oca near Saman (photograph by Adán Umire).

Figure 1.18. A view of numerous cochas (qocha) in the pampa between Cachichupa and Huatasani in the survey area.

Figure 1.19. A cultivated cocha in the pampa near Marcacamarca.

Figure 1.20. A cocha (qocha) in the dry season. Note that the cocha is still wetter than the surrounding area because it tapped into an underground water source.

Figure 1.21. Camelids in the northern Titicaca Basin (photo by Tom Levy).

Figure 1.22. A prehistoric canal in the survey area near Huancanéwichinka.

Figure 1.23. A stand of reeds with its owner near Arapa.

Figure 1.24. A set of harvested reeds near Chucuito.

have since dried out (Henderson 2012). They are distinguishable from boundary walls by their sinuous form near the base of hills where the gradients are steepest. This is a water control feature typical of such agricultural constructions. Inevitably, the former aqueducts have been converted into footpaths or causeways.

Bofedales are small areas of swampy land created by the accumulation of groundwater in the low pampas throughout the region. To a certain extent, a cocha is an altered bofedal. Natural bofedales have stands of sedges and grasses, and are primary grazing areas. They were favored locations for the Archaic hunting and gathering populations, and continue to be very rich and coveted areas for human use as pasture for animals and as settlement locations (Aldenderfer 1989). Bofedales are found in both the puna and suni zones. In the lower areas, it is likely that most bofedales were excavated by farmers to create the cochas seen today.

The terraced hills produce a wide variety of crops, particularly tubers and grains. Houses are also built on terraces, with small hamlets and single-family households built adjacent to agricultural fields. Some of the most fertile land is found on the low hillsides. The terraced hills were optimal from one perspective: they were useful for both agriculture and habitation.

Low grassland pampas are the prime areas for raised field agriculture, particularly where rivers are not entrenched (Figs. 1.25, 1.26). Raised fields are labor-intensive agricultural constructions built in swampy land to improve planting conditions. They are large mounds of earth, raised above water level and designed to provide a moist planting surface. Raised fields were built in a variety of physical forms (see Erickson 1988). They were concentrated along the lake edge, along rivers, and in the low, swampy pampas near the lake and in the river floodplains.[2] Pampas, under the appropriate conditions, can be converted into the most productive agricultural zones with raised field agriculture. The major low grasslands in the Titicaca region include the Pucara area and the Huatta pampas in the north. Water is essential to the successful construction of raised fields, and riverine fields are highly productive. In pampas without rivers, or where rivers are entrenched, raised field segments are associated with canals, aqueducts, and other water-delivery systems.

The immediate lakeshore is the most heavily settled area today; survey data indicate it was intensively occupied in the prehispanic past as well. Littorals provide lacustrine resources, such as fish, totora reeds, and other products. The immediate lake edge is particularly productive when it is adjacent to other environmental zones such as a river or marsh. Totora reed beds represent a very significant resource in the northern Titicaca Basin (Figs. 1.23, 1.24). Reeds are a major industrial plant used for house roof and wall construction, making mats, and building boats to cross Lake Titicaca. The roots are also edible, and are referred to in the sixteenth century and today as *chullu*.

---

2. Raised fields are also known as *waru waru* in Quechua and *suka colla* in Aymara.

Figure 1.25. A set of relict raised fields in the southern part of the survey region, east of Jancomarco.

Figure 1.26. A view of the Rámis River. This is a key area of prehistoric raised fields.

Previous Research and Archaeological Context

Early Colonial Documents

The early chroniclers mention the Titicaca Basin quite frequently. They focused on the great Inca sanctuary on the Island of the Sun and the politically-charged rituals that took place on this great island (Bauer and Stanish 2001). They described the roads—Urcusuyu in the west and Umasuyu in the east—and the various royal *tambos* found along the way. Sixteenth-century documents describe the rich taxes exacted from the towns in the area, including gold, silver, cloth, fish, wool, and other commodities.

As is common in the early documents, the Spaniards were obsessed with religion and politics. The political strife between the Inca and the local inhabitants was one of the principal themes running through many of the early histories. The chroniclers Bernabé Cobo and Pedro Cieza de León, in particular, describe the political struggles in the Inca period. Cieza (1553: Chap. C) says: "Before the Incas reigned, many indians say that in this Colla province there were two kings [*señores*], one call Zapana and the other named Cari, and that these kings conquered many pukaras that are their fortresses." The chroniclers were particularly intrigued by the great political drama involving the more southern Lupaqa (also referred to as "Collas" in many early texts, meaning that they spoke Aymara), the Colla, and the Incas. In the period immediately prior to the conquest of the region by the Inca state, two Aymara-speaking *señoríos* or kingdoms were pitted against each other. The Lupaqa (with the capital in Chucuito) vied for supremacy in the region with the Collas (with the capital in Hatuncolla to the north), who had the misfortune to be located between the Lupaqa to their south and the ever-expanding Inca threat to their north.

After the Inca conquered the Canis and Canchis who lived in the Sicuani area up to the Vilcanota pass, the pressure on the Colla was immense. When the two kings of the Colla and Lupaqa fought a huge battle in what are now the plains of Paucarcolla, the Colla lost, the king losing his life in the battle, and the Lupaqa received the Inca in Chucuito. The Inca and the Lupaqas established a kind of political alliance in which the latter did relatively well even though they were subjects of an empire. The Inca did not interfere too much in Lupaqa affairs but they reworked the Colla territory into a subject province. Cuzco established their main center at the Colla center of Hatuncolla, according to the chroniclers. Archaeological research suggests that the Colla capital was not exactly where Hatuncolla now stands, though the specific location of the Colla capital has not been determined. What we do know is that the Inca built a huge garrison and city at Hatuncolla. Cieza relates that:

> Hatuncolla in past times was the grandest thing in the Collao, and locals affirm that before the Incas subjected them, they were under the authority of Zapana and his descendants . . . and afterward the Inca adorned this town with buildings and many storehouses where by their command the tribute that was brought from the fields were stored, and they had a temple of the Sun with many mamaconas and priests to serve the temple, and a number of mitimaes [colonists] and warriors placed in the frontier. [Cieza de León 1553: CII]

There is little doubt that Hatuncolla was the principal garrisoned town of the Inca and their major administrative center. The Inca also built many more towns and formalized the road system. Towns such as Paucarcolla, Chucuito, Juli, and Copacabana stand out as substantial urban areas, while numerous smaller towns were built across the landscape. The Inca state transformed the heavily populated and exceptionally rich area of Collasuyu into a vast province, but only succeeded in tenuously controlling it for less than 100 years.

Both Cieza and Cobo provide extensive commentary on the Canas and Canchis, ethnic groups located on either side of the pass at Vilcanota, as well as the battles between the Inca and the people in Ayaviri. The conquest of the northern Collao was a hugely significant event in Inca imperial history. Up to that time, they had confined their conquests to the circum-Cuzco region. Setting up the huge city at Raqchi near Sicuani and finally crossing the pass into the Collao was perhaps the principal expansion in their early imperial history. The conquest of the Collao propelled the Inca into an empire of global proportions, substantially increasing the geographical extent and population of their domain.

There is much information about the first Inca move on the Collao under the later emperor Pachacuti. His armies descended from La Raya and attacked the Colla at Ayaviri, chasing them to Pucara where they were massacred. Eventually, the Colla king was killed and the Inca made peace with the Lupaqa. The site and town of Pucara is mentioned prominently in the historical accounts: Cieza (1553: LV), for example, tells us "that everyone says that in the town called Pucara they built a fort and when the Inca arrived they made war . . . and at the end they fought among themselves where many died from both sides and the Collas were conquered and made into prisoners."

The next wave of Inca military incursions into Collasuyu was under Topa Inca in reaction to a series of rebellions. Sarmiento, in 1572, says that in this second major attack by the Inca on the Collas, the locals built four forts, including one in Arapa: "Y los Collas se habian hecho fuertes con cuatro, conviene a saber, en Llallaua, Asilli, Arapa, Pucara" (Cook 1975; And the Collas built four forts in Llallaua, Asilli, Arapa, Pucara). Other chroniclers consistently document the existence of hill forts throughout the region that were built in the pre-Inca periods and used into colonial times.

It was under Huayna Capac that the Inca reconfigured the economic and cultural landscape on a massive scale in the circum-Titicaca Basin (Spurling 1992:126–31). Along with the famous resettlement of Cochabamba in Bolivia, the Inca set up state facilities in Milliraya and perhaps at other locations in the survey area, a set of agricultural lands dedicated to the solar cult in Arapa, and the huge pilgrimage destination on the Island of the Sun. Additional facilities included weavers at Conima, metalworkers at Plateria, Chinchasuyu *mitimaes* in Juli and Ancoraimes, potters in Guaqui and Cupi, and many others throughout the region.

The Inca formalized the Omasuyu road that branched in two at Ayaviri. According to Cieza (1553: LII), the Omasuyu road passed through Asillo and Azángaro and arrived at Lake Titicaca. This road passes through the research area; in fact, we found sections of it in the southeast side of the survey near Huancané. The road must certainly have gone from Azángaro south along the river and then skirted Lake Arapa, passing Samán, Taraco, and Huancané and then climbing over the mountains. Reginaldo de Lizarraga (1968 [1605]: LXXXXIX) describes the town of Arapa in the late sixteenth and early seventeenth century as being situated in a key geographical area near the lake, most likely referring to Lake Arapa to the north as well as to the big lake of Titicaca to the south. Betanzos (1996 [1551]) describes a fortified causeway (and surrounding hills in Arapa) that the Collas fled to after their defeat by Topa Inca in Pucara. The Omasuyu road continued around the lake. There is a beautiful Inca tambo in the town of Carpa (Kidder 1943) that is on the road which then passes through Moho and over the mountains.

Betanzos (1996 [1551]) claims that there were four pre-Inca provinces in the north: Azángaro, Moho, Callabaya, and Chiquicache (and see Spurling 1992). These were most likely culturally part of the Colla area but politically independent and allied with the Colla at Hatuncolla.

The northern Titicaca Basin was a rich source of tribute for the Spanish Crown and *encomenderos*. As seen in the Toledo *Tasa* (Cook 1975), the entire area provided a bounty of goods ranging from gold to chuño. One can argue that the northern Titicaca Basin was the richest area in the entire province, which in turn was one of the richest in all of Tawantinsuyu. Pulling data from the Toledo *Tasa* and the Garci Diez de San Miguel *Visita*, Geoffrey Spurling (1992:72) notes that there were more than 86,000 people in the Colla territories and about 75,000 in the Lupaqa area. This figure is consistent with other censuses conducted since the Colonial period up to the present day (Stanish 2003).

The early chroniclers were also fascinated by the ubiquitous burial towers known as *chulpas*. As with most surveys in the region, we found thousands of chulpa remains across the northern Titicaca Basin (Stanish 2012a). Cieza (1553: C) writes that "[t]he most notable thing to see in this Collao in my opinion is the sepulchers of the dead." The word *chulpa* (or *chullpa*) is in reality a bit of a misnomer as applied to the stone burial towers in the region. In the 1612 dictionary of Ludovico Bertonio (Bk 2:92), a chulpa is described as a basket (*serón*) or burial where the dead were placed. This almost certainly refers to the common basket burials found around the region, from at least La Raya south into Bolivia, northern Chile, and northwest Argentina. The actual word for the burial towers is *amaya uta*. The word *uta* is described as a "covered house." The word *amaya* refers to "dead bodies," "beloved child" (*hijo muy querido*), and, curiously, *almena*, a word that translates as a hole in a wall or battlement or stone in an ancient fortress. What is clear is that at least in the early seventeenth century, there was a distinction between burials in baskets or possibly in below-ground tombs and the houses of the dead. Since the term *chulpa* is so deeply entrenched in the literature, we continue to use it here.

Cieza also briefly described the pyramids of Pucara and the site of Hatuncolla (Cieza de León 1553: CII). Hatuncolla was the most important city in the region according to his informants. In Chapter LXXV he notes that this town was one of the places where the subjects of the Inca Empire would bring their tribute. In this reference, Hatuncolla is one of the four most important Inca installations in the empire. Concerning Pucara, Cieza de León (1553: CII) says that he spent one day there "looking at all of it." He notes that in ancient times the site was a great population center and that today there is almost not a single person living there. He also notes the existence of some stone stelae at the site.

The chronicler Cabello de Balboa (1602–1603) mentions Huancané as the *entrada* to the Omasuyus region to the east. He also notes the road from Huancané south to Moho and into the eastern slopes where there were many gold mines in the Carabaya and Larecaja regions.

Geoffrey Spurling's (1992) ethnohistoric work indicates that people of the northern Titicaca Basin had holdings in the eastern slopes. These regions provided access to coca, gold, honey, feathers, and other forest products. The fact that the Toledo *Tasa* lists gold as a major tribute item from many of these towns is explained by these colonial holdings that most certainly preceded the Inca. Spurling (1992) conducted an outstanding archaeological and historical study of the town of Milliraya just north of Huancané. He discussed documents in the Archivo Nacional that tell of Emperor Huayna Capac placing 1000 weavers and feather workers and 100 potters as mitimae colonists here during his reign (Spurling 1992:4–6).[3]

Archaeological Research in the Northern Titicaca Basin

The cumulative work over a generation allows us to define some broad chronological periods in the region (e.g., Chávez and Mohr Chávez 1975; Cohen 2010; Mohr Chávez 1988; Núñez and Paredes 1978; Plourde 2006; Schultze 2008; Stanish 2003; Steadman 1995; Tantaleán 2005, 2012). The earliest periods in the region are referred to as the Formative—Early, Middle, and Late. The Formative is a long time period that begins with the first settled villages circa 1500 BC and ends with Tiwanaku expansion circa AD 600. The Early Formative dates roughly from 1500 to 800 BC. The Middle Formative dates from around 800 to 400 BC, while the Late or Upper Formative dates from around 400 BC to AD 600. These are all very complex periods of time with a number of distinct pottery and sculptural art styles, such

---

3. The document was apparently discovered by Nathan Wachtel, who told John Murra. The latter published an article with Morris (Murra and Morris 1976).

as previously defined Qaluyu and Pukara, and the more recently defined Huaña. The Tiwanaku state began to expand into much of the Titicaca Basin and surrounding regions around AD 600 and collapsed around AD 1000. The Altiplano period follows Tiwanaku collapse, dating from around AD 1000 to AD 1475, and characterized by regional non-state polities. Finally, Inca control of the Titicaca Basin dates from around AD 1475 to AD 1532. These periods are recognized by pottery styles and ceramic attributes identified over the last generation of archaeological research and formalized in the typology developed by Chávez in Chapter 2 of this monograph.

Formal scientific research in the Titicaca Basin began perhaps with Ephraim Squier but most certainly with Luis Valcárcel, Manuel Chávez Ballón, and Alfred Kidder in the early part of the twentieth century. Valcárcel's work at Pucara demonstrated the sophistication of the stoneworking traditions in the pre-Tiwanaku periods of the region. He showed that this Andean carving tradition extended from Colombia to Bolivia and was represented in the northern Titicaca Basin by early cultures.

Kidder's reconnaissance was concentrated on northern Titicaca (north of Juli to Pucara and east to the other side of the lake near Conima) and was directed at defining the nature of Pucara and possibly earlier sites (Kidder 1943). He, along with Marion Tschopik (1946), discovered a number of sites. Their reports were very sketchy, but they developed ceramic typologies still in use today and helped illustrate the range and variation of archaeological settlement in the northern and western Titicaca Basin.

In the northern extreme of the Titicaca region, Félix Tapia Pineda (1975, 1978) reported a number of sites from Nuñoa. He described a substantial complex of Altiplano period sites, such as Jatun Pukara, Maukka Llajta, and others. Tapia published photographs of well-preserved fieldstone chulpas that appear to date to the Altiplano period. He also described a number of Altiplano period fortified sites, indicating that this site type was found as far north as the Nuñoa region. Likewise, Máximo Neira Avendaño reconnoitered the northern lake region and discovered a number of sites reported on in his preliminary manuscript (Neira Avendaño 1967). Núñez del Prado (1972) discovered Pucara-style monoliths in the far northern Chumbivilcas region, thereby extending the known distribution of that style.

Chávez and Mohr Chávez defined the Yaya-Mama religious tradition (1975) with its monoliths having male and female icons as central themes in the material expression of this ideology. This tradition "is characterized by temples with sunken courts, ritual paraphernalia including ceramic trumpets and burners, and elaborate mythical iconography" (Janusek 2004a:129 and see Burger et al. 2000; Stanish 2012b). Chávez and Mohr Chávez (1975) showed that the famous Arapa stela was actually the missing half of the Thunderbolt stela in Tiwanaku, demonstrating an early case of *huaca* or monument capture in the Titicaca Basin. Elias Mujica worked at Pucara and has published several significant articles on the site and culture (1978, 1985, 1987, 1990).

In the last two decades, there has been a significant amount of work in the northern Titicaca Basin, including five dissertations based upon independent work in the region. Carol Schultze (2008) surveyed and excavated in the Puno Bay, discovering several dozen sites and a major center of silver production from the Formative and Tiwanaku periods. This work drew from the pioneering research of Marion Tschopik (1946), Mario Núñez and Rolando Paredes (1978), and others in the region. Amanda Cohen (2010) surveyed and excavated in the Pukara Valley, discovering sites and the earliest sunken court complex known to date in the entire Titicaca Basin. Elizabeth Klarich (2005) excavated at the site of Pucara and uncovered major residential and feasting areas. Elizabeth Arkush (2005) did an extensive survey of the region and defined the development and consolidation of Altiplano period forts or *pukaras*. Aimée Plourde (2006) excavated the site of Cachichupa in the present survey area, uncovering some very early domestic terraces and feasting episodes with Qaluyu materials. Finally, Abigail Levine (2012) worked at Taraco and demonstrated a rich Qaluyu and Pucara occupation at the site.

Henry Tantaleán (2012) has worked at the town of Ayaviri in the northern Basin. He excavated a large Formative mound known as Balsaspata (also known as Pueblo Libre). Excavations at this site revealed a long sequence of human occupation beginning in the Early Formative (Qaluyu) and continuing through Pucara phases.

Survey Area and Research Design

The Northern Titicaca Basin survey began in the early 1990s with some non-systematic reconnaissance in the region (Stanish, Cohen, and Aldenderfer 2005). Our work at Isla Esteves and the neighboring site of Huajje in 1997 demonstrated that there was a strong Tiwanaku, Qaluyu, and Pucara period presence in the region. The previous research by other scholars, plus our initial work, helped us define our research questions. We were intrigued by the nature and extent of the Pucara polity and its relationship to the earlier Qaluyu culture. The nature of Tiwanaku expansion is a persistent problem in Titicaca Basin archaeology, and the north was poorly known.

Defining the so-called "Collao" pottery and its cultural affiliations was another problem. Luis Lumbreras and Hernán Amat's (1968:84) intriguing suggestion that there was a hiatus in the area during the third through eighth centuries was central to this effort as well. We felt from the beginning that the issue with the hiatus hypothesis was probably more a result of incomplete or inaccurate ceramic chronologies and not the result of a physical abandonment of the area. The northern Titicaca region is simply too rich to abandon unless there was some extraordinary environmental or political event. Finally, the nature of the Inca occupation remains an important research question even though documents give us a decent picture of the political structure.

Settlement archaeology has evolved substantially in the last generation. We pursued a multistage set of methods in this work, consistent with the latest methodologies for ecological zones such as the northern Titicaca Basin.

Figure 1.27. A Google Map view of the survey area.

Stage 1 involved non-intensive reconnaissance to assess the nature and range of archaeological materials in the study area. We conducted non-systematic reconnaissance in 1998, covering the area from the Bolivian border near Conima. These data raised numerous theoretical and empirical questions in Titicaca Basin archaeology. There were many sites with sunken courts. We found vast areas of under-reported raised fields. Archaic sites were discovered along the rivers. Numerous carved stones, including stelae, as well as scores of uncarved monoliths were found throughout the region. Pucara and Qaluyu pottery fragments were scattered, often in dense quantities, over the area. Sites had hundreds of andesite and basalt hoes and adzes. Tombs were everywhere. A major Inca pottery-making area was discovered in the Huatasani region, complete with the kaolin clays of the Sillustani type first defined by Marion Tschopik in 1946. In short, the region promised to help us define the entire sequence from the earliest occupation to the Early Colonial period. We finally settled on the Huancané-Putina area to start the research, given the large number of sites near the lake edge and the Formative period sunken court sites found up the river to the town of Putina.

Stage 2 of the research involved the intensive, full-coverage regional survey. This work began carefully in 1999 and expanded to intensive survey beginning in 2000. We continued full-coverage regional survey around Lake Arapa until 2004.

The survey area is divided into four sections—Putina, Huancané, Arapa, and Taraco, the first two of which are presented in this volume (Figs. 1.27, 1.28). These are largely arbitrary divisions that we used in the survey to create order in our field coverage. The Huancané and Putina areas contain about half of the four sections' sites.

Stage 3 research involved more intensive investigations at selected sites in the region after the survey was completed. We excavated at the site of Taraco for several seasons beginning in 2004, including two areas. Area A was located very near the center of the town, near the river, in an area replete with artifacts. About one kilometer to the north, Cecilia Chávez Justo excavated

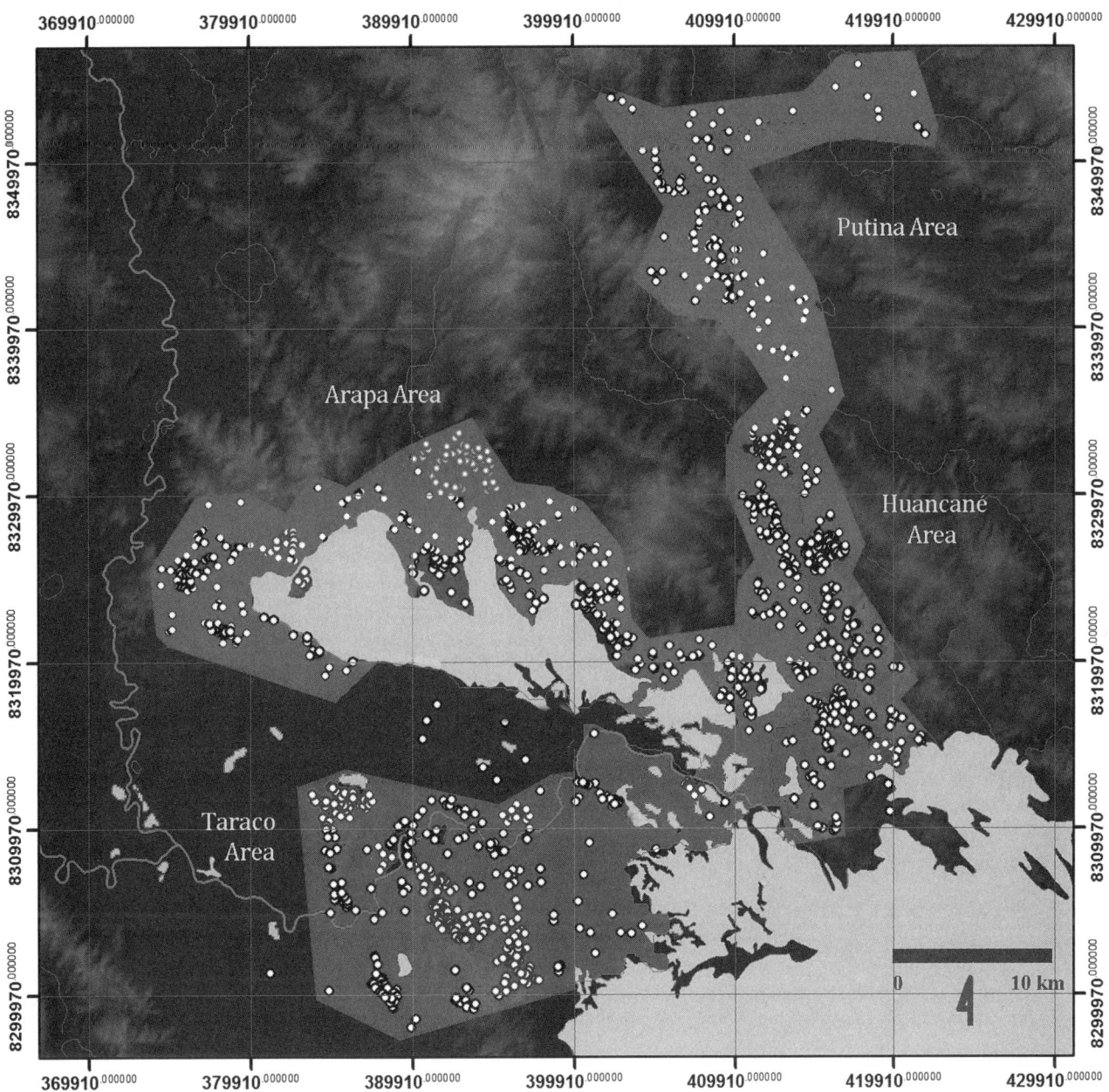

Figure 1.28. A map of the survey limits showing the sites in the region.

the mound at Antamocco, discovering an adobe pyramid with ramps and multiple construction episodes.

The intensive systematic surface collections from some sites within the survey area and the excavation research provided us with the data necessary to construct a viable pottery sequence worked out by Cecilia Chávez over a period of six years.

We based the survey methodology on previous work in the Juli-Pomata, Pucara, and Puno Bay areas. The survey crews were spread 10 to 25 meters apart, depending upon the terrain. We covered 100% of the territory within the survey boundaries, except for a small part of the pampa below Lake Arapa. Sites were recorded using a GPS starting in 2000. The 1999 season was conducted by Stanish and started in the northeastern area east of Putina at Quilcapuncu. We ended near Cachichupa. José Núñez finished the 1999 season ending in the region of Huatasani. From 2000 to 2004, teams headed by Adán Umire and Javier Chalca completed the rest of the survey up to Huancané and around Lake Arapa and Taraco. Stanish revisited all the major sites and many of the smaller ones from 2003 to 2008.

We had worked out all the field procedures in earlier surveys. However, it was clear as early as 2001 that we had a huge problem with the ceramic sequence. In the western Titicaca region, as well as the south, the ceramic chronology was fairly well worked out. Scholars such as Lee Steadman (1995), John Janusek (2004), Szymon Augustyniak (2004), and others had worked out the details of the Formative and Tiwanaku periods in the southern and western Titicaca Basin. In this region, there appears to be a less complex sequence of ceramic styles fitting a more traditional linear trajectory, though, as with all chronologies, there are some overlaps. This is definitely not the case in the northern Titicaca region.

The data from the north simply did not conform to our expectations based on our previous work in the west and south. There were important surprises. Excavations in Taraco by Stanish, Chávez, and Levine indicated substantial overlap between Pucara and Qaluyu styles. In fact, carbon date analysis by Levine, as well as data from unequivocal archaeological contexts, indicated that there were at least three centuries during which Late Qaluyu and Pucara pottery coexisted.

Perhaps even more confusing was the position of Tiwanaku in the north. We knew that there were Tiwanaku sites, such as Maravillas near the river north of Juliaca (Stanish, Cohen, and Aldenderfer 2005), those in the Puno Bay, those reported by Erickson (1988), and so forth. We also found numerous Tiwanaku pottery fragments during the survey and reconnaissance, particularly near the lake, the road, and rivers. But there were huge tracts of land with virtually no Tiwanaku pottery, and certainly no Tiwanaku-occupied sites away from the roads and rivers. Based upon these data, we hypothesized the existence of a local culture that coexisted with late Pucara and Tiwanaku, a culture that we called Huaña.

Sorting out the chronology problem took us many years of analyzing surface collections, carbon dates from excavations, and extrapolations from other areas. After six years and thousands of analyzed pottery fragments, the truly heroic work of Cecilia Chávez Justo resulted in a typology and chronology, based upon a detailed attribute analysis that allows us to make sense of the data (Chávez 2008). This new work is presented in its complete form here in Chapter 2 and is the reason why we are now able to publish the survey results with a much greater degree of confidence.

The following chapters provide this ceramic typology/chronology (Chapter 2), the description of the sites found in the Huancané and Putina sections of the survey (Chapter 3), and a summary of the results (Chapter 4). This monograph provides abundant tables, maps, and figures, illustrating a sample of the vast database created by this research.

2 | Analysis of Ceramics from the Middle and Lower Río Huancané Subdrainage, Department of Puno, Perú

by Cecilia Chávez Justo[1]

The Lake Titicaca Basin is one of the principal areas of indigenous cultural development in the Andes. Our knowledge of this region is the product of various generations of investigators who, through systematic surveys and excavations, have revealed a sequence of more than 10,000 years of human achievement. Part of this history has been informed by the analysis of pottery, which is one of the material remains of a society that is both common and durable through time, even in the wet and cold altiplano. Further, pottery can be considered both an artistic and a technological expression of a people, and, as such, provides a means to study past societies. Indeed, the analysis of ceramic data has a long and distinguished history in Titicaca Basin archaeology.[2]

Many different methods have been employed in ceramic analysis in the central Andes, including type-variety typologies, seriations, attribute analysis, and so forth. These are classifications of the ceramic material based on shared attributes in the sample. Three general observations stand out in the use of these methods.

First, there is a heavy reliance on the use of decorative or morphological criteria applied to "diagnostic" features (rims and decorated body sherds) that come from small sample sizes found in specific contexts such as ritual places or tombs. These criteria are used extensively in the literature of Titicaca Basin ceramic analysis (e.g., Tschopik 1946; Julien 1983; Albarracin-Jordan and Mathews 1990; Stanish et al. 1997).

Second, these classifications often include a highly detailed analysis of pastes incorporating a large number of variables. These variables are derived from attribute differences of the clay inclusions that in turn are derived from a wide range of materials.

Third, in many cases, these typologies can be employed only by the investigator who created them in the first place. In other cases, the majority of the identified paste types are useful only for the site or area from which the sample was derived, making it less useful for comparative purposes for other areas.

Given these observations, I argue that it is important to include samples that do not have any decoration or diagnostic forms. I am referring to the "nondiagnostic" pieces such as plainware body sherds, necks, handles, and bases that are usually much more abundant than diagnostics. It is also useful if the identified pastes are easily recognizable in the field as well as in the laboratory. Furthermore, it is important that the attributes can be used for comparative purposes in areas outside the sampled zone.

In this analysis of the materials from the Huancané-Putina survey, I combine four criteria and analytical levels (Table 2.1). The first criterion is the raw material. This forms the first level

---

1. Translated by Charles Stanish and Sandy Enriquez.
2. See the work of Rowe 1944; Kidder II 1943; Tschopik 1946; Bennett 1948; Mohr 1966; Julien 1983; Mohr Chávez 1992; Alconini 1995; Steadman 1995; Arkush 2005; Klarich 2005.

of analysis in that raw materials fall into different groups based on clay color because the color is related to the clay's source; "groups" in my analysis refer to clay sources. The second criterion focuses on the technical aspects of the manufacture such as clay preparation, firing, and surface treatment that, in total, represents a "ware"; thus, wares incorporate the technological preparation of the clays. The third criterion is morphological, permitting us to classify the vessels according to form and function; this is referred to as "classes." Finally, the fourth analytical level uses decoration as a criterion, allowing us to identify decorative "types." Classes and types reflect the influences or impositions of diverse cultural, political, and ideological factors that modify the iconography and introduce variations in the forms and contours of the vessels.

While it is true that this method can be considered as a kind of typology or seriation, I am less concerned about semantics and more concerned about its utility in the field. Like all analyses of this type, one has to include detailed descriptions of the characteristics of each criterion used because in the final analysis, all of these are hypothetical projections derived from underlying theoretical assumptions and empirical observations. The results obtained from the application of this analysis can also be tested with future collections. It is worth remembering that all typologies are ultimately hypotheses that are constantly tested and refined.

Results

This ceramic methodology was applied to the diagnostic and nondiagnostic material from the middle and lower Huancané sub-basins (Plourde 2006). The survey discovered approximately 500 archaeological sites. In total, a bit more than 15,000 pottery fragments were collected. About 75% of the sample was recovered from sites with architecture, while about 25% came from sites without architecture, indicating that the majority is associated with habitation contexts from different periods. In turn, diagnostics represent approximately 54% of the sample, with the remaining 46% considered nondiagnostic.

In setting up this framework, I first provisionally separated the material in broad periods using the chronology proposed by Stanish (2003:85–90). This chronology covers all the cultural periods in the area—including the supposed "hiatus" discussed by Lumbreras and Amat (1968) and which referred to the supposed lack of Tiwanaku presence after Pucara collapse. The period called "Huaña," proposed by Stanish (2003:159), represents a newly identified cultural group for that time period.

Stanish's framework permitted us to locate our sample within five broad cultural periods as described in Chapter 1. The breakdown of the ceramic sample using these broad cultural periods is as follows: the Formative represents 19.1%, Huaña 2.1%, Tiwanaku 1.8%, Altiplano 58.7%, and the Inca 18.3%. We can see that the ceramic materials associated with the Altiplano period are very abundant, followed by the Formative, the Inca, and smaller quantities of Tiwanaku and Huaña. With these materials now separated into the large groups, we proceeded to apply the four criteria listed above.

First Criterion: Raw Material

Groups represent different clay sources that were hypothetically used by different workshops simultaneously in the area. We defined four groups distinguished by color: orange, red, cream, and brown (Table 2.2). These groups, in turn, have color variants.[3] These variations could be due to the preferential use of a certain clay type or perhaps from differences in the technical production of individual workshops. The groups and their variants are distributed differently in the various periods (Table 2.3). For example, we see that Group 1 (orange) is found only in Huaña, but its variants are found in all periods. Group 2 (red) and its variants are also widely distributed through time. Group 3 (cream) is found only in the late periods from Altiplano to Inca. Group 4 (brown) and its variants are primarily found in the early periods.

Second Criterion: Pottery Technology

Wares were identified in each of the groups and their variants following a three-step analysis: paste identification,[4] the definition of paste groups, and the definition of manufacturing techniques.

The paste identification began with the differentiation of the four clay groups—orange, red, cream, and brown—and their respective variants. The next step was to identify the tempers used in each group. The entire analyzed sample has natural sand temper with quartz grains in different colors. Tempering materials such as mica were used in the early periods (Formative and Huaña), and crushed rock tempers (feldspars, chalk, limestone, andesite, and so forth) were used beginning with the Tiwanaku period.

This initial analysis resulted in the identification of 126 pastes that were then separated within each period by their association with known diagnostic styles (for instance, Tiwanaku *keros*, Inca plates, Pucara flat-bottomed bowls). Based on this analysis, during the Formative period, people used more than 40 different pastes. During the Huaña period, the number dropped to 23, and in the Tiwanaku period there were only 12 pastes. The Altiplano period potters used 26 different pastes while the Inca period peoples used 22.

The second step of this analysis was to form paste groups. The method here is to group individual pastes that share similar characteristics regarding the use of temper and color. I use Roman numerals (I, II, III, IV, and V) to represent the paste groups (Table 2.4). Within these paste groups, Arabic numerals represent the variations and subdivisions within each group. This analysis resulted in a number of pastes that make up each group per period.

---

3. We used the Munsell Color Chart 2000 edition (see Appendix I: Color Key).
4. We initially intended to identify manufacturing techniques but due to the small size of the fragments, we were unable to incorporate these data.

Table 2.1. Criteria and levels of analysis.

	Material	Technology	Morphology	Decoration
Group	X			
Ware	X	X		
Class	X	X	X	
Type	X	X	X	X

Table 2.2. Groups and their variants.

Groups and Their Variants							
1	orange	2	red	3	cream	4	brown
1.1	light orange	2.1	reddish brown	3.1	orange-cream	4.1	light brown
1.2	dark orange						

Table 2.3. Quantities of pastes by group and period.

Group	Formative	Huaña	Tiwanaku	Altiplano	Inca
1	–	1	–	–	–
1.1	17	13	–	7	1
1.2	–	1	7	8	10
2	2	1	5	2	4
2.1	7	3	–	5	–
3	–	–	–	1	2
3.1	–	–	–	3	2
4	3	–	–	–	–
4.1	14	4	–	–	3

Table 2.4. Relationship between groups, pastes, and colors.

Period	Group	Paste	Color
Formative	I-1	2, 3, 7, 8	light orange
	I-1	6	reddish brown
	I-1	1, 4, 5	light brown
	I-2	10, 11	light orange
	I-2	9	light brown
	I-3	12, 13, 14, 15, 16	light orange
	I-4	38, 39, 40	light brown
	I-5	19, 20, 21	red
	I-6	23, 24, 25	reddish brown
	II-1	26, 27, 28	light brown
	II-3	36	light orange
	II-3	33, 34, 35, 37	light brown
	II-5	42	light orange
	II-5	41	light brown
	II-6	43, 44, 45	reddish brown
	II-7	46, 47, 48, 49, 50	brown
	III	52	light orange
	III	51	reddish brown
Huaña	I-1	1, 11	light orange
	I-1	10	dark orange
	I-1	7, 14, 15	reddish brown
	II-1	17	orange
	II-1	4, 5, 20	light orange
	II-1	16	red
	II-1	9	clear brown
	II-2	3, 6, 8, 13, 29, 30, 32	clear orange
	II-2	2, 12, 31	light brown
Tiwanaku	I	1, 2, 3, 4	dark orange
	II	5, 6, 7	dark orange
	III	8, 9, 10, 11, 12	red
Altiplano	I-1	1, 2, 3, 4	dark orange
	I-2	5, 6, 7, 8	dark orange
	I-3	9, 10, 11, 12, 13	light orange
	I-4	25, 26	red
	II	16	cream
	II	14, 15, 17	orange-cream
	III	18, 19, 20, 21, 22	reddish brown
	IV	23, 24	light orange
Inca	I-1	6, 9, 20	dark orange
	I-2	1, 2, 13, 14, 15	dark orange
	I-3	8	dark orange
	I-4	24, 27, 29	dark orange
	II-5	7, 12	red
	II-6	18	red
	III-7	3	cream
	III-8	4	cream
	III-9	5, 16	orange-cream
	IV-10	10	light brown
	IV-11	19, 21	light brown

Combining these attributes teaches us that during the Formative period there were 12 paste groups, in the Huaña and Tiwanaku periods there were 3 paste groups each, in the Altiplano period there were 7 paste groups, and in the Inca period there were 11 paste groups. We see that the Formative has the largest number of paste groups and that the number then remains low until the Inca period. Some paste groups have 2 or more groups differentiated by clay color but which share similar tempers.

Finally, the last step in this phase of the analysis was the definition of the wares. This was achieved by observing the nature of the pastes based upon compactness, hardness, and texture. From this we defined a number of wares of similar technological characteristics within each cultural period, giving the results seen in Table 2.5. There are 3 wares in the Formative, Altiplano, and Inca periods and only 2 in the Huaña and Tiwanaku periods.

Third Criterion: Morphological Analysis

Classes refer not only to morphological criteria of the vessels, but also to their function. This assumes a relationship between the form of vessel and its intended function. Pottery production responds to specific needs such as food preparation (cooking, processing, fermenting, etc.), consumption (eating and drinking), and transport/storage. These tasks all correspond to *functional categories* with which the vessel classes are defined (ollas, jars, pitchers, bowls, etc.) (Table 2.6). These vessel classes can be divided into two categories: open and closed.

Open Vessels

Open vessels are defined as those with a mouth diameter equal to or greater than the vessel's height. The function of these vessels is linked to the consumption of solids or liquids. The identified forms are:

Tazón. A vessel with straight walls that diverge out slightly and a vessel height greater than half of the mouth diameter.

Bowl. A vessel with convex walls, a form close to a hemisphere, and a vessel height less than half the diameter of the mouth.

Plate. A vessel with convex walls and a vessel height less than one-third of the mouth diameter.

Taza. A cup with concave walls, a vessel height half the mouth diameter, and a handle.

Moreover, we can identify the following variants based on the shape of the vessel walls and the form of the lip:

A. With a continuous contour between the base and the highest part of the vessel.
B. With a discontinuous contour occurring in the highest third of the vessel.
C. With a vertical protuberance in the highest third of the vessel.
D. With a flaring protuberance in the highest third of the vessel that significantly widens the mouth diameter.
E. Spherical shapes.

Closed Vessels

These are vessels in which the mouth diameter is less than the vessel's height and the function is associated with food preparation, storage, and/or transport of solids and liquids. The identified forms in the sample are:

Jar. A medium or small vessel with a wide neck and mouth, a wide body, a narrow base, a concave profile, and one or more handles that go from the rim to the body. Its height is greater than half of the mouth diameter.

Pitcher. A large vessel with a narrow mouth, a wide body, a narrow base, a concave profile, and typically one or two handles in the middle part of the body. The height is greater than half of the mouth diameter.

Olla. A large vessel with a wide neck and mouth, a wide body, a narrow base, a concave profile, and typically one or two handles in the middle part of the body. However, there also

Table 2.5. Relationship between groups, wares, and period.

Period	Ware	Group
Formative	I	I-1
		I-6
		II-1
	II	I-4
		II-5
		II-6
		II-7
	III	I-2
		I-3
		I-5
		II-3
		III
Huaña	I	II-1
		II-2
	II	I-1
Tiwanaku	I	III
	II	I
		II
Altiplano	I	I-3
		IV
	II	I-1
		I-2
		II
	III	I-4
		III
Inca	I	I-4
		III-7
		III-8
	II	I-1
		I-2
		I-3
		I-4
		III-9
	III	II-5
		II-6
		IV-10
		IV-11

Table 2.6. Example of the relationship between wares and types of open vessels in different periods.

Period	Ware	Tazones				Bowls				Plates				Cups			
		1	2	3	4	1	2	3	4	1	2	3	4	1	2	3	4
Formative	I	X	X	–	X	X	X	–	X	–	–	–	–	–	–	–	–
	II	X	X	–	X	X	X	–	X	–	–	–	–	–	–	–	–
	III	X	X	–	X	X	X	–	X	–	–	–	–	–	–	–	–
Huaña	I	X	X	–	X	–	X	–	X	–	–	–	–	–	–	–	–
	II	–	X	–	X	–	X	–	X	–	–	–	–	–	–	–	–
Tiwanaku	I	–	X	–	X	–	X	–	X	–	–	–	–	–	–	–	–
	II	–	X	–	X	–	–	–	–	–	–	–	–	–	–	–	–
Altiplano	I	–	X	–	X	–	X	–	X	–	–	–	–	–	X	–	–
	II	–	X	–	X	–	X	–	X	–	X	–	X	–	X	–	–
	III	–	X	–	X	–	X	–	X	–	X	–	X	–	X	–	–
Inca	I	X	X	–	X	–	X	–	X	–	X	–	X	–	–	–	–
	II	–	X	–	X	–	X	–	X	–	–	–	X	–	–	–	–
	III	–	X	–	X	–	X	–	X	–	X	–	X	–	–	–	–

exist ollas without necks (*ollas sin cuello*). The height is greater than half the mouth diameter.

Bottle. A medium or small vessel with a narrow neck and mouth, a wide body, a narrow base, a concave profile, and often one or two handles in the middle part of the body. The height is greater than half the mouth diameter.

Glass. A vessel with concave walls and typically a cylindrical form. The height is greater than half the mouth diameter.

We can also identify the following variants based upon the shape of the vessel walls and the form of the lip:

A. With divergent rims with a continuous contour.

B. With divergent rims with a concave shape. There are two varieties based upon their degree of angle inclination.

C. Vessels with an expanded exterior contour.

D. Spherical vessels without necks.

E. Spherical vessels with short necks.

These classes are found in all the wares; however, formal variants such as "Inca *aryballos*" that are ceremonial in nature are not classed as jars or pitchers. The same can be said for Tiwanaku keros or Pukara incense burners (*incensarios*). The latter are pedestalled bowls that were used to burn incense or a similar material.

"Trumpets" deserve separate mention—these appear only in the Formative and are obviously linked to rituals. Also deserving of separate mention are miniatures, found in all forms; *adornos*, used as ornaments; and, finally, various tools such as spindle whorls and ceramic polishers. These latter are found in a number of periods in the sample and are included in the category of "other" because they cannot be categorized by the functions of food preparation, consumption, storage, and/or transport.

The analyzed sample has a total of 8044 diagnostic fragments. From this, we see that type A and B tazones are common in all periods, but not tazón type C, which is present only in the Altiplano period. On the other hand, type A and type B bowls are found in all time periods, but with lower frequencies in the Huaña and Tiwanaku periods. Type C bowls are found only in the Altiplano and Inca periods. Types D and E are found in the Formative, Altiplano, and Inca periods. The tazas are exclusively in the Altiplano period. The plates are found only during the Altiplano and Inca periods.

Within the category of closed vessels, jar types A and B are found in all periods but type C is not found in the Huaña and Tiwanaku periods. Likewise, pitcher types A and B are found in all periods except Tiwanaku. On the other hand, type A and type B ollas are common in all periods except Huaña and Tiwanaku. Type C and D ollas appear in the Formative and Altiplano periods, while type E ollas are almost exclusively Formative in date with just a few found in Huaña. The bottles are found in all periods except Huaña and the glasses occur from Huaña to Inca.

It should be mentioned that the lack of some closed vessels (ollas and pitchers) from the Tiwanaku sample, as well as the low frequency of jars, could be a sampling size problem or it could be real. If real, it may be due to the nature of Tiwanaku influence in the region, with the appearance of large numbers of keros replacing many of these forms.

This classification system of form and function not only permits the identification of the forms associated with each period but also teaches us about differences in size, the size being the diameter of the rim. The size categories are: miniatures (1–4 mm), very small (5–8 mm), small (9–14 mm), medium (15–17 mm), large (18–22 mm), and very large (23 mm and greater).

All the wares have this range of rim sizes to a greater or lesser degree, indicating that an assemblage was composed of both open and closed vessels of different sizes. In a general sense, the diameters of the ceramic assemblages can provide information on whether the pottery was used for domestic or communal/ritual purposes. For example, a medium-sized tazón was most likely for personal use, while a very large one could have been used in communal events.

Tazones ranged from small to very large in all the Formative and Huaña wares except Huaña Ware II. The very large tazones disappeared in Huaña Ware II and reappeared only in Altiplano Ware I. In Tiwanaku Ware I the tazones are small and medium, while in Ware II there are also very small and large tazones. In all the Altiplano and Inca wares, there are small, medium, and large tazones. Altiplano Ware III and Inca Ware I additionally have very small tazones.

In the case of bowls, all Formative wares range from small to very large, except Ware I, which additionally has very small bowls. The Huaña wares' bowls range from small to large. In the Tiwanaku period there are only small and medium bowls, in Ware I. The Altiplano and Inca wares' bowls range from very small to very large, except Altiplano Ware II, which additionally has miniature bowls, and Inca Ware II, which lacks very large bowls.

Large plates existed in all Altiplano and Inca wares. Altiplano Ware III additionally had medium plates and Altiplano Ware II and Inca Ware I additionally had small and medium plates. The tazas are restricted to the Altiplano wares: Ware I has small to large tazas, Ware II has small and medium tazas, and Ware III has very large tazas.

Moving to the closed vessels, the jars by definition are not large. The Formative wares' jars range from very small to medium. The Huaña period only has small and medium jars in Ware I. Tiwanaku Ware I has very small jars and Tiwanaku Ware II has small and medium jars. The Altiplano wares all have very small to medium jars, and Altiplano Ware II additionally has miniature jars. The Inca wares all have small and medium jars, and Inca Ware I additionally has miniature and very small jars.

The pitchers, as storage vessels, are large and very large in all the wares, except for the Tiwanaku wares, in which this vessel type is not found. The Formative wares' and Huaña Ware I's ollas range from small to very large, and Formative Ware III additionally has very small ollas. The Altiplano wares' ollas range from small to very large, except Ware III, which lacks small ollas. Inca Wares I and II have small and medium ollas.

Formative Wares I and II have very small bottles, and Ware II additionally has miniature and small bottles. Tiwanaku Ware II has miniature bottles, Altiplano Ware II has very small bottles, and Inca Ware II has small bottles. Finally, Huaña Ware II and Altiplano Wares I and II have small glasses. The Tiwanaku wares' glasses range from very small to medium. Inca Ware I has small and medium glasses.

Fourth Criterion: Decoration

The types are derived from the vessel classes present in each cultural period and ware. They are associated with decorative styles known in the existing literature for the area, such as Qaluyu, Pukara, and Tiwanaku. Although the same ceramic vessels can change through time and across space, they can still maintain features and common characteristics that permit the identification of cultural affiliation. Therefore, given that decoration is the basis to define a style, its study and description uses four general aspects: (1) the decorated area, (2) the technical aspects of the decorations, (3) the motifs, and (4) the colors.

The decorated area refers to the used space and the surfaces where the decoration is located. The used spaces are more related to the entire vessels, so since the analyzed sample is composed of ceramic fragments, we could not use this category of analysis. However, if one analyzes both sides of the specimen, that is to say exterior and interior, then the entire sample can be included.

Four decorative techniques were identified and divided into the following two categories: (1) those techniques that alter the surface (incision, slipping, and modeling), and (2) those techniques that add to the surface (painting). These decorative techniques were, in turn, subdivided by motif or decorative style and grouped into three general types: geometric, anthropomorphic, and naturalistic. Finally, the color was analyzed in terms of the quantity and combinations used in each ware.

Within the open vessels, the tazones normally used one or two colors. However, for tazones in Formative Ware II and Huaña Ware II, only one color was used, and in Formative Ware I, Altiplano Ware II, and Inca Ware II, up to three colors were used. One or two colors were used for bowls of the Formative and Altiplano wares, whereas only one color was used for bowls of the Huaña wares and Tiwanaku Ware I. One to three colors were used for bowls of Inca Ware I, one to four colors for those of Inca Ware II, and one or two colors for those of Inca Ware III. The plates of Altiplano Wares II and III and Inca Ware III used one color, those of Inca Ware I used one or two colors, and those of Inca Ware II used three colors. The tazas of the Altiplano wares used only one color.

Moving to the closed vessels, the use of only one color commonly refers to a slip that completely covers the exterior and

Table 2.7. Relationship between types, wares, and period.

	Formative Wares			Huaña Wares		Tiwanaku Wares		Altiplano Wares			Inca Wares		
	I	II	III	I	II	I	II	I	II	III	I	II	III
Qaluyu	X	–	–	–	–	–	–	–	–	–	–	–	–
Qaluyu/Pucara	–	X	–	–	–	–	–	–	–	–	–	–	–
Pucara	–	–	X	–	–	–	–	–	–	–	–	–	–
Huaña/Qaluyu	–	–	–	X	X	–	–	–	–	–	–	–	–
Huaña/Pucara	–	–	–	X	X	–	–	–	–	–	–	–	–
Huaña/Tiwanaku	–	–	–	–	X	–	–	–	–	–	–	–	–
Tiwanaku Local	–	–	–	–	–	X	–	–	–	–	–	–	–
Tiwanaku	–	–	–	–	–	–	X	–	–	–	–	–	–
Huaña/Altiplano	–	–	–	–	–	–	–	X	–	–	–	–	–
Collao	–	–	–	–	–	–	–	X	X	X	–	–	–
Huatasani	–	–	–	–	–	–	–	X	X	X	–	–	–
Inca Collao	–	–	–	–	–	–	–	–	–	–	X	–	–
Inca Huatasani	–	–	–	–	–	–	–	–	–	–	X	–	–
Inca Local	–	–	–	–	–	–	–	–	–	–	–	X	–
Inca Imitation Cuzco	–	–	–	–	–	–	–	–	–	–	–	X	–
Inca Colonial	–	–	–	–	–	–	–	–	–	–	–	–	X

partially covers the interior. One color was used for the jars of the Formative and Huaña wares, except for those of Formative Ware III, which additionally used two colors. The jars of the Altiplano and Inca wares used one or two colors, except for those of Inca Ware III, which used only one color. The pitchers of the Formative wares and Huaña Ware I used one color. The pitchers of Altiplano Ware I and Inca Wares I and III used one color, those of Altiplano Ware III and Inca Ware II used one or two colors, and those of Altiplano Ware II used one to three colors.

The ollas of the Formative wares and Huaña Ware I used one color. Those of the Altiplano wares used one color, except for those of Altiplano Ware I, which additionally used two colors. Those of Inca Ware II used one color. Bottles of the Formative Wares I and II and Altiplano Ware II used one color. The glasses of Huaña Ware II used one color, those of Tiwanaku wares used one or two colors, those of Altiplano Wares I and II used one color, and those of Inca Ware I used one or two colors.

Once these results were derived from the fourth criterion, the next step was to combine them with the classes of vessels and their variants, both open and closed. This permitted us to identify the ceramic styles that were present in the sample: Qaluyu and Pucara (Formative), Tiwanaku (Tiwanaku), Collao and Huatasani (Altiplano), Collao, Huatasani, Taraco, Chucuito, Pacajes, Urcusuyu, Cuzco A and B, and Inca Colonial (Inca).

These styles were then combined with all the wares identified in the analysis (Table 2.7). In the Formative, Ware I is associated with the ceramic style Qaluyu; in Ware II, Qaluyu presence continues but it is combined with Pucara. Formative Ware III is associated with Pucara. In Huaña, meanwhile, Ware I has one of its groups with Formative designs linked to Qaluyu and Pucara and the other only with Pucara. Huaña Ware II is associated with Tiwanaku, Qaluyu, and Pucara. Likewise, in the Altiplano, Ware I is associated with Huaña and the Collao and Huatasani styles, and Wares II and III are associated with Collao and Huatasani. Finally, Inca I is associated with Inca Collao and Inca Huatasani, and Inca II with the local styles Chucuito, Taraco, Pacajes, and the imitation Cuzco types Urqusuyu and Cuzco A and B. Inca Ware III dates to the Colonial period.

Therefore, based upon the presence, absence, or combination of these characteristics, we can differentiate styles that derive from each other, beginning with the earliest periods and ending with the Colonial period. We see gradual changes in the shapes of the vessels as well as the decoration.

Dating the Assemblage

At this point in the analysis, we can combine the number of the ware with the corresponding cultural period to simplify the name. Therefore, Formative Ware I will simply be labeled Formative I and Inca Ware III will be referred to as Inca III. This system offers a general label combining all the criteria used for each of the wares of our sample. Finally, and although this is not a result of the methodology itself, we strengthened the chronological attributions by incorporating some carbon dates from excavated materials in the northern Titicaca Basin as well as ethnohistorical data for the later periods. This allows us to propose a sequence of the analyzed material as seen in Table 2.8. These dates currently stand as the best approximation. They will be tested and refined with future research.

As one can see, the sample begins in the Middle Formative (Formative I) and is associated with the earlier Qaluyu styles and contexts that can be located approximately between 1300 and 750 BC. The Transitional Qaluyu/Pucara (Formative II) would be dated between 750 and 200 BC. The Pucara style or Upper Formative (Formative III) dates between 200 BC and AD 300.

Beyond this, the situation becomes quite complex. The Huaña phenomenon that we have identified is a local tradition that is detectable by at least late Pucara times and it continues up through Tiwanaku. We can provisionally date the initial emergence of Huaña around AD 100 while the Pucara style was contemporaneous and simultaneously flourishing.

We unfortunately have few carbon dates for the Tiwanaku occupation of the northern Titicaca region at this time. Dates from basal levels of the Tiwanaku occupation at a domestic section of Isla Estevez located to the southwest of the survey area indicate an initial settlement between AD 675 and 800.[5] Based on these and other sites in the Puno region, we conclude that Tiwanaku established enclaves around AD 750 to 900 in the Huancané. Huaña I therefore provisionally dates from AD 100 to 750.

The period between Pucara collapse, circa AD 300, and the first Tiwanaku control circa AD 750 was a time of political fragmentation and conflict. The pottery traditions reflect these new cultural circumstances and we see quite a bit of overlap, borrowing, and perhaps even population movements throughout this time.

Huaña II pottery types are contemporary with Tiwanaku in at least the earliest phases. These early Tiwanaku influences date to around AD 750 to 850, a period that we call Tiwanaku I and which of course overlaps with Huaña II. Significant Tiwanaku settlement was most likely well underway by AD 850 and continued up to about AD 950. Tiwanaku II would be this relatively short century-long period. Here we see a significant suppression of Huaña traditions until they reemerge in the post-Tiwanaku political landscape of the Altiplano or Late Intermediate period.

The Late Intermediate period in the northern Titicaca Basin is traditionally represented by the so-called Collao pottery. We can divide this period into three based upon the pottery: the first is associated with Collao and Huatasani, beginning around AD 950 and ending around AD 1275 or so. This period is referred to as Huaña/Altiplano or Altiplano I. The second phase of this period, Altiplano II, dates from AD 1275 to 1400. The third phase, circa AD 1400–1450 and known as Altiplano III, is characterized by the full development of the Aymara señoríos of the ethnohistoric texts.

The pottery is sufficiently sensitive to pick up the initial contact of the Aymara señoríos with the expanding Inca state (for a similar process, see Julien 1983). This Inca I period dates to the brief time from AD 1450 to the actual geopolitical control of the region by the Inca state circa AD 1500. It is associated with the styles Inca Collao and Inca Huatasani or Inca I. The presence of the Inca Empire is associated with local styles and imitation Inca (Inca II) that began around AD 1500 and continued to the Spanish Conquest a generation later in 1533. This Early Colonial period (Inca III) dates to around AD 1533–1600.

Discussion

While we feel very confident that the typology and chronology we offer in this chapter is a robust tool to understand the cultural remains of the northern Titicaca Basin, it also is a working chronological framework that will be tested with future research. Excavations and additional research will serve to refine this chronology and make it useful in as wide a region as possible.

Regarding raw material, it is very clear that three types of clay differentiated by their natural color—orange, red, and brown—were part of the ceramic manufacturing tradition early on, while the fourth—cream—was used in the later periods. Although we have not identified most of the clay sources, we believe that the cream colors are most certainly found in the Huatasani area in the Putina drainage. The dramatic shift from red to cream clays is clearly seen on the road from Huancané to Huatasani, where the landscape literally becomes a white background of kaolins in the pampas. Clay sources are very common in the altiplano. However, it appears that there were superior sources, such as those found at Huatasani, Pucara, Taraco, and other areas. The degree to which these were shared over space and time remains a subject of great interest for future research.

Within the large groups of clay colors, there exists substantial variation in the color of the vessel clays due to the nature of the firing techniques. This variation is common in all cultural periods. It is also important to point out that the sample includes many fragments that are burned or poorly fired. The quantity and dis-

---

5. AA53811 IE 258 charcoal; −21.9 0.8567 ± 0.0046 1243 ± 43
AD 676–882 95.4%
   AA53812 IE 302 charcoal; −22.6 0.8487 ± 0.0046 1317 ± 43
AD 641–802 95.4%

Table 2.8. Suggested absolute dates for types and ware.

Period	Chronology		Phase	Ceramic Type	Ware
Inca	AD	1700	Transition	Inca Colonial	Inca III
		1533			
			Initial	Inca Pacajes	Inca II
				Inca Chucuito	
				Inca Taraco	
				Inca Cuzco	
				Inca Collao	
				Inca Huatasani	
		1500	Transition	Collao	Inca I
				Huatasani	
Altiplano		1450	Initial	Collao	Altiplano III
				Huatasani	
		1400		Collao	Altiplano II
				Huatasani	
		1275	Transition	Huaña/Altiplano	Altiplano I
		1000			
Tiwanaku			Expansive	Tiwanaku	Tiwanaku II
					Tiwanaku I
		700	Initial	Huaña/Tiwanaku	Huaña II
		600	Transition		
		500		Huaña/Pucara	Huaña I
Formative	BCE	AD 300	Initial	Pucara	Formative III
		200 BCE			
		750	Transition	Qaluyu/Pucara	Formative II
		1300	Initial	Qaluyu	Formative I

tribution of these fragments suggest that this was not necessarily due to poor firing, but that the firing/burning was intentional.

The technological criteria not only refers to quantities that reflect the variable quality of the clays and tempers used by the potters, but may also reflect the quantity of pottery workshops seen in the Formative and Altiplano periods (when we see the greatest number of pastes). In other words, for these periods, we can hypothesize that there were many decentralized workshops and that the groups of pastes could represent regional relationships between them.

In the wares, one sees again that the changes in the quality of the paste composition indicate continuity in the use of clays and tempers. The clay sources were probably shared. Changing the quality of a ware and using design motifs that link them to an earlier group or adopting new patterns may allow us to define the means by which these workshops differentiated themselves. Eventually, we may be able to demonstrate the form in which these entities were productively organized, moving from a domestic level of organization to that of a hierarchy or some kind of elite- or state-directed production.

The results from the analysis show us that all wares in all periods contained all types of vessels. This also indicates that potters in all periods had the capacity to make all types of ritual and ornamental vessels.

Regarding the decorative styles, we can say that Formative I incised decoration is related to Qaluyu brown, or black and cream over red. Formative II combines stylistic designs, such as Qaluyu and Pucara. Formative III has strong stylistic links to Pucara, particularly with regard to incised and/or painted on red, black, cream and white. The typical forms are tazones and bowls with an interior bevel that is seen in all ware types.

On the other hand, Huaña I combines the stylistic designs already described for Qaluyu and Pucara; they are not very abundant. They are the typical form for the bowls or tazones with a tripod base. Huaña II, while maintaining Qaluyu and Pucara elements, incorporates some Tiwanaku elements as well.

Tiwanaku I and II are similar in terms of black and/or white over red and/or orange and polychromes, undulating perpendicular lines, and step-fret patterns. The most common shape is the tazón and the kero.

Altiplano I has some of the Tiwanaku shapes, most notably keros, but not all the stylistic elements continue. The motifs that appear in Collao and Huatasani are new. The cream-colored clays appear in Altiplano II and continue to the Inca. An exclusive form is perhaps the taza and tazones with a "comma-shaped" rim.

Finally, one can recognize two great traditions in the Inca period. The first includes types such as Sillustani, Chucuito, Taraco, and Pacajes that correspond more or less to a regional tradition that imitates Inca patterns. A second tradition is similar to the Cuzco types such as Urcusuyu and Cuzco A and B that have Inca stylistic patterns although they are locally manufactured. The presence of Inca control in Inca I is indicated by the gradual adoption of state iconography with some local modifications. For Inca II, the consolidation of Inca state presence is seen in the imposition of its iconographic patterns, including the introduction of new vessel forms. These shapes include plates and bowls with beveled interior rims. The earlier tazón form with Huatasani and Collao decoration, in contrast, endures. The Inca III, during the early Colonial period, witnesses the progressive disappearance of motifs and color combinations typical of the Inca time, and a return to the forms and designs typical of the Altiplano wares. Changes in the shapes of the vessels likewise indicate the new political and cultural regime of the Spanish period.

In sum, the general conclusions of this study and the use of the methods described above indicate that while the clay sources were similar throughout the sequence, there were many changes that were introduced over time in two key areas: technology (firing, slips, etc.) and style.

Summary of the Periods

Formative

The individual pastes produced in this period are all local. Throughout the Formative, the manufacturing quality slowly improves.

There are no pastes that are exclusively dedicated to the production of finewares. That is to say, there does not appear to be any centralized control of the raw materials or of the production.

The commonly assumed difference between Qaluyu and Pucara incisions—that wide ones are Qaluyu and thin ones are Pucara—is not so evident in our sample. There are pastes that have Qaluyu designs that were also used in classic Pucara incensarios with feline motifs.

The production of finewares or "ritual" assemblages is not common. Each ware has examples of fineware vessels.

Likewise we have little to no evidence of foreign vessels. Virtually all finewares are locally produced.

The analyzed sample shows Qaluyu as the dominant style in Formative I, Pucara in Formative III, and a moment when there was a mixing of elements of both styles in Formative II.

There is a final phase, both contemporary and later than Pucara, that is associated with Early Huaña or Huaña I.

Huaña

The case of Huaña deserves special mention. Lumbreras and Amat (1968) suggested that there was a "hiatus" between the collapse of Pucara and the direct presence of the Late Intermediate period or Altiplano period, as is used here. In a later publication with more survey data to draw on, Stanish (2003:159) proposed the term "Huaña" for local populations that coexisted with the late Upper Formative (Pucara) and the first centuries of the Tiwanaku occupation. In the case of early Huaña, which coexisted with Pucara, he suggested that there was a noticeable lack of decorated pottery associated with the noncentralized structure of the political system. The challenge was to test whether such a Huaña pottery assemblage existed and, if so, describe it with the method used here.

In the first case, the sample indicates the existence of this group. Our analysis likewise indicates that Huaña pastes continued into the initial Altiplano period. Huaña I is here divided into two wares, with both open and closed vessels, both plainwares and decorated ones. One of its wares is more related to Pucara, the other to Qaluyu. Forms show some differences from the earlier assemblages.

Hypothetically, I believe that Huaña is a group that was developed during the Middle Formative and continued in the Upper Formative and Tiwanaku, up to the beginnings of the Altiplano period. It was one of the antecedents of Altiplano period Aymara señoríos that the Inca encountered in the region known as the Lupaqa to the west and the Colla to the north. The stratigraphic sequence and ceramic analysis of the materials from recent excavations at the site of Taraco support this reconstruction as well.

Tiwanaku

For Tiwanaku, a principal point is that the distribution of the elite ceramics is outside the political centers. This represents a radical change compared to the Upper Formative in the northern basin. Furthermore, in the Tiwanaku period for the first time we see that these fineware ceramic styles were all derived from a single area, the southern Titicaca Basin. In this case, of course, that area was the Tiwanaku Valley. No other area in the entire region developed "distinctive styles," and all fineware pottery was based upon Tiwanaku canons.

This Tiwanaku assemblage is recognized for its forms and distinctive motifs on keros, tazones, and incensarios, manufactured principally in local pastes although some examples of imported pastes do exist. A major question remains about the coexistence of imported and local finewares, the latter of course imitating Tiwanaku patterns. The sample provides for two distinct wares (I and II) in this period, all made in local pastes.

Altiplano

The Altiplano period that developed after the fall of Tiwanaku is characterized by the development of numerous autonomous entities known as "local señoríos." These polities were composed of kin-based moiety divisions of *ayllus* under chiefs. The diversity in the ceramic assemblage reflects this political scenario in the area occupied by these señoríos. Also, the ceramic manufacture and decoration were much less carefully executed than during preceding periods, indicating a shift away from pottery as an important cultural medium. The most typical vessel forms are *vasos* (glasses) and pitchers that are divided into domestic and ritual.

A point of major interest in the literature centers on the definition of chronological phases during this period, a time characterized by conflict after the fall of Tiwanaku, and expressed in settlement pattern changes. People relocated to the base of high hills and built the famous pukaras that dot the post-Tiwanaku landscape of the northern Titicaca region. Ceramic styles associated with this period include Sillustani, Collao, and Allita Amaya in the north, and Tanka Tanka and Pucarani in the west and south. Based upon work in the Juli-Pomata area, we know that the pukaras were contemporary with lowland, non-defended sites along the sides of the walled settlements as well as in the pampa.

For this timespan, therefore, the analysis produced two distinct periods: (1) one immediately following the collapse of the Tiwanaku state, and (2) one when the Aymara señoríos emerged as distinct, recognizable entities with some degree of centralization (Stanish et al. 1997).

These two phases are recognized by the existence of three wares:

(1) An early one associated with Huaña and referred to as Altiplano I. Here, we see the slow change in the quality and manufacture of the pottery that, while having some similarities to the Tiwanaku tradition in forms such as vasos, does not have the decorative motifs of this earlier state tradition.

(2) An Altiplano II ware that represents groups at the height of inter-ethnic conflict, characterized by an assemblage of both open and closed vessels, and differentiated by new forms such as plates and tazones. We also see the introduction of a new cream clay source.

(3) Altiplano III represents the full establishment of the señoríos encountered by the Inca. This ware reflects the continuity of the Altiplano II elements with some subtle changes.

Inca

Finally, the Inca period represents the reimposition of a centralized political entity in the region after the Altiplano period. The incorporation of Collasuyu is known from numerous historical and archaeological references (see Chapter 1). This incorporation process is reflected in the Inca I wares in which, little by little, canons of Inca style were incorporated into the Altiplano period assemblage. Inca II produced local styles alongside Cuzco ones made in local pastes as well as the wholesale adoption of Inca forms such as aryballoids, bowls, and beveled plates. Finally, Inca III represents the period in which Inca influence gave way to Spanish power. The local groups returned to their stylistic patterns before Inca conquest and simultaneously adopted the new forms and designs of the Spanish regime.

PASTE ANALYSIS

Formative

Paste 1
Color: 5YR5/4 [light brown] (see Fig. 2.1).
Temper:
    White inclusions, subrounded, 1.0 mm, regular, abundant.
    Cross section: Regular. Semi-compact. Smooth. Fine.
Firing: Oxidized [j II] (see Fig. 2.2).
Finish: Wiped, burnished (see Figs. 2.3, 2.4).

Paste 2
Color: 2.5YR5/6 [light orange].
Temper:
    White inclusions, subrounded, 0.5 mm, regular, abundant.
    Gold mica inclusions, laminate, to 1.0 mm, regular, scarce.
    Cut: Exterior-interior (only mica). Regular. Semi-compact. Smooth. Fine.
Firing: Oxidized [a VI].
Finish: Wiped, burnished, polished.

Paste 3
Color: 2.5YR5/6 [light orange].
Temper:
    White inclusions, subrounded, to 1.0 mm, regular, abundant.
    Gold mica inclusions, laminate, 0.1 to 1.0 mm, regular, very scarce.
    Cross section: Exterior-interior (only mica). Regular. Semi-compact. Smooth. Fine.
Firing: Oxidized [a VI].
Finish: Wiped, burnished.

Paste 4
Color: 5YR5/4 [light brown].
Temper:
    White inclusions, subrounded, 0.5 mm, regular, abundant.
    Cross section: Regular. Semi-compact. Smooth. Fine.
Firing: Oxidized [a II].
Finish: Wiped, burnished, polished.

Paste 5
Color: 5YR5/4 [light brown].
Temper:
    White inclusions, subangular, 0.5 mm, regular, abundant.
    Cross section: Regular. Semi-compact. Smooth. Fine.
Firing: Oxidized [a II].
Finish: Wiped, burnished.

Paste 6
Color: 2.5YR5/4 [reddish brown].
Temper:
    White inclusions, subrounded, 0.5 mm, regular, abundant.
    Gold mica inclusions, laminate, 0.1 mm, regular, scarce.
    Black inclusions, subangular, 2.0 mm, irregular, scarce.
    Cross section: Exterior-interior (only mica). Regular. Semi-compact. Smooth. Fine.
Firing: Oxidized [a VII].
Finish: Wiped, burnished.

Paste 7
Color: 2.5YR5/6 [light orange].
Temper:
    Gold mica inclusions, laminate, 0.1 mm, irregular, very scarce.
    Black inclusions, subangular, 0.5 mm, irregular, medium.
    Cross section (interior mica only): Regular. Semi-compact. Smooth. Fine.
Firing: Oxidized [a VI].
Finish: Wiped, burnished.

Paste 8
Color: 2.5YR5/6 [light orange].
Temper:
    White inclusions, subrounded, 0.5 mm, regular, medium.
    Black inclusions, subangular, 0.5 mm, irregular, medium.
    Purplish inclusions, subangular, 0.5 mm, regular, medium.
    Ocher-colored inclusions, subangular, 0.5 mm, irregular, scarce.
    Gold mica inclusions, laminate, 0.1 mm, regular, scarce.
    Cross section (mica exterior-interior): Regular. Semi-compact. Smooth. Fine.
Firing: Oxidized [d VI].
Finish: Wiped, burnished.

Paste 9
Color: 5YR5/4 [light brown].
Temper:
    White inclusions, subrounded, 0.5 mm, regular, abundant.
    Gold mica inclusions, laminate, 0.1 mm, regular, scarce.
    Pink inclusions, subrounded, 0.4 mm, regular, medium.
    Cross section: Exterior-interior (only mica). Regular. Semi-compact. Smooth. Fine.
Firing: Oxidized [a II].
Finish: Wiped, burnished.

Paste 10
Color: 2.5YR5/6 [light orange].
Temper:
    White inclusions, subrounded, 0.5 mm, regular, abundant.
    Gold mica inclusions, laminate, 0.5 mm, regular, scarce.
    Black inclusions, subrounded, 0.5 mm, regular, scarce.
    Cross section: Exterior-interior (only mica). Regular. Semi-compact. Smooth. Fine.
Firing: Oxidized [d VI].
Finish: Wiped, burnished.

Paste 11
Color: 2.5YR5/6 [light orange].
Temper:
    White inclusions, subrounded, 0.1 mm, regular, medium.
    Gold mica inclusions, laminate, 0.1 mm, regular, scarce.
    Cross section (mica exterior-interior): Regular. Semi-compact. Smooth. Fine.
Firing: Oxidized [d VI].
Finish: Wiped, burnished.

RED	CLEAR RED	DARK RED	REDDISH BROWN	BROWN	CLEAR BROWN	DARK BROWN	BLACK
			2.5YR4/3		2.5Y5/2	2.5YR3/3	2.5YR2.5/1
			2.5YR4/4		2.5Y6/2	2.5YR3/4	2.5YR2.5/2
			2.5YR4/6		2.5Y6/3		
			2.5YR5/2		2.5Y7/6		
			2.5YR5/3		2.5YR4/2		
			2.5YR5/4				
		5YR5/2		5YR3/4	5YR5/2	5YR3/2	5YR2.5/1
				5YR4/1	5YR5/3	5YR3/3	5YR2.5/2
				5YR4/2	5YR5/4		5YR3/1
				5YR4/3	5YR5/6		
				5YR4/4			
				5YR4/6			
7.5R3/8	7.5R4/2	7.5R2.5/4		7.5YR4/3	7.5YR4/2	7.5YR3/2	7.5YR2.5/1
7.5R4/8	7.5R4/3	7.5R3/2		7.5YR4/4	7.5YR5/1	7.5YR3/3	
7.5R5/8	7.5R4/4	7.5R3/3		7.5YR4/6	7.5YR5/2	7.5YR3/4	
	7.5R4/6	7.5R3/4		7.5YR5/6	7.5YR5/3		
		7.5R3/6			7.5YR5/4		
					7.5YR6/2		
					7.5YR6/3		
					7.5YR6/4		
10R4/6	10R3/3	10R3/2			10YR4/2	10YR3/2	10YR2/1
10R5/4	10R3/4	10R3/6			10YR4/3		10YR3/1
10R5/6	10R4/2	10R4/3			10YR4/4		
10R6/6	10R4/4				10YR5/2		
10R6/8					10YR5/3		
					10YR5/4		
					10YR5/6		
					10YR6/2		
					10YR6/3		
					10YR6/4		
					10YR6/6		

ORANGE	CLEAR ORANGE	DARK ORANGE	CREAM	ORANGE CREAM	YELLOW CREAM	GRAY	WHITE
	2.5YR5/8	2.5YR7/4	2.5Y7/1	2.5YR7/4	2.5Y6/4	2.5YR3/1	2.5Y8/1
	2.5YR6/3	2.5YR6/6	2.5Y7/3	2.5YR7/6	2.5Y7/2	2.5YR4/1	2.5YR8/2
	2.5YR6/4	2.5YR6/8			2.5Y7/3		
					2.5Y7/4		
					2.5Y8/3		
					2.5Y8/4		
5YR6/8	5YR6/3	5YR5/8		5YR8/3		5YR5/1	5Y8/1
	5YR6/4			5YR8/4			5Y8/3
	5YR6/6						5YR7/1
	5YR7/4						5YR7/3
	5YR7/6						5YR8/1
	5YR7/8						
	7.5YR5/8			7.5YR8/4	7.5YR8/3	7.5R3/1	7.5YR8/1
	7.5YR6/6			7.5YR8/6		7.5YR2.5/1	
	7.5YR6/8			7.5YR8/8		7.5YR4/1	
	7.5YR7/3						
	7.5YR7/4						
	7.5YR7/6						
10R5/8		10R4/8	10YR7/2		10YR7/6	10YR4/1	10YR7/1
			10YR7/3		10YR8/6	10YR5/1	10YR8/1
			10YR7/4		10YR8/8	10YR5/2	10YR8/2
			10YR8/3			10YR6/1	
			10YR8/4				

Figure 2.1. Ceramic color key.

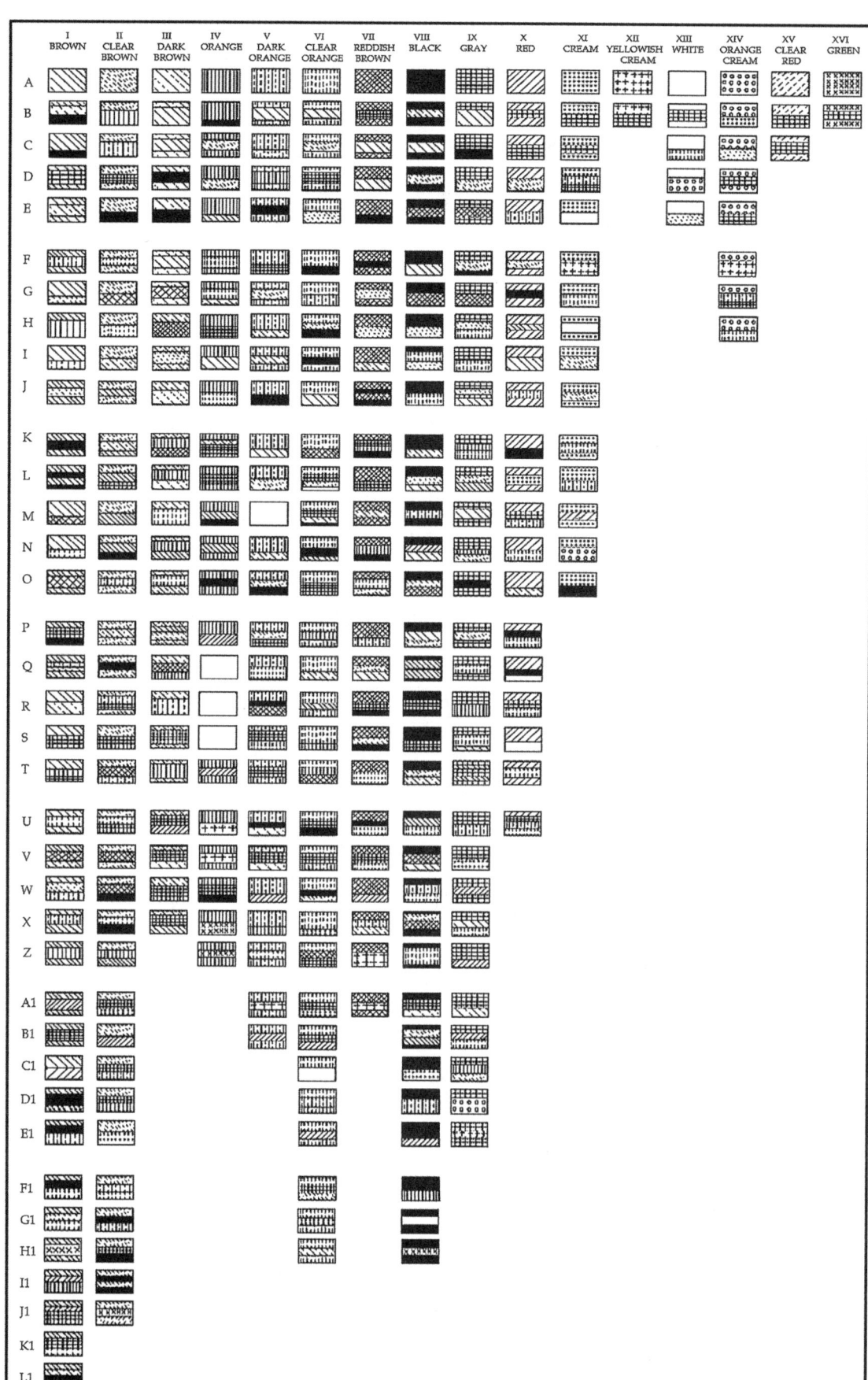

Figure 2.2. Firing color key.

Surface Treatment Key				
Wipe		**Burnish**		**Polished**
A1 Horizontal–Medium		B1 Horizontal–Medium		P1 Complete
A2 Horizontal–Fine		B2 Horizontal–Fine		
A3 Diagonal–Medium		B3 Horizontal–Very Fine		
A4 Diagonal–Fine		B4 Horizontal–Thick		**Not Visible**
A5 Horizontal–Thick		B5 Vertical–Medium		T Rough or "toscos"
A6 Mixed–Fine		B6 Diagonal–Medium		D Deteriorated
A7 Circular–Fine		B7 Vertical–Thick		E Eroded
A8 Without marks		B8 Diagonal–Thick		Q Burned "quemados"
A9 Mixed thick		B9 Vertical–Fine		
		B10 Mixed		
		B11 Circular–Medium		
		B12 Mixed–Medium		

Figure 2.3. Surface treatment key.

1.1. Color
1.2. Temper
    Color
    Form—subrounded, rounded, angular, subangular
    Size expressed in millimeters (mm)
    Distribution—regular, irregular
    Density—scarce, medium, abundant, very abundant
    Visibility—interior, exterior, cut
    Fracture—regular, irregular
    Compaction—compact, semi-compact
    Hardness—soft, semi-soft, semi-hard, hard
    Texture—fine, medium, thick, very thick
1.3. Firing
    Oxidized—orange, brown, reddish brown, cream
    Reduced—dark brown, gray, black
1.4. Surface treatment
    Technique—wiped/smoothed, burnished, polished

Figure 2.4. Paste description key.

Paste 12
Color: 2.5YR5/6 [light orange].
Temper:
    White inclusions, subangular, 0.1 mm, regular, scarce.
    Black inclusions, subangular, 0.1 mm, regular, medium.
    Gold mica inclusions, laminate, 0.1 mm, irregular, scarce.
    Cross section: Exterior-interior (mica). Regular. Semi-compact. Smooth. Fine.
Firing: Oxidized [i VI].
Finish: Wiped, burnished, polished.

Paste 13
Color: 2.5YR5/6 [light orange].
Temper:
    White inclusions, subangular, 0.1 mm, regular, scarce.
    Black inclusions, subangular, 0.1 mm, regular, abundant.
    Gold mica inclusions, laminate, 0.1 mm, irregular, scarce.
    Cross section: Exterior-interior (only mica). Regular. Semi-compact. Smooth. Fine.
Firing: Oxidized [a VI].
Finish: Wiped, burnished, polished.

Paste 14
Color: 2.5YR5/6 [light orange].
Temper:
    White inclusions, subangular, 0.1 mm, regular, abundant.
    Black inclusions, subangular, 0.1 mm, irregular, scarce.
    Gold mica inclusions, laminate, 0.1 mm, irregular, scarce.
    Cross section: Exterior-interior (only mica). Regular. Semi-compact. Smooth. Fine.
Firing: Oxidized [l VI].
Finish: Wiped, burnished.

Paste 15
Color: 2.5YR5/6 [light orange].
Temper:
    Gold mica inclusions, laminate, 0.1 mm, irregular, medium.
    Black inclusions, subangular, 0.1 mm, regular, abundant.
    Cross section: Exterior-interior (only mica). Regular. Semi-compact. Smooth. Fine.
Firing: Oxidized [e VI].
Finish: Wiped, burnished.

Paste 16
Color: 2.5YR5/6 [light orange].
Temper:
    White inclusions, subrounded, 0.1 mm, regular, abundant.
    Gold mica inclusions, laminate, 0.1 mm, irregular, scarce.
    Cross section: Exterior-interior (only mica). Regular. Semi-compact. Smooth. Fine.
Firing: Oxidized [a VI].
Finish: Wiped, burnished.

Paste 19
Color: 10R5/6 [red].
Temper:
    Gold mica inclusions, laminate, 0.1 mm, irregular, very scarce.
    White inclusions, subrounded, 0.5 mm, regular, medium.
    Translucent inclusions, subrounded, 0.1 mm, regular, abundant.
    Ocher-colored inclusions, subrounded, to 3.0 mm, irregular, scarce.
    Cross section: Exterior-interior (only mica). Regular. Semi-compact. Smooth. Fine.
Firing: Oxidized [a X].
Finish: Wiped, burnished.

Paste 20
Color: 10R5/6 [red].
Temper:
    White inclusions, subrounded, 0.1 mm, regular, scarce.
    Black inclusions, subangular, 0.1 mm, irregular, very scarce.
    Gold mica inclusions, laminate, 0.1 mm, irregular, very scarce.
    Cross section: Exterior-interior (mica). Regular. Semi-compact. Smooth. Fine.
Firing: Oxidized [s VI].
Finish: Wiped, burnished.

Paste 21
Color: 10R5/6 [red].
Temper:
    Not visible.
    Gold mica inclusions, laminate, 0.1 mm, irregular, very scarce.
    Cross section: Exterior-interior (mica). Regular. Semi-compact. Smooth. Fine.
Firing: Oxidized [g X].
Finish: Wiped, burnished.

Paste 23
Color: 2.5YR4/6 [reddish brown].
Temper:
    White inclusions, subrounded, 0.1 mm, regular, abundant.
    Gold mica inclusions, laminate, 0.1 mm, regular, medium.
    Cross section: Exterior-interior (only mica). Regular. Semi-compact. Smooth. Fine.
Firing: Oxidized [a VII].
Finish: Wiped, burnished, polished.

Paste 24
Color: 2.5YR4/6 [reddish brown].
Temper:
    White inclusions, subrounded, 0.5 mm, regular, abundant.
    Cross section: Exterior-interior (only mica). Regular. Semi-compact. Smooth. Fine.
Firing: Oxidized [b VII].
Finish: Wiped, burnished.

Paste 25
Color: 2.5YR4/6 [reddish brown].
Temper:
    White inclusions, subrounded, to 1.0 mm, regular, abundant.
    Gold mica inclusions, laminate, 0.1 mm, regular, medium.
    Cross section: Exterior-interior (only mica). Regular. Semi-compact. Smooth. Fine.
Firing: Oxidized [a VII].
Finish: Wiped, burnished.

Paste 26
Color: 10YR6/3 [light brown].
Temper:
    White inclusions, subangular, to 1.0 mm, regular, abundant.
    Gold mica inclusions, laminate, 0.1 mm, regular, medium.
    Translucent inclusions, subangular, to 1.0 mm, regular, medium.
    Cross section: Exterior-interior (only mica). Regular. Semi-compact. Smooth. Medium.
Firing: Oxidized [e II].
Finish: Wiped, burnished.

Paste 27
Color: 5YR5/4 [light brown].
Temper:
    White inclusions, subangular, 0.5 mm, regular, abundant.
    Cross section: Regular. Semi-compact. Smooth. Medium.
Firing: Oxidized [a II].
Finish: Wiped, burnished.

Paste 28
Color: 7.5YR5/3 [light brown].
Temper:
    White inclusions, subrounded, 0.1 mm, regular, medium.
    Black inclusions, subrounded, 0.1 mm, regular, medium.
    Cross section: Regular. Semi-compact. Smooth. Medium.
Firing: Oxidized [d II].
Finish: Wiped, burnished.

Paste 33
Color: 7.5YR5/4 [light brown].
Temper:
    Translucent inclusions, subrounded, 0.1 mm, regular, medium.
    Gold mica inclusions, laminate, 0.1 mm, regular, scarce.
    Cross section: Exterior-interior (only mica). Regular. Semi-compact. Smooth. Fine.
Firing: Oxidized [a II].
Finish: Wiped, burnished.

Paste 34
Color: 7.5YR5/4 [light brown].
Temper:
    White inclusions, subrounded, to 1.0 mm, regular, scarce.
    Black inclusions, subrounded, 0.1 mm, regular, scarce.
    Gold mica inclusions, laminate, 0.1 mm, regular, scarce.
    Cross section: Exterior-interior (only mica). Regular. Semi-compact. Smooth. Fine.
Firing: Oxidized [a II].
Finish: Wiped, burnished.

Paste 35
Color: 7.5YR5/4 [light brown].
Temper:
    White inclusions, subrounded, 0.05 mm, regular, medium.
    Black inclusions, subrounded, 0.05 mm, regular, medium.
    Cross section: Regular. Semi-compact. Smooth. Fine.
Firing: Oxidized [a II].
Finish: Wiped, burnished.

Paste 36
Color: 5YR6/6 [light orange].
Temper:
    White inclusions, subrounded, 0.01 mm, regular, medium.
    Black inclusions, subrounded, 0.05 mm, regular, scarce.
    Gold mica inclusions, laminate, 0.1 mm, regular, scarce.
    Cross section: Regular. Semi-compact. Smooth. Fine.
Firing: Oxidized [a VI].
Finish: Wiped, burnished.

Paste 37
Color: 5YR5/4 [light brown].
Temper:
    Translucent inclusions, subrounded, 0.1 mm, regular, medium.
    Black inclusions, subrounded, 0.1 mm, regular, medium.
    Cross section: Regular. Semi-compact. Smooth. Medium.
Firing: Oxidized [h II].
Finish: Wiped, burnished.

Paste 38
Color: 5YR5/4 [light brown].
Temper:
    Gray inclusions, angular, to 1.0 mm, regular, abundant.
    Gold mica inclusions, laminate, 0.1 mm, regular, medium.
    Cross section: Exterior-interior (only mica). Regular. Semi-compact. Smooth. Medium.
Firing: Oxidized [a II].
Finish: Wiped, burnished.

Paste 39
Color: 5YR5/4 [light brown].
Temper:
    Gray inclusions, angular, 1.0 mm, regular, abundant.
    Purplish inclusions, angular, 1.0 mm, regular, medium.
    Cross section: Exterior-interior (only mica). Regular. Semi-compact. Smooth. Medium.
Firing: Oxidized [d II].
Finish: Wiped, burnished.

Paste 40
Color: 5YR5/4 [light brown].
Temper:
    Purplish inclusions, angular, 1.0 mm, regular, abundant.
    Cross section: Regular. Semi-compact. Smooth. Medium.
Firing: Oxidized [l II].
Finish: Wiped, burnished.

Paste 41
Color: 5YR5/4 [light brown].
Temper:
    Pink inclusions, subangular, to 1.0 mm, regular, abundant.
    Gold mica inclusions, laminate, 0.1 mm, regular, medium.
    Translucent inclusions, subangular, 0.5 mm, regular, medium.
    Cross section: Exterior-interior (only mica). Regular. Semi-compact. Smooth. Medium.
Firing: Oxidized [a II].
Finish: Wiped, burnished, polished.

Paste 42
Color: 2.5YR5/6 [light orange].
Temper:
    Pink inclusions, subangular, to 1.0 mm, regular, abundant.
    Gold mica inclusions, laminate, 0.1 mm, regular, very abundant.
    Black inclusions, subangular, 0.5 mm, irregular, scarce.
    Cross section: Exterior-interior (only mica). Regular. Semi-compact. Smooth. Medium.
Firing: Oxidized [a VI].
Finish: Wiped, burnished.

Paste 43
Color: 2.5YR5/4 [reddish brown].
Temper:
    Gray inclusions, subangular, 0.1 mm, regular, abundant.
    Gold mica inclusions, laminate, 0.1 mm, regular, abundant.
    Cross section: Exterior-interior (only mica). Regular. Semi-compact. Smooth. Fine.
Firing: Oxidized [a VII].
Finish: Wiped, burnished.

Paste 44
Color: 2.5YR5/4 [reddish brown].
Temper:
    Purplish inclusions, angular, 0.1 mm, regular, abundant.
    Cross section: Exterior-interior (only mica). Regular. Semi-compact. Smooth. Fine.
Firing: Oxidized [a VII].
Finish: Wiped, burnished.

Paste 45
Color: 2.5YR5/4 [reddish brown].
Temper:
    Gray inclusions, subangular, 0.1 mm, regular, abundant.
    Gold mica inclusions, laminate, 0.1 mm, regular, abundant.
    Cross section: Exterior-interior (only mica). Regular. Semi-compact. Smooth. Fine.
Firing: Oxidized [a VII].
Finish: Wiped, burnished.

Paste 46
Color: 5YR4/4 [brown].
Temper:
    Gold mica inclusions, laminate, 0.8 mm, regular, medium.
    Black inclusions, subangular, 0.5 mm, regular, scarce.
    Translucent inclusions, subrounded, to 1.0 mm, regular, abundant.
    Cross section: Exterior-interior (only mica). Regular. Semi-compact. Smooth. Fine.
Firing: Oxidized [a I].
Finish: Wiped, burnished.

Paste 47
Color: 7.5YR4/3 [brown].
Temper:
    Gold mica inclusions, laminate, 0.1 mm, regular, scarce.
    White inclusions, subrounded, 0.1 mm, regular, abundant.
    Black inclusions, subangular, 0.1 mm, regular, medium.
    Cross section: Exterior-interior (only mica). Regular. Semi-compact. Smooth. Fine.
Firing: Oxidized [a I].
Finish: Wiped, burnished, polished.

Paste 48
Color: 5YR4/4 [brown].
Temper:
    Gold mica inclusions, laminate, 0.1 mm, regular, abundant.
    White inclusions, subrounded, 0.1 mm, regular, abundant.
    Cross section: Exterior-interior (only mica). Regular. Semi-compact. Smooth. Fine.
Firing: Oxidized [a I].
Finish: Wiped, burnished.

Paste 49
Color: 2.5YR5/6 [light orange].
Temper:
    Gold mica inclusions, laminate, 0.1 mm, regular, medium.
    White inclusions, subrounded, 0.1 mm, regular, abundant.
    Cross section: (Mica exterior-interior.) Regular. Semi-compact. Smooth. Fine.
Firing: Oxidized [d VI].
Finish: Wiped, burnished.

Paste 50
Color: 2.5YR5/6 [light orange].
Temper:
    White inclusions, subrounded, 0.5 mm, regular, medium.
    Pink inclusions, angular, 0.5 mm, regular, scarce.
    Cross section: Regular. Semi-compact. Smooth. Fine.
Firing: Oxidized [a VI].
Finish: Wiped, burnished.

Paste 51
Color: 2.5YR4/6 [reddish brown].
Temper:
    White inclusions, subrounded, 0.1 mm, regular, abundant.
    Black inclusions, subrounded, 0.1 mm, regular, abundant.
    Cross section: Regular. Semi-compact. Smooth. Fine.
Firing: Oxidized [a VII].
Finish: Wiped, burnished.

Paste 52
Color: 2.5YR5/6 [light orange].
Temper:
    White inclusions, subrounded, 0.5 mm, regular, abundant.
    Cross section: Regular. Semi-compact. Smooth. Fine.
Firing: Oxidized [a VI].
Finish: Wiped, burnished.

Huaña

Paste 1
Color: 2.5YR5/6 [light orange].
Temper:
    White inclusions, subrounded, 0.05 mm, regular, abundant.
    Cross section: Regular. Semi-compact. Smooth. Fine.
Firing: Oxidized [a VI].
Finish: Wiped.

Paste 2
Color: 5YR5/4 [light brown].
Temper:
    Translucent inclusions, subrounded, 0.05 mm, regular, medium.
    Black inclusions, subrounded, 0.05 mm, regular, medium.
    Cross section: Regular. Semi-compact. Smooth. Fine.
Firing: Oxidized [a II].
Finish: Wiped.

Paste 3
Color: 5YR6/6 [light orange].
Temper:
    White inclusions, subangular, 0.1 mm, regular, medium.
    Translucent inclusions, subrounded, 0.05 mm, regular, medium.
    Black inclusions, subrounded, 0.05 mm, regular, scarce.
    Cross section: Regular. Semi-compact. Smooth. Fine.
Firing: Oxidized [b VI].
Finish: Wiped, burnished.

Paste 4
Color: 5YR6/6 [light orange].
Temper:
    White inclusions, subrounded, 0.1 mm, regular, medium.
    Black inclusions, subrounded, 0.1 mm, irregular, scarce.
    Gold mica inclusions, laminate, 2.0 mm, regular, scarce.
    Cross section: (Exterior-interior mica.) Regular. Semi-compact. Smooth. Fine.
Firing: Oxidized [a VI].
Finish: Wiped.

Paste 5
Color: 2.5YR5/6 [light orange].
Temper:
    White inclusions, subrounded, 0.05 mm, regular, abundant.
    Translucent inclusions, subrounded, 0.05 mm, regular, abundant.
    Gold mica inclusions, laminate, 0.1 mm, regular, scarce.
    Cross section: (Exterior-interior mica.) Regular. Semi-compact. Smooth. Fine.
Firing: Oxidized [a VI].
Finish: Wiped, polished.

Paste 6
Color: 5YR6/4 [light orange].
Temper:
    White inclusions, subangular, 0.05 mm, regular, scarce.
    Black inclusions, subangular, 0.05 mm, irregular, scarce.
    Ocher-colored inclusions, subrounded, 0.05 mm, irregular, scarce.
    Cross section: Regular. Semi-compact. Smooth. Fine.
Firing: Oxidized [a VI].
Finish: Wiped.

Paste 7
Color: 7.5YR5/4 [reddish brown].
Temper:
    White inclusions, subrounded, 0.05 mm, regular, scarce.
    Purplish inclusions, subangular, 0.1 mm, regular, scarce.
    Ocher-colored inclusions, subrounded, 0.05 mm, regular, scarce.
    Gold mica inclusions, laminate, 0.1 mm, irregular, very scarce.
    Cross section: (Exterior-interior mica.) Regular. Semi-compact. Smooth. Fine.
Firing: Oxidized [a VII].
Finish: Wiped, burnished.

Paste 8
Color: 5YR6/4 [light orange].
Temper:
    White inclusions, subangular, 0.05 mm, irregular, scarce.
    Black inclusions, subangular, 0.05 mm, irregular, scarce.
    Cross section: Regular. Semi-compact. Smooth. Fine.
Firing: Oxidized [a VI].
Finish: Burnished.

Paste 9
Color: 5YR5/4 [light brown].
Temper:
    White inclusions, subrounded, 0.1 mm, regular, abundant.
    Black inclusions, subrounded, 0.05 mm, regular, abundant.
    Cross section: Regular. Semi-compact. Smooth. Fine.
Firing: Oxidized [a II].
Finish: Wiped.

Paste 10
Color: 2.5YR6/8 [dark orange].
Temper:
    White inclusions, subrounded, 0.05 mm, regular, scarce.
    Purplish inclusions, subrounded, 0.05 mm, regular, scarce.
    Black inclusions, subrounded, 0.05 mm, irregular, scarce.
    Cross section: Regular. Semi-compact. Smooth. Fine.
Firing: Oxidized [s V].
Finish: Wiped, burnished.

Paste 11
Color: 2.5YR5/6 [light orange].
Temper:
    White inclusions, subrounded, 0.1 mm, regular, scarce.
    Translucent inclusions, subangular, 0.1 mm, irregular, scarce.
    Purplish inclusions, subangular, 0.1 mm, regular, medium.
    Cross section: Regular. Semi-compact. Smooth. Fine.
Firing: Oxidized [i VI].
Finish: Wiped, burnished.

Paste 12
Color: 5YR5/4 [light brown].
Temper:
    White inclusions, subrounded, 0.05 mm, regular, medium.
    Gold mica inclusions, laminate, 0.05 mm, irregular, very scarce.
    Cross section: (Exterior-interior mica.) Regular. Semi-compact. Smooth. Fine.
Firing: Oxidized [a II].
Finish: Wiped, burnished.

Paste 13
Color: 5YR6/4 [light orange].
Temper:
    White inclusions, subangular, 0.1 mm, regular, scarce.
    Purplish inclusions, subangular, 0.1 mm, regular, scarce.
    Gold mica inclusions, laminate, 0.1 mm, regular, medium.
    Cross section: (Exterior-interior mica.) Regular. Semi-compact. Smooth. Fine.
Firing: Oxidized [a VI].
Finish: Wiped, burnished.

Paste 14
Color: 7.5YR5/4 [reddish brown].
Temper:
    Black inclusions, subangular, 0.1 mm, regular, medium.
    White inclusions, subrounded, 0.1 mm, regular, medium.
    Ocher-colored inclusions, subrounded, 2.0 mm, regular, scarce.
    Gold mica inclusions, laminate, 0.1 mm, regular, medium.
    Cross section: Exterior-interior (mica). Regular. Semi-compact. Smooth. Fine.
Firing: Oxidized [a VII].
Finish: Wiped, burnished.

Paste 15
Color: 2.5YR5/4 [reddish brown].
Temper:
    Translucent inclusions, subrounded, 0.1 mm, regular, scarce.
    Cross section: Regular. Semi-compact. Smooth. Fine.
Firing: Oxidized [a VII].
Finish: Wiped.

Paste 16
Color: 10R6/8 [red].
Temper:
    Translucent inclusions, subrounded, 0.1 mm, regular, medium.
    Black inclusions, subrounded, 0.1 mm, regular, medium.
    Cross section: Regular. Semi-compact. Smooth. Fine.
Firing: Oxidized [a X].
Finish: Wiped.

Paste 17
Color: 10R5/8 [orange].
Temper:
    White inclusions, subrounded, to 1.0 mm, regular, abundant.
    Black inclusions, subrounded, 0.5 mm, irregular, scarce.
    Gold mica inclusions, laminate, 0.1 mm, regular, medium.
    Cross section: Exterior-interior (mica). Regular. Semi-compact. Smooth. Fine.
Firing: Oxidized [a IV].
Finish: Wiped, burnished.

Paste 20
Color: 2.5YR5/6 [light orange].
Temper:
    White inclusions, subrounded, 0.1 mm, regular, abundant.
    Translucent inclusions, subrounded, 0.1 mm, regular, medium.
    Black inclusions, subrounded, 0.1 mm, irregular, scarce.
    Gold mica inclusions, laminate, 0.1 mm, regular, medium.
    Cross section: (Exterior-interior mica.) Regular. Semi-compact. Smooth. Fine.
Firing: Oxidized [a VI].
Finish: Wiped, burnished.

Paste 29
Color: 5YR6/4 [light orange].
Temper:
    White inclusions, subrounded, 0.1 mm, irregular, scarce.
    Black inclusions, subangular, 0.1 mm, irregular, scarce.
    Red inclusions, subangular, 0.1 mm, irregular, scarce.
    Gold mica inclusions, laminate, 0.1 mm, irregular, scarce.
    Cross section: Exterior-interior (mica). Regular. Semi-compact. Smooth. Fine.
Firing: Oxidized [a VI].
Finish: Wiped, burnished.

Paste 30
Color: 5YR6/4 [light orange].
Temper:
    White inclusions, subrounded, 0.1 mm, regular, medium.
    Ocher-colored inclusions, subrounded, 0.1 mm, irregular, scarce.
    Translucent inclusions, subrounded, 0.1 mm, irregular, scarce.
    Gold mica inclusions, laminate, to 1.0 mm, regular, medium.
    Cross section: Exterior-interior (mica). Regular. Semi-compact. Smooth. Fine.
Firing: Oxidized [h VI].
Finish: Wiped, burnished.

Paste 31
Color: 7.5YR6/3 [light brown].
Temper:
    White inclusions, subrounded, 0.1 mm, regular, abundant.
    Black inclusions, subrounded, 0.1 mm, regular, medium.
    Gold mica inclusions, laminate, to 1.0 mm, regular, medium.
    Cross section: Exterior-interior (mica). Regular. Semi-compact. Smooth. Fine.
Firing: Oxidized [a II].
Finish: Wiped, burnished.

Paste 32
Color: 7.5YR7/4 [light orange].
Temper:
    Translucent inclusions, subangular, 0.1 mm, irregular, scarce.
    Black inclusions, subangular, 0.1 mm, irregular, scarce.
    Gold mica inclusions, laminate, 0.1 mm, regular, scarce.
    Cross section: Exterior-interior (mica). Regular. Semi-compact. Smooth. Fine.
Firing: Oxidized [a VI].
Finish: Wiped, burnished, polished.

Tiwanaku

Paste 1
Color: 2.5YR6/6 [dark orange].
Temper:
　Not visible.
　Cross section: Regular. Compact. Semi-hard. Very fine.
Firing: Oxidized [a V].
Finish: Wiped, burnished, polished.

Paste 2
Color: 2.5YR6/6 [dark orange].
Temper:
　Gray inclusions, subangular, 2.0 mm, irregular, very scarce.
　Reddish inclusions, subangular, 2.0 mm, irregular, very scarce.
　Cross section: Regular. Compact. Semi-hard. Very fine.
Firing: Incompletely oxidized [l IV].
Finish: Wiped, burnished.

Paste 3
Color: 2.5YR6/6 [dark orange].
Temper:
　Translucent inclusions, subrounded, 0.1 mm, regular, abundant.
　Black inclusions, subrounded, 2.0 mm, irregular, scarce.
　Cross section: Regular. Compact. Semi-hard. Very fine.
Firing: Oxidized [g V].
Finish: Wiped, burnished.

Paste 4
Color: 2.5YR6/6 [dark orange].
Temper:
　Translucent inclusions, subrounded, 0.1 mm, regular, abundant.
　Cross section: Regular. Compact. Semi-hard. Very fine.
Firing: Oxidized [a V].
Finish: Wiped, burnished, polished.

Paste 5
Color: 2.5YR6/6 [dark orange].
Temper:
　White inclusions, subrounded, 0.1 mm, regular.
　Black inclusions, subrounded, 0.1 mm, irregular, scarce.
　Cross section: Regular. Compact. Semi-hard. Very fine.
Firing: Oxidized [a V].
Finish: Wiped, burnished.

Paste 6
Color: 2.5YR6/6 [dark orange].
Temper:
　White inclusions, subrounded, 0.1 mm, regular, very scarce.
　Cross section: Regular. Compact. Semi-hard. Very fine.
Firing: Oxidized [a V].
Finish: Wiped, burnished.

Paste 7
Color: 2.5YR6/6 [dark orange].
Temper:
　White inclusions, subrounded, 0.1 mm, irregular, very scarce.
　Gold mica inclusions, laminate, 0.1 mm, regular, scarce.
　Cross section: Exterior-interior (only mica). Regular. Compact. Semi-hard. Very fine.
Firing: Oxidized [e V].
Finish: Wiped, polished.

Paste 8
Color: 10R6/6 [red].
Temper:
　White inclusions, subrounded, 0.5 mm, regular, medium.
　Black inclusions, subrounded, 0.5 mm, regular.
　Cross section: Regular. Compact. Semi-hard. Very fine.
Firing: Oxidized [a X].
Finish: Wiped, burnished, polished.

Paste 9
Color: 10R6/6 [red].
Temper:
　White inclusions, subrounded, 0.1 mm, regular, scarce.
　Black inclusions, subrounded, 0.1 mm, regular, scarce.
　Purplish inclusions, subangular, 0.1 mm, irregular, scarce.
　Cross section: Regular. Compact. Semi-hard. Very fine.
Firing: Oxidized [a X].
Finish: Wiped, burnished.

Paste 10
Color: 10R6/6 [red].
Temper:
　White inclusions, subrounded, 0.1 mm, regular, scarce.
　Cross section: Regular. Compact. Semi-hard. Very fine.
Firing: Oxidized [a X].
Finish: Wiped, burnished.

Paste 11
Color: 10R6/6 [red].
Temper:
　White inclusions, subrounded, 0.5 mm, regular.
　Black inclusions, subrounded, 0.5 mm, regular, scarce.
　Cross section: Regular. Compact. Semi-hard. Very fine.
Firing: Oxidized [a X].
Finish: Wiped, burnished, polished.

Paste 12
Color: 10R6/6 [red].
Temper:
　White inclusions, subrounded, 0.1 mm, irregular, very scarce.
　Cross section: Regular. Compact. Semi-hard. Very fine.
Firing: Oxidized [b X].
Finish: Wiped, burnished.

Altiplano

Paste 1
Color: 2.5YR6/6 [dark orange].
Temper:
    White inclusions, subangular, to 1.0 mm, regular, abundant.
    Ocher-colored inclusions, subangular, to 1.0 mm, irregular, scarce.
    Gray inclusions, subangular, to 1.0 mm, irregular, scarce.
    Cross section: Exterior-interior white. Regular. Semi-compact. Semi-smooth. Medium.
Firing: Oxidized [l V].
Finish: Wiped, burnished, polished.

Paste 2
Color: 2.5YR6/6 [dark orange].
Temper:
    White inclusions, subangular, to 2.0 mm, regular, abundant.
    Cream inclusions, subangular, to 2.0 mm, regular, medium.
    Ocher-colored inclusions, subangular, 1.0 mm, irregular, scarce.
    Black inclusions, subangular, 0.8 to 1.0 mm, irregular, scarce.
    Cross section: Exterior-interior. Regular. Semi-compact. Semi-smooth. Fine.
Firing: Incompletely oxidized [h V].
Finish: Wiped, burnished.

Paste 3
Color: 2.5YR6/6 [dark orange].
Temper:
    White inclusions, subangular, 1.0 mm, regular, abundant.
    Reddish/purple inclusions, subangular, 1.0 mm, irregular, scarce.
    Black inclusions, subangular, 1.0 mm, irregular, scarce.
    Cross section: Exterior-interior. Regular. Semi-compact. Semi-smooth. Medium.
Firing: Oxidized [a V].
Finish: Wiped, burnished.

Paste 4
Color: 2.5YR6/6 [dark orange].
Temper:
    White inclusions, subangular, to 3.0 mm, regular, abundant.
    Cross section: Exterior-interior. Regular. Semi-compact. Semi-smooth. Medium.
Firing: Oxidized [a V].
Finish: Wiped, burnished.

Paste 5
Color: 2.5YR6/6 [dark orange].
Temper:
    Purplish inclusions, subangular, to 1.0 mm, regular, medium.
    Black inclusions, subangular, to 1.0 mm, regular, medium.
    White inclusions, subangular, to 1.0 mm, regular, medium.
    Gray inclusions, subangular, 0.5 mm, irregular, scarce.
    Ocher-colored inclusions, subangular, to 1.0 mm, irregular, scarce.
    Cross section: Exterior-interior. Regular. Semi-compact. Semi-smooth. Thick.
Firing: Oxidized [g V].
Finish: Wiped, burnished, polished.

Paste 6
Color: 2.5YR6/6 [dark orange].
Temper:
    Purplish inclusions, subangular, 1.0 mm, regular, abundant.
    White inclusions, subangular, 0.6 mm, regular, scarce.
    Black inclusions, subangular, 0.6 mm, irregular, scarce.
    Cross section: Exterior-interior. Regular. Semi-compact. Semi-smooth. Thick.
Firing: Oxidized [a V].
Finish: Wiped, burnished.

Paste 7
Color: 2.5YR6/6 [dark orange].
Temper:
    White inclusions, subangular, 1.0 mm, regular, scarce.
    Gray inclusions, subangular, to 4.0 mm, irregular, abundant.
    Cross section: Exterior-interior white. Regular. Semi-compact. Semi-smooth. Thick.
Firing: Oxidized [h V].
Finish: Wiped, burnished.

Paste 8
Color: 2.5YR6/6 [dark orange].
Temper:
    White inclusions, subangular, to 1.0 mm, regular, medium.
    Black inclusions, subangular, to 1.0 mm, irregular, scarce.
    Reddish inclusions, subangular, to 2.0 mm, irregular, scarce.
    Cross section: Exterior-interior white. Regular. Semi-compact. Semi-smooth. Thick.
Firing: Oxidized [f V].
Finish: Wiped, burnished.

Paste 9
Color: 5YR6/6 [light orange].
Temper:
    White inclusions, subangular, to 1.0 mm, regular, medium.
    Opaque inclusions, subangular, 1.0 mm, regular, medium.
    Cross section: Exterior-interior white. Regular. Semi-compact. Semi-smooth. Fine.
Firing: Oxidized [d VI].
Finish: Wiped, burnished, polished.

Paste 10
Color: 5YR6/6 [light orange].
Temper:
    White inclusions, subangular, to 1.0 mm, regular, scarce.
    Gray inclusions, subangular, 0.5 to 4.0 mm, regular, medium.
    Ocher-colored inclusions, subangular, 1.0 mm, irregular, scarce.
    Cross section: Exterior-interior white. Regular. Semi-compact. Semi-smooth. Fine.
Firing: Oxidized [e VI].
Finish: Wiped, burnished.

Paste 11
Color: 5YR6/6 [light orange].
Temper:
    White inclusions, subangular, to 3 mm, regular, abundant.
    Cross section: Exterior-interior white. Regular. Semi-compact. Semi-smooth. Fine.
Firing: Oxidized [o VI].
Finish: Wiped, burnished.

Paste 12
Color: 5YR6/4 [light orange].
Temper:
    Gray inclusions, subangular, 1 to 2.0 mm, regular, scarce.
    Reddish inclusions, subangular, 1.0 mm, regular, medium.
    Cross section: Exterior-interior. Regular. Semi-compact. Semi-smooth. Fine.
Firing: Oxidized [c VI].
Finish: Wiped, burnished.

Paste 13
Color: 5YR6/4 [light orange].
Temper:
    White inclusions, subangular, to 1.0 mm, regular, abundant.
    Gray inclusions, subangular, 0.5 to 1.0 mm, regular, medium.
    Cross section: Exterior-interior. Regular. Semi-compact. Semi-smooth. Fine.
Firing: Oxidized [l VI].
Finish: Wiped, burnished.

Paste 14
Color: 2.5YR7/6 [cream orange].
Temper:
    White inclusions, subangular, to 1.0 mm, regular, abundant.
    Cross section: Exterior-interior. Regular. Semi-compact. Semi-smooth. Medium.
Firing: Oxidized [a XIV].
Finish: Wiped, burnished, polished.

Paste 15
Color: 2.5YR7/6 [cream orange].
Temper:
    White inclusions, subangular, to 1.0 mm, regular, medium.
    Cream inclusions, subangular, to 1.0 mm, regular, medium.
    Ocher-colored inclusions, subangular, 0.8 mm, irregular, scarce.
    Cross section: Exterior-interior white. Regular. Semi-compact. Semi-smooth. Medium.
Firing: Oxidized [a XIV].
Finish: Wiped, burnished, polished.

Paste 16
Color: 10YR7/4 [cream].
Temper:
    White inclusions, subangular, to 1.0 mm, regular, abundant.
    Cross section: Exterior-interior. Regular. Semi-compact. Semi-smooth. Medium.
Firing: Oxidized [a XI].
Finish: Wiped, burnished.

Paste 17
Color: 2.5YR7/6 [cream orange].
Temper:
    White inclusions, subangular, 1.0 mm, regular, medium.
    Black inclusions, subangular, 0.5 mm, irregular, scarce.
    Cross section: Exterior-interior white. Regular. Semi-compact. Semi-smooth. Medium.
Firing: Oxidized [c XIV].
Finish: Wiped, burnished.

Paste 18
Color: 2.5YR5/4 [reddish brown].
Temper:
    Black inclusions, subangular, 1.0 mm, regular, abundant.
    Ocher-colored inclusions, subangular, 1.0 mm, irregular, scarce.
    Cross section: Regular. Semi-compact. Semi-hard. Thick.
Firing: Oxidized [a VII].
Finish: Wiped, burnished.

Paste 19
Color: 2.5YR5/4 [reddish brown].
Temper:
    Black inclusions, subangular, 1.0 mm, regular, medium.
    Reddish inclusions, subangular, 1.0 mm, regular, medium.
    Cross section: Exterior. Regular. Semi-compact. Semi-hard. Thick.
Firing: Oxidized [a VII].
Finish: Wiped, burnished, polished.

Paste 20
Color: 2.5YR5/4 [reddish brown].
Temper:
    White inclusions, subangular, 0.1 mm, irregular, scarce.
    Cross section: Exterior. Regular. Compact. Semi-hard. Thick.
Firing: Oxidized [a VII].
Finish: Wiped, burnished, polished.

Paste 21
Color: 2.5YR5/4 [reddish brown].
Temper:
    White inclusions, subangular, 0.1 mm, regular, medium.
    Cross section: Interior. Regular. Semi-compact. Semi-hard. Thick.
Firing: Incompletely oxidized [t VII].
Finish: Wiped, burnished.

Paste 22
Color: 2.5YR4/4 [reddish brown].
Temper:
    Black inclusions, subangular, 1.5 mm, regular, abundant.
    White inclusions, subangular, 1.0 mm, regular, medium.
    Ocher-colored inclusions, subangular, 2.0 mm, irregular, scarce.
    Cross section: Exterior-interior white. Regular. Semi-compact. Semi-hard. Thick.
Firing: Incompletely oxidized [f VII].
Finish: Wiped, burnished.

Paste 23
Color: 5YR6/6 [light orange].
Temper:
    White inclusions, subangular, to 1.0 mm, regular, abundant.
    Translucent inclusions, subangular, 0.5 mm, irregular, scarce.
    Black inclusions, subangular, 0.5 mm, irregular, very scarce.
    Cross section: Exterior-interior. Regular. Semi-compact. Semi-smooth. Thick.
Firing: Oxidized [a VI].
Finish: Wiped, burnished.

Paste 24
Color: 5YR6/6 [light orange].
Temper:
    White inclusions, subangular, to 5 mm, regular, abundant.
    Black inclusions, subangular, 0.5 to 1.0 mm, irregular, medium.
    Cross section: Exterior-interior. Regular. Semi-compact. Semi-smooth. Thick.
Firing: Oxidized [b VI].
Finish: Wiped, burnished.

Paste 25
Color: 10R5/6 [red].
Temper:
    White inclusions, subangular, 1.0 mm, regular.
    Cross section: Regular. Semi-compact. Semi-smooth. Medium.
Firing: Oxidized [f X].
Finish: Wiped, burnished.

Paste 26
Color: 10R5/6 [red].
Temper:
    White inclusions, subrounded, to 1.0 mm, regular, abundant.
    Cross section: Regular. Semi-compact. Semi-smooth. Medium.
Firing: Oxidized [a X].
Finish: Wiped, burnished.

Inca

Paste 1
Color: 2.5YR6/6 [dark orange].
Temper:
    Pink inclusions, subangular, to 1.0 mm, regular, abundant.
    Black inclusions, subangular, 0.5 mm, irregular, very scarce.
    Cross section: Exterior-interior. Regular. Semi-compact. Semi-hard. Fine.
Firing: Oxidized [a V].
Finish: Wiped, burnished.

Paste 2
Color: 2.5YR6/6 [dark orange].
Temper:
    White inclusions, subangular, 1.0 mm, regular, scarce.
    Ocher-colored inclusions, subangular, to 1.0 mm, irregular, scarce.
    Cross section: Exterior-interior. Regular. Semi-compact. Semi-hard. Fine.
Firing: Oxidized [a V].
Finish: Wiped, burnished, polished.

Paste 3
Color: 10YR7/4 [cream].
Temper:
    Gray inclusions, subangular, 0.8 mm, regular, abundant.
    Black inclusions, subangular, to 1.0 mm, irregular, medium.
    Cross section: Exterior-interior. Regular. Semi-compact. Semi-hard. Fine.
Firing: Oxidized [a XI].
Finish: Wiped.

Paste 4
Color: 10RR7/3 [cream].
Temper:
    Not visible.
    Cross section: Not visible. Regular. Semi-compact. Semi-smooth. Fine.
Firing: Oxidized [o XI].
Finish: Wiped, burnished, polished.

Paste 5
Color: 7.5YR8/4 [cream orange].
Temper:
    White inclusions, subrounded, 0.5 mm, regular, medium.
    Cross section: Exterior-interior. Regular. Semi-compact. Semi-smooth. Fine.
Firing: Oxidized [a XIV].
Finish: Wiped, burnished.

Paste 6
Color: 2.5YR6/8 [dark orange].
Temper:
    White inclusions, subrounded, 0.5 mm, regular, abundant.
    Black inclusions, subangular, 0.5 mm, irregular, scarce.
    Cross section: Exterior-interior. Regular. Semi-compact. Semi-hard. Fine.
Firing: Oxidized [a V].
Finish: Wiped, burnished, polished.

Paste 7
Color: 10R5/6 [red].
Temper:
    White inclusions, subrounded, 0.6 mm, irregular, very scarce.
    Cross section: Regular. Compact. Semi-hard. Very fine.
Firing: Oxidized [f X].
Finish: Wiped, burnished.

Paste 8
Color: 2.5YR6/6 [dark orange].
Temper:
    White inclusions, subangular, 0.5 mm, regular, abundant.
    Cross section: Not visible. Regular. Semi-compact. Semi-hard. Fine.
Firing: Oxidized [a V].
Finish: Wiped, burnished, polished.

Paste 9
Color: 2.5YR6/6 [dark orange].
Temper:
    White inclusions, subangular, 0.5 mm, regular, very abundant.
    Black inclusions, subangular, 0.5 mm, irregular, scarce.
    Cross section: Regular. Semi-compact. Semi-hard. Fine.
Firing: Oxidized [a V].
Finish: Wiped, burnished.

Paste 10
Color: 5YR5/4 [light brown].
Temper:
    White inclusions, subrounded, 4.0 mm, irregular, scarce.
    Cross section: Regular. Compact. Semi-hard. Fine.
Firing: Oxidized [d II].
Finish: Wiped, burnished.

Paste 12
Color: 10R6/6 [red].
Temper:
    White inclusions, subrounded, 0.6 mm, irregular, very scarce.
    Cross section: Regular. Compact. Semi-hard. Very fine.
Firing: Oxidized [a X].
Finish: Wiped, burnished.

Paste 13
Color: 2.5YR6/6 [dark orange].
Temper:
    White inclusions, subangular, 0.5 mm, regular, abundant.
    Black inclusions, subangular, 0.5 mm, irregular, scarce.
    Translucent inclusions, subangular, 0.8 mm, irregular, very scarce.
    Cross section: Exterior. Regular. Semi-compact. Semi-hard. Fine.
Firing: Oxidized [o V].
Finish: Wiped, burnished.

Paste 14
Color: 2.5YR6/6 [dark orange].
Temper:
    White inclusions, subangular, 0.5 mm, regular, abundant.
    Translucent inclusions, subangular, irregular, medium.
    Black inclusions, subangular, 0.5 mm, irregular, scarce.
    Cross section: Interior. Regular. Semi-compact. Semi-hard. Fine.
Firing: Oxidized [a V].
Finish: Wiped, burnished.

Paste 15
Color: 2.5YR6/6 [dark orange].
Temper:
    White inclusions, subangular, 0.5 mm, regular, very abundant.
    Black inclusions, subangular, 0.5 mm, irregular, scarce.
    Black mica inclusions, laminate, 0.5 mm, regular, medium.
    Cross section: Interior (mica). Regular. Semi-compact. Semi-hard. Fine.
Firing: Oxidized [c V].
Finish: Wiped, burnished.

Paste 16
Color: 7.5YR8/4 [cream orange].
Temper:
    White inclusions, subrounded, 0.5 mm, irregular, scarce.
    Cross section: Regular. Compact. Smooth. Fine.
Firing: Oxidized [a XIV].
Finish: Wiped, burnished.

Paste 18
Color: 2.5YR6/6 [dark orange].
Temper:
    White inclusions, subrounded, 0.5 mm, regular, abundant.
    Black inclusions, subrounded, 0.5 mm, irregular, scarce.
    Cross section: Regular. Semi-compact. Semi-hard. Very fine.
Firing: Oxidized [a V].
Finish: Wiped, burnished.

Paste 19
Color: 5YR5/4 [light brown].
Temper:
    White inclusions, subrounded, 4.0 mm, regular, medium.
    Cross section: Regular. Compact. Semi-hard. Fine.
Firing: Oxidized [a II].
Finish: Wiped, burnished.

Paste 20
Color: 2.5YR6/6 [dark orange].
Temper:
    White inclusions, subangular, 0.5 mm, regular, abundant.
    Black inclusions, subangular, 0.5 mm, irregular, scarce.
    Cross section: Regular. Semi-compact. Semi-hard. Fine.
Firing: Oxidized [a V].
Finish: Wiped, burnished.

Paste 21
Color: 5YR5/4 [light brown].
Temper:
    White inclusions, subrounded, 4.0 mm, regular, medium.
    Cross section: Regular. Compact. Semi-hard. Fine.
Firing: Oxidized [a II].
Finish: Wiped, burnished.

Paste 24
Color: 2.5YR6/6 [dark orange].
Temper:
    Black inclusions, subangular, 0.5 mm, irregular, medium.
    Cross section: Regular. Semi-compact. Semi-hard. Fine.
Firing: Oxidized [a V].
Finish: Wiped, burnished.

Paste 27
Color: 2.5YR6/6 [dark orange].
Temper:
    White inclusions, subangular, to 1.0 mm, regular, medium.
    Purplish inclusions, subangular, to 1.0 mm, regular, medium.
    Gray inclusions, subangular, to 1.0 mm, regular, medium.
    Cross section: Exterior-interior. Regular. Semi-compact. Semi-hard. Medium.
Firing: Oxidized [a V].
Finish: Wiped, burnished.

Paste 29
Color: 2.5YR6/6 [dark orange].
Temper:
    White inclusions, subangular, 0.5 mm, regular, very abundant.
    Black inclusions, subrounded, subangular, 0.5 mm, irregular, scarce.
    Cross section: Exterior-interior. Regular. Semi-compact. Semi-hard. Medium.
Firing: Oxidized [a V].
Finish: Wiped, burnished.

DESCRIPTION OF WARES (Figs. 2.5–2.10)

Formative I (Figs. 2.11–2.26)

Group I-1/1, 2, 3, 4, 5, 6, 7, 8

The paste colors are light brown, light orange, and reddish brown. They are characterized by the use of white inclusions, subrounded, 0.5 mm to 1.0 mm in size, with a regular dispersion and with a density of medium to heavy. They can also include black subangular inclusions, 0.2 mm to 0.5 mm, with an irregular dispersion and with a density of medium to low. There are also purple subangular inclusions, 0.5 mm in size, with regular dispersion and medium density. Also there are ocher-colored inclusions, subangular, 0.5 mm in size, with low density and irregular dispersion. These pastes also have gold laminated mica, up to 1.0 mm in size, with a regular dispersion and a density of low to very low. The pastes are characterized by a regular fracture and are semi-compacted with a soft and fine texture. Surface finishes are wiped, burnished, and polished.

Group I-6/23, 24, 25

The paste color is reddish brown. It contains white inclusions, subrounded from 0.1 mm to 1.0 mm in size. The white inclusions are regularly dispersed and abundant. They also have gold mica, laminated, 0.1 mm in size, with regular dispersion and medium density. The inclusions are visible in the cross section: the fracture is regular. The pastes are regular, semi-compact, and soft with a fine texture. The finish is wiped and polished.

Group II-1/26, 27, 28

The pastes are light brown. These pastes have white inclusions, are subangular, 0.5 mm to 1.0 mm in size, and the dispersion of inclusions is regular and abundant. Other inclusions are translucent, subangular, up to 1.0 mm in size with a regular dispersion and medium density; and black inclusions that are subrounded, up to 0.1 mm in size, and regularly dispersed with a medium density. The pastes can also have laminate gold mica, up to 0.1 mm in size, and regularly dispersed with a medium density. The inclusions are visible in cross sections. The fracture is regular, semi-compact, soft, and with a medium texture. The finish is wiped and burnished.

Associated Style: Qaluyu

Associated Assemblage:

Open Vessels

Tazones, type A, variants 1, 2, 3, 4, and 5 (Figs. 2.11, 2.12).

These can be small, medium, large, and very large vessels. Decorated vessels are usually burnished, although some are polished, and the flat areas are wiped. Decorative slips include external and internal colors in reds, oranges, browns, or creams. Type A4 also uses painted decoration combined with two colors (black and cream or red over red slip or orange); in type A5, there are examples with incised decoration over red slips. The designs are geometric (horizontal lines).

Tazones, type B, variants 1, 2, 3, 4, 5, 6, 7, and 8 (Figs. 2.13, 2.14).

These are small, medium, large, and very large. Decorated vessels typically are burnished with the flat areas wiped. They are decorated with external and/or internal slips in red and orange. They also use incised decorations and/or are painted in a color (cream over red) or in two colors (black and red over cream). The designs are geometric (horizontal lines, vertical lines, diagonal lines, circles, squares, and crosshatched).

Bowls, type A, variants 1, 2, 3, 4, 5, 6, 7, and 9 (Figs. 2.15, 2.16).

These are very small, small, medium, large, and very large. In the decorated vessels, the most common finish is polished, with plain areas being wiped. This type is slipped, both exterior and interior, in red, orange, and brown. Types A3, A4, and A7 can have lateral appendixes (rounded protuberances) under the rim.

Bowls, type B, variants 1, 2, 3, 4, 5, and 6 (Figs. 2.17, 2.18).

These are very small, small, medium, large, and very large. In the decorated vessels, the most common finish is polished, with flat areas being wiped. This type is slipped both on the exterior and interior in red; there are also painted types with black over red on the exterior or in brown near the internal rim.

Bowls, type D, variants 1 and 3 (Fig. 2.19).

These are small, medium, large, and very large. In the decorated vessels, the most common finish is polished, with flat areas being wiped. This type is slipped both exterior and interior in red or brown. Exterior and interior slips are red or brown. Exterior decoration is also characterized by a cream color over red, with spaces separated or with incised geometric decorations (lines and ovals) on the internal rim on a red slip.

Bowls, type E, variant 1 (Fig. 2.19).

These are medium sized and are burnished. The decoration is painted in the exterior with brown over red slip. The motifs are geometric (horizontal lines, circles, and crosshatched).

Closed Vessels

Jars, type A (Fig. 2.20).

In general there are three sizes: very small, small, and medium. They are wiped on the exterior and interior; however, there are some burnished examples when there is decoration. Plainwares are the most common but there also are decorated ones with red and orange slips and incised decoration on the rim (oval grooves).

Jars, type B, variants 1 and 2 (Fig. 2.20).

In general there are three sizes: very small, small, and medium. These are wiped on the interior and exterior although there are some decorated burnished examples. The plainwares are the most common, but there are also decorated ones with exterior red slips and/or interior red slips and incised decoration on the rim (oval grooves).

Jars, type C, variants 1, 2, and 3 (Fig. 2.21).

There are two sizes: small and medium. These are wiped on the interior and exterior although there are some decorated burnished examples. The plainwares are the most common, but there are also decorated ones with interior and exterior red and orange slips; only in type C3 are there incised decorations on the rim (oval grooves).

Pitchers, type A, variants 1, 2, and 3 (Fig. 2.22).

There are two sizes: large and very large. These are wiped on the interior and exterior although there are some decorated burnished examples. There are plainwares and decorated ones with exterior red and orange slips and/or interior red slips. In type A3, there is incised decoration on the rim (oval grooves).

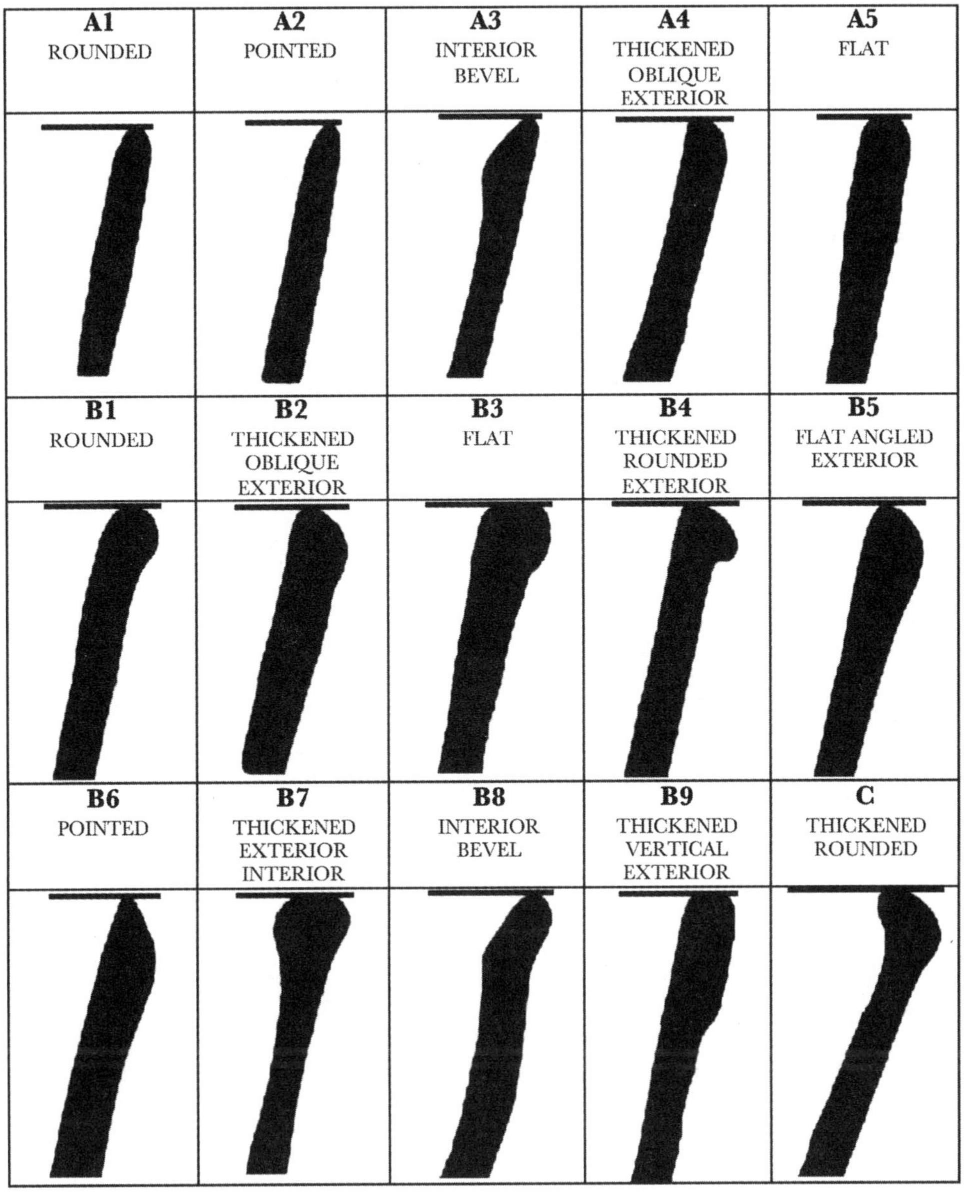

Figure 2.5. Rim shape typology—tazones.

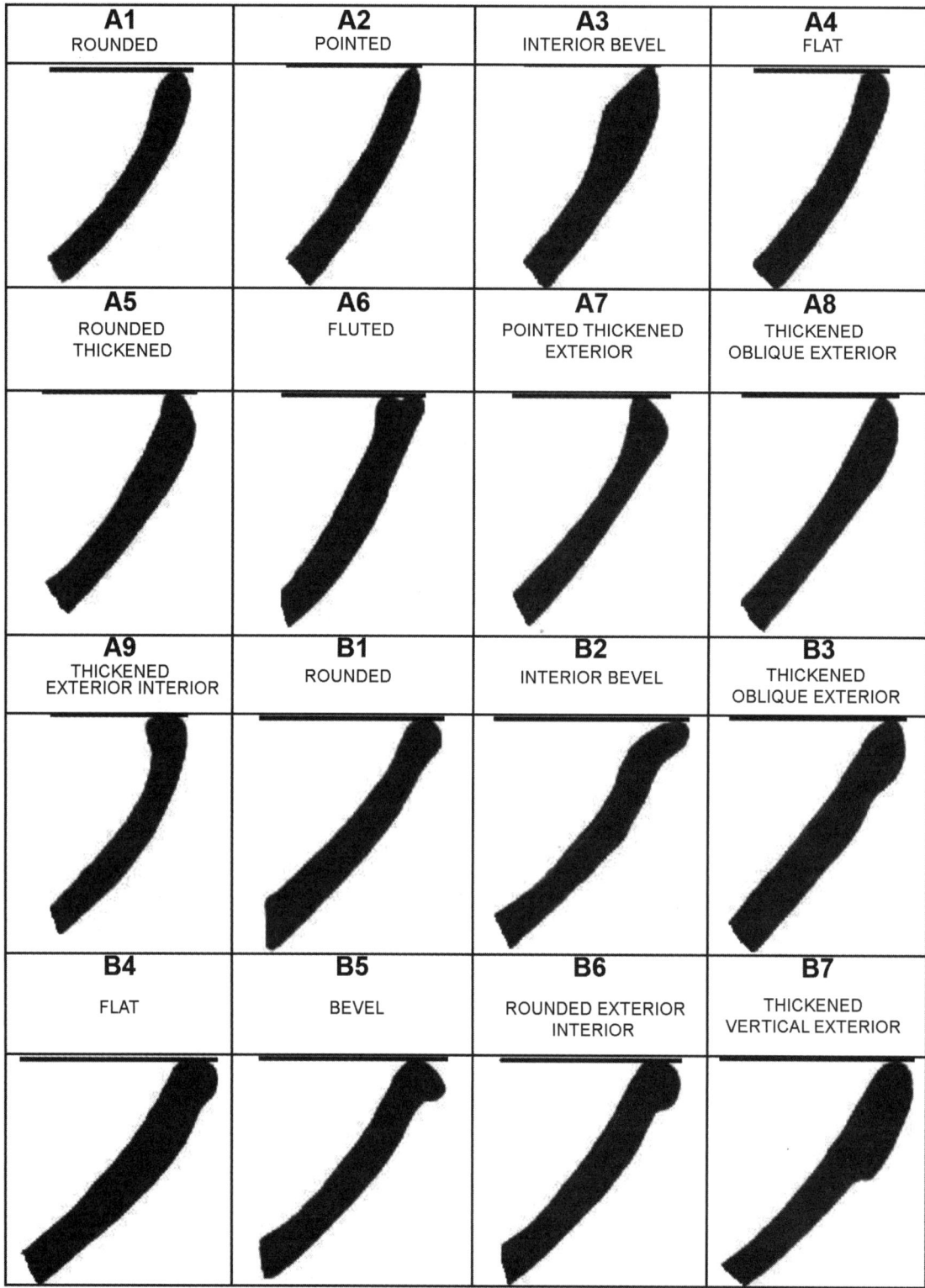

Figure 2.6. Rim shape typology—bowls, types A and B.

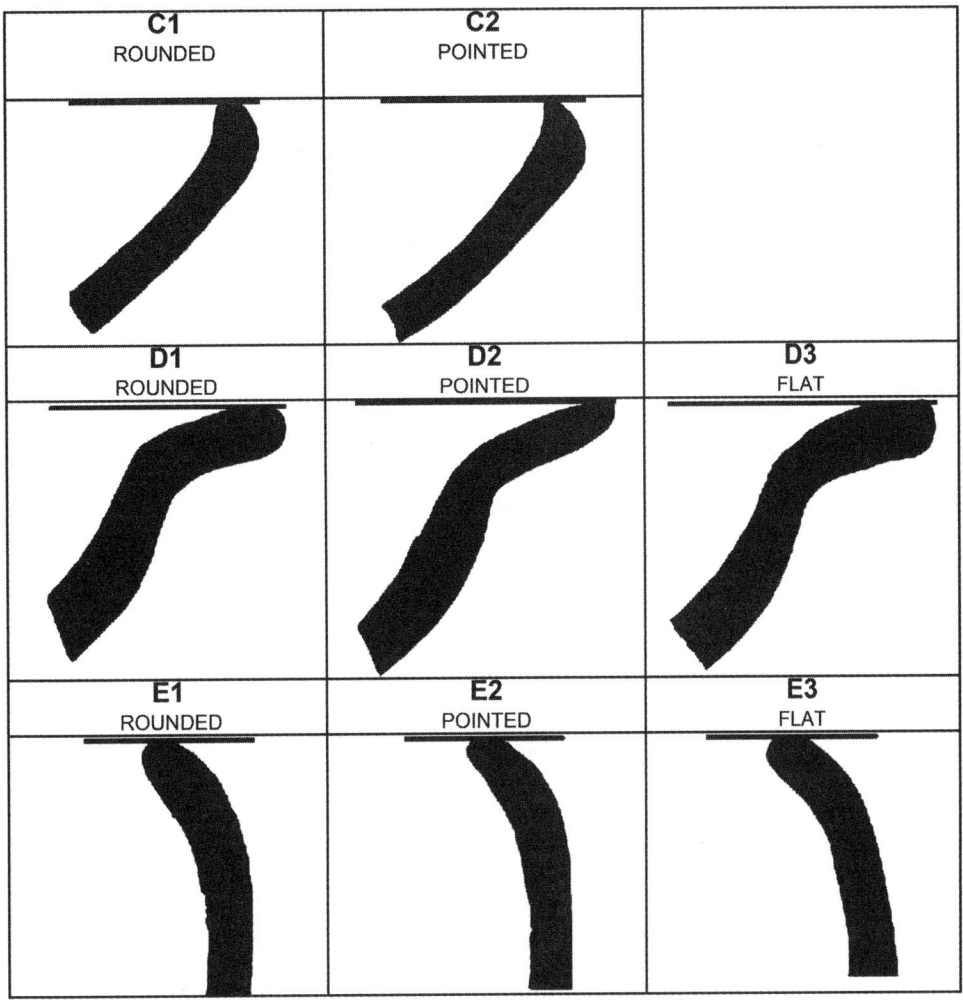

Figure 2.7. Rim shape typology—bowls, types C, D, and E.

Pitchers, type B, variants 1 and 2 (Fig. 2.23).

There are two sizes: large and very large. These are wiped on the interior and exterior although there are some decorated burnished examples. In general this type is plain but they can also be decorated with exterior and interior red and orange slips.

Ollas, type A, variants 1, 2, and 3 (Fig. 2.24).

There are four sizes: small, medium, large, and very large. These are wiped on the interior and exterior although there are some decorated burnished examples. In general this type is plain but they can also be decorated with exterior and interior red and orange slips.

Ollas, type B, variant 2 (Fig. 2.25).

There are five sizes: very small, small, medium, large, and very large. These are wiped on the interior and exterior although there are some decorated burnished examples. In general, they are plain but they can be decorated with interior and exterior red and orange slips.

Ollas, type D, variants 1, 2, 3, and 4 (Fig. 2.25).

There are four sizes: small, medium, large, and very large. These are wiped on the interior and exterior although there are some decorated burnished examples. In general, they are plainwares that can be decorated with interior and exterior red and orange slips.

Ollas, type E, variants 1, 2, and 3 (Fig. 2.26).

There are three sizes: small, medium, and large. These are wiped on the interior and exterior although there are some decorated burnished examples. In general, they are plain but can be decorated with external and internal red slips.

Bottles, type A, variant 1 (not shown).

This is a small vessel; it has a wiped surface, and has no decoration.

Other Forms Associated with the Assemblage: Cups

Ritual Elements: Incense burners, trumpets

Productive Tools: Polishing tools

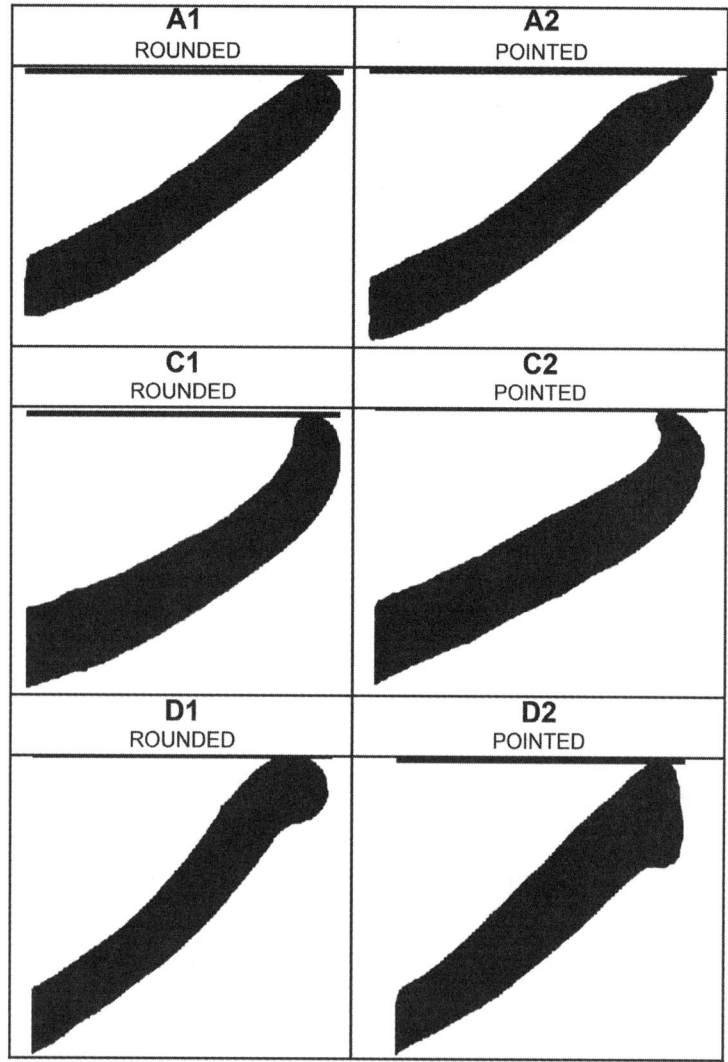

Figure 2.8. Rim shape typology—plates.

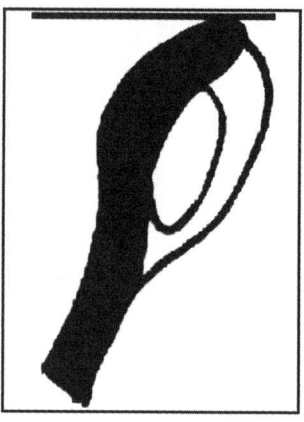

Figure 2.9. Rim shape typology—cup.

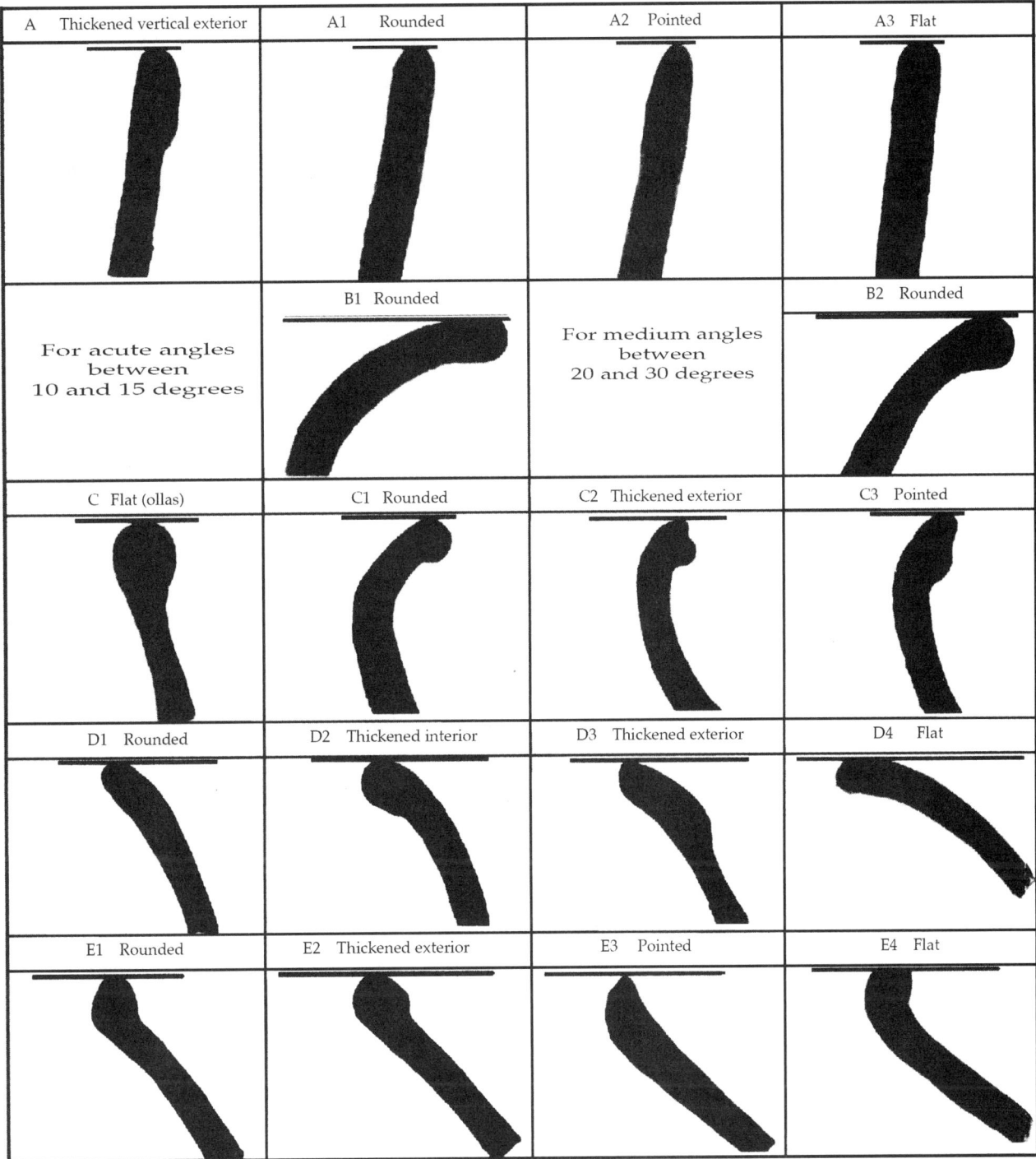

Figure 2.10. Rim shape typology—ollas.

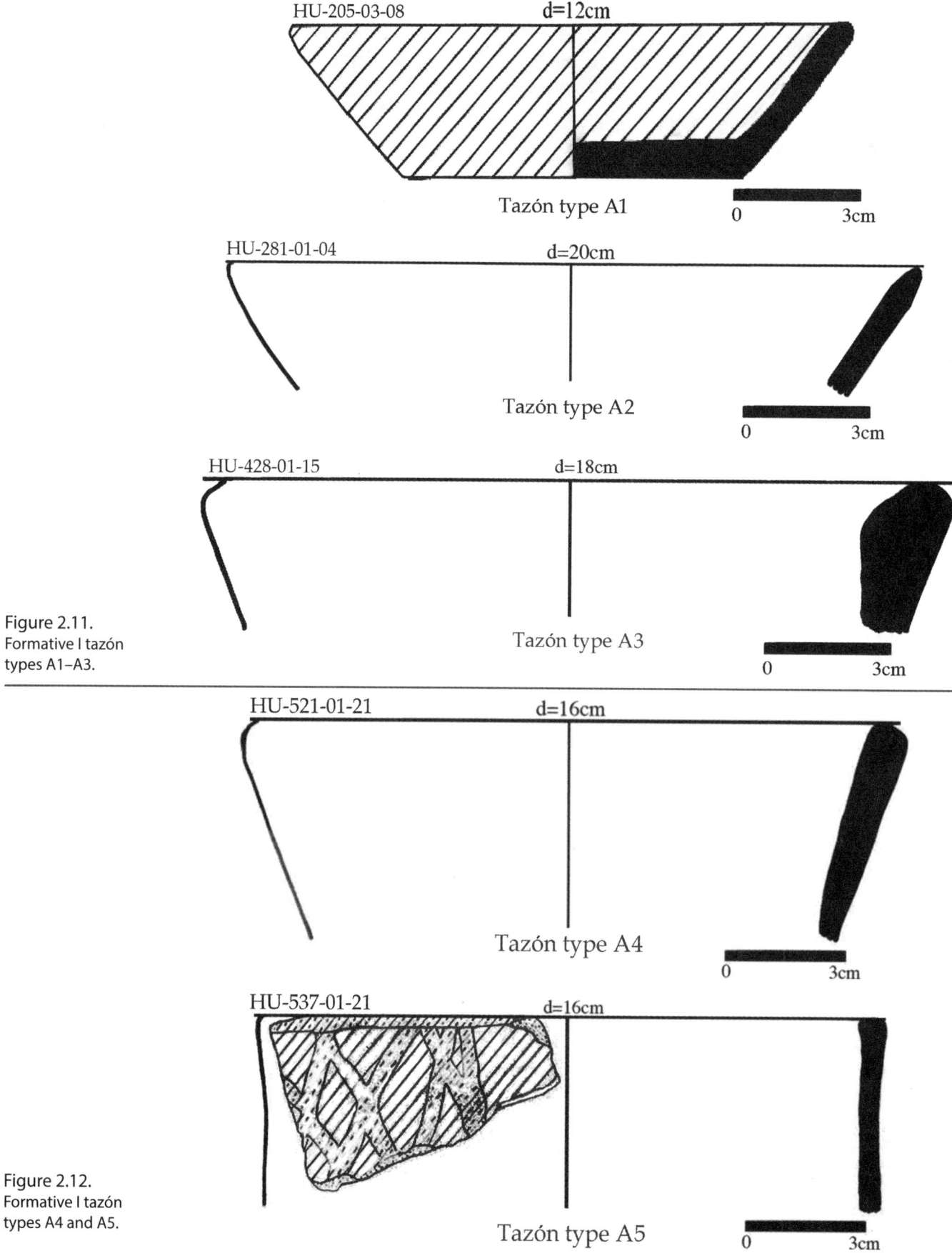

Figure 2.11. Formative I tazón types A1–A3.

Figure 2.12. Formative I tazón types A4 and A5.

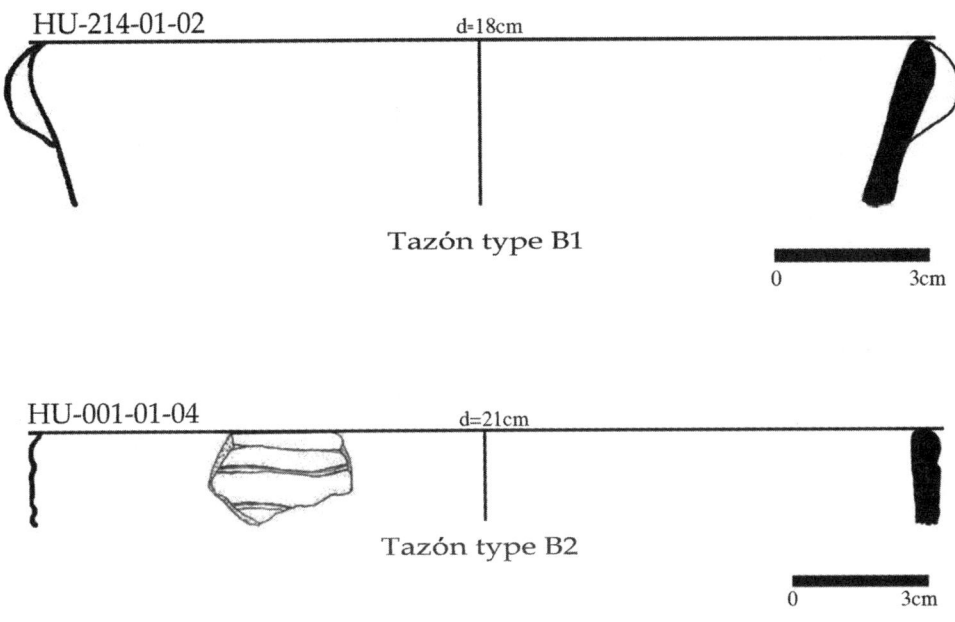
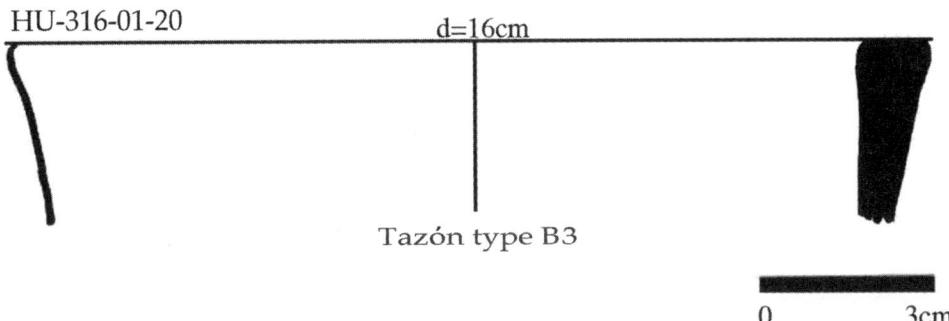
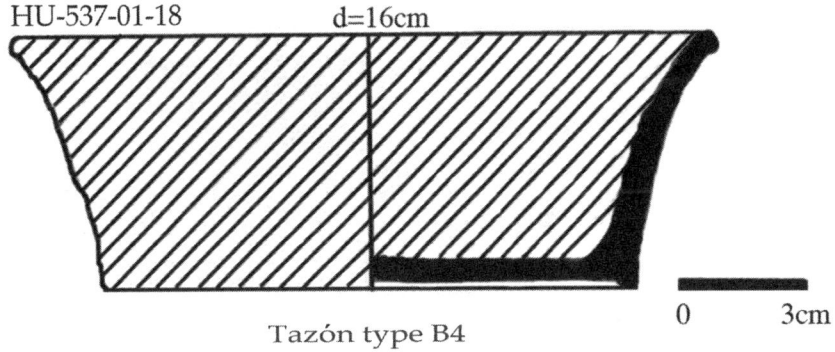

Figure 2.13. Formative I tazón types B1–B4.

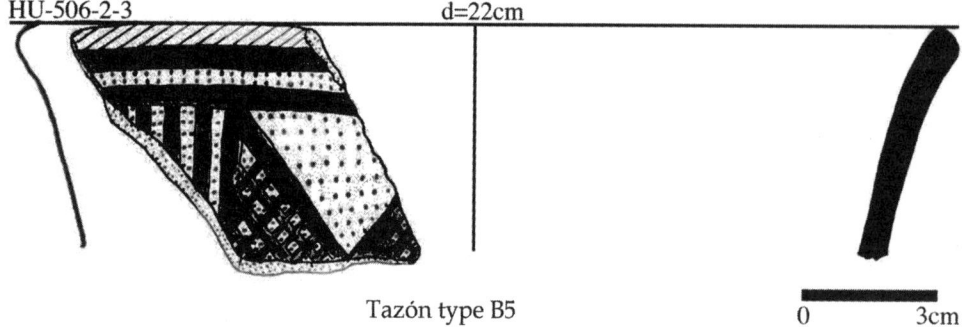

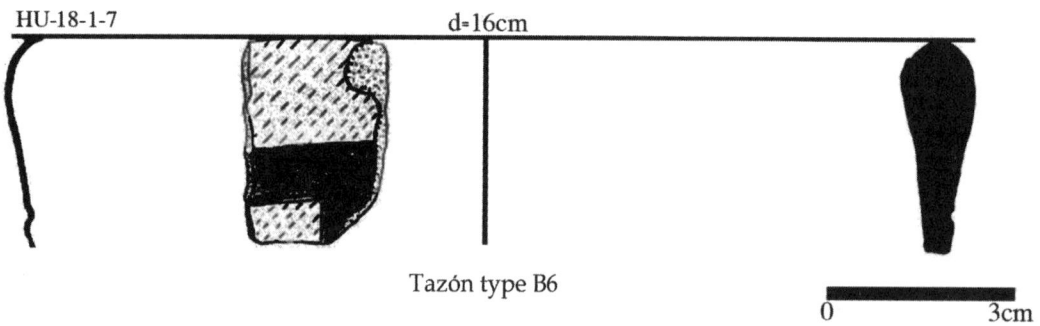

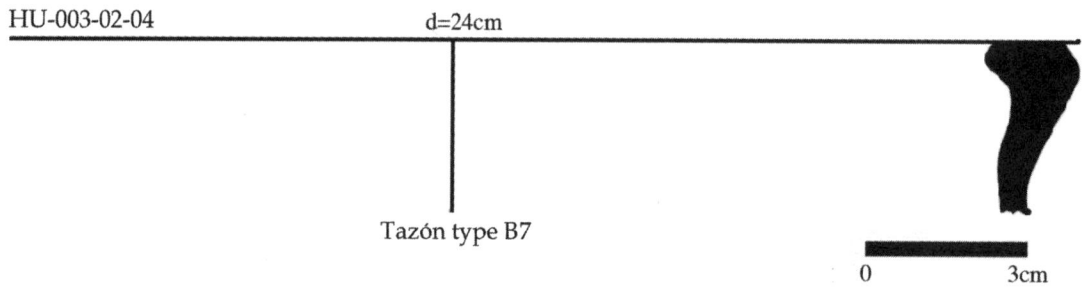

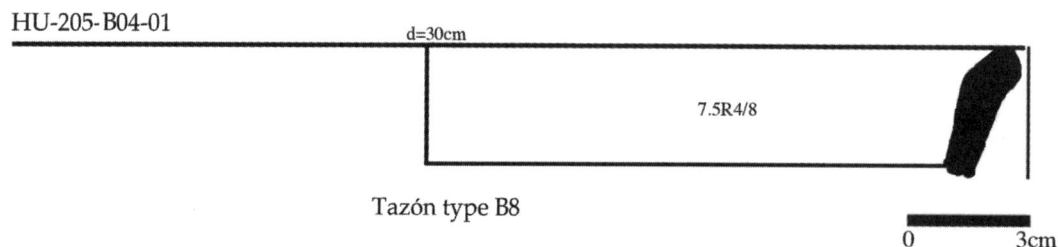

Figure 2.14. Formative I tazón types B5–B8.

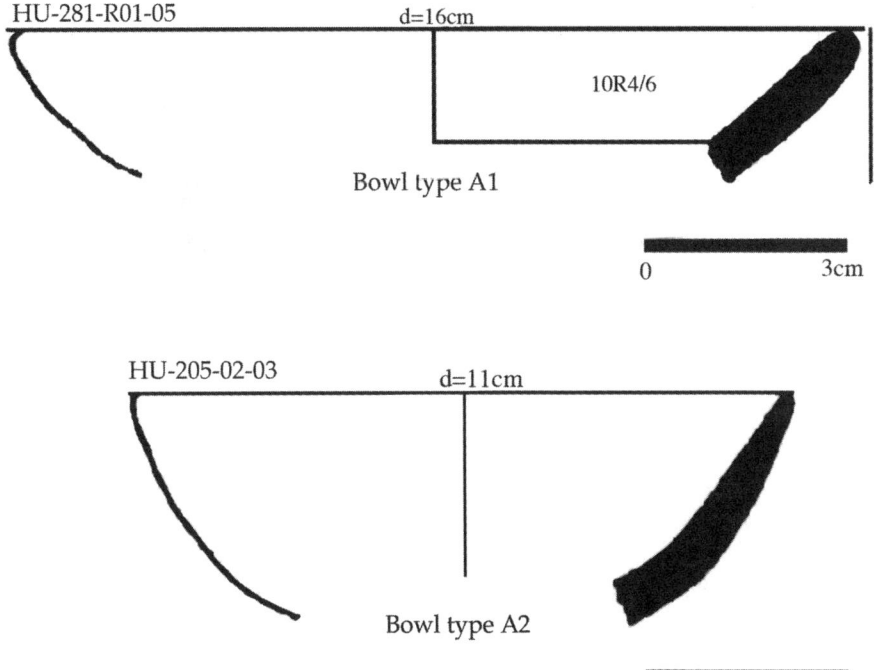

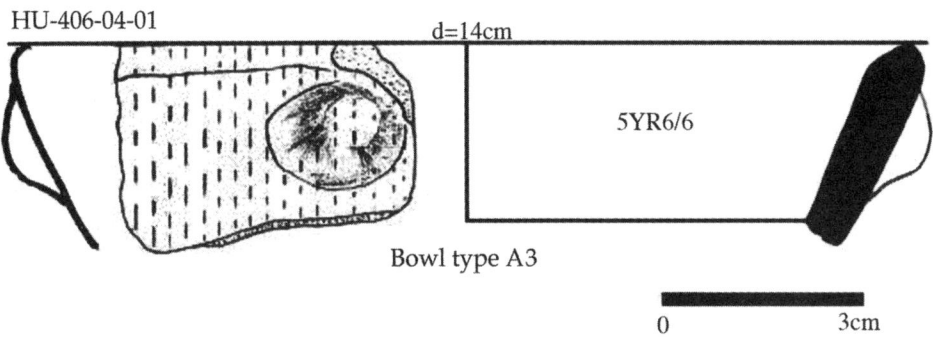

Figure 2.15. Formative I bowl types A1–A3.

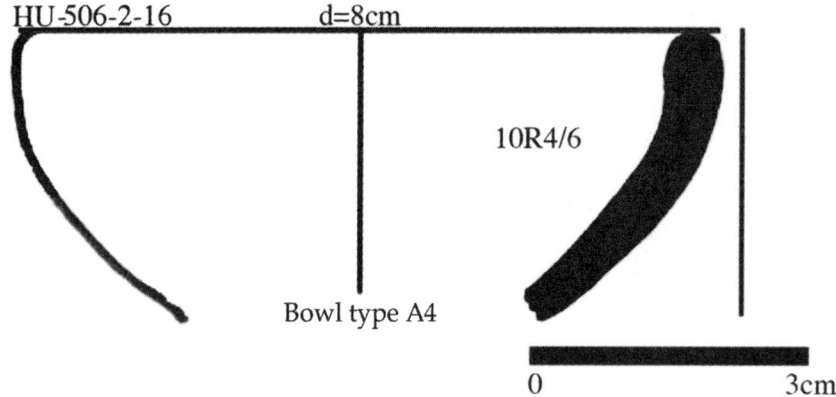
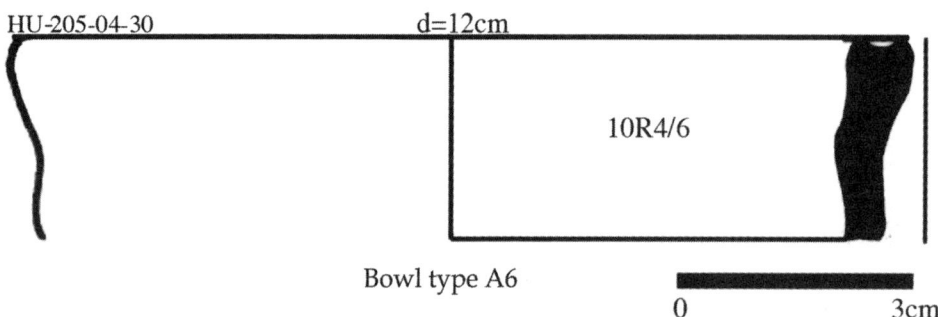
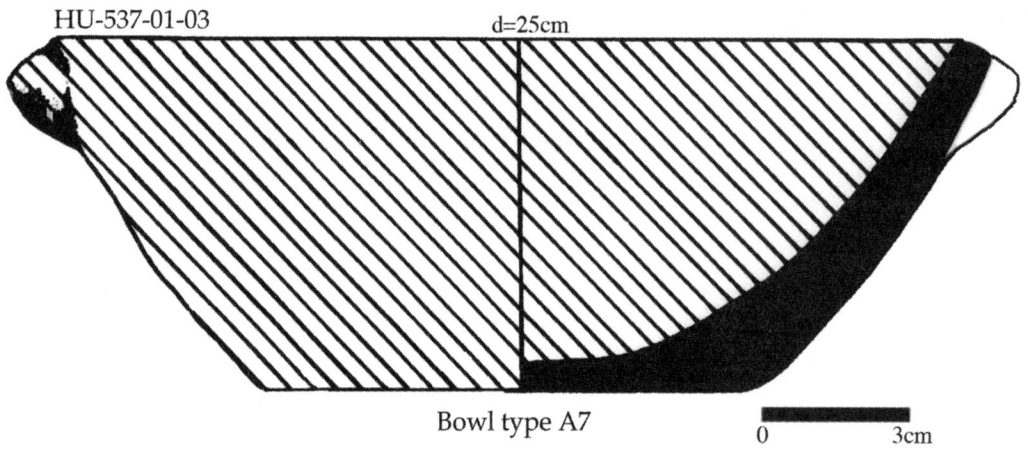
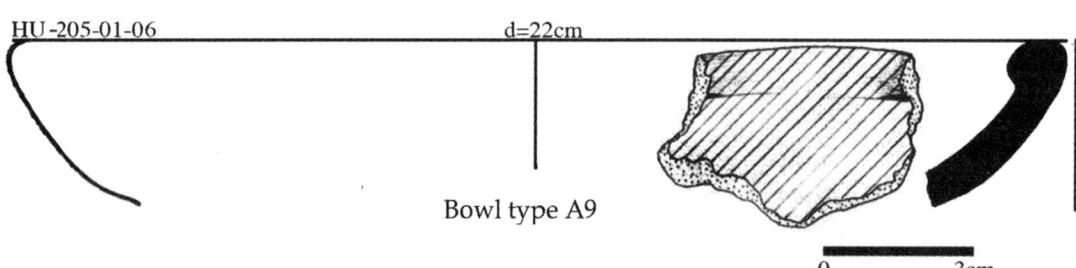

Figure 2.16. Formative I bowl types A4, A6, A7, and A9.

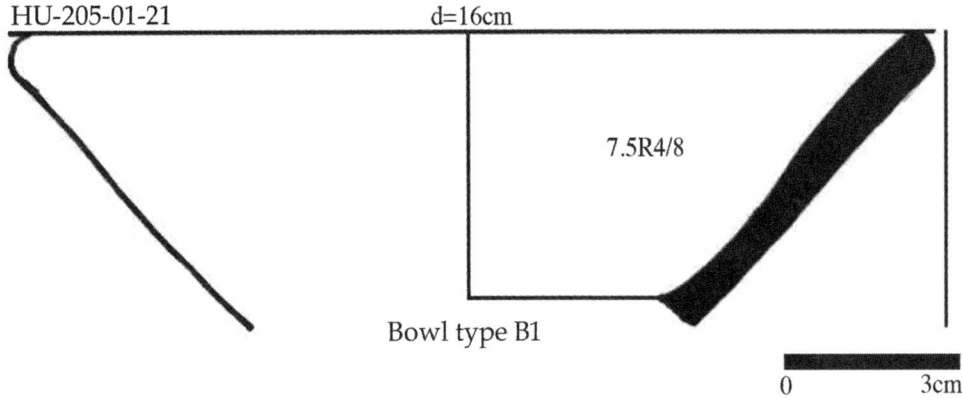

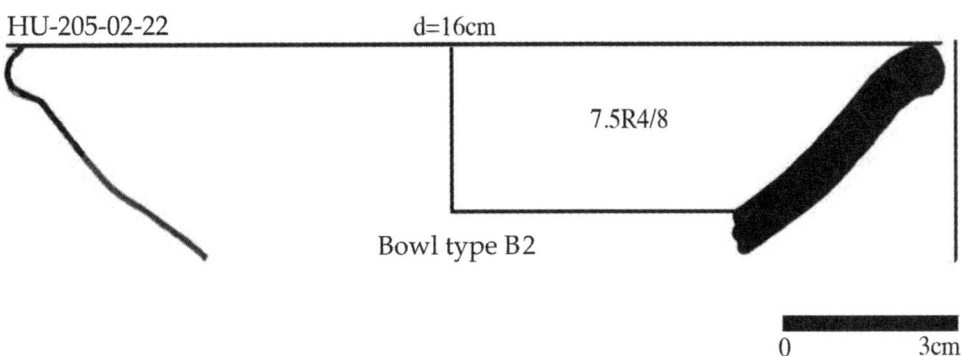

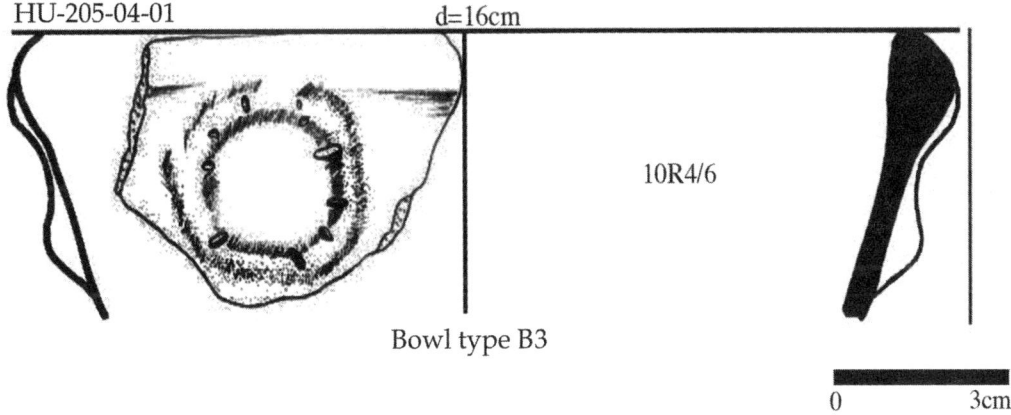

Figure 2.17. Formative I bowl types B1–B3.

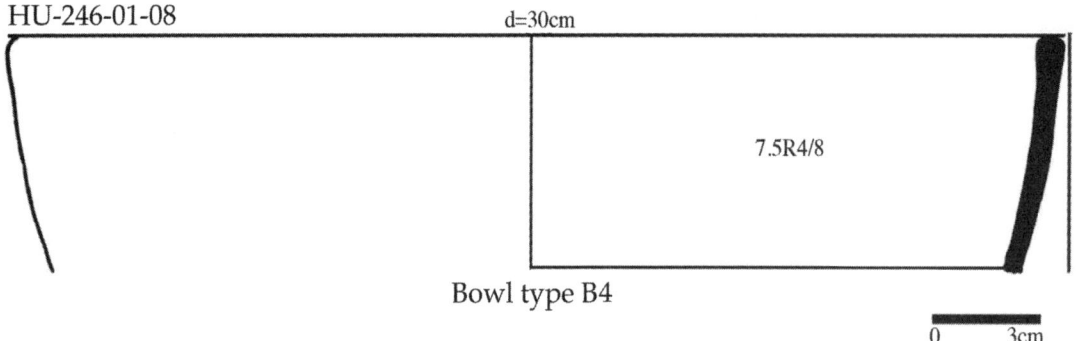
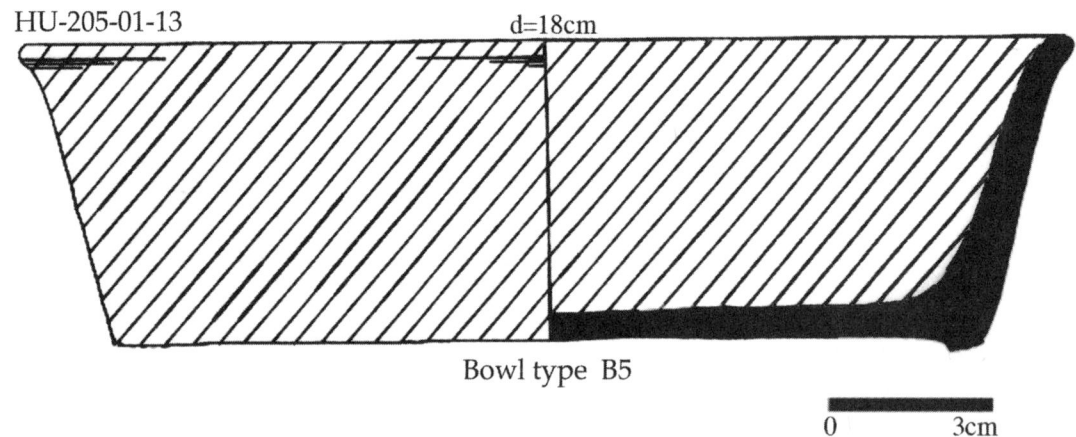
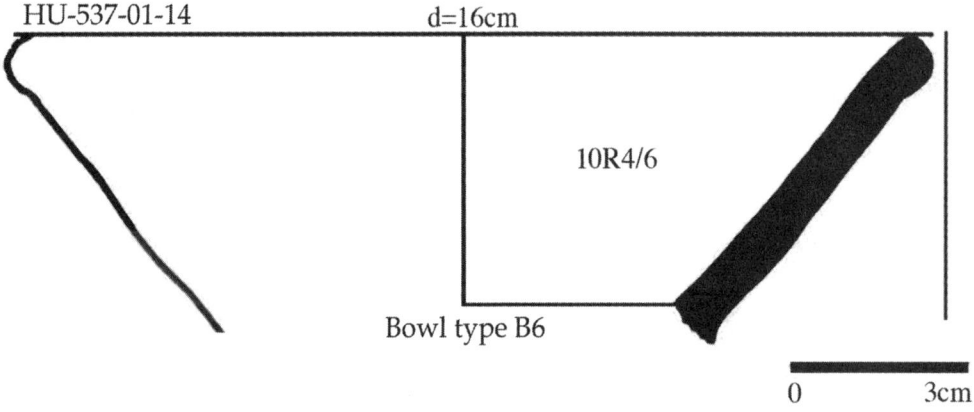

Figure 2.18. Formative I bowl types B4–B6.

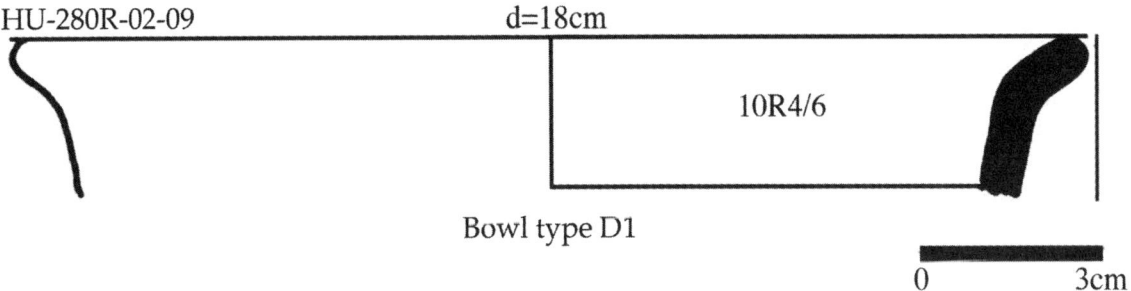
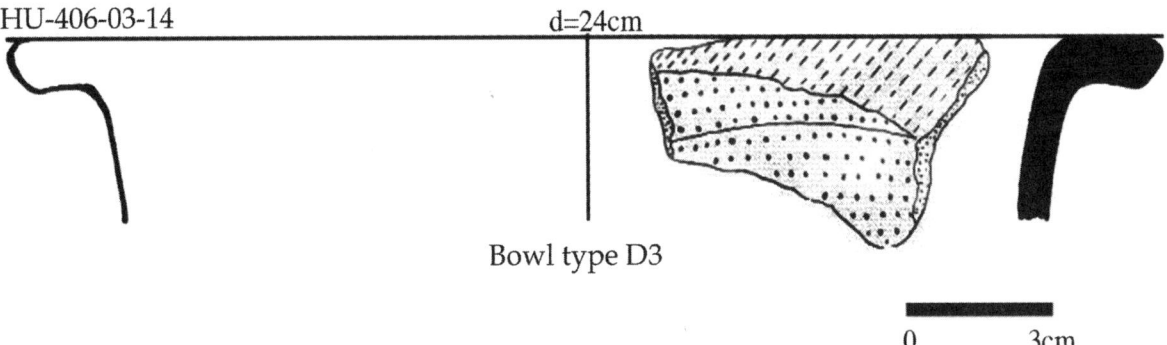
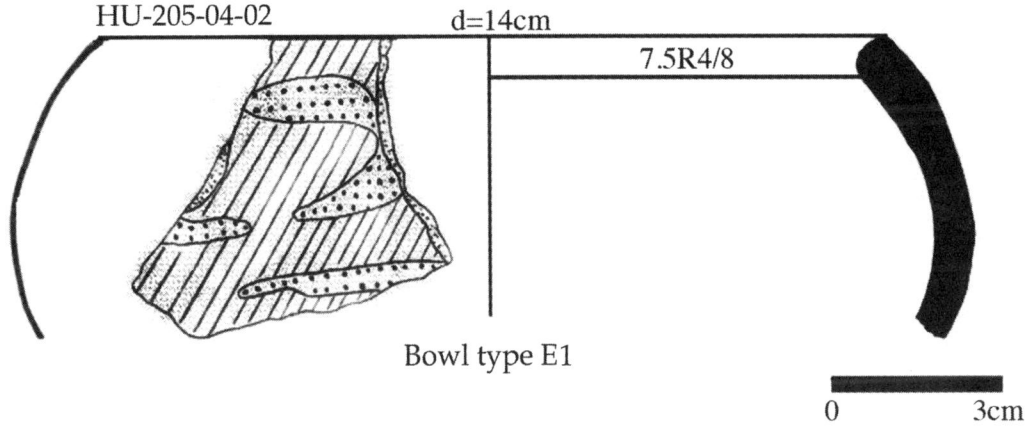

Figure 2.19. Formative I bowl types D1, D3, and E1.

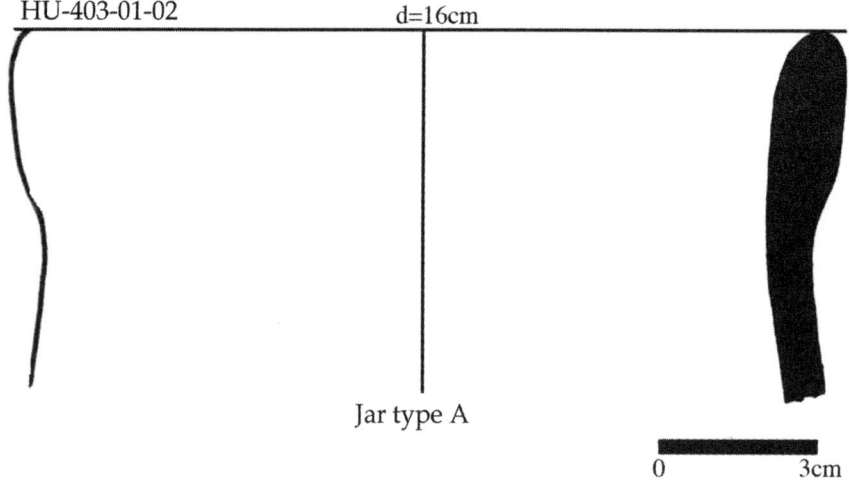

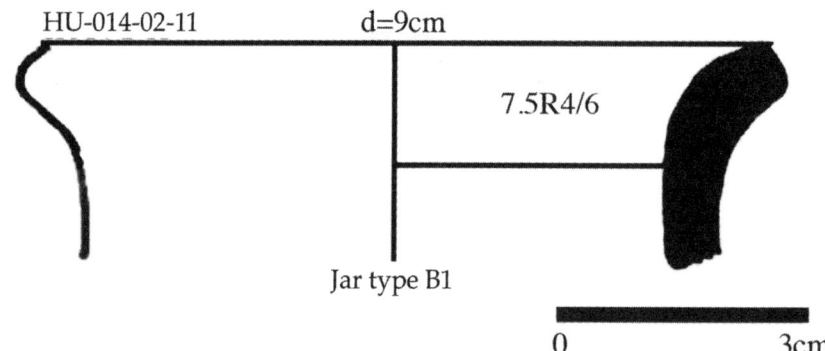

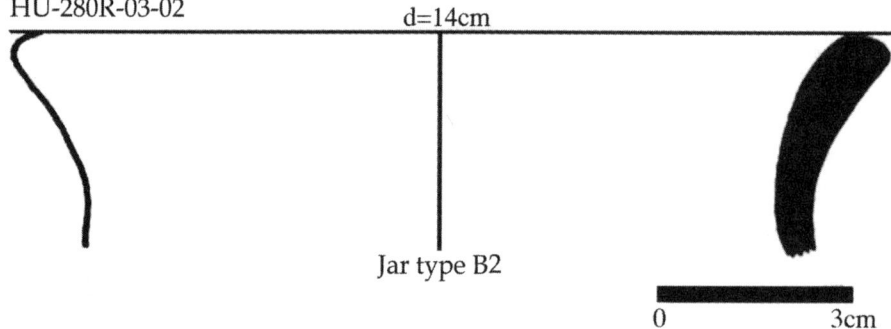

Figure 2.20. Formative I jar types A, B1, and B2.

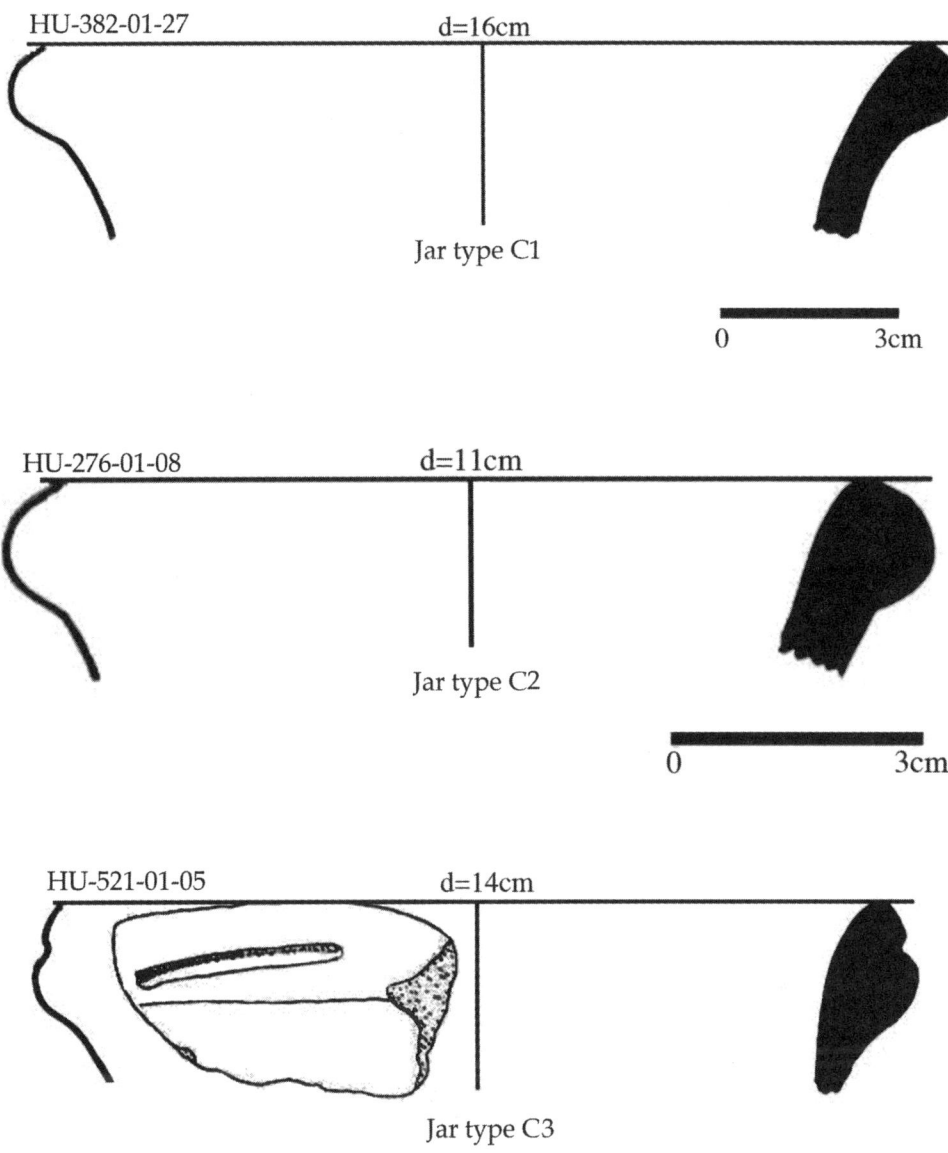

Figure 2.21. Formative I jar types C1–C3.

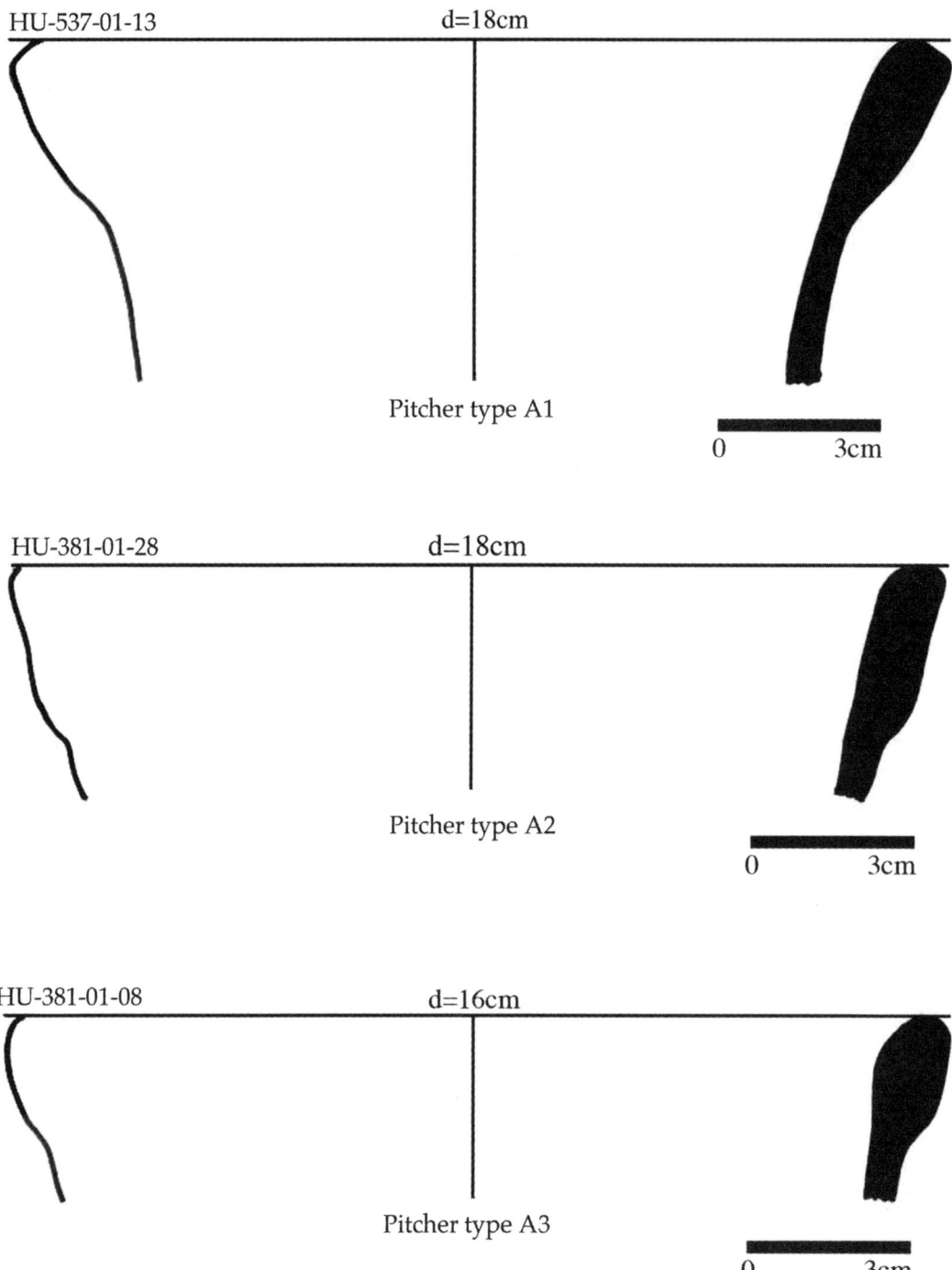

Figure 2.22. Formative I pitcher types A1–A3.

Analysis of Ceramics

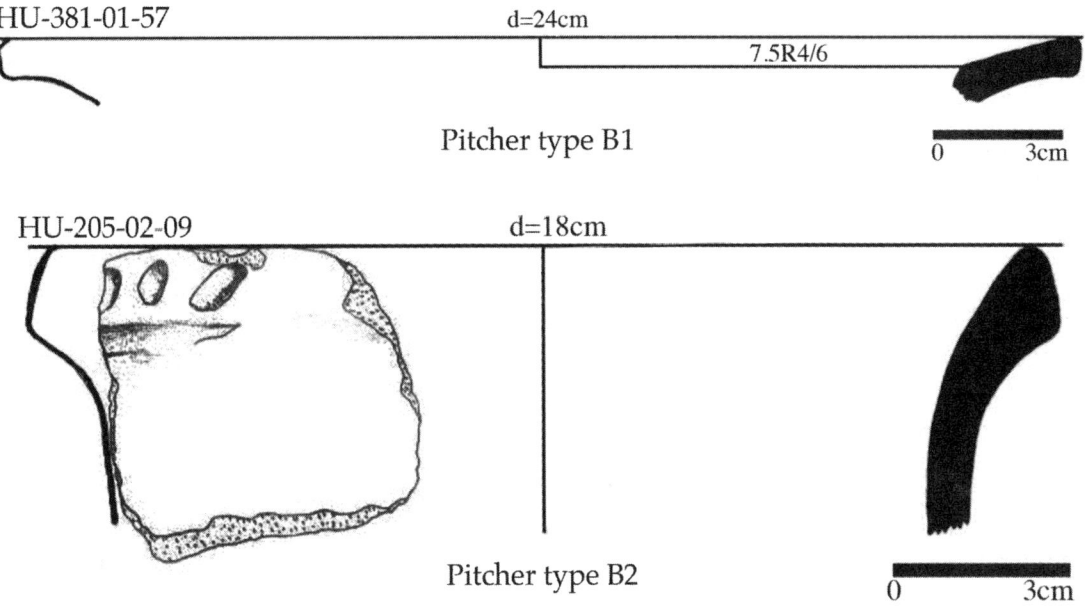

Figure 2.23. Formative I pitcher types B1 and B2.

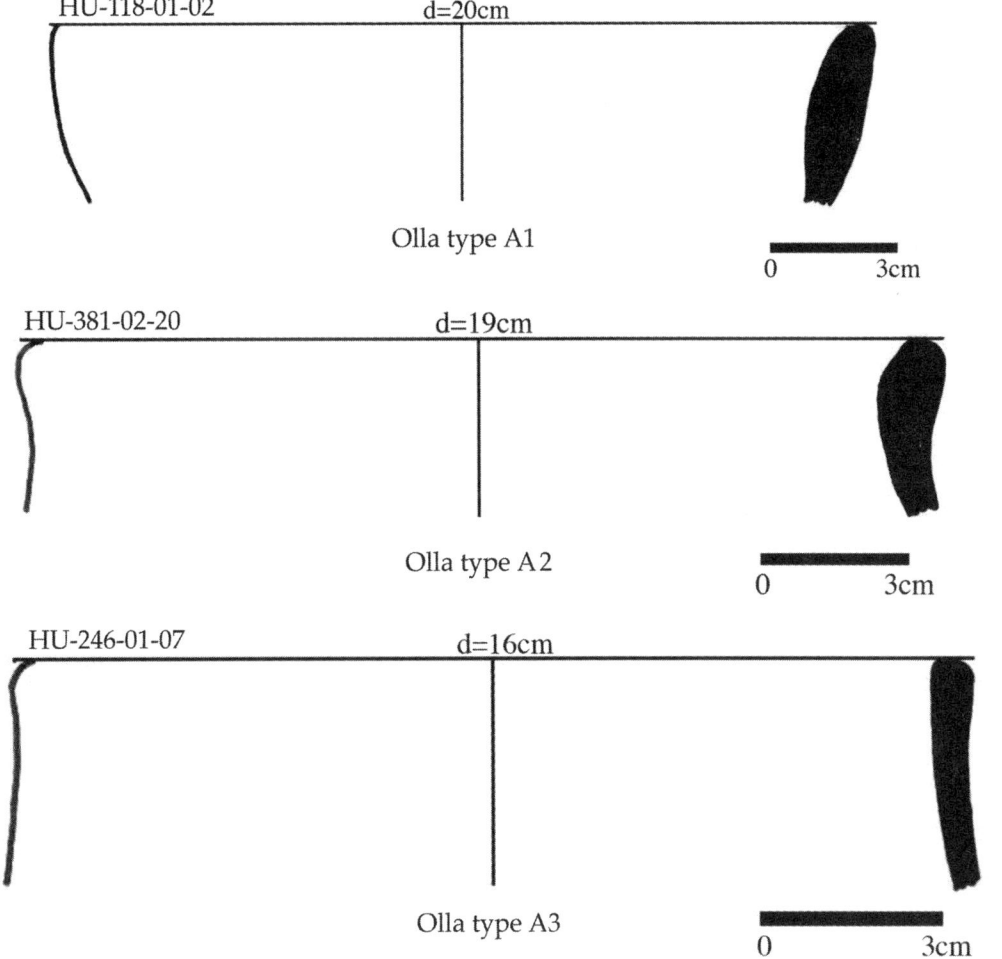

Figure 2.24. Formative I olla types A1–A3.

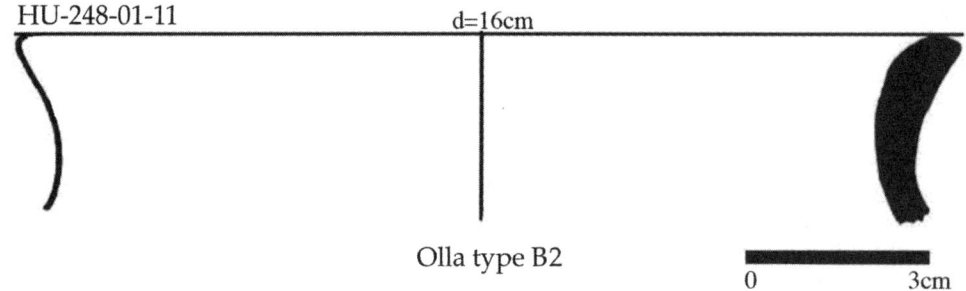
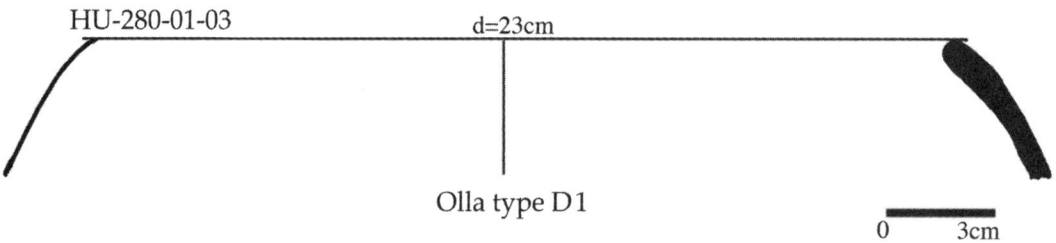
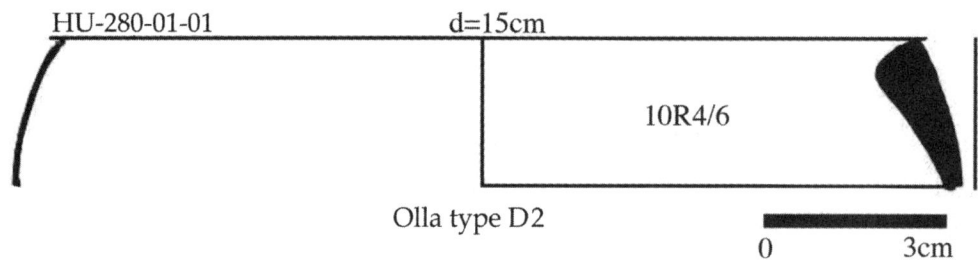

Figure 2.25. Formative I olla types B2, D1, and D2.

Analysis of Ceramics

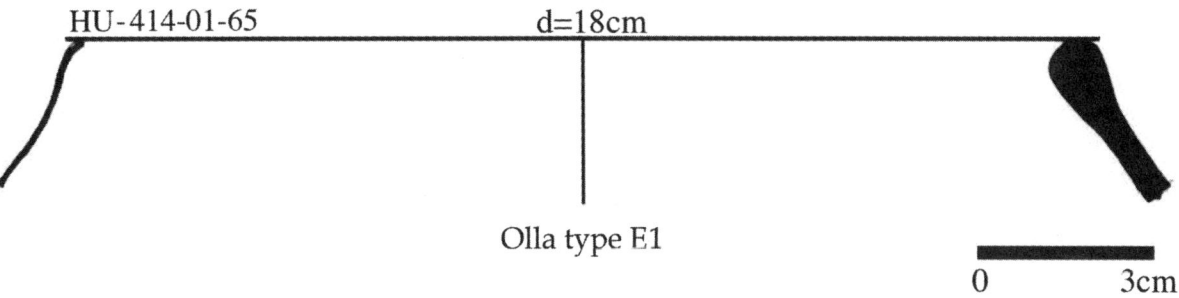

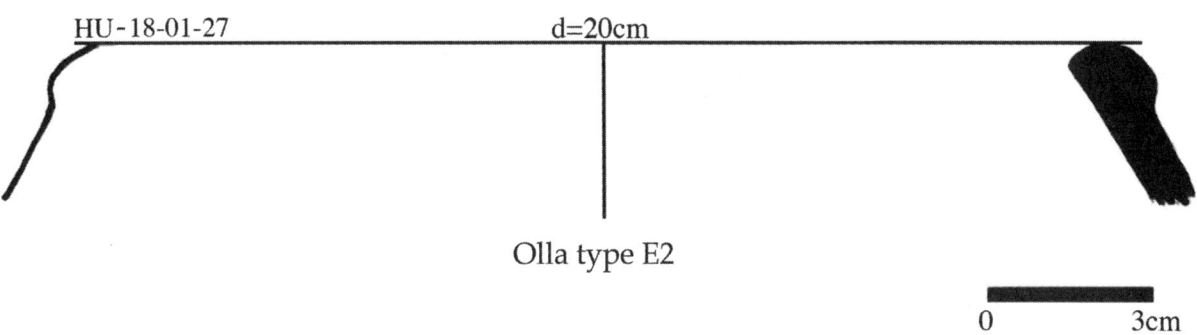

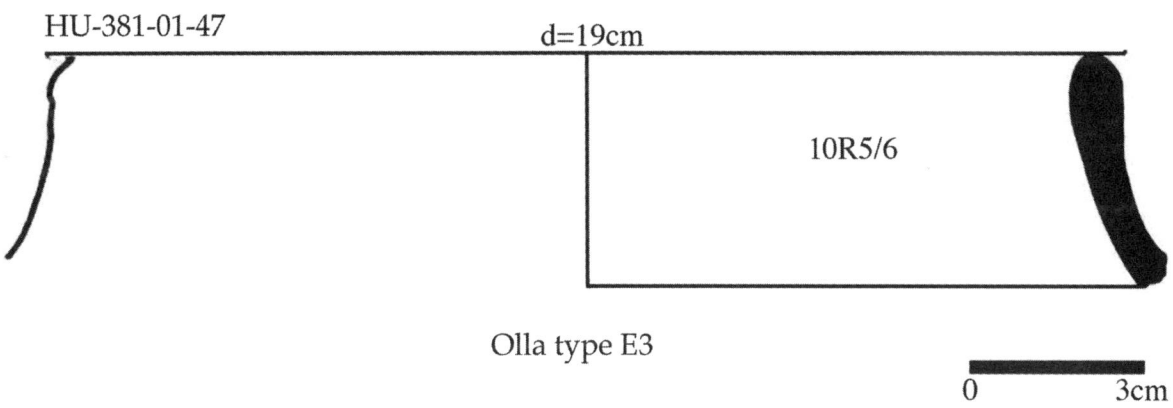

Figure 2.26. Formative I olla types E1–E3.

Formative II (Figs. 2.27–2.38)

Group II-4/38, 39, 40

Paste color is light brown. It is characterized by gray angular inclusions, up to 1.0 mm in size with a regular, high-density dispersion. It can also have purple angular inclusions up to 1.0 mm with a regular dispersion and a medium density. There is also gold laminar mica up to 0.1 mm in size, with a regular dispersion and medium density. The inclusions are visible in the cross section: the paste has a regular fracture, and is semi-compact, soft with a medium texture. Surface finish is wiped and burnished.

Group II-5/41, 42

The colors are light brown and light orange. There are pink subangular inclusions, up to 1.0 mm with a regular dispersion and abundant density. Translucent inclusions are subangular and are 0.5 mm with a regular dispersion and medium density. Black inclusions are subangular, of 0.5 mm with irregular dispersion and sparse density. There is also gold laminar mica up to 0.1 mm with a regular dispersion and medium to very abundant density. The inclusions are visible in the cross section and the mica is on the exterior and interior surfaces. The paste has a regular fracture, is semi-compact, soft, and of medium texture. Surface finish is wiped, burnished, and polished.

Group II-6/43, 44, 45

The color is reddish brown. It is characterized by gray inclusions, subangular, of 0.1 mm size, regular dispersion and high density. There are also purple angular inclusions, of 0.1 mm with a regular dispersion and abundant density. There is also gold laminar mica, of 0.1 mm, with a regular dispersion and abundant density. The inclusions are visible in the cross section and the mica is visible only on the exterior and interior surface. The fracture is regular, semi-compact, soft, and of fine texture. Surface finish is wiped and burnished.

Group II-7/46, 47, 48, 49, 50

The pastes are light brown and light orange. They are characterized by subrounded white inclusions of 0.1 mm size, with a regular dispersion and abundant density. There can also be black subangular inclusions of 0.1 mm to 0.5 mm sizes with a regular dispersion and medium to sparse density. Pink angular inclusions of 0.5 mm are present with a regular dispersion and medium to sparse density. There are translucent inclusions, subrounded, up to 1.0 mm with a regular dispersion and abundant density. There is also gold laminar mica of 0.1 mm to 0.8 mm with a regular dispersion and abundant to sparse density. The inclusions are visible in the cross section and the mica only in the exterior and interior. The fracture is regular, semi-compact, soft, and of fine texture. Surface finish is wiped and burnished.

Associated Style: Qaluyu/Pucara

Associated Assemblage:

Open Vessels

Tazones, type A, variants 1, 4, and 5 (Fig. 2.27).

There are four sizes: small, medium, large, and very large. These decorated vessels are most commonly burnished with the flat areas wiped. Decorations include red external and internal slips. There are also painted decorations on the exterior in one color (red or white over red or brown slips) and internal incised decorations defining areas painted in black over red. The A1, A4, and A5 types have exterior incised decorations combining one color (cream or brown over red). The designs are geometric (horizontal and diagonal lines, squares).

Tazones, type B, variants 1, 2, 4, 5, 6, and 8 (Fig. 2.28).

There are four sizes: small, medium, large, and very large. The most common finish is burnished with the flat areas wiped. They can be decorated with red, orange, or cream slips. They can also have incised decorations with or without exterior black paintings. The designs are geometric (horizontal and vertical lines, squares).

Bowls, type A, variants 1, 2, 3, 4, 5, 7, and 8 (Fig. 2.29).

There are three sizes: small, medium, and large. The most common finish is burnished with the flat areas wiped. They use red, brown, and orange slips on the exterior and interior. The A1 and A4 types have lateral appendixes close to the rim (rounded protuberances).

Bowls, type B, variants 1, 2, 3, and 4 (Fig. 2.30).

There are three sizes: small, medium, and large (only in type B4 is there an example of very large). The most common surface finish is burnished with the flat areas wiped. Decorations include interior and exterior red slips. The type B3 has lateral appendixes under the rim (rounded protuberances).

Bowls, type D, variants 1 and 3 (Fig. 2.31).

These are very large, and only in type D1 is there an example of a small size. The most common finish is burnished with the flat areas wiped and external and internal red slips for decorations. Type D1 has incised decorations on the exterior defining red painted areas over a cream internal rim. The designs are geometric (diagonal lines and ovals).

Bowls, type E, variants 1, 2, and 3 (Fig. 2.32).

These are small, medium, large, and very large. The most common finish is burnished with the flat areas wiped. Exterior decorations include black paints or incisions over red or two colors (brown plus cream). The designs are geometric (horizontal and diagonal lines). Type E3 has lateral protuberances under the rim (rounded protuberances).

Closed Vessels

Jars, type A (Fig. 2.33).

They are small and medium. They have handles from the rim to the body. The most common finish is wiping, but they are also sometimes burnished when decorated. The majority is plain; others are decorated on the exterior and close to the interior rim with common red slips, although some are also orange and brown. Some have incised geometric decorations (oval grooves) with or without rounded protuberances on the rim combined with lines that form squares.

Jars, type B, variants 1 and 2 (Fig. 2.33).

They are small and medium, and only in type B2 are there very small ones. The most common finish is wiping; only in type B2 are there examples of burnishing when decorated. The majority is plain; the decorated ones have exterior slips and red-toned slips near the interior rim.

Jars, type C, variants 1, 2, and 3 (Fig. 2.34).

They are small and medium. The general finish is wiping, but in types C1 and C2 they can be burnished. The majority is plain; only in type C2 are there examples of exterior slips and red slips near the internal rim.

Pitchers, type A, variants 2 and 3 (Fig. 2.35).

They are generally large, although in type A3 they may be very large. The most common finish is wiping, and only in type A3 are some

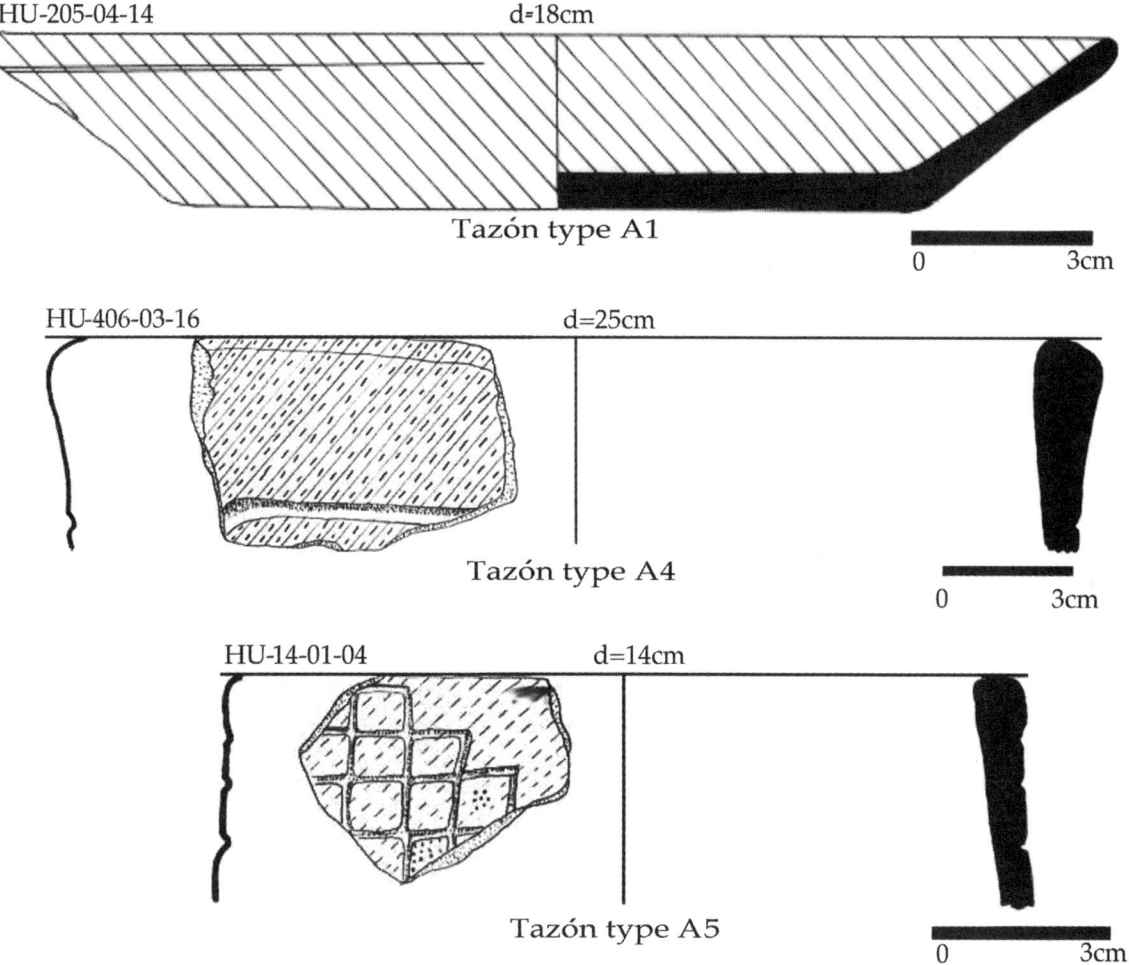

Figure 2.27. Formative II tazón types A1, A4, and A5.

burnished. There are examples of plainwares; others are decorated with external slips and red or orange slips near the internal rim.

Pitchers, type B, variant 2 (Fig. 2.35).
They are large and very large. Wiping is used as a finish, and burnishing when decorations are present. There are plain examples and others decorated with red-toned slips on the exterior and near the interior rim.

Ollas, type A, variants 1, 2, and 3 (Fig. 2.36).
They are medium, large, and very large (only in A3 is there a small example). The common finish is wiping and, when decorated, burnishing. There are plain examples and others decorated with red exterior slips and interior slips near the rim.

Ollas, type B, variant 2 (not shown).
They are small, medium, and large. They use wiping as a finish and, when decorated, burnishing. In general they are plain, or have red slips on the exterior and near the interior rim.

Ollas, type C (not shown).
They are medium and large; they only have burnished finishes. They can be plain or have red/orange external slips near the rim as the only decoration.

Ollas, type D, variants 1, 2, 3, and 4 (Fig. 2.37).
They are small, medium, large, and very large. They use burnishing as a finish, although some are also wiped. They can be plain or decorated with red or orange slips on both the exterior and near the internal rim. Some also have incised geometric decorations near the rim (rounded grooves).

Ollas, type E, variants 1, 2, and 3 (Fig. 2.38).
They are small, medium, and large (only in type E2 are there very large examples). The most common finish is wiping, although some are burnished. Generally they are plain; others are decorated with external red slips and orange or brown slips near the interior rim.

Bottles, type A, variants 1 and 3 (not shown).
They are small and miniature. The finish is wiping (with the flat areas wiped) and burnishing for those decorated with red-toned exterior slips.

Other Forms Associated with the Assemblage: Cups, spoons

Ritual Elements: Incense burners

Productive Tools: Polishing tools

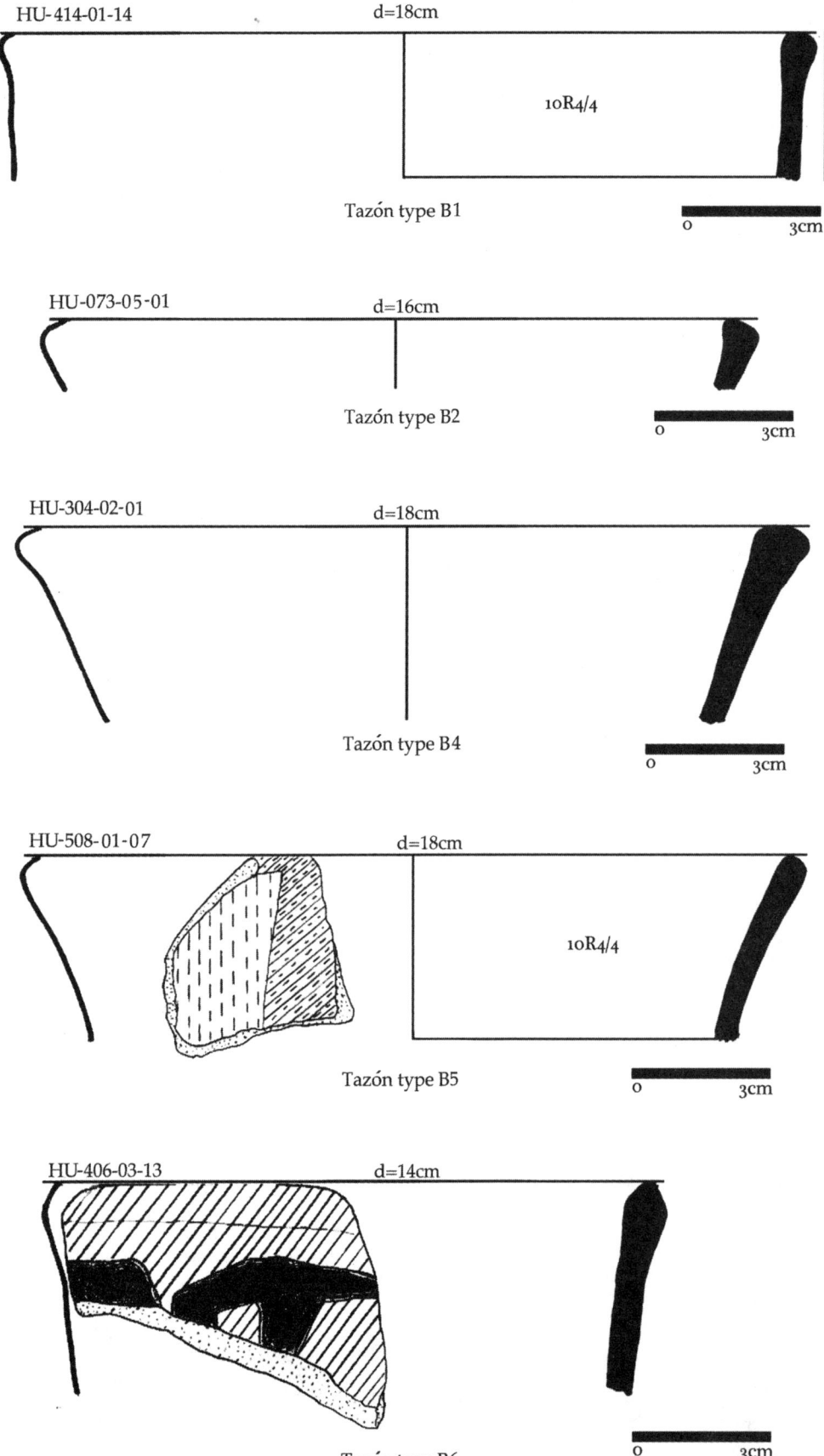

Figure 2.28. Formative II tazón types B1, B2, and B4–B6.

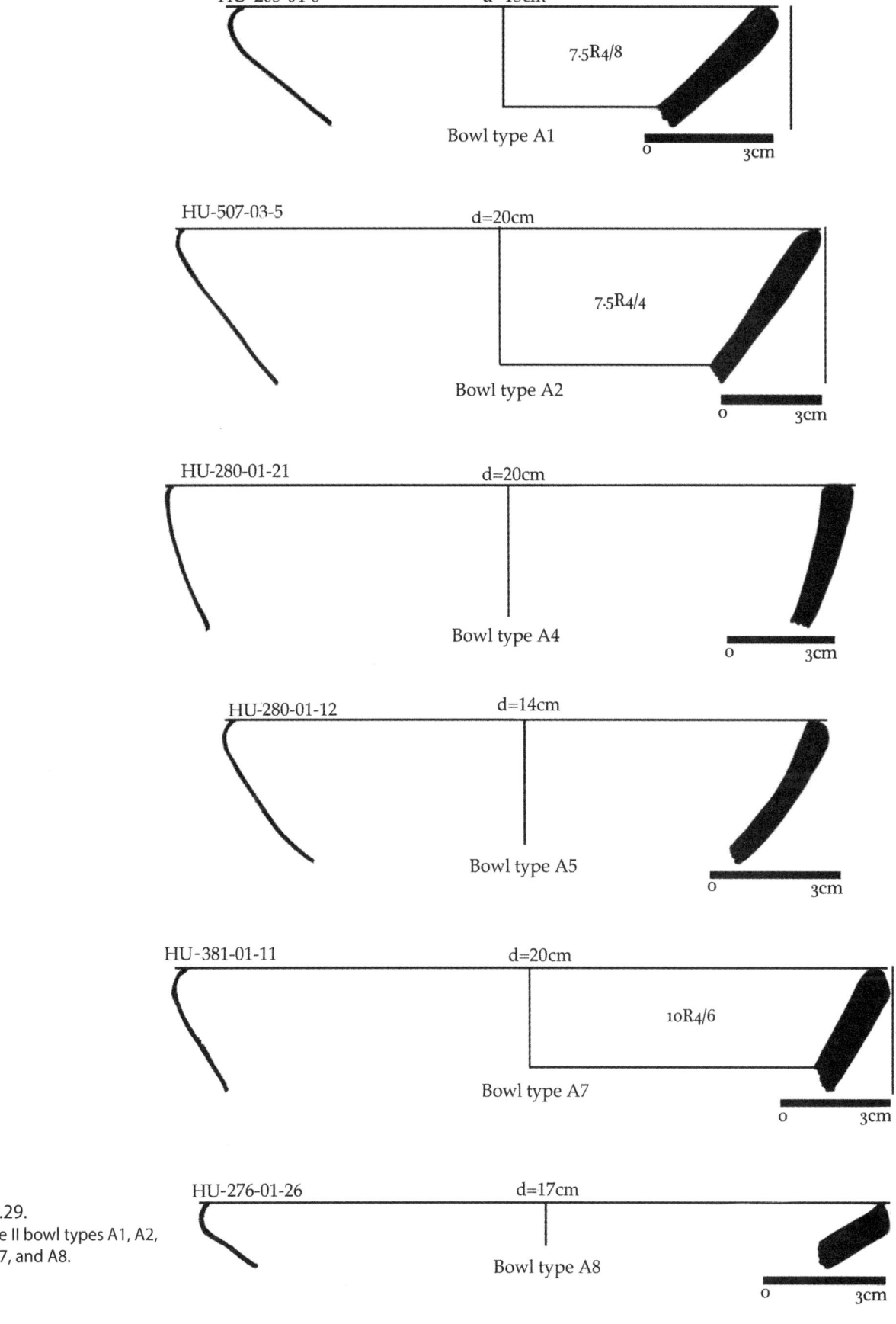

Figure 2.29.
Formative II bowl types A1, A2, A4, A5, A7, and A8.

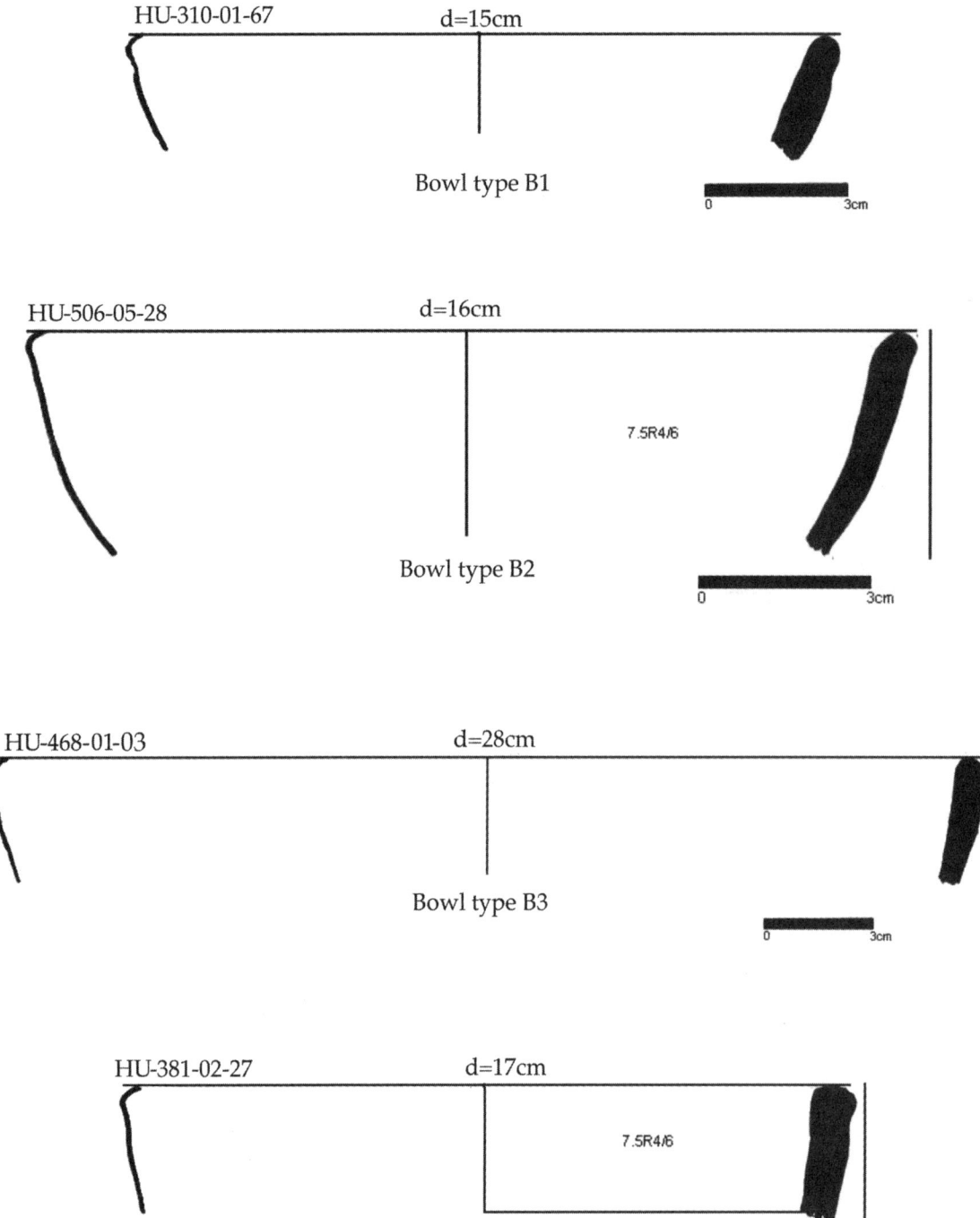

Figure 2.30. Formative II bowl types B1–B4.

Analysis of Ceramics

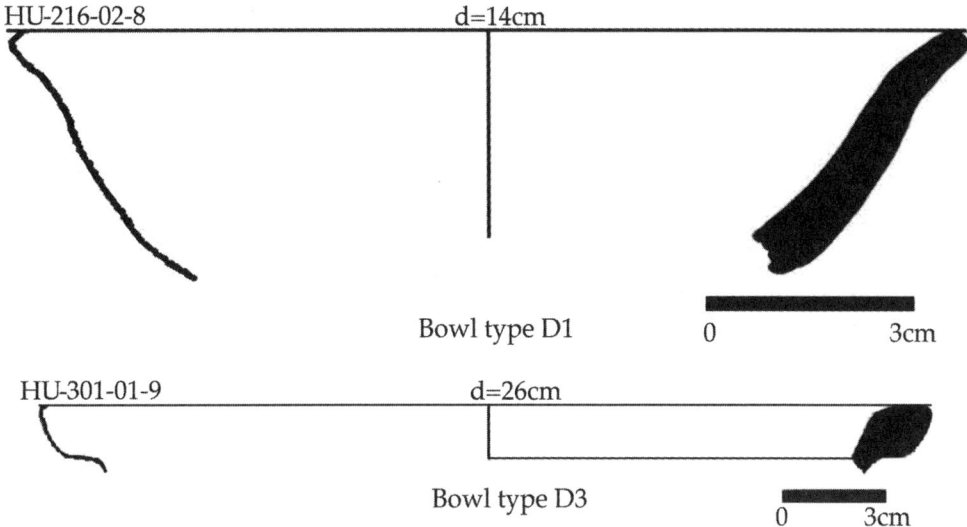

Figure 2.31. Formative II bowl types D1 and D3.

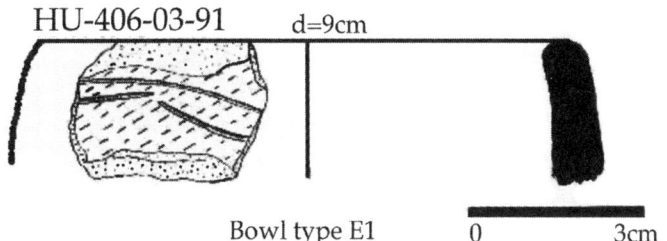

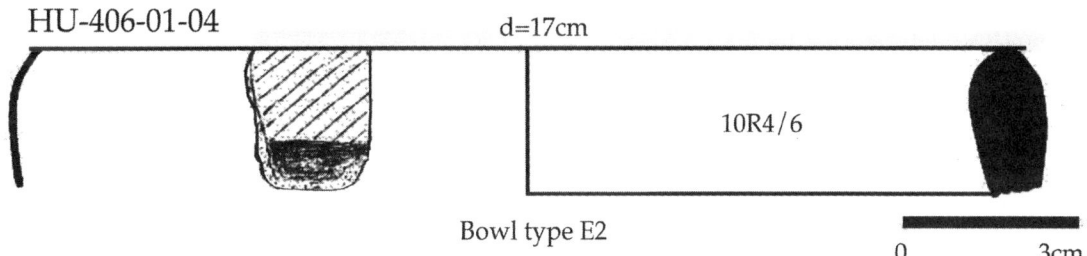

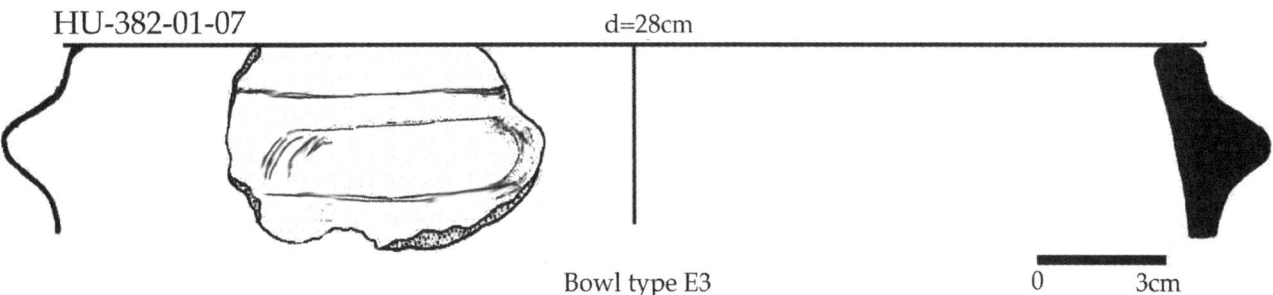

Figure 2.32. Formative II bowl types E1–E3.

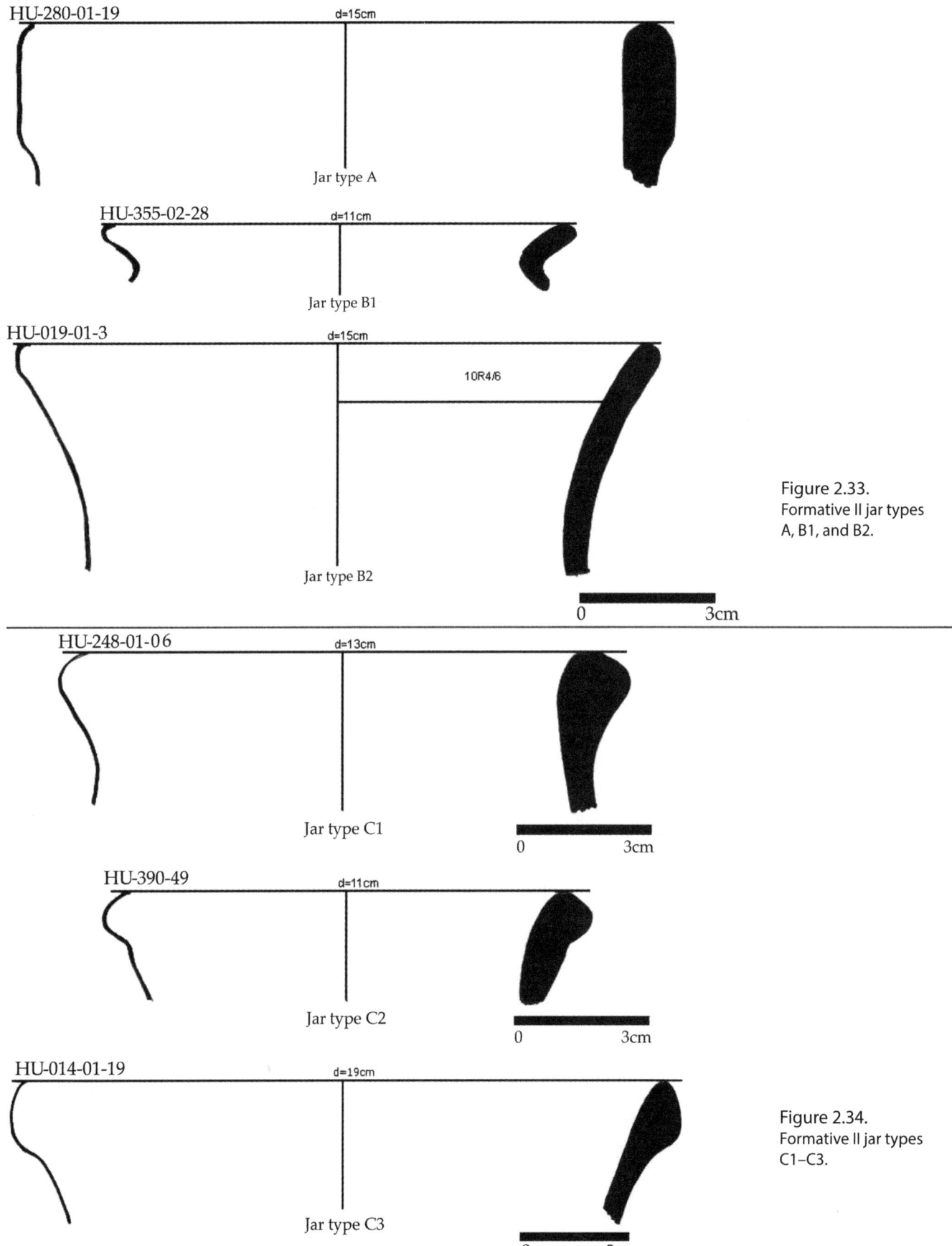

Figure 2.33. Formative II jar types A, B1, and B2.

Figure 2.34. Formative II jar types C1–C3.

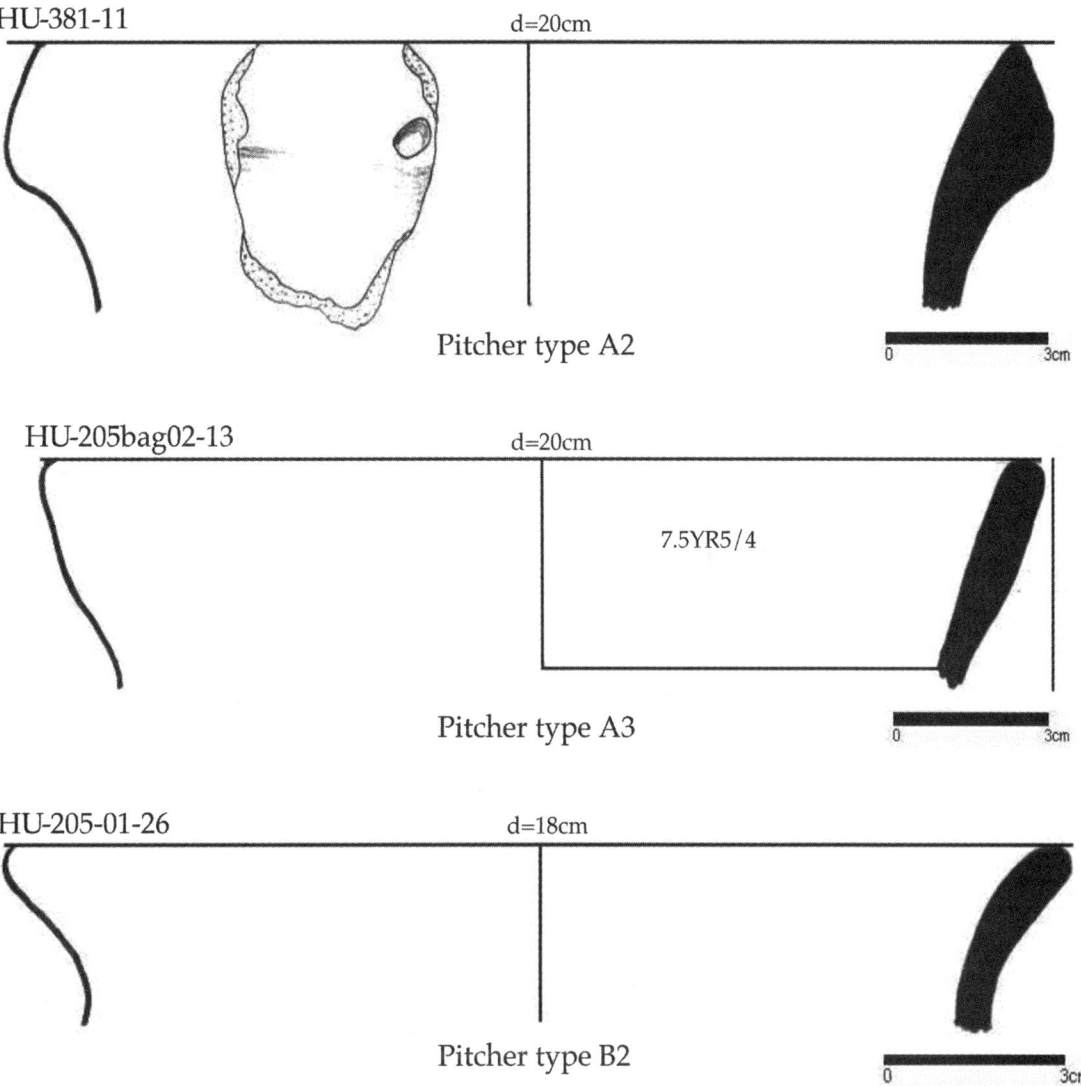

Figure 2.35. Formative II pitcher types A2, A3, and B2.

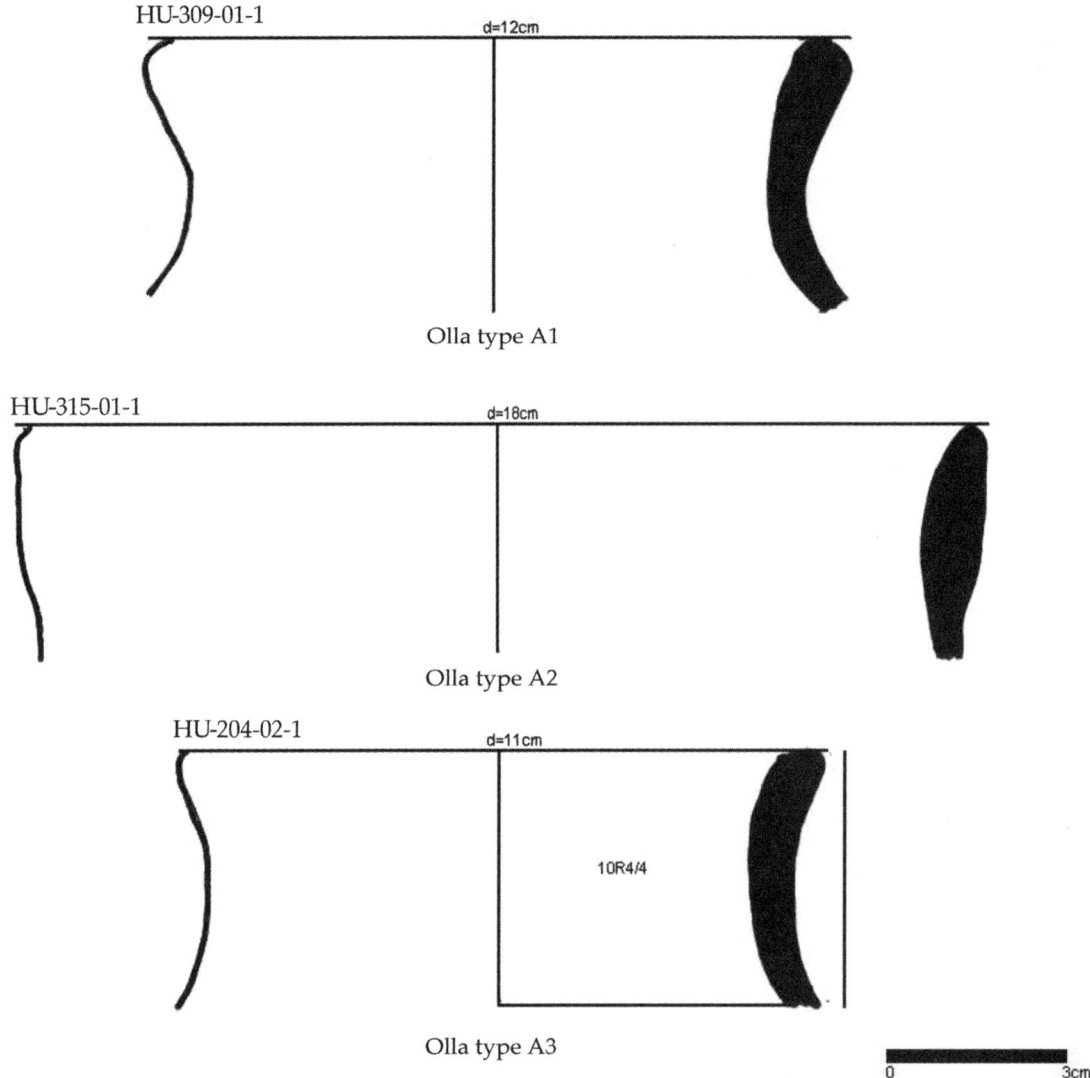

Figure 2.36. Formative II olla types A1–A3.

Analysis of Ceramics 77

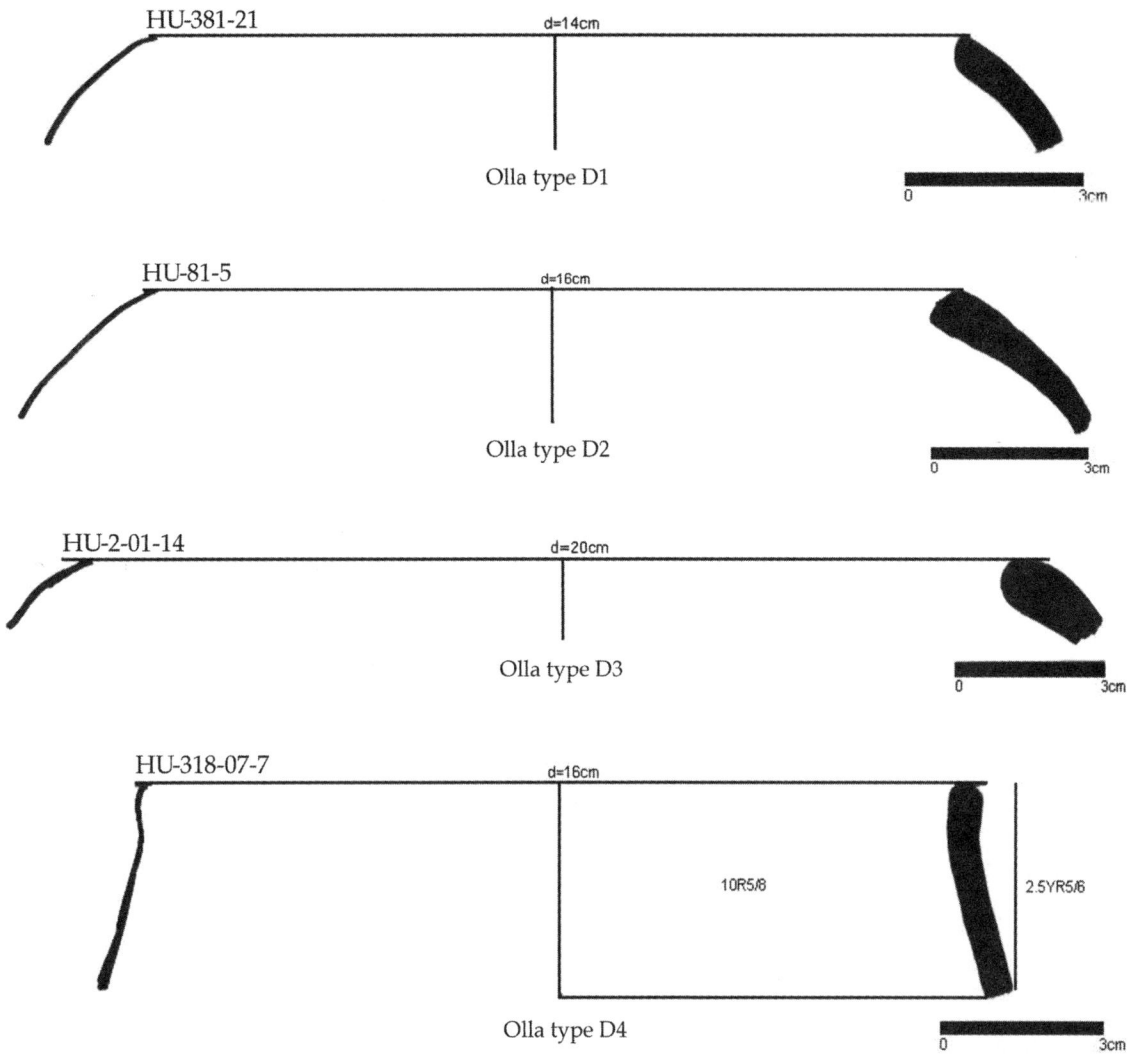

Figure 2.37. Formative II olla types D1–D4.

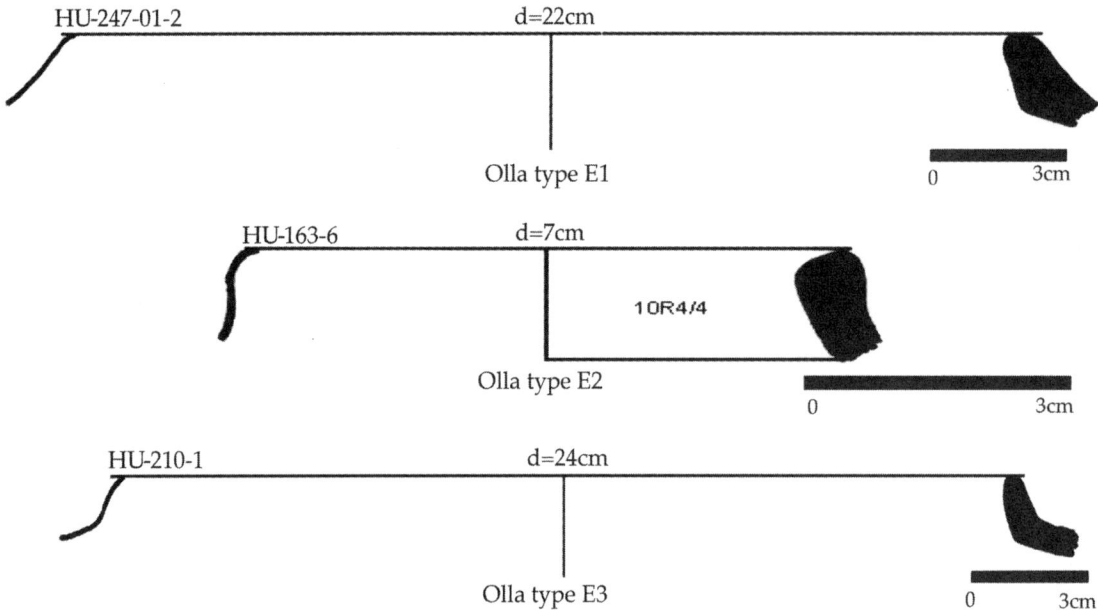

Figure 2.38. Formative II olla types E1–E3.

Formative III (Figs. 2.39–2.50)

Group I-2/9, 10, 11

The paste colors are light brown and light orange. They are characterized by white subrounded inclusions of 0.1 mm to 0.5 mm with a regular dispersion and medium to abundant density. They can also include pink subrounded inclusions of 4.0 mm with a regular dispersion and density. Black subrounded inclusions of 0.5 mm with regular dispersion and density are also found. They also include gold laminated mica of 0.1 mm with a regular dispersion and sparse density. The inclusions are visible in the cross section and the mica only in the exterior and interior. The fracture is regular, semi-compacted, with a soft and fine texture. The finish is wiped and burnished.

Group I-3/12, 13, 14, 15, 16

The pastes are light orange. They have white subangular inclusions of 0.1 mm with a regular dispersion and abundant to sparse density. They can also have black subangular inclusions of 0.1 mm with a regular dispersion and abundant to sparse density. There is also gold laminated mica of 0.1 mm with an irregular dispersion and sparse density. The inclusions are visible in the cross section and the mica only in the exterior and interior. They have a regular fracture, and are semi-compacted, with a soft and fine exterior. The finish is wiped, burnished, and eventually polished.

Group I-5/19, 20, 21

The paste color is red. It is characterized by white subrounded inclusions of 0.1 mm to 0.5 mm with a regular dispersion and medium to sparse density. It can also include translucent subrounded inclusions of 0.1 mm with a regular dispersion and abundant density. Ocher-colored subrounded inclusions of 3 mm with an irregular dispersion and sparse density are also present. There is also gold laminated mica of 0.1 mm with an irregular dispersion and sparse density. The inclusions are visible in the cross section and the mica only in the exterior and interior. They have a regular fracture, semi-compacted, with a soft and fine texture. The finish is wiped and burnished.

Group II-3/33, 34, 35, 36, 37

The pastes are brown and light orange. They contain white subrounded inclusions of 0.05 mm with a regular dispersion and medium density. There are also subrounded black inclusions of 0.05 mm with a regular dispersion and medium to sparse density. There are translucent subrounded inclusions of 0.1 mm with a regular dispersion and medium density. There is also gold laminated mica of 0.1 mm with a regular dispersion and sparse density. The inclusions are visible in the cross section and the mica only in the exterior and interior. The fracture is regular, semi-compacted, with a soft and fine texture. The finish is wiped and burnished.

Group III/51, 52

The paste colors are reddish brown and light orange. This group is composed of white subrounded inclusions of 0.5 mm size with a regular dispersion and abundant density. Others are black subrounded inclusions of 0.1 mm with an even dispersal and high density. The inclusions are visible in the cross section: they have a regular fracture, semi-compact, with a soft and fine texture. The finish is wiped and burnished.

Associated Style: Pucara

Associated Assemblage:

Open Vessels

Tazones, type A, variants 1, 3, 4, and 5 (Figs. 2.39, 2.40).
There are four sizes: small, medium, large, and very large. The most common finish is burnished for the decorated ones and wiped flat areas. The decoration includes red external and/or internal slips. The types

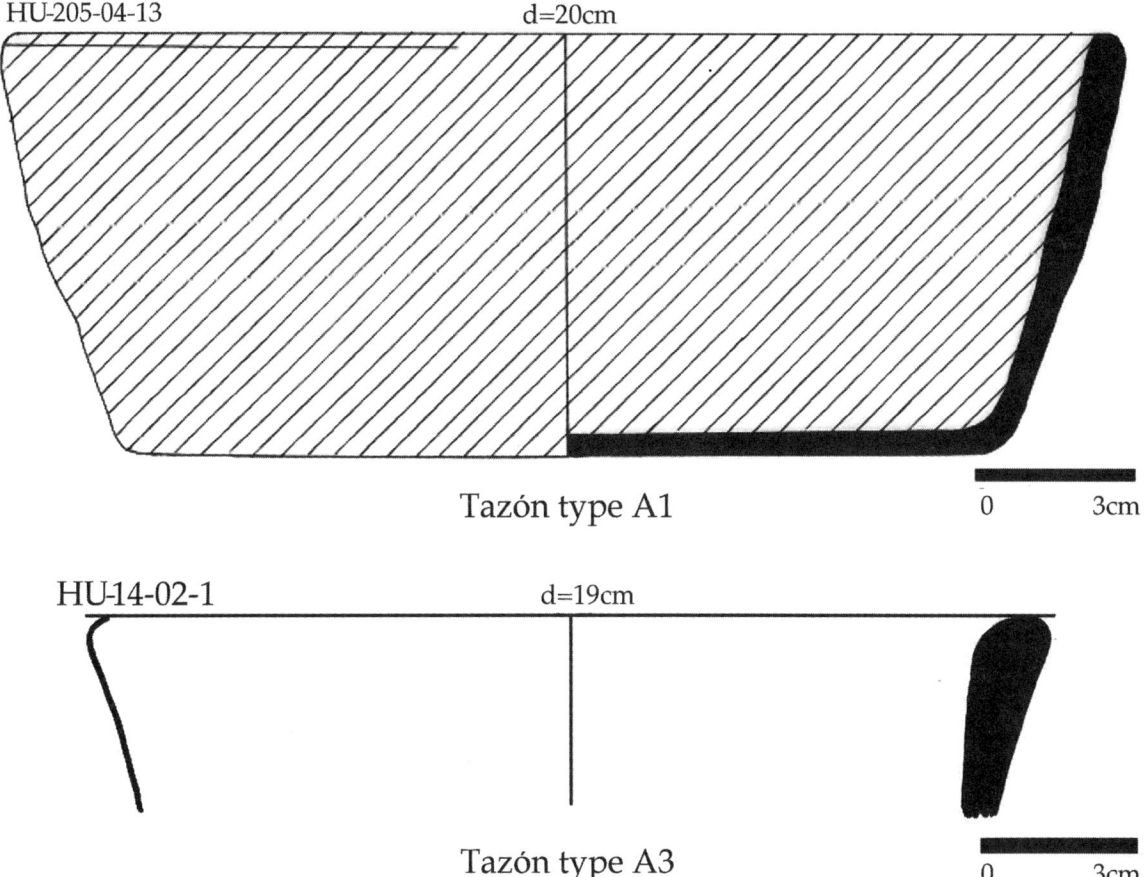

Figure 2.39. Formative III tazón types A1 and A3.

A1, A4, and A5 have incised exterior decorations, but the type A4 also includes exterior incisions delimiting areas painted cream over red. The type A5 has parts painted black over red. The designs are geometric (squares, circles, and stepped).

Tazones, type B, variants 2, 3, 4, 5, 6, 7, and 8 (Figs. 2.41, 2.42).

They are small, medium, large, and very large. The decorated ones are commonly burnished and the plainwares are wiped. The decorations include red, orange, and brown external and/or internal slips. There are also incised decorations with or without paint on the exterior (with only one interior example) in one color (black, cream, or tones of orange over distinct slips) or a combination of two colors (black + red over cream or black + cream over red). The designs are geometric (horizontal, vertical, diagonal, and stepped, circles, and squares).

Bowls, type A, variants 1, 2, 3, 4, 5, 6, 7, and 9 (Fig. 2.43).

They are small, medium, large, and very large. The most common finish is burnishing on the decorated vessels and wiping on the plainwares. The decorations include red or orange slips on the exterior and/or interior. Types A3, A4, and A5 have lateral appendixes under the rim (rounded protuberances).

Bowls, type B, variants 1, 2, and 4 (Fig. 2.44).

They are small, medium, large, and very large. In general the decorated ones are burnished and the plain ones are wiped. The decorations include red or orange slips on the exterior and/or interior. Only type B1 has decorations painted on the interior over one color (black + cream over red or brown over orange) and type B2 can have geometric shapes (horizontal lines) incised on the exterior over different slips as decorations.

Bowls, type D, variants 1 and 3 (Fig. 2.45).

They are large and very large. They are burnished when decorated and wiped when they are plain. The decorations use red, orange, and brown external and/or internal slips. Decorations also include external incisions with or without paints in one color (black or red over cream). The motifs are geometric (diagonal lines, triangles, circles).

Bowls, type E, variant 3 (Fig. 2.45).

They are medium and large. The decorated ones are burnished and plain ones are wiped. The only decoration is an exterior orange slip.

Closed Vessels

Jars, type A (Fig. 2.46).

They are very small, small, and medium. They commonly use wiping for the flat areas and burnishing for the decorated ones. They use red and orange slips on the exterior and interior surfaces near the rim. They can have incised decorations on the rim (oval grooves) or can be painted one color (black over red). In many cases, the designs are geometric (horizontal and stepped).

Jars, type B, variants 1 and 2 (Fig. 2.46).

They are small and medium, although in type B2 there can be very small examples. The common finishes are wiping and burnishing for the decorated vessels. Decorations include red and orange exterior slips and interior slips near the rim. The type B1 also has decorations painted in two colors (black + reddish brown over red) with geometric designs (horizontal lines).

Jars, type C, variants 1 and 2 (Fig. 2.46).

They are only small and medium plainwares, generally wiped as a finish.

Pitchers, type A, variants 1, 2, and 3 (Fig. 2.47).

They are large and very large. The most common finish is wiping. Some are plainwares and others are decorated with external red slips.

Pitchers, type B, variant 2 (Fig. 2.47).

They are large and generally wiped. They can be plainwares or decorated with red-toned external slips.

Ollas, type A, variants 1, 2, and 3; type B, variants 1 and 2 (Fig. 2.48).

They are small, medium, large, and very large, generally burnished. They can be plainwares or decorated with external red or orange slips.

Ollas, type D, variants 1, 2, 3, and 4 (Fig. 2.49).

They are large or very large; only in type D1 are there small and medium. Generally they are burnished. There are examples of both plainwares and decorated wares with red-toned slips on the exterior and interior lips.

Ollas, type E, variants 1, 2, and 3 (Fig. 2.50).

They can be small, medium, large, and very large. They are commonly burnished. They can be plainwares or decorated with external brown or red slips.

Other Forms Associated with the Assemblage: Cups

Ritual Elements: Incense burners, trumpets

Productive Tools: Polishing tools

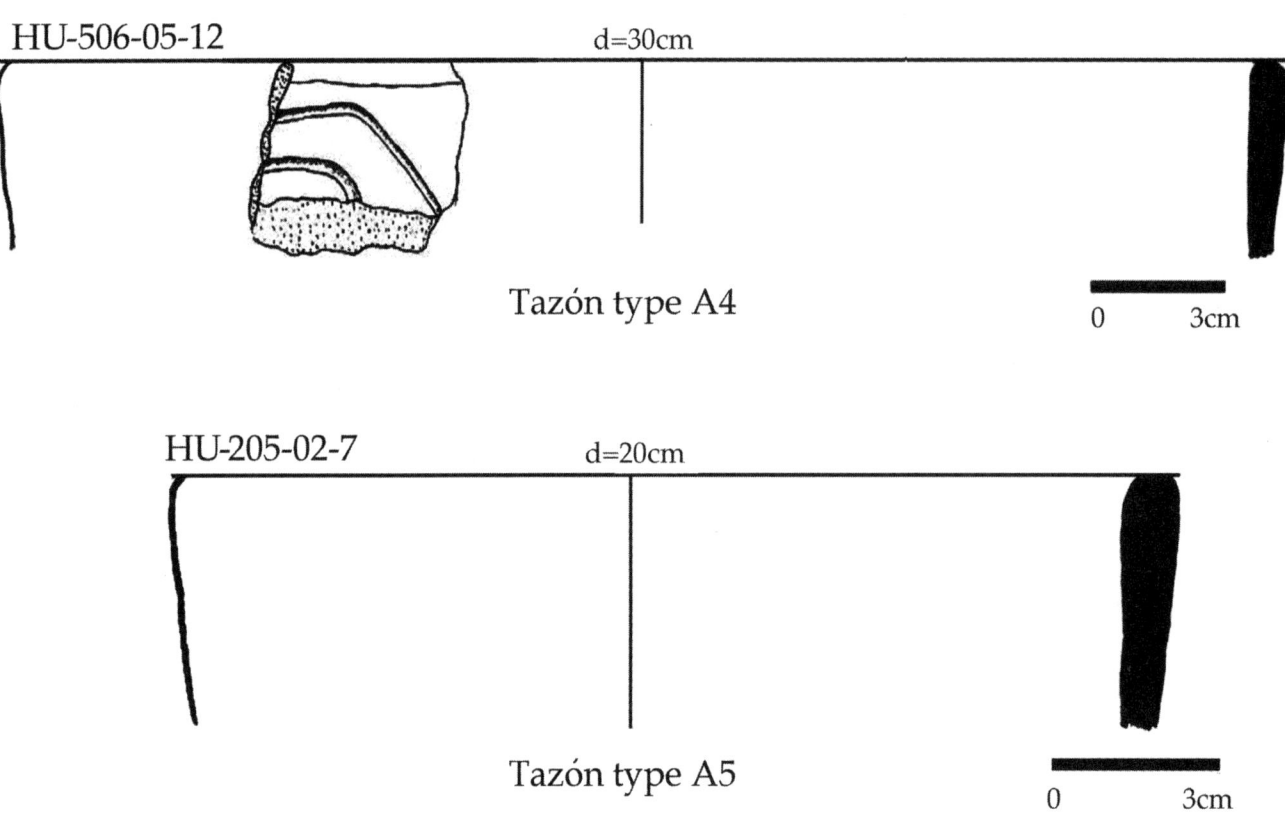

Figure 2.40. Formative III tazón types A4 and A5.

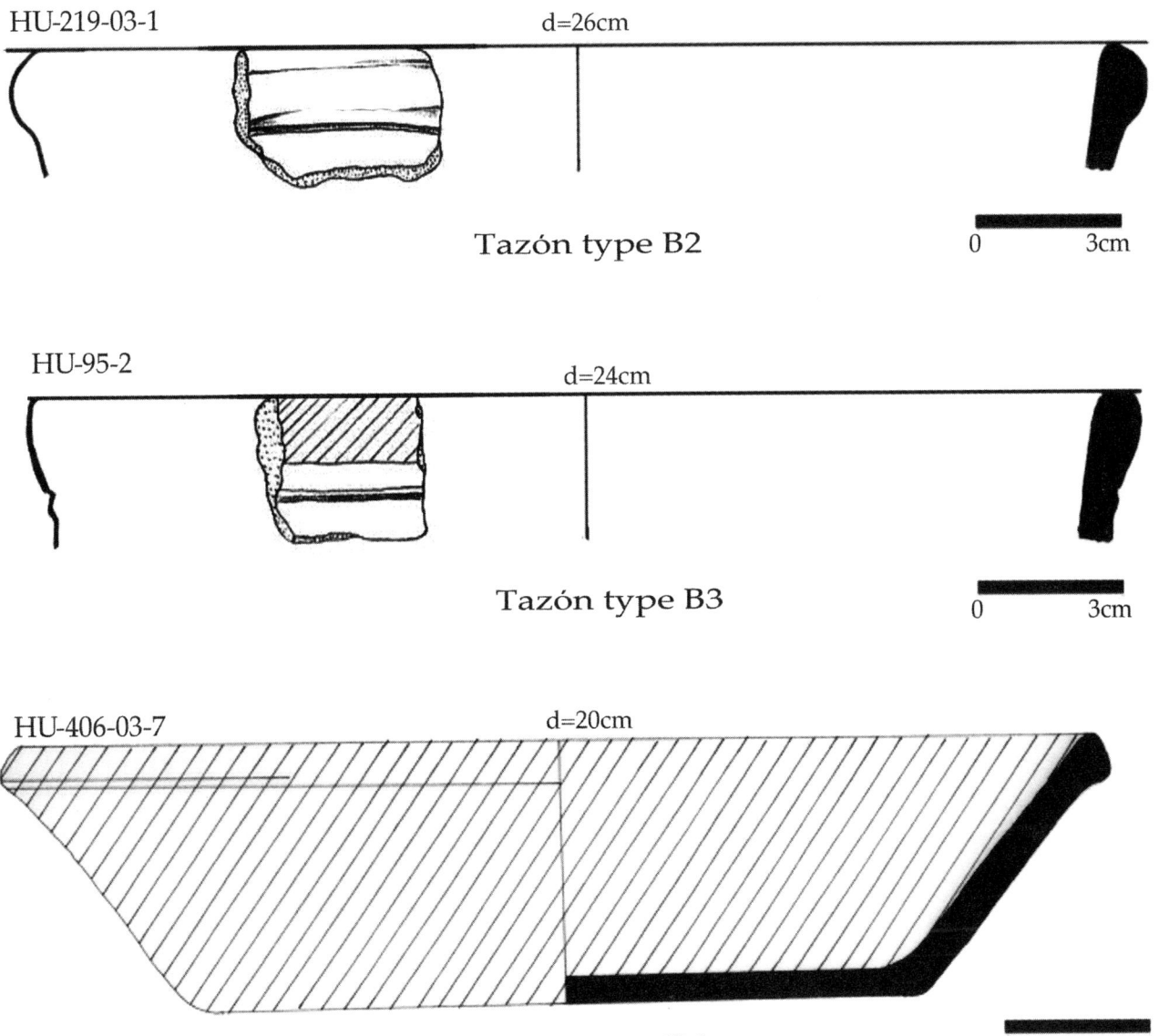

Figure 2.41. Formative III tazón types B2–B4.

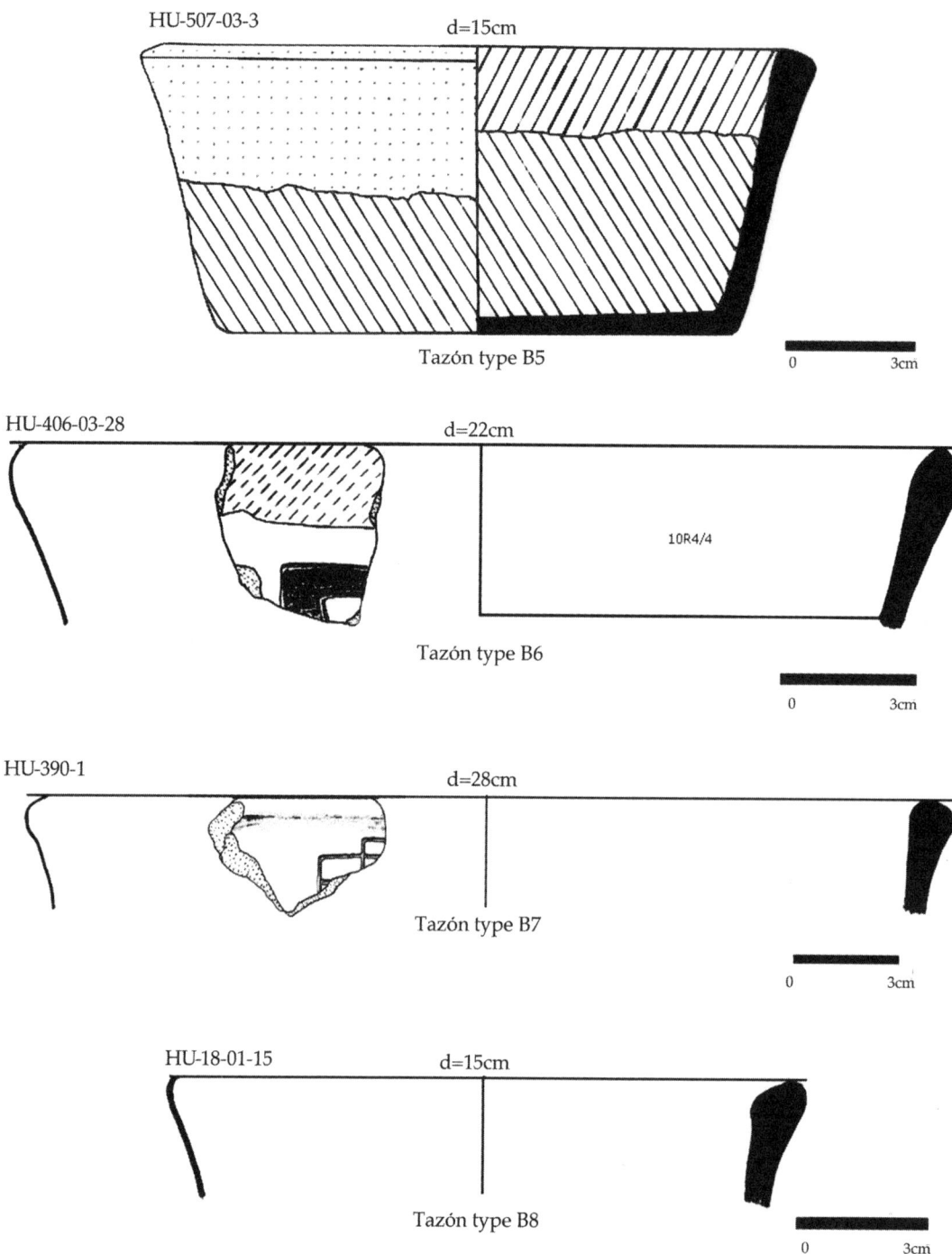

Figure 2.42. Formative III tazón types B5–B8.

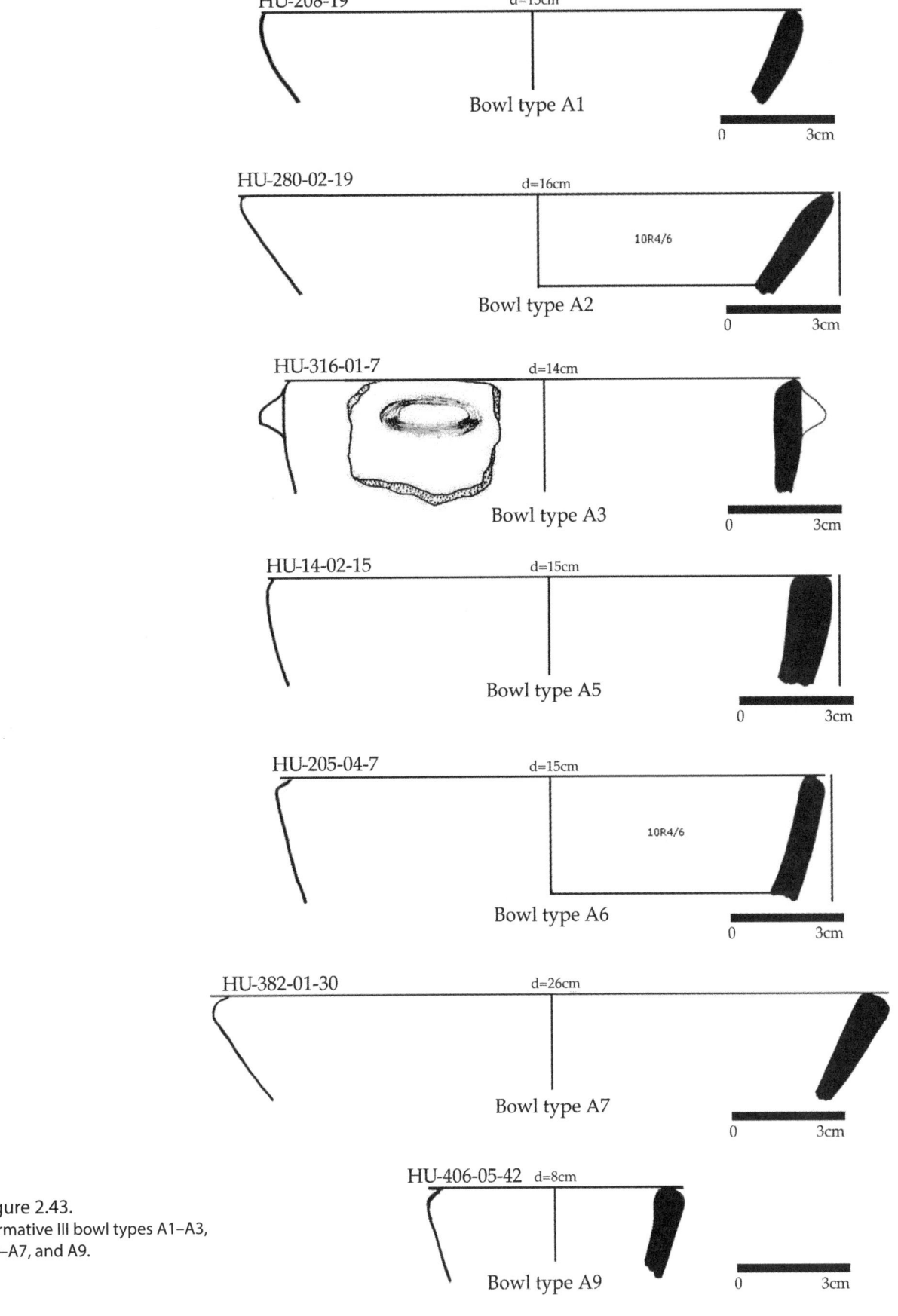

Figure 2.43.
Formative III bowl types A1–A3, A5–A7, and A9.

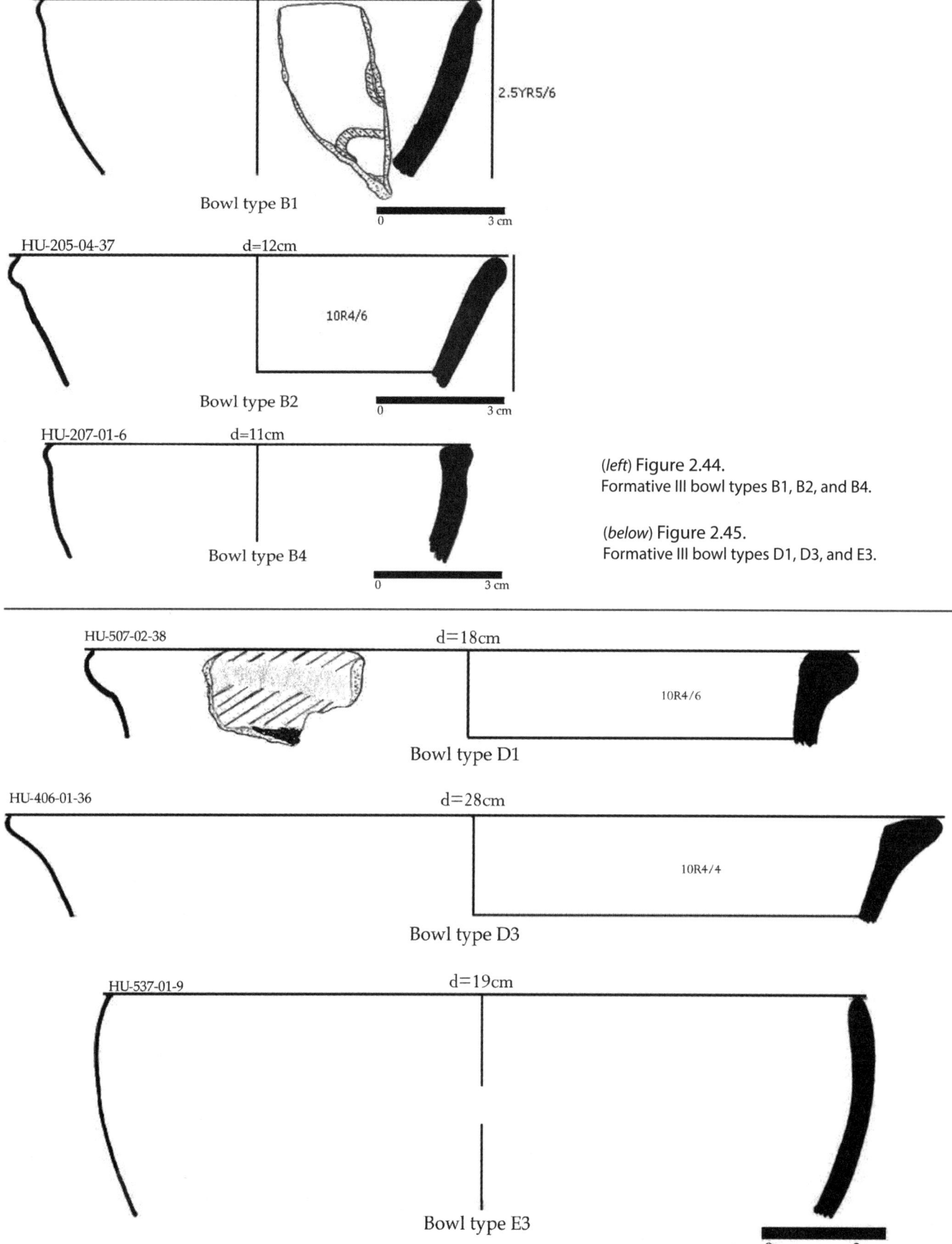

(*left*) Figure 2.44.
Formative III bowl types B1, B2, and B4.

(*below*) Figure 2.45.
Formative III bowl types D1, D3, and E3.

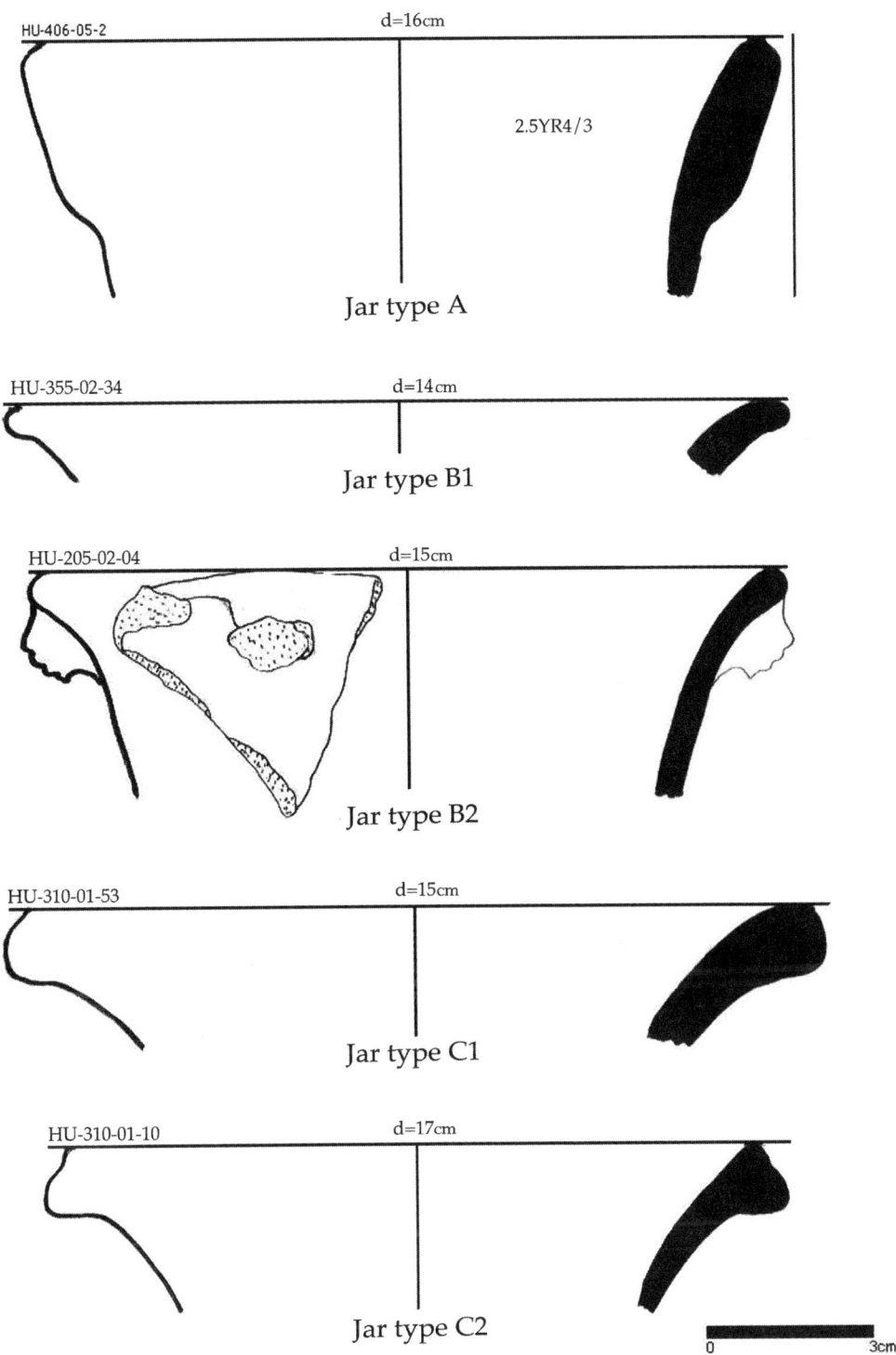

Figure 2.46. Formative III jar types A, B1, B2, C1, and C2.

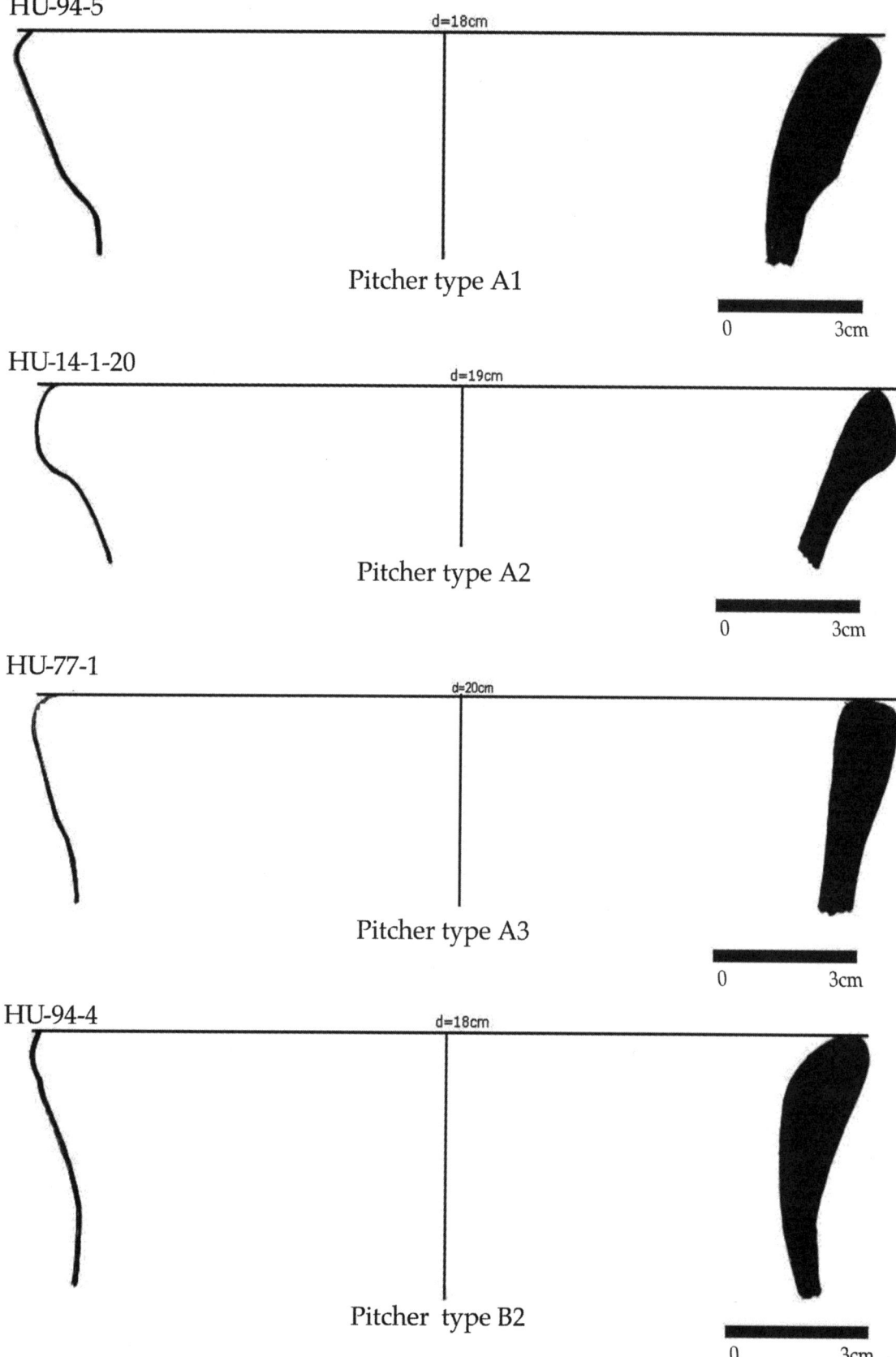

Figure 2.47. Formative III pitcher types A1–A3 and B2.

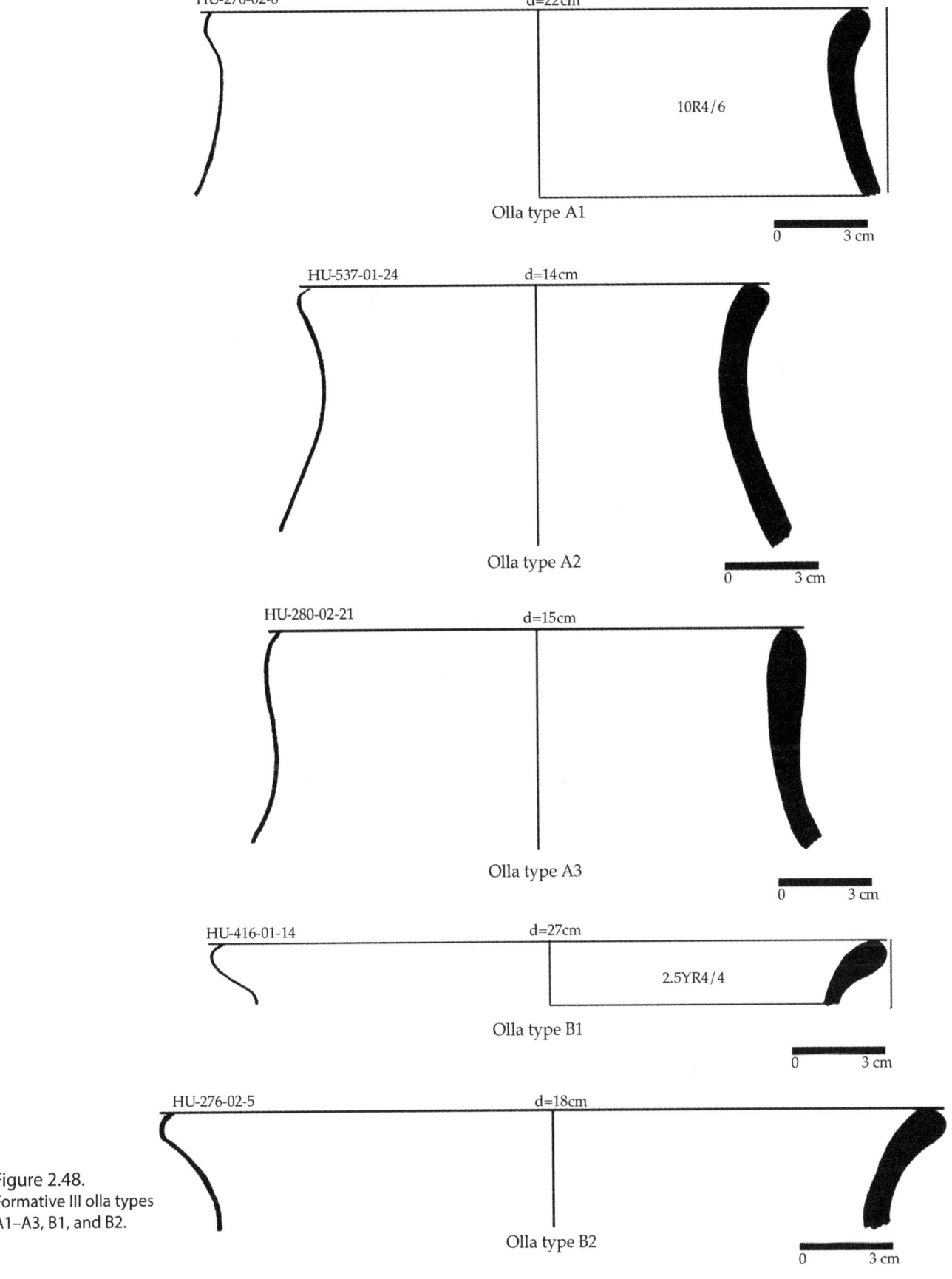

Figure 2.48. Formative III olla types A1–A3, B1, and B2.

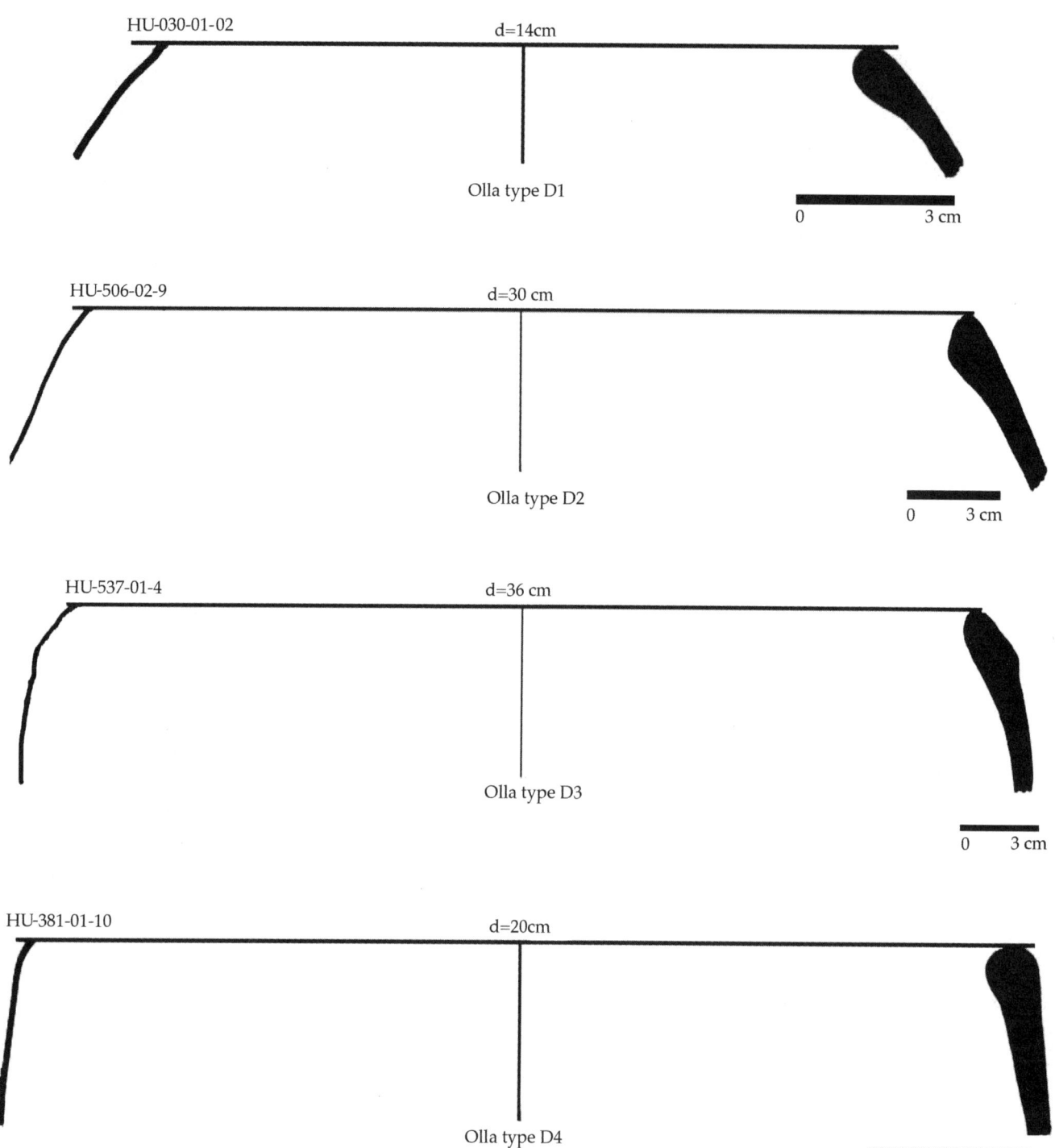

Figure 2.49. Formative III olla types D1–D4.

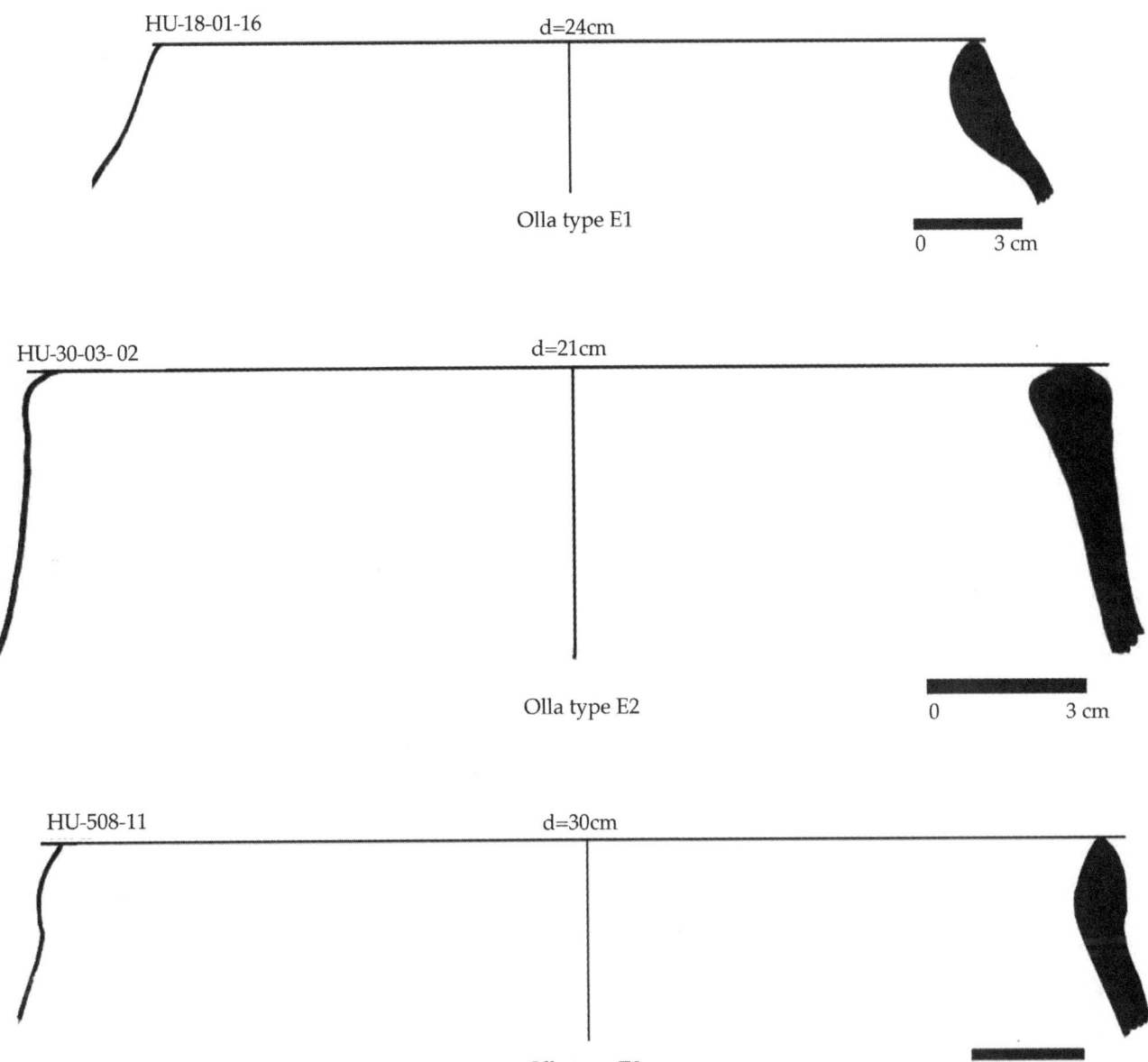

Figure 2.50. Formative III olla types E1–E3.

Huaña I (Figs. 2.51–2.59)

Group II-1/4, 5, 9, 16, 17, 20

The pastes are light brown, orange, light orange, and red colored. They are characterized by white subrounded inclusions of 0.1 mm with a regular dispersion and medium density. They can also have black subrounded inclusions of 0.05 mm to 0.1 mm with a regular dispersion and abundant to sparse density. Translucent subrounded inclusions are also present, of 0.05 mm to 0.1 mm with a regular dispersion and medium to abundant density. There is also gold laminated mica of 2.0 mm with a regular dispersion and sparse density. The inclusions are visible in the cross section and the mica only in the exterior and interior. They have a regular fracture, semi-compact, with a soft and fine texture. The finish is wiped with exceptional polish.

Group II-2/2, 3, 6, 8, 12, 13, 29, 30, 31, 32

The pastes are light brown and light orange. They are composed of white subangular inclusions of 0.05 mm to 0.1 mm with a regular dispersion and medium to sparse density. Others include subrounded translucent and/or black inclusions of 0.05 mm with a regular dispersion and medium density. Red subangular inclusions of 0.1 mm are also present with an irregular dispersion and sparse density. There is also gold laminated mica of 0.05 mm with an irregular dispersion and very sparse density. The inclusions are visible in the cross section and the mica only in the exterior and interior. They have a regular fracture, semi-compact, with a soft and fine texture. The finish is wiped and burnished.

Associated Style: Qaluyu/Pucara

Associated Assemblage:

Open Vessels

Tazones, type A, variants 1, 3, 4, and 5 (Fig. 2.51).

They are small, medium, and large. They are commonly burnished as a finish. There are examples of plainwares; others are decorated with red or orange external and/or internal slips. In type A5, they can have incised decorations on the exterior delimiting areas painted in black over orange or only painted decorations combining two colors (black and orange over red). The designs are geometric (horizontal or vertical lines).

Tazones, type B, variants 1, 3, 4, 5, 7, and 8 (Fig. 2.52).

They are medium, large, and very large. Only in type B5 are there small examples (14 cm). The finish is generally burnished for the decorated vessels and wiped for the flat areas. They use red or orange slips on the exterior and/or interior. They can also have painted decorations combining one color (black over red) with geometric designs (horizontal lines).

Bowls, type A, variants 1, 4, and 5 (Figs. 2.53, 2.54).

They are small, medium, and large. They are commonly wiped, although some are burnished. The decorations include red slips on the exterior and/or interior. Only in type A5 is there evidence of painted geometric designs (horizontal lines) decorating the interior in one color (black) over the natural color of the vessel.

Bowls, type B, variants 1, 3, and 4 (Figs. 2.54, 2.55).

They are small, medium, and large. The most common finish is wiping, although some are burnished. There are plainwares and others decorated with red or orange slips on the exterior and/or interior. Decorations also include geometric designs (horizontal lines) painted in black over orange.

Closed Vessels

Jars, type A; type B, variants 1 and 2; type C, variants 1, 2, and 3 (Fig. 2.56).

They are small and medium. Those of types A and B are finished by wiping and eventually burnishing; those of type C are only wiped. There are examples of plainwares and decorated wares with red and orange slips on the exterior and near the interior rim. Type A shows incised geometric designs (oval grooves) and type B has lateral appendixes (rounded protuberances), while type C only has red slips.

Pitchers, type A, variants 1, 2, and 3; type B, variants 1 and 2 (Fig. 2.57).

They are large and very large. They commonly use wiping as a finish. There are examples of plainwares and others decorated with red slips on the exterior and near the interior rim.

Ollas, type A, variants 1, 2, and 3 (Fig. 2.58).

They are medium, large, and very large. The most common finish is wiping. The majority are plainwares and others are decorated with red slips on the exterior and near the interior rim.

Ollas, type B, variants 1 and 2 (Fig. 2.58).

They are large and very large. Generally, they use wiping as a finish. The majority are plainwares and others are decorated with red or orange slips on the exterior and near the interior rim.

Ollas, type D, variant 1 (Fig. 2.59).

They are large and very large wiped plainwares.

Ollas, type E, variants 1 and 2 (Fig. 2.59).

They are small and medium, using wiping as a finish. There are examples of plainwares and decorated wares with orange slips on the exterior and near the interior rim.

Other Forms Associated with the Assemblage: Cups

Ritual Elements: Incense burners, trumpets

Productive Tools: Polishing tools

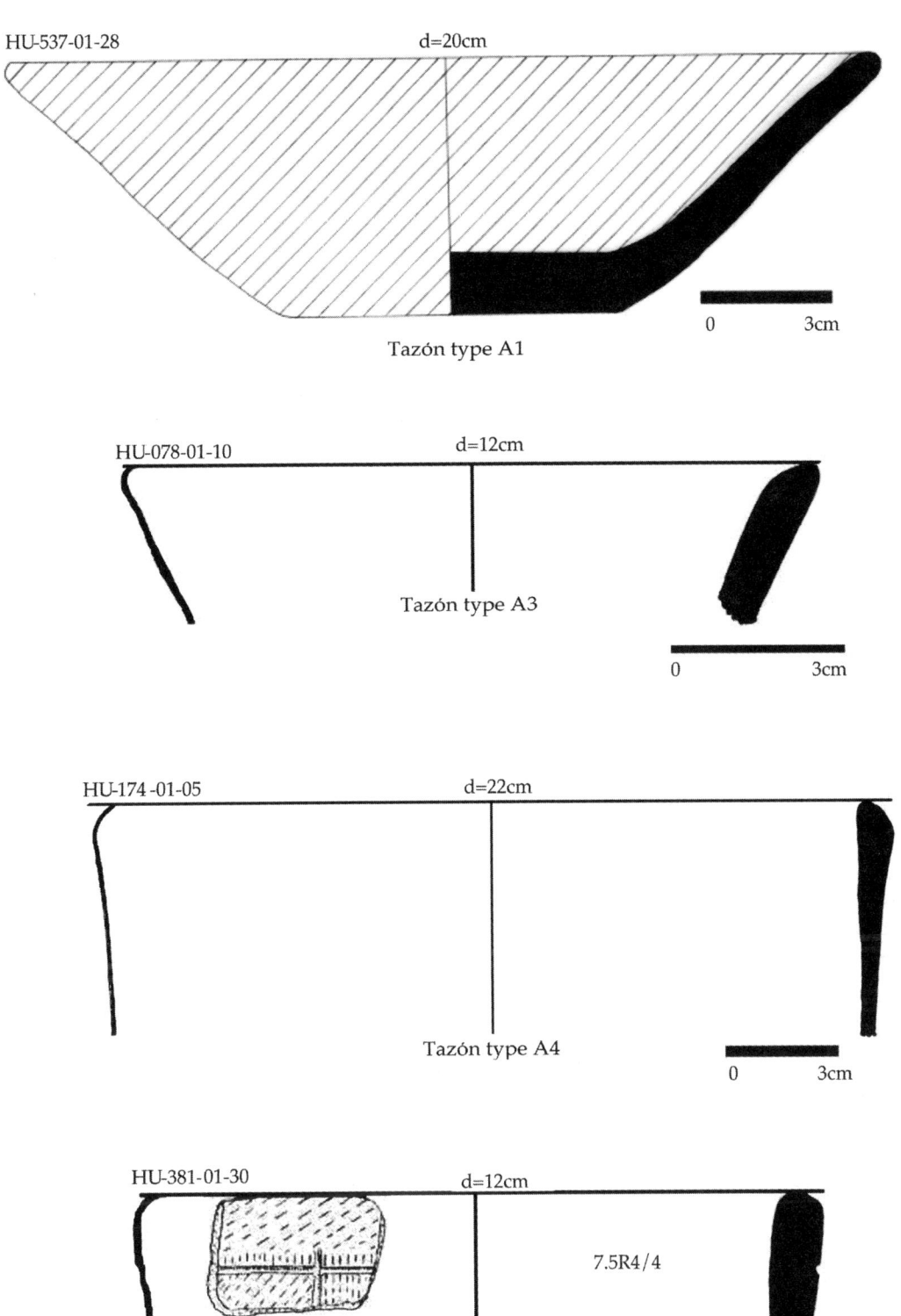

Figure 2.51. Huaña I tazón types A1 and A3–A5.

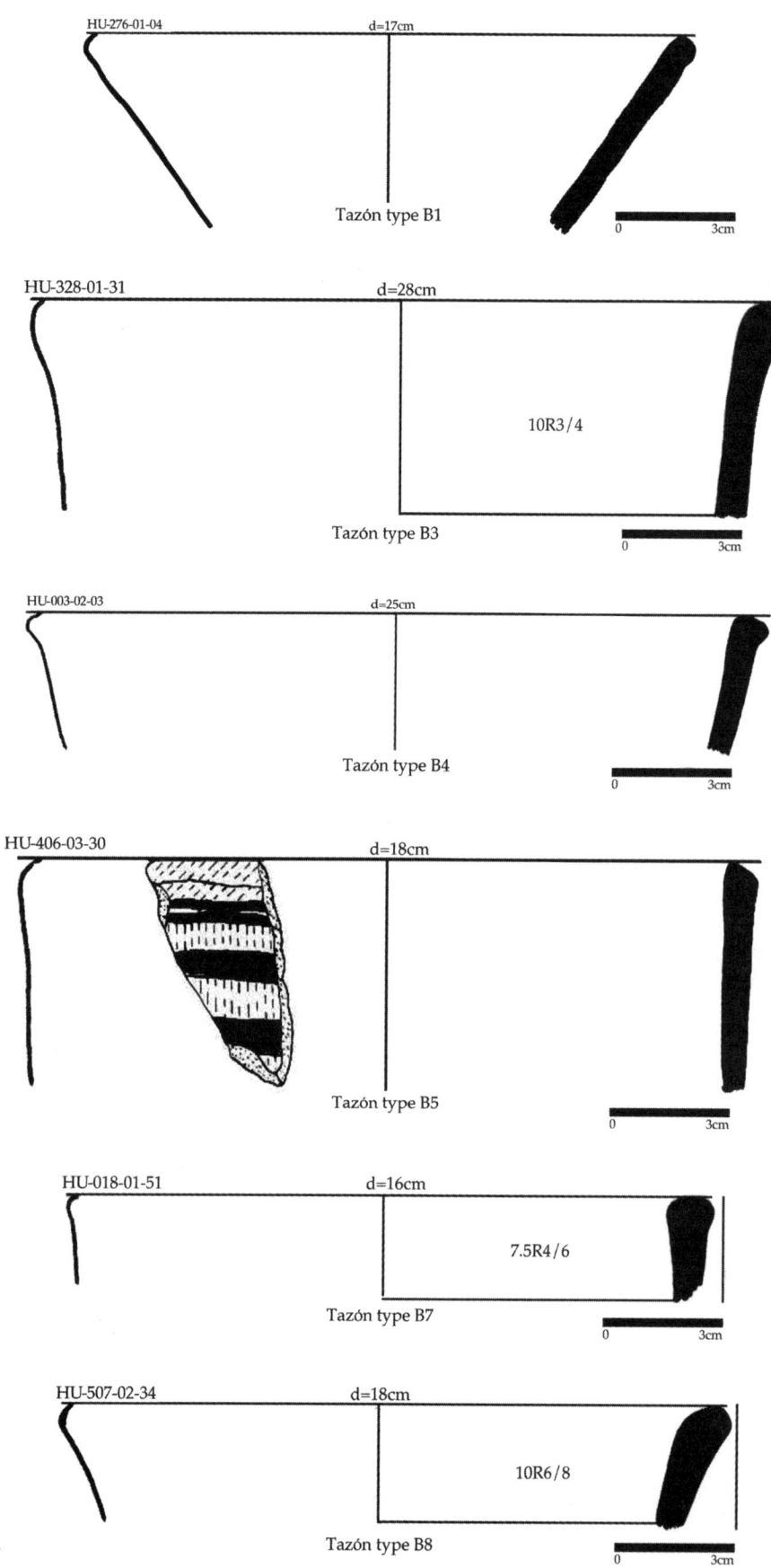

Figure 2.52. Huaña I tazón types B1, B3–B5, B7, and B8.

Analysis of Ceramics

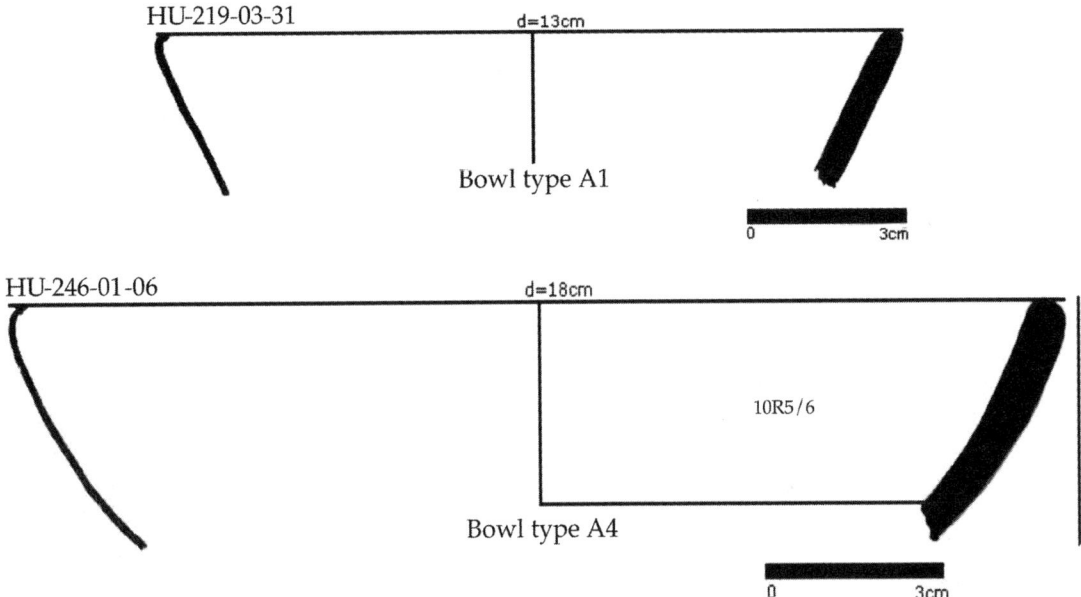

Figure 2.53. Huaña I bowl types A1 and A4.

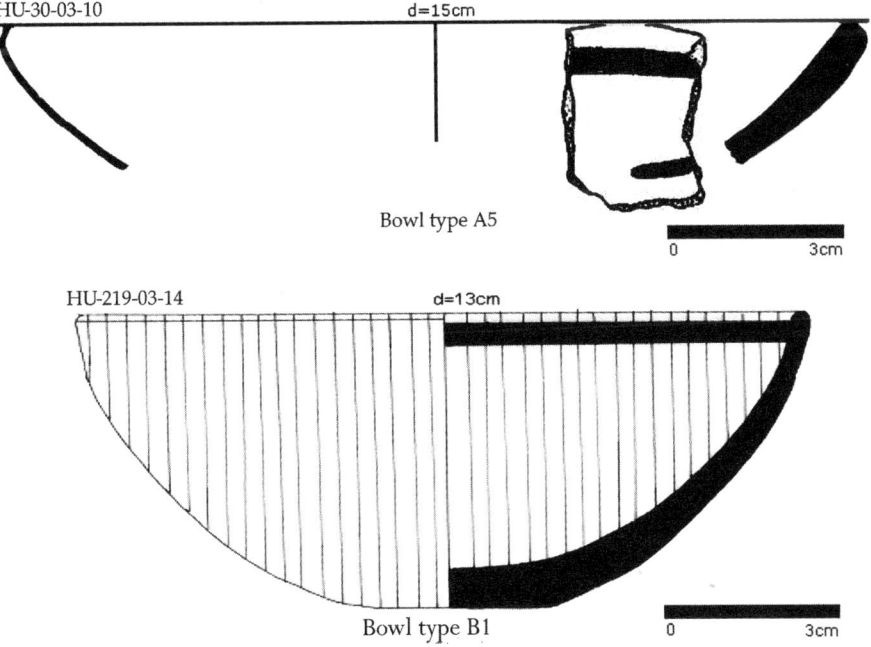

Figure 2.54. Huaña I bowl types A5 and B1.

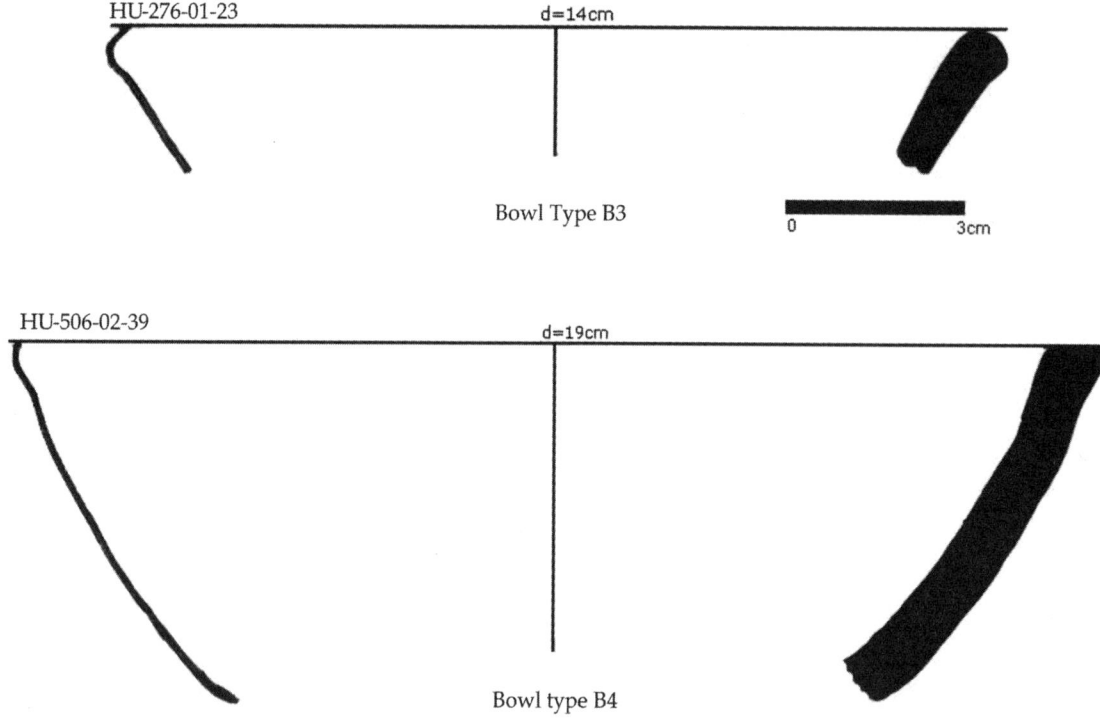

Figure 2.55. Huaña I bowl types B3 and B4.

Analysis of Ceramics 95

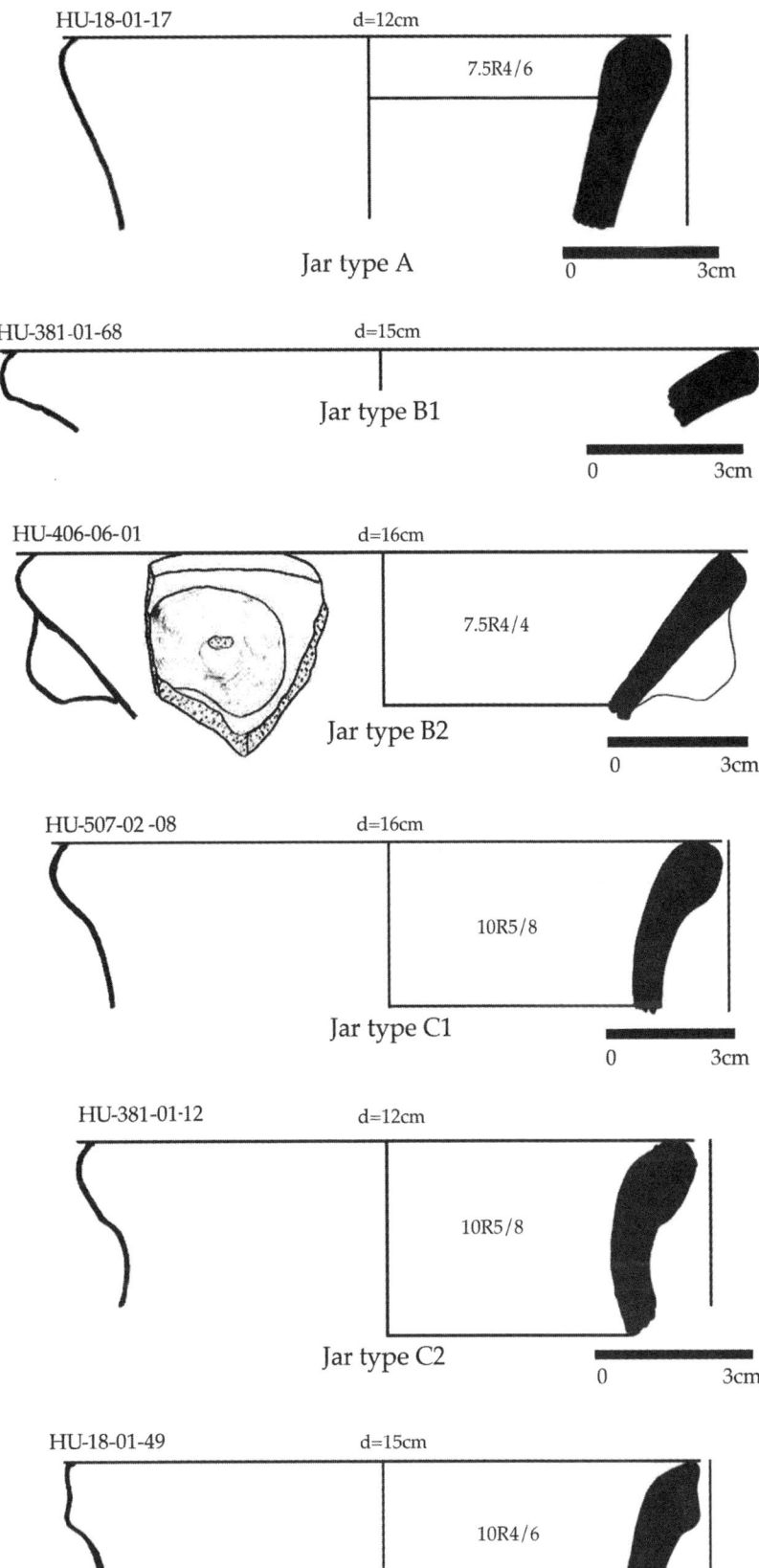

Figure 2.56.
Huaña I jar types A, B1, B2, and C1–C3.

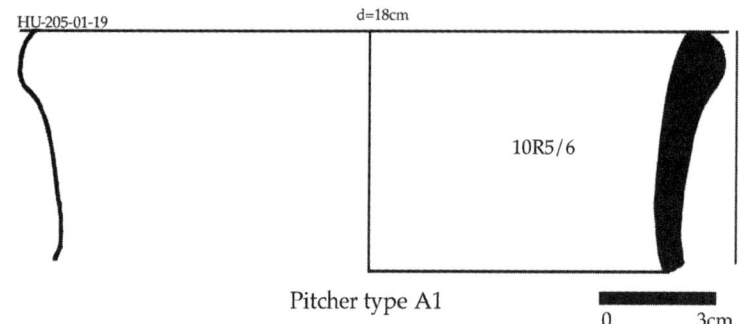
Pitcher type A1

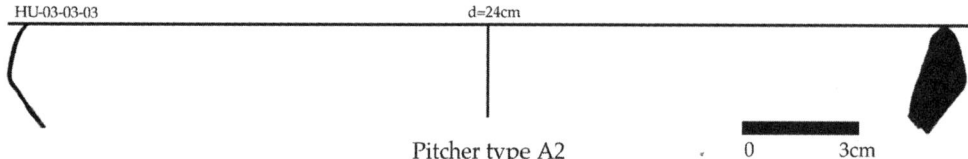
Pitcher type A2

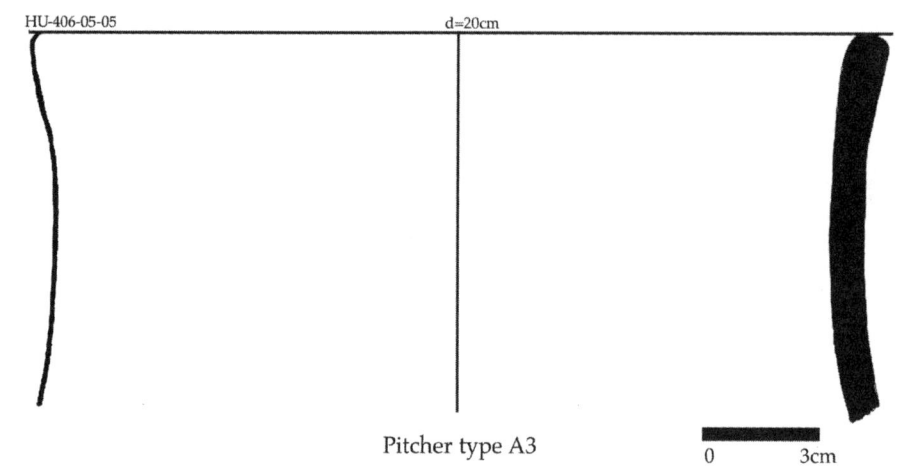
Pitcher type A3

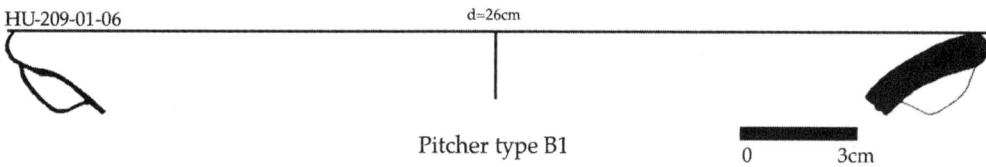
Pitcher type B1

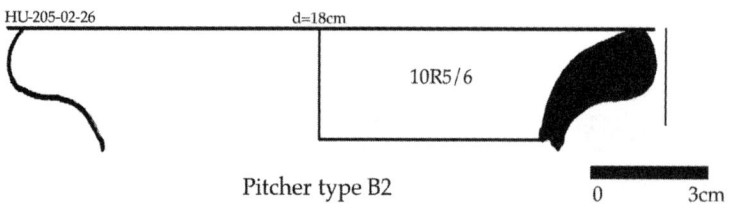
Pitcher type B2

Figure 2.57. Huaña I pitcher types A1–A3, B1, and B2.

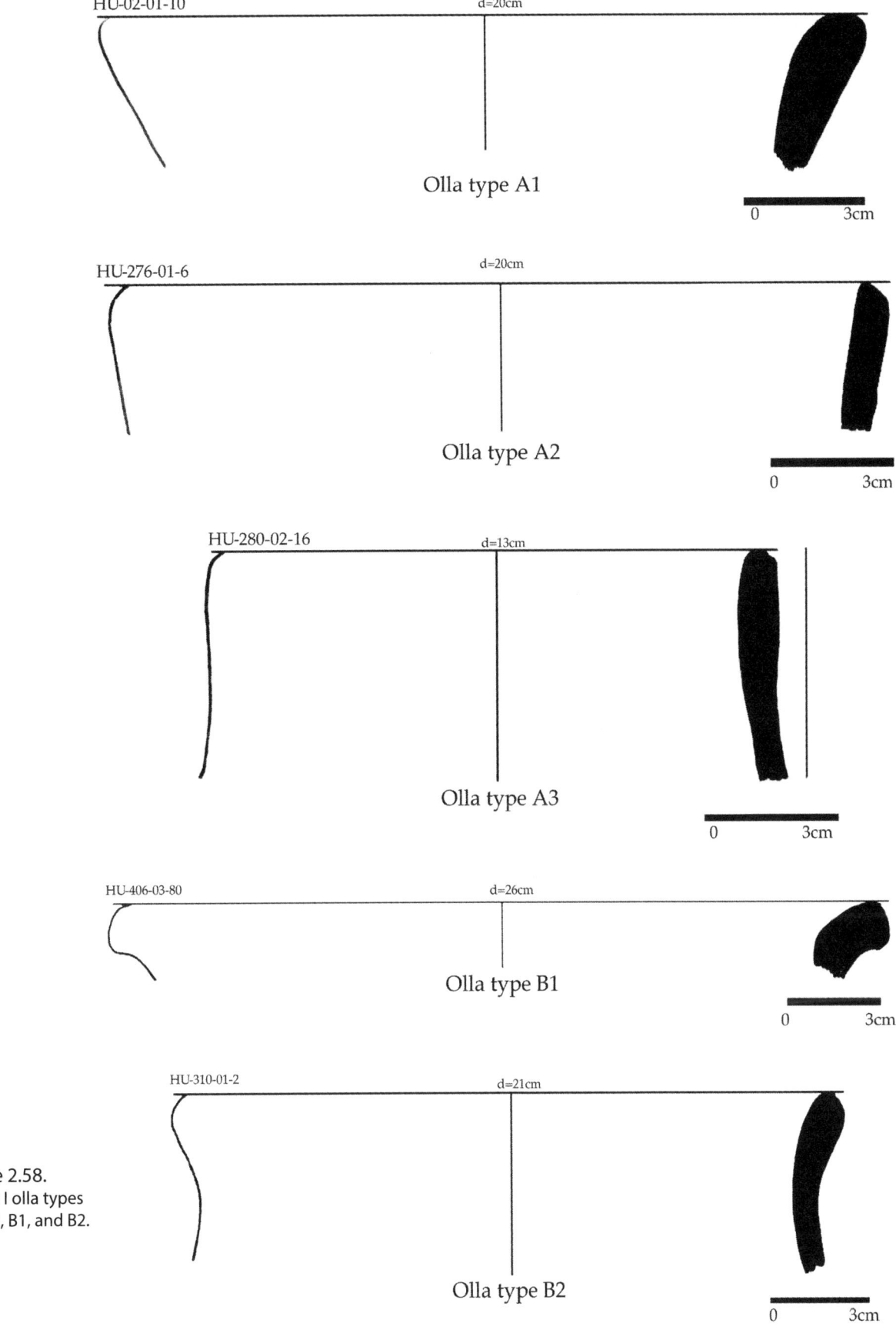

Figure 2.58. Huaña I olla types A1–A3, B1, and B2.

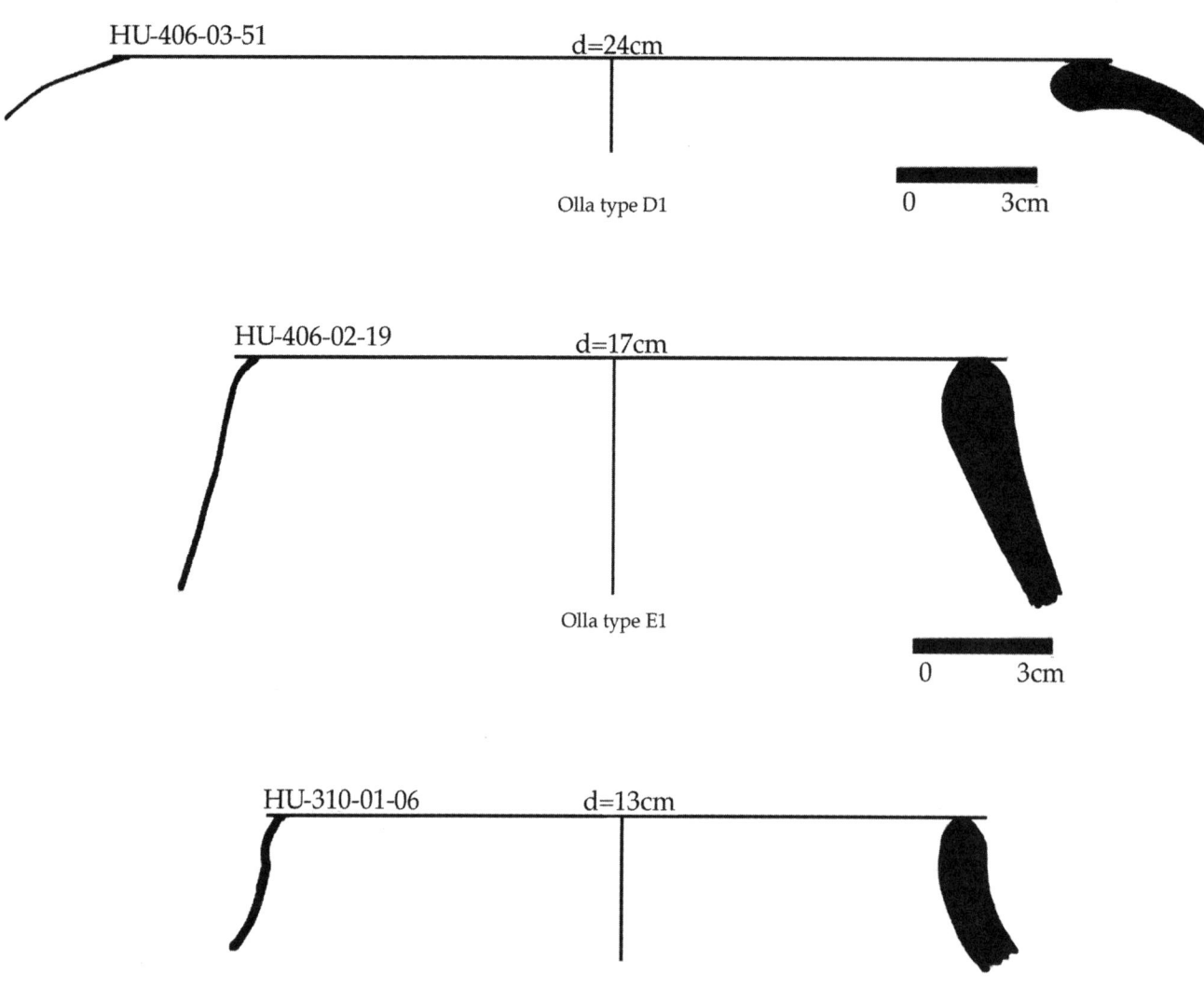

Figure 2.59. Huaña I olla types D1, E1, and E2.

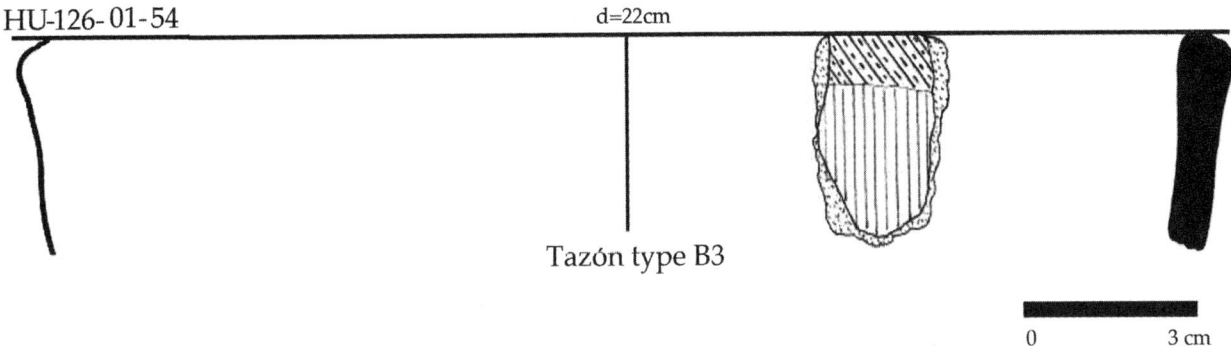

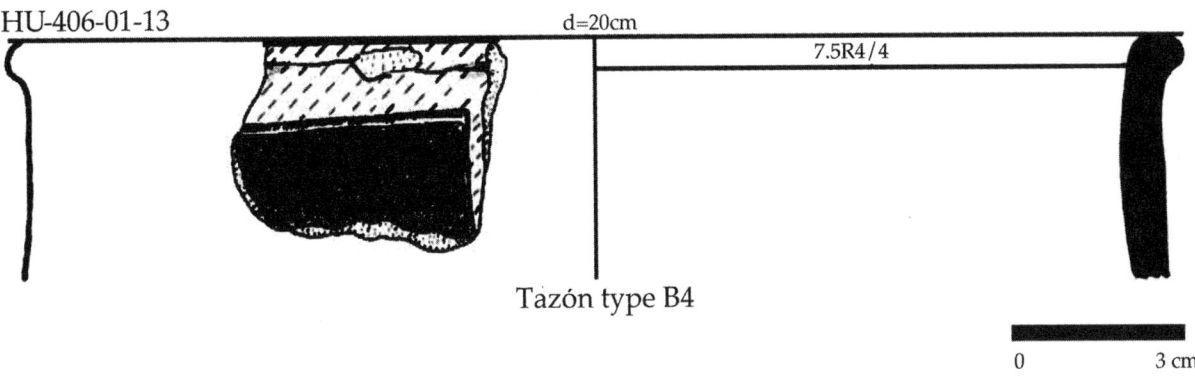

Figure 2.60. Huaña II tazón types B3 and B4.

Huaña II (Figs. 2.60–2.63)

Group I-1/1, 7, 10, 11, 14, 15

The pastes are light orange, dark orange, red, and reddish brown. They are characterized by the presence of white subrounded inclusions of 0.05 mm with a regular dispersion and abundant to sparse density. Others include ocher-colored subrounded inclusions of 0.05 mm to 2.0 mm with a regular dispersion and sparse density. Purple subangular inclusions of 0.1 mm to 0.5 mm are also present with a regular dispersion and sparse density. Translucent subangular inclusions of 0.1 mm with an irregular dispersion and sparse density are found, in addition to black subrounded inclusions of 0.05 mm with an irregular dispersion and sparse density. There is also laminated gold mica of 0.1 mm with an irregular dispersion and very sparse density. The inclusions are visible in the cross section and the mica only in the exterior and interior. The fracture is regular, semi-compact, with a soft and fine texture. The finish is wiped and burnished.

Associated Style: Qaluyu/Pukara/Tiwanaku

Associated Assemblage:

Open Vessels

Tazones, type B, variants 3 and 4 (Fig. 2.60).
They are large; only in type B4 are there small examples. They commonly use burnishing as a finish. There are examples of plainwares while others are decorated with red or brown slips on the exterior and/or interior. There are also decorations painted on the exterior separating black spaces over the cream or red slips.

Bowls, type A, variants 4 and 7 (Fig. 2.61).
They are small, medium, and large. The common finish is wiping. Some are plain; others are decorated with external red slips or with painted black decorations separating spaces on the exterior and/or interior in black over red or orange.

Bowls, type B, variants 1 and 5 (Fig. 2.61).
They are medium and are burnished. They can be plainwares or decorated with red slips on the exterior and/or interior.

Bowls, type D, variant 2 (Fig. 2.61).
They are large and burnished; they are decorated with red slips on the exterior and interior.

Closed Vessels

Jars, type B, variant 1 (Fig. 2.62).
They are very small and wiped. They are decorated with red slips on the exterior and near the interior rim.

Pitchers, type B, variants 1 and 2 (Fig. 2.63).
They are large and very large, wiped and plain.

Vasos, type A, variant 1 (Fig. 2.63).
They are small and medium, wiped, and plain.

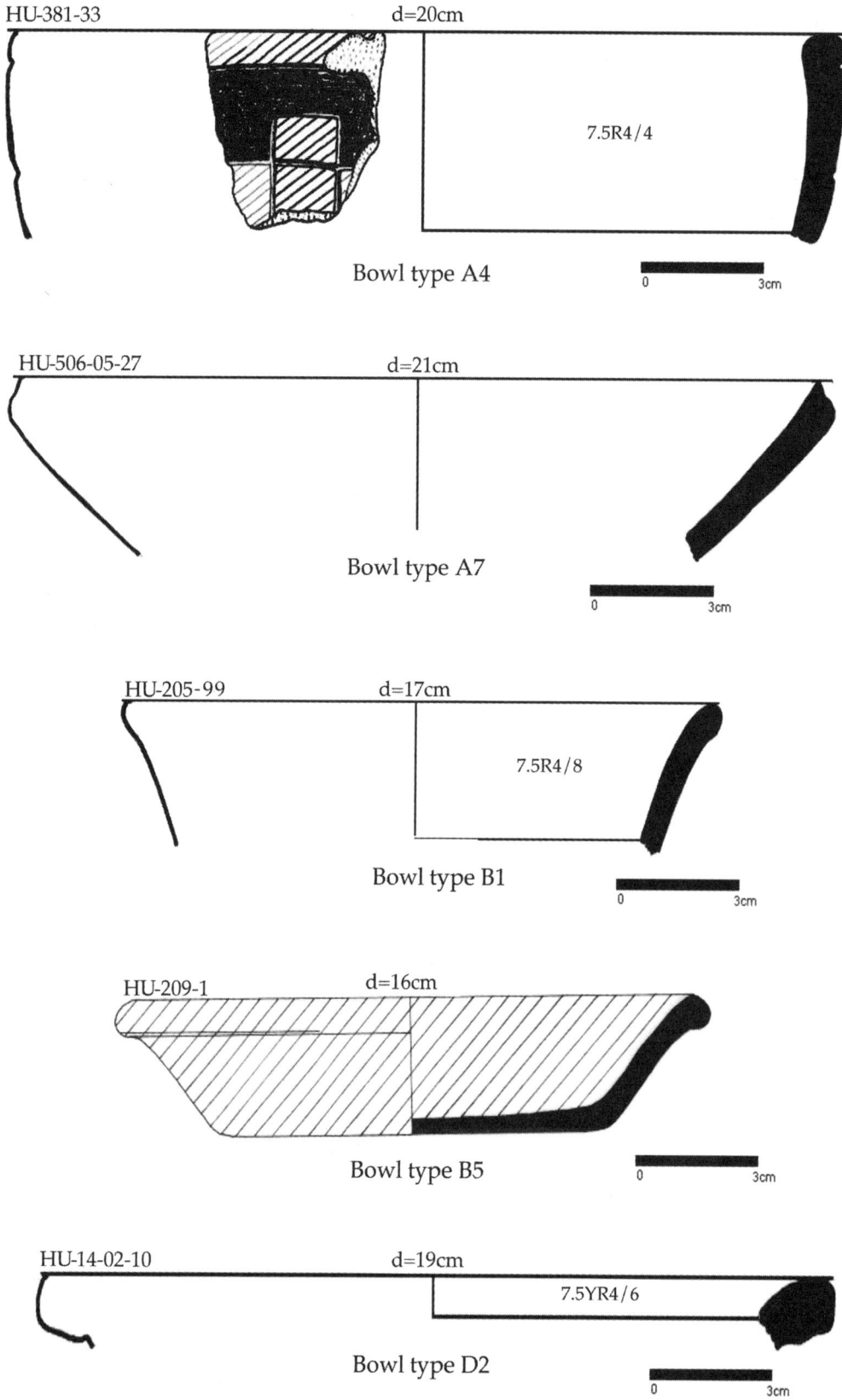

Figure 2.61. Huaña II bowl types A4, A7, B1, B5, and D2.

Analysis of Ceramics

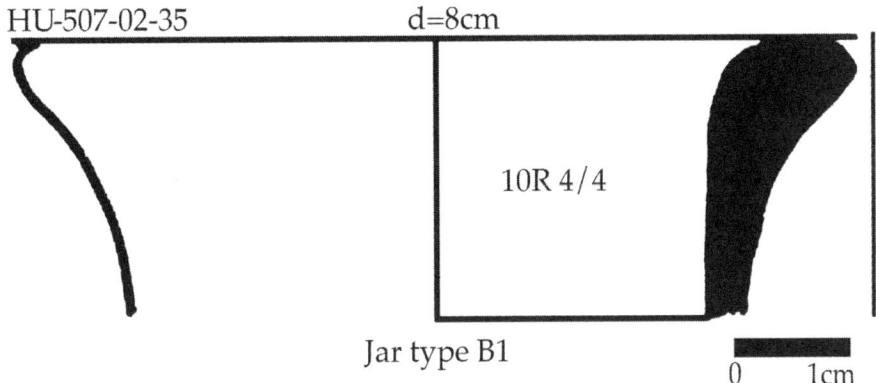

Figure 2.62. Huaña II jar type B1.

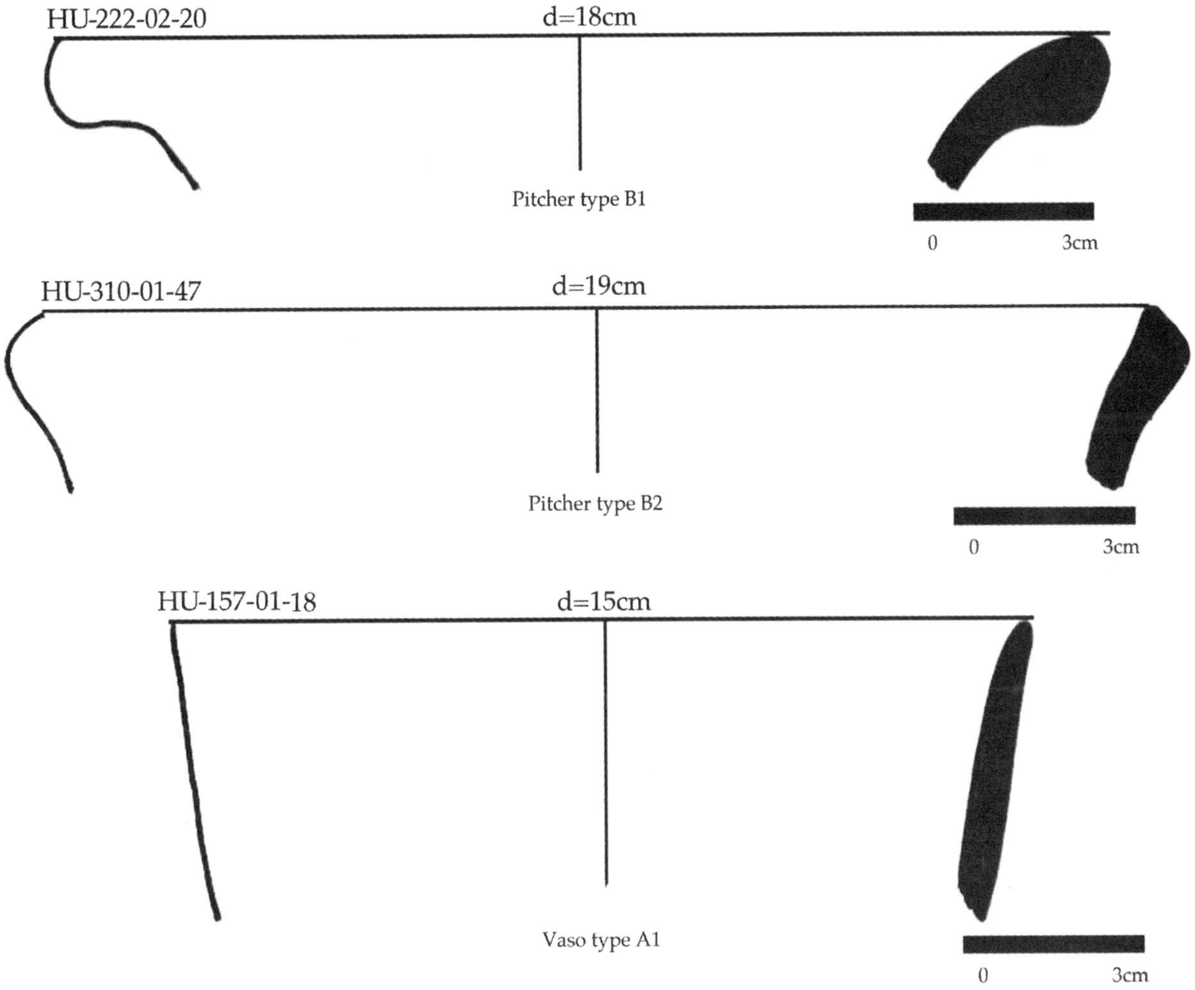

Figure 2.63. Huaña II pitcher types B1 and B2 and vaso type A1.

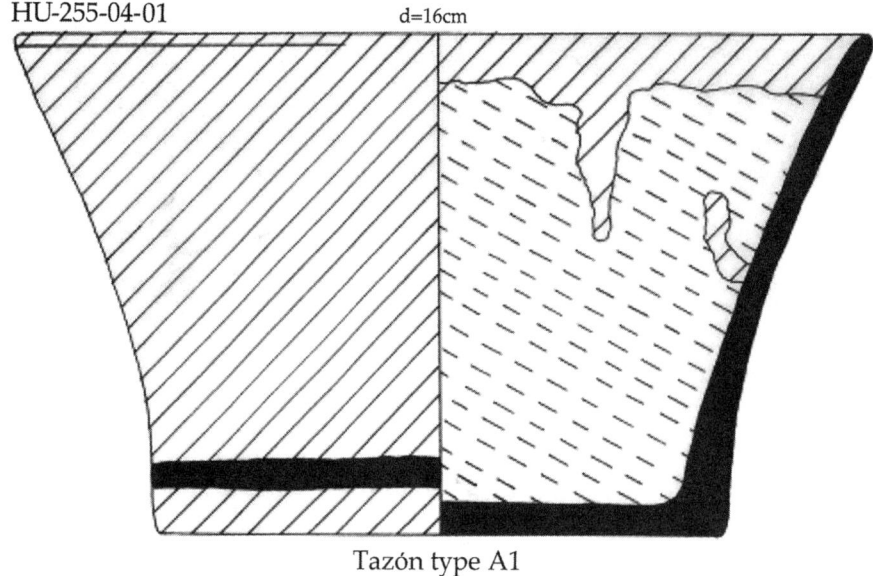

Figure 2.64. Tiwanaku I tazón types A1 and A2.

Tiwanaku I (Figs. 2.64–2.66)

Group III/8, 9, 10, 11, 12

The pastes are red in color. They are characterized by white subrounded inclusions of 0.5 mm size to 0.1 mm with a regular dispersion and medium to very sparse density. Other inclusions are black, subrounded, of 0.5 mm size with a regular dispersion. Purple subangular inclusions of 0.1 mm with an irregular dispersion and sparse density are also present. The inclusions are visible in the cross section: the fracture is regular, compact, and semi-hard with a fine texture. The finish is wiped, burnished, and polished.

Associated Style: Tiwanaku Local

Associated Assemblage:

Open Vessels

Tazones, type A, variants 1 and 2 (Fig. 2.64).

They are small and medium. They generally use burnishing as a finish. There are examples of plainwares (perhaps due to deterioration) although the majority have painted decorations on the exterior combining black over red with geometric (crosshatched) or naturalistic (birds) designs. Type A1 combines two colors (black + cream over red) with a red slip on the interior.

Bowls, type A, variants 1, 4, and 5 (Fig. 2.65).

They are medium and large. They have a wiped finish. They are decorated with exterior and/or interior red slips or with painted black over orange interiors. The designs are geometric (horizontal and diagonal lines).

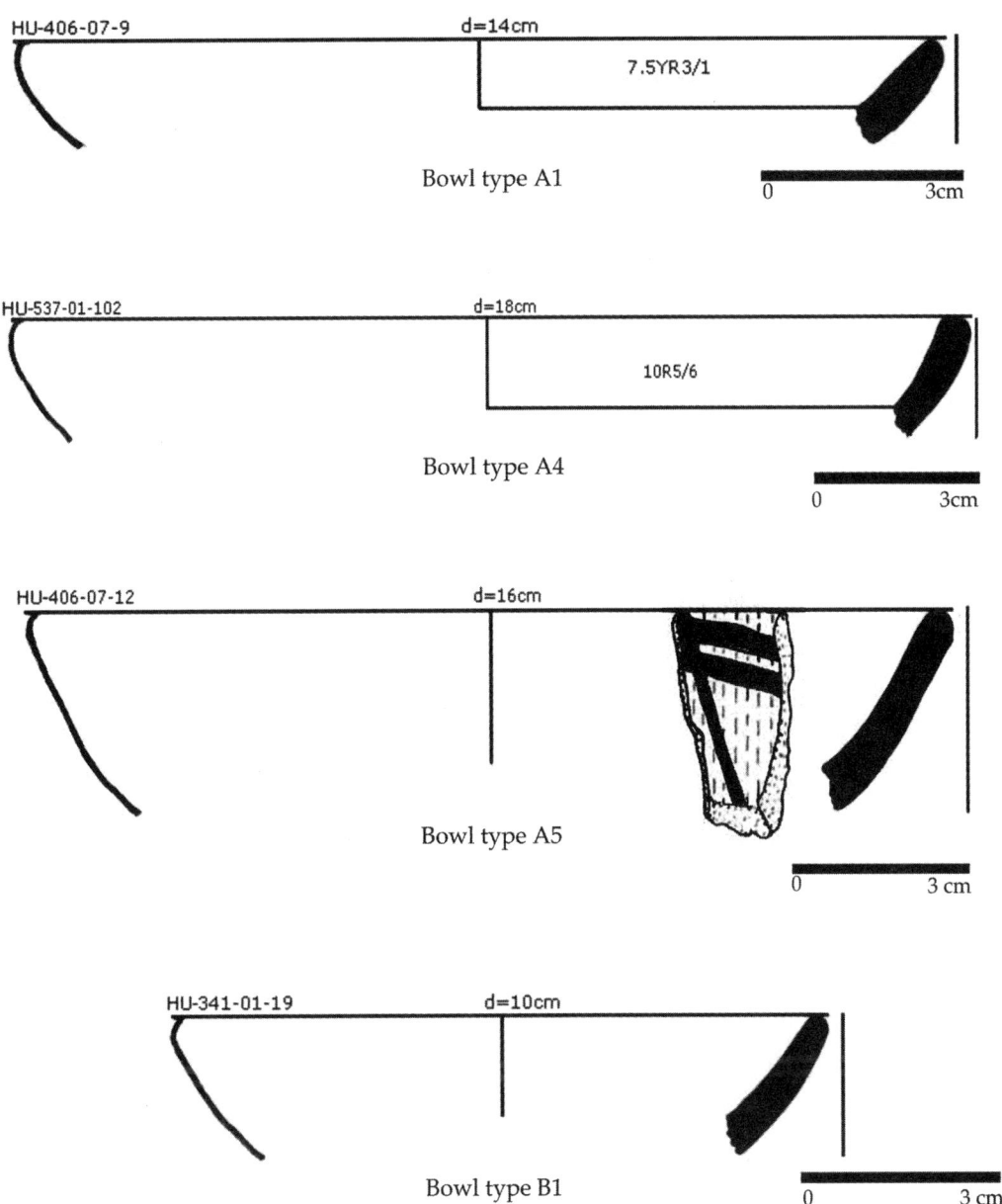

Figure 2.65. Tiwanaku I bowl types A1, A4, A5, and B1.

Bowls, type B, variant 1 (Fig. 2.65).
They are small and wiped, decorated with a red slip on the exterior.

Closed Vessels

Jars, type A (Fig. 2.66).
They are small, burnished, and plain.

Vasos, type A, variants 1 and 2 (Fig. 2.66).
They are very small, small, and medium. They are commonly burnished as a finish, although some are polished. They are decorated with red or orange slips on the exterior and interior. They are also decorated with black over red or orange paint on the exterior. There is one example of decorative black over red paint in the interior. The designs are geometric (undulating and horizontal lines).

Ritual Elements: Incense burners

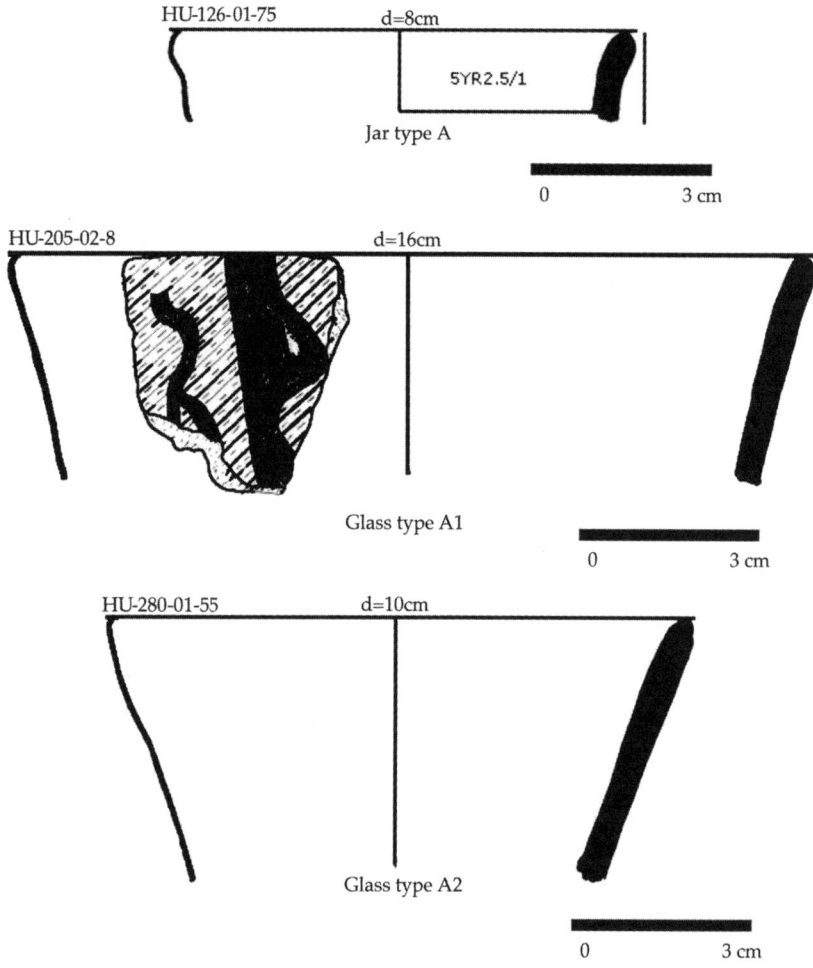

Figure 2.66. Tiwanaku I jar type A and glass types A1 and A2.

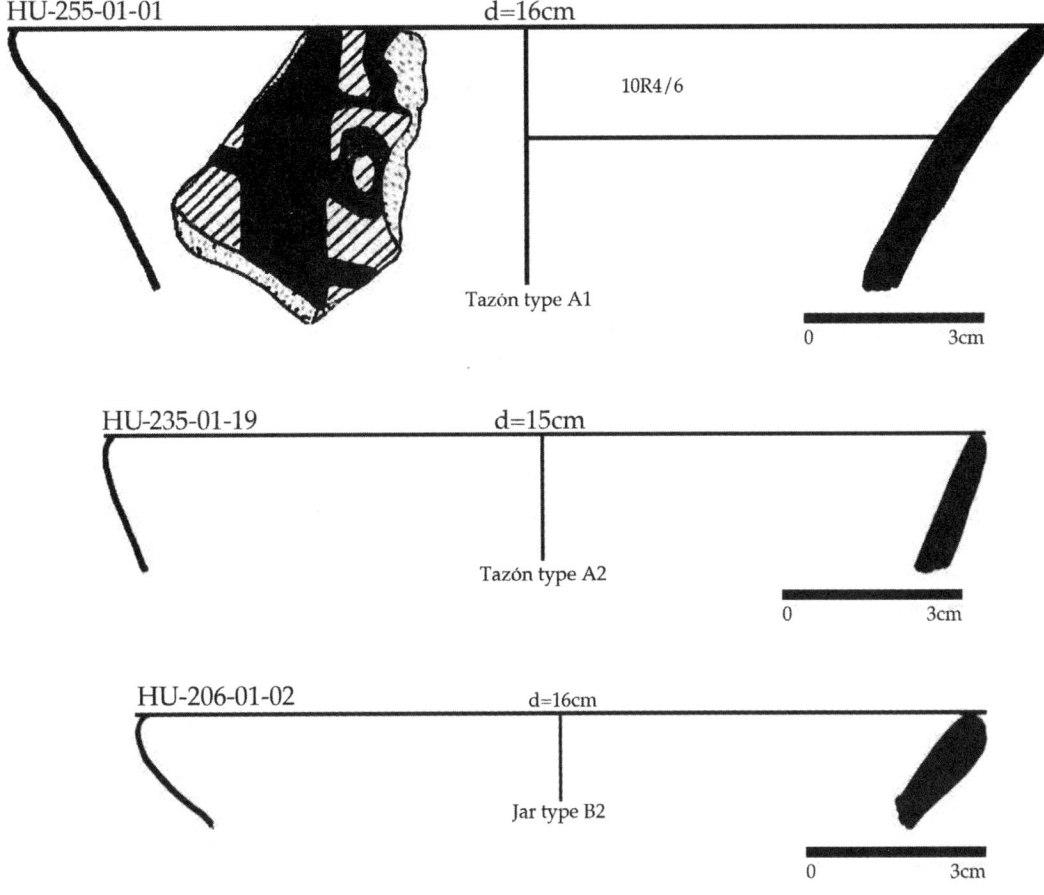

Figure 2.67. Tiwanaku II tazón types A1 and A2 and jar type B2.

Tiwanaku II (Figs. 2.67–2.69)

Group II/1, 2, 3, 4

They have a dark orange color. They contain translucent subrounded inclusions of 0.1 mm with a regular dispersion and abundant density. In addition, there are gray, black, and/or reddish subangular inclusions of 2.0 mm with an irregular dispersion and sparse density. The inclusions are visible in the cross section: they have a regular fracture, compact, semi-hard and very fine. The firing process is complete oxidation. The finish is wiped, burnished, and polished.

Group II/5, 6, 7

They are a dark orange color. They are composed of white subrounded inclusions of 0.1 mm with a regular dispersion and medium to very sparse density. Others include subrounded black inclusions of 0.1 mm with an irregular dispersion and sparse density. There is also laminated gold mica of 0.1 mm with a regular dispersion and sparse density. The inclusions are visible in the cross section and the mica on the exterior and interior. They have a regular fracture, compact, semi-hard and with a very fine texture. The finish is wiped and burnished.

Associated Style: Tiwanaku Local

Associated Assemblage:

Open Vessels

Tazones, type A, variants 1, 2, and 4 (Fig. 2.67).
They are small and medium, but in type A1 some examples of very small (6–8 cm) and large (18 cm) are present. They use burnishing and wiping (which may be due to erosion) as finishes. They can be plainwares or decorated with red or orange slips on the exterior and/or interior; they also use painted decorations on the exterior in one color (black) or two colors (black + cream) over red with geometric motifs (diagonal, vertical, and undulating lines, and crosshatched).

Closed Vessels

Jars, type B, variant 2 (Fig. 2.67).
They are small and medium, wiped and plain.

Vasos, type A, variants 1 and 2 (Fig. 2.68).
They are very small, small, and medium. They can be burnished or wiped, although there are some examples of polished finishes. They use red slips as decorations on the exterior and interior or painted decorations on the exterior and/or interior in one color (black or orange) over

red, brown, or orange. Decorations may also include a combination of colors (black + cream) over red. The designs are geometric (horizontal and undulating lines).

Bottles, type A (Fig. 2.69).

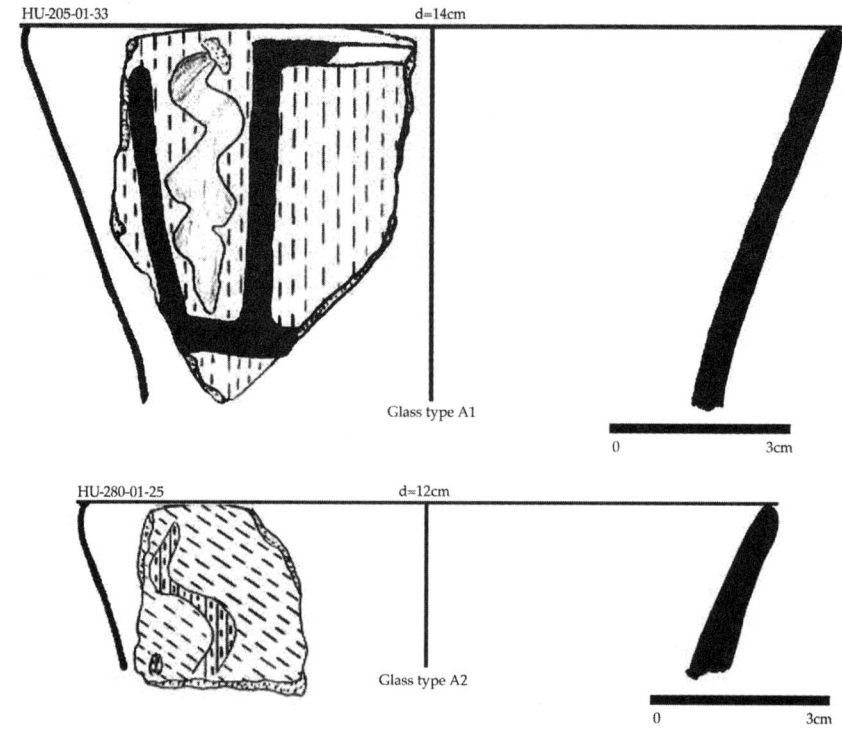

(*right*) Figure 2.68. Tiwanaku II glass types A1 and A2.

(*below left*) Figure 2.69. Tiwanaku II bottle type A.

(*below right*) Figure 2.70. Altiplano I tazón types A1, A2, and A4.

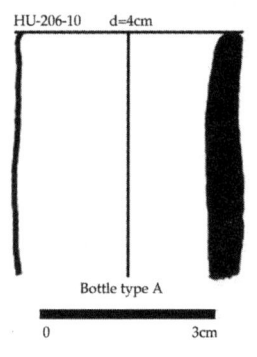

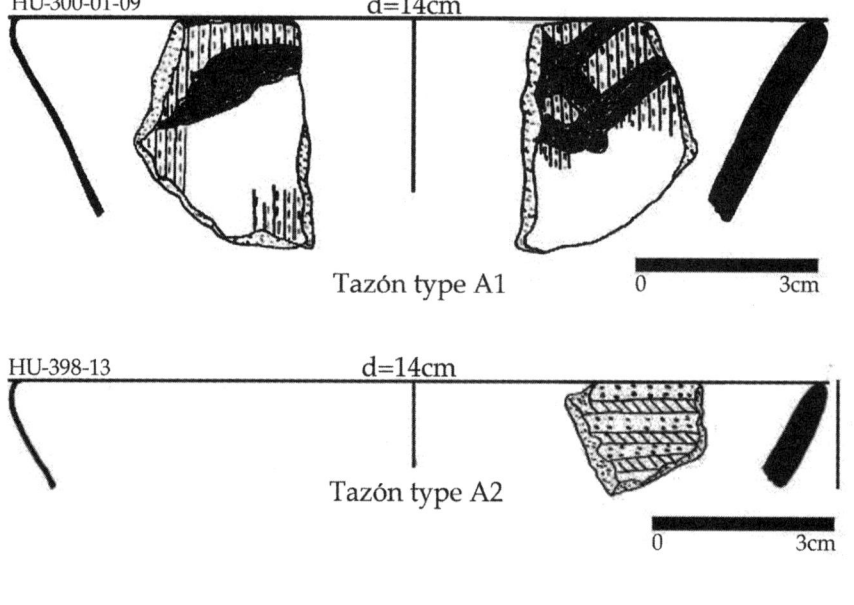

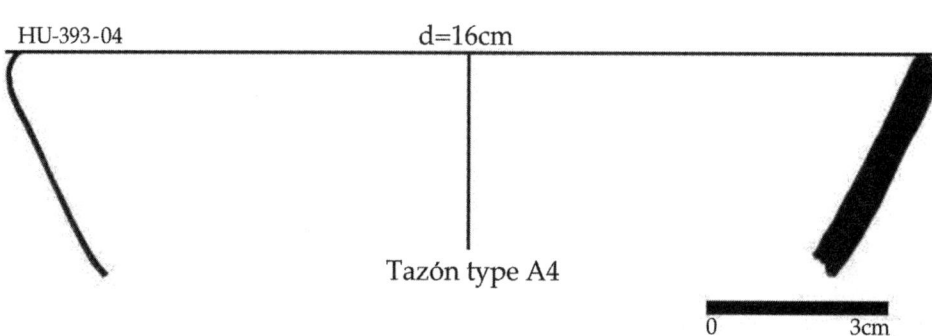

Altiplano I (Figs. 2.70–2.81)

Group I-3/9, 10, 11, 12, 13

The color of the pastes is light orange. They are composed of white subangular inclusions up to 1.0 mm with a regular dispersion and medium to abundant density. There are also opaque subangular inclusions of 1.0 mm, and gray subangular inclusions from 0.5 mm up to 4.0 mm, both with a regular dispersion and medium density. There are ocher-colored subangular inclusions of 1.0 mm with an irregular dispersion and medium density. They have a regular fracture, are semi-compact, and semi-soft with a fine texture. The inclusions are visible in the cross section: exterior and interior. The finish is wiped, burnished, and eventually polished.

Group IV/23, 24

They are light orange colored and integrated with white subangular inclusions up to 5 mm with a regular dispersion and abundant density. In addition, there are black subangular inclusions of 0.5 mm size with an irregular dispersion and medium to very sparse density. Translucent subangular inclusions of 0.5 mm size with an irregular dispersion and sparse density are also present. The inclusions are visible in the cross section: exterior and interior. The fracture is regular, semi-compact, and semi-soft with a thick texture. The finish is wiped and burnished.

Associated Style: Late Huaña/Collao

Associated Assemblage:

Open Vessels

Tazones, type A, variants 1, 2, and 4 (Fig. 2.70).
They have three sizes: small, medium, and large. The predominant finish is wiping, although some are burnished (especially the decorated ones). There are plainware examples. Others are decorated with red or cream slips on the exterior and/or interior. They may also have painted decorations on the exterior and/or interior in one color (black) over red, brown, or cream. The designs are geometric (lines) and naturalistic (branches).

Tazones, type B, variants 1, 2, 3, 4, 5, and 7 (Fig. 2.71).
They are small, medium, and large. Only type B7 has a very large (26 cm) example. They use wiping as a finish. Plainware examples exist; others are decorated with red or orange slips on the exterior and/or interior. They also have one color (black over brown or orange, or brown over cream or orange) painted decorations on the interior. They also combine two colors (black + brown over orange) and use geometric (horizontal, vertical, and diagonal lines) and naturalistic designs.

Tazones, type C (not shown).
They are large, wiped, and plain.

Bowls, type A, variants 1, 2, 3, 4, 5, 7, 8, and 9 (Figs. 2.72, 2.73).
They are very small, small, medium, and large. They commonly use wiping for a finish, although some examples are burnished. They can be plain or decorated with red, orange, cream, or brown slips on the exterior and/or interior. They have painted interior decorations (possibly exterior) of black over red, orange, or brown. They also have brown over white or orange, or red over orange, and in addition may combine two colors (black + brown over a cream or orange slip, or white + orange over brown). The designs are geometric (horizontal, vertical, diagonal, and undulating lines) and naturalistic (branches).

Bowls, type B, variants 1, 2, 3, 4, 5, and 6 (Figs. 2.74, 2.75).
They are very small, small, medium, large, or very large. They use wiping as a finish, although type B1 has sparse burnished examples. They can be plain or decorated with red, orange, brown, or cream slips on the exterior and/or interior. They also have interior painted decorations in one color (black, brown, or red over red brown or orange slips). They also combine two colors (black + brown over cream or orange). The designs are geometric (horizontal, vertical, undulating lines crosshatched, and circles); some have holes in the body, and possibly protuberances on the rim.

Bowls, type C, variants 1 and 2 (Fig. 2.76).
They are small or medium. They use wiping as a finish. They can be plain or decorated with orange slips on the exterior and/or interior. They can also have painted interior decorations in black over orange or black over brown. The designs are geometric (vertical and horizontal lines).

Bowls, type D, variant 2 (Fig. 2.76).
They are small, medium, large, and very large. The finish is wiped. There are plainwares, but others are decorated with red or orange slips on the exterior and/or interior. They can also have interior painted decorations in brown over orange. The designs are geometric (horizontal and diagonal lines).

Bowls, type E, variants 2 and 3 (Fig. 2.76).
They are small, medium, and large. The common finish is wiped, although type E3 has sparse burnished examples. They can be plain or decorated with red or orange slips on the exterior and/or interior.

Plates, type D, variant 1 (Fig. 2.77).
They are plain, wiped, and large.

Tazas (Fig. 2.77).
They are small, medium, and large, and are wiped. They can be plain or decorated with red or orange slips on the exterior and interior.

Closed Vessels

Jars, type A (Fig. 2.78).
They are very small, small, and medium. They are wiped and can be plain or decorated with orange slips on the exterior and near the interior rim. Some specimens have painted interior decorations in black or brown over orange, brown, or cream. The designs are geometric (undulating lines) and possibly have appendixes flat on the rim with or without perforation.

Jars, type B, variants 1 and 2 (Fig. 2.78).
They are very small, small, and medium. They generally use wiping for a finish, although some are burnished. They can be plain or decorated with orange, brown, or cream slips on the exterior and near the interior rim. Some specimens have painted one-color decorations on the exterior (black or brown over red or cream) or a combination of two colors (black + brown over cream). The designs are geometric (horizontal, vertical, and diagonal lines). They also have incised decorations on the exterior near the rim (oval grooves) or flat appendixes without perforation on the rim.

Jars, type C, variants 1, 2, and 3 (Fig. 2.79).
They are small and medium. They commonly use wiping as a finish, although type C3 contains some burnished specimens. They can

108 *The Northern Titicaca Basin Survey*

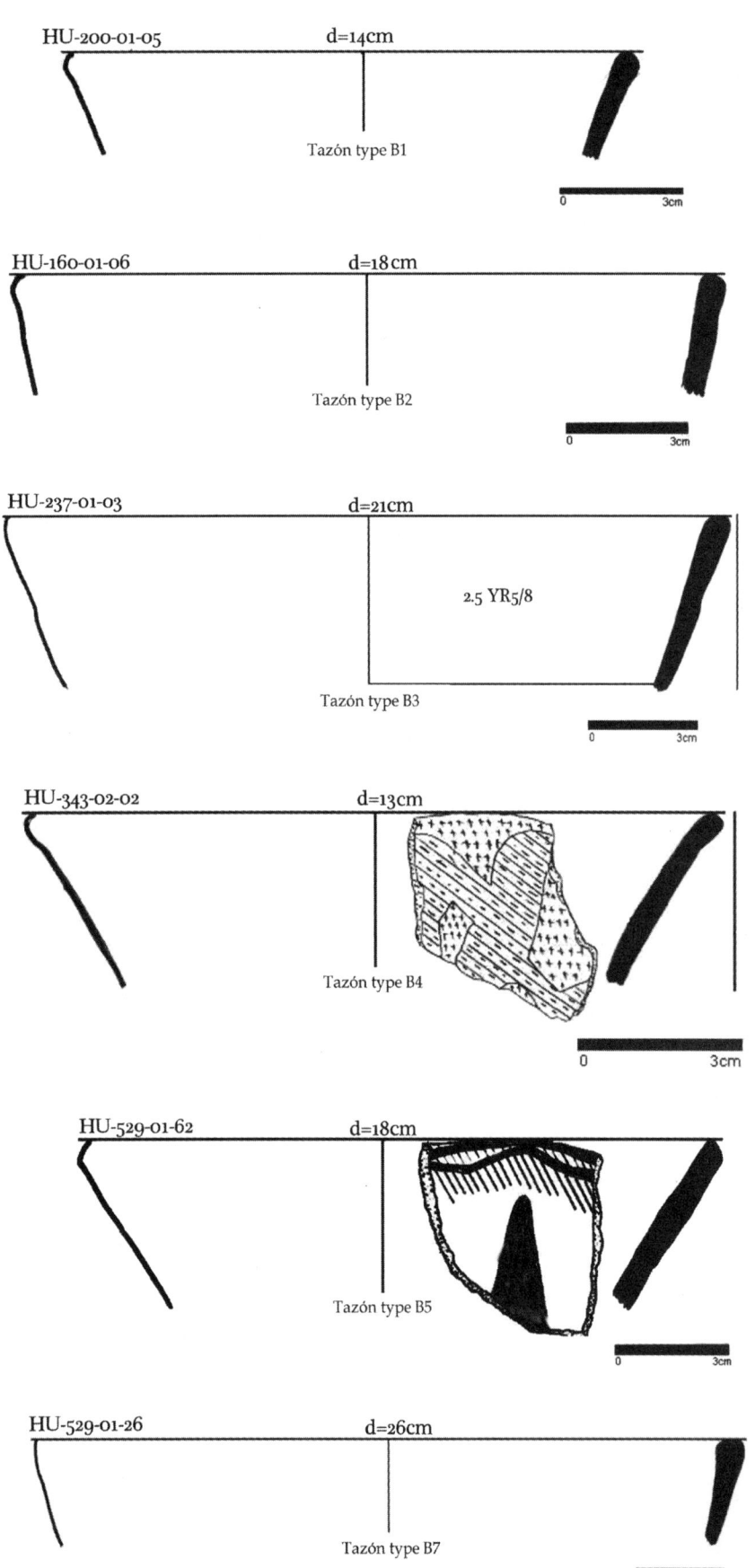

Figure 2.71.
Altiplano I tazón types B1–B5 and B7.

Analysis of Ceramics

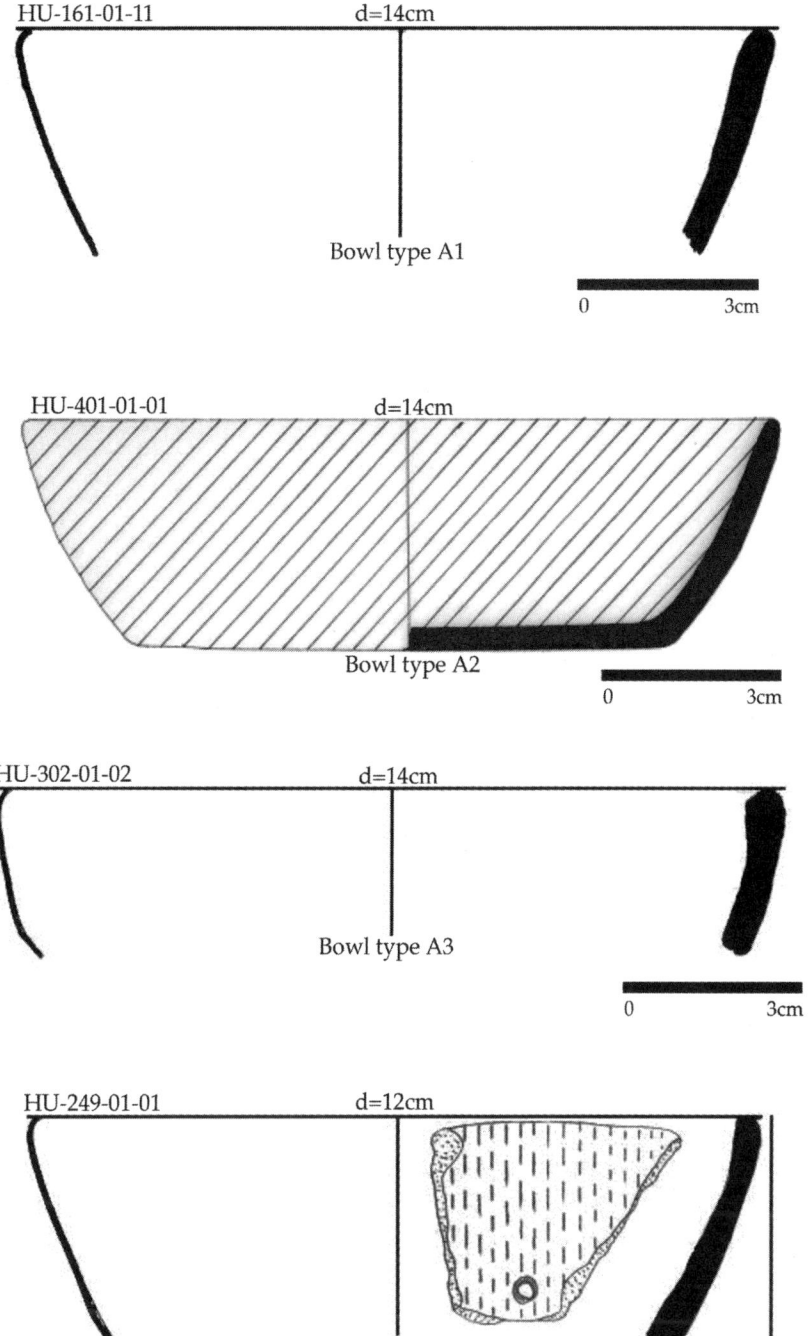

Figure 2.72. Altiplano I bowl types A1–A4.

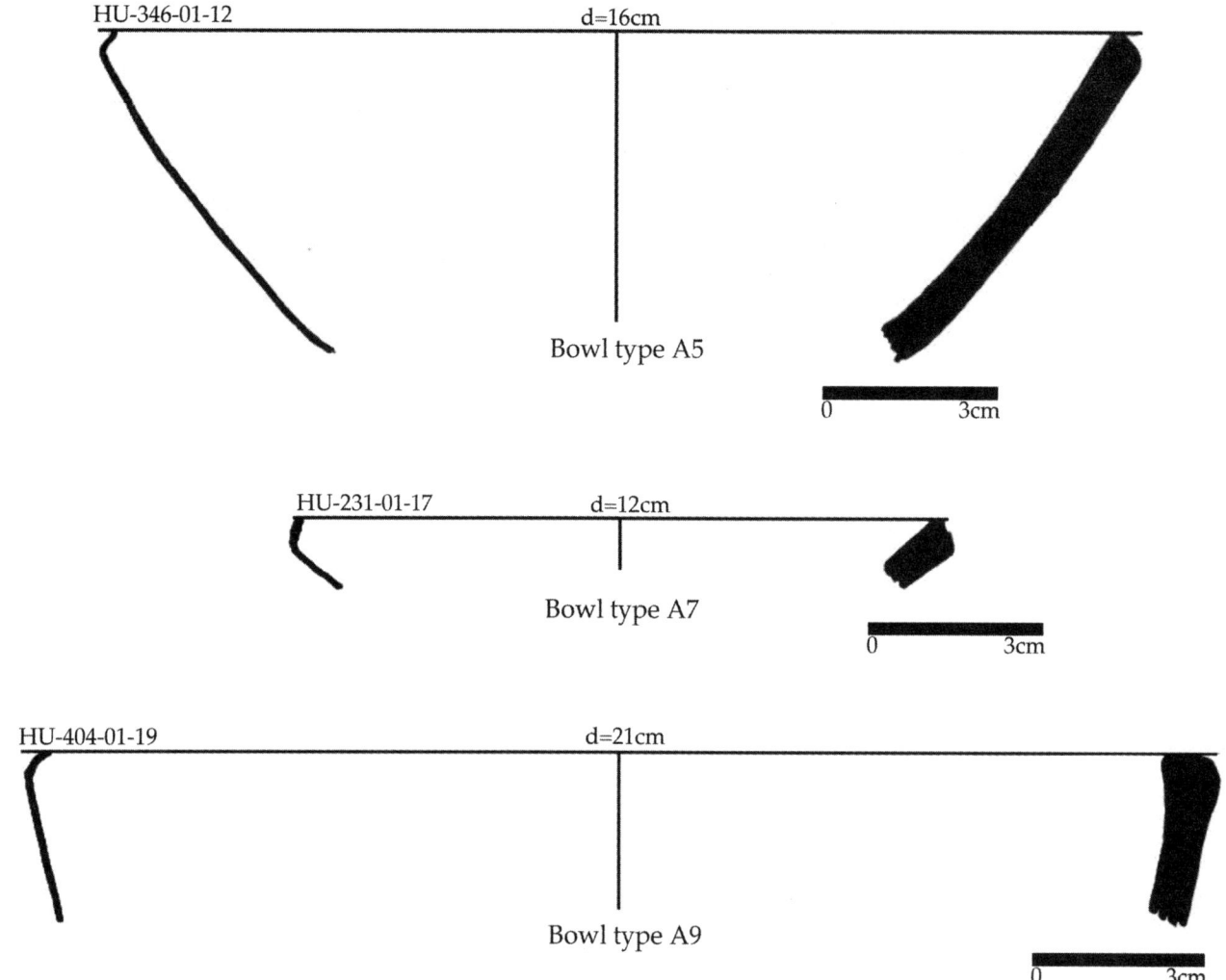

Figure 2.73. Altiplano I bowl types A5, A7, and A9.

be plain and only in type C3 are they decorated with exterior/interior red or orange slips. They also have painted decorations on the exterior of white over red or black over orange. The designs are geometric (horizontal lines).

Pitchers, type A, variant 3 (Fig. 2.80).
They are large, wiped, and unslipped.

Pitchers, type B, variants 1 and 2 (Fig. 2.80).
They are large and very large. They use wiping as a finish. There are plainwares and also decorated vessels with external (and near the internal rim) red, brown, and orange slips. They also have painted decorations on the exterior in black over orange or red, brown over orange, orange over brown, and possibly black over red in the interior. The designs are geometric (horizontal, vertical, and undulating lines, plus circles). They can also have flat appendixes without perforation on the rim.

Ollas, type A, variant 2 (Fig. 2.81).
They are large and wiped. They can be plain or possibly decorated with internal orange-toned slips near the rim.

Ollas, type B, variant 2 (Fig. 2.81).
They are plain, small, and large. They are wiped. Some are decorated with black and white over brown paint. The designs are geometric (horizontal lines).

Ollas, type D, variants 1 and 3 (Fig. 2.81).
They are medium, wiped, and plain.

Vasos [base].

Other Forms Associated with the Assemblage: Spoons

Ornamental Elements: Beads

Productive Tools: Polishing tools, spindle whorls

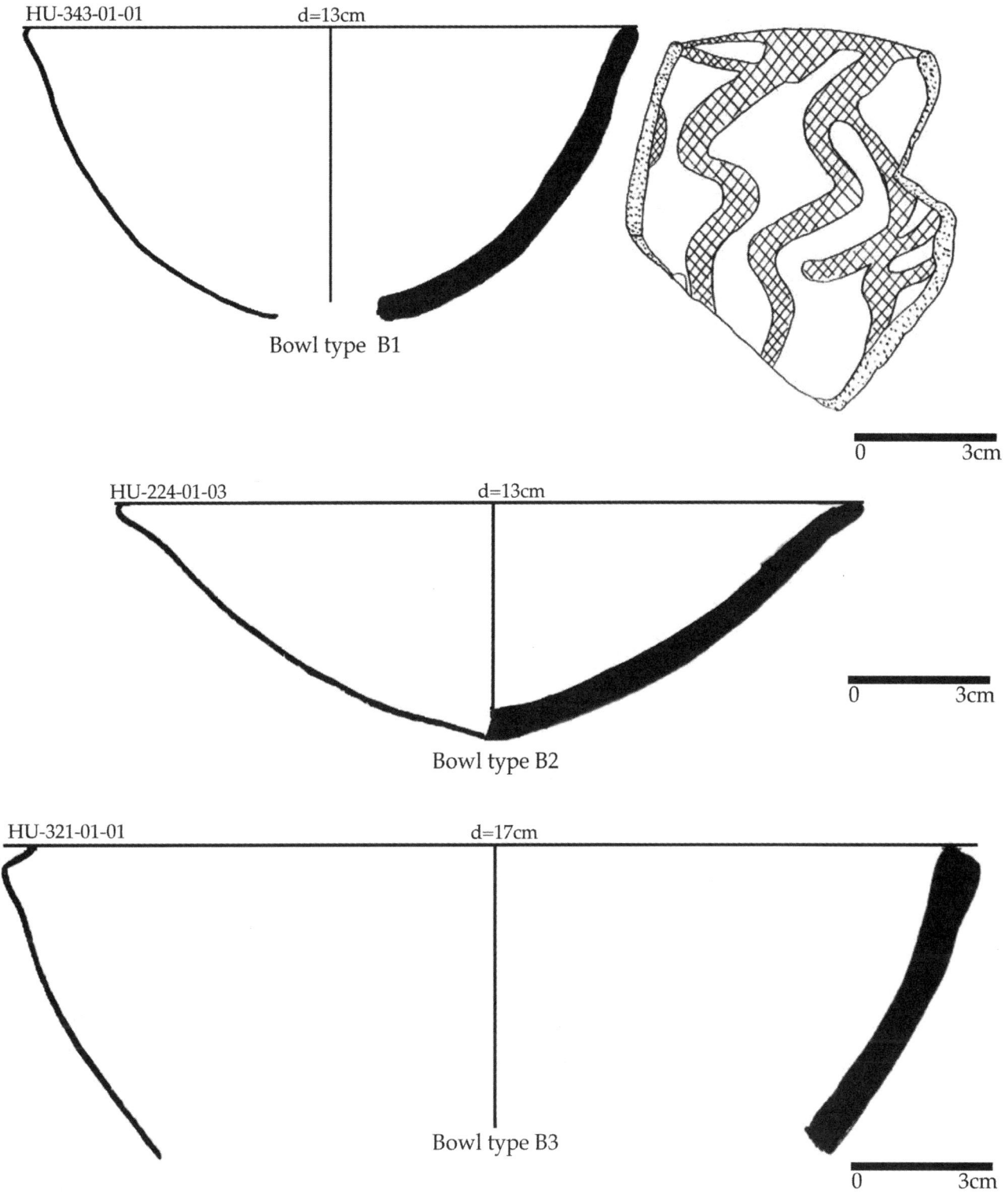

Figure 2.74. Altiplano I bowl types B1–B3.

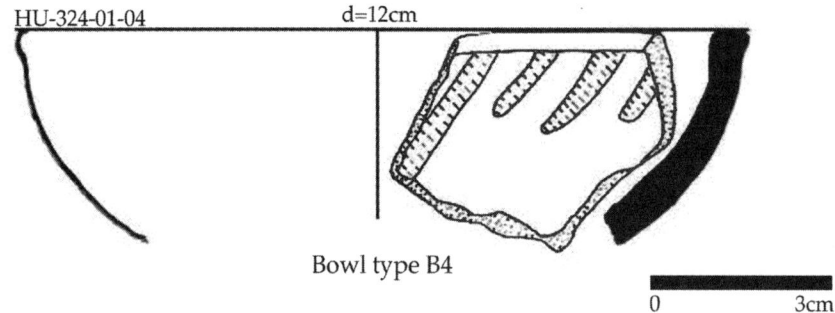
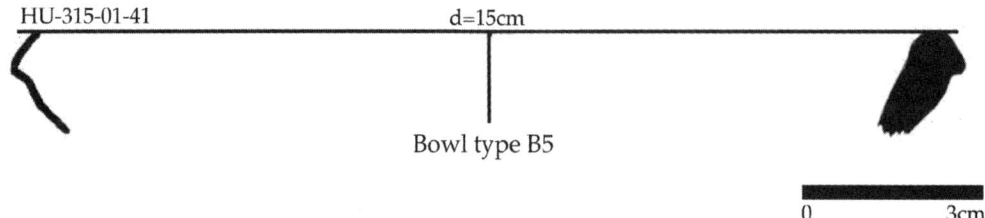
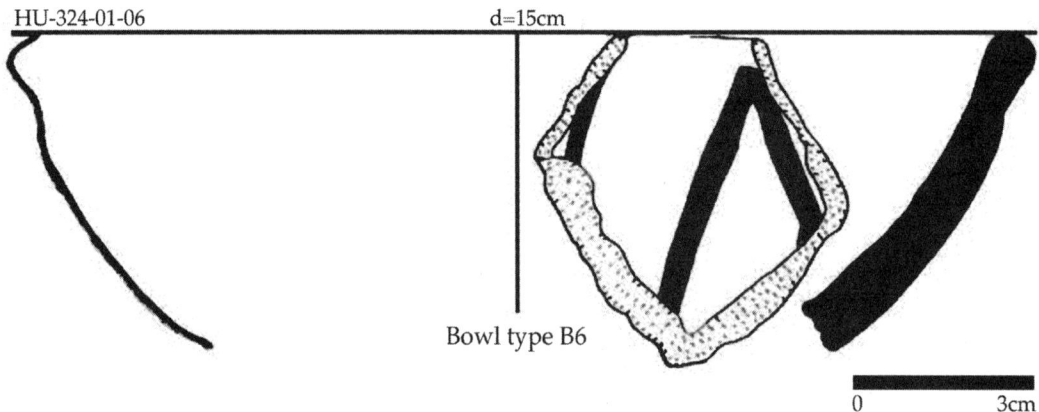

Figure 2.75. Altiplano I bowl types B4–B6.

Analysis of Ceramics 113

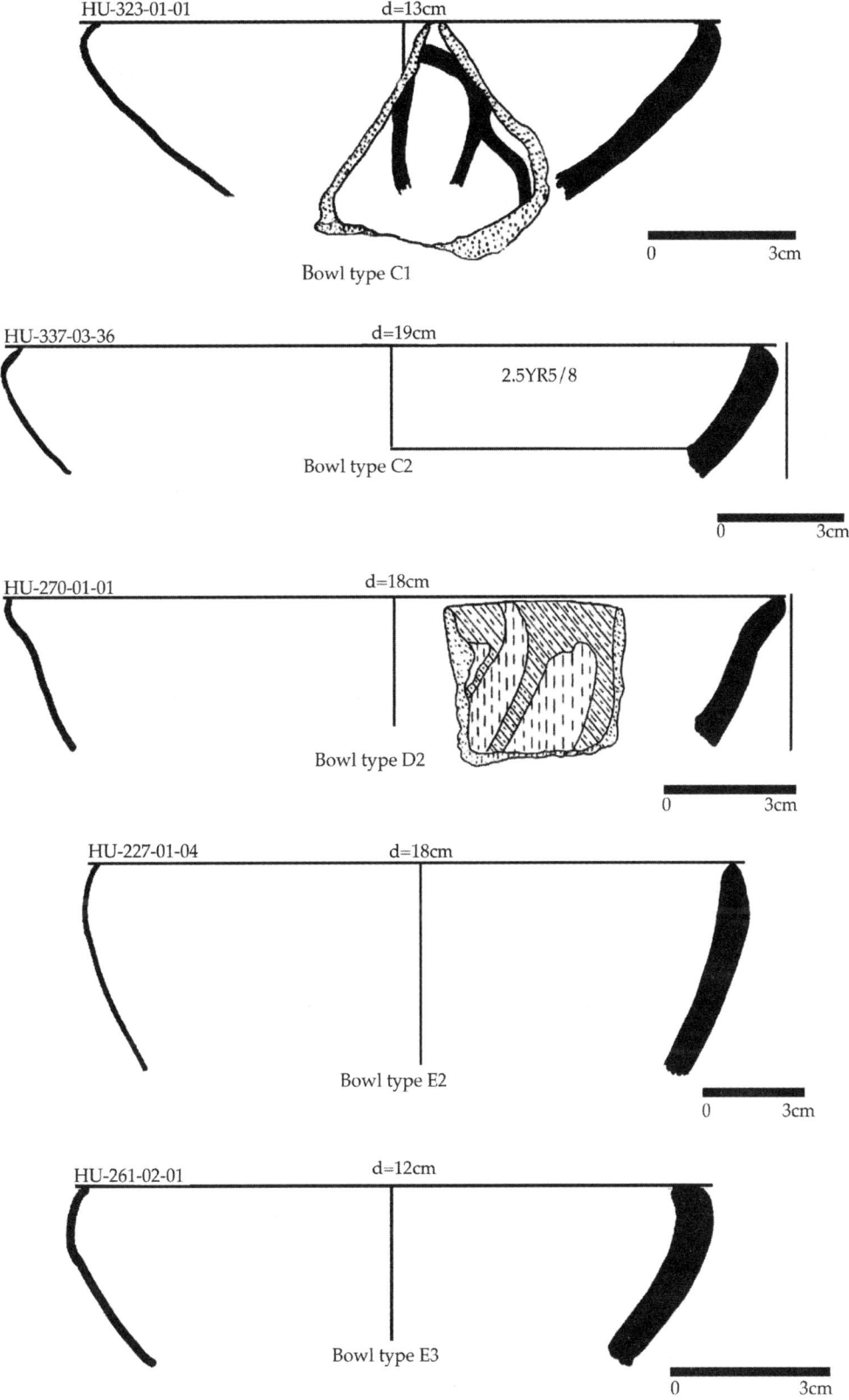

Figure 2.76. Altiplano I bowl types C1, C2, D2, E2, and E3.

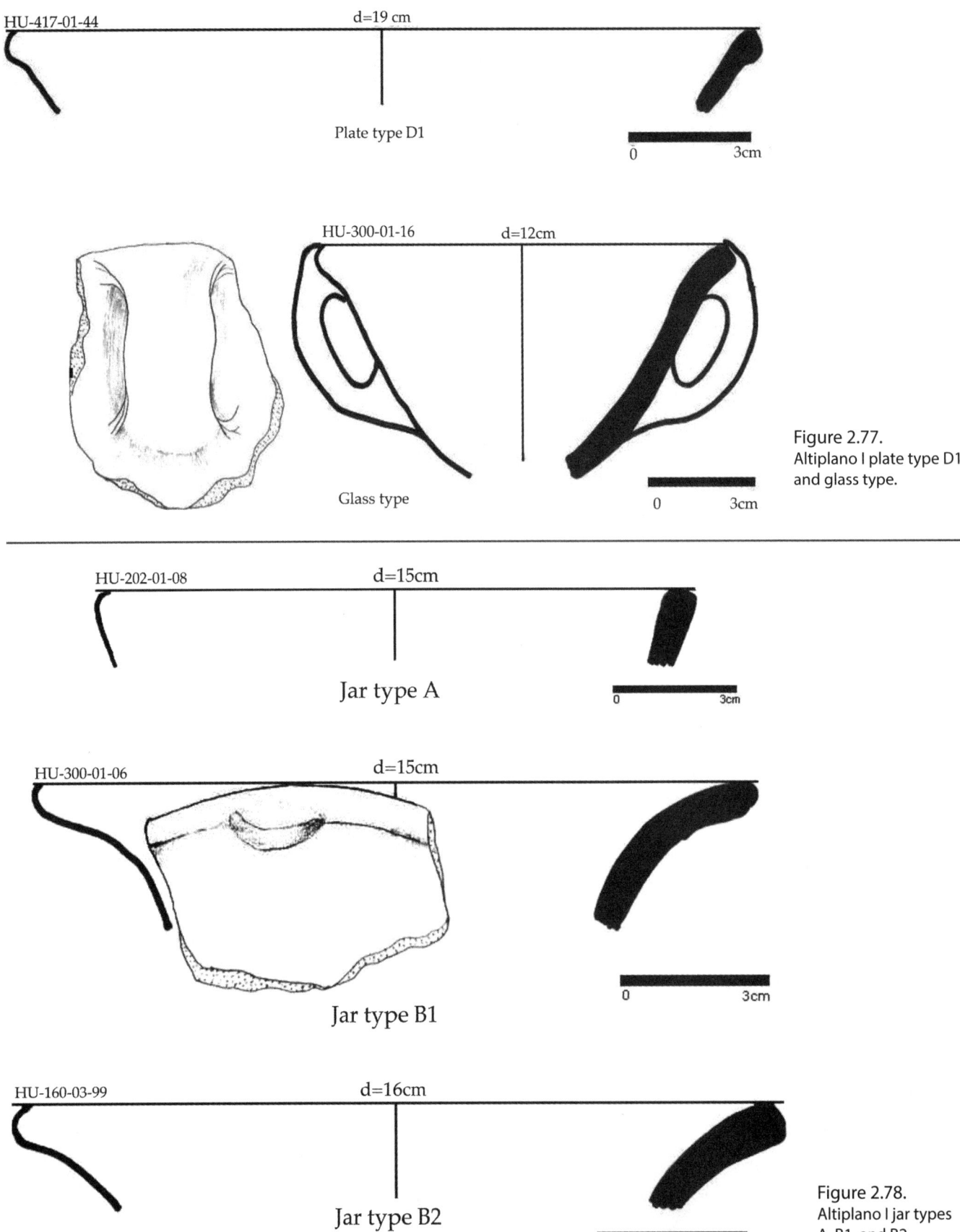

Figure 2.77. Altiplano I plate type D1 and glass type.

Figure 2.78. Altiplano I jar types A, B1, and B2.

Analysis of Ceramics

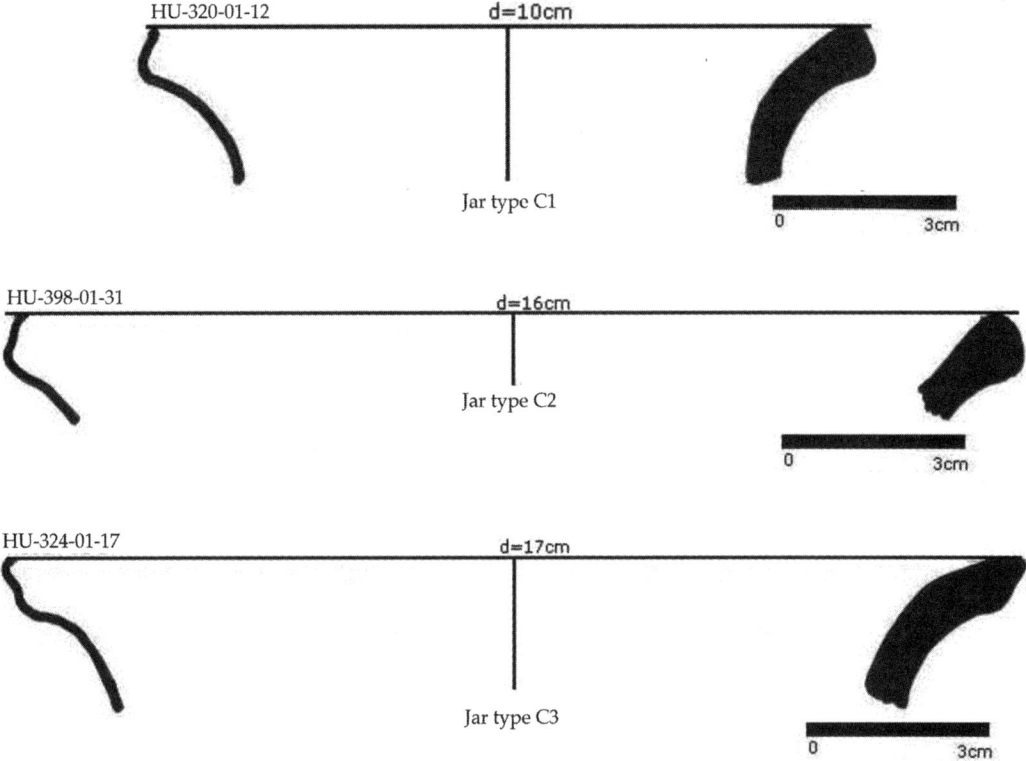

Figure 2.79. Altiplano I jar types C1–C3.

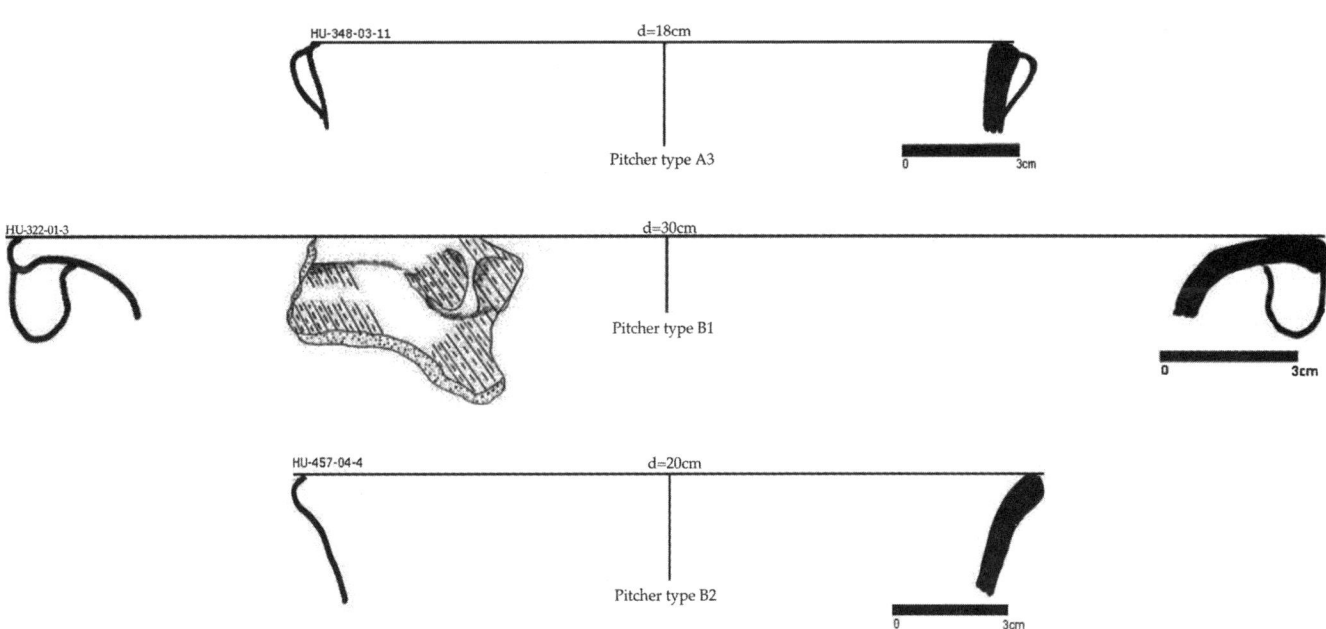

Figure 2.80. Altiplano I pitcher types A3, B1, and B2.

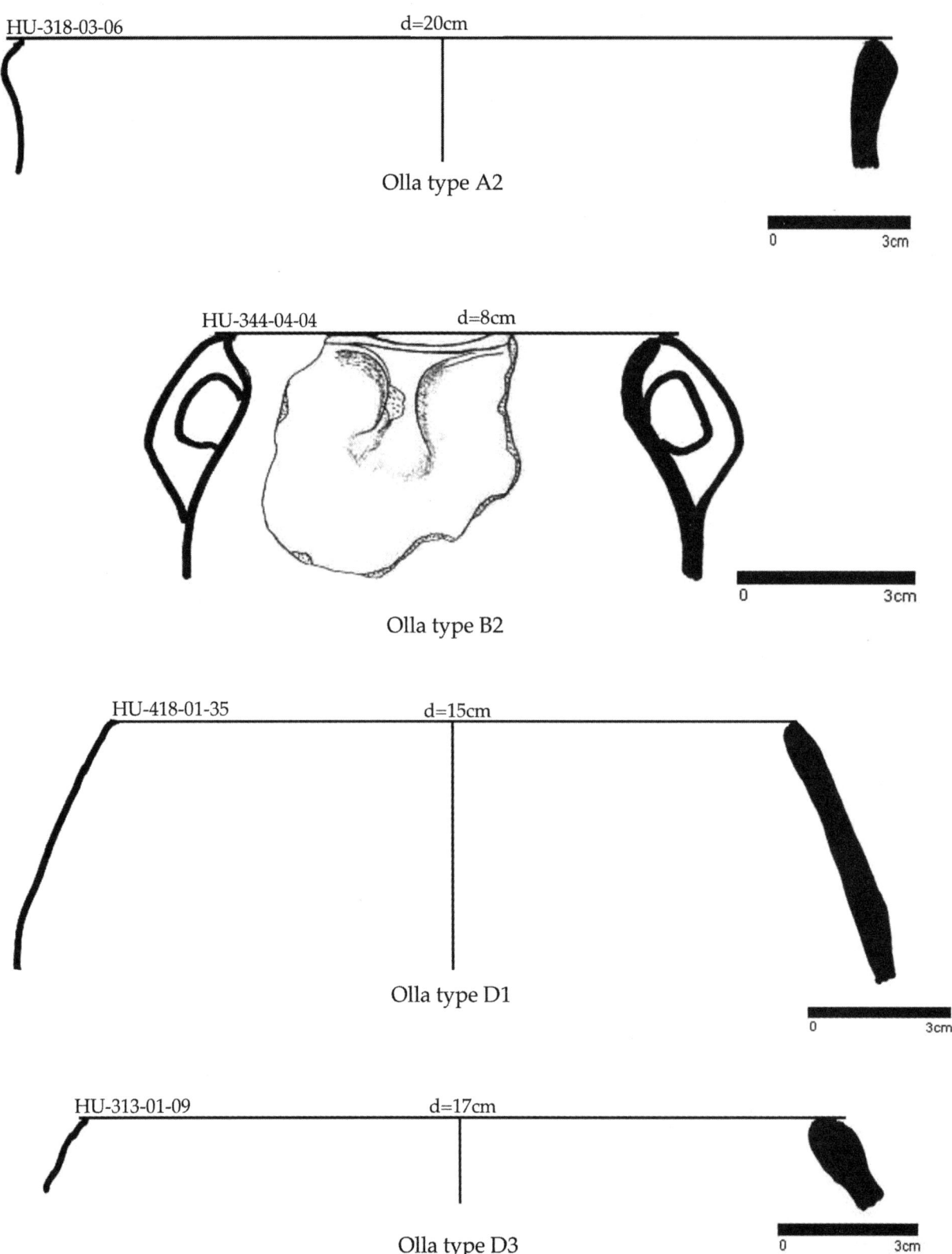

Figure 2.81. Altiplano I olla types A2, B2, D1, and D3.

Altiplano II (Figs. 2.82–2.97)

Group I-1/1, 2, 3, 4

The paste color is dark orange. It is composed of white subangular inclusions of 3 mm, regular dispersion, and abundant density. There can also be subangular red/purple, ocher-colored, and gray inclusions up to 1.0 mm with an irregular dispersion and sparse density. The cream subangular inclusions are up to 2.0 mm with a regular dispersion and medium density. The black inclusions are subangular, range from 0.8 mm to 1.0 mm, and have an irregular dispersion and sparse density. The inclusions are visible in the cross section: exterior and interior. The fracture is regular, semi-compact, semi-soft, and with medium texture. The finish is wiped, burnished, and occasionally polished.

Group I-2/5, 6, 7, 8

The pastes are dark orange in color. They are characterized by white subangular inclusions of 0.6 mm to 1.0 mm with a regular dispersion and medium to sparse density. They can also have purple inclusions that are subangular, up to 1.0 mm, with a regular dispersion and medium to abundant density. The gray subangular inclusions are from 0.5 mm to 4.0 mm with an irregular dispersion and abundant to sparse density. The ocher-colored subangular inclusions are up to 1.0 mm in size with an irregular dispersion and sparse density. Black subangular inclusions from 0.6 mm to 1.0 mm with an irregular dispersion and sparse density are also present. There are also reddish subangular inclusions up to 2.0 mm in size with an irregular dispersion and sparse density. The inclusions are visible in the cross section: exterior and interior. The fracture is regular, semi-compact, and semi-soft with a thick texture. The finish is wiped, burnished, and occasionally polished.

Group II/14, 15, 16, 17

The color is cream orange and cream. They are integrated with white subangular inclusions up to 1.0 mm in size with a regular dispersion and medium to abundant density. They can also have ocher-colored subangular inclusions approximately 0.8 mm in size with an irregular dispersion and sparse density. Cream subangular inclusions up to 1.0 mm with a regular dispersion and medium density are also present. Black subangular inclusions of 0.5 mm size with an irregular dispersion and sparse density were found. The inclusions are visible in the cross section: exterior and interior. The fracture is regular, semi-compact, and semi-soft with a medium texture. The finish used is wiping, burnishing, and possibly polishing.

Associated Style: Collao and Huatasani

Associated Assemblage:

Open Vessels

Tazones, type A, variants 1, 2, 3, 4, and 5 (Fig. 2.82).
They are small and medium, although type A1 has some large (18–22 cm) examples. The predominant finish is wiping, and only in type A1 are some burnished. They can be plain or decorated with red, orange, cream, or brown slips. They are also decorated with paint generally in the exterior and, in some cases, both the exterior and the interior. They use one color (black, cream, white, or brown) or two colors (black + red, black + brown, black + white) over the different slips. The motifs are geometric (diagonal, vertical, horizontal lines, crosshatched) and also naturalistic.

Tazones, type B, variants 1, 3, 6, and 7 (Fig. 2.83).
They are small, medium, and large. They use wiping as a finish; only in type B1 are some burnished. They can be plain or decorated with red, orange, or brown slips. They can also be decorated with paint on the interior in one color (black or brown over orange, brown over cream) or a combination of three colors (black + brown + red over light brown). The designs are geometric (horizontal, vertical, diagonal, and undulating lines) and naturalistic (branches).

Tazones, type C (Fig. 2.83).
They are medium, wiped, and plain.

Bowls, type A, variants 1, 2, 3, 4, 5, 6, 7, and 9 (Figs. 2.84–2.86).
They are very small, small, medium, and large. They commonly use wiping as a finish, although types A1, A3, A4, and A5 have burnished specimens. They can be plain or decorated with red, orange, or brown slips. They can also have interior or possibly exterior paint decorations in one color (black, brown, or red over the red/orange/white/brown slips) or a combination of two colors (white + orange over brown or black + brown over orange). The designs are geometric (horizontal, diagonal, undulating lines, circles, and crosshatched) and naturalistic (branches) with possible lateral appendixes (rounded protuberances) on the rim.

Bowls, type B, variants 1, 2, 3, 4, 5, and 6 (Figs. 2.87, 2.88).
They are very small, small, medium, large, and very large. They use wiping as a common finish in types B1 and B2 although some are burnished. Some are plain and others are decorated with red, orange, brown, or cream slips. They can also be decorated with paint in the interior and possibly exterior in one color (black, brown, red, or orange) over different slips or in two colors (black + brown) over a cream or orange slip. The designs are geometric (horizontal, vertical, diagonal, and undulating lines, crosshatched) and naturalistic (branches).

Bowls, type C, variants 1 and 2 (Fig. 2.88).
They are small, medium, and large. They use wiping as a finish; only in type C1 are there burnished examples. They can be plain or decorated with exterior and/or interior orange slips. They also use interior paint decorations in black over orange or brown. The designs are geometric (diagonal lines).

Bowls, type D, variants 1, 2, and 3 (Fig. 2.89).
They are small, medium, large, and very large. They use wiping as a finish; only in type D2 are some burnished. They can be plain or decorated with exterior and/or interior red, orange, or brown slips. Some also have interior paint decorations in brown over orange. The designs are geometric (diagonal and undulating lines).

Bowls, type E, variants 1, 2, and 3 (Fig. 2.89).
They are small, medium, and large. They are commonly wiped, although some in types E1 and E3 may have been burnished. There are plain examples and others decorated with exterior and/or interior orange slips or painted decorations in black over red with geometric designs (horizontal and diagonal lines).

Plates, type D, variants 1 and 2 (Fig. 2.90).
They are large and wiped. They are commonly plain, although some have interior decorations in black over orange paint.

Tazas (Fig. 2.91).
They are small, medium, and large; are wiped; and can be plain or decorated with exterior/interior orange slips.

118 The Northern Titicaca Basin Survey

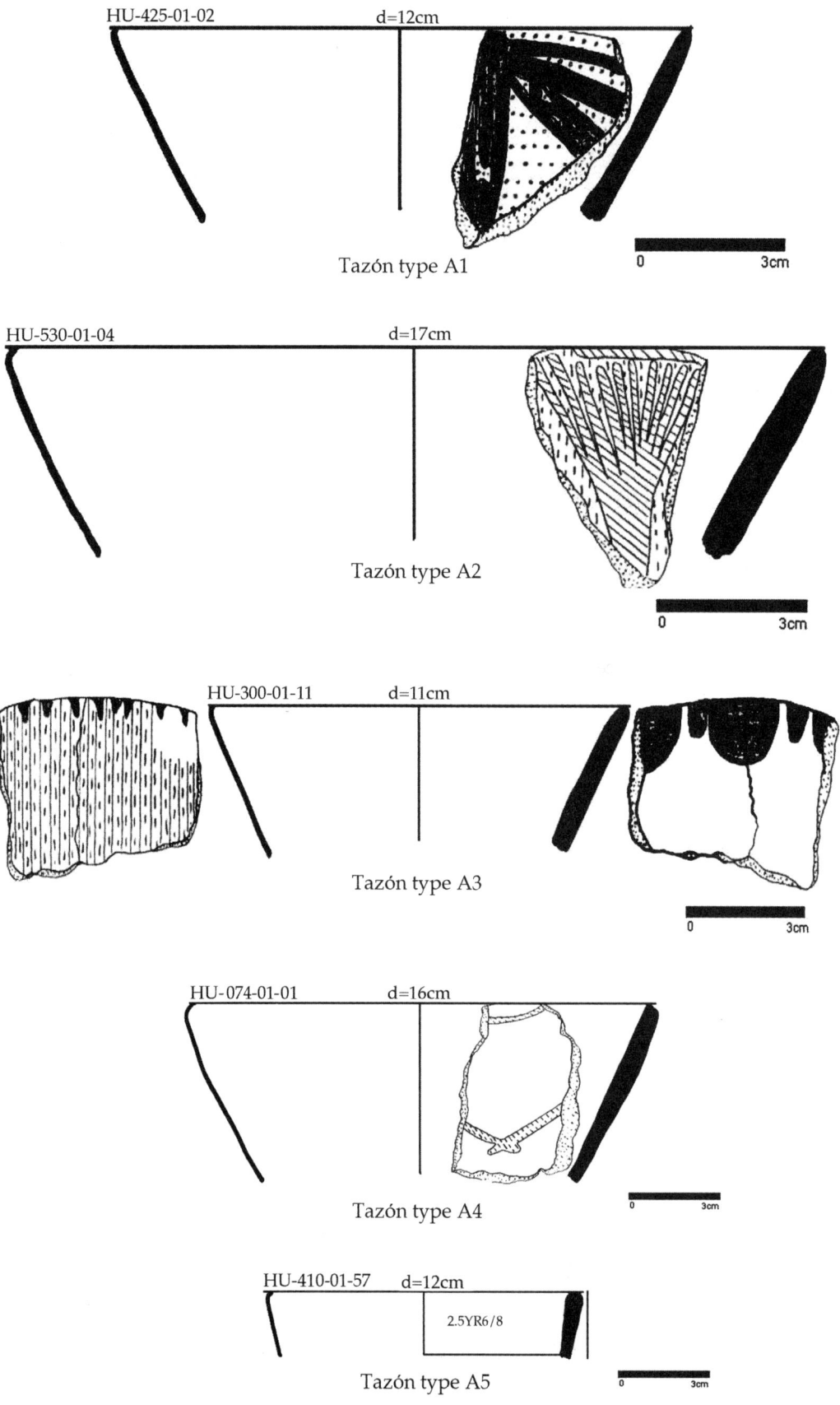

Figure 2.82. Altiplano II tazón types A1–A5.

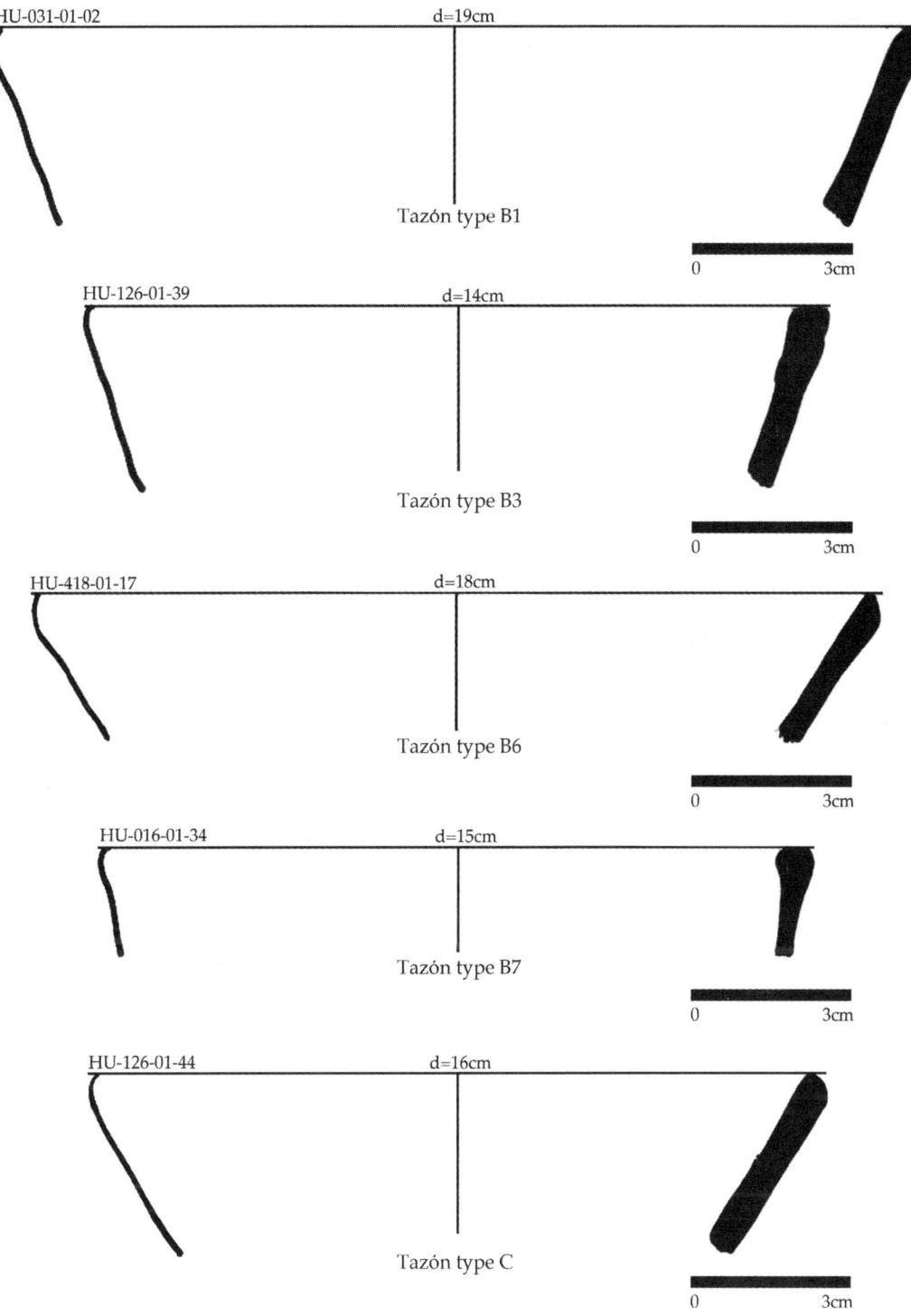

Figure 2.83. Altiplano II tazón types B1, B3, B6, B7, and C.

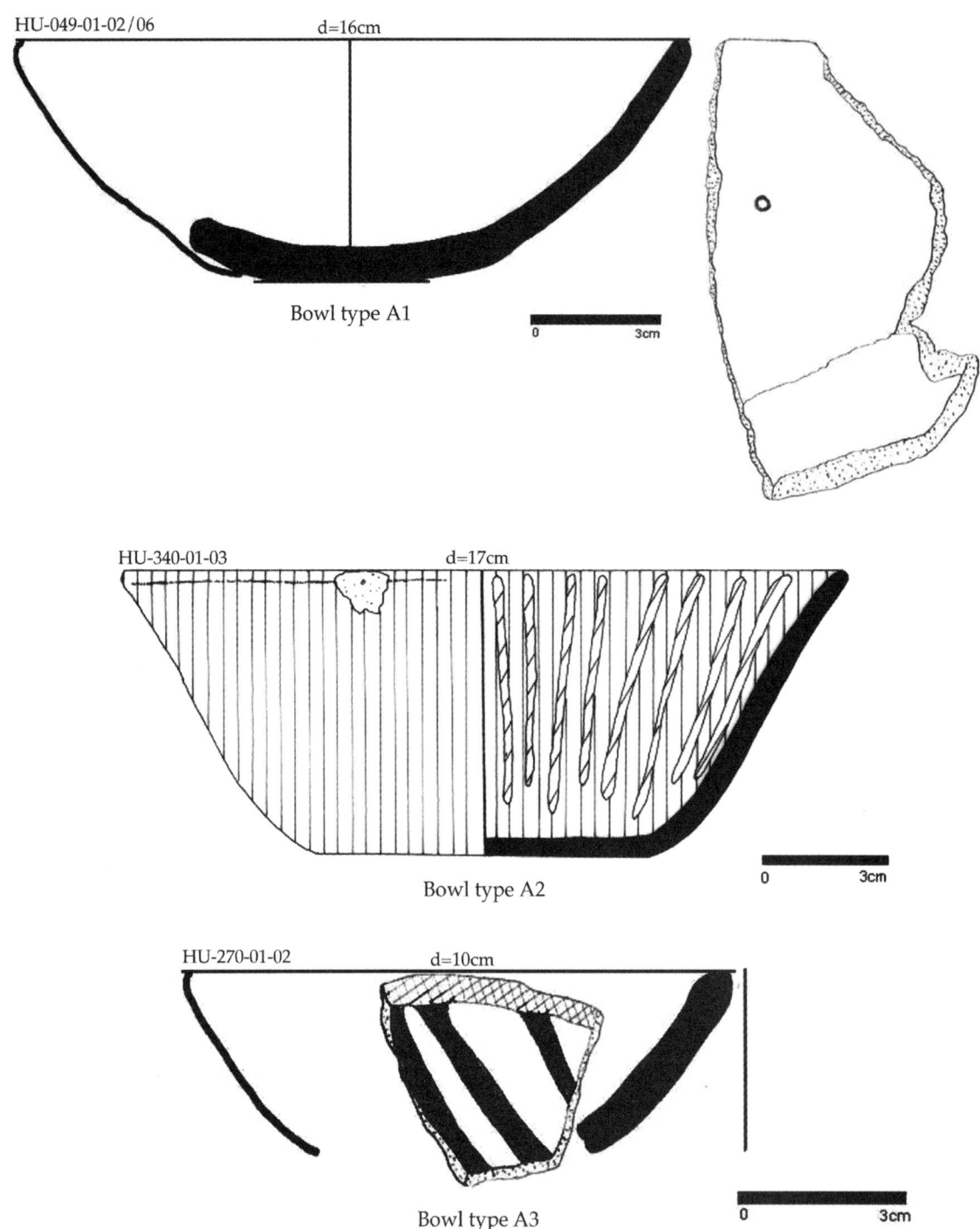

Figure 2.84. Altiplano II bowl types A1–A3.

Closed Vessels

Jars, type A (Fig. 2.91).

They are very small, small, or medium, although there are some miniature examples. They use wiping as a finish. There are plain specimens while others are decorated with orange or red slips. Some are also decorated with paint on the exterior in dark brown over brown or on the interior in black over orange. The designs are geometric (horizontal and vertical lines); they can also have exterior incised decorations (rounded grooves) on the rim.

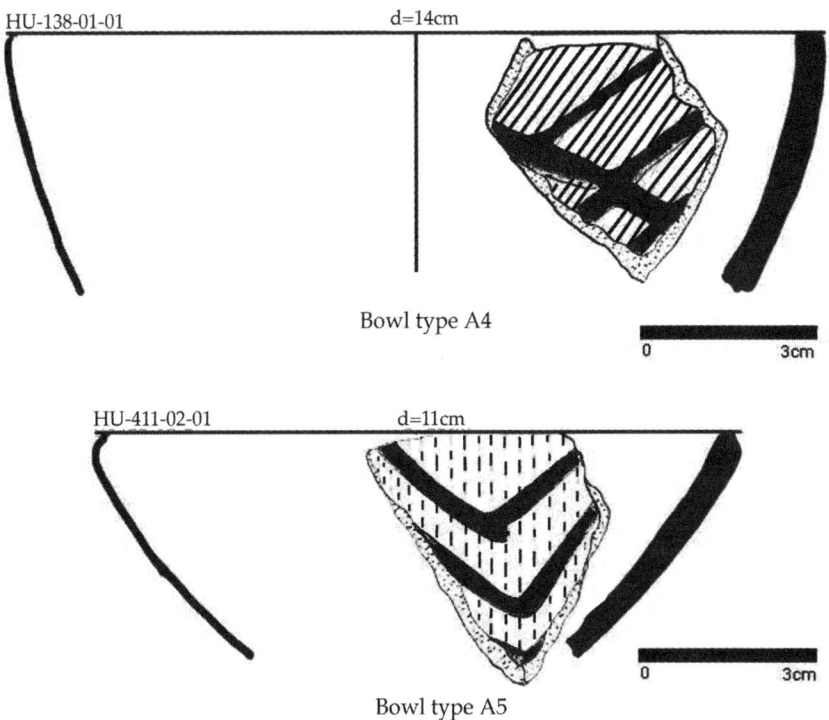

Figure 2.85. Altiplano II bowl types A4 and A5.

Jars, type B, variants 1 and 2 (Fig. 2.92).

They are very small, small, and medium. They are generally wiped although some are burnished. They can be plain or decorated with orange, brown, red, or cream slips. Some also have exterior and/or interior paint decorations in one color (black or brown over different slips) or in two colors (black + white or black + brown over red or orange slips, or red + orange over cream). The designs are geometric (circles, horizontal lines, and crosshatched). They can be decorated with exterior incisions (rounded grooves) or flat appendixes without perforation on the rim.

Jars, type C, variants 1, 2, and 3 (Fig.2.92).

They are very small, small, and medium. They use wiping as a finish, and only in type C1 are there scarce burnished specimens. They are plain and only in type C1 do some have exterior/interior red or orange slips. In type C3, some slips have interior painted decorations in black over red, using geometric designs (diagonal lines).

Pitchers, type A, variants 1, 2, and 3 (Fig. 2.93).

They are large, wiped, and plain. Only in type A3 is there a specimen decorated with an exterior red slip over the natural color of the vessel.

Pitchers, type B, variants 1 and 2 (Fig. 2.94).

They are large and very large. They use wiping as a finish. They can be plain or decorated with orange, brown, red, or cream slips. They can also have exterior paint decorations in one color (black or brown over orange, red, or brown slips) or a combination of three colors (black + cream + red over an orange slip). The designs are geometric (horizontal lines, crosshatched, and circles) and there are flat appendixes on the rim decorated with incisions that may be perforated.

Ollas, type A, variants 2 and 3 (Fig. 2.95).

They are medium and large. They are wiped for a finish. They can be plain or have white slips on the exterior.

Ollas, type B, variants 1 and 2 (Fig. 2.95).

They are small, medium, large, and very large. The finish is wiping. They can be plain or decorated with orange, red, or brown slips on the exterior and/or interior.

Ollas, type C; type D, variants 1 and 2 (Fig. 2.96).

They are large and very large. They are wiped and can be plain or decorated with exterior orange slips.

Glasses, type A, variants 1 and 2 (Fig. 2.97).

They are very small or small. They are wiped and sometimes burnished. They can be plain or have painted decorations on the exterior in black over brown with geometric circle designs.

Other Forms Associated with the Assemblage: Spoons, miniatures

Ritual Elements: Incense burners

Productive Tools: Polishing tools, spindle whorls

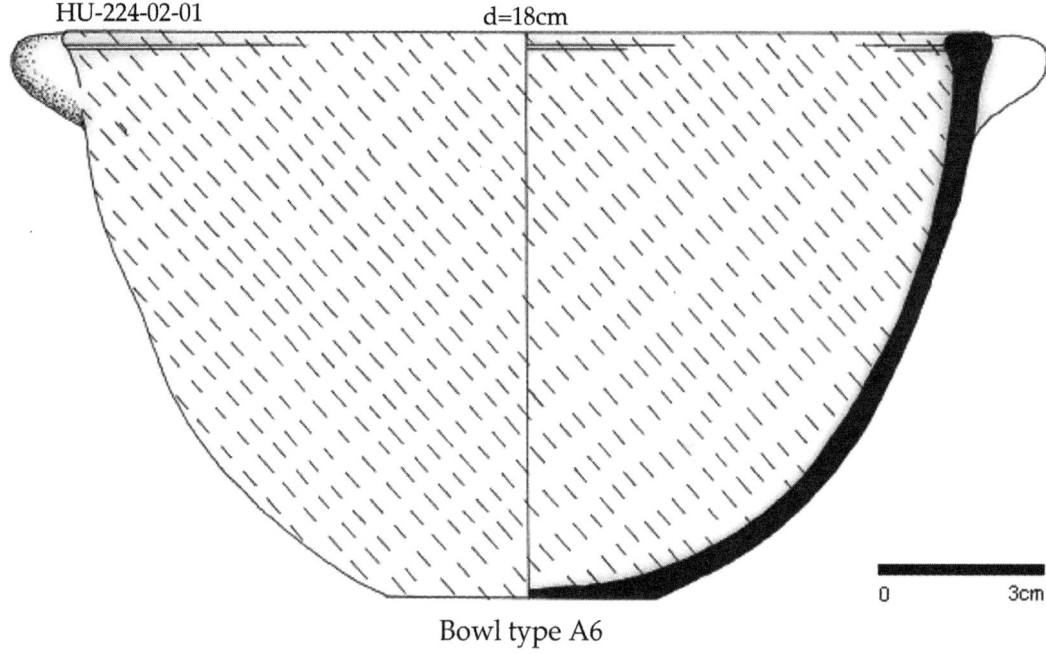
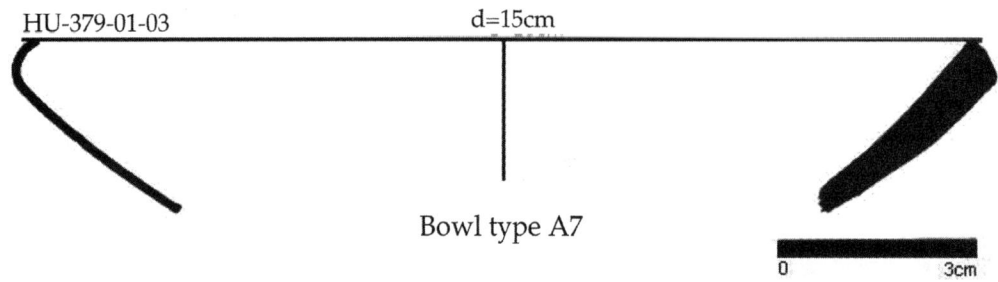
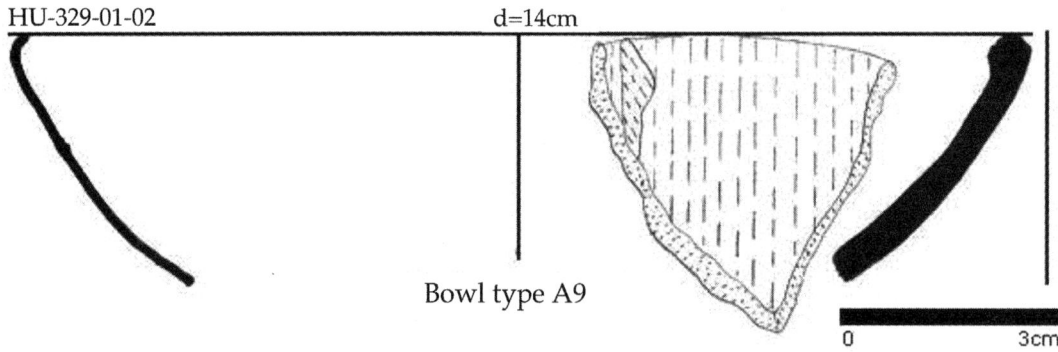

Figure 2.86. Altiplano II bowl types A6, A7, and A9.

Analysis of Ceramics

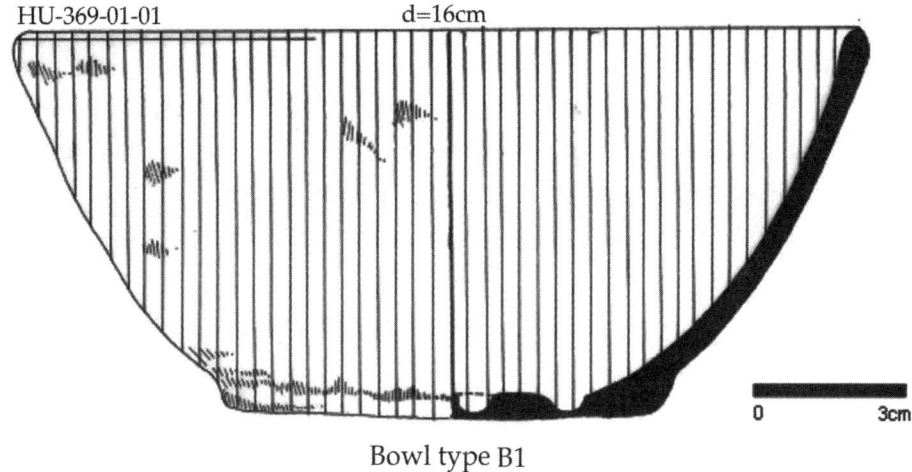

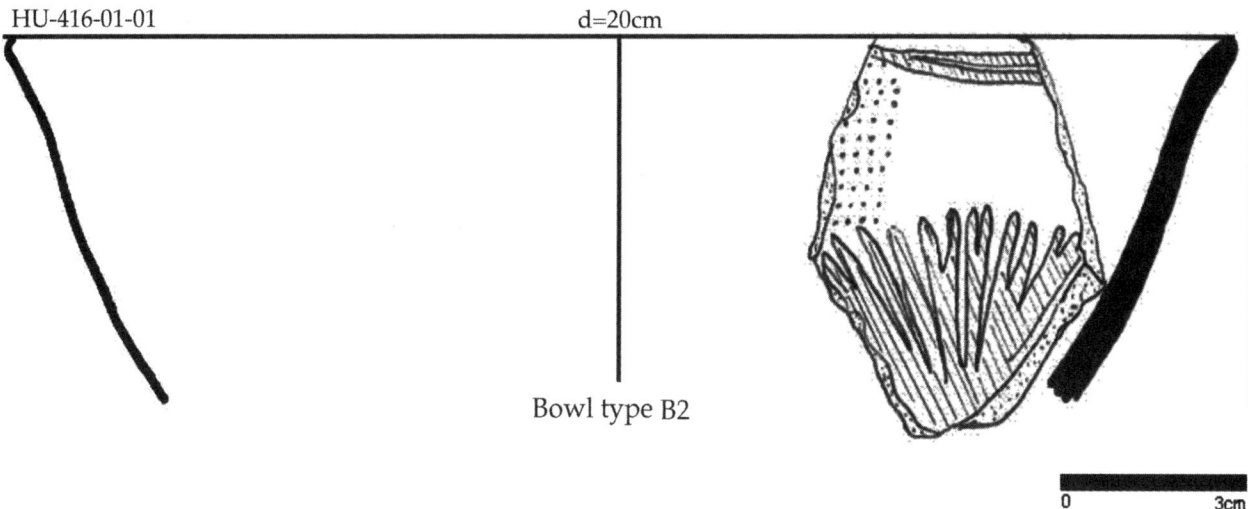

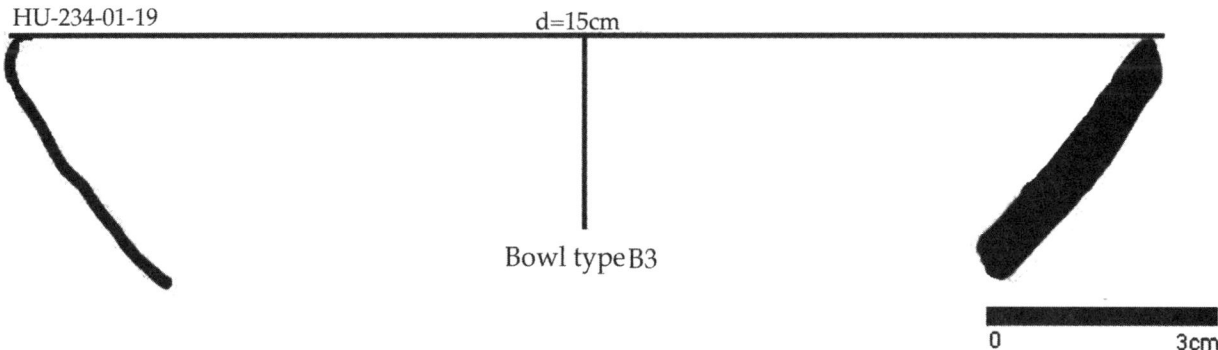

Figure 2.87. Altiplano II bowl types B1–B3.

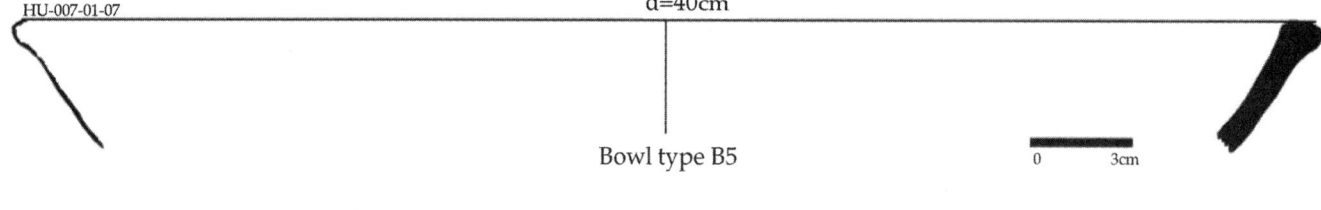
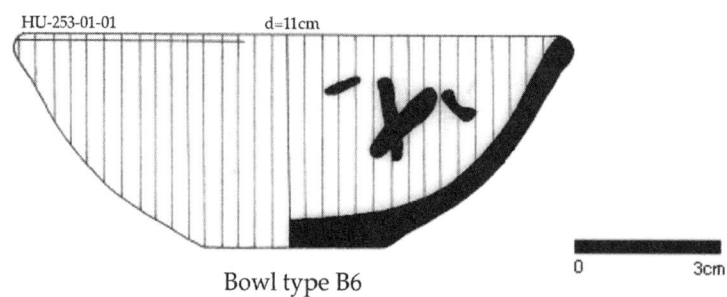
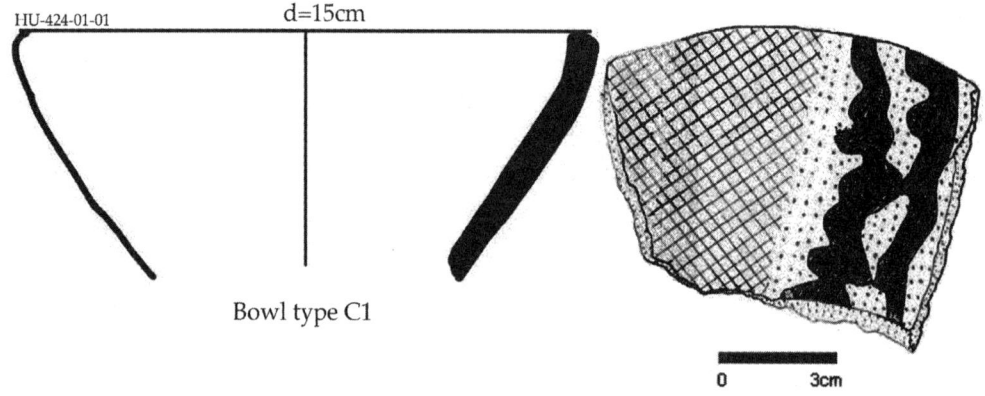
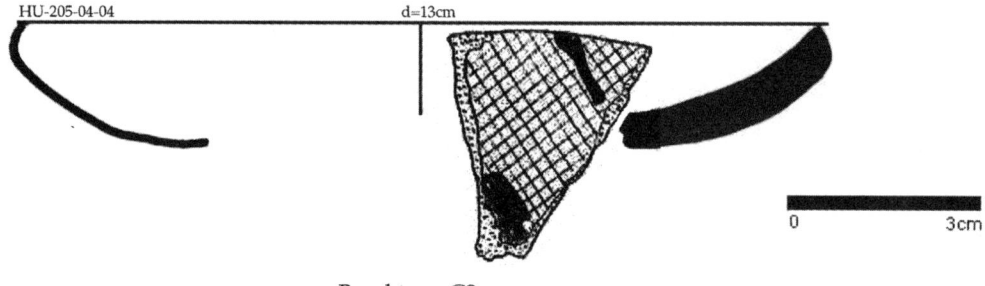

Figure 2.88. Altiplano II bowl types B5, B6, C1, and C2.

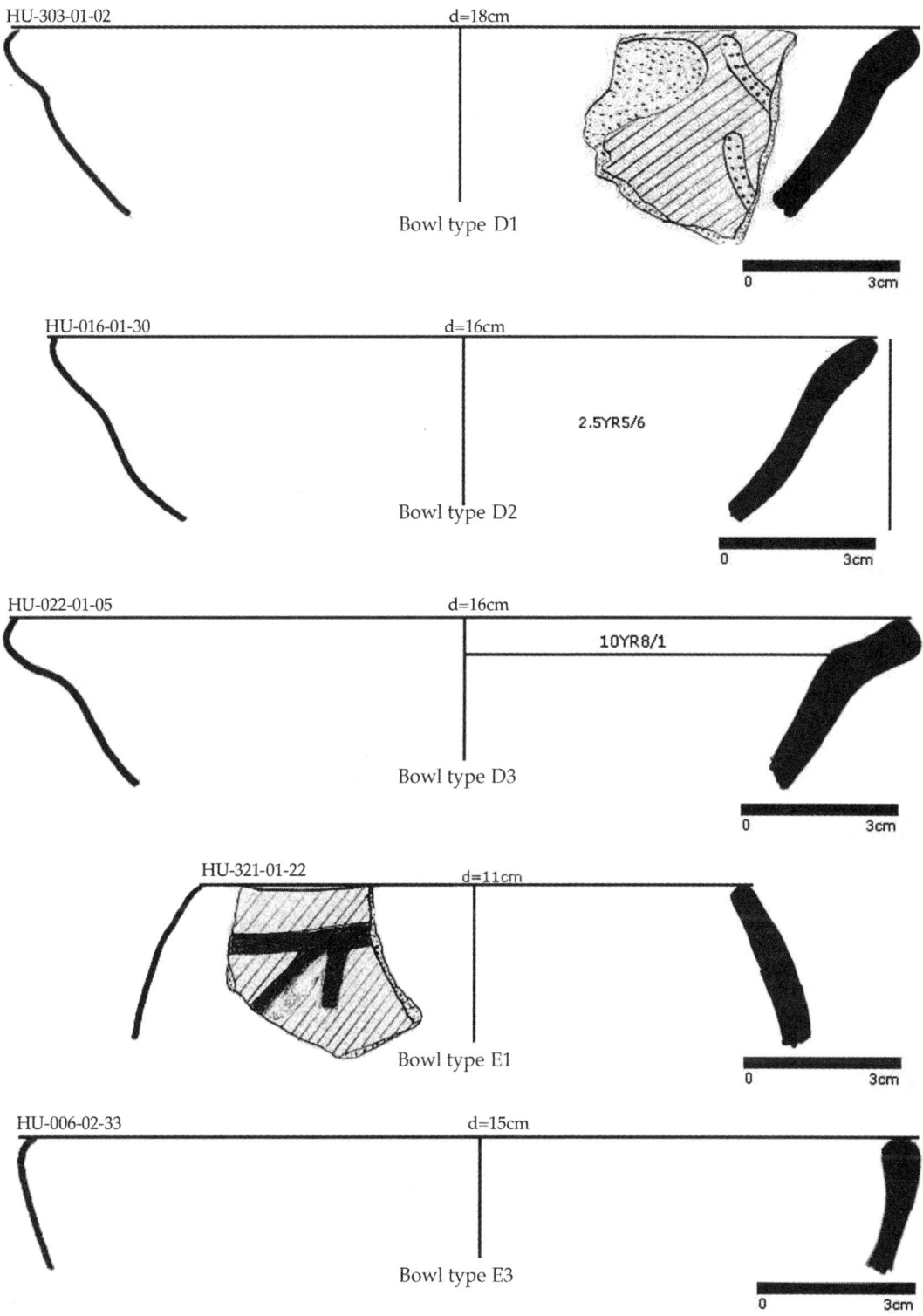

Figure 2.89. Altiplano II bowl types D1–D3, E1, and E3.

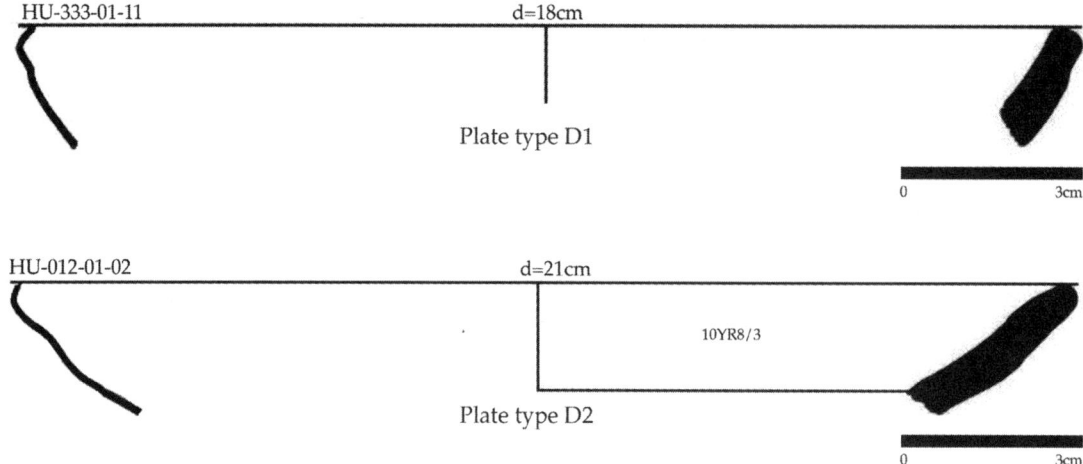

Figure 2.90. Altiplano II plate types D1 and D2.

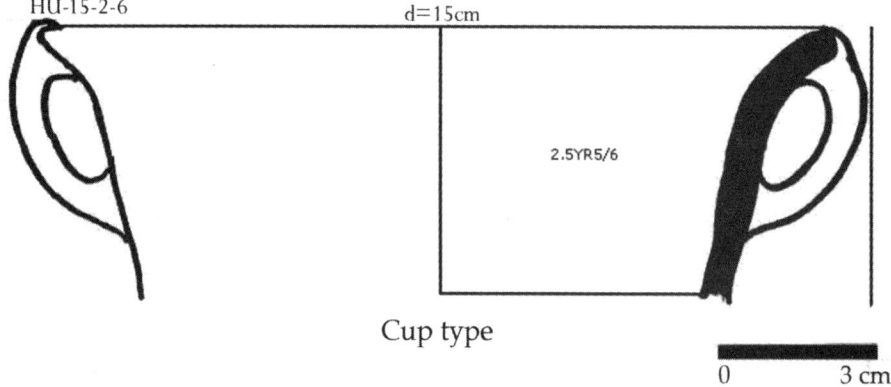

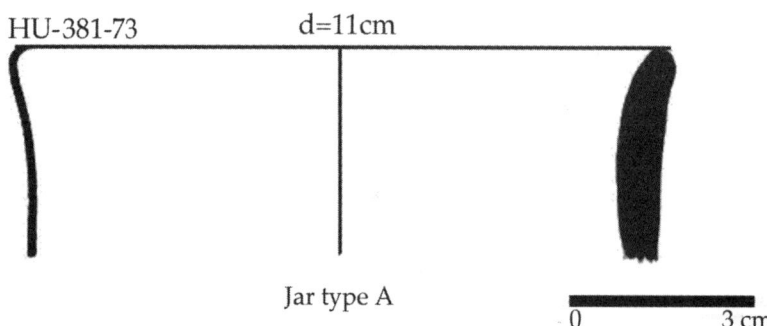

Figure 2.91. Altiplano II cup and jar type A.

Analysis of Ceramics

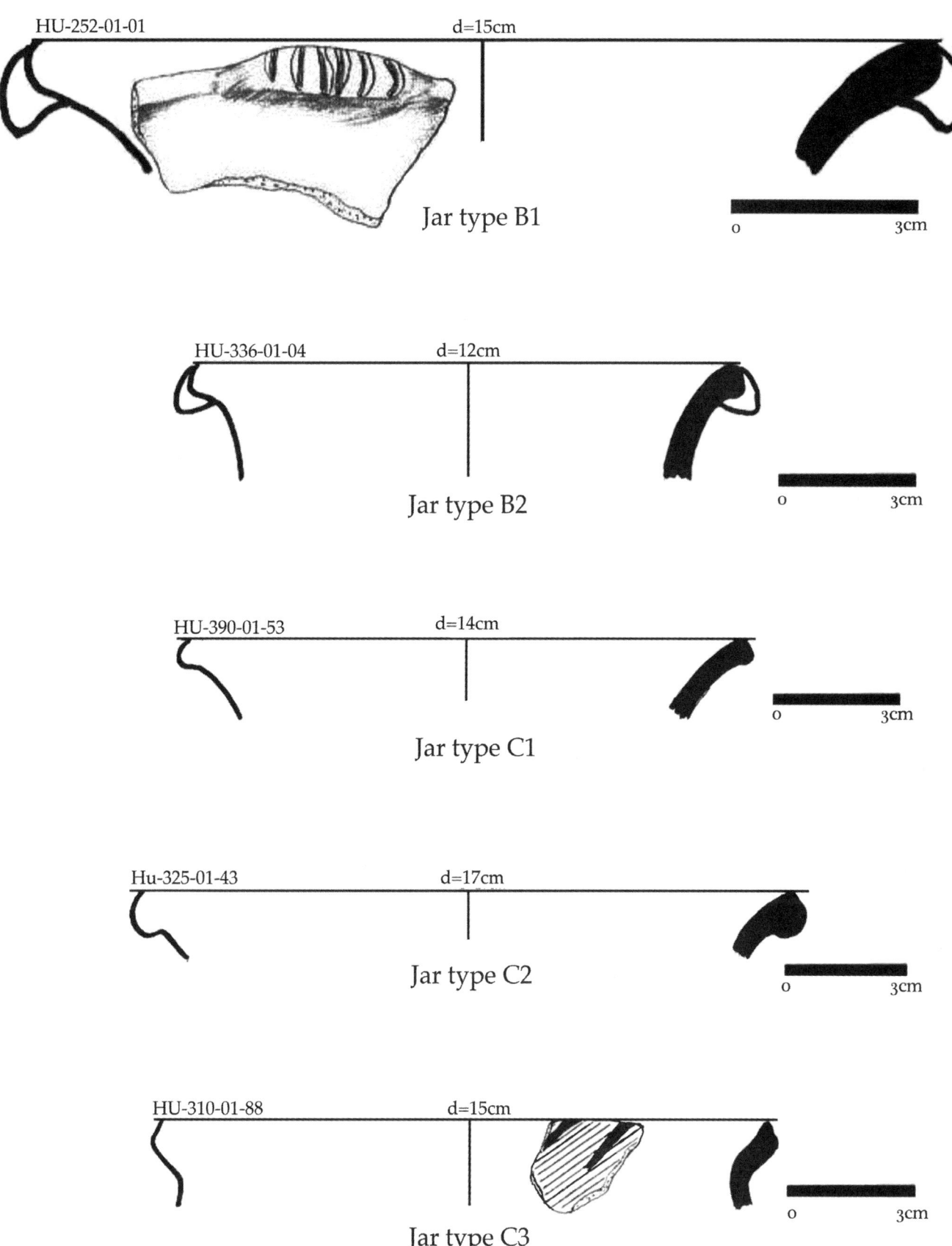

Figure 2.92. Altiplano II jar types B1, B2, and C1–C3.

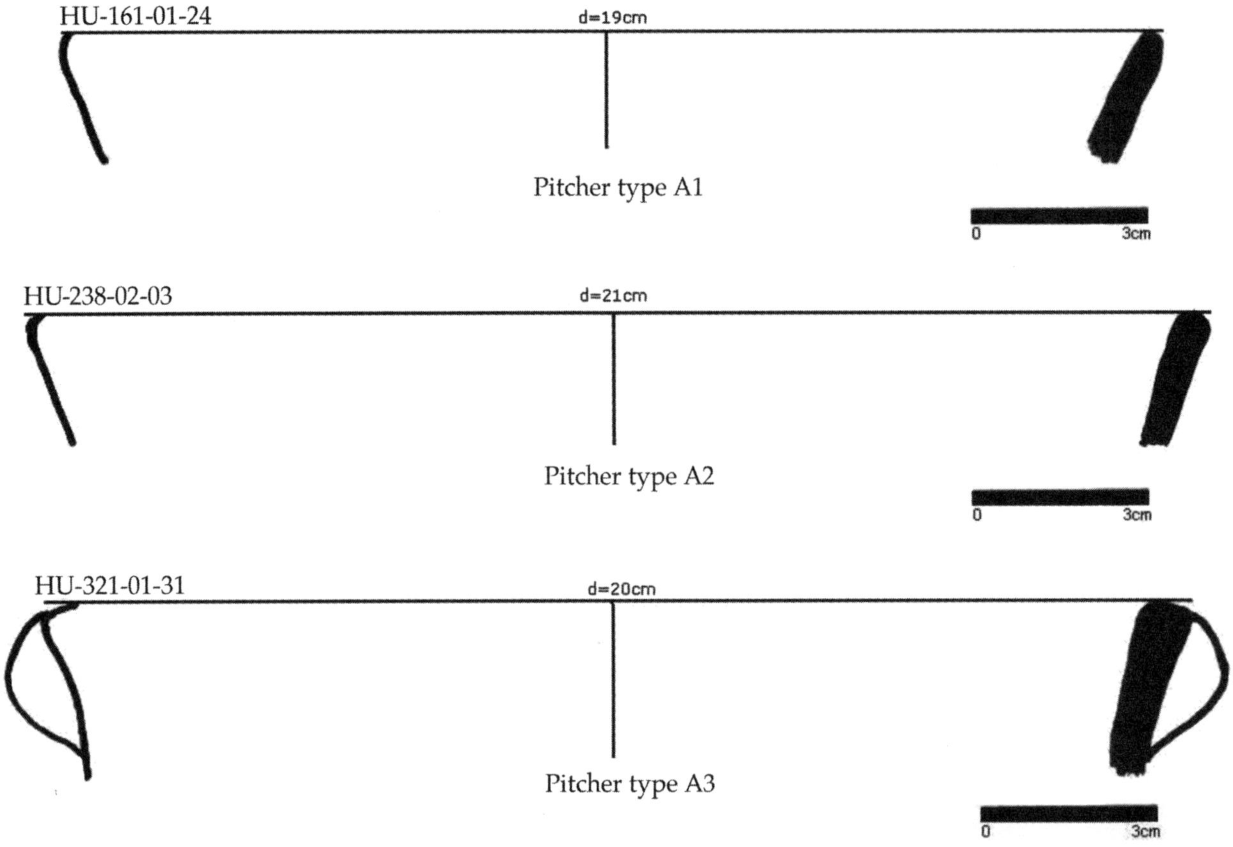

128   *The Northern Titicaca Basin Survey*

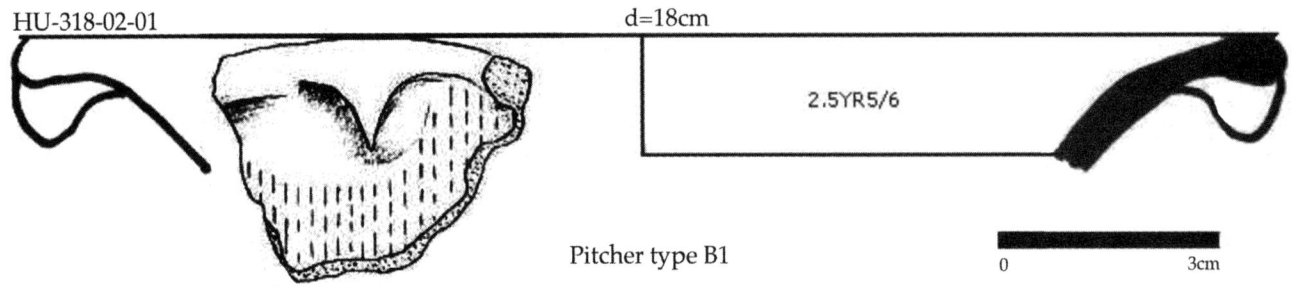

Figure 2.93. Altiplano II pitcher types A1–A3.

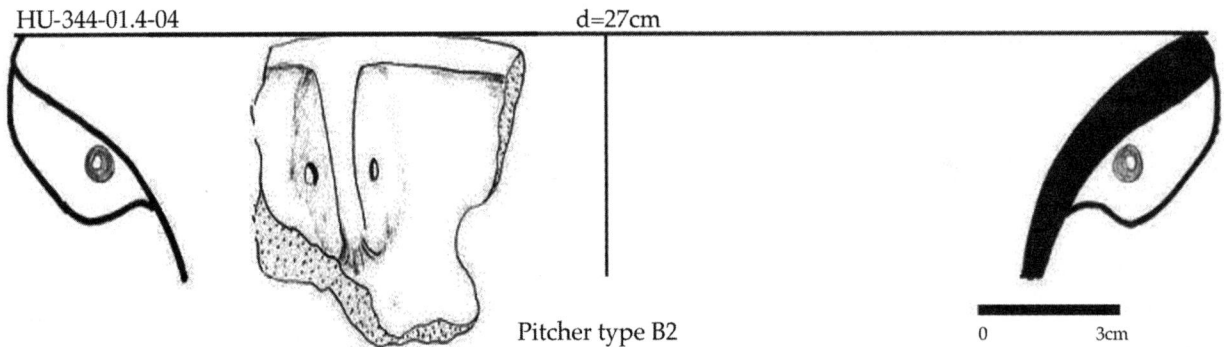

Figure 2.94. Altiplano II pitcher types B1 and B2.

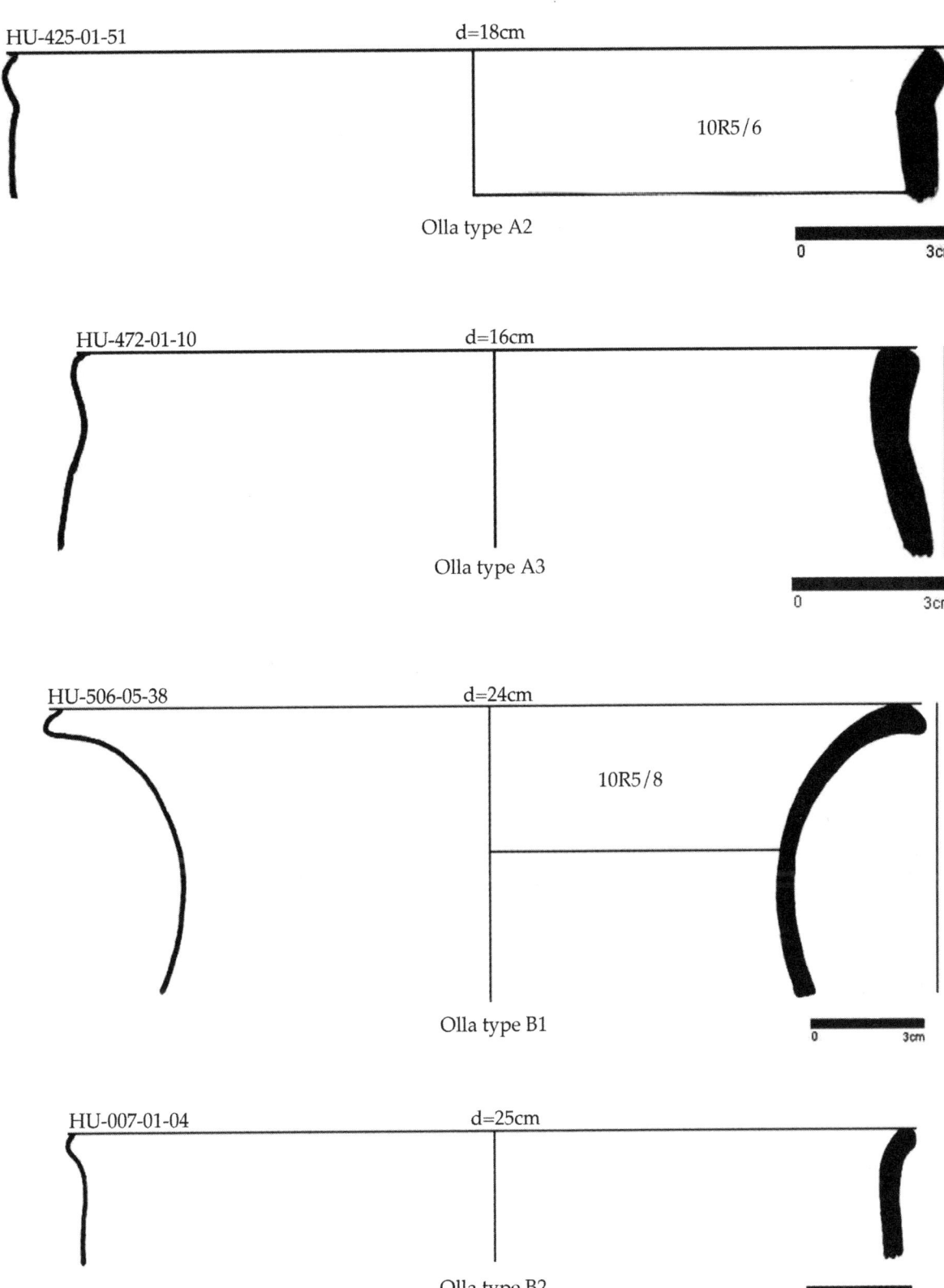

Figure 2.95. Altiplano II olla types A2, A3, B1, and B2.

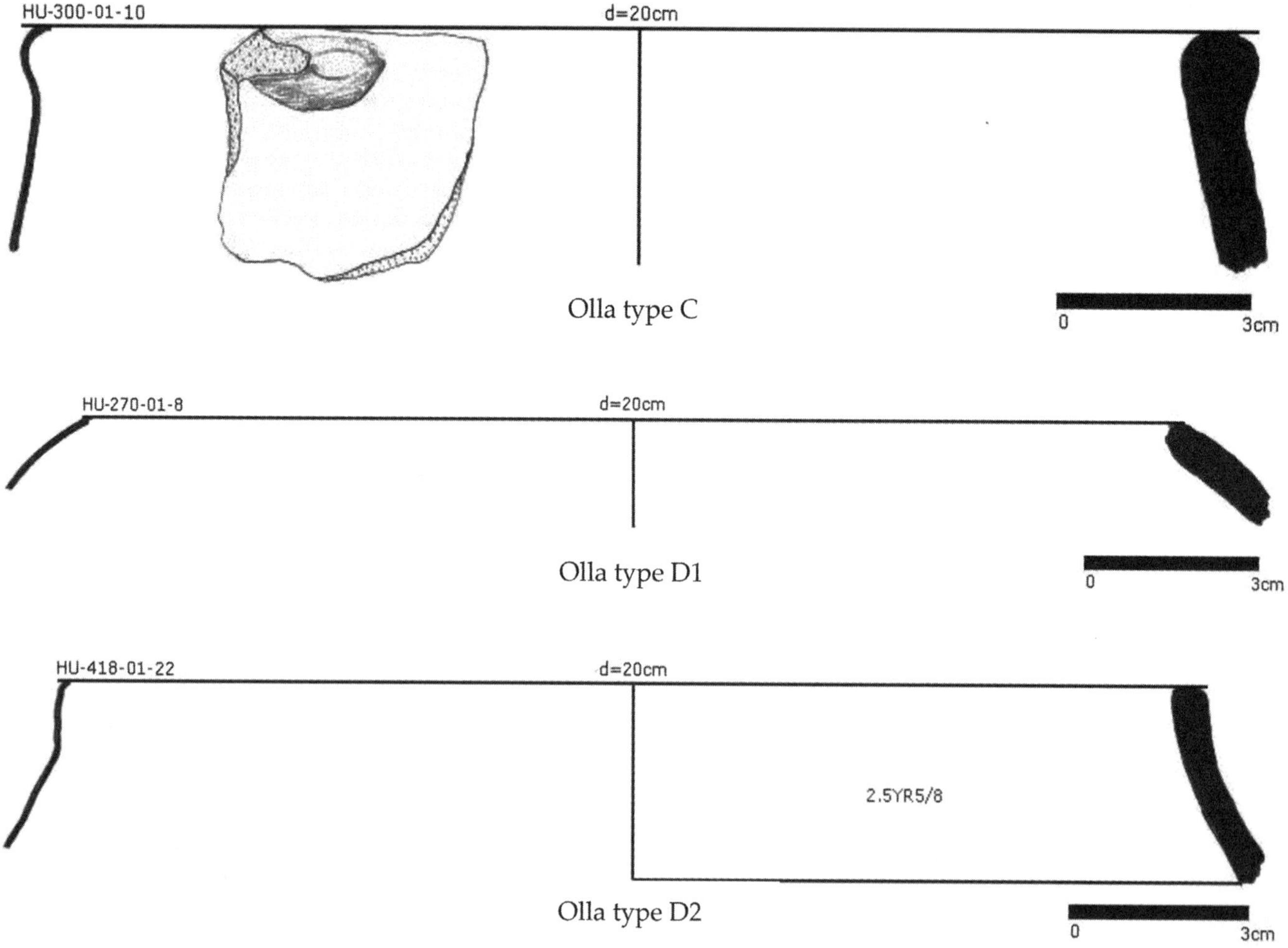

Olla type C

Olla type D1

Olla type D2

Figure 2.96. Altiplano II olla types C, D1, and D2.

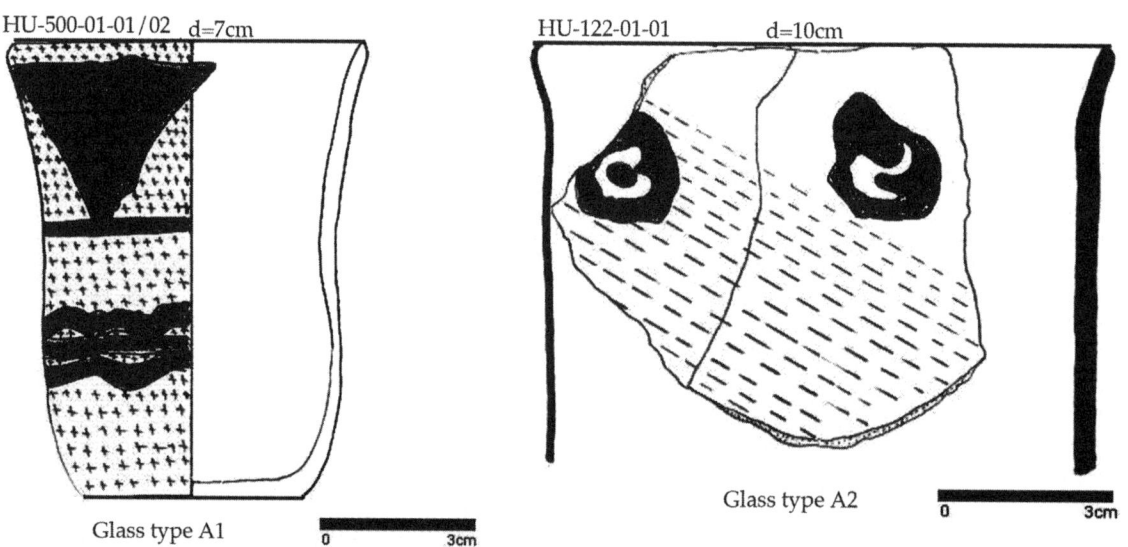

Figure 2.97. Altiplano II glass types A1 and A2.

ALTIPLANO III (Figs. 2.98–2.111)

Group I-4/25, 26

The color is red. They are composed of white subrounded inclusions up to 1.0 mm in size with a regular dispersion and abundant density. The fracture is regular; they are semi-compact and semi-soft with a medium texture. The inclusions are visible in the cross section: exterior and interior. The finish is wiped and burnished with occasional polishing.

Group III/18, 19, 20, 21, 22

The pastes are reddish brown in color. They include black subangular inclusions up to 1.5 mm in size with a regular dispersion and medium to abundant density. There are also ocher-colored subangular inclusions up to 2.0 mm in length with an irregular dispersion and sparse density. Reddish subangular inclusions of 1.0 mm with a regular dispersion and medium density are also present. White subangular inclusions of 0.1 mm with an irregular dispersion and medium to sparse density were also found. The inclusions are visible in the cross section: exterior and interior. The fracture is regular, semi-compact, and semi-hard with a thick texture. The finish is wiped and burnished.

Associated Style: Collao and Huatasani

Associated Assemblage:

Open Vessels

Tazones, type A, variants 1, 2, 3, 4, and 5 (Figs. 2.98, 2.99).

They typically have only size small and medium; only in type A1 are there very small and large specimens in small quantities. They use wiping as a finish, although very few are burnished. A few are plain; others are decorated with red, orange, brown, or cream slips. They can also have interior paint decorations although some have both interior and exterior paint. They use one color (black or brown) or two colors (black + brown) over different slips. The designs are geometric (diagonal, vertical, horizontal, and undulating lines).

Tazones, type B, variants 1, 3, 6 and 8 (Figs. 2.99, 2.100).

They are small, medium, large, and very large. They are commonly wiped as a finish; only in type A1 are some burnished. They are generally plain while others are decorated with orange, red, and cream slips. They may also have painted interior decorations in black or brown over different slips. The designs are geometric (horizontal, vertical, and diagonal lines).

Tazones, type C (Fig. 2.100).

They are medium, wiped, and plain.

Bowls, type A, variants 1, 2, 3, 4, 5, 6, 7, and 9 (Figs. 2.101, 2.102).

They are small, medium, and large. The most common finish is wiping, although some are burnished. There are plain specimens and others are decorated with orange, red, cream, or brown slips. There are also some with painted decorations on the interior using one color (black, brown, or red) or a combination of two colors (black + red, black + orange, black + brown, or black + cream) over different slips. The designs are geometric (horizontal, vertical, diagonal, zigzag lines, crosshatched) and anthropomorphic.

Bowls, type B, variants 1, 2, 3, 4, 5, and 6 (Figs. 2.103, 2.104).

They are very small, small, medium, large, and very large. The most common finish is wiping; only in type B1 do some appear burnished. They can be plain or decorated with red, orange, cream, or brown slips. They are also decorated with paint on the exterior and/or interior in one color (black, red, white, or brown over diverse slips) or a combination of two colors (black + brown over orange or brown + red over orange or black + reddish brown over red). The designs are geometric (horizontal, vertical, diagonal, undulating lines, and circles) and naturalistic (camelids).

Bowls, type C, variants 1 and 2 (Fig. 2.105).

They are small and medium. They use wiping as a finish. They can be plain or decorated with orange-toned slips. They can also have paint decorations in black, brown, or red over orange, red, or cream slips. The designs are geometric (horizontal, diagonal lines, and circles).

Bowls, type D, variants 1 and 2 (Fig. 2.105).

They are small, medium, and large. The most common finish is wiping; although some are burnished, they are scarce. They can be plain or decorated with orange or brown-toned slips. They can also have painted decorations on the interior in black over red. The designs are geometric (horizontal and vertical lines).

Bowls, type E, variants 1, 2, and 3 (Fig. 2.106).

They are very small, small, medium, large, and very large in size. They are only wiped. The specimens are plain, but some are also decorated with orange slips. They may also have interior painted decorations of black over white or orange. The designs are geometric (vertical lines and circles).

Plates, type A, variant 1 (Fig. 2.107).

They are large, wiped, and unslipped.

Cups (Fig. 2.107).

They are large, wiped, and decorated with red and/or orange slips.

Closed Vessels

Jars, type A (Fig. 2.107).

They are very small, small, and medium. The only finish is wiped. They are commonly plain, although some are decorated with orange slips. They may also have painted decorations on the interior of black over orange or brown over red on both the exterior and interior.

Jars, type B, variants 1 and 2 (Fig. 2.108).

They are very small, small, and medium. The majority of these fragments are wiped, although some are burnished. They can be plain or decorated with red, orange, or brown slips. They may also have interior and/or exterior painted decorations in one color (black, brown, or red over different slips) or a combination of two colors (black + brown over red). The designs are geometric (horizontal, vertical, and diagonal lines). In addition, there are incised decorations that form triangles on the neck, as well as oval grooves on the rim and appendixes with or without perforation beneath the rim.

Jars, type C, variants 2 and 3 (Fig. 2.109).

They are small and medium. The only finish is wiping. They can be plain or decorated with orange or red slips on both the exterior and interior.

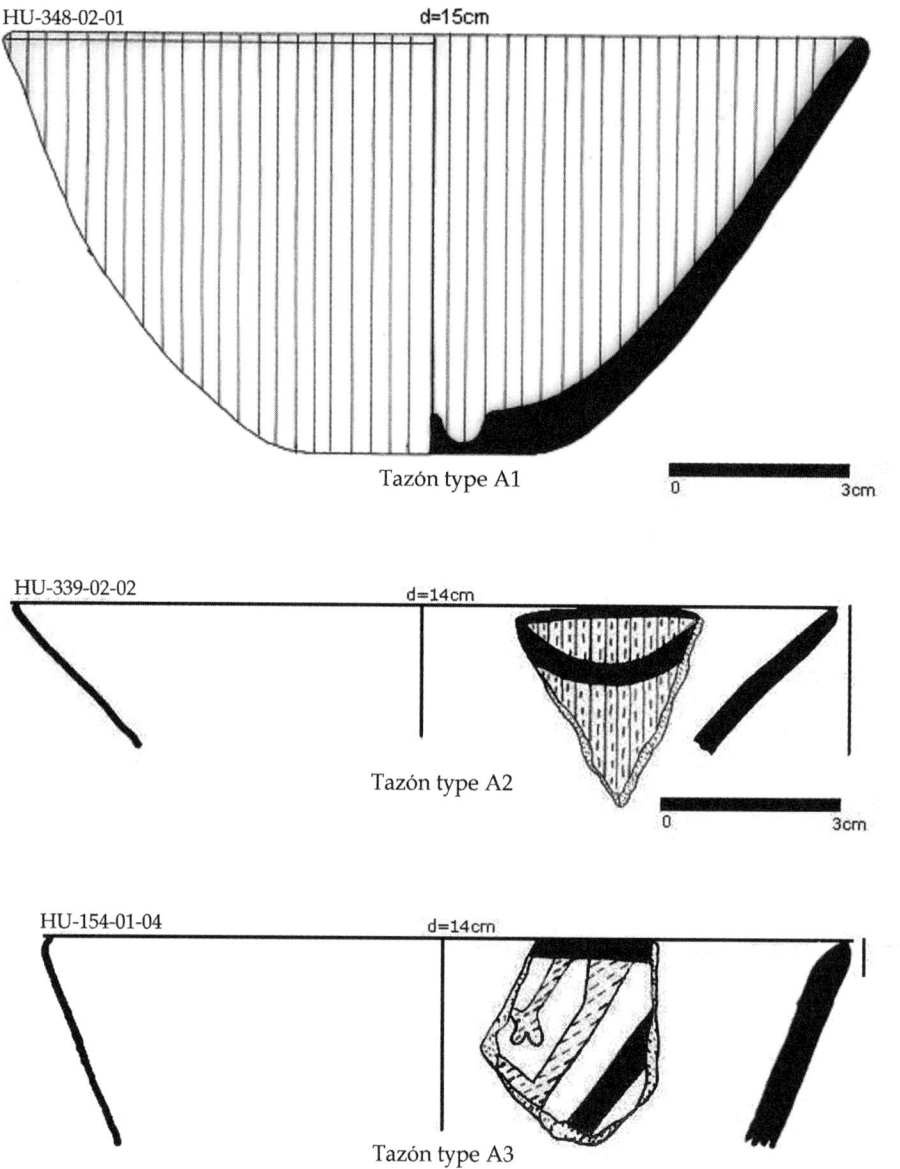

Figure 2.98. Altiplano III tazón types A1–A3.

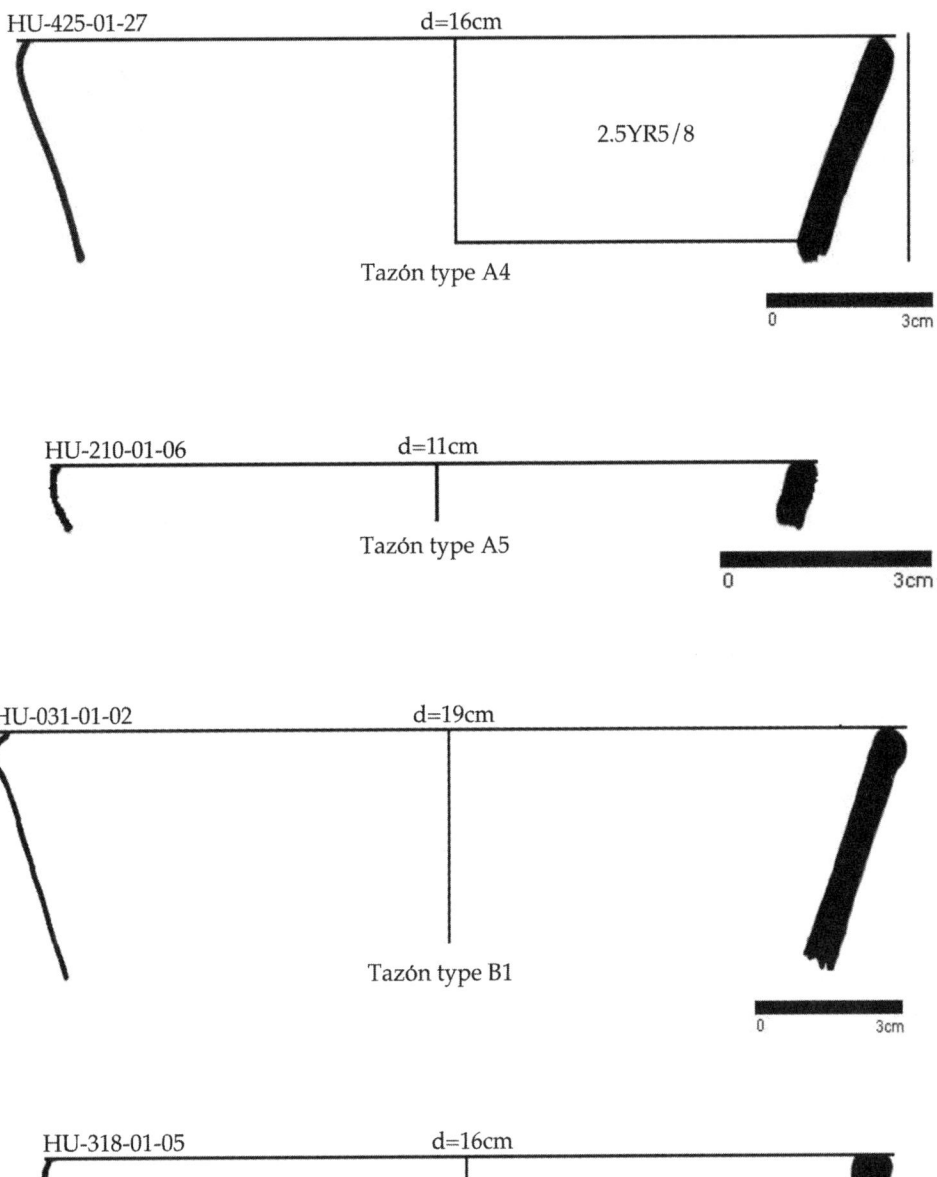

Figure 2.99. Altiplano III tazón types A4, A5, B1, and B3.

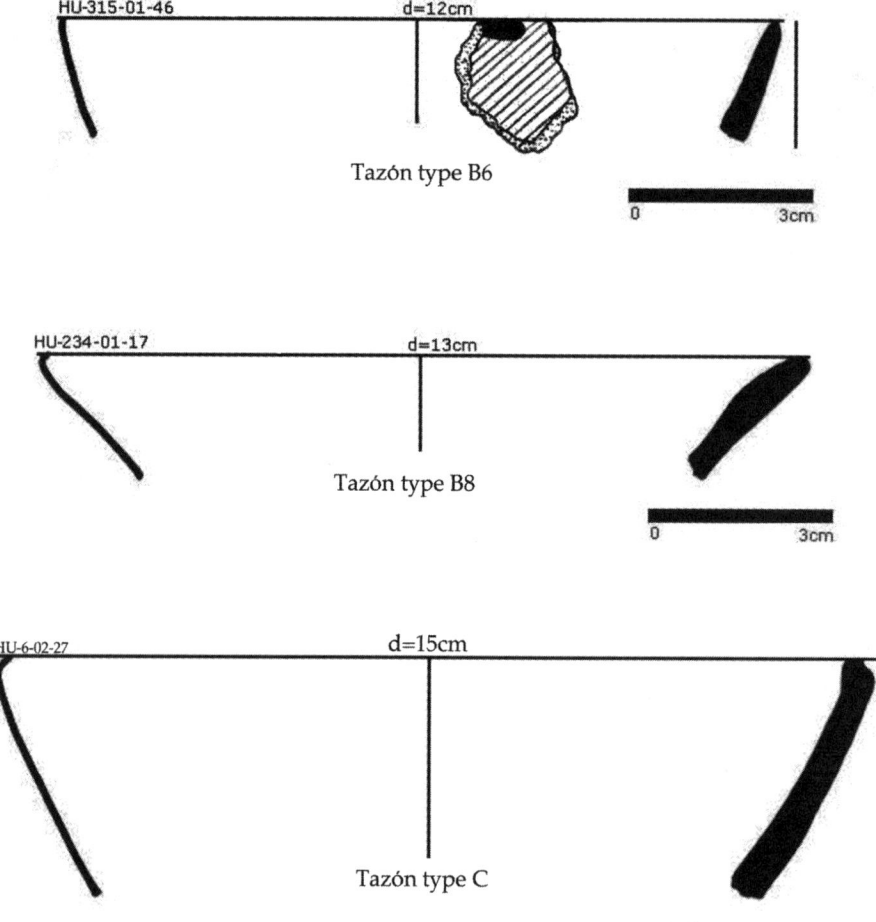

Figure 2.100. Altiplano III tazón types B6, B8, and C.

Analysis of Ceramics

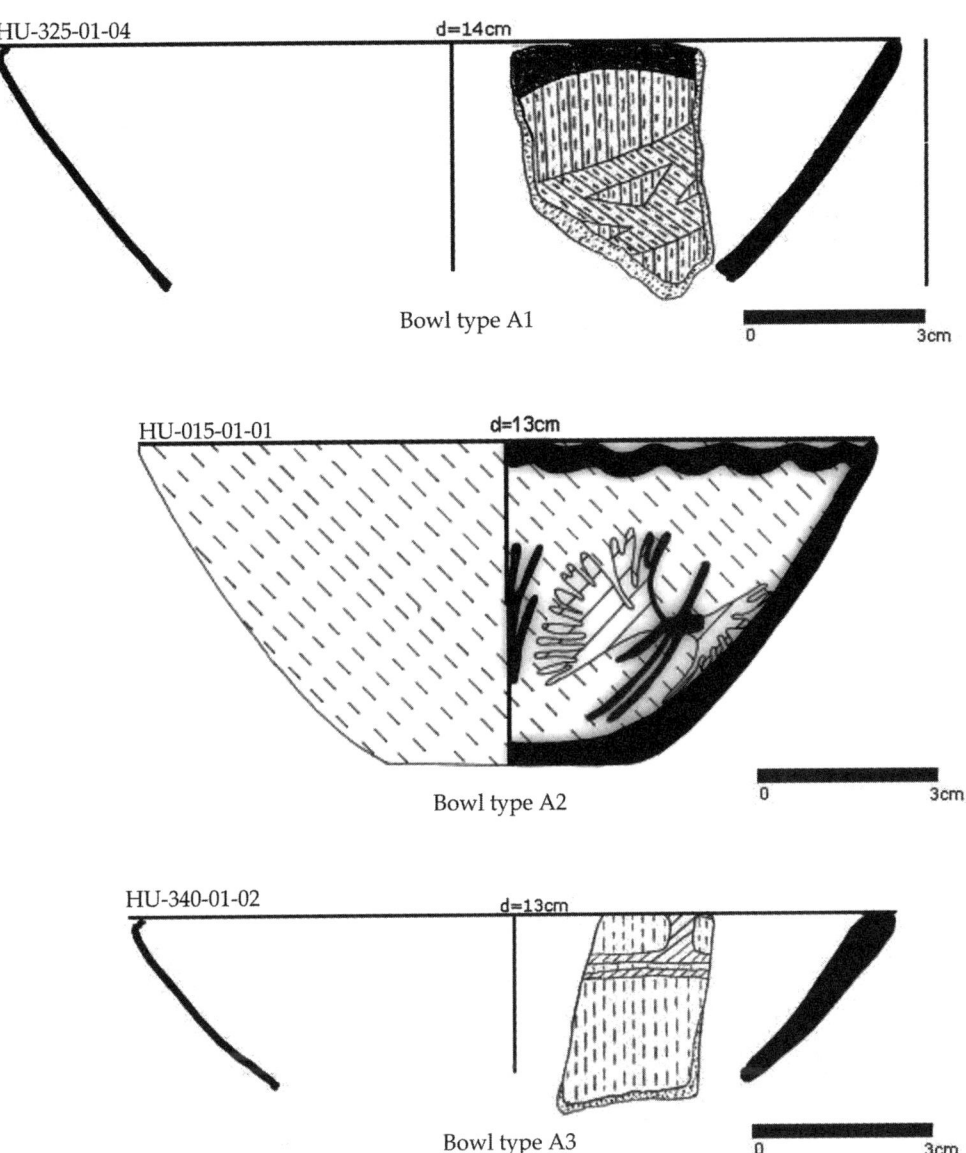

Figure 2.101. Altiplano III bowl types A1–A3.

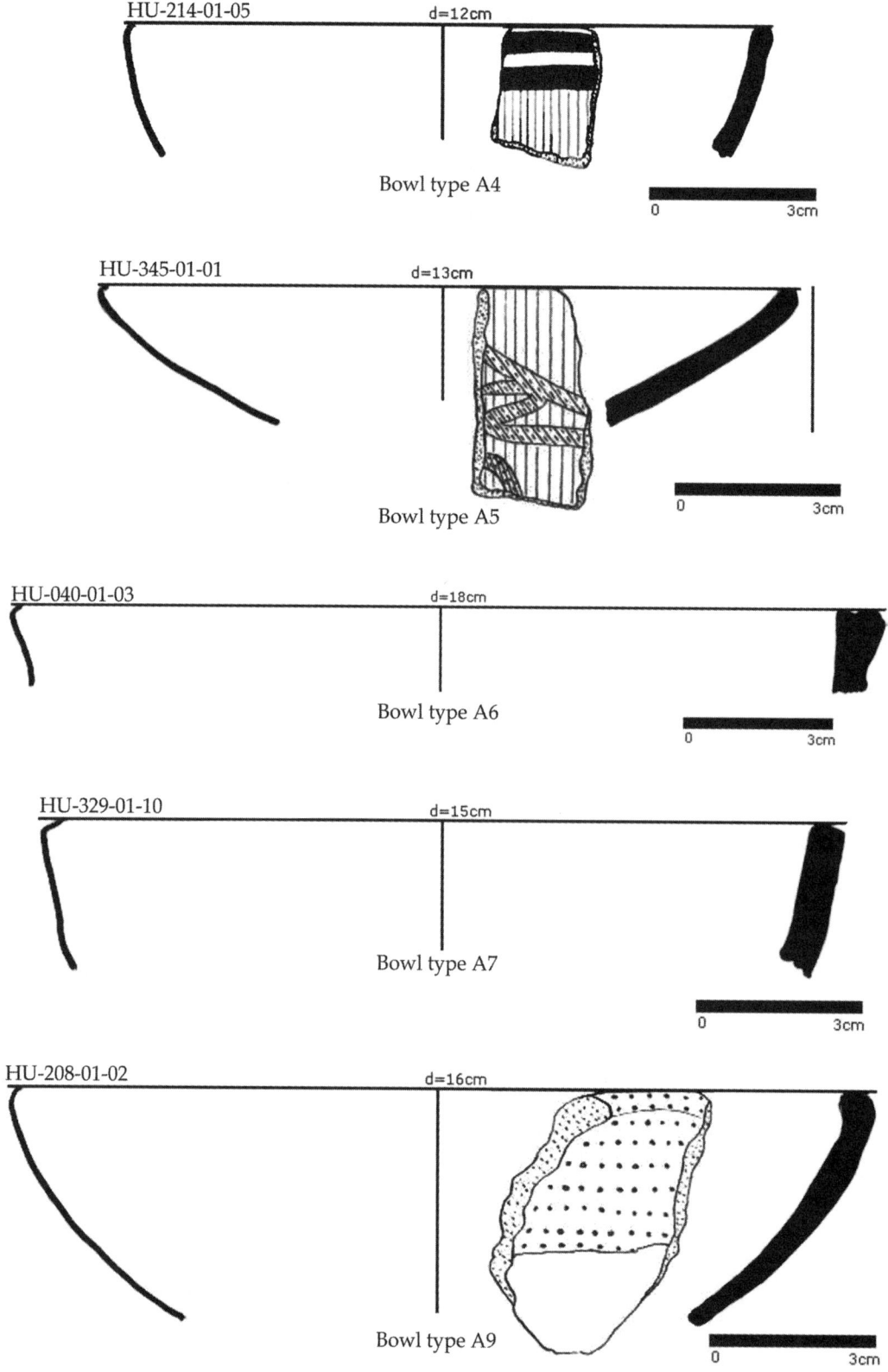

Figure 2.102. Altiplano III bowl types A4–A7 and A9.

Analysis of Ceramics 137

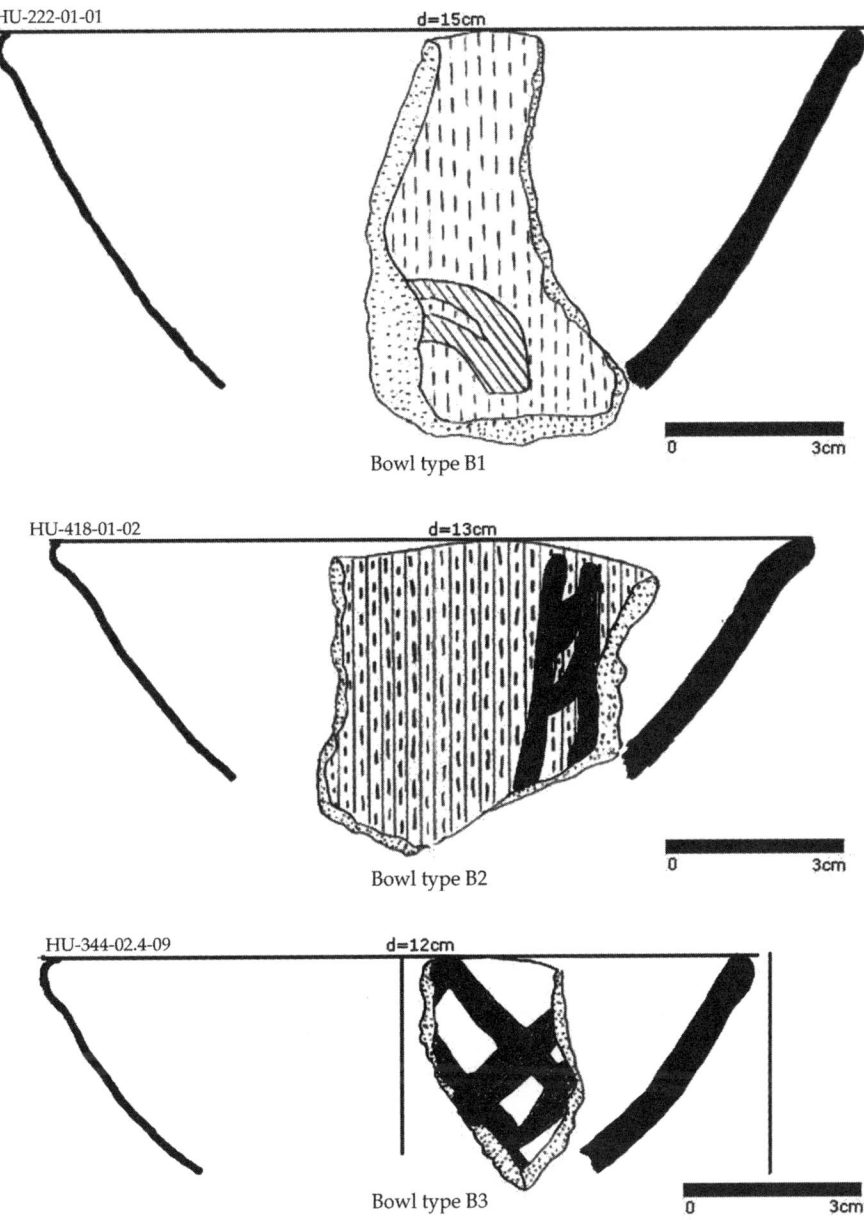

Figure 2.103. Altiplano III bowl types B1–B3.

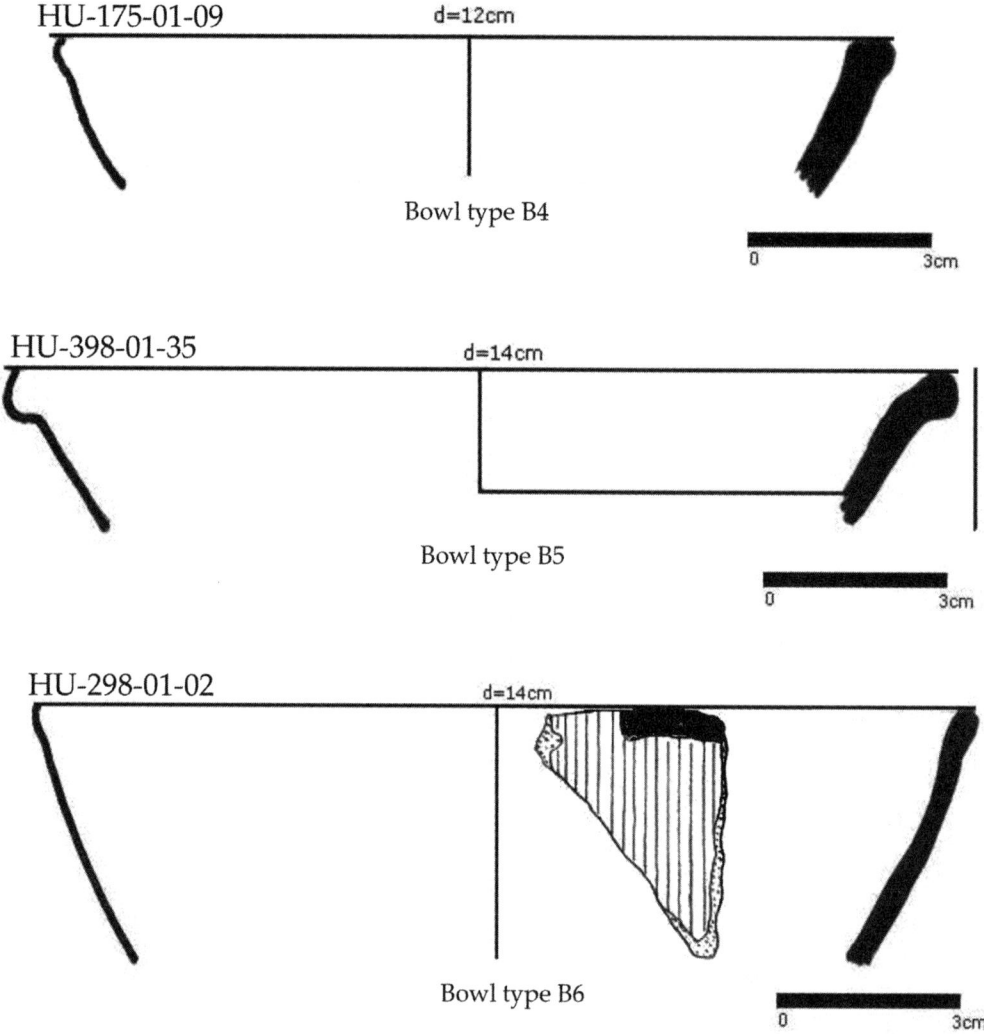

Figure 2.104. Altiplano III bowl types B4–B6.

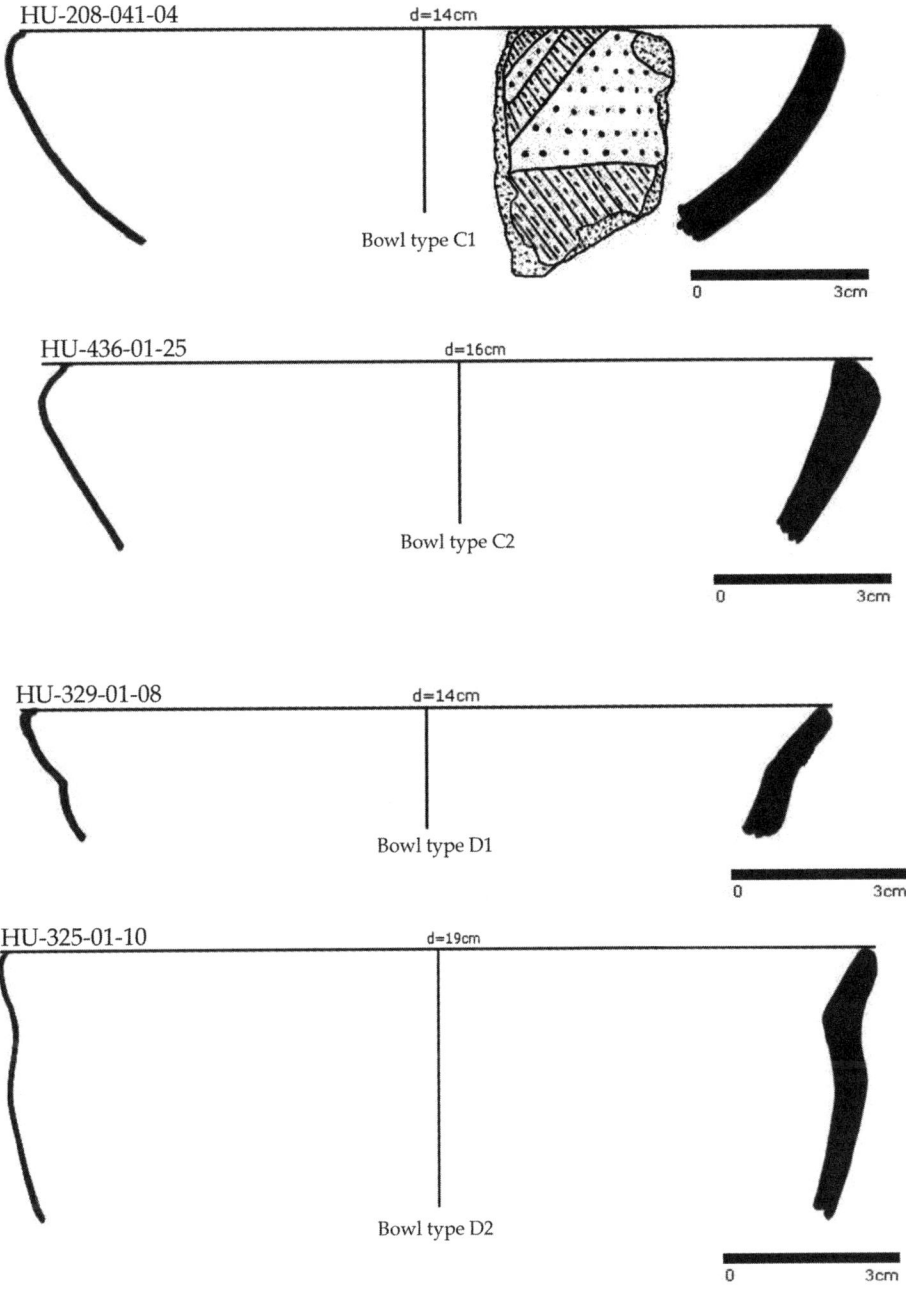

Figure 2.105. Altiplano III bowl types C1, C2, D1, and D2.

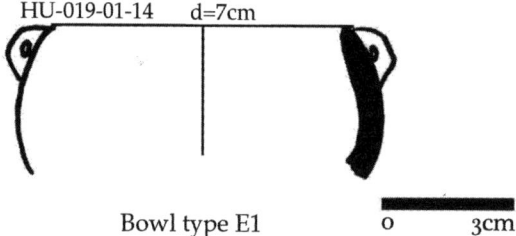

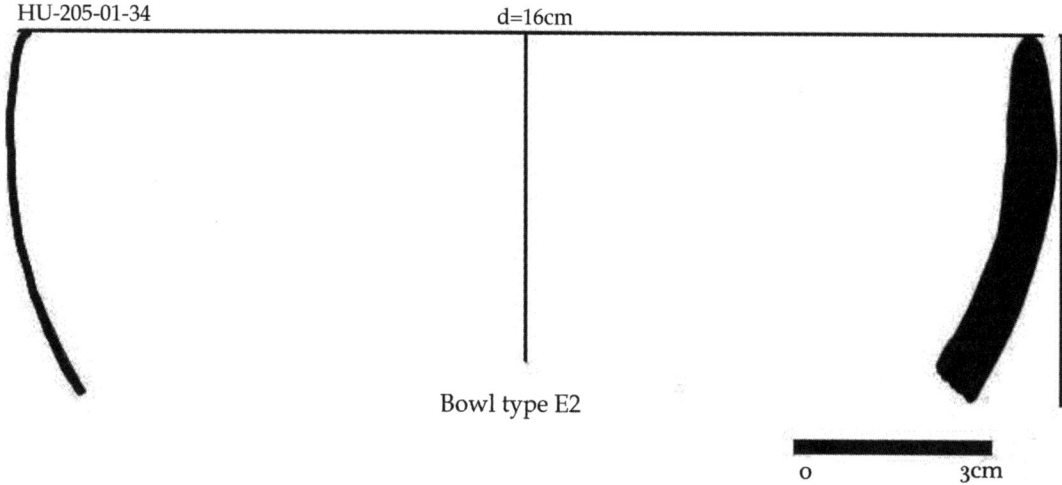

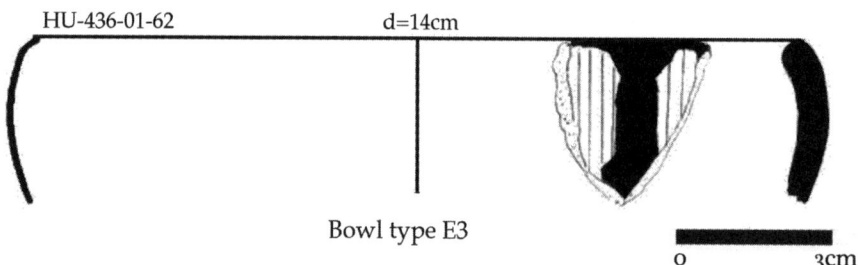

Figure 2.106. Altiplano III bowl types E1–E3.

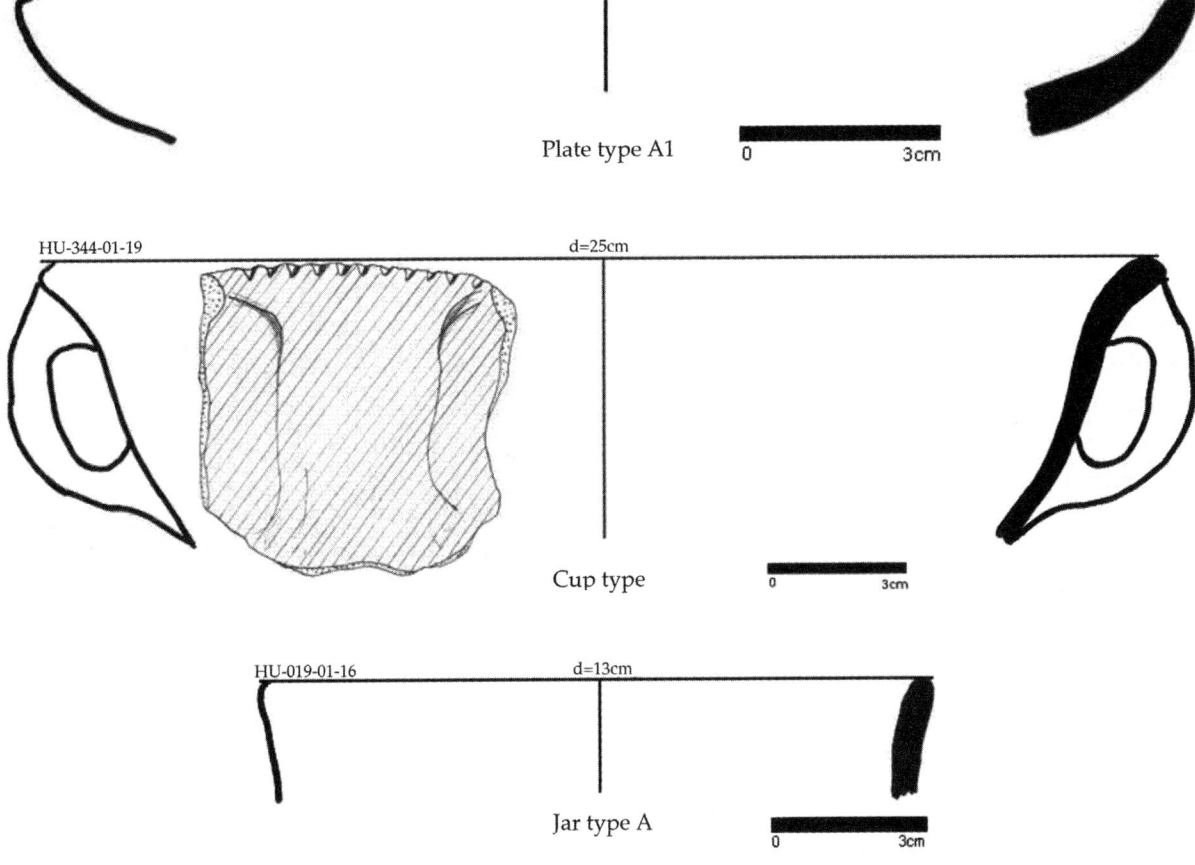

Figure 2.107. Altiplano III plate type A1, cup type, and jar type A.

Pitchers, type A, variant 3 (Fig. 2.110).
They are large, wiped, or burnished. They are decorated with orange slips on the exterior and possibly geometric incisions (diagonal lines).

Pitchers, type B, variants 1 and 2 (Fig. 2.110).
They are large and very large. They are commonly wiped, although some specimens are burnished. They can be plain or decorated with orange, red, or brown slips. They may also have interior and/or exterior painted decorations in one color (black, brown, or red over different slips) or a combination of two colors (brown + red over cream). The designs are geometric (horizontal, vertical, and diagonal lines). They may also have incised decorations on the exterior rim composed of oval grooves and/or flat appendages with or without perforation.

Ollas, type A, variants 2 and 3 (Fig. 2.111).
They are large and very large. They are only wiped and are plain.

Ollas type B, variant 2 (Fig. 2.111).
They are medium, large, and very large. The only finish used is wiping. The majority are plain, but some specimens have complete or partial slips in orange tones as decorations.

142 *The Northern Titicaca Basin Survey*

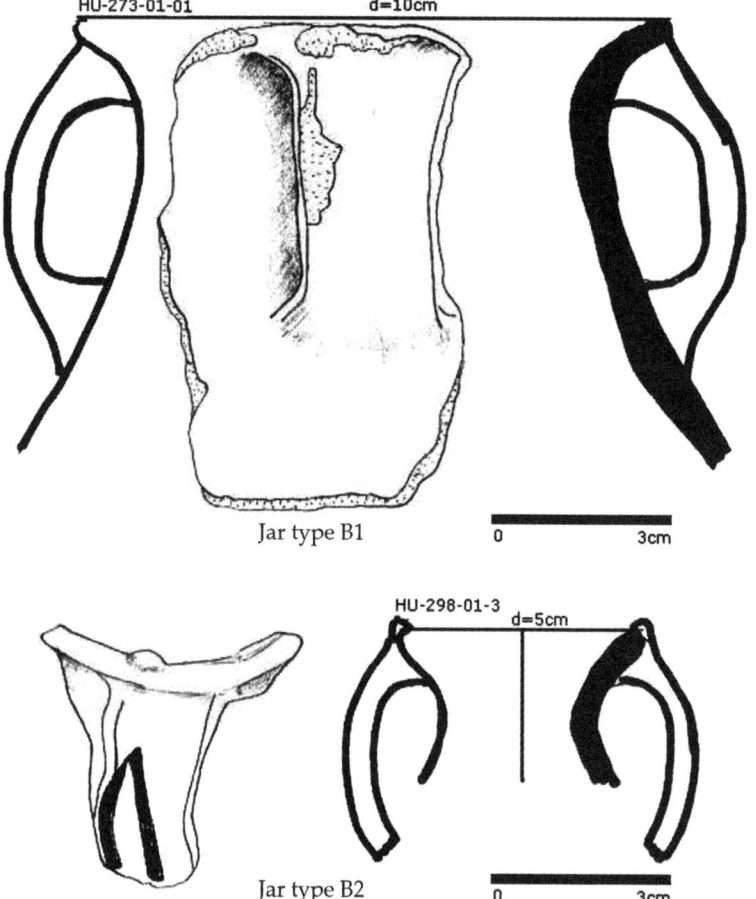

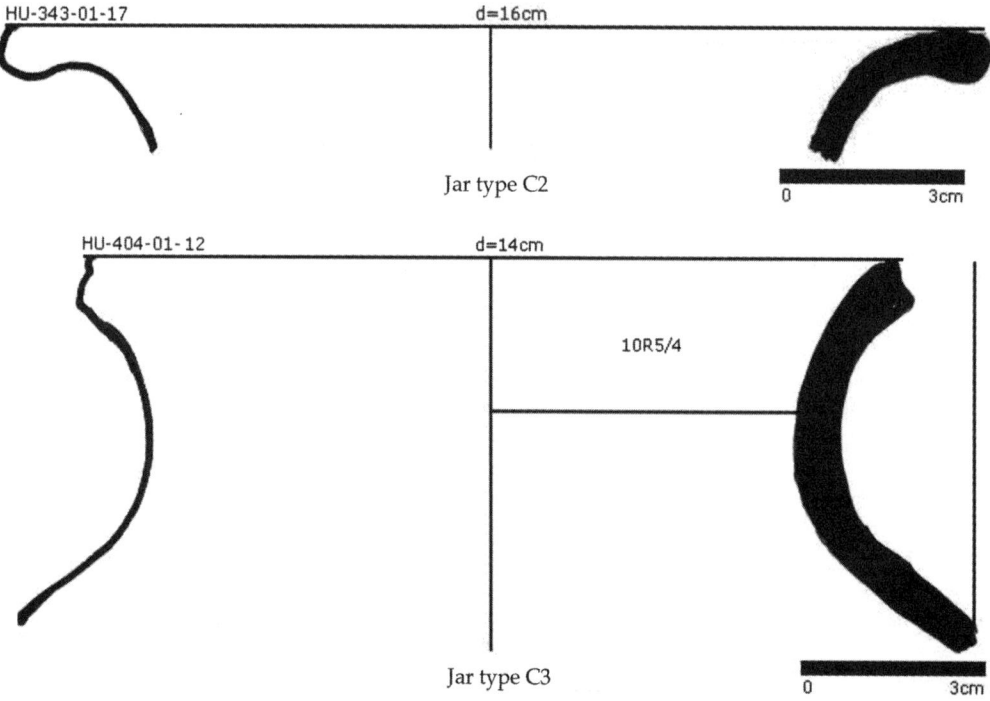

(*left*) Figure 2.108. Altiplano III jar types B1 and B2.

(*below left*) Figure 2.109. Altiplano III jar types C2 and C3.

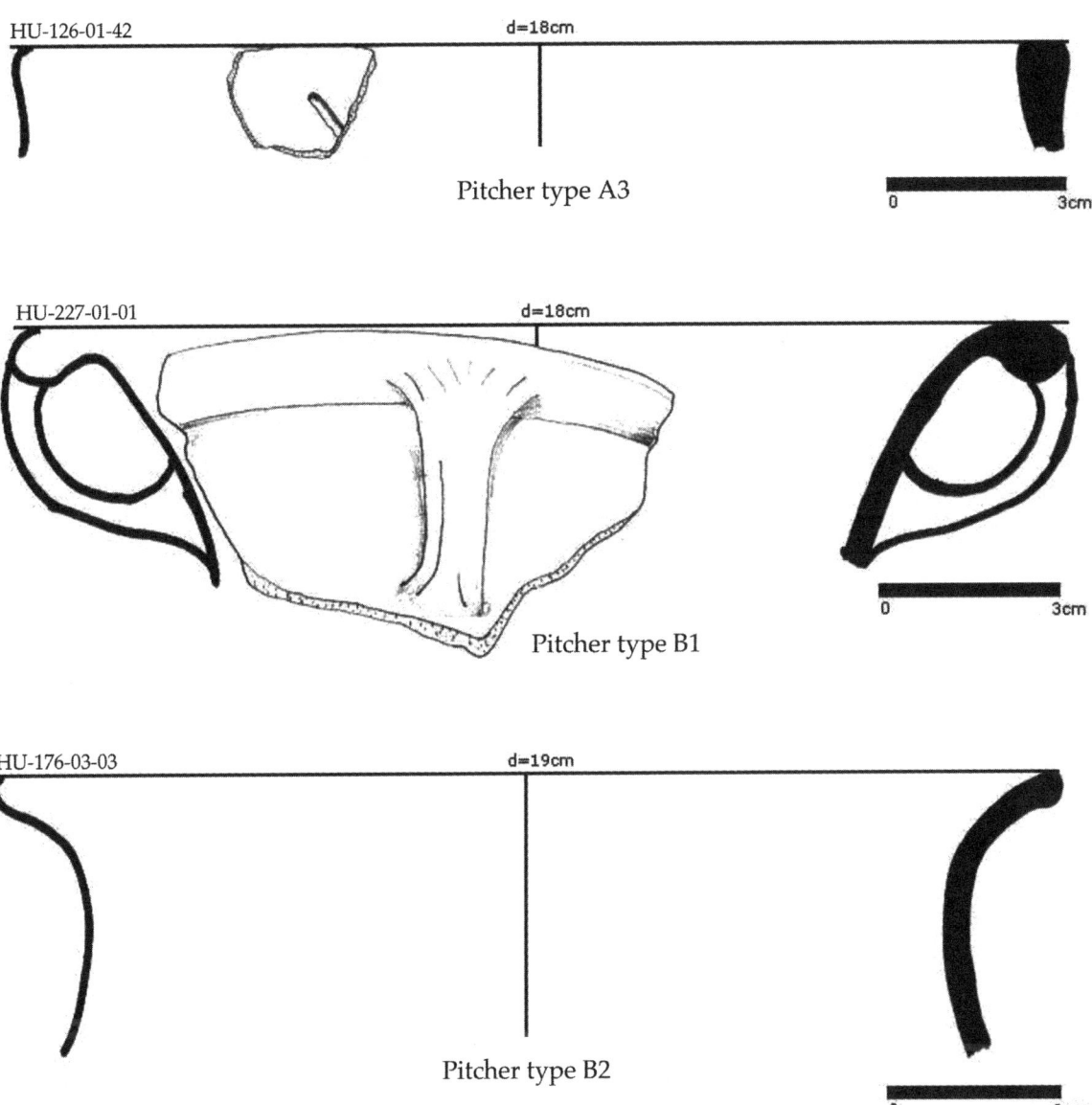

Figure 2.110. Altiplano III pitcher types A3, B1, and B2.

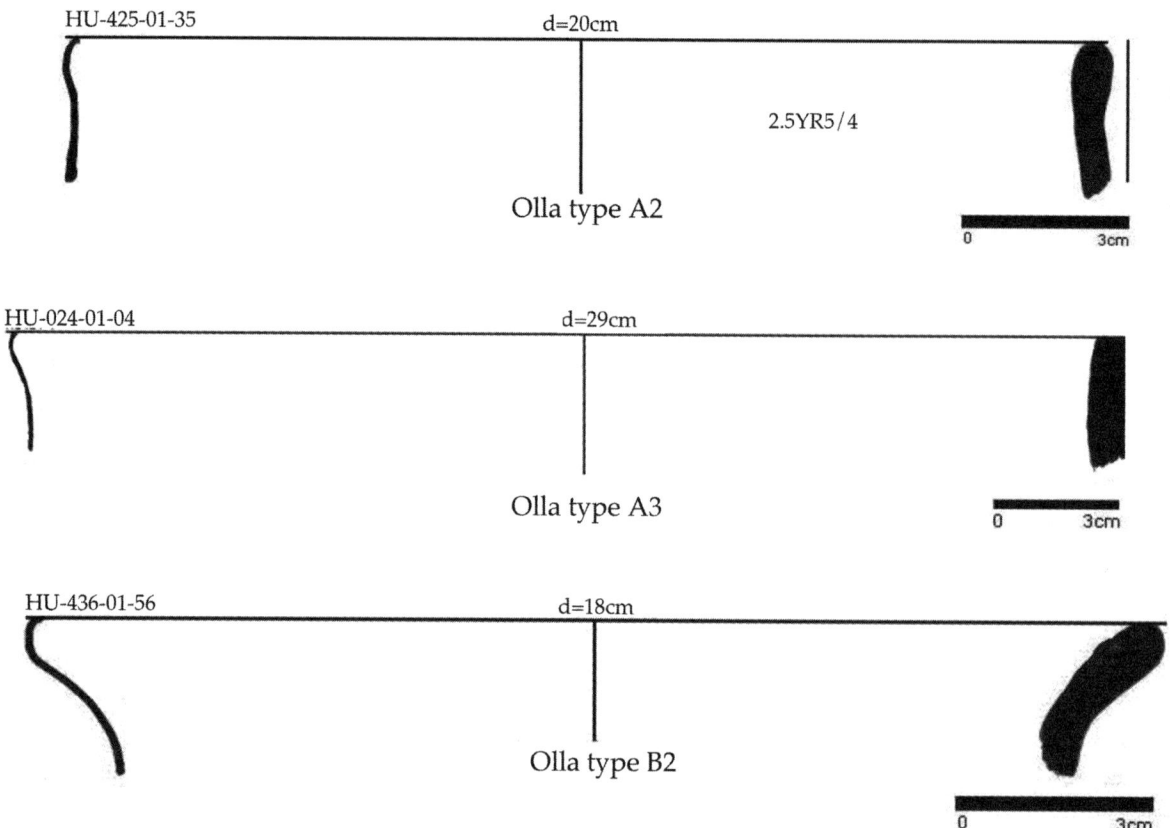

Figure 2.111. Altiplano III olla types A2, A3, and B2.

Inca I (Figs. 2.112–2.124)

Group I-4/27, 29

The color of the pastes is dark orange. They are composed of white subangular inclusions up to 1.0 mm in length with a regular dispersion and medium to abundant density. They may also have black subrounded inclusions of 0.5 mm with an irregular dispersion and sparse density. Purple and/or gray subangular inclusions of 1.0 mm with a regular dispersion and medium density are also present. The inclusions are visible in the cross section: exterior and interior. The fracture is regular, semi-compact, semi-hard, and of a medium texture. The finish is wiped and burnished.

Group III-7/3

The color of the pastes is cream. They are integrated with gray subangular inclusions of 0.8 mm with a regular dispersion and abundant density. There are also black subrounded inclusions up to 1.0 mm in size with an irregular dispersion and medium density. The inclusions are visible in the cross section: exterior and interior. The fracture is regular, semi-compact, and semi-soft with a fine texture. The finish is wiped.

Group III-8/4

The color of the pastes is cream. There are no visible inclusions. The fracture is regular, semi-compact, semi-soft, and of a fine texture. The finish is wiped, burnished, and occasionally polished.

Associated Style: Inca Collao and Inca Huatasani

Associated Assemblage:

Open Vessels

Tazones, type A, variants 1, 2, 3, and 4 (Fig. 2.112).

They have two sizes: small and medium, although only in type A2 are there very small specimens (8 cm). They are wiped. There are few plainwares; the others are decorated with red, orange, brown, or cream slips. There are also internal paint decorations, although one specimen has a combination of internal and external and another only with external paint. They use one color (black, brown, or red) or a combination of two colors (black + red, black + orange, or black + brown) over different slips. The designs are geometric (horizontal, undulating lines, crosshatched) and naturalistic (branches).

Tazones, type B, variants 1, 5, and 6 (Fig. 2.113).

They are very small, small, and medium. The majority are wiped; only in type B1 are there burnished specimens. They can be plain, although some are decorated with orange, red, or cream slips. There can also be internal paint decorations (possibly even on the exterior) in one color (black, brown, or red over different slips) or in two colors (black + brown over cream). The designs are geometric (horizontal, diagonal, undulating lines, and crosshatched circles).

Bowls, type A, variants 1, 2, 3, 4, 5, 6, 7, and 9 (Figs. 2.114, 2.115).

They may be very small, small, medium, and large. The common finish is wiping, although types A1, A2, A3, and A4 also have burnished finishes. They can be plain or decorated with orange, red, brown, and cream slips. They may also have interior paint decorations (possibly exterior) in one color (black, brown, or red over different slips) or a combination of two colors (black + brown or black + orange or black + red over cream, then brown + white or brown + red or brown + orange over orange or cream). There can also be three color combinations (black + orange + red or brown + red + orange over cream). The designs are geometric (horizontal, diagonal, undulating lines, crosshatched, and triangles).

Bowls, type B, variants 1, 2, 3, 4, 5, and 6 (Figs. 2.116, 2.117).

They are small, medium, and large. In general, the finish is wiped although some are also burnished. They can be plain or decorated with orange, red, cream, or brown slips on the interior and exterior. They may also have painted decorations on the interior (and possibly exterior) in one color (black, brown, or red over different slips) or can be a combination of two or three colors (black + brown or black + red or black + brown + red over cream or black + orange + red over cream). The designs are geometric (horizontal, diagonal, and undulating lines).

Bowls, type C, variants 1 and 2 (Fig. 2.118).

They are small, medium and (only in type C1) very large. The common finish is wiping although some specimens are also burnished. They are plain, but some are decorated with orange, red, or cream slips. They may also have interior paint decorations in one color (black or brown over different slips) or a combination of two colors (black + brown over cream or red). The designs are geometric (horizontal, vertical lines, and triangles). They can also have lateral appendixes on the rim (protuberances).

Bowls, type D, variants 1, 2, and 3 (Fig. 2.118).

They are small and medium. The finish is wiped, although in type D2 there are burnished specimens. They can be plain or decorated with interior paints in one color (black or brown over orange, red, cream, and white slips) or a combination of two colors (black + brown or red + white over orange and cream, black + white over orange). The designs are geometric (horizontal, vertical lines).

Bowls, type E, variants 1, 2, and 3 (Fig. 2.119).

They are small, medium, large, and very large. The finish is wiped, although in type E2 there are some burnished specimens. They can be plain (especially in type E1) or decorated with red or orange slips on the interior and exterior. They may have painted decorations on the interior in black over the slips. The designs are geometric (horizontal lines, crosshatched, circles, and triangles).

Plates, type A, variant 1 (Fig. 2.120).

They are small and wiped. For decorations, they have cream or white slips and interior painting in brown over cream or black + red over cream. The designs are geometric (horizontal lines and triangles). They can also have a handle modeled with naturalistic motifs (birds).

Plates, type C (Fig. 2.120).

They are medium and large. They can be wiped or burnished and use exterior slips in cream as decoration. There are interior paintings in one color (brown over cream or black over red) or a combination of two colors (brown + orange over red). The designs are geometric (horizontal, vertical, and undulating lines, and triangles).

Plates, type D, variants 1 and 2 (Fig. 2.120).

They are large, wiped, and plain.

Closed Vessels

Jars, type A (Fig. 2.121).

They are very small, small, and medium. Generally, the finish is wiping although some are also burnished. They can be plain or decorated with interior red slips near the rim and exterior paint decorations in black over red or cream. The designs are geometric (vertical lines).

Jars, type B, variants 1 and 2 (Fig. 2.121).

They are very small, small, and medium. They are wiped and sometimes burnished as a finish. They can be plain or decorated with orange, red, brown, cream, or white slips. There are also some exterior and/or interior painted decorations in one color (black or red over different slips) or a combination of two colors (black + red over brown). The designs are geometric (horizontal, vertical lines, and triangles) or naturalistic (chilies).

Jars, type C, variants 1, 2, and 3 (Fig. 2.122).

They are small and medium. They are generally wiped; only in types C2 and C3 are there burnished specimens. They can be plain or decorated with red or orange slips (only in type C2 are there also cream slips and painted decorations in black, brown, or red over orange or red). The designs are geometric (horizontal lines, crosshatched). They can also have flat appendixes with or without perforation near the rim.

Pitchers, type B, variants 1 and 2 (Fig. 2.123).

They are large and very large. The finish is wiped, although some specimens are also burnished. They can be plain or decorated with exterior and interior slips in orange, red, brown, or cream. They also have exterior painted decorations and, in type B1, interior decorations in black or red over different slips. The designs are geometric (horizontal lines). They possibly have flat appendixes with perforation near the rim.

Ollas, type B, variant 2 (Fig. 2.123).

They are small and medium, wiped, and plain.

Vasos, type A, variant 1 (Fig. 2.124).

They are small or medium, found wiped or burnished. They have interior and/or exterior painted decorations in black over brown or black with brown over cream. The designs are geometric (circles and crosshatched). They may also have decorations modeled naturalistically (birds).

Other Forms Associated with the Assemblage: Miniatures

Productive Tools: Polishing tools, spindle whorls

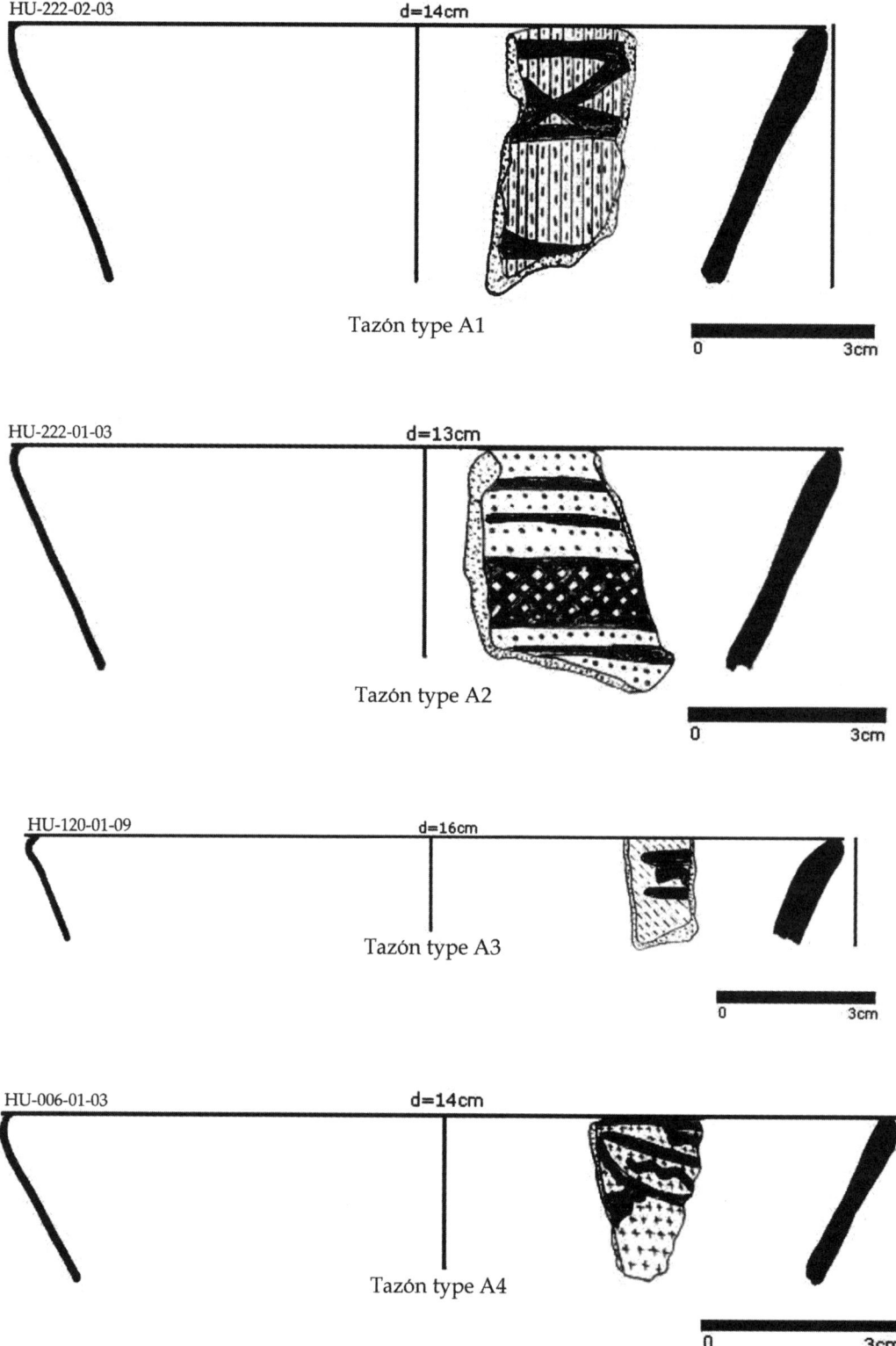

Figure 2.112. Inca I tazón types A1–A4.

Analysis of Ceramics

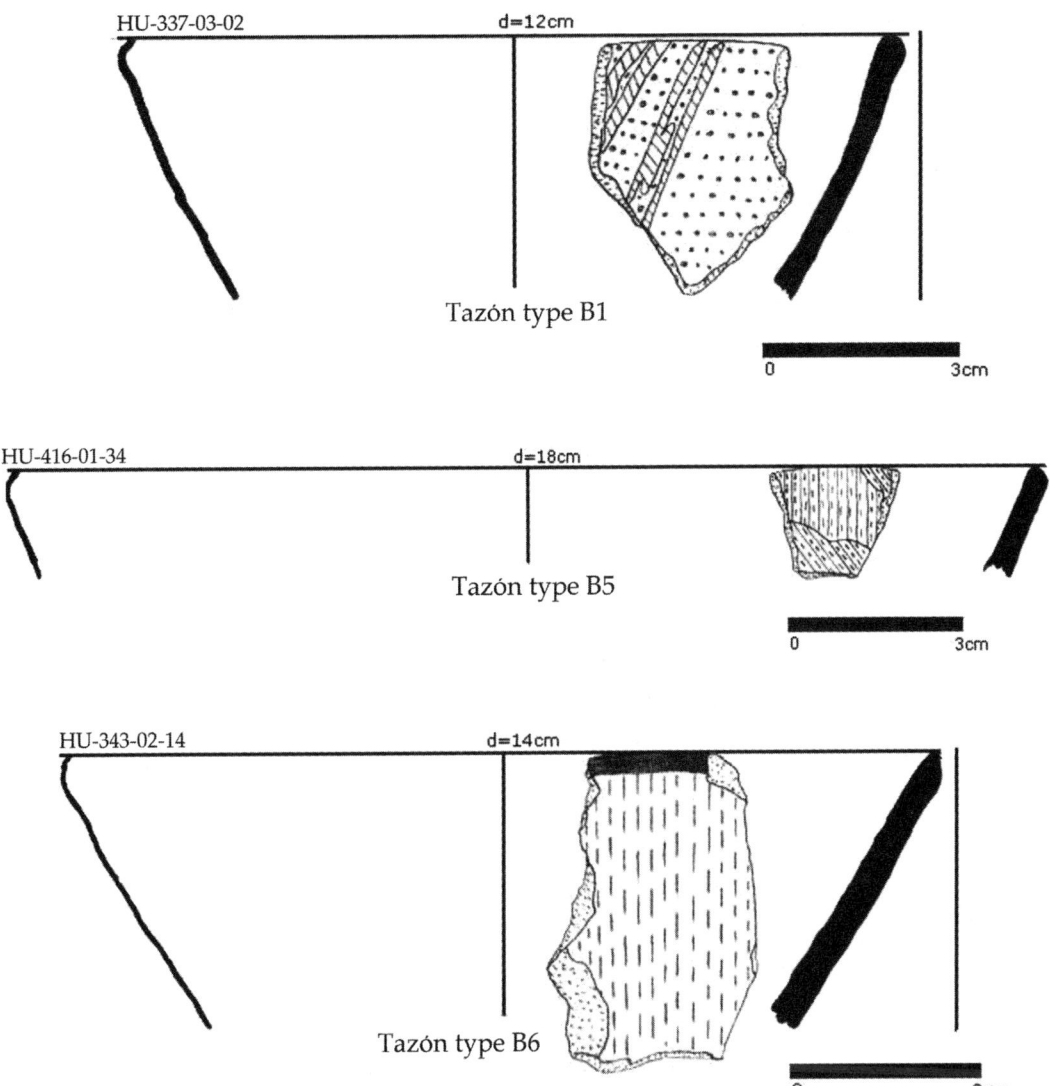

Figure 2.113. Inca I tazón types B1, B5, and B6.

148   *The Northern Titicaca Basin Survey*

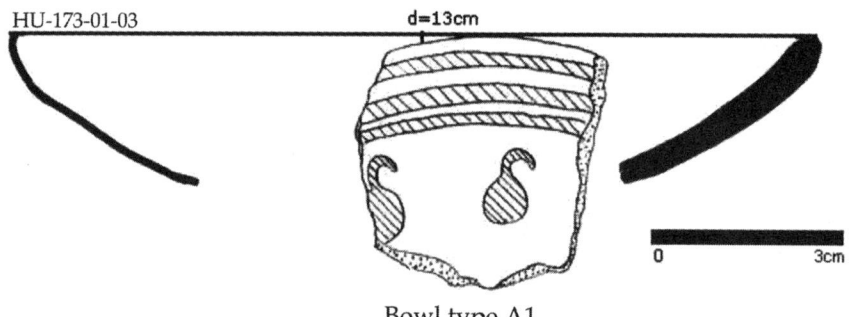

Bowl type A1

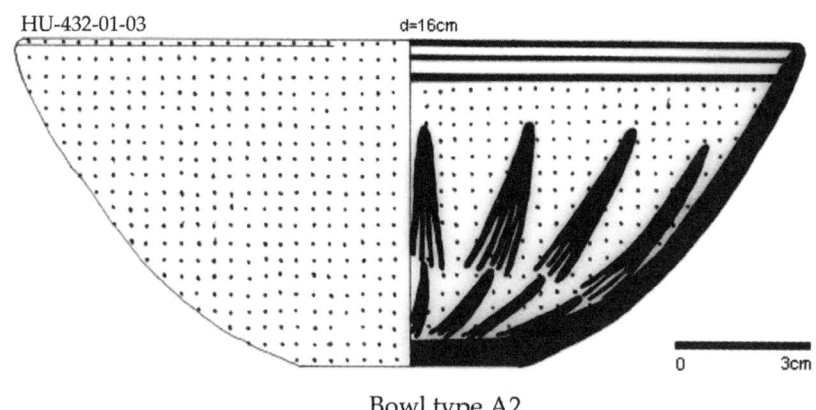

Bowl type A2

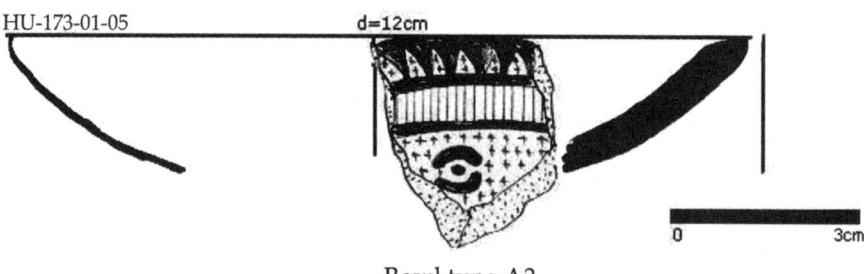

Bowl type A3

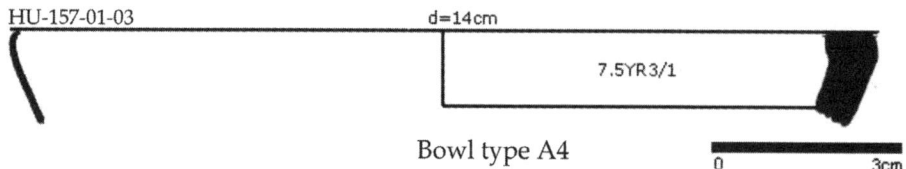

Bowl type A4

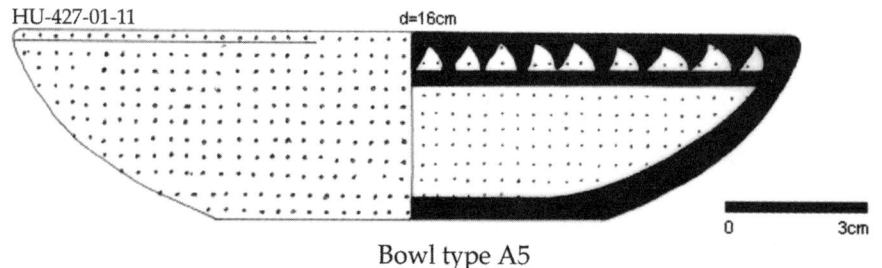

Bowl type A5

Figure 2.114. Inca I bowl types A1–A5.

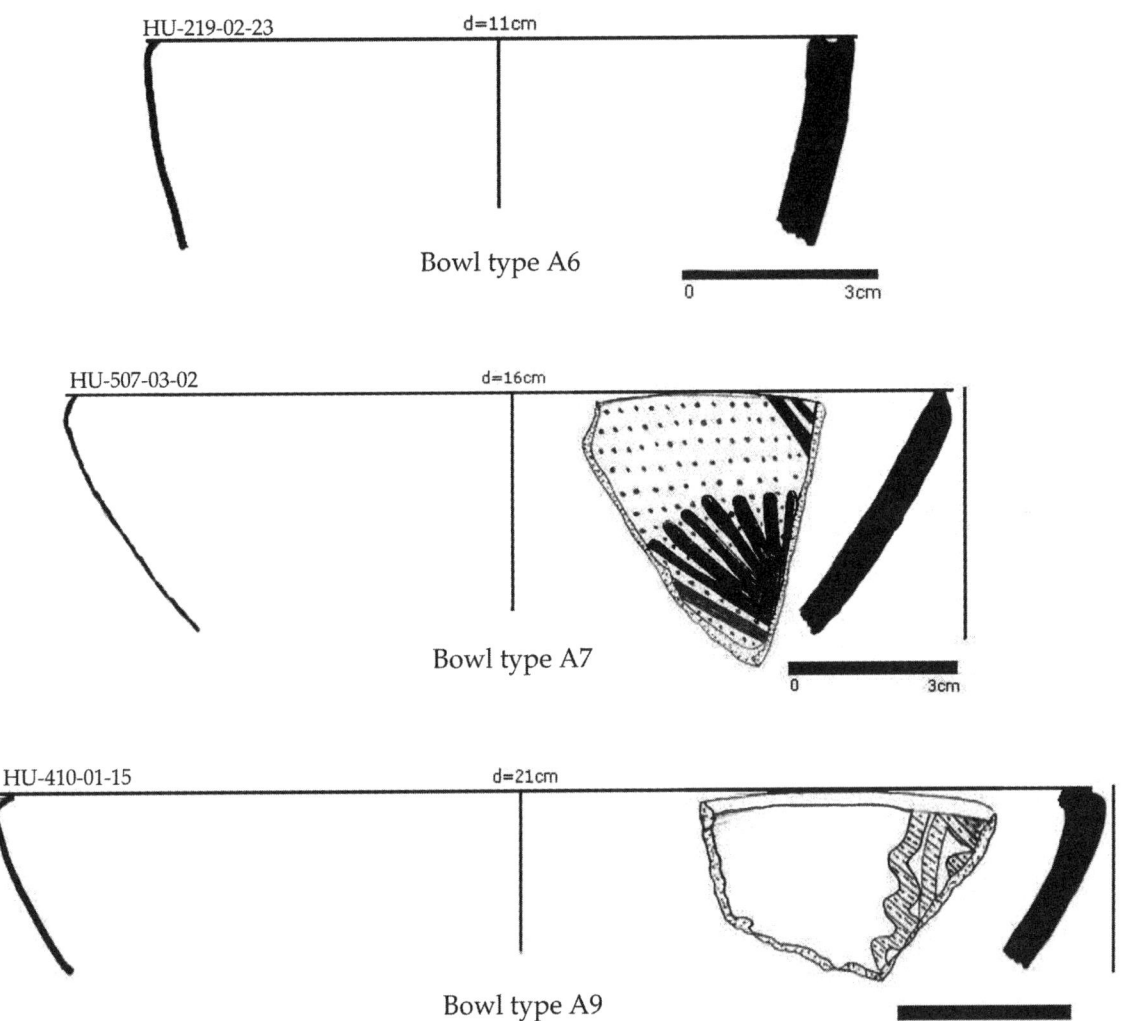

Figure 2.115. Inca I bowl types A6, A7, and A9.

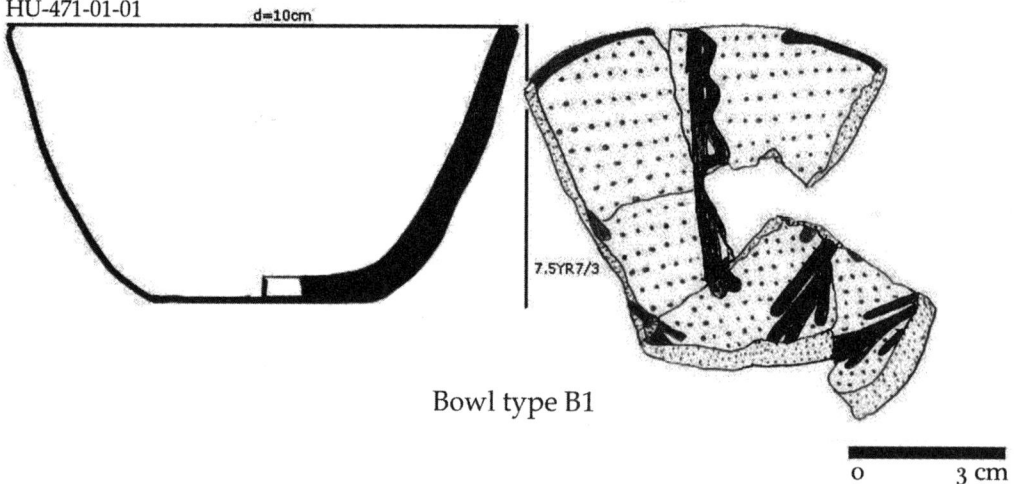

Bowl type B1

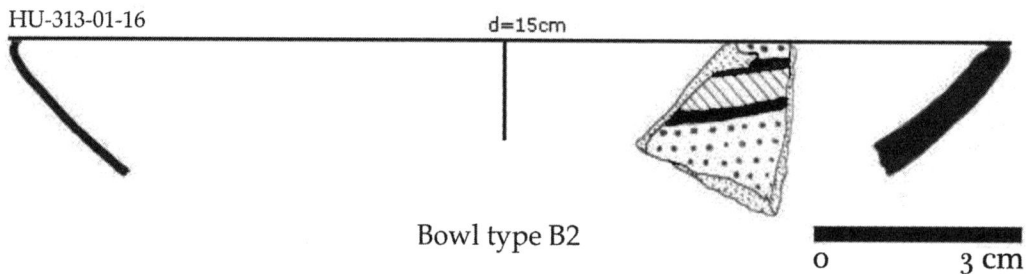

Bowl type B2

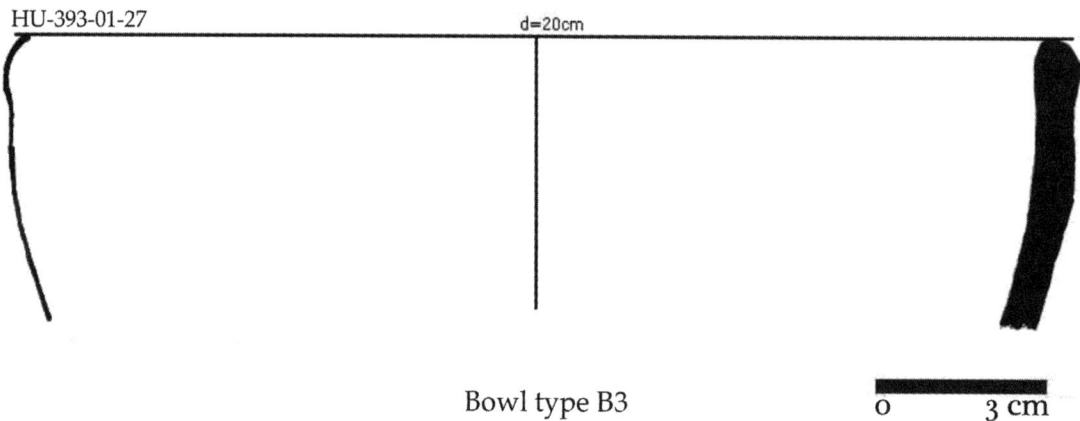

Bowl type B3

Figure 2.116. Inca I bowl types B1–B3.

Analysis of Ceramics 151

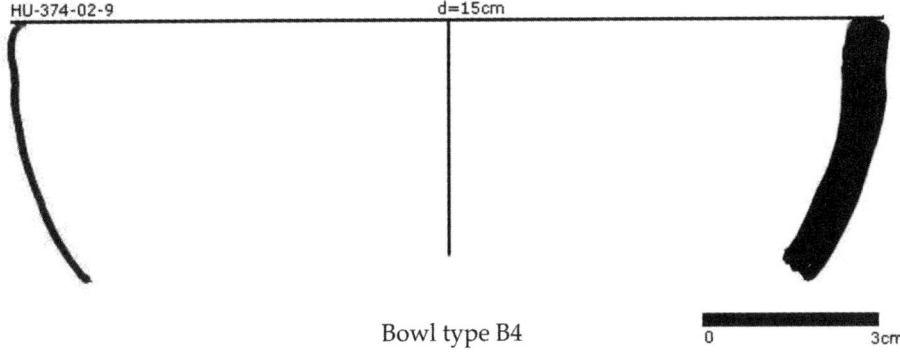

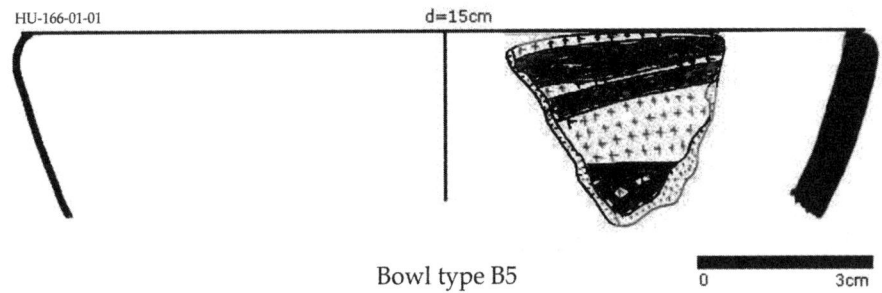

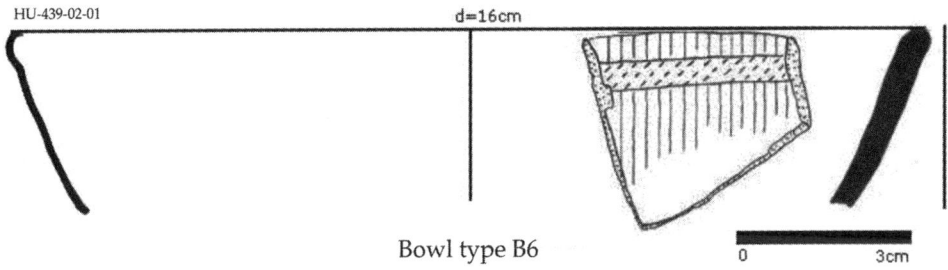

Figure 2.117. Inca I bowl types B4–B6.

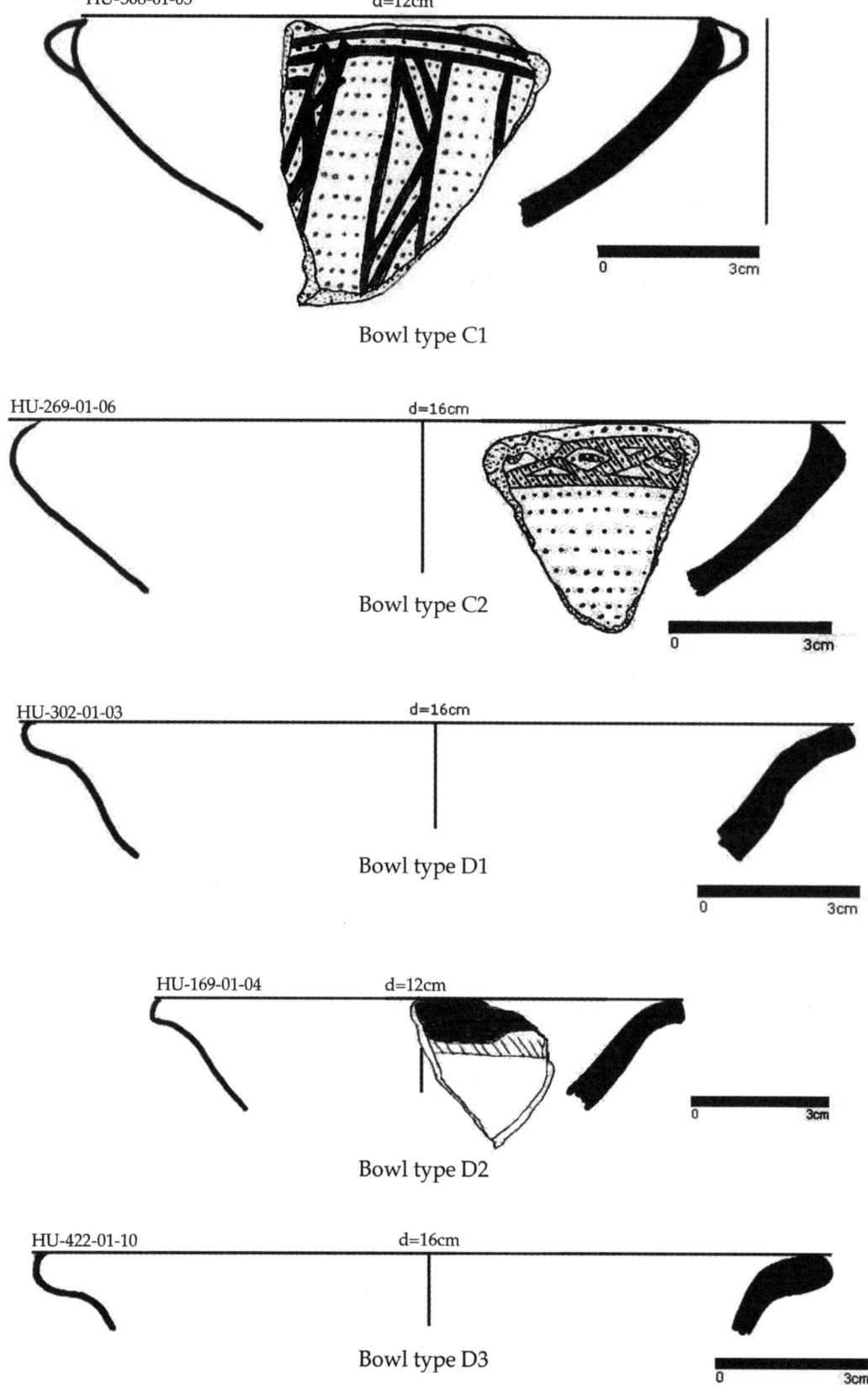

Figure 2.118. Inca I bowl types C1, C2, and D1–D3.

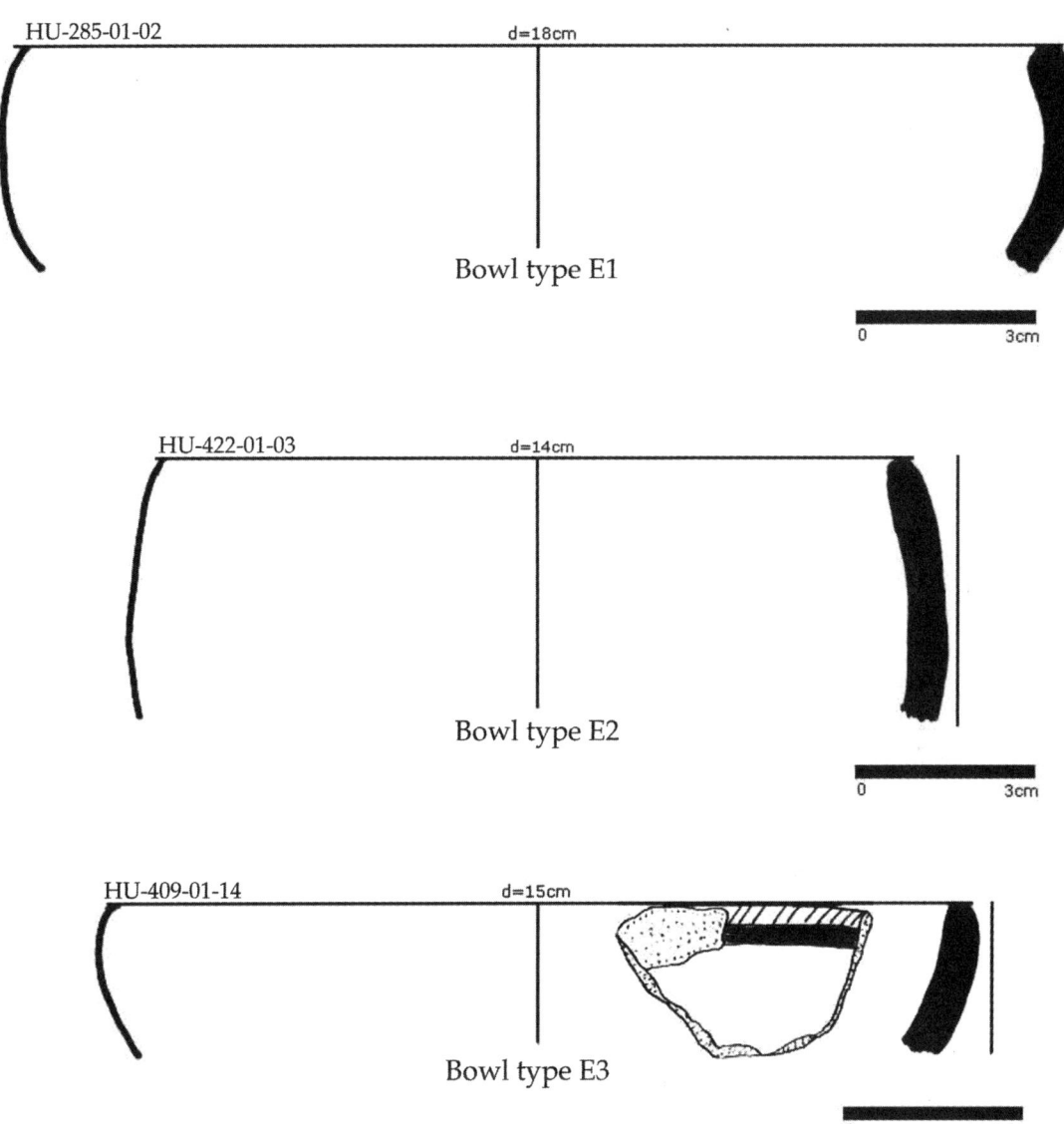

Figure 2.119. Inca I bowl types E1–E3.

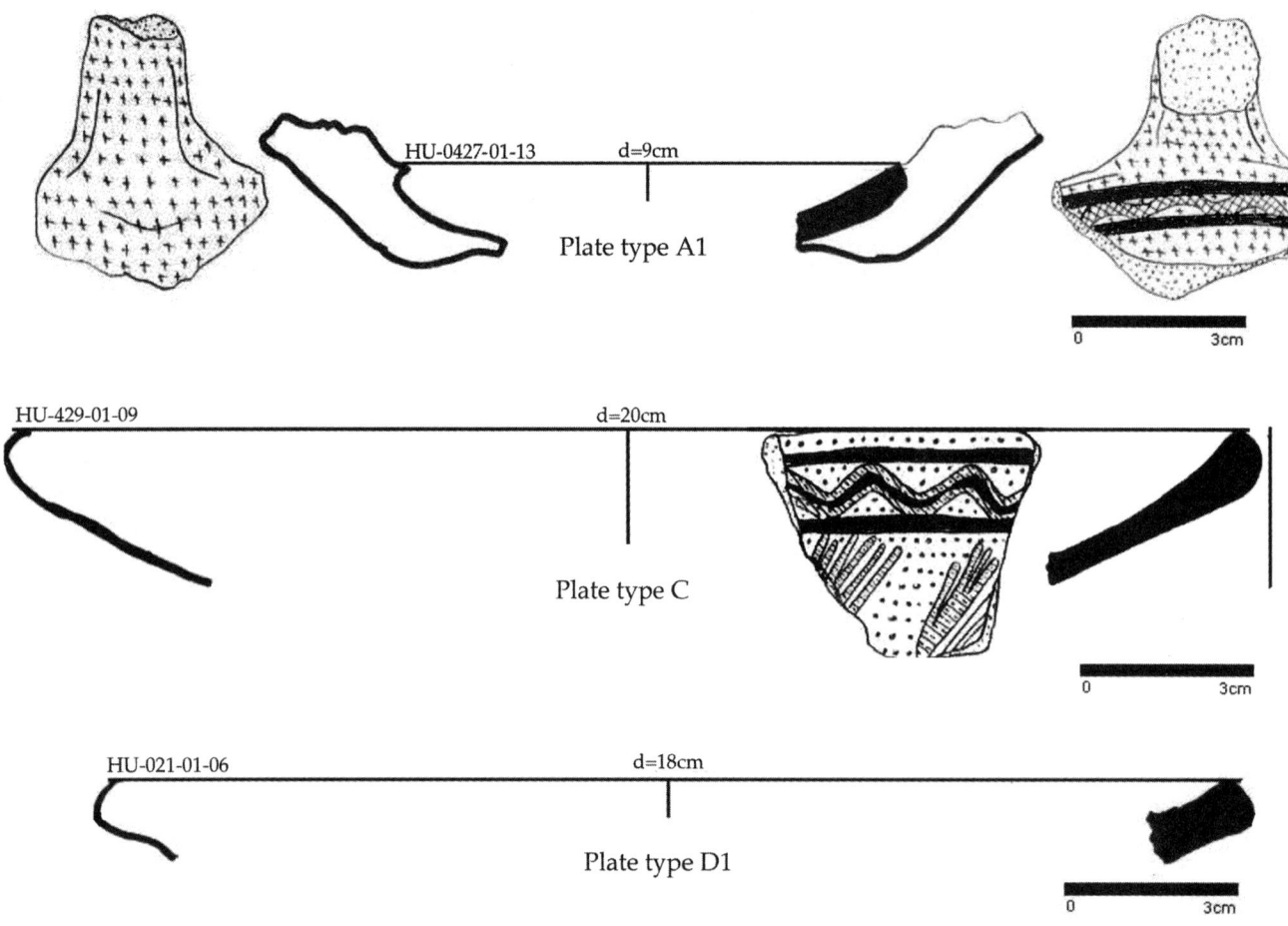

Figure 2.120. Inca I plate types A1, C, and D1.

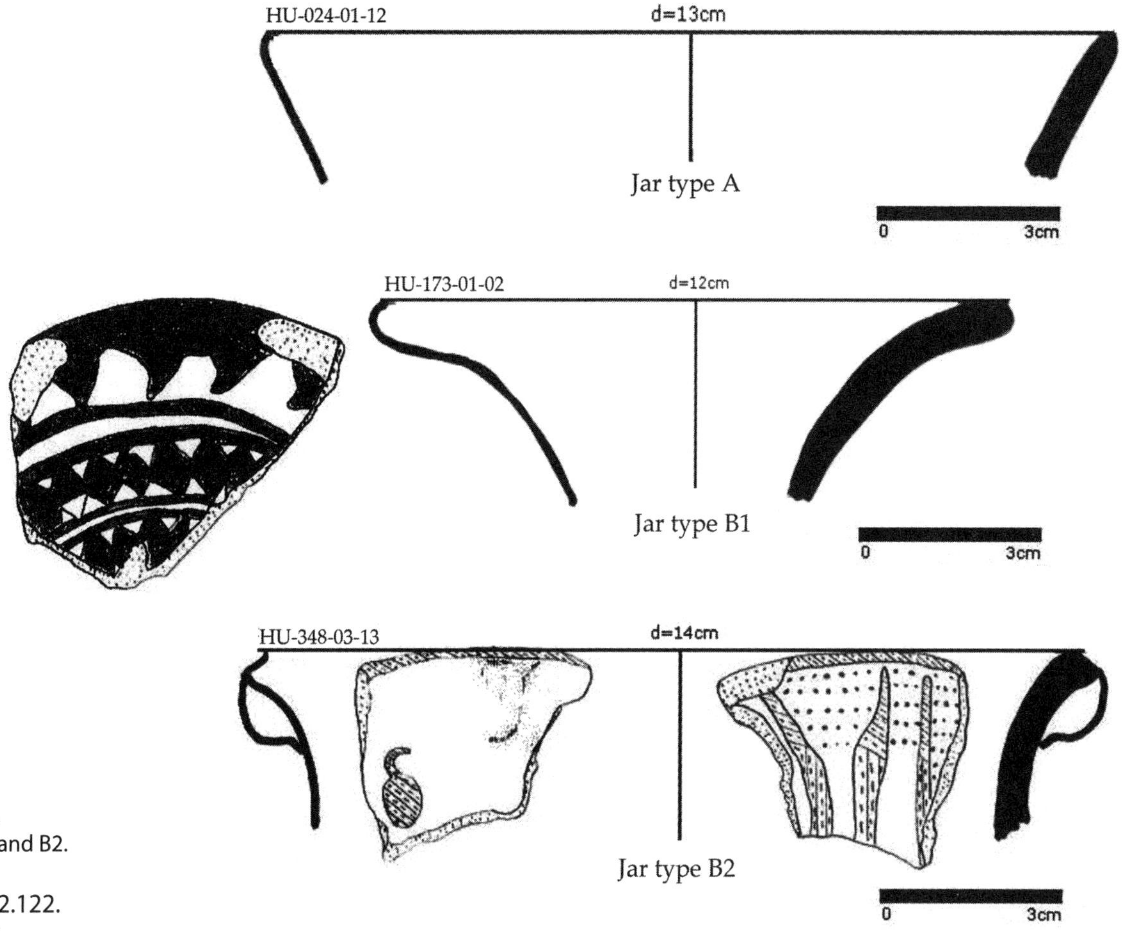

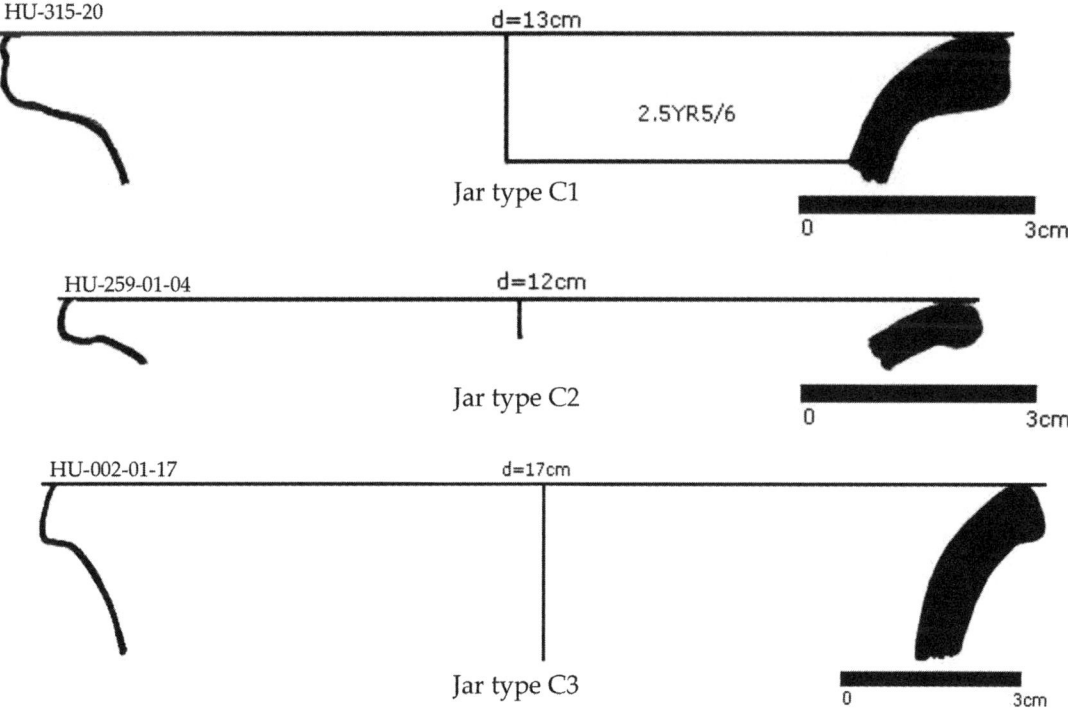

(*right*) **Figure 2.121.**
Inca I jar types A, B1, and B2.

(*below right*) **Figure 2.122.**
Inca I jar types C1–C3.

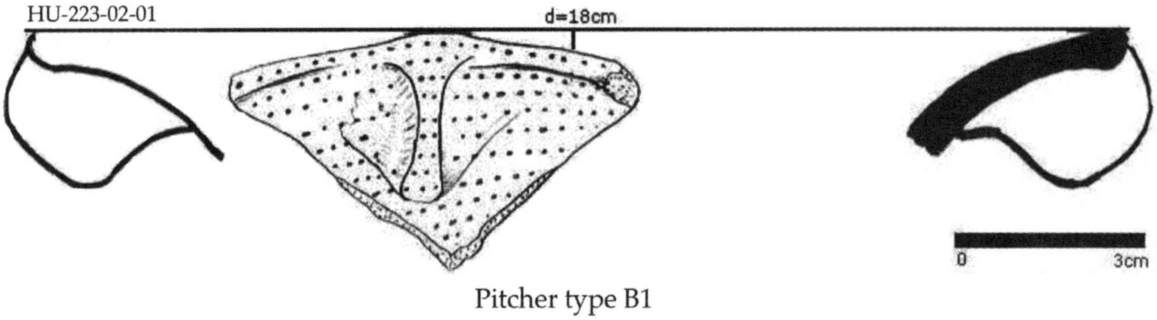

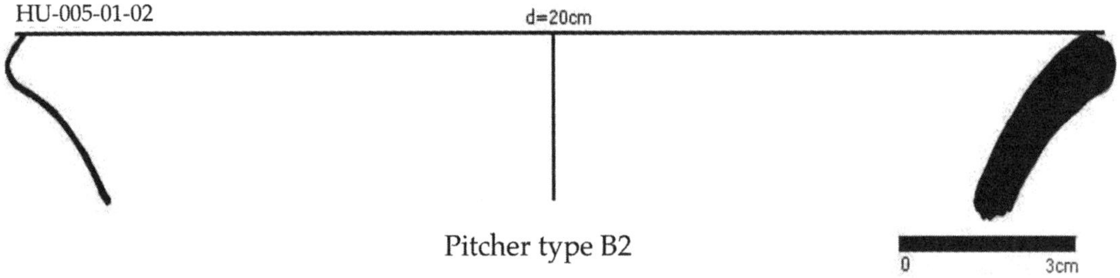

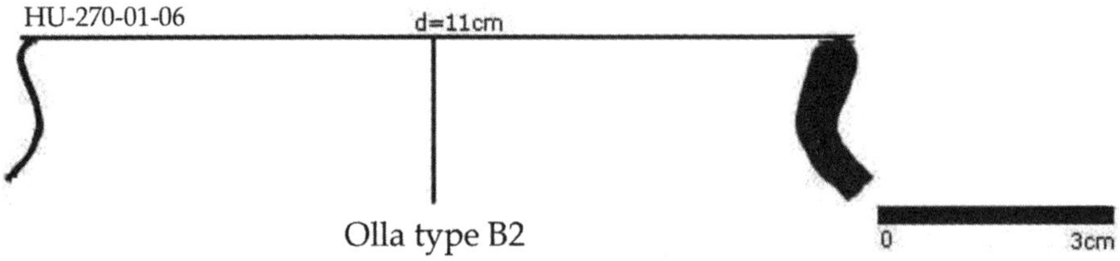

156 The Northern Titicaca Basin Survey

HU-223-02-01 d=18cm

Pitcher type B1

HU-005-01-02 d=20cm

Pitcher type B2

HU-270-01-06 d=11cm

Olla type B2

Figure 2.123. Inca I pitcher types B1 and B2 and olla type B2.

HU-348-01-01 d=15cm

Glass type A1

Figure 2.124. Inca I glass type A1.

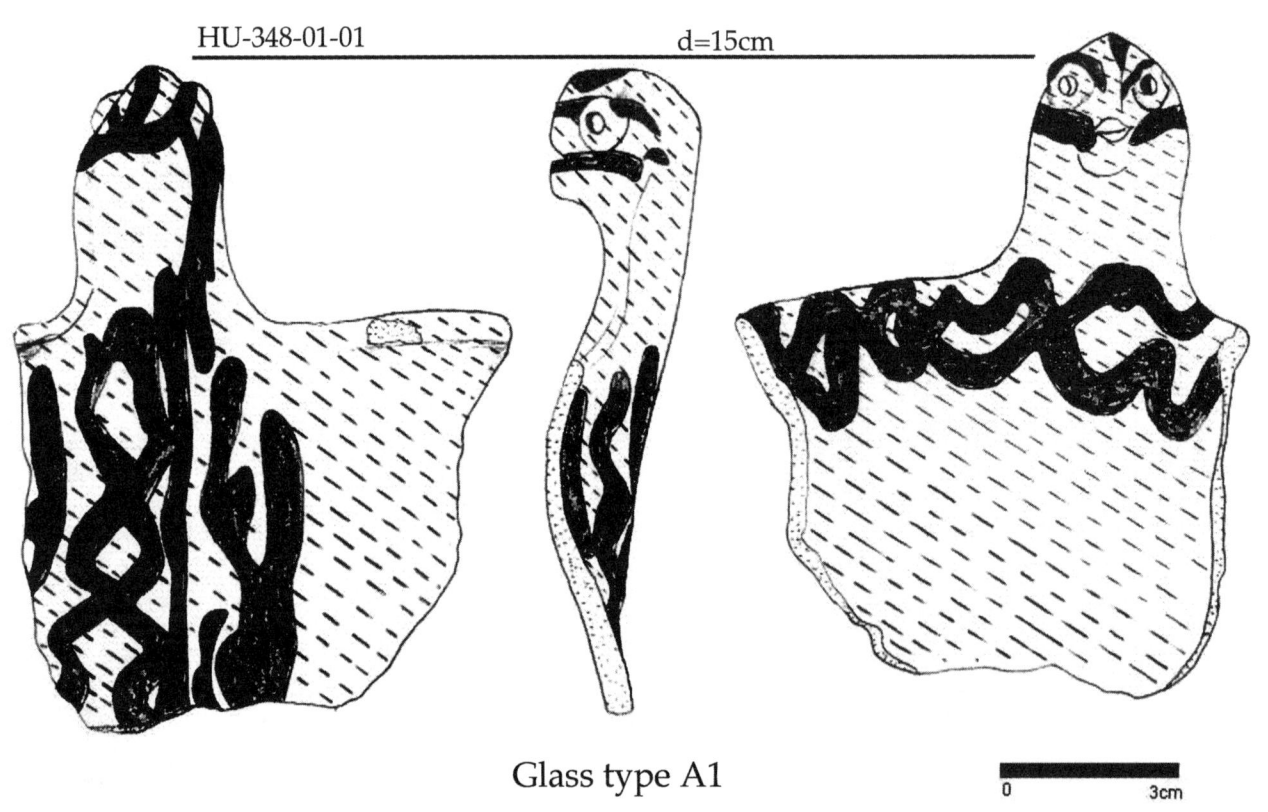

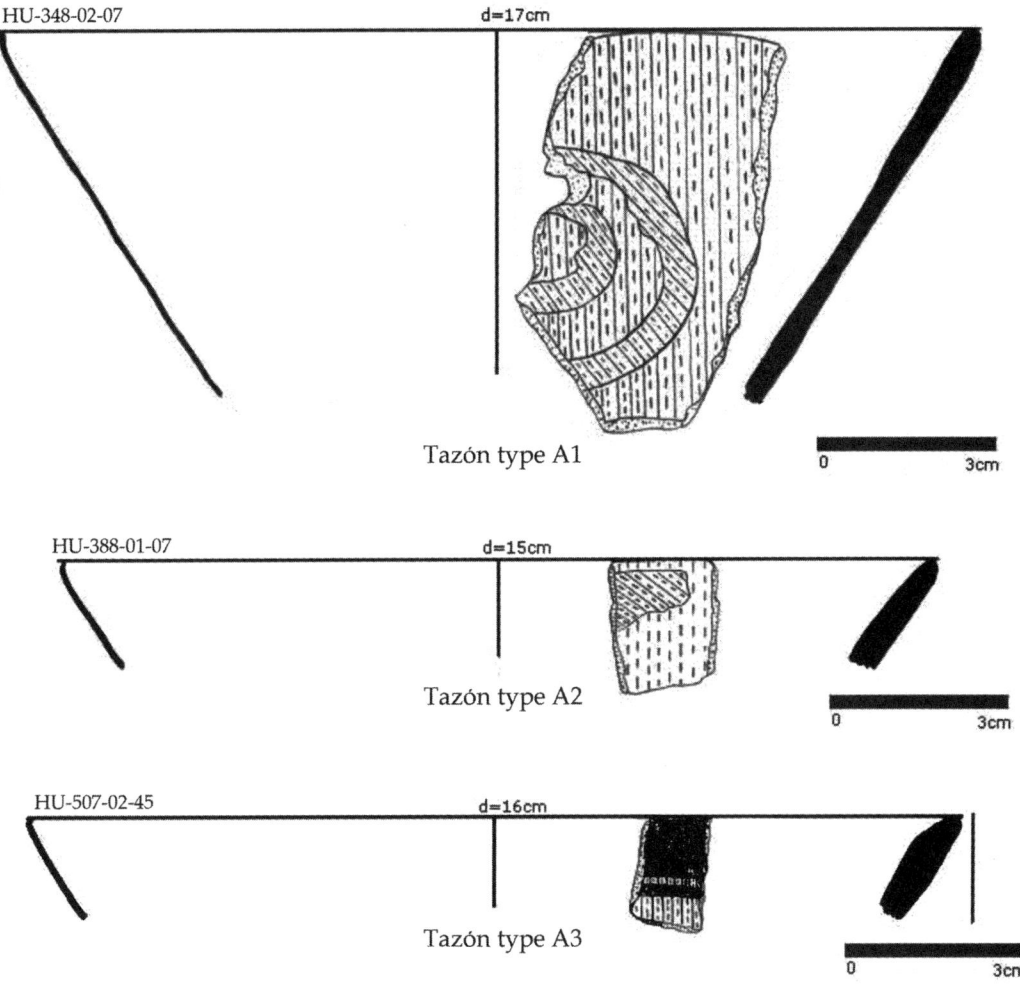

Figure 2.125. Inca II tazón types A1–A3.

Inca II (Figs. 2.125–2.133)

Group I-1/1, 2, 6, 8, 9, 13, 14, 15, 20, 24

The paste colors are dark and light orange. They are composed of white subangular inclusions of 0.5 mm to 1.0 mm with a regular dispersion and abundant to sparse density. There are also pink subangular inclusions up to 1.0 mm in size with a regular dispersion and abundant density. Black subangular inclusions from 0.5 mm to 1.0 mm in size with an irregular dispersion and medium to sparse density are also present. Ocher-colored subangular inclusions up to 1.0 mm in size with an irregular dispersion and sparse density are found, in addition to gray subangular inclusions of 0.8 mm with a regular dispersion and abundant density. There are also translucent subangular inclusions from 0.5 mm to 0.8 mm in size with an irregular dispersion and medium to sparse density. Black laminated mica of 0.5 mm with a regular dispersion and medium density are also found. The inclusions are visible in the cross section and the mica only in the exterior and interior. The fracture is regular, semi-compact, and semi-hard with a fine texture. The finish is wiped, burnished, and polished.

Group III-9/5, 16

The paste color is cream orange. They have a regular quantity of white inclusions 0.5 mm in size, subrounded, with a regular dispersion and sparse density. The inclusions are visible in the cross section: the fracture is regular, semi-compact, and semi-soft with a fine texture. The primary finish is burnishing.

Associated Style: Inca Regional: Taraco, Sillustani, Chucuito; Pacajes Inca Cusqueño: Urcusuyu, Cuzco A and B.

Associated Assemblage:

Open Vessels

Tazones, type A, variants 1, 2, and 3 (Fig. 2.125).

They are only medium. They use wiping and burnishing as finishes, although in type A3 there are some polished specimens. There is one plain specimen (perhaps due to erosion); the others are decorated with red, orange, or cream slips. The internal painted decorations (only one specimen uses external decorations) are black or brown over different slips. The designs are geometric (horizontal and undulating lines and circles).

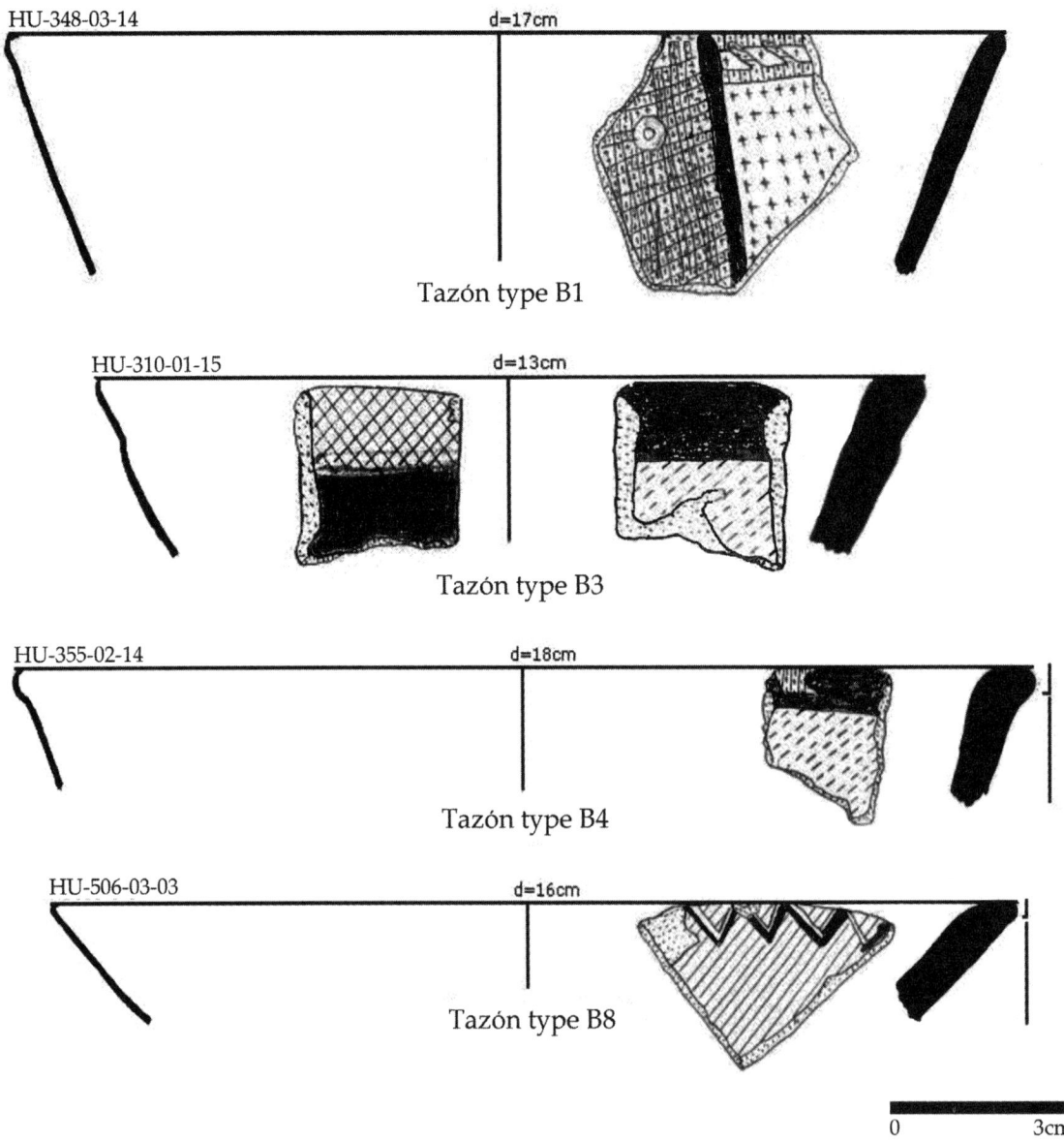

Figure 2.126. Inca II tazón types B1, B3, B4, and B8.

Tazones, type B, variants 1, 3, 4, and 8 (Fig. 2.126).

They are small, medium, and large. They are burnished as a finish; only in type B1 are a few wiped. They have painted interior and/or exterior decorations in one color (black over orange, cream, or red). They may also have two colors (black + orange or black + white over different slips). The designs are geometric (horizontal and vertical lines, crosshatched, and triangles).

Bowls, type A, variants 1, 2, 3, 4, and 5 (Fig. 2.127).

They are very small, small, medium, and large. Generally, they are burnished with few examples of wiping. They can be plain or have an interior and/or exterior orange, red, brown, or cream slip. They may also have interior and/or exterior painted decorations in one color (black, brown, or red), two colors (black + white, black + red, brown + orange, brown + white, white + orange, white + red), three colors (black + orange + red, black + brown + orange) and up to four colors (black + brown + orange + red) over different slips. The designs are geometric (horizontal, vertical, diagonal, undulating lines, triangles, circles, crosshatched). There are also anthropomorphic and naturalistic designs.

Bowls, type B, variants 1, 2, 3, and 5 (Fig. 2.128).

They are small, medium, and large. The most common finish is burnished, although some are also wiped. They can be plain or decorated with interior and/or exterior pink, orange, or cream slips. They may combine one color (black or brown), two colors (black + brown, black + white) or three colors (black + red + cream) over three different slips. The designs are geometric (horizontal, vertical, diagonal lines, and triangles) or naturalistic (branches).

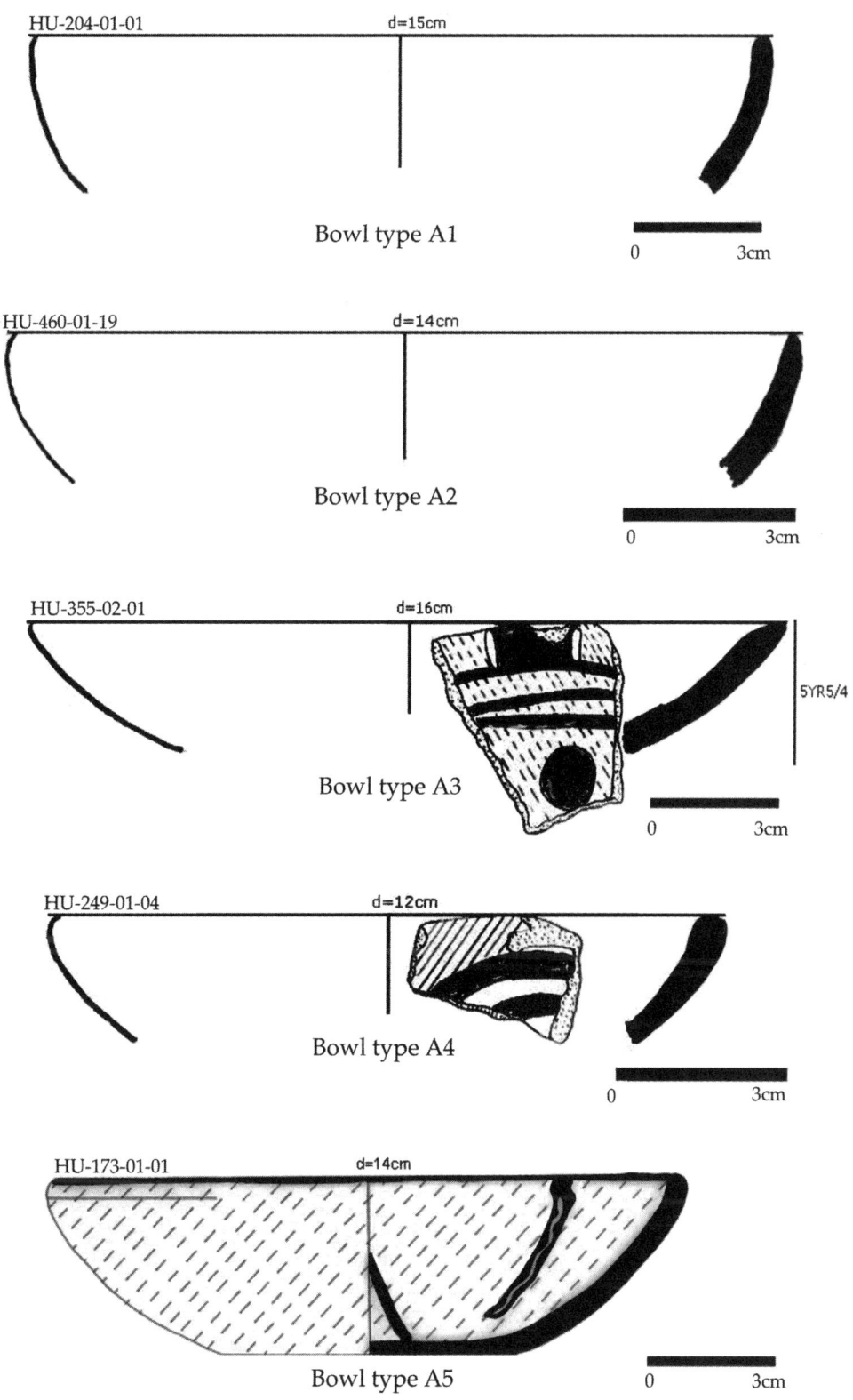

Figure 2.127. Inca II bowl types A1–A5.

160 *The Northern Titicaca Basin Survey*

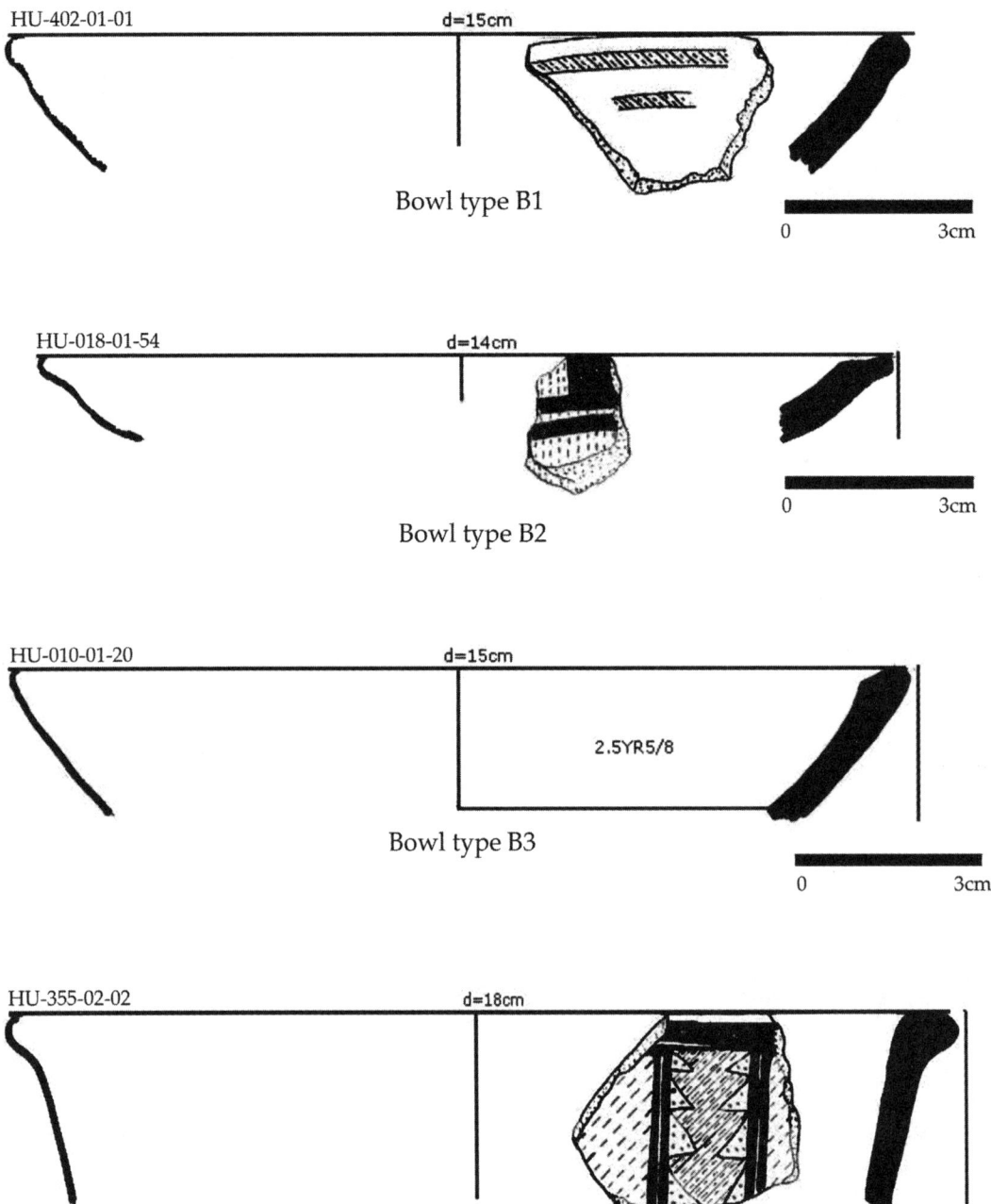

Figure 2.128. Inca II bowl types B1–B3 and B5.

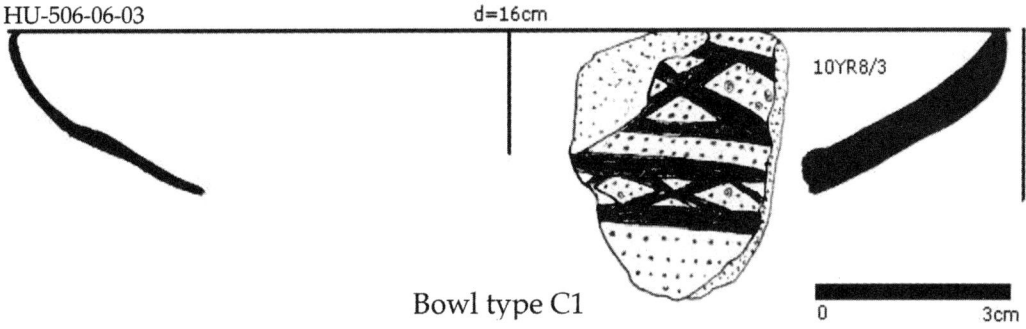

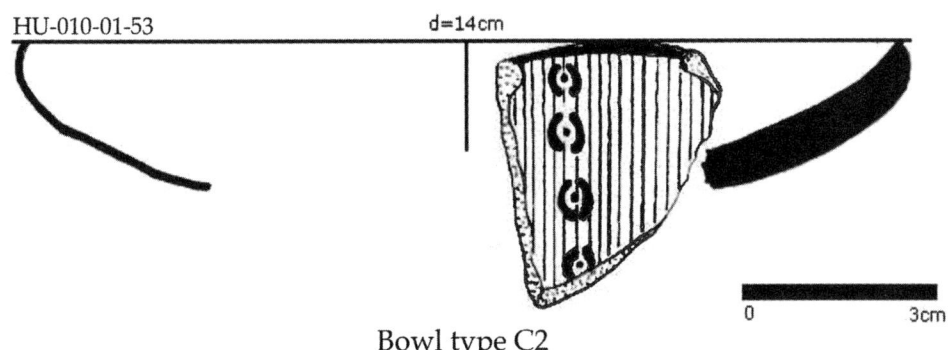

Figure 2.129. Inca II bowl types C1 and C2.

Bowls, type C, variants 1 and 2 (Fig. 2.129).

They are small or medium in size, burnished and decorated with interior and/or exterior red, brown, orange, or cream slips. They may combine one color (black) or two colors (black + brown) over different slips. The designs are geometric (horizontal lines).

Plates, type A, variant 2; type C (Fig. 2.130).

They are large and utilize burnishing or wiping. The decorations painted on the interior combine three colors (black + brown + red) over cream or red slips. The designs are geometric (horizontal lines and triangles) or naturalistic (chilies).

Closed Vessels

Jars, type A (Fig. 2.131).

They are small and burnished with red slips on the exterior and parts of the interior.

Jars, type B, variants 1 and 2 (Fig. 2.131).

They are small or medium. Generally, they are wiped although some are burnished. They are decorated with a red or orange slip on the exterior (and near the interior rim). They can also have painted decorations on the exterior and/or interior with one color (black, brown, or red) or two colors (black + white) over different slips. The designs are geometric (horizontal lines). They can have flat appendixes with perforation near the rim.

Jars, type C, variant 3 (Fig. 2.131).

They are medium and wiped. They are decorated with a red slip on the exterior and part of the interior rim. They can have flat appendixes on the rim.

Pitchers, type B, variants 1 and 2 (Fig. 2.132).

They are large and very large. Generally, they are burnished although scarce specimens are wiped. They can be plain or decorated with external and/or possibly internal (near the rim) red, orange, or brown slips. They also have painted decorations in one color (black, brown, white, or red) or two colors (black + red) over different slips. The designs are geometric (horizontal lines). They can have flat appendixes with perforation near the rim.

Ollas, type A, variant 2 (Fig. 2.133).

They are medium, burnished, and plain.

Ollas, type B, variant 2 (Fig. 2.133).

They are small or medium. The finishes are wiped or burnished. Generally, they are plain, but can be decorated with a red exterior slip.

Bottles, type A, variant 2 (Fig. 2.133).

They are small, wiped, and plain.

Productive Tools: Polishing tools, spindle whorls

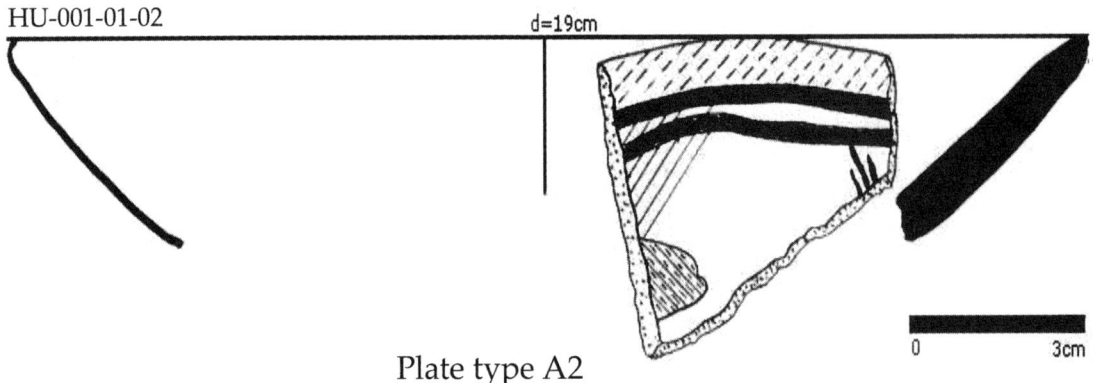

Plate type A2

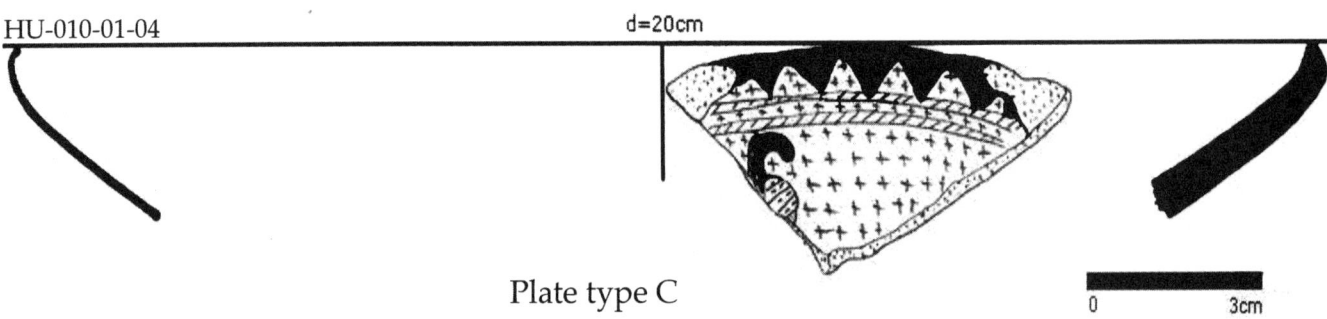

Plate type C

Figure 2.130. Inca II plate types A2 and C.

Analysis of Ceramics

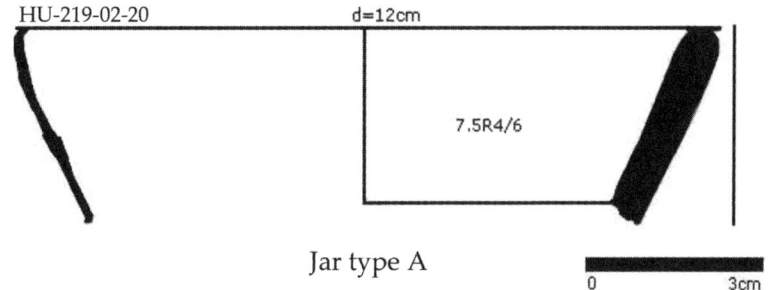

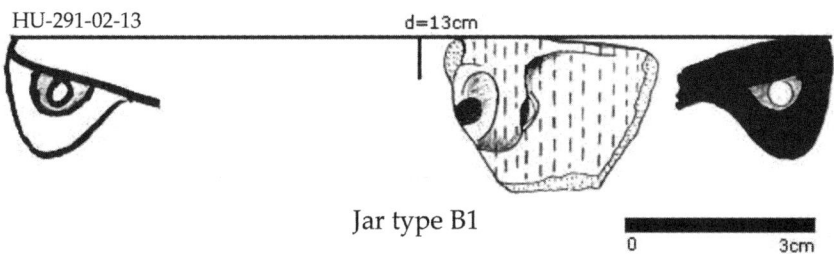

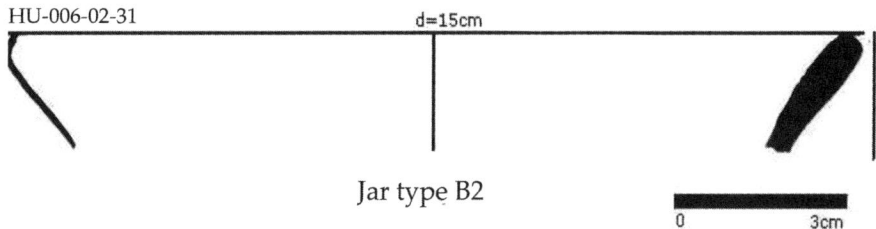

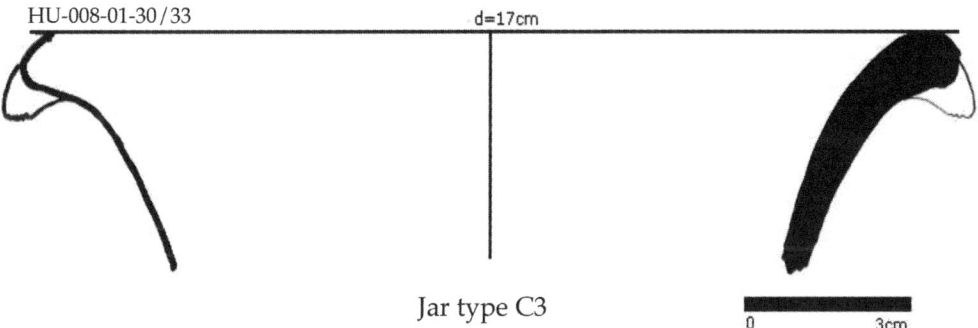

Figure 2.131. Inca II jar types A, B1, B2, and C3.

164 *The Northern Titicaca Basin Survey*

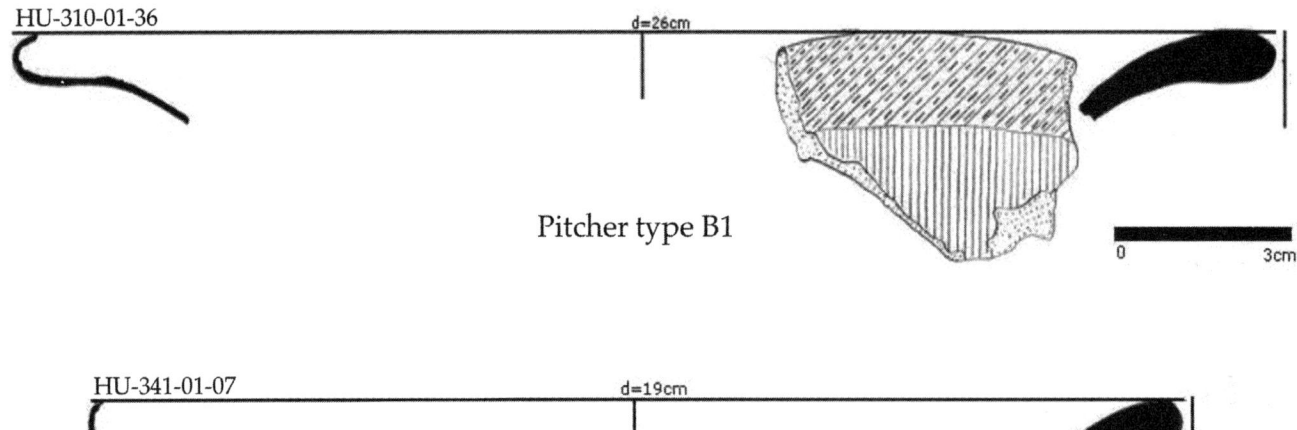

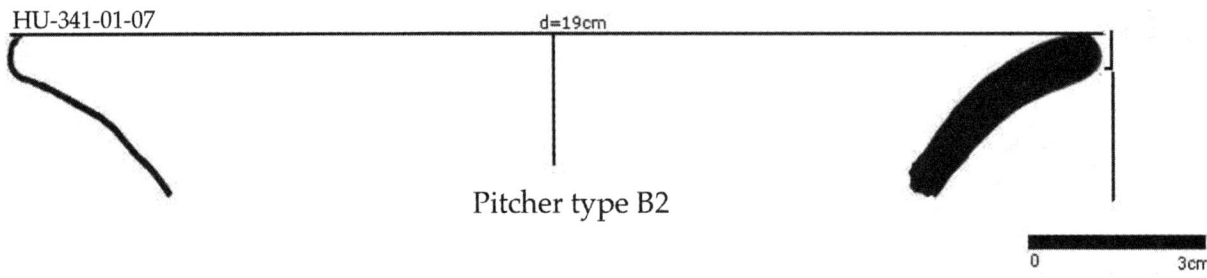

Figure 2.132. Inca II pitcher types B1 and B2.

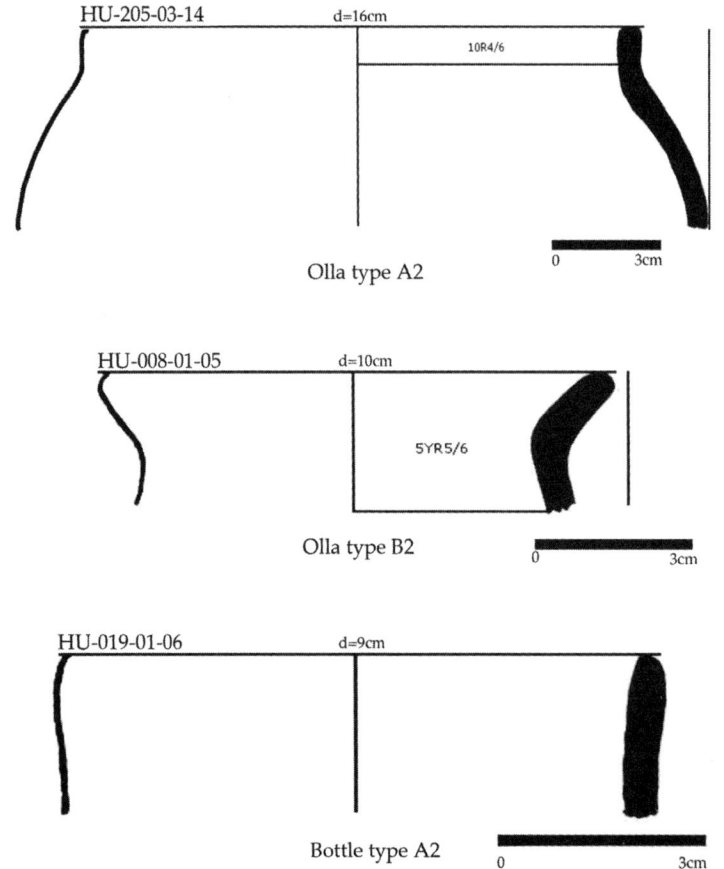

Figure 2.133. Inca II olla types A2 and B2 and bottle type A2.

Inca III (Figs. 2.134–2.141)

Group II-5/7, 12

The pastes are red colored. There are white subrounded inclusions of 0.6 mm size with an irregular dispersion and very sparse density. The inclusions are visible in the cross section: the fracture is regular, compact, and semi-hard with a very fine texture. The finish is wiped and burnished.

Group II-6/18

The paste color is red. It is composed of white subrounded inclusions of 0.5 mm size with a regular dispersion and abundant density. Others include black subrounded inclusions that measure 0.5 mm with an irregular dispersion and sparse density. The inclusions are visible in the cross section: the fracture is regular, compact, and semi-hard with a fine texture. The finish is wiped and burnished.

Group IV-10/10

The paste is a light brown color. It is composed of white subrounded inclusions of 4.0 mm size with an irregular dispersion and sparse density. The inclusions are visible in the cross section: the fracture is regular, compact, and semi-hard, with a fine texture. The finish is wiped and burnished.

Group IV-11/19, 21

The paste is light brown. It is integrated with white subrounded inclusions of 4.0 mm size with a regular dispersion and medium density. The inclusions are visible in the cross section: the fracture is regular, compact, and semi-hard with a fine texture. The finish is wiped and burnished.

Associated Style: Inca Colonial and Early Colonial

Associated Assemblage:

Open Vessels

Tazones, type A, variants 1, 2, 3, and 4 (Fig. 2.134).

They are medium size and only in type A3 are there large specimens. The finishes used are wiping and burnishing. They also have red, orange, or brown slips with interior painted decorations (only one specimen has exterior painted decorations) in one color (black or brown) or a combination of two colors (black + white) over different slips. The designs are geometric (horizontal and diagonal lines, circles, and dots).

Tazones, type B, variants 1 and 7 (Fig. 2.135).

They are medium and burnished. They are plain or decorated with brown slips on the interior and exterior.

Bowls, type A, variants 1, 2, 3, 4, 5, 6, and 7 (Figs. 2.136, 2.137).

They are very small, small, medium, and large. Generally they are burnished, although some are also wiped. They are plain and sometimes decorated with interior and/or exterior red, orange, brown, cream, or white slips. They also have interior and/or exterior painted decorations in one color (black, brown, or red) or two colors (black + red, black + brown, black + white, brown + cream) over different slips. The designs are geometric (horizontal, vertical, diagonal, undulating lines, concentric circles, triangles) or naturalistic (chiles).

Bowls, type B, variants 1, 2, 3, 4, and 6 (Fig. 2.138).

They are small, medium, and large. They are burnished and possibly wiped. They are plain, though some are decorated with red, orange, or brown slips. They may also have interior and/or exterior painted decorations in one color (black, brown, or cream) or two colors (black + white) over different slips. The designs are geometric (horizontal and vertical lines, ovals) and/or naturalistic.

Bowls, type C, variants 1 and 2 (Fig. 2.139).

They are small, medium, and large. They are burnished and wiped. They are plain, though some are decorated with an interior and/or exterior red or orange slip. They may also have interior and/or exterior painted decorations in one color (black) or two colors (black + brown) over different slips. The designs are geometric (horizontal, vertical lines, and circles).

Bowls, type D, variants 1, 2, and 3 (Fig. 2.139).

They are small, medium, and large. They are burnished and wiped. They are plain, though some are decorated with red, orange, or brown slips on the interior and/or exterior. They can also have painted decorations on the interior and/or exterior in black or brown over different slips. The designs are geometric (horizontal lines).

Bowls, type E, variants 1, 2, and 3 (Fig. 2.140).

They are small, medium, and large. They are commonly burnished; only in type E3 are some also wiped. They may be plain or decorated with red, orange, or brown slips on the interior and/or exterior. They can also have painted decorations on the interior and/or exterior in one color (black or white) over the slips. The designs are geometric (vertical lines, circles).

Plates, type A, variant 1 (Fig. 2.140).

They are large and burnished. They can be decorated with red slips or have interior painted decorations in black over red. The designs are geometric (crosshatched).

Closed Vessels

Jars, type A (Fig. 2.141).

They are small or medium. They are burnished as a finish. The decorations are red slips on the exterior and part of the rim/neck of the interior.

Jars, type B, variants 1 and 2 (Fig. 2.141).

They are medium, burnished or wiped. They can be decorated with a red slip on the exterior and part of the interior rim/neck. They can also have exterior painted decorations in black over red. The designs are geometric (horizontal lines, triangles).

Pitchers, type B, variants 1 and 2 (Fig. 2.141).

They are large and very large. They utilize burnishing and wiping as a finish. They can be plain or decorated with red or orange slips on the exterior and part of the interior rim/neck. They may also have painted exterior decorations in black, orange, brown, or red over different slips. The designs are geometric (diagonal or vertical lines, and triangles).

Productive Tools: Polishing tools, spindle whorls

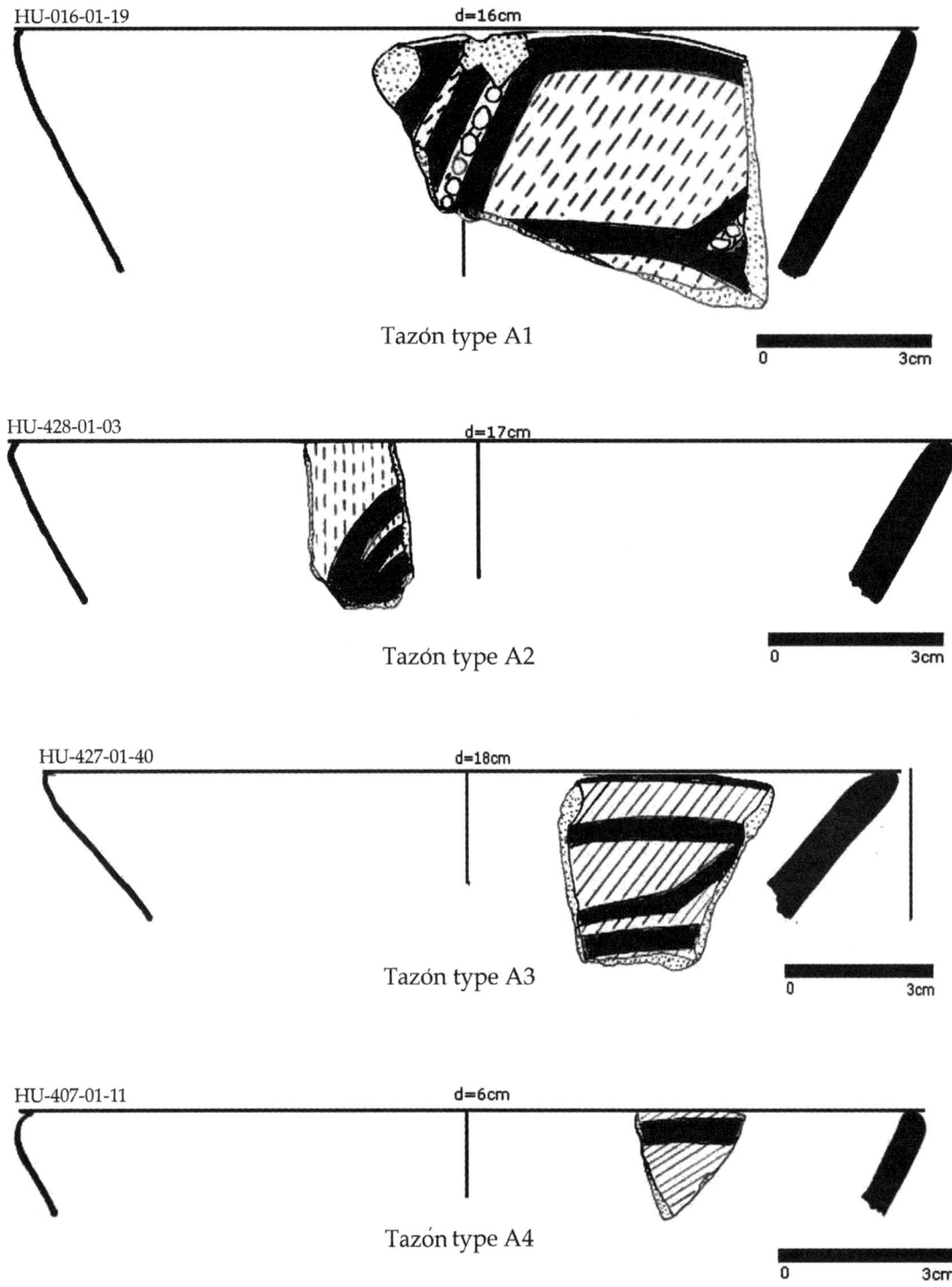

Figure 2.134. Inca III tazón types A1–A4.

Analysis of Ceramics

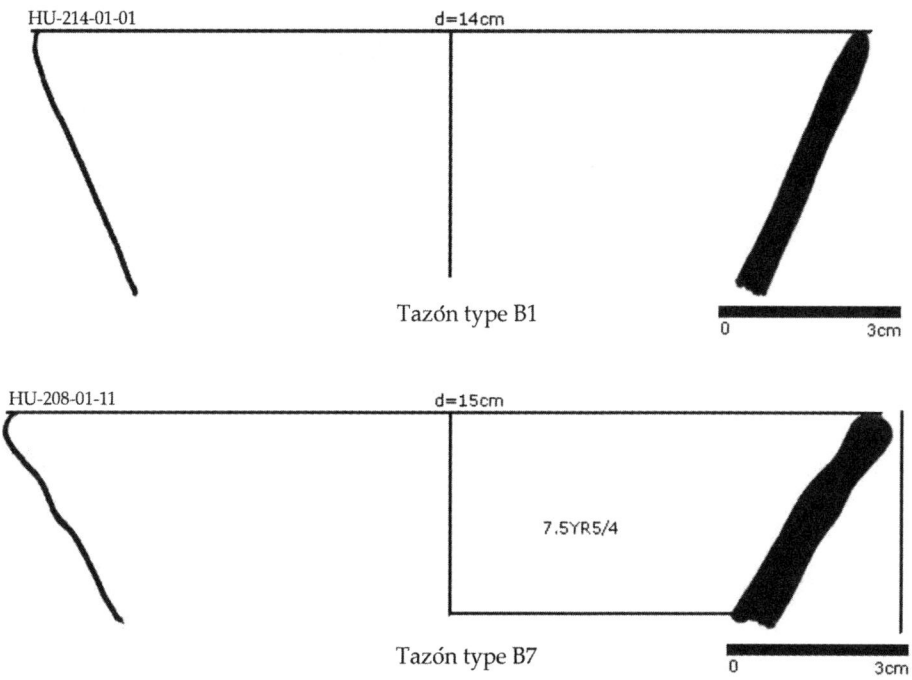

Figure 2.135. Inca III tazón types B1 and B7.

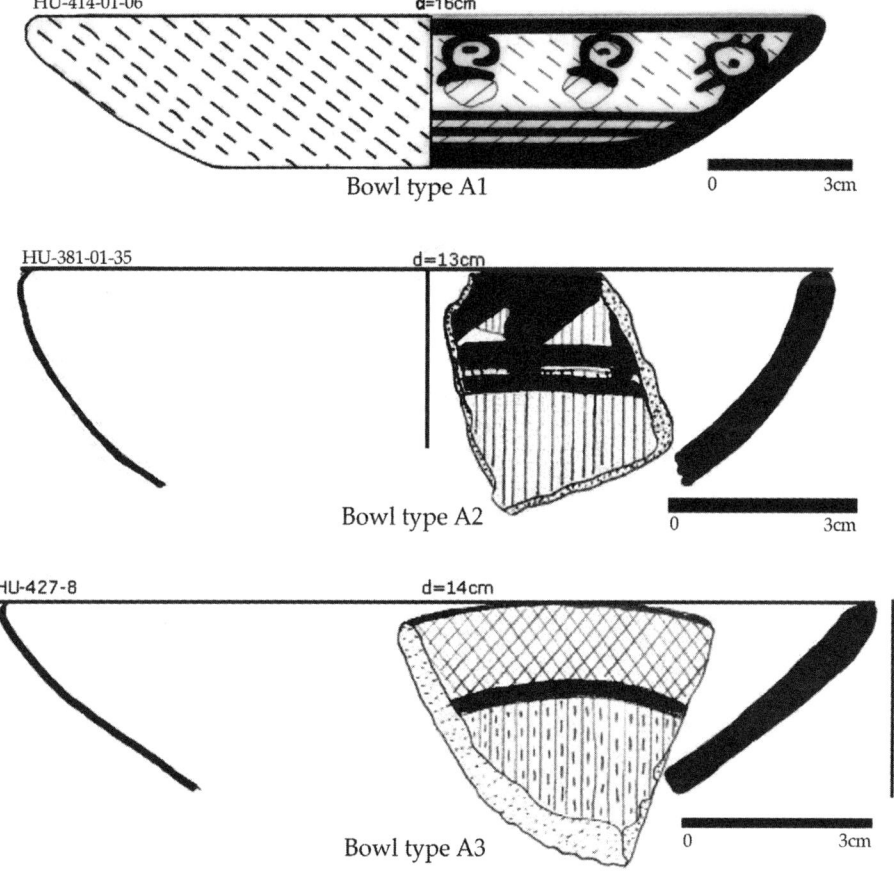

Figure 2.136. Inca III bowl types A1–A3.

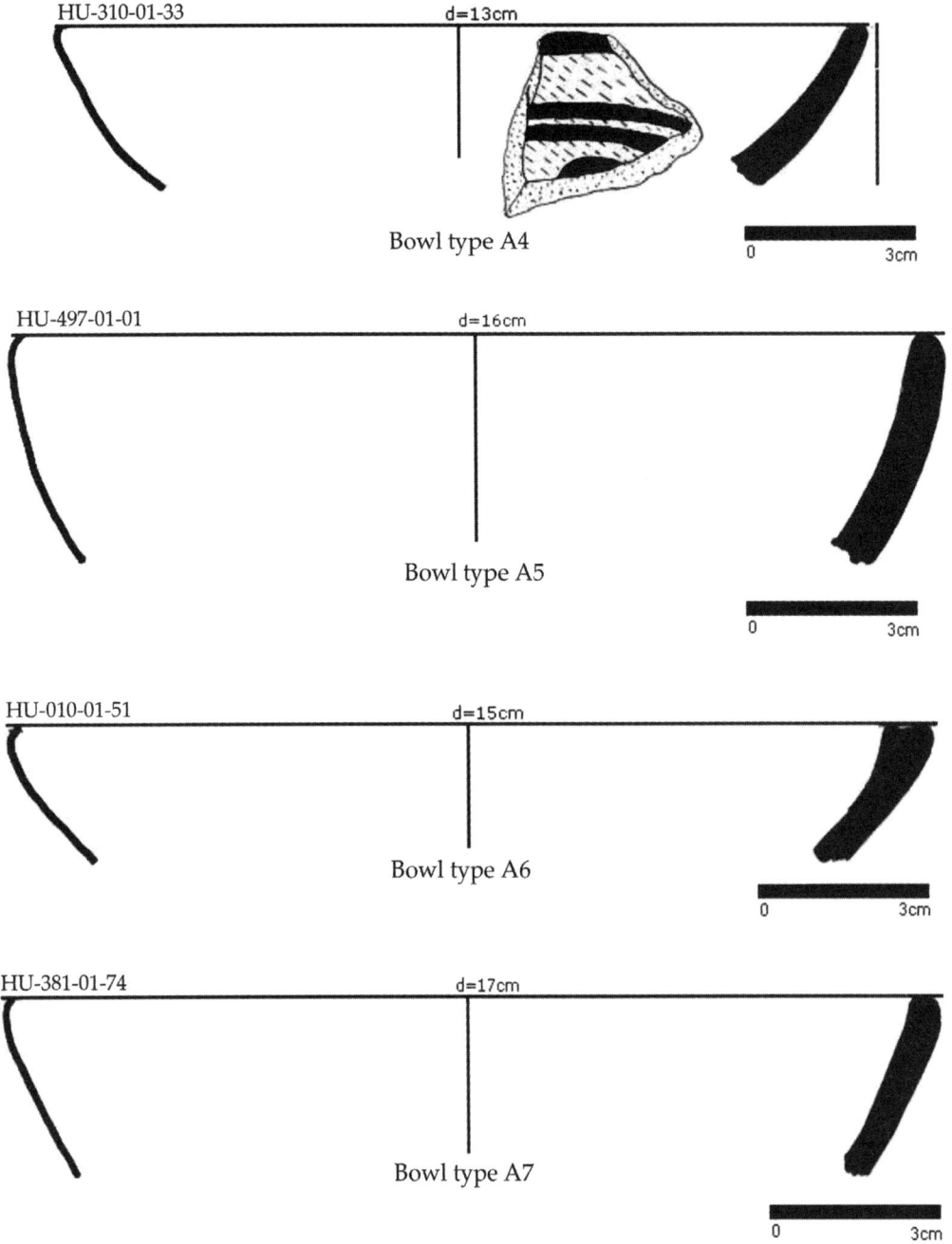

Figure 2.137. Inca III bowl types A4–A7.

Analysis of Ceramics

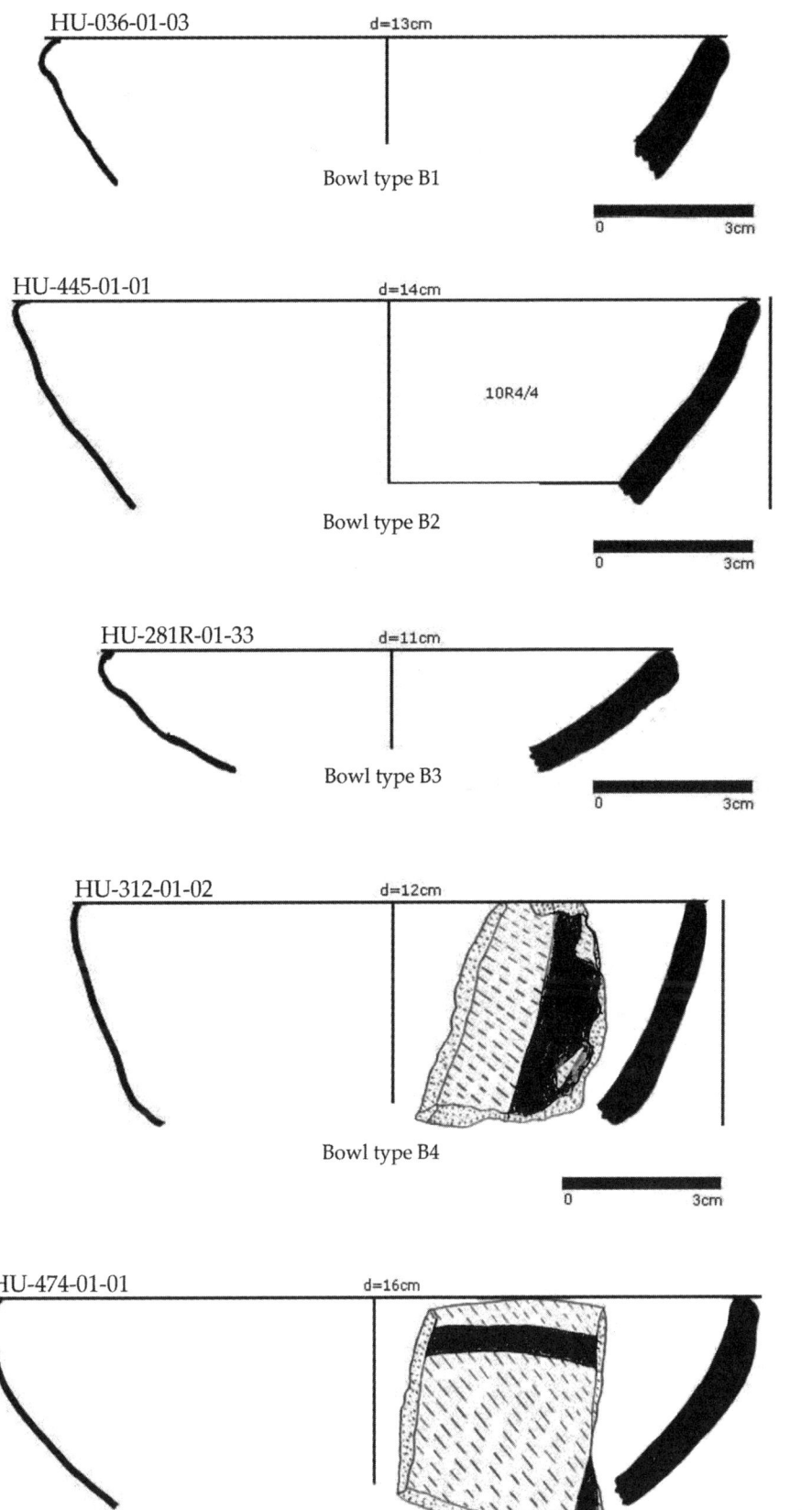

Figure 2.138. Inca III bowl types B1–B4 and B6.

170   *The Northern Titicaca Basin Survey*

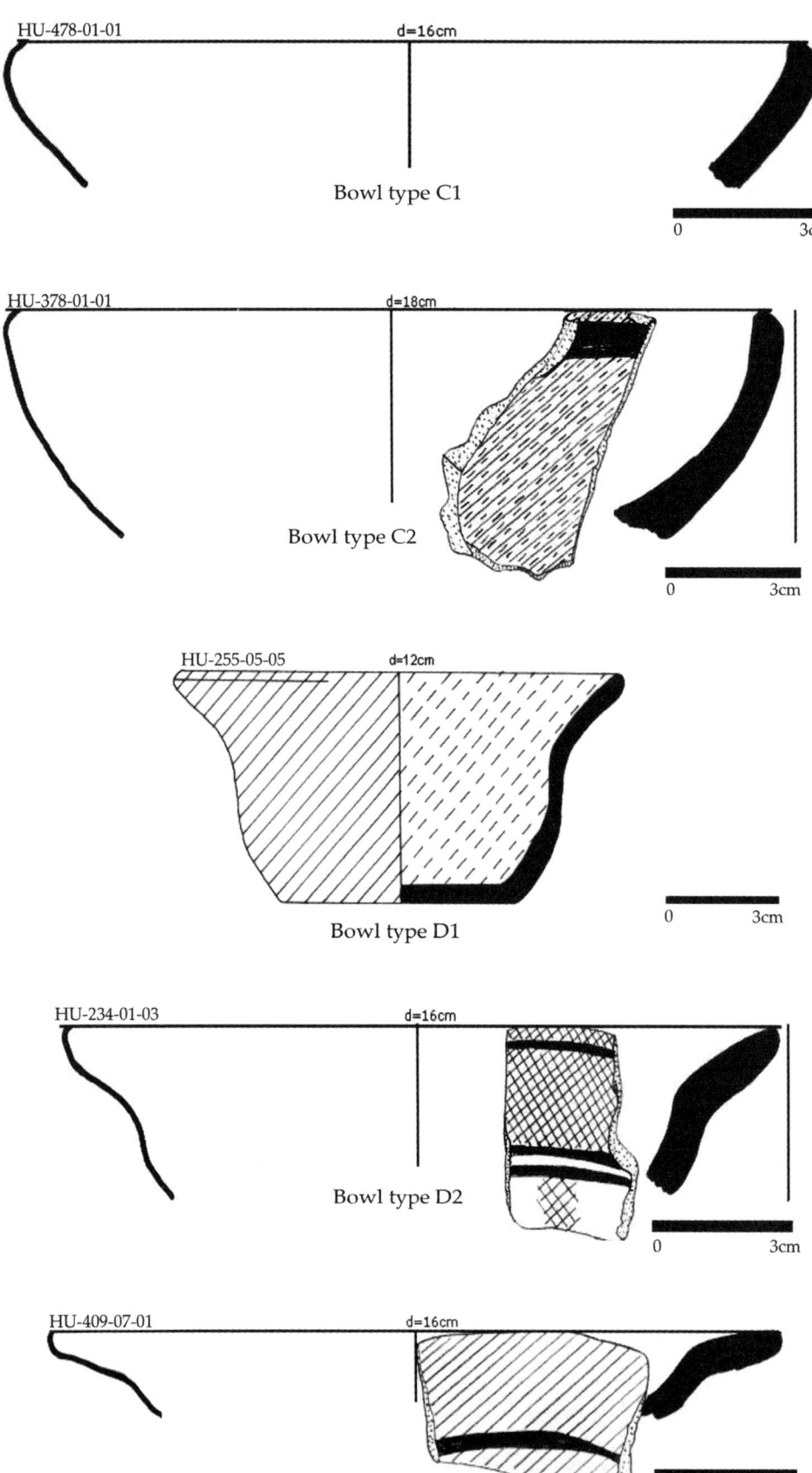

Figure 2.139.
Inca III bowl types C1, C2, and D1–D3.

Analysis of Ceramics

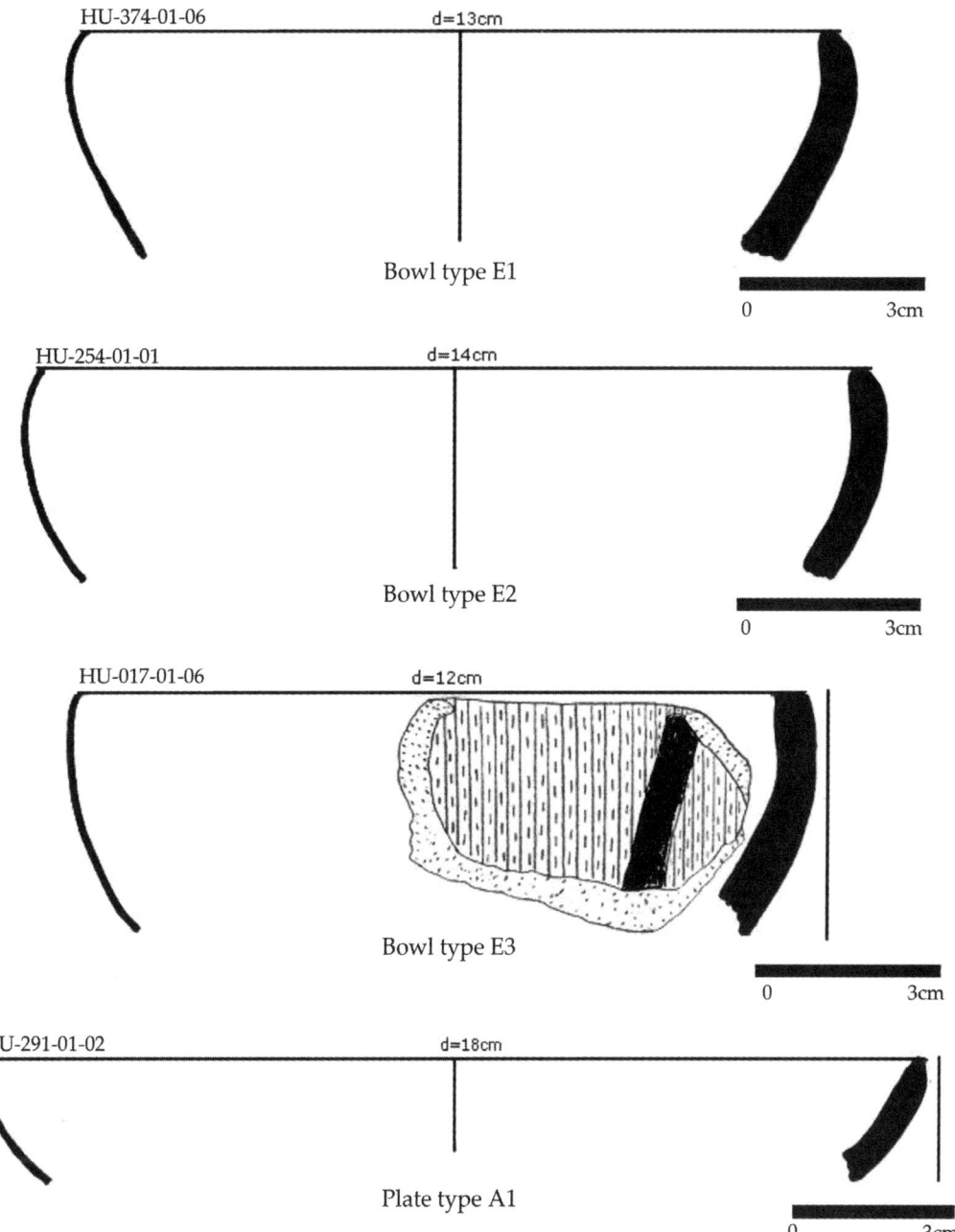

Figure 2.140. Inca III bowl types E1–E3 and plate type A1.

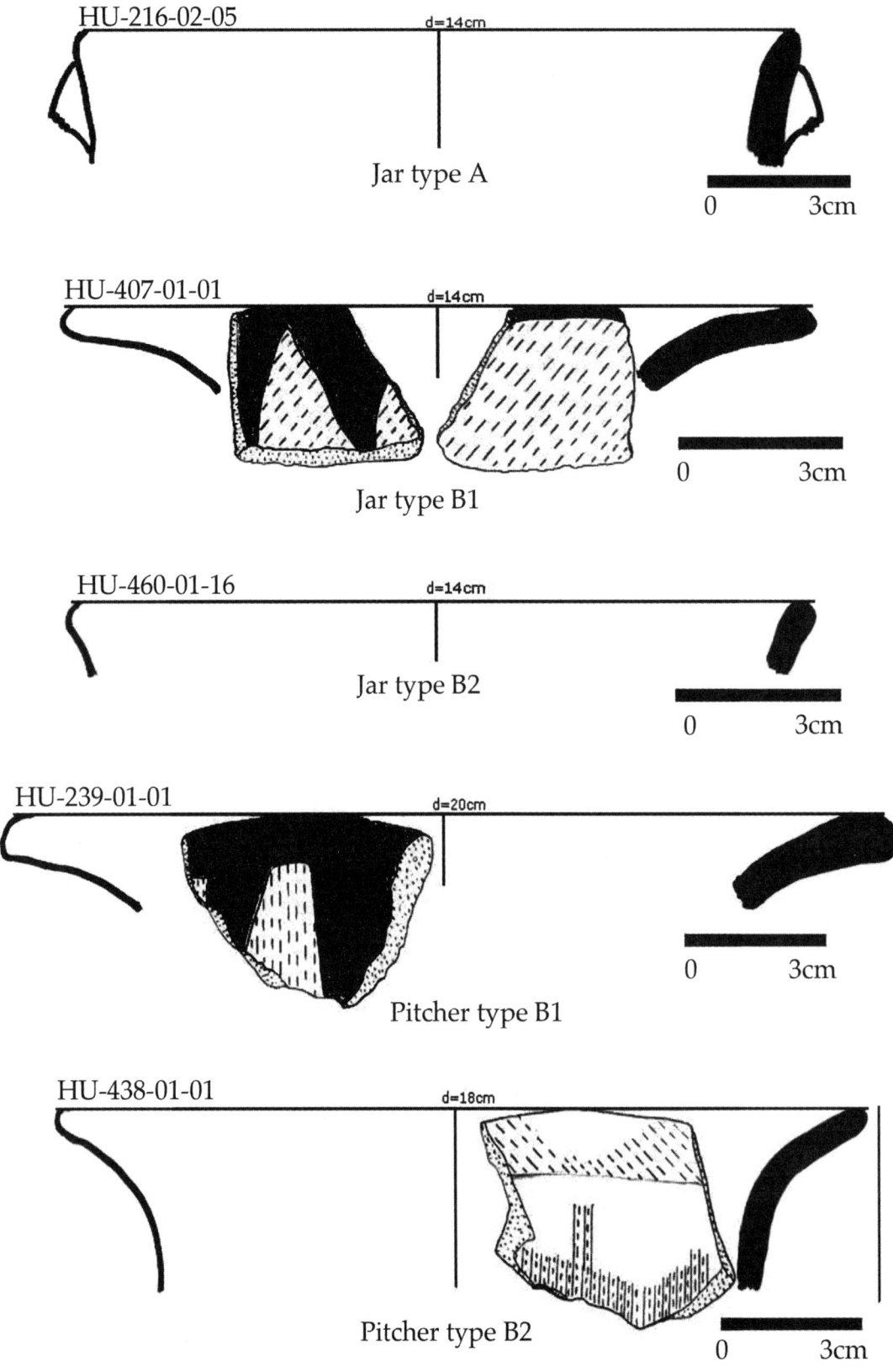

Figure 2.141. Inca III jar types A, B1, and B2, and pitcher types B1 and B2.

3 | Site Descriptions

This chapter describes the sites found on survey. For us to assign a period designation to a site, we required at least two diagnostics for the pre-Altiplano periods, and at least three diagnostics for the Altiplano and Inca periods. As a result, there will occasionally be a sherd illustrated or described from a time period not listed in Tables 3.1 or 3.2, simply because it is the only diagnostic from the collection associated with that site.

Table 3.1. Sites with a habitation component in the Huancané-Putina survey.

Site #	Site Name	Elevation (masl)	Site Size	Type*	Form I	Form II	Form III	Huaña I	Huaña II	Tiw I	Tiw II	Alt I	Alt II	Alt III	Inca I	Inca II	Inca III
3	Huancahuichinca	3855	9–11 ha	H/C/R	1								1	1	1	1	1
4	Huancané Pueblo	3840	5–10 ha	H		1	1						1	1	1	1	1
6	Miyuraya	3853	2 ha	H/C									1	1	1	1	1
7		3954	40 × 70 m	H/C									1	1	1	1	1
8	Pucara	4020	10 ha	H/C								1	1		1		
9		3857	<1.0 ha	H								1	1	1	1	1	1
10	Huatasane Sur	3855	1 ha	H/C								1	1	1	1		
11		3852	40 × 40 m	H								1	1	1	1	1	1
12		3840	0.25 ha	H									1		1		
13		3842	50 × 50 m	H													
14	Cachichupa	3842	7 ha	H/C/R	1				1						1	1	
15	Santa Rosa Cochapampa Sur	3851	1.3 ha	H/C								1	1	1	1	1	1
16		3858	1 ha	H/C									1	1			
17		3853	0.25 ha	H													
18	Inchuyu (see Hu-406)	4060															
19	Totorani	3829	3 ha	H/C	1				1								
20		3830	0.75 ha	H		1							1	1	1		
22		3971	20 × 35 m	H				1									
30	Putina Pueblo	3867	4–7 ha	H/C/R	1		1							1	1	1	1
33		3859	3 ha	H/C													
35	Comunidad Mijani	3877	60 × 60 m	H		1							1	1	1		
36		3918	10 × 70 m	H													
39	Condortañani	3947	100 × 100 m	H								1	1	1	1	1	
40	Condortañani	3950	100 × 90 m	H								1			1		
41	Comunidad Huyllapata	3963	90 × 70 m	H													
42	Wichoqollo Quilcapunku	3921	100 × 75 m	H/C													
44	Jacha Chuco	4035	250 × 90 m	H						1							
45	Chiquiria	3988	40 × 50 m	H/C									1	1	1		
49	Kaka chupa	3882	50 × 50 m	H													
50		3888	50 × 70 m	H								1	1	1	1	1	1
51		3865	20 × 50 m	H													
52		3861	30 × 50 m	H										1			
53		3848	100 × 100 m	H										1	1		1
56		3946	30 × 30 m	H													
58	part of 011, 059, 129	3846	3 ha	H/T/D/C													
60		3854	50 × 75 m	H/D													
61		3856	25 × 25 m	H											1		
62		3925	25 × 40 m	H		1									1		
67		3860	50 × 100 m	H		1											
68		3967	3 ha	H													
69	Incachupa	3895	50 × 50 m	H													
70	Huasunta	3908	75 × 150 m	H/D									1				1
71		3846	50 × 50 m	H		1	1							1	1		
72		3876	25 × 35 m	H		1	1										
73	Torrance Sur	3875	25 × 100 m	H	1		1	1									
74		4049	70 × 70 m	H			1										
75		3950	50 × 200 m	H			1										
76		4011	50 × 100 m	H			1	1						1			
77		3934	50 × 50 m	H/D									1	1	1		1
78		3904	10 × 20 m	H									1	1			
79		4028	50 × 70 m	H/D										1			
81		4090	2–3 ha	H/C/D									1				
91**		3950	20 × 20 m	H		1	1								1		
92**		3950	26 × 32 m	H/R	1	1	1	1						1			
94		3900	4 ha	H/R	1	1	1										
95		3883	2 ha											1	1		

Site Descriptions 175

Table 3.1 cont.

Site #	Site Name	Elevation (masl)	Site Size	Type*	Form I	Form II	Form III	Huaña I	Huaña II	Tiw I	Tiw II	Alt I	Alt II	Alt III	Inca I	Inca II	Inca III
96		3880	70 × 50 m	H													
99		3875	40 × 40 m	H/T		1											
103		3885	25 × 40 m	H/T			1										
107		3891	40 × 40 m	H/T											1		
108		3880	20 × 20 m	H/C													
109		3877	20 × 20 m	H													1
110**		3872	25 × 25 m	T/C													
111		3958	20 × 20 m	H											1		
112		3901	20 × 50 m	H/C													
113	Pampa Mijani	3869	30 × 30 m	T/H											1		
114		3861	30 × 30 m	H/T													
115	T'ojopata	4100	50 × 50 m	T/H													
118	Cantacanta	4349	10 × 10 m	H/C										1			
119	Cheqtaq'ollo	3870	4 ha	H/C										1			
120**	Comunidad Caya-caya	3893	40 × 30 m	H/C	1	1	1					1	1	1	1	1	
121		3855	30 × 50 m	H	1							1	1		1	1	
125	Laq'oni	4101	0.8 ha	H									1				
126	Acapana	3866	50 × 50 m	H									1	1	1		
127	Comunidad Caya-caya	3864	70 × 100 m	H			1						1	1	1		
128**	Marumpuncu	3840	50 × 70 m	T/H									1	1	1	1	1
130		3885	2 ha	H						1	1			1	1	1	1
131		3890	70 × 70 m	H	1							1	1	1	1		
132	Catarani Haja	3855	60 × 200 m	H		1	1							1			
133	Subida a Catarani	3875	60 × 120 m	H													
134	Tuquni Q'ocho	3905	50 × 70 m	H											1		1
135		3877	100 × 70 m	H				1									
136	Catarani Nuñomoq'o	3894	1 ha	H/R											1		
137	Santa Cruz de Catarani	3936	1.5 ha	H			1						1	1	1		1
138	Pojsorunipata	3870	50 × 50 m	H		1	1						1	1	1	1	1
139	Pucachaca	4022	40 × 50 m	H		1								1	1		1
154	Buena vista	3887	250 × 200 m	H/C		1			1			1	1	1	1	1	1
156	Comunidad Torno	3876	80 × 70 m	H		1									1		1
157	Qlocho	3904	2 ha	H													
158	Wilaqarqa	3957	100 × 50 m	H/C									1				1
159	Wilaqarqa Chupa	3884	0.25 ha	H/C									1	1	1		1
161	Comunidad Torno	3866	1 ha	H		1							1	1	1		1
162	Chijora	3838	20 × 70 m	H									1	1	1		1
163	Caya-caya	3874	0.5 ha	H/C		1		1						1			
167	Cerro Cuñuna	3948	100 × 120 m	H/C					1					1	1		1
168	Comunidad Ajarani	4008	40 × 40 m	H		1	1	1					1	1	1		1
169		3944	1–2 ha	H/R/D									1	1	1		1
172		3840	3–4 ha	H		1							1	1			
173	Kulqupunku	3870	20 × 20 m	H/C										1	1		
174	Cerro Amayapata	3889	1.5 ha	H/C		1									1		1
175	Quilapuncu	3836	40 × 40 m	H		1								1			1
200	Tintiña Pata-Luriata	3834	80 × 50 m	H										1	1		1
201	Tintiña Pata	3825	60 × 80 m	H/T											1		1
202	Tintiña Pata	3832	100 × 80 m	H/T											1		1
203	Parcialidad Luriata	3825	70 × 40 m	H											1		1
204	Parcialidad Luriata	3827	30 × 70 m	H											1		1
205	Queajachi	3834	100 × 300 m	H/C		1	1	1						1	1	1	1
206	Iglesia Adventista	3833	70 × 20 m	H		1		1						1	1	1	1
207	Parcialidad Luriata	3834	50 × 30 m	H		1	1							1	1		1
208	Parcialidad Luriata	3834	150 × 80 m	H		1								1	1		1
209	Tintiña Pata	3830	10 × 40 m	H/C		1								1	1		1
211		3830	80 × 40 m	H/T													
213**		3832	50 × 75 m	H/C			1										
214	Tintiña Pata	3826	90 × 50 m	H	1	1						1	1	1	1		1

Table 3.1 cont.

Site #	Site Name	Elevation (masl)	Site Size	Type*	Form I	Form II	Form III	Huaña I	Huaña II	Tiw I	Tiw II	Alt I	Alt II	Alt III	Inca I	Inca II	Inca III
215		3825	100 × 70 m	H													1
216		3829	100 × 100 m	H										1		1	
217		3829	50 × 100 m	H/T										1		1	1
218	Siaquello Parcialidad	3831	50 × 50 m	H													
219	Cerro Cacachi	3894	4–5 ha	H/C/D	1	1	1	1									
222	Cerro Chojachi	3941	4 ha	H/C/D	1	1											
225		3970	10 × 40 m	H/R/D													
226		4028	2–3 ha	H/C/D										1			1
227		4067	250 × 100 m	H/C/D										1			1
228		4069	20 × 60 m	H		1								1			1
230	Parq'a	4014	75 × 75 m	H										1			
231		3825	40 × 50 m	H										1			
232		3833	20 × 30 m	H	1									1			
233		3858	100 × 20 m	H/C										1			1
234	Mullawipata	3840	70 × 40 m	H		1				1				1			1
236		3832	40 × 40 m	H										1			1
237	Aqo Pukro	3846	50 × 25 m	H										1			1
239	Barrios Altos	3846	40 × 45 m	H/C		1											
240		3913	120 × 100 m	H/C	1	1	1				1			1		1	1
241		3971	60 × 40 m	H/D	1	1	1							1		1	
242**	Pueblo de Vizcachane	3893	25 × 25 m	H						1							
243	Cerro Vizcachane	4112	300 × 150 m	H/D/C						1			1	1		1	1
244	Cerro Vizcachane	4082	50 × 50 m	H/D/C						1			1	1			
246	Pampa de Quella'huyo	3846	70 × 80 m	H								1					
247	Saltocarca	3839	40 × 40 m	H/T							1						
248	Huata	3831	2 ha	H/C/R/T		1	1										
249	Pampa de Quella'huyo	3823	50 × 50 m	H													
250		3838	20 × 20 m	H/T		1	1										1
251	Pampa Cacajache	3825	40 × 40 m	H							1			1			1
252	Pampa Cacajache	3835	80 × 80 m	H/C		1						1		1			1
254		3826	20 × 20 m	H										1			
255		3829	30 × 20 m	C/H													
261		3834	100 × 100 m	H		1											1
265	Cerro Vizcachane	4082	80 × 40 m	H													
266	Cerro Sotisani	4021	40 × 40 m	H/C	1												
267	Cerro Sotisani	4020	30 × 70 m	H													
268	Cerro Sotisani	4017	100 × 30 m	H/D													
269	Cerro Sotisani	3893	200 × 60 m	H/C	1	1					1			1	1	1	
270	Parcialidad Chijuyo	3826	80 × 100 m	H										1			
271		3837	20 × 25 m	H		1											
273	Cerro Pecosani	3934	2 ha	H/C													
274	Cerro Pecosani	3918	2 ha	H		1	1		1								
275	part of Hu-003	3847	20 × 20 m	H/R													
276	Santiaquillo	3830	3–6 ha	H	1	1								1	1		1
278		3832	3–4 ha	H										1	1	1	1
279	Huarisa	3917	2–3 ha	H/D										1			1
280		3879	4–7 ha	H/C	1	1	1							1	1		
281		3871	4–5 ha	H/C		1	1							1	1		1
283	Chacacruz	3835	40 × 40 m	H													
285	Juntuma	3854	30 × 30 m	H/T		1								1			
288		3845	40 × 30 m	H		1								1			
289		3830	30 × 30 m	H										1			
291	Chuseqa sayaña pata	3828	100 × 20 m	H/C			1					1	1	1			
293		3830	30 × 30 m	H								1	1	1			
295		3833	20 × 20 m	H								1	1	1			
296		3833	25 × 50 m	T/C						1		1	1	1			
297		3854	80 × 80 m	H								1	1	1		1	

Site Descriptions 177

Table 3.1 cont.

Site #	Site Name	Elevation (masl)	Site Size	Type*	Form I	Form II	Form III	Huaña I	Huaña II	Tiw I	Tiw II	Alt I	Alt II	Alt III	Inca I	Inca II	Inca III
298	Cerro Quequecani	3878	300 × 40 m	H/C/D													
299		3863	50 × 50 m	H												1	
300		3872	200 × 30 m	H/C										1			
302		3830	30 × 30 m	H													1
304		3963	300 × 70 m	H/C										1	1		1
306	Tumuku/Upani Pata	3949	2 ha	H/R													
308		3849	20 × 20 m	H		1	1	1					1	1		1	1
309		3832	30 × 20 m	H	1	1		1					1	1			1
310		3843	3 ha	H	1	1							1	1			1
312		3966	30 × 20 m	H	1									1			
313		3950	60 × 60 m	H	1								1				
314		3852	20 × 20 m	H									1				
315		3884	1 ha	H/T	1	1							1	1			
316	Machacamarca	3918	1 ha	H/R/D/C	1	1	1						1	1			
317		3838	100 × 50 m	H		1								1			
318		3846	100 × 40 m	H/C			1						1	1			
319		3847	80 × 60 m	H/C									1	1			
320		3848	100 × 100 m	H/C									1	1			1
321		3855	80 × 80 m	H/C	1	1							1	1			
322		3847	1.5–2 ha	H									1	1			
324		3848	100 × 100 m	H/C									1	1			
325		3848	2 ha	H									1	1			
327		4094	2.5 ha	H									1	1			
328		3866	80 × 80 m	H									1	1			1
329		3901	100 × 100 m	H/C									1				1
333		3862	60 × 30 m	H									1	1			
337		3851		H/C									1	1			
340		3857	100 × 100 m	H/C									1	1			
345		3852	50 × 50 m	H/C									1	1			
348		3847	100 × 150 m	H/C					1				1	1			
349		3837	40 × 80 m	H/C									1	1			
351	Collpa Huata	3849	100 × 30 m	H/C									1	1			1
359		3834	20 × 10 m	T									1	1			
361	Cerro Coacollo	4139	300 × 100 m	H/D				1					1	1			
370		3846	60 × 30 m	H				1					1	1			
376		3876	40 × 30 m	H/C									1	1			
378		3857	30 × 30 m	H									1	1			
380		3839	30 × 30 m	T/H									1	1			
381	Cerro Kuyuraya	3848	100 × 100 m	H/C	1	1	1			1			1	1			
382	Cerro Kuyuraya	3843	2 ha	H/C	1		1						1	1			1
384		3855	70 × 70 m	H	1								1				
385		3866	20 × 20 m	H/C									1	1			1
387		3848	30 × 30 m	H/T													
388	Jarjamase/Sustia	3851	30 × 30 m	H/C		1							1	1		1	
390		4020	100 × 50 m	H/C									1	1			
392		3836	30 × 30 m	H									1	1			
396		3854	40 × 50 m	H/T									1	1			
398	Comunidad Jurata	3835	120 × 150 m	H		1	1						1	1			1
399		3835	100 × 100 m	H	1								1	1			
400		3836	50 × 50 m	H/C									1	1			1
402	Comunidad Azangarillo	3846	20 × 20 m	H									1	1			
404		3835	200 × 50 m	H		1							1	1			
406	Jinchu huichinka/Inchuyu	3837	200 × 100 m	H/C	1		1						1	1	1	1	
407		3830	30 × 40 m	H										1	1	1	1
408	Comunidad Azangarillo	3844	50 × 50 m	H									1	1	1		1
409		3836	100 × 70 m	H/C		1	1						1	1	1		1
411		3862	80 × 15 m	H/C/D	1								1	1	1	1	1
412	part of 414	3889	50 × 50 m	H/C/T/D	1	1	1			1			1	1	1	1	1

Table 3.1 cont.

Site #	Site Name	Elevation (masl)	Site Size	Type*	Form I	Form II	Form III	Huaña I	Huaña II	Tiw I	Tiw II	Alt I	Alt II	Alt III	Inca I	Inca II	Inca III
414	Comunidad Machacamarca	3841	300 × 100 m	H/C	1												1
415	Comunidad Jurata	3843	30 × 30 m	H		1									1	1	
416		3844	100 × 100 m	H/C			1								1		
417		3843	100 × 100 m	H/C	1										1	1	1
418		3839	80 × 40 m	H/C	1	1									1	1	
419	Comunidad Azangarillo	3838	70 × 70 m	H										1	1	1	1
420	Callapani	3848	10 × 10 m	H/T											1	1	
422		3855	70 × 20 m	H/T										1	1		
423		3843	80 × 50 m	H										1	1		1
424		3832	100 × 50 m	H/C		1								1	1	1	
425		3834	40 × 40 m	H										1	1		
426		3829	50 × 40 m	H										1	1		
427	Comunidad Jurata	3834	100 × 50 m	H/T	1									1	1		1
428	Comunidad Jurata	3834	100 × 40 m	H/R	1	1								1	1	1	1
429	Comunidad Jurata	3827	70 × 70 m	H/C	1									1	1		
430	Callapani	3859	80 × 20 m	H/C											1		
431	Cerro Pucara	3891	150 × 200 m	H/C		1	1							1	1		1
432	Comunidad Callapani	3960	200 × 300 m	H/C		1	1							1	1		1
433	Comunidad Callapani	3970	200 × 200 m	H/C		1								1	1		
434	Comunidad Quencha	3860	40 × 30 m	H										1	1		
435	Mun. Condorena	3870	80 × 20 m	H		1		1									
436	Cerro Choquechambi	3857	300 × 80 m	H/C				1	1		1						
439		3856	60 × 30 m	H/C										1	1		1
442		3851	30 × 30 m	H										1			
443		3846	100 × 40 m	H		1								1	1		
445		3845	200 × 50 m	H											1		
446		3832	40 × 40 m	H									1	1	1		
447	Quishuarani	3845	80 × 40 m	H									1	1	1		1
449	Comunidad Tahurauta	3837	40 × 60 m	H/T									1	1			
450		3851	25 × 25 m	H										1	1		
451		3888	25 × 25 m	H/R									1				
452	Pichacane	4049	70 × 70 m	H/C/T/D										1	1		
453	Pichacane	4073	100 × 60 m	H/C			1										
454		4031	80 × 150 m	H									1	1	1	1	
455		4075	60 × 60 m	H/D											1	1	
456		4257	100 × 60 m	H									1	1			
457	Cerro Condorhuachani	4168	70 × 50 m	H/D									1	1	1	1	1
459		3872	80 × 20 m	H/C									1	1	1	1	1
460		3874	50 × 40 m	H									1	1	1		1
461	Comunidad Tahurauta	3870	30 × 30 m	H									1	1			
464		3872	100 × 50 m	H/C										1	1		
465		3857	100 × 50 m	H										1	1	1	
466		3861	80 × 20 m	H/C										1	1		
467		3864	100 × 40 m	H									1	1	1	1	1
468		3866	100 × 100 m	H									1	1	1	1	1
472		3868	150 × 50 m	H/C									1	1	1	1	1
474		3902	30 × 30 m	H/C										1	1		
475		3910	40 × 40 m	H									1		1		
480		3851	100 × 40 m	H/C										1	1		
481		3856	50 × 40 m	H/C										1	1		
482		3839	25 × 25 m	H/T										1	1		
483**		3839	25 × 30 m	T/H										1	1		
484		3847	20 × 50 m	T/H										1	1		
485		3847	50 × 30 m	T/H										1	1		
486		3846	50 × 30 m	T/H											1		
488		3868	80 × 80 m	T/H										1	1		
489		3846	60 × 40 m	T/H										1	1		
490	Río Cala Cala	3844	30 × 30 m	T/H											1		

Site Descriptions 179

Table 3.1 cont.

Site #	Site Name	Elevation (masl)	Site Size	Type*	Form I	Form II	Form III	Huaña I	Huaña II	Tiw I	Tiw II	Alt I	Alt II	Alt III	Inca I	Inca II	Inca III
491	Río Cala Cala	3846	40 × 20 m	T/H													
492	Río Cala Cala	3845	30 × 30 m	T/H													
493		3856	25 × 25 m	T/H													
494		3837	40 × 60 m	T/H													
495		3862	60 × 60 m	H		1									1		1
496	Comunidad Queallo	3888	80 × 80 m	T/H											1		1
497		3860	60 × 50 m	H		1									1	1	
498	Comunidad Queallo	3865	80 × 80 m	H/C											1		
500		3969	90 × 40 m	H/C													
501		3968	80 × 80 m	H													
502		3859	40 × 50 m	H													
506	Tupu huyu	3884	100 × 80 m	H/C	1	1	1	1	1				1		1	1	1
507	Comunidad Queallo	3894	100 × 80 m	H/C	1	1	1	1	1			1	1		1	1	
508	Comunidad Queallo	3885	60 × 40 m	H/C								1	1				
509		3923	80 × 40 m	H		1		1				1	1	1	1		1
510	Cerro Trallate	3941	50 × 50 m	H		1							1				1
511	Cerro Ikejanani	3888	100 × 100 m	H/C	1	1	1					1	1	1	1		1
512	Cerro Ikejanani	3869	100 × 100 m	H	1	1		1		1		1	1	1	1	1	1
513	Comunidad Cohasia	4074	60 × 60 m	H		1	1	1					1	1	1	1	1
515		4104	100 × 100 m	H/D/C									1	1	1	1	
517	Cerro Trallate	3988	150 × 70 m	T/H		1		1				1	1	1	1		1
520		4004	60 × 50 m	H	1	1	1	1		1			1				
521		3999	150 × 100 m	H													
524		3874	25 × 25 m	H/U													
527		3950	120 × 80 m	H/C													
530		4053	150 × 100 m	H/C										1		1	
531		4001	150 × 100 m	H/C	1	1											
532		3948	100 × 150 m	H/R/C	1	1	1	1									
536	Comunidad Sunuoco	3830	100 × 100 m	H/R/C	1	1	1	1									
537	Ninacarca	3824	100 × 100 m	H/C						1							

*A: agriculture; C: cemetery; T: temporary camp; D: defensive; R: ritual; U: unknown; H: habitation
**No surface sherds or no collection

Table 3.2. Cemetery-only sites in the Huancané-Putina survey.

Site #	Site Name	Elevation (masl)	Site Size	Type*	Form I	Form II	Form III	Huaña I	Huaña II	Tiw I	Tiw II	Alt I	Alt II	Alt III	Inca I	Inca II	Inca III
21		3846	20 × 20 m	C													
32		3890	0.5 ha	C								X	X	X	X		
38	Huayllapata	3878	70 × 50 m	C									X		X		
48	Hapujapupata	3925	30 × 30 m	C								X	X	X			
54		3861	10 × 20 m	C													
57		3851	6 m diam	C													
63				C													
66	part of 081	3887	3–4 m diam	C								X	X	X			
80			2.5 m diam	C													
85		4229	2 m diam	C													
88		4175	0.5 ha	C													
93		3950	10 × 10 m	C													
97		3869	4 × 10 m	C													
98		3875	30 × 30 m	C								X	X	X	X		
100	Comunidad Caya-caya	3968	30 × 30 m	C													
122	Huayyapata	3862	50 × 70 m	C								X	X				
123		3875	50 × 50 m	C								X	X	X			
155		3888		C													
160	Challwanipata	3932	25 × 25 m	C		X						X	X	X	X	X	
176	Huatasani area	3851	30 × 50 m	C		X						X	X	X	X	X	X
210	Tintiña Pata	3845	20 × 40 m	C								X	X	X			
212		3837	60 × 60 m	C	X					X							
220	Cerro Cacachi	3866	4 × 4 m	C													
221	Cerro Cacachi	3860	20 × 20 m	C								X	X	X			
223		3841	80 × 50 m	C							X	X	X	X			
224		3855	30 × 40 m	C							X	X	X	X	X	X	
235	Tiqaparki	3848	40 × 40 m	C	X							X	X	X			
238	Soaquillo parcialidad	3858	40 × 25 m	C								X	X	X	X	X	
245	Cerro Vizcachane	4097	20 × 20 m	C								X	X	X			
256		3859	40 × 40 m	C						X		X	X		X		
257		3861	100 × 75 m	C	X	X						X	X	X			
258		3847	15 × 10 m	C								X	X				
259		3922	10 × 10 m	C								X	X				
260		3842	20 × 20 m	C								X	X	X		X	
262		3851	100 × 100 m	C								X	X	X	X		
263		3855	35 × 40 m	C								X	X	X			
264	Santiaguillo	3853	10 × 10 m	C									X	X	X		
272		3871	1.5 × 1.5 m	C													
277		3854	5 × 5 m	C								X	X		X		
286		3863	30 × 10 m	C	X							X	X	X	X	X	
287		3858	20 × 20 m	C									X	X	X		
290		3838	1 × 1 m	C													
292		3839	10 × 10 m	C								X	X		X		
303		3843	30 × 20 m	C			X					X	X	X	X		
305		3898	20 × 10 m	C	X							X	X	X	X	X	
311		3950	5 × 5 m	C													
323		3861	6 × 14 m	C								X	X	X	X		
330		3879	20 × 20 m	C									X	X			
331		3878	20 × 20 m	C			X					X	X	X	X	X	
332		3873	100 × 40 m	C			X					X	X	X	X		
334		3877	25 × 25 m	C									X	X	X		
335	Muñani Pata	3867	30 × 30 m	C								X	X	X	X		
336		3862	80 × 50 m	C								X	X	X	X	X	
338		3860	30 × 30 m	C								X	X	X	X		
339		3858	80 × 50 m	C								X	X	X	X	X	
341		3930	30 × 30 m	C			X					X	X	X	X		
342		3928	30 × 30 m	C					X		X	X	X	X	X	X	X
343		3858	50 × 50 m	C							X	X	X	X	X	X	X
344		3866	100 × 100 m	C			X					X	X	X	X		

Table 3.2 cont.

Site #	Site Name	Elevation (masl)	Site Size	Type*	Form I	Form II	Form III	Huaña I	Huaña II	Tiw I	Tiw II	Alt I	Alt II	Alt III	Inca I	Inca II	Inca III
346		3860	30 × 30 m	C													
347		3884	70 × 20 m	C								X	X	X			
350	Collpa Huata	3858	20 × 20 m	C								X	X	X			
352		3843	10 × 10 m	C													
353		3902	30 × 30 m	C								X	X		X	X	X
354		3864	20 × 25 m	C									X	X	X	X	X
355		3887	10 × 10 m	C								X	X	X			
356		3894	5 × 5 m	C													
358			10 × 10 m	C													
360	Cerro Coacollo	3989	2.3 × 2.3 m	C									X		X		
362		4154	10 × 10 m	C								X	X				
363	Cerro Jarjamase	4100	60 × 60 m	C										X			
369	Comunidad Kuyuraya	3869	25 × 20 m	T/C								X					
374		3880	60 × 80 m	C													
375		3880	20 × 20 m	C								X	X	X		X	X
377		3811	60 × 60 m	C								X	X				
383		3881	40 × 20 m	C													
386		3852	10 × 10 m	C													
389		4066	5 × 5 m	C													
393		3860	10 × 10 m	C								X	X	X	X		X
394		3867	5 × 5 m	C								X	X	X	X		
397		3810	100 × 70 m	C								X	X	X	X		X X
403		3853	30 × 30 m	C								X	X	X	X		X
408	Comunidad Tumata Huichinca	3852	30 × 40 m	C					X			X	X	X	X		
410		3862	80 × 60 m	C									X	X	X		
413		3876	20 × 20 m	C									X				
421	Callapani Machacamarca	3865	5 × 5 m	C	X	X					X	X	X	X		X	
437		3874	100 × 50 m	C	X							X	X	X	X	X	
438		3874	70 × 40 m	C		X	X					X	X	X	X		
440	Cerro Choquechambi	3878	150 × 50 m	C								X	X	X	X		
441	Cerro Choquechambi	3870	20 × 20 m	C								X	X	X	X		
444	Cerro Acocollo	3871	120 × 80 m	C								X	X	X	X		
448	Comunidad Tahurauta	3871	30 × 30 m	C								X	X	X			
462	Amayuta	3902	10 × 10 m	C								X	X	X	X		
469		3880	20 × 20 m	C								X	X	X	X		
471		3940	70 × 70 m	C								X	X	X	X		
473		3891	50 × 40 m	C									X	X	X		X
476		3904	25 × 20 m	C									X	X			
478		3883	10 × 10 m	C									X		X		
479		3884	15 × 15 m	C								X	X		X		
499		3935	20 × 20 m	C								X	X	X	X	X	X
503		3884	20 × 20 m	C								X	X	X	X	X	
504		3880	10 × 10 m	C			X										
505		3884	60 × 40 m	C													
514		4103	100 × 100 m	C													
516	Cerro Trallate	4122	20 × 20 m	C								X	X		X	X	X
518		4026	50 × 50 m	C									X	X	X	X	
522		3923	10 × 10m	T/C												1	
523		3918	5 × 5 m	C													
525		3906	5 × 5 m	C													
526		3903	40 × 40 m	C									X			X	
528		3977	20 × 20 m	C									X				
529		3990	20 × 30 m	C									X				
533		3876	50 × 70 m	C			X						X				
534	Yapupampa	3840	10 × 10 m	C			X						X	X			
535	Yapupampa	3840	10 × 10 m	C													
538		3845	40 × 40 m	C									X	X			

*A: agriculture; C: cemetery; T: temporary camp; D: defensive; R: ritual; U: unknown; H: habitation
**No surface sherds or no collection

Hu-003/Hu-276. Huancahuichinka; Wankawichinca. (Figs. 3.1–3.4)

This hilltop terraced site was found in 1998 during the first reconnaissance of the region by de la Vega, Chávez, Plourde, and Stanish. During the intensive survey of 2000 and 2001, we discovered the sunken court section to the north and gave the site the designation Hu-276. Called "Huancahuichinka" by the landowners and other residents, the site was most likely a regional center during the Early through Upper Formative periods. There is a large and impressive sunken court at the top of the ridge.

It is difficult to accurately measure the dimensions of the sunken court because the walls themselves are covered by at least a meter of wall fall and topsoil. As a result, the outline of the wall is ambiguous, creating a one- to two-meter-wide wall outline above the depression. The court also has a roundish appearance that we believe is due to the fact that it was quadrangular but not square. The long side measures about 23 m (top of wall fall to top of wall fall), while the shortest side is 17 m and the opposite side is 21 m. These measurements are approximate and they may be off by as much as 2 m. At 23 m on one side, this is one of the largest courts in the northern Titicaca Basin outside Pucara. The court does not appear to be oriented to the cardinal directions. We were asked by the landowner to not take any more measurements right at the time we were taking out our Brunton compasses, and we complied with the request from the landowner. We estimate that the court is oriented about 15–20 degrees west of north.

Two farmers discovered one broken monolith directly in the center of the court, standing upright. In 1998, we happened to arrive when they were digging it out. The visible parts of the two pieces were more than 130 cm long. They were carved with what appeared to be a bird (perhaps a parihuana), a circle or "doughnut" motif, and other designs that were largely hidden because they occurred on the section that was lying below the surface. These motifs are also known from monoliths found at Pukara and Taraco and would traditionally be described as "Qaluyu" in style. The monolith was still there at Huancahuichinka in situ until at least 2004. When we last checked in 2010, the monolith had been looted. The hole left behind by the looters was a little more than 2 m deep, suggesting a monolith of that length.

The highest area of the site is the original Hu-003 section. It is a typical "type 3" site, as defined in the Juli-Desaguadero region, in the southwest Titicaca region (Stanish et al. 1997). These sites are characterized by corporate architecture at the top of the hill or crest and domestic terraces around the hillslope below. The terraces are broad and wide with abundant pottery and other evidence of domestic use and occupation, notably lithic artifacts and eroding middens. The sector called Hu-003 runs into Hu-276 and in reality forms a single complex. The Hu-003 site area covers about 9–11 ha, while the Hu-276 area is about 3–6 ha in extent. Hu-276 has an apparent cruciform mound with at least one odd sunken court. This sector is described below as Hu-276.

Hu-003 has an Altiplano and Inca period occupation throughout the site area as well. This site, located in the bend of the river, is in one of the most fertile spots in the valley. It is logical that there would be a continuous occupation on this area throughout the region's prehistory and history.

Hu-004. Huancané Pueblo. (Fig. 3.1)

This is the town of Huancané, a large, paved city with few remains on the surface. The entire town today, excluding the military base, is approximately 800 by 1500 m in size. We estimate the Inca period occupation to be around 5 to 10 ha, but this estimate is based simply on observations in the streets and surface scatters of artifacts. We found a number of fine Inca pieces in some excavated earth used for modern building materials. There were the usual Late Horizon sherds in the few adobe bricks that were not painted. There is little question that the town had a substantial Inca occupation.

We collected materials from the streets and in ditches and discovered materials beginning with Formative II, and a large amount of Altiplano and Inca material. It is likely that the town was similar to Putina (Hu-030) in the Formative period, the center of a major settlement. Given the urban sprawl covering the ancient settlement, this is impossible to determine.

Hu-006. Milliraya; Miyuraya.

Geoffrey Spurling (1992) investigated this site and reported that this was a pottery workshop of mitima colonists. We visited the site during our reconnaissance in 1998 and confirmed his observations. The main part of the archaeological site lies under the modern town. Late Horizon pottery is found throughout the area.

Below the modern town of Milliraya is a natural terrace that looms over the river. There is a scatter of pottery fragments and chipped stone from the modern road to the terrace. The majority of the ceramic diagnostics are late in date—Altiplano and Inca. Likewise, we discovered some tombs along the edge of the natural terrace, a pattern typical for late burials in the region.

Hu-007.

This is a small site typical of the Altiplano and Inca periods of the region. It is located near Hu-008, a major fortified site located on a tall ridge above Hu-007. The site of Hu-007 itself sits on the low hillslope of the ridge and consists of a series of three well-made large terraces and a number of smaller ones. Altiplano period terraces are located at the top of the site, where there is also a shallow cave with small walls at the cave's opening. Inside the cave area is at least one burial, and there are probably more in the area. All the materials in the cave area are Altiplano and Inca in style.

Hu-008. Pucara. (Figs. 3.1, 3.5, 3.6, 3.67)

This fortified site is located on the top of a large ridge, and extends onto the sides of the ridge toward the western side of the valley. There are nine terraces that average about 2 m in height. These terraces join with natural outcrops on the north and south sides of the ridge, a classic defensive pattern in the Titicaca Basin.

On the surface of the lowest terrace of the pukara, we found four circular structures, about 2 to 3 m in diameter, with stone foundations. There are many more circular structures on the higher terraces. These are about 2 m in diameter and are constructed with pink sandstone blocks, some of which are vertical and appear to be rectangular in form. All these terraces have a low density of artifacts. At the top of the ridge there was a moderate scatter of pottery.

At the top of the site, there were a number of rectangular structures about 4 to 5 m on a side. There is a natural depression between the outcrops on the east side of the pukara. This area forms a "plaza," 120 m east-west and 35 m north-south. On the north side is a square area approximately 15 m on a side.

To the south of this plaza, there is an area with some cut rocks adjacent to the southern outcrop. One of the cut rocks, approximately 1 m on a side and with a flat and smooth top, has two circular depressions carved into its top. These depressions are 5 cm in diameter and 2 cm deep.

East of the plaza, near the top of the ridge, are two large chulpas. Each chulpa is approximately 7 m in diameter; they are about 10 m apart. There are many smaller tombs in the east and south sides of the ridge. There is no visible architecture. The hillsides in the middle and lower part of the ridge have terraces as well.

Site Descriptions

Figure 3.1. This is a view of the lower part of the survey area from above Hu-008 looking southeast past Huancané Pueblo. Lake Titicaca begins behind Huancané Pueblo just over the hill.

Figure 3.2. Huancahuichinka, site Hu-003.

Figure 3.3. A monolith found by farmers in the sunken court at Hu-003. The stone has broken apart. It was in its original location, standing upright in the court. It has unfortunately been removed by looters in the last several years and its present location is unknown.

Figure 3.4. The site of Hu-003 and its relationship to the sunken court formerly designated as Hu-276. The photograph was taken from Hu-408.

Figure 3.5. The pukara of Hu-008 and other sites in the pampa and along the base of the fortified hill.

Figure 3.6. A circular chulpa on the pukara of Hu-008.

Hu-009.

This is a small domestic site, less than 1 ha in size. It consists of a low-density scatter of Altiplano II artifacts that cover terraces at the base of a hillslope on the edge of the river. A modern structure was found at the base of the slope as well.

Hu-010. Huatasani Sur.

This site is located southwest of the modern town of Huatasani and probably represents the remains of an Inca tambo on the road, near the river. It is part of the large Inca complex in the Huatasani area. The site consists of a high density of artifacts and sits between the base of the ridge and the edge of the river on the site's south side. The site covers approximately 1.0 ha. There are both Altiplano period and Inca diagnostics on the surface. There is no visible domestic architecture. There is a below-ground cist tomb in the center of the site that had been looted recently. There are other tombs on the edge of the ridge to the north of the site. The diagnostic ceramics are largely Altiplano III and Inca in date, and the quality of the Late Horizon pottery is quite high. There is a small amount of Altiplano II pottery.

Hu-011. (Fig. 3.7)

Hu-011 is one of a cluster of sites associated with Hu-059 and other sites. Sector Hu-011 has Altiplano and Inca I pottery. There is no evidence of architecture. This sector is composed of terraces built inside a large rock outcrop. Hu-059, in turn, is the flat section in front with a large wall of a structure.

Hu-012.

This is a small site, about 0.25 ha in size. There is a low-density scatter of artifacts eroding from a midden on the natural terrace that follows the contours of the river. There are artifacts on the top of the natural terrace as well. The diagnostics are all Altiplano period in date, with one Inca II fragment. This one fragment was not sufficient to designate an Inca II occupation in Table 3.1.

Hu-013.

Hu-013 is a small domestic site, located on a natural mound in the eastern side of the valley in the pampa. The site has a low-density scatter of Altiplano II artifacts that covers the top of the mound and continues for 110 m on top of the mound to the side of the valley. There were two Inca II fragments as well. These two fragments were not sufficient to designate an Inca II occupation in Table 3.1. The scatter of artifacts is about 50 m in width. A canal runs on the north side of the mound. On the valley side of the mound are two canals that run parallel to each other to the edge of the site, where they unite. A single canal continues on the side of the mound, about halfway up the side. Here it changes direction to the west and continues for at least 130 m. The major canal is 30 cm wide and 15–20 cm deep.

Hu-014. Cachichupa. (Figs. 3.8, 3.9)

This site has been mapped and test excavated by Aimée Plourde (2006). A full description of the site can be found in this source. Cachichupa is one of the most important sites in the survey area. It is located

Figure 3.7. The site of Hu-011 on a natural mound at the base of a hill. The site is naturally terraced among vertical natural strata.

Figure 3.8. A view of the location of Hu-014 from the south. The site is located at the base of a hill next to the river. The site is strategically located to control access through this valley.

Figure 3.9. An uncarved monolith on the site of Hu-014. The monolith was originally in the sunken court area of the site but was moved by road construction activities.

in an extremely strategic position in the half kilometer-wide opening to the Putina Valley. The contemporaneous site of Putina (Hu-030) is similarly located at the other end of the valley.

Cachichupa is composed of a series of artificial terraces that ascend the outcrop. Plourde excavated one of these terraces and discovered a cache of Qaluyu vessels in what looks like a feasting/ceremonial pit. Below the terraces are a series of compounds and sunken courts that measure around 20 × 20 m up to as much as 50 × 50 m in size. Excavations by Plourde in one of these structures indicate that they were used in at least the Pucara period. Several undecorated monoliths were found on the site in 2002 but many have since disappeared, probably due to the road construction that has destroyed a significant portion of the site.

Hu-015. Santa Rosa Cochapampa Sur. (Fig. 3.10)

This site is located just south of the town of Huatasani, near the road. It was most likely part of the Inca complex described in Hu-010. It is located about 200 m from Hu-016 and more or less 200 m to the north of another scatter of artifacts. The site of Hu-015 has a very high density of Altiplano and Inca pottery and lithic artifacts that cover a natural river terrace. There are various burials eroding out of the edge of the terrace.

Hu-016. Santa Rosa Cochapampa Norte. (Fig. 3.11)

Hu-016 is a domestic habitation site located on the sides and edges of a natural ridge. This site has a very high density of Altiplano and Inca pottery as well as lithic artifacts. The scatter extends for about 1 ha up to the crest of the ridge. Below-ground cist burials are found on the highest edge of the site. Like Hu-015, it is close to the road. We interpret this site as a tambo in this cluster of Inca sites near Huatasani.

Hu-017.

This is a small site that is less than 0.25 ha in size. It consists of a low-density dispersal of late ceramics and chipped stone. A number of terraces were constructed in the sides of the ridge. These terraces have few artifacts.

Hu-018.

This site was first recorded as Hu-018 in reconnaissance and later revisited by the systematic survey crew and given the site number Hu-406. A few artifacts retain the designation Hu-018. Please see Hu-406 for a fuller discussion.

Hu-019. Totorani.

Totorani is a relatively large 3 ha site located at the base and on the sides of a small ridge. It consists of well-made terraces covered with a low-density scatter of artifacts. The majority of the pottery is late, with a few Inca pieces discovered on the surface. In front of the ridge are large, squarish terraces. There are some cist tombs here, plus an active cocha in the pampa in front of these terraces.

Hu-020.

This small Altiplano site is characterized by a low to moderate density of artifacts eroding from a midden on a natural river terrace. The site is less than 1 ha and the surface artifact density varies from low to moderate throughout the area. There are remains of a rectangular structure that measures 9 × 22 m. The date of this structure is unknown, but is most likely post-Inca.

Hu-021.

This Altiplano and early Inca period site is located approximately 600 m north of Hu-019. It is composed of at least four above-ground tombs and a moderate scatter of pottery near the tombs. These tombs have been looted. They were constructed from reddish sandstone blocks. They are circular, approximately 1 m in diameter. Some of the blocks are still vertical. The tombs are oriented in a line that is approximately north-south. It is most likely that this is a cemetery site that has been looted.

Hu-022.

This Altiplano period site is located on top of a natural ridge on the west side of the valley. It has a low density of pottery on the surface. A large area of the site has been destroyed by heavy construction equipment and it was therefore not possible to determine the full size of the site, though it is at least 20 × 35 m and probably larger, but no more than 50 × 50 m.

Hu-023.

This was the original number of Hu-205.

Hu-024. Cerro Pucara.

There is a scatter of late pottery over the side of the hill called Pucara. This does not appear to have been a habitation area, but perhaps a temporary camp.

Hu-025. Alta Gracia.

There is a scatter of late pottery over the side of the hill called Pucara. There are some modern *pagos* ("payments" or offerings) evident here. This site does not appear to have been a habitation area, but perhaps was a temporary camp or ritual area.

Hu-026–Hu-029.

These numbers were not used.

Hu-030. Putina Pueblo. (Figs. 3.12–3.16)

The town of Putina is built over a large Middle Formative through modern settlement. The site was most likely a major center occupied during Huaña II times, contemporary with Tiwanaku but without any significant contact with the Tiwanaku peoples. It is very reminiscent of the site of Balsas Pata or Pueblo Libre located outside Ayaviri and numerous other contemporary sites in the region. The settlement is located above a river in a strategic position to control traffic going through the narrow pass. Numerous monoliths were found in the street as late as 2003. However, as of 2009 almost all of these had been covered with concrete or removed for new street construction. Areas of exposed midden were found in the south and southwest sides of the town. These middens, again very similar to sites such as Balsas Pata and Qaluyu, were rich in Formative diagnostics, bone, stone tools and debris, and evidence of walls. It is likely that at one time this site looked like the Qaluyu type site, since monoliths and cut stone of this variety are usually found with such sunken courts. It is difficult to estimate the total size of the settlement, but it is between 4.0 and 7.0 ha.

The site of Putina offers a cautionary note to survey archaeologists. In 1999 and up to at least 2003, there was substantial surface evidence for a major occupation at the site. As the economy of the region has substantially improved, there has been much construction activity. All the monoliths that were once found on the street are gone—removed or paved over with concrete and asphalt. Buildings or roads now cover the midden areas. Much fill has been brought in from a few kilometers away. The adobe walls that previously held many ceramic diagnostics have been plastered and painted. In short, much of the surface evidence for a major occupation in the town has disappeared in the ten years between 1999 and 2009. Putina, from an archaeological perspective, is reminiscent of Huancané and the other urban areas in the northern Titicaca Basin. Excavation is the only way to fully understand these settlements.

Figure 3.10.
A view of the location of Hu-015 just south of Huatasani in the pampa. The site is located on the low, natural hill.

Figure 3.11.
The site of Hu-016 just south of Huatasani. The site is a terraced natural hill.

Figure 3.12.
The modern town of Putina located strategically between the ends of two ridges. The site of Hu-030 is found under the modern town.

Hu-031. (Fig. 3.14)

This is a small site, about 20 × 30 m, located above the town of Putina. There is a typical Christian pilgrimage path with stations that winds its way up the hill. At the very top is this site, characterized by a light scatter of pottery and two obsidian fragments. The pottery was largely Altiplano period II and III, with a small number of Altiplano I fragments. There was no visible architecture on the surface, though the site itself was in a very low depression no more than 25 cm deep. This is most likely a temporary camp. It could also be a ritual area.

Hu-032. (Fig. 3.17)

This is a very small, single slab cist tomb, 1.5 m in diameter. There were no artifacts on the surface. This kind of tomb is typical of the region.

Hu-033.

This is a large, dispersed site on the pampa with abundant late pottery. This site stretches over 3.0 ha and appears to be a combination of a residential area with tombs. There are numerous chulpa bases and likely structure foundations on the surface. The pottery indicates Altiplano I, II, and Inca I occupations.

Hu-034. Comunidad Mijani.

This is a small open-air Archaic site composed of a low-density scatter of lithic debris. It has obsidian, jasper, basalt, and chert waste material. There are no ceramic artifacts on the surface.

Hu-035. Comunidad Mijani.

This site has Altiplano pottery mixed in among modern and Colonial period structures and foundations at the base of a hill.

Hu-036.

This small site is located in the pampa and has some lithic debris and Altiplano period pottery.

Hu-037. Mijani.

This is a small 20 × 70 m Archaic site in the pampa with jasper, chert, obsidian, basalt, and quartz artifacts. There are no ceramic artifacts on the surface.

Hu-038. Huayllapata.

This Altiplano period site has a number of below-ground cist tombs. The density of the artifacts on the surface is very high, probably due to the extensive looting of the tombs. We cannot determine if this is a habitation site as well but it does not appear to be the case, given the general absence of stone tools. According to our local informants, pottery is manufactured in the area today, given the presence of good clay sources.

Hu-039. Condortañani.

This Altiplano period site has a number of terraces or platforms, open areas, and circular structures. It is located on the top of a high hill about 4000 m above sea level.

Hu-040. Condortañani.

This is a purely Altiplano II site with a scatter of artifacts over an area a bit under 1 ha. There is little surface evidence, although some structures can be discerned on the hillside of Cerro Quimsacuyo.

Figure 3.13. A view of Putina from a distance.

Figure 3.14. A closer view of Putina and Hu-030. The small site of Hu-031 is on top of the hill behind the town, near the towers.

Figure 3.15. An exposed section in a construction cut in the mound at Putina. A large wall can be seen in the profile.

(*right*) Figure 3.16. An uncarved monolith in Putina in 2001. Dimensions: 310 × 41 × 20 cm.

(*below*) Figure 3.17. Small, looted tomb on Hu-032. Internal diameter approximately 35 cm.

Hu-041. Comunidad Huayllapata.

This late site is located in a high area alongside a quebrada. Today, there is a bofedal or swampy area at the base of the terraces. The quebrada was terraced and used for a small habitation area.

Hu-042. Wichoqollo quilcapunku.

This is a dispersed site with very low and wide artificial terraces. Hu-042 is located at the eastern end of the survey area on a pass into the Macusani area from Putina. One of the more significant features of this site is that it has a Tiwanaku occupation, evidenced by a half dozen or so plainware kero fragments. This site represents one of just a few settlements this far from the lake with evidence of Tiwanaku pottery. It is almost certainly along a road into the forested Carabaya region. The site was founded in the Tiwanaku period and continued through the Inca period.

Hu-043. Quilcapunku.

This is a rockshelter with some lithic and ceramic artifacts. There is a light Archaic component, along with some Altiplano pottery. The site area is only about 12 m long by 5 m wide. It is a low rockshelter, located about 1 km from the river. There is no visible water source today. It represents a very transient Altiplano period occupation in this region.

Hu-044. Hachachuko; Jacha Chuco.

This is a major Altiplano period and Late Horizon site. The site spreads over almost 2.5 ha. It includes terraces and circular structures. It is on the highest part of the hill with an encircling wall about 1.30 m in width. The height of the wall was at least 5.0 m. It is not certain whether this was a defensive wall or a corral, or functioned as both.

Hu-045. Chiquiria.

This is a minor late site with a low density of Altiplano period artifacts on a few low artificial terraces. This is a typical small hamlet settlement for this period.

Hu-046. Rosaqniyoq Q'ocha.

This is a minor Altiplano period site with a low density of artifacts spread over a small area. It likely was a temporary campsite for pasturing animals.

Hu-047.

This site number was not used.

Hu-048. Hapujapupata.

The extent of the site was difficult to define. By the topography, it would appear to be about 1 ha, but judging by the surface evidence the areal extent is about half. There are two circular structures about 2 m in diameter and some fragments of Altiplano II pottery. This is most likely a lightly looted Altiplano II cemetery.

Hu-049. Kaka chupa.

There are at least six cist tombs on this site. We also noted obsidian flakes, as well as other lithic debris. The chipped stone debris suggests domestic use, but there is no other evidence for this on the surface of this nondisturbed site. The pottery is Altiplano and Inca period in date, suggesting a small hamlet.

Hu-050.

This is a small Altiplano period and Inca domestic site located on a low crest on a hill. There are two well-made artificial terraces with artifacts that extend to the top of the ridge. The terraces are between 1.0 and 1.5 m high. There were no tombs evident. The sandstone blocks used in the modern field structure were most likely obtained from Hu-014, located just below the site on the pampa.

Hu-051.

This is a low, domestic terrace site with a scatter of late artifacts. The site is set in rocks above good agricultural land. There is a modern *capilla* (chapel) today, along with a modern cemetery and corrals.

Hu-052. (Fig. 3.18)

This is a small domestic terrace site directly below some beautiful cliffs. There is midden eroding out of the terraces. This Altiplano and Inca period settlement was dispersed over a small area, and probably represented a hamlet of a few house compounds at most.

Hu-053.

This 1 ha Altiplano period site is close to the river. There is a high density of artifacts on the surface eroding out of midden accumulations. No surface architecture is evident, apart from the terraces that were possibly ancient. The area is used for net fishing today. No tombs are evident.

Hu-054.

This ridgetop has Altiplano period chulpa bases and/or slab cist tombs. It is heavily looted. There are at least four tombs, all of them round and all about 2 m in diameter. They are too badly looted to take precise measurements. The tombs are fieldstone constructions.

Hu-055. Pukara.

This is a minor Altiplano period pukara that covers about 1 ha. There is a light scatter of Altiplano II and III pottery on the surface with one Inca I sherd. There is at least one encircling wall at the top with some very poorly preserved structures. There are no tombs evident on the surface of the site. There is no evidence of permanent habitation (but see Hu-056).

Hu-056.

This site is most likely a habitation area associated with the pukara at Hu-055. There are only Altiplano period II diagnostics on what is probably a single compound. One low artificial terrace was noted on the surface, and was used as a platform for a house.

Hu-057. (Fig. 3.19)

This is a single chulpa base located on the ridge spur that drops below Hu-055. It is about 150 m from Hu-056. This chulpa is built with fieldstones and is round and quite large, about 6 m in diameter, with a 2.5 m diameter chamber.

Hu-058. (Figs. 3.19, 3.20)

The site is composed of a number of domestic terraces built on the sides of a line of vertically tilted natural ridges. There is a scatter of artifacts on the terraces, and the density of the artifacts is higher in the upper terraces. The site is located next to a river that runs through a line of ridges. The diagnostic pottery is both Formative and late in date. There are several agricultural implements and some chipped stone debris on the surface. These andesite groundstone tools are usually associated with Formative settlements.

Hu-059. (Figs. 3.19, 3.21)

This is a single feature associated with sites Hu-011, Hu-058, and Hu-129. It is a 3 × 5 m set of upright, uncut stones that resembles a large

Figure 3.18.
The site area of Hu-052.

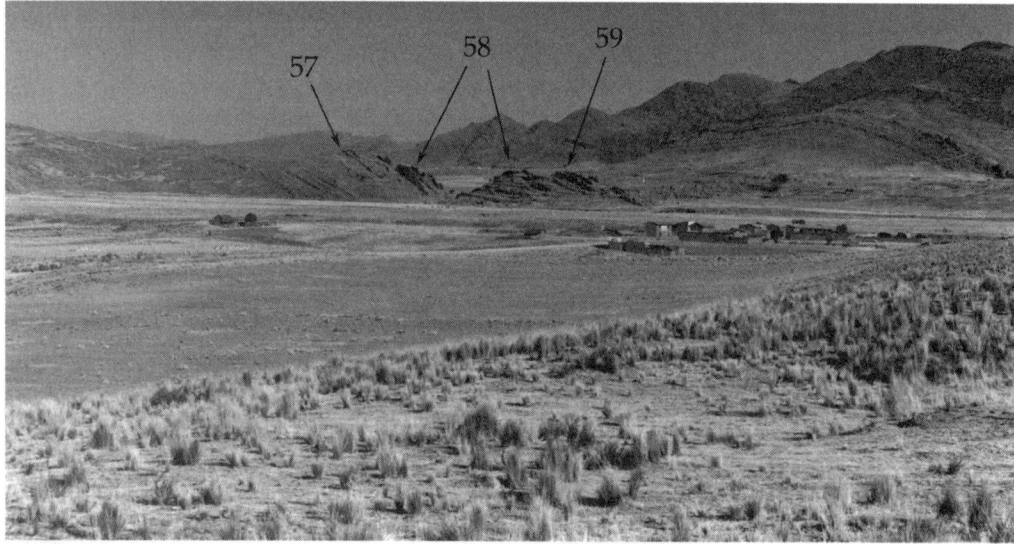

Figure 3.19.
Site locations of Hu-057, Hu-058, and Hu-059.

Figure 3.20.
A close-up of the site area of Hu-058.

Figure 3.21. A close-up of the site area of Hu-059.

chulpa, but not a very carefully built one. This feature is in the same complex as Hu-058. It is larger than slab cist tombs and the spacing between the stones is rare. The function of this feature is unknown but it is curious that there are diagnostics from all Altiplano types as well as Inca I. This suggests that this was an area continuously visited or utilized by pastoralists for a long period of time.

Hu-060.
This is an Altiplano period site located near the modern, and probably ancient, road. There are five artificial terraces, about 75 m long and built about 10 m apart.

Hu-061.
This is a small scatter of Altiplano period I and II pottery with some modern or Colonial period structures. It is likely that some of the rocks used in these structures were quarried from an earlier site.

Hu-062.
This is a small Altiplano period scatter that represents a single household.

Hu-063.
This is a small Late Horizon cemetery.

Hu-064.
These are linear raised fields, not in use today. These raised fields cover an area of at least 50 × 200 m.

Hu-065.
This is a minor pukara that has a very light scatter of Formative III and Altiplano period pottery. The hill looks like a classic minor pukara with several encircling walls. Also, there are a number of well-made enclosures and structures on the surface. The surface artifacts are very light, supporting the observation that this is a minor pukara that was not inhabited. The existence of Late Formative pottery suggests that this site served defensive purposes during this time.

Hu-066.
This is a single slab cist tomb or chulpa base about 3–4 m in diameter. There is a 1–1.5 m internal chamber evident in this fieldstone tomb. It is an isolated tomb on a remote hill.

Hu-067. (Fig. 3.22)
This is a moderately-sized Altiplano period and Early Colonial habitation site associated with a modern occupation. The site is built underneath and adjacent to a natural rock face. Some grinding stones were noted on the surface of the site.

Hu-068. (Figs. 3.23, 3.24)
This is a large Formative and late site scattered over a hilltop and hillsides. It is likely that the Formative occupation was also fortified and that at least the later use of the site was as a typical pukara. There are several encircling walls and a number of structures on the top of the hill. The structures are poorly preserved and appear to be square or rectangular in construction style. On the north side of the hill is a series

Figure 3.22. The site of Hu-067.

Figure 3.23. Site location of Hu-068.

Figure 3.24. Hu-068 from the base of the hill.

of artificial terraces that have a light scatter of artifacts. The top of the hill contains a much denser artifact scatter, including many andesite hoes or hoe fragments. Such hoe fragments are common at Formative sites.

There is a quebrada at the northern end of the site. This quebrada has water today and there is a trail that follows it up into the hillside that informants say leads to the large antenna outside Putina. Below the quebrada is a canal that draws water to the pampa below.

Hu-069.

This is a late site adjacent to and below Hu-068. (It also has one Formative II sherd.) It is located at the edge of the quebrada. The inhabitants of this site most likely utilized the defensive walls of Hu-068.

Hu-070. Incachupa.

This is a large pukara on a low area. There is a set of defensive walls with many large, circular structures inside. This is a major pukara, in our typology, with permanent habitation inside. The defensive walls are double-coursed, with a rubble fill, a construction technique consistent with the ceramics dating to Altiplano periods I and II and early Inca (Inca I). The circular structures are approximately 2 to 4 m in diameter.

Hu-071. Huasunta.

This is a small scatter of Altiplano II pottery. There is a possible ancient spring nearby. There are no artificial terraces, just a scatter of artifacts.

Hu-072.

This is a scatter of Formative and Altiplano period pottery located adjacent to a rock outcrop. There is a quebrada nearby that discharges water into the pampa. In the rainy season, it creates a bofedal or swampy area right below the site.

Hu-073. Torrance Sur.

This small site, which has a scatter of Formative and Altiplano pottery, is located on the top of a ridge. There is little evidence of tombs or structures, though some of the Inca I pottery may be associated with a badly looted tomb. The site is located directly above a swampy area in the pampa. There is a transverse wall built to hold water in a crude reservoir. The date of this wall is unknown. The owner of the land has a cousin who lives in Torrance, California.

Hu-074.

This is a scatter of Altiplano period II artifacts on a high hill above the pampa. There is no evidence of tombs or structures.

Hu-075.

This site is located on a rocky crest of a hill above the pampa. It has Formative III and Altiplano II and III diagnostics. There is a curious long wall that runs roughly northeast-southwest, cutting across the rock face. This Formative and Altiplano period site is a light occupation without evidence of tombs or structures.

Hu-076.

This is a light scatter of Altiplano period pottery on three artificial terraces. There is no evidence of tombs or structures.

Hu-077. (Fig. 3.25)

This Formative and Altiplano site is located in a very high location on the side of a steep mountain. The site sits on a natural ridge that juts out of the hill and provides a flat living space. Surface artifact density is light. There is a large wall that runs perpendicular to the mountain side. The wall fall is wide, about 2 m in diameter. There are at least two rectangular structures still surviving. One is 4 × 3 m, and the second is 3.5

Figure 3.25. The high mesa sites of Hu-077 and Hu-078 on the side of the ridge that leads to Putina.

× 4.0 m. Below the structures on a narrow ridge is a wall that appears to be defensive, in that it cuts across the only access to the structures. This wall could also be used to corral animals. This is additional evidence that the Formative period had defensive sites.

Hu-078. (Figs. 3.25, 3.26)

This site is located on the side of a steep mountain. It sits in a natural ridge that juts out of the mountainside. There is a moderate density of artifacts on the surface, including many agricultural implements. There are a number of upright, unshaped stones that may have been from a larger structure. One stone structure is still visible. It measures 3.0 × 3.5 m. The entire site is Formative in date although the area is currently cultivated. It is possible that the structure is later in date than the occupation, having functioned as a field house for cultivation. This is additional evidence that the Formative period witnessed an investment in defending their settlements.

Hu-079.

This is a small Formative and Altiplano period II site located in a natural depression on a ridgetop. There is a moderate surface artifact density. There is a wall that may have blocked access to the site for defensive purposes.

Hu-080.

See Hu-081.

Hu-081. (Fig. 3.27)

This is a large Formative site located on a high location. The surface artifact density is high, and all diagnostic sherds are Formative in date. The site sits on a natural saddle on a point where the mountain ridge widens out. The site has a series of low, artificial terraces in the saddle and on the sides of the hills surrounding the saddle. There is a large domestic component on the site, but no evidence of corporate architecture. There are abundant agricultural implements, particularly hoes, on the site surface. Surrounding the habitation area of the site is a number of agricultural terraces that are still utilized today. The agriculture is supported by rainfall, not irrigation. There is little evidence of defensive walls, with the exception of Hu-082, but the high location would have been naturally defensible. A single carbon date collected by Lisa Cipolla from a basal feature in a structure on the site was 1994 +/- 42 BP.[1] This date confirms the ceramic diagnostic evidence. Hu-081 is outstanding evidence that defense played a key role in settlement location and overall settlement patterning in the Formative periods.

Site number Hu-080 was originally assigned to a single slab cist tomb, 2.5 m in diameter, that was on the edge of Hu-081. The tomb was built with fieldstone masonry. No artifacts were associated with the tomb.

Hu-082.

This was assigned to a large wall, about 1.0 m in width and up to 1.0 m high in some sections. The wall is in the site area of Hu-081.

Hu-083.

This is a small group of linear raised fields. They are not in use today and cover about 1.0 ha.

Hu-084.

This is a modern, abandoned structure.

---

1. AA53817, Charcoal, Hu-081.P11, 1994 +/- 42; 108 calBC (94.2%) 87 calAD using IntCal 09, OxCal 4.1.

Figure 3.26. A close-up of structures on the site area of Hu-078.

Figure 3.27. A view of the site area of Hu-081.

Hu-085.

This is an Altiplano or Inca period chulpa base, about 2 m in diameter. The chulpa was fieldstone and there was no pottery associated with the tomb area.

Hu-086, Hu-087.

These two site numbers were assigned to sets of ancient agricultural terraces that were notable for their isolation and lack of any associated habitation areas detectable from the surface.

Hu-088.

These are two isolated cists, 1.5 m in diameter, located on the crest of a hill. Both were looted, and did not have any associated artifacts on the surface nearby. These are almost certainly tombs.

Hu-089.

This number was assigned to a single, one-course wall oriented to 130/310 degrees. It was roughly parallel to the present trail. It is essentially an ancient wall on a high ridge without any associated tombs or structures evident from the surface.

Hu-090.

There were a number of curious features in this area even though there was no pottery or other artifacts on the surface. There was a set of eroded, ancient agricultural terraces built with low walls. About 30 m below these on the valley side of the ridge was a set of two large terraces. These latter artificial terraces were also quite old and surprisingly high, about 0.75 to 1.0 m. There is also another isolated, single wall similar to Hu-089. This raises that possibility that there was a road on this ridge with abutting walls on the low sides, a typical construction technique in other areas of the Titicaca Basin for roads in high rainfall areas.

Hu-091.

This is a very small, late scatter of late artifacts. There are no tombs or other structures evident on the surface. We did not make a collection.

Hu-092.

This is a rectangular structure, 26 × 32 m in size and on top of a low hill. The structure is poorly made with walls that come out at 45-degree angles. Below the structure are some terraces oriented to fit the contour of the hill. There is no pottery on the surface. It is possibly a corral, and is certainly late in date.

Hu-093.

This site consists of three slab cist tombs or chulpa bases that measure 2.0 m, 2.2 m, and 3.0 m in diameter. We did not make a collection.

Hu-094.

Reminiscent of Hu-077, this site has a long wall on top of the ridge on the southern end of the site that meets a set of walls that flare out and encircle the rest of the site. This is similar to a type 3 site with a series of terraces up the hill. There appears to be a single court here, about 30 × 30 m in dimension. This would make it a very large court indeed, perhaps one of the largest in the region. On the upper part are high mounds of rocks that look similar to the rubble at Hu-014. The platform and terraces are well made. The court is close to cardinally oriented. The site is about 4.0 ha in size.

The northern side of the site has a beautiful set of terraces, about seven in total. At the base is a rectangular platform, 90 × 135 m. It is quite large, well prepared, and flat. There is little pottery. This platform is almost cardinally oriented, about 5 degrees off magnetic north.

On the west side of the site is another platform, about 28 × 90 m, with internal divisions of 7 × 14 m, 10 × 14 m, 13 × 14 m, and so forth. The divisions are obviously not even. Between the north and west platforms is another platform, 40 × 65 m and oriented 288/108 degrees. On this one, there are no internal divisions.

The entire effect of the architecture is to give a low, terraced hill with a series of platforms at its base. The platforms appear to be structure compounds. The site has Formative and later occupations. The lower platforms are reminiscent of Hu-014 and are probably Formative in date. A possible exception is the western platform with the more regular (14 m long) units. This could be late. The pottery is Formative and Altiplano, indicating a Formative period construction with a later reoccupation.

Hu-095.

This site is a 2.0 ha settlement with Formative and Altiplano period occupations. There are irregular structures and a probable sunken court at the top. The court area is characterized by a depression that is difficult to accurately measure, but it is not larger than 20 × 20 m, and is probably smaller.

Hu-096.

This is a small, dispersed Late Horizon site with no visible architecture or tombs.

Hu-097.

This is a set of at least four late cist tombs, all about 1.0 m in diameter. There were no artifacts on the surface.

Hu-098.

This site is composed of a small set of disturbed late period tombs or possibly a very small domestic area without evidence of habitation or other structures.

Hu-099.

This is an Archaic locus with materials eroding off a natural terrace above the river on the flat pampa. There is an area below the site and adjacent to the river that would have been an ideal location for animals—low and swampy. This locus has a high density of lithic debris and a high variety of materials. There is a scatter of Formative sherds as well. See Hu-101 to Hu-106.

Hu-100.

This pampa site consists of at least two heavily eroded and looted cist tombs with Altiplano period pottery.

Hu-101–Hu-106.

These are all loci of high artifact concentrations that make a sprawling area of Archaic sites on the pampa along the river on the first natural terrace (Table 3.3). A test excavation by Lisa Cipolla at the site of Hu-105 provided a basal date of 5091+/- 47 BP.[2]

Hu-107.

This is a light scatter of Altiplano period and Late Horizon pottery with no evidence of structures or tombs.

---

2. AA53818, Charcoal, Hu-105.P.10, 5091 +/- 47; 3979 (95.4%) 3778 calBC using IntCal 09, OxCal 4.1.

Table 3.3. All Archaic sites recorded in the survey.*

Site #	Site Name	Elevation (masl)	Type**	Und. Arc	EA	MA	LA	TA	Un TA-LH
3	Huancahuichinca	3855	H/C/R					X	X
6	Miyuraya	3853	H/C				X		
14	Cachichupa	3842	H/C/R				X		X
34	Comunidad Mijani	3924	T	X				X	
37	Mijani	3951	T	X					
43	Quilcapunco	3973	T	X					
99		3875	H/T	X		X	X	X	
101		3850	T	X					
102		3855	T	X			X	?	
103		3860	H/T	X		X	X	X	
104		3860	T	X					
105		3863	T	X			X		
106		3860	T						X
113	Pampa Mijani	3869	T/H	X		X	X		X
114		3861	T	X					
115	T'ojopata	4100	T/H						X
117	Comunidad Caya-caya	4165	T						X
128	Marumpuncu	3830	T/H	X					
165	Qapuya	3885	T	X					
176	Huatasani area	3851	T	X					
201	Tintiña Pata	3821	H/T	X					
202	Tintiña Pata	3835	H/T	X					
211		3850	H/T	X					
217		3829	H/T	X					
246	Pampa de Quella'huyo	3873	H	X					
247	Saltocarca	3839	T	X			X		X
248	Huata	3856	H/C/R/T	X					
250		3823	T	X					
253		3845	T/C	X					
263		3904	C/R/T	X					
276	part of Hu-003	3840	H/R	X					
280	Huarisa	3890	H/C	X			X		X
285	Chacacruz	3854	H/T	X					
286		3863	T	X					
296		3833	T/C	X					
297		3854	H	X					
300		3922	H/C						X
304		4005	H/C	X					
310		3851	H	X					X
315		3880	H/T						X
316	Machacamarca	3927	H/R/D/C				X		
326		4187	T					?	
343		3858	C/T	X					
349		3851	H/C	X					X
359		3849	T	X		X	X		
364		4100	T				X		X
367		3839	T	X					
368		3837	T				X		X
373		3853	T	X					
374		3880	T/C	X					
379		3868	T/C	X					
380		3849	T				X		X
381	Cerro Kuyuraya	3864	H/C			X	X		X
382	Kulluraya	3866	H/C						X
385		3866	H/C	X					
387		3868	H						X
391		3848	T			X			
396		3868	H/T	X					
406	Jinchu huichinka/Inchuyu	3861	H/C	X	X	X		X	X
412		3963	H/C/T/D	X		X			X
417		3869	H/C						X
420	Callapani	3873	H/T	X					
422		3877	H/T	X					
427	Comunidad Jurata	3858	H/T	X					
428	Comunidad Jurata	3857	H/R	X					
448	Comunidad Tahurauta	3871	C			X		?	
452	Pichacane	4058	H/C/T/D				X		
457	Cerro Condorhuachani	4148	H/D				X		
458		4069	T	X					
459		3869	T/C	X					
463	Comunidad Tahurauta	3891	T	X					
480		3872	H	X					
481		3880	H	X					
482		3859	T		X		X		
483		3848	T/H				X	?	
484		3847	T		X	X			
485		3847	T		X		X	X	X

Table 3.3 cont.

Site #	Site Name	Elevation (masl)	Type**	Und. Arc	EA	MA	LA	TA	Un TA-LH
486		3846	T/H		X		X		X
487		3845	T				X	?	
488		3845	T		X		X	?	X
489		3846	T/H			X	X		
490	Río Cala Cala	3844	T			X	X		
491	Río Cala Cala	3846	T				X	?	
492	Río Cala Cala	3845	T	X					
493	Río Salto	3856	T/H			X			X
494		3860	T/H						
495		3878	H				X		
496	Comunidad Queallo	3879	T/H						X
497		3871	H	X					
498	Comunidad Queallo	3868	H	X					
502		3899	H	X					
506	Tupu huyu	3922	H/C					X	X
507	Comunidad Queallo	3909	H/C	X					X
508	Comunidad Queallo	3924	H/C						X
517	Cerro Trallate	4045	T/H	X					
521		4029	H						X
522		3923	C/T			X			X
537	Ninacarca	3853	H						X

*The Archaic component of multi-period sites tends to be very small. Elevations taken on the Archaic scatters within larger sites are usually different than the elevations taken in the center of the entire site listed in Table 3.1 or Table 3.2. The elevations in this table were taken on the Archaic component only.
**C: cemetery; T: temporary camp; D: defensive; R: ritual; U: unknown; H: habitation

Hu-108.
This is a small chipped stone workshop on the pampa with Altiplano period II sherds. There is an upright, uncarved rock standing in the middle of the site that may or may not be culturally significant.

Hu-109. (Fig. 3.28)
This is a modest Altiplano period and Inca period site with walls that have the look and feel of a tambo. It is located at the base of a hill in Bellavista, a small, well-watered area with a number of houses tucked up in a fertile section of the research area. There is a standing, uncarved monolith in the area. There are very few objects on the surface but the existing ones date to the later periods.

Hu-110.
This is a very light scatter of nondiagnostic pottery fragments. It is most likely late in date.

Hu-111.
This is a typical Altiplano period site on a ridgetop with a scatter of Altiplano II sherds. There are two round structures that measure approximately 3.0 and 3.5 m in diameter. These may be unlooted slab cist tombs or structure foundations for temporary dwellings.

Hu-112. (Fig. 3.29)
This modest Altiplano period site is located in a high, flat area. It has a number of circular structures and tombs and was a modest hamlet during this period. The structures measure between 3 and 4 m in diameter.

Hu-113. Pampa Mijani. (Fig. 3.30)
This is a very important Archaic site located in the Pampa Mijani. It is located on a very low knoll in the middle of a periodically inundated pampa. The site is small, about 30 m on a side, but has a very high density of lithic flakes and chipping debris. This is clearly a workshop area with substantial debris on the surface. This would have been an ideal area to hunt during the rainy season. There is also a small scatter of Altiplano II sherds on this site.

Hu-114.
This is an Archaic site. It is, like Hu-113, located on a low hill in the pampa with a full range of lithic flakes and chipping debris on the surface. Like Hu-113, this site would have been an ideal area to hunt during the rainy season. There is also an Altiplano II occupation on the site.

Hu-115. T'ojopata.
This is a small Archaic and reoccupied Altiplano period site with a set of poorly preserved, squarish structures about 2.0 × 2.0 m in dimension. There are also some very irregular structures, and one possible slab cist tomb, about 1.3 m in diameter. The site is located high, at about 4100 m above sea level, on the side of a hill near a small quebrada.

Hu-116. Laq'oni.
This is a small Altiplano period and Late Horizon site with a set of poorly preserved, circular structures about 2 m in diameter. The site is very high, over 4300 m above sea level, on the side of the mountain. The site is on a low hill on a flat area on the mountainside and appears to be ritual in nature. There is no evidence for tombs and the pottery was nondescript but obviously Altiplano and Inca.

Hu-117. Comunidad Caya-Caya.
This is a single Archaic point found at more than 4100 m above sea level.

Hu-118. Cantacanta.
This Formative and Altiplano period site is very high, at about 4400 m above sea level. It is on the hilltop where today there are a large number of modern ritual remains. The site is covered with structures, cist tombs, slab cist tombs, and possible chulpa bases. There are more than 40 structures evident on the surface of the site. There is also a large quantity of

Figure 3.28. Standing, uncarved monolith at Hu-109.

bola stones on the surface. The site is 1 ha in size and has Formative I and III and Altiplano II materials. While the site is very high up, and in a defensive location, there are no walls. The existence of bola stones may indicate a defensive function. It appears to be a largely ritual site.

Hu-119. Cheqtaq'ollo.
This site has a high quantity of artifacts on the surface, including ceramics and lithic fragments. There is a substantial Formative period occupation. The quality of the Inca pottery is impressive. We also recovered a number of modern glass fragments and pottery wasters. There is a dense occupation of circular houses, tombs, open areas, and large terrace walls.

Hu-120. Comunidad Caya-Caya.
This small site is a dispersal of late pottery from some disturbed below-ground tombs and small habitation structures.

Hu-121.
This very small site with a few nondiagnostic sherds is located on the pampa near the river. The ceramics all looked late or modern. We did not make a collection. There is a modern cocha nearby.

Hu-122. Comunidad Caya-Caya.
This very small Altiplano period cemetery is located on a low ridge. It has a number of cist tombs on a low rise in the pampa.

Hu-123. Huayyapata.
This very small Altiplano period cemetery is located on a low ridge. It has a number of cist tombs on a low rise in the pampa. We did not make a collection.

Hu-125.
This small hilltop site has a very low dispersal of late sherds associated with circular structures around open areas. This site is a habitation area.

Hu-126. Acapana.
This curiously-named locality is a natural mound with what appears to be an artificially-flattened area on top. The entire mound is covered with some Formative and later pottery. There are two fragments of Tiwanaku pottery that suggest an occupation here. This is similar to the surveys in the Juli-Pomata and Mazocruz regions where we find sites with substantial numbers of Formative fragments and a few Tiwanaku ones. As in these cases, the sites are located on the road near a river. There does not appear to be any corporate architecture on the site, although this would have to be tested. There are a number of lithic fragments and agricultural implements on the site surface. The Tiwanaku occupation is significant, being one of the northernmost sites of this time period in the survey area. The site is on the road, and the occupation would constitute a site with Tiwanaku materials on the route to the eastern slopes.

Figure 3.29. Site area of Hu-112 showing partial remains of a circular structure.

Figure 3.30. Site area of Hu-113.

Hu-127. Comunidad Caya-Caya.

This is a pampa mound close to the river, about 150 m away, with Formative and later occupations. The natural mound appears to be artificially modified on top, to give a truncated pyramid form. The mound is heavily eroded. Lithic debris—including jasper, chalcedony, and more common materials—is scattered on the surface. There are no evident tombs or other structures visible.

Hu-128. Marumpuncu.

Marumpuncu is located in a natural outcrop with a number of artificial terraces and very poorly-preserved structures. It is near the river. This site has a number of occupations, from the Archaic through modern. Diagnostic pottery includes Formative, Huaña, Altiplano, and Late Horizon. There are numerous lithic fragments on the surface, including obsidian and other exotic raw materials, indicating an Archaic component. Unfortunately, the collection bags never appeared in the lab and were most likely lost in Huancané.

Hu-129.

This site was renumbered as Hu-058.

Hu-130.

This is a dispersed site below a natural rock outcrop. There are a number of fragments on the surface and a series of very low terraces. The curious feature about this site is that there are at least two depressions that could be sunken courts. The area is badly damaged now, but these deserve intensive investigations. The collection for this site was also lost. The period attributions are based upon the field observations.

Hu-131. Laq'oni.

This late site has a scatter of pottery and a number of lithic fragments scattered over an area of about 1.75 ha. There are agricultural implements on the surface. A series of artificial terraces gives the impression of an access to a higher platform area.

Hu-132. Catarani Haja.

This is a natural mound in the pampa that has Formative artifacts scattered on the surface. It is close to the river. There is no evidence of corporate construction and there are no structures or tombs visible on the surface.

Hu-133. Subida a Catarani.

This is a natural mound in the pampa that has a late occupation. The site is next to the river. There is no evidence of corporate construction and there are no structures or tombs visible on the surface.

Hu-134. Tuquni Q'ocho.

This small site has a few fragments of Late Horizon pottery and some lithic artifacts. There is one artificial terrace with some open areas and possible structures. The structures are circular, but are very badly preserved. There is no evidence of corporate construction and there are no structures or tombs visible on the surface.

Hu-135.

This late site is a pampa mound with a large quantity of Local Inca and Altiplano period diagnostic pottery on the surface.

Hu-136. Catarani Nuñomoq'o.

This Formative and Huaña period site is located on a low natural mound at the base of a hill. The site has a likely sunken court or other corporate construction as evidenced by an obvious platform with lines of walls forming rectangular and square irregular structures. Fragments of decorated pottery and lithic debris are found over the site area.

Hu-137. Santa Cruz de Catarani.

This moderately sized late site has a few artificial terraces that are now agricultural. It is located near a quebrada. There is no evidence of tombs. The pottery is late in style.

Hu-138. Pojsorunipata.

This is a natural mound on the side of the pampa with a scatter of late artifacts.

Hu-139. Pucachaca.

This is a small late site with a scatter of pottery and lithics. There is no evidence for tombs.

Hu-140. Condorwachana.

This site is located on the top of the highest mountain in the community of Caya Caya, at almost 4500 m above sea level, clearly deserving its name. It is an "apu" for this community. The site has a small Altiplano period component spread over a 0.25 ha area. This site is almost certainly ritual in nature.

Hu-154. Buena Vista.

This is a major site that was occupied during the Formative and late periods. The site is now a village with houses and open areas. In the north side of the site are some terraces with abundant pottery and lithics on the surface. Small, circular looted tombs are noted across the settlement. The site is located within 300 m of the river and there is a bofedal about 200 m to the south. The modern occupation has obscured most of the site's architecture.

Hu-155.

This is a single circular chulpa base made with fieldstones. It is about 3.0 m in diameter. There were no artifacts on the surface.

Hu-156. Comunidad Torno.

This site is located in the pampa on a small natural mound. There is a depression on top of the hill that could be a sunken court. This speculation is supported by the presence of Formative II and III and Huaña I pottery. There is a high quantity of lithic debris, including obsidian points, quartz, and other nonlocal raw materials.

Hu-157. Qlocho.

This is a late site with several low artificial terraces. It is located at the base of a hill adjacent to a small quebrada.

Hu-158. Wilaqarqa.

This is an Altiplano through Inca site with several low artificial terraces. Some of the stones in the terraces are slabs that were probably pulled from an earlier construction. There is at least one cist tomb, less than 1.0 m in diameter.

Hu-159. Wilaqarqa Chupa.

This habitation site has a number of cist tombs, circular structures of approximately 1.20 m, and terraced platforms. There is a Formative occupation and an Altiplano/Inca reoccupation. There is a natural mica source on this site. A possible uncarved stela is found on a natural rocky area above. Near the possible stela is a possible sunken court as evidenced by a small depression. It is virtually impossible to estimate, but the court would most likely be small, 12 m long or less.

Hu-160. Challwanipata.

This cemetery site has a number of circular cist tombs and slab cist tombs. The site also has a worked natural rock with small depressions. A few Formative II sherds were found in an otherwise largely Altiplano and Inca period site.

Hu-161. Comunidad Torno.

This is a natural mound in the pampa with a scatter of Altiplano and Inca period artifacts over the elevated part of the mound. There are a number of obsidian fragments, along with other nonlocal raw materials. There are no artifacts on the pampa off the mound. This is a pattern typical of Archaic sites, yet we found no diagnostics from that period. One Formative sherd was collected as well.

Hu-162. Chijora.

This is a natural mound in the pampa with a scatter of late artifacts over the elevated part of the mound. There are a number of obsidian fragments, along with other nonlocal raw materials.

Hu-163. Caya caya.

This is a small, natural mound in the pampa about 50 m from the river with Formative and later materials. There are a number of lithic artifacts on the surface, including debris from nonlocal raw materials. The mound has a group of cist tombs as well.

Hu-164. Caya caya.

This site number was assigned to a set of large walls with large blocks. There are no artifacts or other structures on the surface.

Hu-165. Qapuya.

This is an Archaic site located below a rock outcrop. It is located near a bofedal. There are a number of lithic artifacts on the surface, including debris from nonlocal raw materials. There are no diagnostic bifaces and the lithic assemblage suggests a workshop.

Hu-166. Pampa de Wilaqalqa.

This location is characterized by a number of cochas on both sides of the Putina River. There are a few fragments of diagnostic pottery near the cochas including Formative and late types. It does not appear to be a habitation site.

Hu-167. Cerro Cuñuna.

This is a Huaña site area that includes some rockshelters and a hilltop. There are cist tombs in the shelters, as well as tombs along the crest of the hill. There are some very large blocks that may have been used in another construction that has been destroyed.

Hu-168. Comunidad Ajarani.

This is a scatter of late diagnostics over the sides and top of a low hill about 600 m from the river. There are no evident tombs or other structures.

Hu-169.

This is a late site at the base of a hill, next to a quebrada, that covers at least 1, and possibly 2, ha. The site is composed of a number of *canchas* and terraces with a low density of artifacts on the surface.

Hu-172. Calvario. (Figs. 3.31, 3.32)

This is a Formative regional center located at the top of a high hill above the town of Huatasani. There is a sunken court at the top made with red sandstones. The court appears to be trapezoidal in shape. The dimensions from the surface indicate a court about 11 m long on the short width, 13 m on the two even sides, and 18 m on the long wall of the trapezoid. Like the classic type 3 sites in the region, Hu-172 has a large number of terraces that surround the temple on the top. The site is located in a highly defensible location, but there are no obvious defensive walls as seen on the later pukaras. There is a substantial Altiplano occupation. The landowner requested no measuring so we could not take the precise orientation of the court but the alignment is about 5 degrees off north.

Hu-173. Kulqupunku.

This is a small mound next to the river below site Hu-172. It is a small Formative and late site associated with the Huatasani complex.

Hu-174. Cerro Amayapata.

This site has a number of artificial terraces with round structures, on the sides up to the top of a hill. Fragments of Formative, Tiwanaku I, Altiplano, and Inca pottery were found on the site as well as a large quantity of lithic debris and agricultural implements.

Hu-175. Quilcapuncu. (Fig. 3.33)

This is a small scatter of late pottery on the surface at the base and on the side of a low hill. There is a double-coursed wall that runs roughly east-west. The remains of recent pagos are found on this site. This is the far eastern end of the survey area and represents a major pass into the Macusani area and then into the eastern lowlands.

Hu-176.

This is a series of Altiplano and Inca period tombs on a low ridge. These are small, slab cist tombs with a moderate level of ancient and modern debris. There are some nondiagnostic Archaic materials as well.

Hu-200. Tintiña Pata-Lariata.

This is a dispersed site on a low rise above a periodically inundated area. There are a number of lithic artifacts on the surface. The site represents a Formative and late habitation area.

Hu-201. Tintiña Pata.

This is a dispersed site on a low rise above a periodically inundated area. There are a number of lithic artifacts on the surface. The site has a habitation area with Archaic, Formative, and late occupations.

Hu-202. Tintiña Pata.

This is a dispersed site on a low rise above a periodically inundated area. There are a number of lithic artifacts on the surface. The site has an Archaic component and Altiplano period and Late Horizon occupations.

Hu-203. Tintiña Pata.

This is a dispersed site on a low rise above a periodically inundated area. There are a number of lithic artifacts on the surface. The site represents a late habitation area.

Hu-204. Parcialidad Lariata. (Figs. 3.34, 3.37)

This small but important Formative period site is located at the base of a major hill, Luriata. Two broad terraces that start at the base of the hill and climb up the sides characterize the site area. There are numerous lithic artifacts, including obsidian and other artifacts of nonlocal raw materials. It is part of the complex that includes Hu-205.

Site Descriptions

Figure 3.31. Sunken court on Hu-172 outlined in white.

Figure 3.32. Wall of sunken court on Hu-172.

Figure 3.33. Site area of Hu-175.

Figure 3.34. Site area of Hu-204.

Hu-205. Queajachi. (Figs. 3.35–3.39)

This 3.0 ha site is a major Formative, Huaña, and Tiwanaku settlement with a late component located at the base of Cerro Luriata. It is at the end of the hill as it flattens onto the pampa on the edge of the Río Huancané. The site is located adjacent to the modern road and almost certainly was on the ancient road system for movement between the Huancané area and the northwestern side of the lake. The edge of this hill was artificially modified to make a platform mound with two levels. The river curves around the site and artifacts are found up to the river's edge. Notable surface artifacts include Tiwanaku pottery, decorated Formative pottery, a wide variety of stone raw materials, agricultural implements, and copper fragments.

There is a large number of cut stones on the surface that suggests that there was a sunken court or some other kind of corporate construction at this site that was destroyed in the past.

This site was originally numbered Hu-023.

Site Descriptions

Figure 3.35. Hu-205 from a distance.

Figure 3.36. Sites Hu-205, Hu-526, Hu-527, Hu-532, and Hu-533 from a distance.

Figure 3.37. Site area of Hu-204 and Hu-205.

Figure 3.38. Site of Hu-205.

Figure 3.39. Cut stone on the site of Hu-205.

Hu-206. Iglesia Adventista.

This is a small site located on a low mound in the pampa with a substantial Tiwanaku and later occupation. There is a Formative II fragment on the site as well. There are a number of lithic artifacts on the surface and a scatter of pottery fragments. The site represents a habitation area. Two whole vessels, one an Inca I piece and the other either Altiplano or Inca I, were shown to the crew and drawn on the sketch map. These were not collected.

Hu-207. Parcialidad Lariata.

This is a very small Huaña I and late site located on a low mound in the pampa. There are a number of lithic artifacts on the surface and a scatter of late pottery fragments. The site represents a late habitation area.

Hu-208. Parcialidad Lariata.

This is a Formative III and late site located on a low mound in the pampa. There are a number of lithic artifacts on the surface and a scatter of late pottery fragments. The site represents a late habitation area.

Hu-209. Tintiña Pata.

This is a small site located on the top of a small promontory. There are also intrusive tombs on the site. The pottery from the primary occupation is Formative in date, and there are later diagnostics from the intrusive tombs. There is one Huaña II and one Tiwanaku II sherd in the collection, but these were insufficient to assign an occupation.

Hu-210. Tintiña Pata.

This is most likely a disturbed Altiplano period cemetery site located on a low rise in the pampa.

Hu-211.

This is a late site with an Archaic component, located on a low mound in the pampa. There are a number of lithic artifacts on the surface and a scatter of late pottery fragments. The site represents a late habitation area.

Hu-212.

This is a late cemetery site located on a low mound in the pampa. There are a number of human bones on the surface and a scatter of late pottery fragments associated with slab cist tombs. The site represents a disturbed late cemetery area.

Hu-213.

This is a late site located on a low mound in the pampa with some badly disturbed structure walls, most likely late tombs. The site is either a habitation area or a disturbed cemetery. No artifacts were found on the surface.

Hu-214. Tintiña Pata.

This is a late site located on a low mound in the pampa. There are a number of lithic artifacts on the surface and a scatter of late pottery fragments. The site has Formative, Altiplano period, and Late Horizon occupations in a habitation area.

Hu-215.

This is a Formative and late site located on a low mound in the pampa. There are a number of lithic artifacts on the surface and a scatter of late pottery fragments and a few Formative ones.

Hu-216.

This is a Formative, Huaña II, Tiwanaku II, and late site located on a low mound in the pampa. There are a number of lithic artifacts on the surface and a scatter of late pottery fragments. The site represents a habitation area occupied throughout a long sequence.

Hu-217.

This is a site located on a low mound in the pampa and has Formative, Tiwanaku, and late pottery. There are a number of lithic artifacts on the surface that represent an Archaic occupation.

Hu-218. Siaquello Parcialidad.

This site is located on a low mound in the pampa. There are a number of lithic artifacts on the surface and a scatter of late pottery fragments. The site represents an Altiplano period and Late Horizon habitation area with a possible Huaña occupation as well.

Hu-219. Cerro Cacachi. (Figs. 3.40, 3.41)

This very significant settlement has occupations from Qaluyu through Pucara, Huaña I, Tiwanaku, Altiplano period, and Late Horizon. The site area covers 4 to 5 ha on a hill in the middle of the pampa. The hill is covered with well-made terraces. Some of the terrace walls are clearly defensive walls that have been converted into modern agricultural planting surfaces. The walls follow the classic pattern of protecting the weakest areas with the largest walls while using the natural cliffs to augment the defense. One wall actually has an "indented trace" or zigzag pattern, a feature rarely seen in Titicaca Basin pukaras (though this is found in Inca sites such as Sacsahuaman and Inkallacta in Bolivia). There are numerous chulpas and cist and slab cist tombs on the site. Artifacts are found over the entire site. There are agricultural implements, grinding stones, obsidian, and substantial quantities of lithics made from local chert. Likewise, there are a number of Formative and Tiwanaku diagnostics, along with the more common Altiplano period and Late Horizon types.

At the top of the hill, there is a depression and shaped stones suggestive of a sunken court. It is very difficult to determine the size give substantial disturbance.

We made numerous smaller collections over the entire hill and sides. Collection 219-03 was made at the top of the hill and it contained a high percentage of Formative sherds. The existence of a very dense Formative I through Huaña I occupation on the top of the hill reinforces the idea that defensive considerations were significant settlement determinants in these early periods.

Hu-220. Cerro Cacachi. (Fig. 3.42)

This is a single, circular, fieldstone, chulpa base, approximately 2.8 m in diameter. It has a double-row stone wall. There were no artifacts on the surface of this site. Most curious is the large Formative monolith associated with the chulpa. The monolith, approximately 4 m long and made of sandstone, is in a classic Middle Formative style with the typical indentation at the top. It was most likely dragged from Hu-219 and either was used in the construction of the chulpa (unlikely) or was ritually associated with the chulpa (more likely). Alternatively, the most prosaic interpretation is that the monolith was simply piled up with the rest of the rocks to clear the field for cultivation.

Hu-221. Cerro Cacachi.

This site has two chulpas, both of fieldstone construction and circular in shape. One chulpa is 3.5 m in diameter, while the other is too badly disturbed to measure, but it is probably similar in size to the first. There were no artifacts on the surface of this site.

Hu-222. Cerro Chojachi. (Fig. 3.40)

This large 4.0 ha site has Formative, Altiplano and Inca diagnostics and is located on a terraced hilltop. There are a number of chulpas and slab cist tombs. There are no existing habitation structures. There is much Altiplano and Inca pottery as well as grinding stones, lithic flakes, and some metal fragments. This was an important fortified site.

Hu-223.

This is a small Altiplano period and Late Horizon site, probably a disturbed cemetery. There are a number of slab cist tombs and there is no significant lithic debris. The site is used today as a location for pagos.

Hu-224.

This is a small Altiplano period and Late Horizon site, probably a disturbed cemetery. There are a number of slab cist tombs and a possible chulpa. There are also human bones on the surface from recent looting. Two sherds—Huaña I and Tiwanaku I—were also discovered in the collection from this site.

Hu-225. (Fig. 3.43)

This is an Altiplano period and Late Horizon scatter of pottery near the top of a ridge. There are some likely habitation structures. The site is on the trail and today there is a modern *apacheta*. It was most likely a ritual area in the past. It is part of the same settlement area as Hu-227.

Figure 3.40. Site locations of Hu-219 and Hu-222.

Site Descriptions

Figure 3.41. Site of Hu-219 showing collapsed chulpa from stones quarried off a fortified site.

Figure 3.42. Uncarved sandstone monolith on Hu-220. Dimensions: 380 x 77 x 22 cm.

Figure 3.43. Site of Hu-225.

Hu-226. (Figs. 3.44, 3.45)

This is a habitation and cemetery site on the ridge that is actually part of the settlement complex including Hu-225 and Hu-227. There are over 300 structures, all circular, that range from 1.0 to 6.0 m in diameter. The site is a significant settlement in a defensive location. There are defensive walls below, and a number of structure clusters suggesting patio groups. The pottery assemblage is consistently Altiplano I, II, and III plus Inca I for all the associated sites in this complex. This fits extremely well with a model of forced resettlement to the valley bottom with the conquest of the area by the Inca in the Inca II period.

Hu-227. (Fig. 3.46)

This is a very large site on the side and top of a ridge and is part of the settlement complex including Hu-225 and Hu-226. There are a number of terraces with circular structures and tombs. A large defensive wall cuts across the ridge at the ridge's southern end. There are no basalt or andesite hoes or adzes recorded on the site.

Hu-228.

This is a small scatter of late pottery and a few lithic artifacts.

Hu-229. (Fig. 3.47)

This is a single, very well made circular structure next to a modern apacheta. The structure is 4.0 m in diameter. There is a light scatter of artifacts over a broad area of about 0.50 ha. Today, there is also a large amount of pago remains on the surface. This was most likely a ritual area associated with the ridgetop settlements during the Altiplano period.

Hu-230. (Fig. 3.48)

This is a curious site. It includes a line—about 46 m long—of ten round structures. Each structure is between 3.5 and 4.0 m in diameter. The alignment is 130/310 degrees. There is a perimeter wall that runs parallel to the line of structures. Below this are three other lines of structures with four, four, and five structures respectively. All the structures are circular. There is another line of structures on the opposite side. The alignment of round structures is similar to that seen in Hu-265. Like this latter site, Hu-230 has pottery from only the Altiplano period. If there had been an Inca occupation, it would be tempting to describe these as colcas. However, this was most likely a more formal kind of Altiplano period habitation area, though this remains to be tested.

Hu-231.

This is a small scatter of Formative period and late artifacts. The site is located in the pampa on a low mound. There are no tombs evident. It appears to be a fairly typical small Formative site reoccupied in the Altiplano period.

Hu-232.

This is a small scatter of Altiplano period artifacts. The site is located in the pampa on a low mound. There are no tombs evident. This appears to be a habitation site that was abandoned after Inca conquest.

Hu-233.

This is a scatter of late artifacts with one Formative III period sherd. The site is located at the base of a low mound in the pampa. There are slab cist and cist tombs.

Hu-234. Parq'a.

This is a scatter of late artifacts. The site is located in the pampa on a low mound. Unlike Hu-232, this site was not abandoned after Inca conquest.

Figure 3.44. Modern apacheta on Hu-226.

Figure 3.45. Circular structure on Hu-226.

Figure 3.46. Site area of Hu-227.

Figure 3.47. Circular structure on Hu-229.

Figure 3.48. Circular structure on Hu-230.

Hu-235. Tiqaparki.
This is a light scatter of late artifacts and human bone. The site is located in the pampa on a low mound. According to an informant, there used to be tombs here but they had been recently plowed under.

Hu-236. Mullawipata.
This is a light scatter of Altiplano II. The site is located in the pampa on a low mound.

Hu-237.
This is a light scatter of Altiplano period artifacts. The site is located at the base of Cerro Luriata.

Hu-238. Soaquillo Parcialidad.
This is an area of at least seven disturbed Altiplano II slab cist tombs on a small hill.

Hu-239. Aqo Pukro.
This is a small scatter of late artifacts. The site is located at the base of Cerro Luriata.

Hu-240. Barrios Altos. (Fig. 3.49)
This is a late habitation site with four rectangular structures on what are now agricultural terraces. There are also a few chulpa bases. There is a 2.5 m wide road that runs through the site. The road is Inca in style. The site was heavily cultivated and we were not permitted to collect artifacts. The pieces that we did see were Inca II in style.

Hu-241.
This is a scatter of Formative and late artifacts on a small promontory in the middle of Cerro Vizcachane. The site is at about 4000 m above sea level. There are large sandstone blocks associated with possible domestic terraces. The existence of a Formative II occupation on this defensible area is very significant.

Hu-242. Pueblo Vizcachane.
This is a light scatter of pottery on a hillside. We were not permitted to make a collection by the landowner, but the pottery appears to be all Altiplano period and Late Horizon in date.

Hu-243. Cerro Vizcachane. (Figs. 3.50, 3.51)
This is a major ridgetop habitation and cemetery site associated with Hu-244. At around 4100 m above sea level, this is one of the highest large habitation sites in the survey area. There are a number of circular structures that average from 3.5 to 4.0 m in diameter. Almost all the diagnostics are Altiplano period II in date. This is a classic Altiplano period habitation site located in what is an obvious defensive location (and see site Hu-265).

Hu-244. Cerro Vizcachane.
This site is part of the complex with Hu-243. There are approximately thirty round structures, 3.5–4.0 m in diameter, and a few slab cist and chulpa bases. There are no surface artifacts here, due to the sediments that have covered this area and the total lack of looting or other disturbances. However, we date this site based upon its proximity to Hu-243.

Figure 3.49. Site area of Hu-240.

Figure 3.50. Circular structures on Hu-243.

Figure 3.51. Defensive wall on Hu-243.

Hu-245. Cerro Vizcachane.
This site has a circular chulpa and slab cists. The double-row chulpa has a diameter of 2.5 m. There were no sherds on the surface.

Hu-246. Pampa de Quella'huyo.
This site is located near the village of Quella'huyo and is about 400 m from the lake. There is a series of very low terraces on very flat land. These terraces are cultivated today but were most likely habitation areas in the past. Diagnostics from the Formative, Huaña, Tiwanaku, and Late Horizon are found on the surface. There is an indeterminate Archaic occupation as well. Along with Hu-248, this area, adjacent to or very near the lake edge, constituted one of the key Tiwanaku settlements in the region.

Hu-247. Saltocarca; Saltocucho. (Figs. 3.52, 3.53)
This is an Archaic, Formative, and Tiwanaku site located adjacent to an outcrop near the lake. The site is small and is confined to the area at the base of the natural rocks. There is a wide variety of lithic raw materials on the surface including artifacts made from obsidian, basalt, chert, and quartzite. There are lots of flakes from an obvious lithic workshop area. There are also agricultural implements that are typically Formative. These data suggest that this was a stone tool workshop area with a habitation component from the Archaic to the Formative III period.

Hu-248. Huata. (Fig. 3.52)
This site is located near the lake on the promontory that juts into the water. The entire area is now agricultural terraces with some large natural rocks piled up seemingly at random near the site. There is a scatter of Formative, Altiplano, Tiwanaku, and Late Horizon period diagnostics on the surface along with some nondiagnostic Archaic scatters of lithics. There are also chulpas and slab cist tombs with evidence of recent looting in the form of a large scatter of human bone. There is an andesite outcrop with cupules carved into the rock, a clear ritual feature of unknown date and use (see Arkush 2005b for a comparison to the western Titicaca Basin).

Hu-249. Pampa de Quella'huyo. (Fig. 3.54)
This is an Altiplano period and Late Horizon site in the Pampa de Quellahuyo. There is no existing architecture. There is a moderate density of lithic debris. The most significant aspect of this site is the road as seen in Figure 3.54. This is a classic Inca-style road, about 2.5–3.0 m wide, well made, with steps and small canals for drainage. There is one Tiwanaku sherd, but it is not sufficient to designate a period.

Hu-250.
This is an undated scatter of lithics with a wide variety of raw materials. This is usually indicative of an Archaic workshop. There was a light scatter of Altiplano II pottery that was not collected. There are no other surface features such as structures or tombs.

Hu-251. Pampa Cacajache.
This is a scatter of Tiwanaku through Inca III diagnostics located in a cultivated field on the pampa about 60 m from the edge of Lake Titicaca. There are no other surface features such as structures or tombs; this appears to be a habitation site.

Figure 3.52. Site location of Hu-247 and Hu-248.

Figure 3.53. Site location of Hu-247.

Figure 3.54. Prehispanic road above Hu-249.

Hu-252. Pampa Cacajache.

This is a scatter of Altiplano through Inca III diagnostics in a cultivated field about 100 m from the lake edge and adjacent to Cerro Chojachi where Hu-222 is located. There is a possible slab cist tomb on a low wall.

Hu-253. (Fig. 3.55)

This is an Altiplano I and II period cemetery site on two low mounds in the pampa. There is also an Archaic component to the site. There are approximately fourteen slab cist tombs in this site area. This find is very significant because the mound is at least partially artificial. This "tumulus" type of burial is extremely rare in the Titicaca Basin, though some have been found in the Ilave River area in the western lake area. It is likely that this kind of tumulus was much more common but that most have been destroyed. It is also likely that many of the Altiplano period scatters on low mounds that we find throughout the research area were originally tombs like this but have since been flattened by agricultural land use and the sacking of the slabs for later construction.

Hu-254.

This is a small scatter of Altiplano period and Inca III diagnostics in a cultivated field.

Hu-255.

This is a line of at least five tombs on the first natural terrace above the lake. This was clearly a favored cemetery location for millennia, beginning in the earliest Formative periods. It is significant that there are Tiwanaku cist tombs at this site. There is also a scatter of chert flakes and obsidian that suggests a habitation or workshop. This site is no more than 8.0 m above the present lake level, and part is lower. The existence of this site indicates that the lake level was not significantly higher at any point since the Formative period for any appreciable period of time.

Hu-256.

This is a small rise with eroded tombs located about 25 m from Hu-255. It is therefore part of the cluster of tombs in the sites Hu-255 to Hu-262. The site is in an elevated area in the pampa like the other tombs in this lake-edge zone, and has Tiwanaku I, Altiplano II, and Inca I pottery.

Hu-257. (Fig. 3.56)

This site has a few Altiplano period slab cist tombs in the group Hu-255–Hu-262. The site is in an elevated area in the pampa. There are also Formative sherds in the area, indicating either Formative period above-ground tombs or an earlier habitation site.

Hu-258.

This is a set of Altiplano period slab cist tombs associated with Hu-255–Hu-262. The site is in an elevated area in the pampa. There is one Inca diagnostic but we did not use this to assign a period.

Hu-259.

This is a set of slab cist tombs associated with Hu-255–Hu-262. The site is in an elevated area in the pampa.

Hu-260.

This is a set of slab cist tombs associated with Hu-255–Hu-262. The site is in a naturally elevated area in the pampa. This is the typical pattern in which a low natural hill was used by Altiplano period people to bury their dead. One Inca sherd was also found in this collection but not used to assign a period.

Hu-261.

This is a scatter of artifacts on a field in the pampa associated with the cemetery areas from Hu-255 to Hu-262. This is probably a habitation site, including a Tiwanaku I occupation.

Hu-262.

This is a scatter of artifacts on a field in the pampa associated with the cemetery areas from Hu-255 to Hu-262. There are a number of slab cist tombs that are probably the source of the pottery.

Hu-263.

This site consists of a low, terraced hill with a few slab cist and chulpa tombs on the top of the hill. The pottery is all Altiplano period. There are three principal terraces about 100 m long and between 20 and 40 m wide. The slab cist tombs range from 1.0 to 2.0 m in diameter. There is also evidence of an Archaic use of the site area. We found the remains of recent pagos from the top of the hill where the prehispanic tombs are located.

Hu-264. Santiaguillo. (Figs. 3.57, 3.58)

This is a single, large, circular chulpa with quarried and carved andesite and sandstone rocks. It is located in the pampa in a flat area. Some of the blocks reach 1 m on a side. The chulpa is about 6.0 m in diameter. The chulpa's style is usually considered Late Horizon in date, although the associated ceramic fragments are curiously all Formative III. It is possible that this was a Formative period site with a structure that was reutilized by Late Horizon masons to build the chulpa.

Hu-265. Cerro Vizcachane.

This small, late habitation site has three rows of circular structures similar and related to Hu-243. The structures range from 3.0 to 4.0 m in diameter on the outside rows, with those in the middle around 1.0–1.3 m in diameter. The surface evidence suggests that the structures in the middle are tombs, while those on the outside are for habitation, storage, or both. The site is located on a ridgetop below Hu-243, and is most likely part of this complex. The pottery is consistently Altiplano period. The lines of structures are reminiscent of Inca colcas, but there is no Late Horizon pottery at all. The alignment of structures is similar to that seen at Hu-230.

Hu-266. Cerro Sotisani. (Fig. 3.1)

This small, Altiplano period site is located on a ridgetop at over 4000 m above sea level. There are at least four round structures, about 5.0 m in diameter, in a pattern similar to those at Hu-265. A number of structures have been disturbed for the planting of eucalyptus trees.

Hu-267. Cerro Sotisani. (Fig. 3.1)

This habitation and cemetery site is on a ridgetop. It has a number of circular structures and at least one chulpa with a double row of stones that measures approximately 2.0 m in diameter. These structures are similar to those at Hu-266.

Hu-268. Cerro Sotisani. (Fig. 3.1)

This ridgetop habitation and cemetery site has about a dozen large structures, about 5.0–6.0 m in diameter, similar to Hu-266. There are also slab cist tombs in the site area.

Hu-269. Cerro Sotisani. (Fig. 3.1)

This ridgetop and hillside habitation site is composed of a number of artificial terraces. The presence of a Formative occupation is significant here since the site is in a very defensible location.

Figure 3.55. Pampa mound of Hu-253.

Figure 3.56. Chulpa at Hu-257.

(*right*) Figure 3.57. Large chulpa at Hu-264.

(*below*) Figure 3.58. Close-up of large limestone slab at Hu-264.

Figure 3.59. Sunken court at Hu-276.

Hu-270. Parcialidad Chijuyo.

This late site has materials from Altiplano I to Inca III and is located on the pampa among some modern houses. There are a number of terraces that are still used today as house platforms. There are also lithic artifacts.

Hu-271.

This small Formative hamlet site is located on a small natural mound in the pampa.

Hu-272.

This is a small, double-row fieldstone chulpa, 1.5 m in diameter. It is located on a low hilltop.

Hu-273. Cerro Pecosani.

This is an artificial terrace on a hill with a light scatter of Altiplano period pottery and at least four slab cist tombs. All the tombs are approximately 1.5 m in diameter.

Hu-274. Cerro Pecosani.

This is a 2 ha Altiplano period habitation site on a hill. There are some low terraces. The hill is currently planted with eucalyptus, so there is very little surface material.

Hu-275.

This site is a small Altiplano period and Inca I hamlet at the base of Cerro Pecosani. Surface materials are very sparse.

Hu-276. (Fig. 3.59)

This part of the Hu-003 complex is a half-cruciform mound located to the northwest side of the hill. This area, originally listed as Hu-276, is about 3–6 ha in size and has a sunken court. This is an odd court, if it is a sunken court at all. First, it is rectangular, approximately 13 m on the long side and 7 on the short. Rectangular courts are virtually unknown in the northern Titicaca Basin. The court is not oriented to the cardinal directions (it is about 40 degrees off magnetic north). It is also located in an odd area for a court of this style and complexity. Other courts like this are found on or near hilltops. On the other hand, the interior walls are very similar in building style to those at Pucara. The pottery is dense and consistent with a major Formative period center. Also, numerous slabs similar to those found at Pucara that faced the walls are found in the area near this stone-lined rectangular depression. Finally, the court is located on what could be the interior mound of a half-cross-shaped construction. The impression of the senior author is that this is not a Formative sunken court, or alternatively, it is the first rectangular court documented in the northern Titicaca Basin. There is an Archaic component as well, but we did not find any diagnostics.

Hu-277.

This is a single, very badly disturbed slab cist tomb. The diameter is between 3.0 and 4.0 m.

Hu-278. Santiaquillo.

The modern village sits on an Altiplano and Inca period site. There are some cut stone blocks on the surface and incorporated into houses. The quality of the Inca pottery is quite good. The site would have been a small Inca village.

Hu-279.

This is a classic Altiplano period pukara with defensive walls and terraces up to the top of the hill. The top of the hill has a moderate scatter of artifacts. There are no obvious structures, though some areas show possible badly looted habitations.

Hu-280. Huarisa.

This is one of the major settlements in the region. Huarisa is located on a low hill with a number of well-made terraces and a high density of artifacts on the surface. The site has Archaic, Formative, and Tiwanaku occupations. There are some small quantities of ceramics from later occupations as well, but these are not very intense. There is a large quantity of obsidian and other exotic lithic raw materials on the site. Fragments of copper were also found. The quality and quantity of Formative and Tiwanaku finewares, plus the large site size, suggest that Huarisa was a settlement of considerable importance in the past. The top of the hill is very rocky and narrow. There is no evidence of any sunken courts or other corporate architecture on the site.

Hu-281.

This is one of the major settlements in the region. This site is about 400 m from the lakeshore and is located on a low hill among the modern urban village area. The site has about ten well-made artificial terraces that were habitation areas. There is a substantial distribution of pottery and other diagnostics on the surface.

Hu-282.

This site number was used to designate about 1 ha of raised fields.

Hu-283.

This late site is a small dispersal of Tiwanaku I and Altiplano I and II pottery near Hu-282's raised fields.

Hu-284. Chacacruz. (Figs. 3.60, 3.61)

This is a petroglyph with a number of small circular depressions. There are two rocks with obvious carvings. The length of the rocks is about 1.30 m while the width varies, but it is around 50 cm in the center. The petroglyph is located adjacent to a spring and the road. There are no artifacts associated with this site, but this is very likely an Inca huaca.

Hu-285. Chacacruz.

This small mound in the pampa has a very long occupation, from the Formative through the Late Horizon. There are also a number of lithic artifacts on the surface that represent a nondiagnostic Archaic component.

Hu-286.

This site is composed of three groups of slab cist tombs on a promontory. The groups are about 5 m apart from each other. The diagnostics are Formative II and Altiplano period in date. There also is a nondiagnostic Archaic component.

Hu-287.

This small Altiplano I–III and Inca I mound site was probably a cemetery that was disturbed by modern road construction. There are some human bones scattered on the surface.

Hu-288. Juntuma.

This is a natural mound in the pampa that has Formative II and a late occupation. It is close to the river. There is no evidence of corporate construction and there are no structures or tombs visible on the surface.

Hu-289.

This is a small mound in the pampa with a late occupation. There are no tombs evident. There are lithic artifacts on the surface.

Hu-290.

This is a single slab cist tomb in the pampa that is late in date as indicated by the construction type. The tomb is 1 m in diameter. There are no artifacts.

Hu-291. Chuseqa Sayaña pata. (Fig. 3.62)

This is a cemetery and habitation settlement with at least one chulpa with a 2.10 m diameter and a number of slab cist tombs. The site is located on a mound in the pampa that also had a Formative III period occupation, most likely a residential and possibly a ritual one. There are few lithic flakes, although a fragment of a hoe was found that is most likely Formative in date as well. There is a single, large sandstone monolith and a number of cut sandstone blocks on the surface. The monolith—a little under 4 m in length, 60 cm wide, 35 cm thick, and made of sandstone—is in a classic Middle Formative style. The existence of a Formative III occupation combined with these cut stones suggests that there was a sunken court near the site. The landowner said that he dragged the monolith from the side of the nearby hill to make a bench.

Hu-292.

This is a very small scatter of pottery and human bones. It is most certainly a destroyed tomb that dated to the Altiplano or Inca II period.

Hu-293.

This is a small mound in the pampa with an Altiplano I, II, and III occupation. There are no tombs evident. There are no lithic artifacts on the surface.

Hu-294.

This is a nondiagnostic lithic scatter, about 25 × 25 m in size, on a natural terrace on the river along with some Altiplano I and II pottery fragments. The pottery is most likely from a looted set of tombs.

Hu-295.

This is a small mound in the pampa with an Altiplano period occupation. There are no tombs evident. There are no lithic artifacts on the surface.

Hu-296.

This is an Archaic lithic scatter with Altiplano and Inca I period pottery eroding out of a low hill about 300 m from the river. The site is on the first natural river terrace. It also has some intrusive tombs. It is possible that this is an Archaic locus of a larger site that is largely buried, with intrusive Altiplano period tombs.

(*right*) Figure 3.60. Site area of Hu-284.

(*below left*) Figure 3.61. Carved limestone block on Hu-284.

(*below right*) Figure 3.62. Uncarved sandstone monolith on Hu-291.

Hu-297.

This is a small mound in the pampa with a Tiwanaku and later occupation on or near a nondiagnostic Archaic component. There are no tombs evident. There are a number of lithic artifacts on the surface.

Hu-298. Cerro Quequecani. (Figs. 3.63, 3.64)

This Tiwanaku and late site is on a hill with a number of artificial terraces and a moderate density of surface artifacts. There are also a number of slab cist tombs and a possible chulpa base. There are at least three circular structures about 5.0–6.0 m in diameter that are aligned. There are a number of chert flakes as well as some obsidian fragments. The location on a hill with what appear to be defensive walls makes this a probable fortification or refuge site.

Hu-299. (Fig. 3.64)

This is a small and late habitation area on the Cerro Quequecani site. It is part of the site complex of Hu-298 and Hu-300.

Hu-300. (Figs. 3.1, 3.64)

This Altiplano and Late Horizon period habitation and cemetery site is found on a hilltop. There are a number of terraces around the hill with artifacts and eroding midden. There are also circular structures of 5.0–6.0 m diameter. There are some lithic artifacts on the surface that we interpret as an undiagnostic Archaic occupation.

Hu-301.

This is a set of raised fields. We found some Formative I and later sherds in disturbed areas, suggesting there was a habitation or cemetery site that was converted into this agricultural feature later in the sequence.

Hu-302.

This is a small pampa site with Altiplano and Inca I components. There are few lithic artifacts on the surface.

Hu-303.

This is a small pampa site with a Late Horizon component. There is a single chulpa base, 3.0 m in diameter, at the edge of the site. There are few lithic artifacts on the surface.

Hu-304.

This is a Formative I through Huaña I and Altiplano period habitation and cemetery site that covers over 2 ha. The site is located on a hilltop and hillside. There are a number of habitation terraces. There are also a number of slab cist tombs and some chulpas. Significantly, there are hoe and adze artifacts on the site that are typically Formative in date. There is also a nondiagnostic Archaic component on this hilltop site.

Hu-305.

This is a small Altiplano II and Inca I period cemetery site on the side of a hill on a promontory. There are slab cists and some chulpas in an area of about 10 × 20 m.

Hu-306. Tumuku; Upani pata.

This 2.0 ha Formative and late site is located on the sides and top of a hill. This site has a number of large habitation terraces. There is a scatter of lithic artifacts. Sandstone blocks are found scattered over the surface, indicating that there was a sunken court. It is not possible to determine the size of the court.

Hu-307.

This is a possible prehispanic construction in the middle of the pampa. The structure is 20 × 30 m with a double-rowed wall. Inside the large structure is a smaller one in the center. There are no artifacts to date the structure.

Hu-308.

This is a small pampa mound site with late materials.

Hu-309.

This is a small scatter of Formative and Altiplano period artifacts on a pampa mound. There are a few lithic artifacts on the surface, mainly chert flakes.

Hu-310.

This multicomponent site has Archaic, Formative, Huaña, Tiwanaku, Altiplano, and Late Horizon occupation. The 3.0 ha site is located at the base and on the side of a hill. There are about five artificial terraces with a high density of artifacts on the surface. Lithic artifacts include obsidian, chert, and quartzite plus fragments of agricultural implements. This was a major habitation area throughout the sequence. There are springs nearby today, and the site is next to the road in this side of the valley.

Hu-311.

This is an isolated slab cist tomb, 3.5 m in diameter. The tomb has unusually large blocks that may have been quarried from an earlier site, now gone.

Hu-312.

This is a small late site on a natural mound. It is located in the pampa.

Hu-313.

This is a small Formative and later site located on the sides of a hill.

Hu-314.

This is a small Altiplano III and Inca III site located on the sides of a hill.

Hu-315. (Fig. 3.65)

This is a scatter of lithics and pottery on three large artificial terraces below Hu-316. This area has Formative and Tiwanaku pottery and a scatter of Archaic lithics with a large number of late diagnostics. Hu-315 is clearly associated with the sunken court complex on the hill of Machacamarca (Hu-316).

Hu-316. Machacamarca. (Figs. 3.65–3.74)

This is one of the principal Formative and Huaña I period centers, with a sunken court and monolith. The site covers most of the east side of Cerro Machacamarca with artificial terraces. There is a trapezoidal sunken court with a "key-shaped" entrance that measures about 17 × 20 m. The court is not cardinally oriented. Rather, the orientation of the court and the narrow "stairs" to the east is about 60–65 degrees. Curiously, this orientation hit the rising sun during the June solstice two millennia ago. The courts at Amantani Island and Incatunuhuiri are oriented to the same direction. The uncarved stela is found in the center of the court, apparently very close to its original location. The monolith is 2.30 m long and about 35 cm wide. We cannot measure the third side because it is buried. On the hill above the court on the west side are several chulpas, approximately 3.0 m in diameter. The chulpas are Altiplano period in date.

Figure 3.63. Site area of Hu-298; view of east side. Note encircling walls on the east side of the site. View is from south to north.

Figure 3.64. Site area of Hu-298, Hu-299, and Hu-300; view of west side.

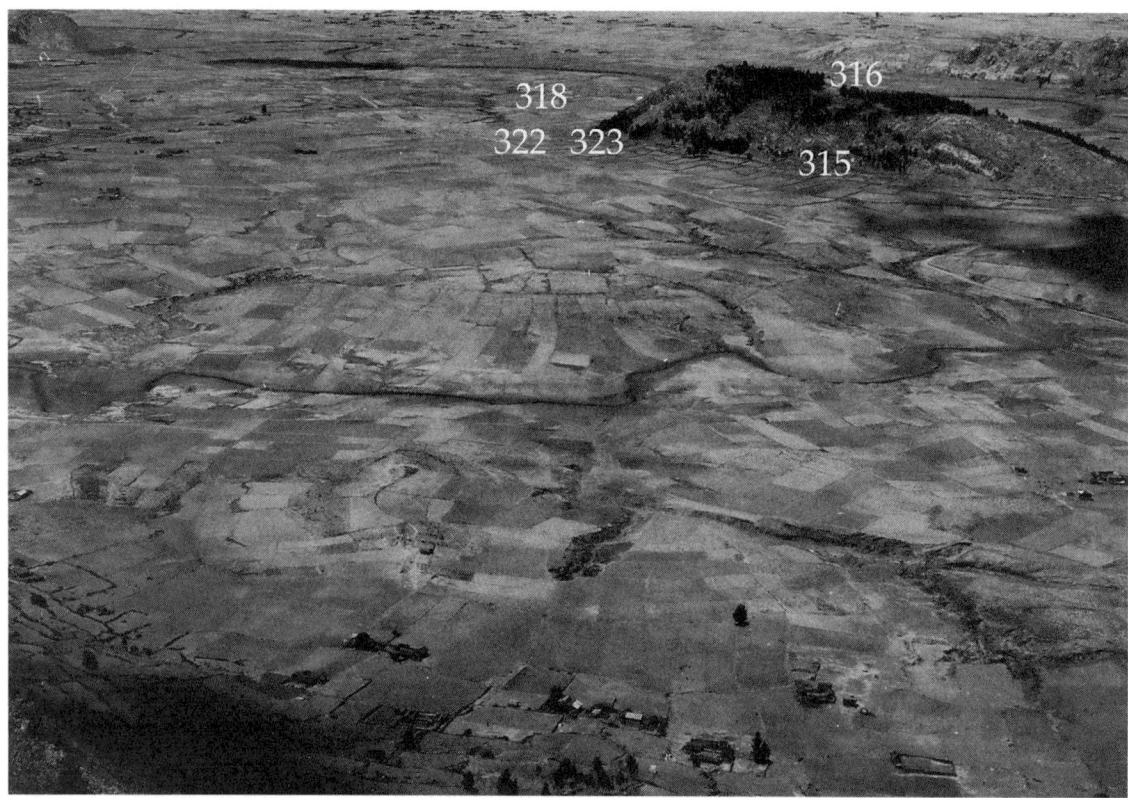

Figure 3.65. Relationship between Hu-315, Hu-316, Hu-318, Hu-322, and Hu-323.

Figure 3.66. Site area of Hu-316.

Site Descriptions

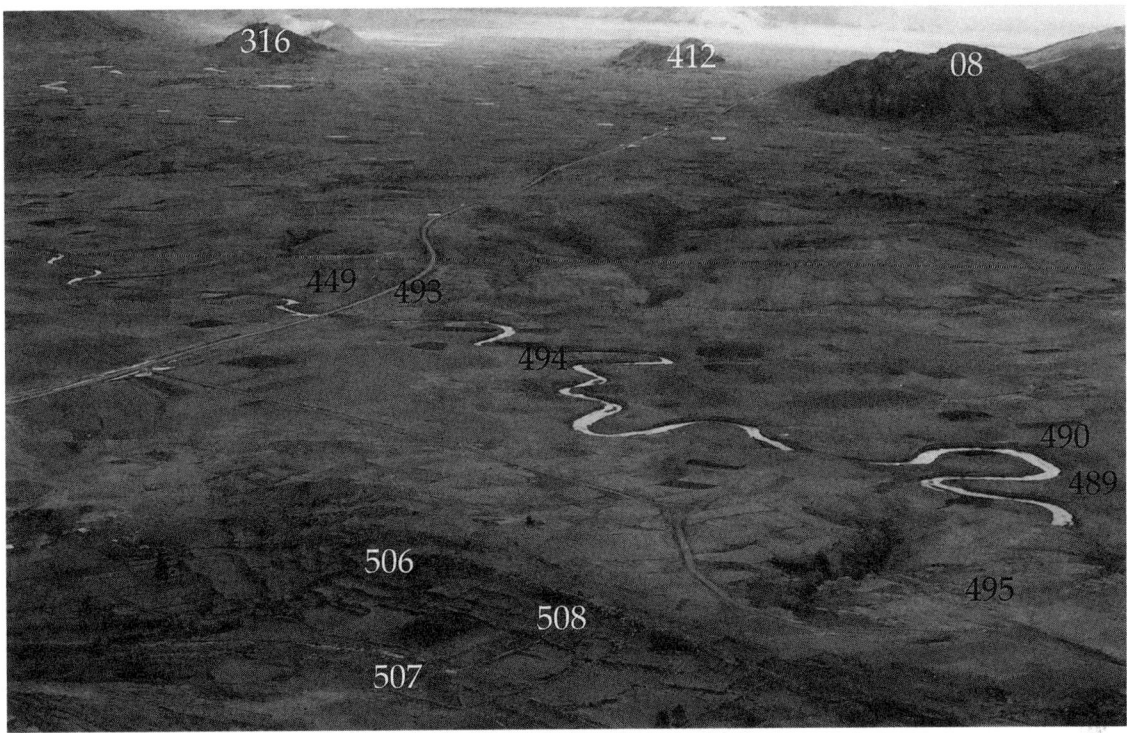

Figure 3.67. View of mid-Huancané Valley.

Figure 3.68. Distance view of Hu-316.

Figure 3.69. Location of sunken court on Hu-316.

Figure 3.70. View of sunken court on Hu-316.

Figure 3.71. View of monolith in the middle of the sunken court on Hu-316.

Figure 3.72. Close-up view of notch on the monolith in the sunken court on Hu-316.

Figure 3.73. Cut limestone block on Hu-316.

Figure 3.74. Cut limestone block on Hu-316.

Virtually all the pottery found in the sunken court area is Formative and Huaña I period in date. The Altiplano III pottery is associated with the large chulpas above the court. The sites of Hu-315, Hu-317, and Hu-414 each have substantial Formative and Altiplano period occupations. It is therefore likely that the court was built in the Formative with associated occupations on the sides and below the hill. The Formative period complex collapsed in the Huaña period after which people continued to live on the pampa sites but abandoned the hilltop, except for using it as a cemetery area and a pukara for defense.

Hu-316 also has a Late Archaic component.

Hu-317.
This Formative, Altiplano, and Inca period site is located on a pampa mound. No tombs are evident. There are abundant lithic artifacts.

Hu-318. (Figs. 3.65, 3.75)
This Formative and Altiplano period site is located on a natural pampa mound. There are a number of tombs, all slab cist, on the surface. There are abundant lithic artifacts as well.

Hu-319.
This Altiplano period site is located on a natural pampa mound. There are some slab cist tombs and abundant lithic artifacts.

Hu-320. (Fig. 3.75)
This Altiplano period site is located on a natural pampa mound. There are some slab cist tombs and abundant lithic artifacts.

Hu-321. (Fig. 3.75)
This site has Altiplano I–III and Inca I occupations. The site is found in the pampa with a scatter of lithic artifacts on the surface, along with some slab cist tombs.

Hu-322. (Figs. 3.65, 3.75)
This is a Formative and late habitation site in the pampa on one of the low ridges that cuts across the plain. There are a number of lithic flakes, but few agricultural tools. No tombs are noted on this site, but slab cist tombs are found in other sites near Hu-322.

Hu-323. (Figs. 3.65, 3.75, 3.76)
This is an Altiplano period tumulus with a high quantity of pottery. The tumulus is 6 × 14 m. One slab cist is 2.0 m in diameter. There are other smaller tombs found in the tumulus as well. This is a rare form of burial in the region. It is possible that these were much more common in the past and have been destroyed for farming or other economic activities.

Hu-324. (Fig. 3.75)
This is a 1.0 ha Altiplano period site. It is a scatter of Altiplano period pottery and lithic artifacts, plus some small groups of slab cist tombs. The tombs are grouped into three areas.

Hu-325. (Fig. 3.75)
This is a 2.0 ha late habitation site. There is a high density of pottery and other artifacts, including lithics, grinding stones, hoes, and some copper. There are also a number of slab cist tombs on the surface.

Hu-326.
This is a single projectile point fragment found on a hilltop. This is a probable Terminal Archaic point.

Hu-327.
This is a large Altiplano I and II period habitation site. There are a number of quadrangular structures made with large blocks. The site has platforms and terraces. There are a number of lithic artifacts on the surface. The site is odd in that such large blocks are usually associated with either Formative II, Formative III, or Inca occupations, yet we found no sherds from these periods. The site deserves more attention and certainly the data suggest a level of complexity not usually seen in Altiplano period settlements. It is possible that the Altiplano I occupation, so close in space and time to Tiwanaku II, could explain this anomaly.

Hu-328.
This is a small Altiplano period and Inca I and III habitation site with three artificial terraces and some lithic artifacts on the surface.

Hu-329.
This is a small Altiplano period and Inca I habitation site with three artificial terraces and some lithic artifacts on the surface.

Hu-330.
This is a small pampa mound cemetery site. There are three slab cist tombs, approximately 2.0 m in diameter. There are also human bones and some pottery fragments on the surface associated with the tombs.

Hu-331.
This is a small pampa mound cemetery site with a few slab cist tombs.

Hu-332.
This is a small pampa mound with a number of slab cist tombs. There are also human bones and some nondiagnostic pottery fragments on the surface associated with the tombs. We did not make a collection.

Hu-333.
This is a light scatter of late pottery and lithics on the pampa.

Hu-334.
This is a light scatter of Late Horizon pottery and lithics on the pampa, probably a cemetery area.

Hu-335. Muñani pata.
This is a light scatter of Late Horizon pottery and lithics on the pampa, probably a cemetery area.

Hu-336.
This is a natural pampa mound with a few slab cist tombs.

Hu-337.
This is a natural pampa mound with habitation and cemetery components. The site is a large site, approximately 2.0 ha. There are a number of slab cist tombs and some chulpas. There are also a number of lithic artifacts, including some grinding stones.

Hu-338.
This site is at least three slab cist tombs with a scatter of pottery and human remains on the surface from recent looting.

Hu-339.
This is a disturbed slab cist tomb on the pampa.

Figure 3.75. Survey region in the Machacamarca area.

Figure 3.76. Chulpa on Hu-323 using blocks quarried from Hu-322.

Hu-340. (Fig. 3.77)

This is a pampa site with Late Horizon and Tiwanaku diagnostics. This 1 ha site contains a number of lithic artifacts, including grinding stones and agricultural implements. A fragment of copper was found on the surface. There are also a number of tombs, including slab cists and chulpas. The slab cists are large, up to 2.0 m in diameter.

Hu-341.

This is a scatter of artifacts on a few artificial terraces. There are some eroding tombs near the surface.

Hu-342.

This is a scatter of artifacts on a few artificial terraces. It appears to be a cemetery area.

Hu-343.

This is a pampa mound with a number of slab cist tombs. There are human bones on the surface associated with the tombs. There are also a number of lithics that represent an undiagnostic Archaic occupation.

Hu-344.

This late site is a pampa mound with a very high density of artifacts on the surface. There are abundant lithics and pottery. We also found some metal artifacts. There are slab cist tombs with human bones on the surface.

Hu-345.

This is a small pampa mound with slab cist tombs and square structures. The latter are either domestic structures or square chulpas.

Hu-346.

This is a small site on the side of the Putina River that has a number of slab cist tombs eroding out of the river cut. There are fine polished lithic artifacts along with Altiplano period pottery.

Hu-347.

This site is at the base and sides of a hill. It has about twenty-five cist and slab cist tombs aligned roughly north-south.

Hu-348.

This is a habitation and cemetery site on the edge of the pampa. It has a scatter of Altiplano period and Late Horizon pottery associated with slab cist tombs.

Hu-349.

This is a habitation and cemetery site on the edge of the pampa. It has a scatter of Altiplano period and Late Horizon pottery associated with slab cist tombs. There are also a number of lithics that represent an undiagnostic Archaic occupation.

Hu-350.

This is a pampa mound with a number of slab cist tombs. There are human bones on the surface associated with the tombs.

Hu-351. Collpa Huata.

This late site is located in the pampa along the base of a low hill. There are some low, artificial terraces and some slab cist tombs. Human bones are associated with the tombs. The terraces are most likely designed for habitation areas. There are a number of lithic remains on the surface.

Figure 3.77. Intact bowl found in situ on slab cist tomb on Hu-340.

Hu-352.

This is a small, late cemetery on the pampa. There is a low density of pottery on the surface and at least three tombs with associated human bones.

Hu-353.

This is a small scatter of late artifacts on a few low terraces at the base of a hill. This most likely represents a disturbed cemetery.

Hu-354.

This is a small scatter of late artifacts on a few low terraces on the side of a hill. This most likely represents a disturbed cemetery.

Hu-355.

This is a small scatter of late artifacts on a few low terraces at the base of a hill. There are two chulpas, 1.50 m in diameter. There is a possible structure associated with this site.

Hu-356.

This site has at least four slab cist tombs on a small rise at the edge of a hill. There are no artifacts on the surface.

Hu-357.

This small late site is a scatter of artifacts on a small pampa mound, most likely from some looted tombs.

Hu-358.

This small late site is a scatter of artifacts on a small pampa mound, most likely from some looted tombs.

Hu-359.

This site is a scatter of lithic and ceramic artifacts on the side of the Chusca River. There were two projectile points found, one basalt and one quartzite. The pottery is Altiplano period. There is also a Middle and Late Archaic site with a later Altiplano period reoccupation.

Hu-360. (Fig. 3.78)

This is a well-preserved but looted chulpa, 2.30 m in diameter, with human bones in the chamber. Part of the roof still exists. Small amounts of Altiplano period pottery are found on the surface outside the tomb. Inside, there is no pottery with the bone scatter.

Hu-361. Cerro Coacollo.

This is a moderately sized site with a habitation zone and terrace walls that also most likely functioned as defensive. There is very little disturbance and therefore few artifacts on the surface. The architecture and layout of the site suggest an Altiplano period date, but there were no diagnostics. We did not make a collection but identified the pottery as Altiplano I and II.

Hu-362.

This is a single slab cist tomb that has been badly disturbed. Only one slab remains while the others have been incorporated into a boundary marker.

Hu-363.

This site has a chulpa of 2.0 m diameter. There are also some enigmatic, semicircular walls that are barely visible.

Hu-364.

This is an isolated Archaic projectile point.

Hu-365. (Fig. 3.79)

This is a nondiagnostic lithic scatter in the pampa located adjacent to the river near site.

Figure 3.78. Chulpa on Hu-360.

Hu-366. (Fig. 3.79)

This is a nondiagnostic lithic scatter in the pampa located adjacent to the river near site.

Hu-367.

This is an Archaic lithic scatter in the pampa, with a projectile point fragment.

Hu-368. (Fig. 3.66)

This is an Archaic lithic scatter in the pampa, with two projectile points.

Hu-369.

This is a site with at least twelve slab cist tombs on a low rise in the pampa. There are a number of lithic artifacts as well.

Hu-370.

This is a small scatter of Altiplano II pottery and lithics on the surface of a low mound in the pampa.

Hu-371. (Fig. 3.66)

This is a small scatter of nondiagnostic lithic artifacts in the pampa near the river Chusca.

Hu-372.

This is a small scatter of lithic artifacts in the pampa.

Hu-373.

This is an Archaic lithic scatter in the pampa, with a projectile point.

Hu-374.

This is an Archaic lithic scatter in the pampa, with a projectile point. There are also some slab cist tombs.

Hu-375.

This is a late cemetery site. There are a number of tombs and human bones.

Hu-376.

This is a late habitation and cemetery site on a low mound. There are a number of slab cist tombs and lithic debris.

Hu-377. (Fig. 3.80)

This late site is located on a small rise next to a mountain. There is a shrine on the site at present. The site has a scatter of late pottery and a few lithic flakes. It was most certainly a ritual area in the Inca and possibly Altiplano times.

Hu-378. (Figs. 3.79, 3.80, 3.81)

This is a site with a scatter of late diagnostics. There are no lithics on the site.

Hu-379. (Figs. 3.79, 3.81)

This is a lithic scatter with some slab cist tombs. Human bones are on the surface. It is on the pampa. It is likely that this was an Archaic scatter on a low natural rise with some intrusive Altiplano period or Late Horizon tombs.

Hu-380. (Fig. 3.79)

This is a site at the base of a hill. It has a number of Archaic diagnostic points and many waste flakes and other lithic artifacts.

Hu-381. Cerro Kuyuraya. (Figs. 3.80–3.83)

This is a site on the side of a hill with a number of habitation terraces. It is a continuation of Hu-382 but it has a Huaña and Tiwanaku component not found in that sector of the complex. Hu-381 is about 2.0 ha in size, and combined with Hu-382, the site complex reaches about 4.0 ha. There are abundant eroding midden and diagnostic pottery on the surface. There are also a number of points on the surface, several of which were Archaic. Slab cist tombs are found on the surface as well. There is a possible sunken court that is heavily damaged.

Hu-382. Cerro Kuyuraya. (Figs. 3.81, 3.82)

This is a continuation of Hu-381. The site is about 2.0 ha in size, and when combined with Hu-381, reaches about 4.0 ha. There are wide terraces that have eroding midden. There are many diagnostics from the eroding middens. Hu-381 and Hu-382 represent a significant settlement from the Archaic period.

Hu-383. (Fig. 3.81)

This site is a set of slab cist tombs with human bones. There is late pottery along with some Formative diagnostics. This site is also used today for modern rituals as evidenced by the broken glass and other signs of a pago.

Hu-384.

This is a small, late scatter of pottery and some lithics on a pampa hill base.

Hu-385. (Figs. 3.84, 3.85)

This is a small Altiplano period site on the side of a hill in the pampa that has at least ten slab cist tombs. Human bones are found dispersed around the site. There are also some agricultural implements and other lithics, suggesting an earlier habitation site. There is likewise an Archaic lithic assemblage.

Hu-386.

This is a light scatter of human bones at the edge of the pampa. There are no upright stones or other surface indications of tombs.

Hu-387.

This site is composed of two agricultural terraces with a scatter of pottery. There is also a light scatter of Archaic lithics. At the edge of the site, we discovered an obsidian projectile point.

Hu-388.

This is a small, late scatter of pottery and some lithics on a pampa hill base.

Hu-389.

This is an isolated slab cist tomb with very little diagnostic material.

Hu-390. Cerro Sustia. (Fig. 3.84)

This site has a number of tombs and an associated habitation area that covers about a half hectare. The tombs are large slab cists, about 2.5–3.0 m in diameter. There is a heavy scatter of artifacts and some eroding midden. Both grinding stones and chipped stone were found on the surface.

Hu-391.

This is an isolated Archaic projectile point that we date to the Middle Archaic.

Site Descriptions

Figure 3.79. View showing relationship between Hu-365, Hu-366, Hu-378, Hu-379, and Hu-380.

Figure 3.80. View showing relationship between Hu-377, Hu-378, and Hu-381.

Figure 3.81. View showing relationship between Hu-378, Hu-379, Hu-381, Hu-382, and Hu-383.

Figure 3.82. View showing site area of Hu-381 and Hu-382.

Figure 3.83. Sunken court structure on Hu-381.

Figure 3.84. View showing relationship between Hu-385, Hu-390, Hu-397, Hu-503, and Hu-504.

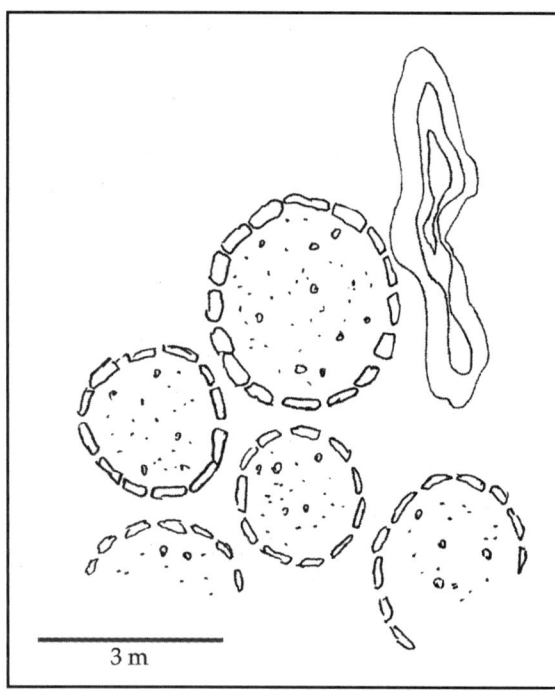

Figure 3.85. Sketch map showing structures on Hu-385.

Hu-392.
This is a light scatter of late pottery on a small site. There are some obsidian fragments as well as other lithic artifacts.

Hu-393.
This is a set of slab cist tombs at the edge of the pampa. There are associated human bones on the surface. The pottery is late in date.

Hu-394.
This is a set of slab cist tombs at the edge of the pampa. There are associated human bones on the surface. The pottery is late in date.

Hu-395.
This is a small natural rock outcrop with some dispersed late pottery.

Hu-396.
At this site there is a scatter of late pottery on the surface of several artificial terraces. There is also an isolated projectile point that is Archaic.

Hu-397. (Fig. 3.84)
This is a small pampa mound with slab cist tombs and associated human bones. The tomb diameters vary between 1.0 and 1.5 m. There are very few lithics and other domestic artifacts, suggesting that this is a cemetery site.

Hu-398. Jurata.
This is a scatter of late artifacts over a 1.0 to 1.5 ha site with no visible architecture.

Hu-399.
This is a scatter of late pottery on the surface of several artificial terraces.

Hu-400.
This is a scatter of late pottery on the surface of several artificial terraces.

Hu-401.
This is an isolated projectile point.

Hu-402.
This is a light scatter of late artifacts on a low rise in the pampa. This most likely represents a disturbed cemetery.

Hu-403.
This is a light scatter of late artifacts at the edge of the pampa. This most likely represents a disturbed cemetery.

Hu-404.
This is a 1.0 ha late site at the edge of the pampa. There is a light density of artifacts. There are few lithic artifacts and no evident tombs.

Hu-405.
This is a light scatter of late artifacts at the edge of the pampa. There are abundant lithics, including many nonlocal raw materials. This is a possible Archaic site without any diagnostic points.

Hu-406 (formerly Hu-018). Inchuyu; Jinchu huichinka. (Figs. 3.86, 3.95)
This is a 2 ha mound in the pampa that was originally reconnoitered in 1998 and given the site number Hu-018. It was found again in the systematic survey several years later and was given the number Hu-406. We never alter site numbers, so the artifacts listed as Hu-018 in the figures remain labeled as such. The mound is located near the Huancané River. The mound is at least 4 m high, probably much higher. It seems likely that it originally formed a substantial U-shape comprising a classical high-status pyramid structure typical of the Late Formative. Hu-406 is in one of the richest locations in the survey area. It has diagnostics from virtually every time period beginning in the Early Archaic and continuing up to the present. The quality of the Formative pottery is extremely high. The site has a very rare feline-faced trumpet fragment (Hu-406-03-27 in Fig. A113) plus numerous flat-bottomed bowls.

Hu-407. (Fig. 3.95)
This is a small late site on a low natural mound in the pampa. Like Hu-408, it is a late component part of the site complex including Hu-406–Hu-408 and Hu-505.

Hu-408. Tumata. (Fig. 3.95)
This is a small late site on a low natural mound in the pampa. It is part of the Hu-406 site complex but was collected as a separate site due to the different ceramic assemblage, which was late. This area most likely represents a late cemetery at the end of the mound and natural hill.

Hu-409. Azangarillo.
This is a light scatter of Altiplano I and Late Horizon artifacts in a cultivated area on a low mound in the pampa.

Hu-410. Huichinca.
This is a late site on a natural mound in the pampa. Informants from the area say that there used to be slab cist tombs that have since been plowed under.

Hu-411. (Figs. 3.87, 3.88)

This site is located on a low hilltop. There are a number of slab cist tombs, human bones, and lithic debris over a small area. This is a habitation site with tombs.

Hu-412. (Figs. 3.1, 3.67, 3.88)

This site is located on a hilltop. There are three Archaic projectile points; fragments of agricultural tools; a substantial amount of lithic debris, including many nonlocal raw material types; and chulpas. The chulpas are 3 m in diameter. The site is in a defensive location with habitation debris and a small encircling wall, though this wall is not a typical defensive construction. The site itself is not that large, being 50 × 50 m at most. Hu-412 most likely served as a refuge and probably a ceremonial area in different periods throughout prehistory. The Tiwanaku occupation atop a high hill on a small site is quite rare.

Hu-413. (Figs. 3.1, 3.88)

This is a light scatter of artifacts and human bones associated with some badly eroded slab cist tombs. The site is located on the side of a large hill below Hu-412.

Hu-414. Machacamarca. (Figs. 3.1, 3.89)

This site is composed of a series of artificial terraces with eroding midden near the river.

Hu-415. (Fig. 3.90)

This is a small scatter of largely late pottery at the base of a rock outcrop in the pampa.

Hu-416. (Figs. 3.90, 3.91)

This is a 1.0 ha Formative through Late Horizon site located from the base to the top of a large rock outcrop. There are some Tiwanaku diagnostics though there is no Huaña. The late period occupation is part of Hu-415. At the base, there are some terraces and eroding midden. There are also chulpas at the top of the hill. These chulpas have diameters of between 2.0 and 3.0 m. Note that this outcrop is different from the one in Hu-417.

Hu-417.

This is a 1.0 ha Archaic and Formative and late site located from the base to the top of a large rock outcrop. At the base, there are some terraces and eroding midden. There are also chulpas at the top of the hill. These chulpas have diameters of between 2.0 and 3.0 m. Note that this outcrop is different from the one in Hu-416.

Hu-418.

This is a low rise on the pampa. There is at least one chulpa with a diameter of 3.0 m. There is evidence of other tombs. The pottery is Altiplano and Inca period along with a substantial collection of Formative I. It appears to be originally a Middle Formative habitation mound in the pampa that was subsequently used as a cemetery in the later periods.

Hu-419. Azangarillo.

This is a light scatter of late artifacts on a small mound at the edge of the pampa.

Hu-420. Parcialidad Collapani.

This site is a light scatter of late pottery on a natural mound on the pampa. There is also an isolated projectile point near the site that is Archaic in date.

Hu-421.

This is an Altiplano period tomb site on the pampa.

Hu-422.

This is a very light scatter of late pottery on top of a natural rock outcrop with an undiagnostic Archaic assemblage on the surface.

Hu-423.

This is a light scatter of late artifacts on a small mound at the edge of the pampa.

Hu-424.

This is a light scatter of late artifacts on a small mound at the edge of the pampa plus a few Formative II sherds. There are also some slab cist tombs on the site.

Hu-425.

This is a light scatter of pottery fragments on an eroding natural terrace at the edge of the pampa.

Hu-426.

This is a moderate scatter of pottery and a few lithic artifacts at the edge of the pampa.

Hu-427.

This is a set of terraces at the base of a rock outcrop with a scatter of lithic and ceramic artifacts. The lithic artifacts include nonlocal raw materials and grinding stones. The assemblage is undiagnostic Archaic. The site is a relatively large Formative I and II settlement of around 0.5 ha.

Hu-428.

This is a scatter of late artifacts on artificial terraces along with an undiagnostic Archaic assemblage. There are also natural rocks with pecked circular depressions. The pottery is early with a number of late diagnostics in the collection.

Hu-429.

This is a light scatter of artifacts at the base of a rock outcrop. At the top of the outcrop there are a number of badly disturbed chulpas with very large stones. The remains of slab cist tombs are also found at the top. The site has mainly Altiplano II and II pottery on the surface.

Hu-430. (Fig. 3.93)

This is a light scatter of late Formative artifacts on a small mound in the pampa. There are also slab cist tombs.

Hu-431. Cerro Pucara. (Figs. 3.92, 3.93)

This is a scatter of late artifacts on a number of artificial terraces that end at the top of the hill in a large platform. The platform is approximately 10 × 15 m in dimension. There are slab cist tombs with diameters between 1.10 and 1.50 m. This site is part of the complex including Hu-432 and Hu-433.

Hu-432. Comunidad Collapani; Cerro Pucara. (Figs. 3.92, 3.93)

This large and complex 6.0 ha site has Formative through Late Horizon occupations with an apparent hiatus in Huaña II and Tiwanaku times. The site is located at the top and sides of a hill. Artifacts include non-Archaic projectile points, many hoe and axe fragments, and Formative, Altiplano period, and Late Horizon pottery. There are small chulpas at the top of the hill with diameters of about 1.30 m, a number of slab cist

Figure 3.86.
View of lower valley from Hu-406.

Figure 3.87.
Site area of Hu-411.

Figure 3.88.
Site area of Hu-411 and Hu-412 in relation to Hu-413 and Hu-436.

Site Descriptions

Figure 3.89. Site area of Hu-414.

Figure 3.90. Site area of Hu-415 and Hu-416.

Figure 3.91. Site area of Hu-416.

tombs, defensive walls, platforms, quadrangular structures, and circular structures. This site is part of the complex including Hu-431 and Hu-433.

Hu-433. (Fig. 3.92)

This is a site located on the side of a hill. The site has occupations from the Formative phases plus some late sherds. There are artificial terraces with eroding midden. Likewise, there are well-made structures with selected fieldstones. In the lower part of the site are some chulpas and slab cist tombs. The terraces of this site are related to site Hu-432 and form a single settlement. This site is part of the complex including Hu-431 and Hu-432.

Hu-434. Quencha.

This is a light scatter of late artifacts on the base of a hill in the pampa.

Hu-435. Condorena. (Fig. 3.93)

This ridgetop site has circular structures between 4.0 and 6.0 m in diameter. There is a light scatter of late pottery on the surface.

Hu-436. Choquechambi. (Figs. 3.88, 3.94)

This is a scatter of pottery fragments and other artifacts on a series of low terraces at the base of a hill on the pampa. There are a number of slab cists with diameters between 1.0 and 1.5 m. The site has Formative, Tiwanaku, Altiplano period, and Late Horizon occupations. It is part of the site complex including Hu-413, Hu-437, and Hu-440.

Hu-437. Machacamarca.

This is a series of slab cist and cist tombs and a possible habitation site in the pampa. The slab cists are about 1.0 m in diameter. There are Formative, Altiplano period, and Late Horizon ceramic diagnostics on the surface. There is very little lithic debris, suggesting a series of disturbed tombs. It is part of the site complex including Hu-413, Hu-436, and Hu-440.

Hu-438.

This is a series of slab cist and cist tombs and a possible habitation site in the pampa. The lack of lithic debris suggests a series of disturbed tombs. The surface diagnostics are largely Altiplano period and Late Horizon in date. There are a few Tiwanaku diagnostic fragments on the surface as well.

Hu-439.

This is a series of slab cist and cist tombs on the pampa. The slab cists measure 1.3 and 2.0 m in diameter with large slabs 60 cm in height. The site area has Altiplano period and Late Horizon diagnostics. There is also some chert lithic debris on the surface.

Hu-440. Base de Cerro Choquechambi.

This is a large area of Altiplano period chulpas and slab cist tombs on the pampa. In one area, the slab cists are approximately 2.0 m in diameter with large blocks and in another area there are smaller slab cists (approximately 1.0 m in diameter).

Hu-441.

This is a series of slab cist and cist tombs on the pampa. The lack of lithic debris suggests a series of disturbed tombs. The surface diagnostics are largely Altiplano period in date.

Site Descriptions

Figure 3.92. Site area of Hu-431, Hu-432, and Hu-433.

Figure 3.93. Site area of Hu-430, Hu-431, Hu-432, and Hu-435, showing survey limit.

Figure 3.94. Slab cist on Hu-436.

Hu-442.
This is a light scatter of Altiplano period and Late Horizon pottery on a low rise on the pampa above the river. There are a few fragments of hoes on the surface and some other lithic debris, suggesting a habitation area.

Hu-443.
This is a light scatter of Altiplano period and Late Horizon pottery on a low rise on the pampa above the river. There are a few lithic tool fragments, suggesting a habitation area. There are no visible tombs or structures.

Hu-444. Comunidad Acocollo.
This appears to be a cemetery area in the pampa, located near a number of modern cochas. The pottery is largely Altiplano period with some possible Late Horizon. There are no lithic fragments. We did not make a collection.

Hu-445.
This is a moderately dense scatter of lithic and ceramic artifacts at the edge of a pampa. There are abundant lithic flakes, fragments of agricultural implements, and Altiplano period and Late Horizon pottery. There are some badly disturbed slab cist tombs in this site area. The site is located near some cochas.

Hu-446.
This is a very light scatter of Formative, Altiplano period, and Late Horizon pottery and some lithics on a low pampa mound. The site is located approximately 150 m from the river. There is no visible architecture on the surface.

Hu-447.
This is a very light scatter of Altiplano period pottery and some lithics on the side of a pampa. The site is located approximately 200 m from the river. There is no visible architecture on the surface.

Hu-448. Comunidad Tahurauta. (Fig. 3.99)
This is a very small site, about 30 × 30 m in size, with an abundant scatter of lithics and some Middle Archaic diagnostics. There are many different raw materials represented. There are at least six point fragments. The site is located at the edge of the pampa. There are very few pottery fragments on the surface, all late in date. The site is a very old lithic workshop.

Hu-449. (Figs. 3.67, 3.95, 3.99)
This is a scatter of some lithics and Altiplano period pottery. There are no lithic bifaces or other diagnostic material that indicate an Archaic occupation, but the type of raw materials and flake characteristics suggest a possible Archaic site. The site is located at the edge of the pampa. This site was accidentally numbered twice and is also listed as Hu-493.

Hu-450.
This is a scatter of some Altiplano period pottery. The site is small, located next to a very large modern cocha in the pampa. There is no visible architecture or tombs on the surface.

Hu-451.
This is a high hilltop site on Cerro Pichacane, about 25 × 25 m in size. It is a nondescript scatter of pottery on some poorly made terraces and there are just a few fragments of Altiplano period pottery plus some Formative I. The site is used today for pagos and may have had some ritual significance in the past. The existence of an early Formative occupation is very significant in this defensive location.

Hu-452.
This is a high hilltop and hillside site on Cerro Pichacane, about 70 × 70 m in size. It is a nondescript scatter of Altiplano period pottery and one Late Archaic projectile point (Fig. B4). The site has typical slab cist tombs and approximately six terraces. There is no evidence of ritual at this site.

Hu-453.
This half-hectare site is located on the side of a hill. There are some semicircular structures and some chulpas with diameters of about 2.0 m. There is very little material on the surface.

Hu-454.
This is a moderately sized Inca site with squarish structures, mostly similar to those at Hu-453 and Hu-456, located on a series of low terraces. There is a round structure with a diameter of about 4–6 m.

Hu-455.
This small site has Formative III and Altiplano period diagnostics. It is located on the top of a small hill at over 4075 m above sea level. Clearly in a defendable location, it is significant that there is a Formative point in the collection.

Hu-456.
This site has only one ceramic type—Huaña I—that is spread over a small area of about 0.60 ha. This site has rectangular structures similar to those at Hu-453 and Hu-454 and at least one circular structure with a diameter of about 4 to 6 m.

Hu-457.
This is a largely Altiplano period site with a Late Archaic component on top of a mesa or *peñón*. There is a single decorated Tiwanaku fragment as well on this high and defendable area.

Hu-458.
This is a single Archaic projectile point located on the top of a high hill.

Hu-459.
This is a late site located at the base of a large hill. There is also one nondiagnostic Archaic point. On some low terraces, the site has chulpas with average diameters around 2.5 to 3.0 m and slab cist tombs with large upright slabs and diameters of approximately 0.80 m.

Hu-460.
This small, late site is a scatter of a modest number of artifacts over a presently cultivated surface in the pampa.

Hu-461. (Fig. 3.5)
This small, late site is a scatter of a modest number of artifacts over a presently cultivated surface in the pampa.

Hu-462. (Fig. 3.5)
This site consists of at least two chulpas, approximately 1.20 m in diameter, located on the pampa. The associated material is all late in date.

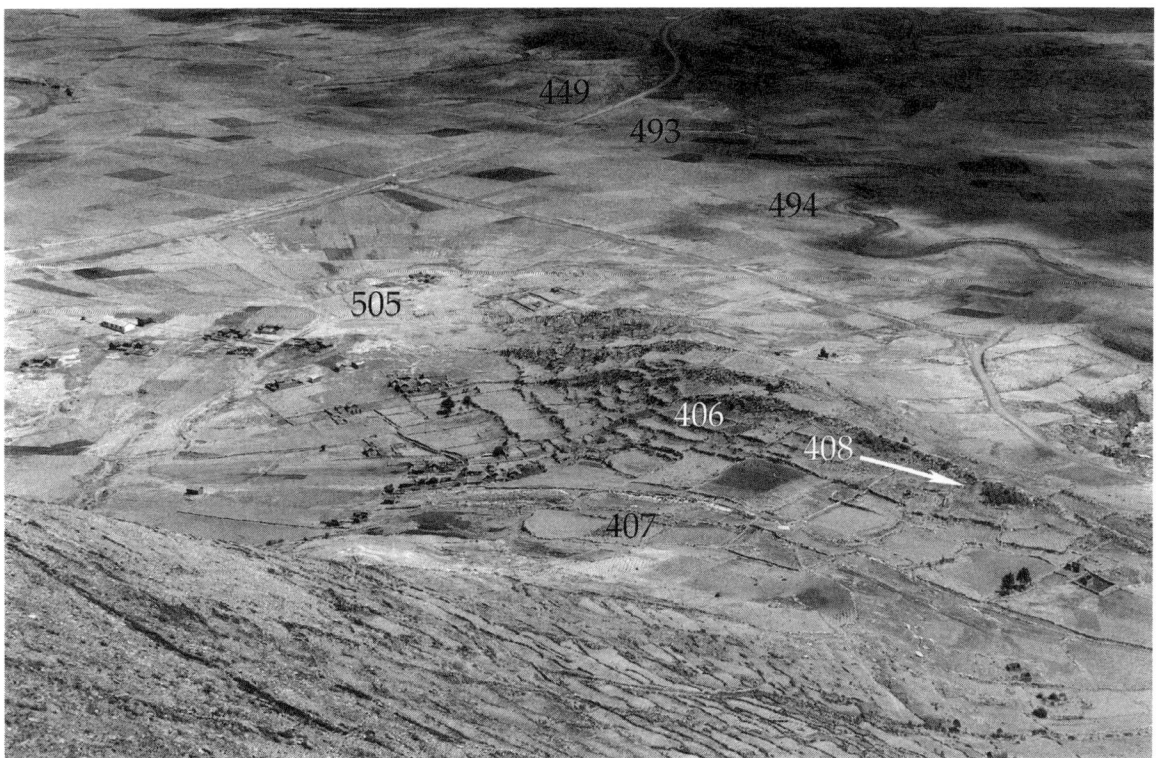

Figure 3.95. Site area around Hu-505 and its relation to various adjacent sites.

Hu-463.
This is a single Archaic projectile point in the pampa.

Hu-464.
This half-hectare site has Formative and late period components in the form of a light scatter of diagnostics on the side of a hill.

Hu-465. (Fig. 3.5)
This is an artifact concentration, over about a half hectare, on the pampa near the road. There are chert flakes amid late period ceramic diagnostics.

Hu-466. (Fig. 3.5)
This site is a series of slab cist tombs and chulpas in the pampa. There are also some highly disturbed round structures.

Hu-467. (Fig. 3.5)
This is a light scatter of late diagnostics near the road in the pampa.

Hu-468. (Fig. 3.5)
This 1.0 ha site has abundant Formative and Altiplano diagnostics on the surface on the pampa adjacent to a hill. There is also a high density of andesite and basalt agricultural tools, a diagnostic of Formative sites. Likewise, the site has a wide range of lithic materials including obsidian, chert, and quartzite artifacts.

Hu-469.
This is a very small concentration of late artifacts associated with a number of slab cist tombs on a small natural mound. The diameters of these slab cists are approximately 0.80 to 1.20 m.

Hu-470.
This is a piece of rock art with small cupules about 2–3 cm in diameter.

Hu-471.
These are slab cist tombs and one chulpa in the pampa associated with late diagnostics. The chulpa is about 1.20 m in diameter while the slab cists are around 0.80 m in diameter.

Hu-472.
This moderately sized late site is located at the base of a hill. There is lithic debris on the surface of this site.

Hu-473.
These are slab cist tombs and one chulpa in the pampa associated with late diagnostics. The slab cists are around 0.80–1.20 m in diameter. See Hu-477.

Hu-474.
This is a small scatter of late diagnostics on the side of Cerro Pichacane. This most likely represents a disturbed cemetery.

Hu-475.

This is a small scatter of late diagnostics on the pampa. This most likely represents a disturbed cemetery.

Hu-476.

These are slab cist tombs and two chulpas on a small peñón at the base of Cerro Pichacane, associated with late diagnostics. The slab cists are around 0.80–1.00 m in diameter and the chulpas are around 1.40 m in diameter.

Hu-477.

This is a small concentration of Altiplano period diagnostic ceramics and lithics associated with Hu-473. In reality, they compose a single site complex. Hu-477 has abundant lithic debris indicating a workshop near and around a rockshelter. The site has obsidian, chert, quartzite, jasper, and basalt. This site is a lithic working area next to the domestic component in Hu-473. These two areas are good evidence that the Altiplano period peoples were working and using a wide variety of lithic raw material sources, as in the Archaic period.

Hu-478.

This small cemetery site has a number of slab cist tombs and at least one chulpa. Most of the tombs are larger, about 1.20 m in average diameter.

Hu-479.

This is a small scatter of Altiplano period artifacts near a cocha in the pampa.

Hu-480.

This is a small scatter of late pottery and lithics in a quebrada in the pampa. The pottery is Altiplano period in date. Lithics include some obsidian and chert that represent an undiagnostic Archaic component. There is no evidence of tombs or other architecture, although the site is heavily disturbed.

Hu-481.

This is a small scatter of late pottery and Archaic lithics on the pampa edge. The pottery is Altiplano period and Late Horizon in date. No lithics were recovered.

Hu-482. (Fig. 3.96)

This site has a rare Early Archaic component, a Late Archaic component, and Altiplano period pottery scattered at the edge of a river in the pampa. This Early Archaic site is most likely associated with Hu-484–Hu-486. There is a large quantity of lithic debris, suggestive of a workshop. There are no agricultural tools. There is no surviving architecture on the site.

Hu-483. (Fig. 3.98)

This site has a Middle Archaic component and a possible Altiplano period occupation, based upon the round structures present. At least seven points or point fragments were recovered along with obsidian, quartz, chert, and basalt flakes plus other lithic tools. The quantity of lithic debris is impressively high, suggestive of a workshop. The site is located on the edge of the Cala Cala River.

Hu-484. (Fig. 3.98)

This site has a rare Early Archaic component, a Middle Archaic component, and Altiplano period pottery scattered at the edge of a river in the pampa. At least ten points were recovered from the surface along with obsidian, basalt, chert, and quartz plus other lithic tools. This Early Archaic site is most likely associated with Hu-482–Hu-486.

Hu-485. (Fig. 3.98)

This site has a rare Early Archaic component, plus Middle Archaic and Late Archaic occupations along with some Altiplano period pottery scattered at the edge of a river in the pampa. At least twenty-four points were recovered from the surface along with obsidian, basalt, chert, and quartz plus other lithic tools. This Early Archaic site is most likely associated with Hu-482–Hu-486.

Hu-486. (Figs. 3.96, 3.98)

This site has a rare Early Archaic component, a Late Archaic component, and Late Horizon pottery scattered at the edge of a river in the pampa. At least eleven points were recovered from the surface along with obsidian, basalt, chert, and quartz plus other lithic tools. This Early Archaic site is most likely associated with Hu-482–Hu-485.

Hu-487. (Figs. 3.96, 3.98)

This Late Archaic site is located on the edge of the Cala Cala River. There were at least twenty-four points along with a large quantity of obsidian, quartz, chert, and basalt flakes plus other lithic tools.

Hu-488. (Figs. 3.96, 3.97)

This site has Middle and Late Archaic components along with Altiplano period pottery. The site is located next to the Cala Cala River. At least nine points were recovered from the surface along with obsidian, basalt, chert, and quartz flakes plus other lithic tools.

Hu-489. (Figs. 3.67, 3.96, 3.97)

This site has Middle and Late Archaic components along with Late Horizon pottery. The site is located next to the Cala Cala River. At least fifteen points were recovered from the surface along with obsidian, basalt, chert, and quartz flakes plus other lithic tools.

Hu-490. (Figs. 3.67, 3.96, 3.97)

This site has Middle and Late Archaic components along with Altiplano and Late Horizon pottery. The site is located next to the Cala Cala River. A few point fragments were recovered from the surface along with obsidian, basalt, chert, and quartz flakes plus other lithic tools.

Hu-491.

This site has a Late Archaic component along with Late Horizon pottery. The site is located next to the Cala Cala River. Two points were recovered from the surface along with basalt, chert, and quartz flakes plus other lithic tools.

Hu-492.

This site has a Late Archaic component along with Altiplano period pottery. The site is located next to the Cala Cala River. One basalt point was recovered from the surface along with basalt and chert plus other lithic tools.

Hu-493. (Figs. 3.67, 3.95, 3.97, 3.99)

This site has a Late Archaic component along with Late Horizon pottery. The site is located next to the Cala Cala River. Five points were recovered from the surface along with basalt and obsidian flakes. This site was accidentally numbered twice and is also listed as Hu-449.

Site Descriptions

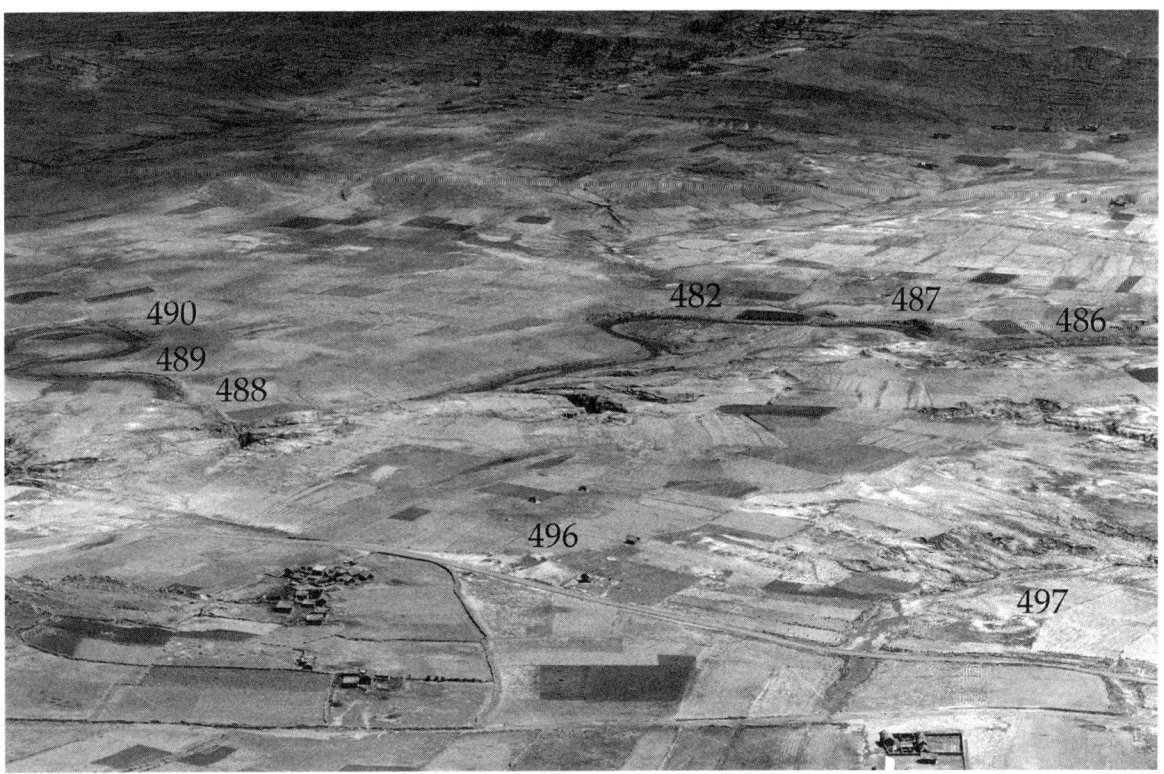

Figure 3.96. Relationship between sites Hu-482, Hu-486, Hu-487, Hu-488, Hu-489, Hu-490, Hu-496, and Hu-497.

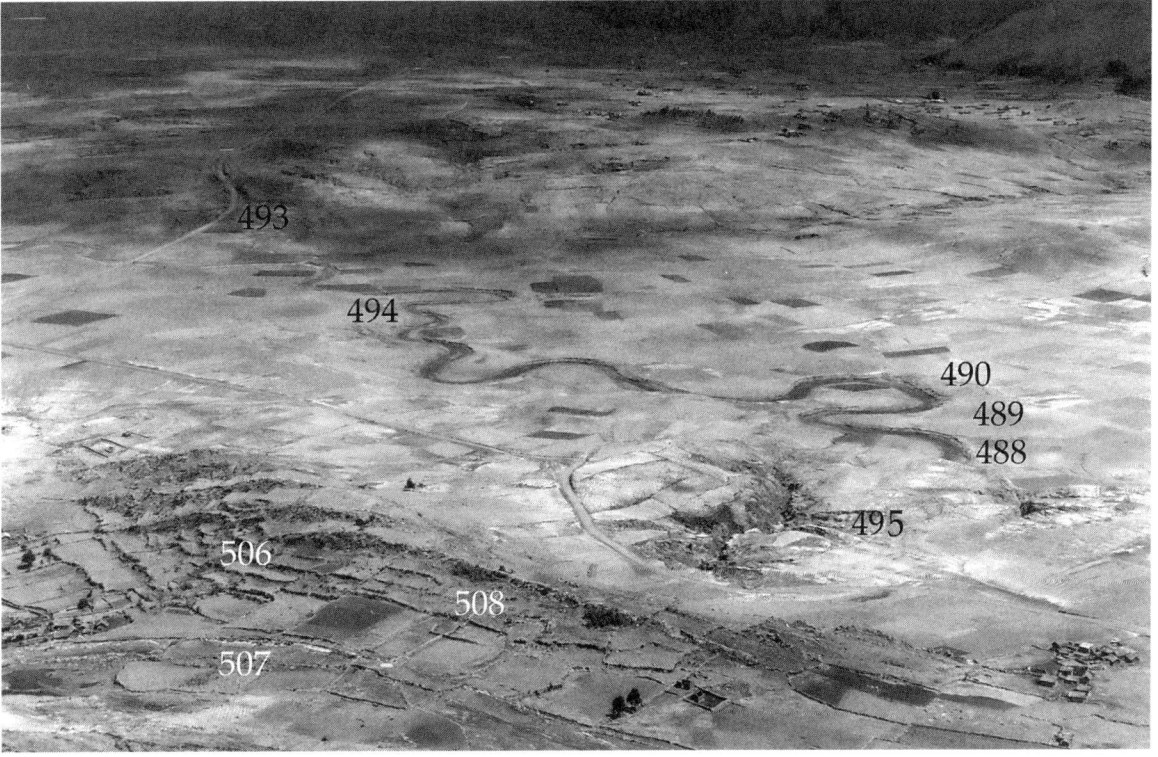

Figure 3.97. Site area around Hu-506 and its relation to various adjacent sites.

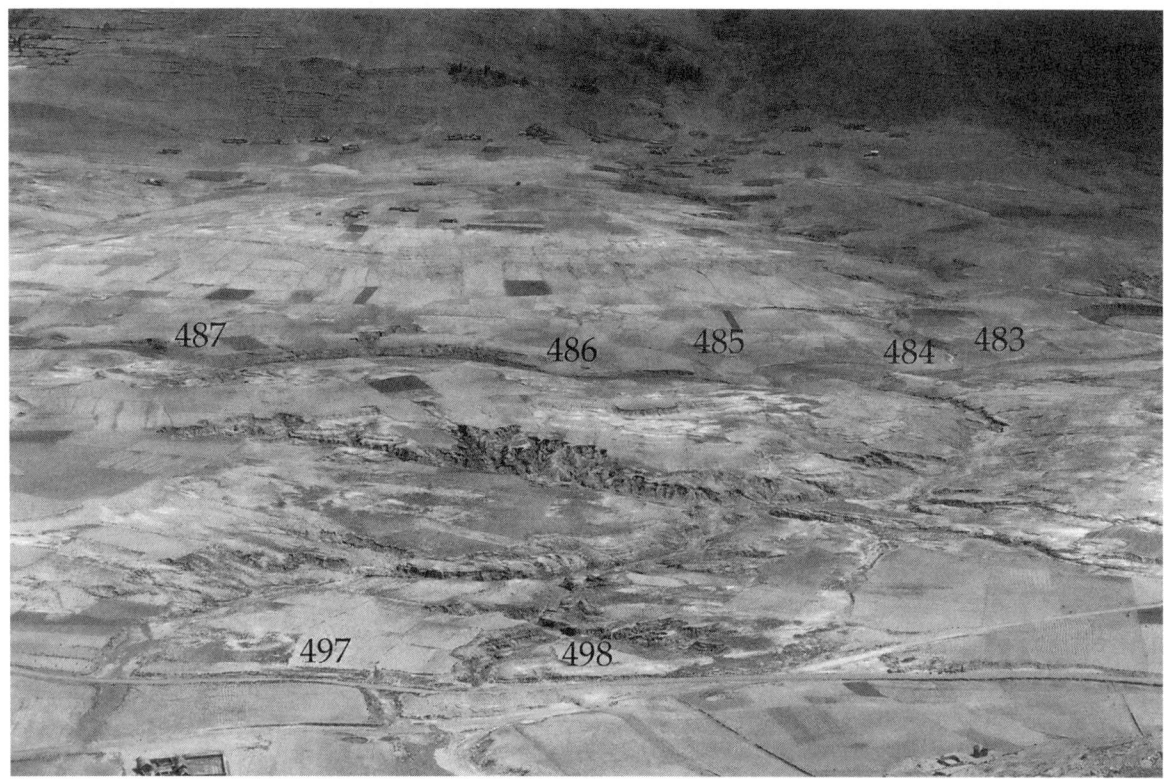

Figure 3.98. Relationship between sites Hu-483 through Hu-487, Hu-497, and Hu-498.

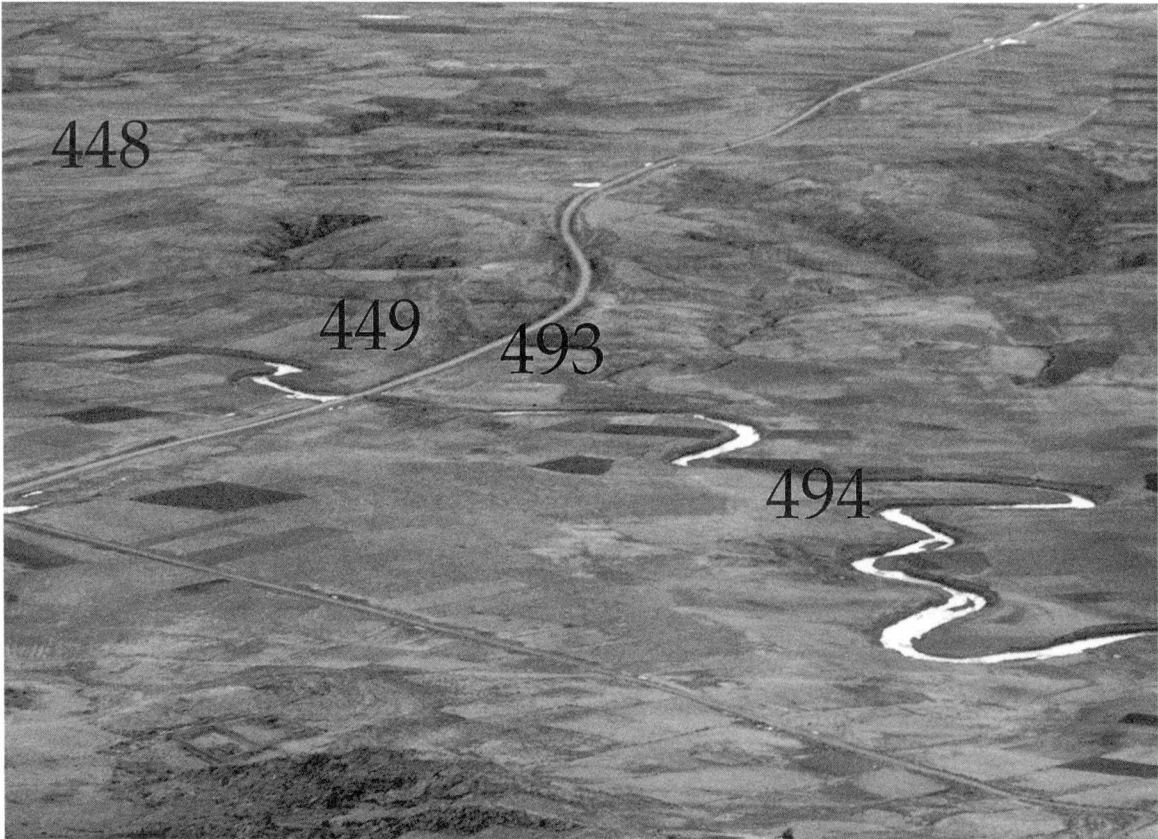

Figure 3.99. Mid-valley view showing the relationship of major and minor sites.

Hu-494. (Figs. 3.67, 3.95, 3.97, 3.99)
This small site is located at the edge of the pampa. There is a small scatter of Archaic lithics and some Altiplano period pottery.

Hu-495. (Figs. 3.67, 3.97)
This small site is located at the edge of the pampa. There is a small scatter of Formative II and Late Horizon pottery and a small amount of Archaic lithic debris.

Hu-496. (Fig. 3.96)
This area has a Late Archaic lithic scatter along with some Late Horizon pottery on the edge of the pampa. One Archaic obsidian point was recovered.

Hu-497. (Figs. 3.96, 3.98)
This small scatter of Formative II and late pottery is located on the pampa. There is no surviving architecture or tombs. There is a small amount of Archaic lithic debris as well.

Hu-498. (Fig. 3.98)
This small scatter of Late Horizon pottery is located on the pampa. There is no surviving architecture but there are the remains of a few slab cist tombs. There is a small amount of Archaic lithic debris as well.

Hu-499. (Fig. 3.100)
This site is located on top of a low hill in the pampa. There are a number of slab cist tombs over a 20 × 20 m area with associated Late Horizon pottery. The slab cists have diameters of around 0.80 m. There is also an existing chulpa, 1.30 m in diameter.

Hu-500. (Fig. 3.100)
This site is located on the side of a hill on the pampa. There are a number of slab cist tombs on artificial terraces. The associated pottery is Altiplano period in date. There are a number of human bones scattered on the surface, indicating that the tombs were disturbed in the last few years.

Hu-501.
This is a light scatter of Late Horizon pottery at the base of a hill. There are some circular structures 4.0–5.0 m in diameter. There are no lithics or other artifacts on the surface of the site.

Hu-502.
This is a light scatter of Altiplano II pottery at the base of a hill with a small Archaic component.

Hu-503. (Fig. 3.84)
This area is characterized by a number of slab cist tombs on a small promontory that rises in the pampa. The tomb diameters average around 0.80 m. The site is also an area of modern pagos.

Hu-504. (Fig. 3.84)
This site is located on the second natural terrace above a quebrada. This is a cemetery site with at least seven slab cists with diameters of about 0.90 m. The pottery is late in date.

Hu-505. (Fig. 3.95)
This is a site associated with the complex at Hu-406–Hu-408. It is an area of late pottery located on a natural terrace below the main mound area. This is a cemetery site with a number of slab cists that are heavily disturbed.

Hu-506. (Figs. 3.67, 3.97)
This site is about 1 ha in size and is located adjacent to and on the Llamaccani hill. There are a number of artificial terraces that rise up to a natural rock outcrop. It is an important site with occupations from the Terminal Archaic through Qaluyu, Pucara, Tiwanaku, Late Huaña, Altiplano period, and Late Horizon. The pottery is dense and well made with diagnostics from each of these periods. We recovered over thirty points, hoe fragments, lithic flakes, grinding stones, and a number of metal artifacts. There are also a number of slab cist tombs with eroding human bone. There are eroding middens on the terraces. This is a small but important site that was continually occupied for several millennia.

Hu-507. (Figs. 3.67, 3.97)
This site is about 1 ha in size and is located on the sides of the Llamaccani hill. There are a number of artificial terraces that rise up to a natural rock outcrop. It is an important site with occupations from the Archaic, Qaluyu (Formative I) through Pucara, Huaña, Altiplano period, and Late Horizon. The pottery is dense and well made with diagnostics from each of these periods. There are obsidian, chert, quartz, and basalt flakes and other lithic fragments and agricultural implements. There are a number of slab cist tombs that range between 0.80 and 1.20 m in diameter.

Hu-508. (Figs. 3.67, 3.97, 3.100)
This is a small scatter of Formative, Altiplano period, and Late Horizon materials on the side of a hill near and inside a rock outcrop. There is a chulpa with a 2.50 m diameter and a scatter of human bones plus some disturbed slab cist tombs. Lithic materials include obsidian and basalt point fragments and a quantity of lithic debris of various raw materials. There is a small Archaic component as well.

Hu-509.
This is a light scatter of Altiplano II artifacts on some low terraces. There are no lithic artifacts on the surface.

Hu-510.
This is a small Formative II site located on a low hill. The pottery is overwhelmingly characterized by domestic wares.

Hu-511.
This is a 1 ha Formative and late site located on a low hill. The Formative occupation is probably restricted to some low domestic terraces that are now cultivated, while the late artifacts come from some slab cist tombs on the site. There were no lithic artifacts on the surface.

Hu-512.
This is a 1 ha Formative and late site located on top of a low hill about 400 m from the present edge of Lake Titicaca. The site has a number of low domestic terraces around a rock outcrop. There are some shaped blocks on the site as well. The site has a number of obsidian, chert, and quartz flakes and other debris along with some agricultural tool fragments.

Hu-513.
This is a small scatter of late diagnostics on a hilltop with some lithic debris.

Hu-514. (Figs. 3.101, 3.102)
This is a large 1 ha cemetery with Altiplano period diagnostics. The site contains a number of slab cist tombs and chulpas. The diameters of the slab cists average around 0.80 m while the chulpas are approximately 1.20 m in diameter. There were no lithic artifacts noted on the surface.

Hu-515. (Figs. 3.101, 3.103)

This is a 1 ha fortified site with Formative, Altiplano period, and Late Horizon occupations. There are a number of circular structures between 3.0 and 4.0 m in diameter on four large terraces that lead to a platform. There are also chulpa bases and a possible square chulpa. Lithic artifacts include hoe fragments and chert.

Hu-516. (Fig. 3.103)

This is small Altiplano period cemetery site with a few badly disturbed slab cist tombs and at least one chulpa. The site is on a low hilltop. The pottery is Altiplano period in style. We did not make a collection.

Hu-517. (Fig. 3.104)

This site has one Early–Middle Archaic transitional biface, a scatter of lithic debris and flakes, and a scatter of late pottery. The site is a little over 1.0 ha in size, is built on artificial terraces, and has some circular structures.

Hu-518. (Fig. 3.105)

This is a small Altiplano period cemetery site with a number of disturbed slab cist tombs and at least one chulpa. The chulpa is 3.0 m in diameter. The slab cist tombs range from 0.80 to 1.20 m in diameter. The site is on the sides and top of a low hill. It is most likely associated with the pukara at Hu-519.

Hu-519.

This probable pukara is built on the top of a low hill with at least two, and possibly three, circular walls. There is a low density of Altiplano period pottery and no additional visible structures. This is a minor pukara, one not used as a permanent habitation but rather as a refuge site.

Hu-520. (Fig. 3.103)

This is a small site with a few circular structures that are badly disturbed. The diagnostic pottery is late in date. There are some basalt and chert flakes.

Hu-521. (Figs. 3.103, 3.106)

This moderately sized village site is built with artificial terraces. There is a possible sunken court with a monolith. The court is approximately 20 × 20 m in size. It is badly disturbed and it is difficult to determine with any precision the direction. A conservative estimate is that it is between 320 and 333 degrees or about 35 degrees off north. The monolith measures approximately 1.60 × 0.40 × 0.18 m. Diagnostic pottery on the surface includes Qaluyu, Pucara, Tiwanaku, and Late Horizon. There are abundant lithic materials including three Formative points, fragments of agricultural implements, and chert, obsidian, and quartz flakes. There is an Archaic scatter as well.

Hu-522. (Fig. 3.107)

This site is located on the sides of a hill. It has three chulpas, one in "Cuzco" style, and two built with fieldstone masonry along the side of the hill. These round chulpas are 1.20 m in diameter. Hu-522 also has an Archaic component. It is the only Middle Archaic site found near the lake.

Hu-523.

This is a badly eroded chulpa, 2.50 m in diameter. There was no associated pottery on the surface.

Hu-524.

This is a small Altiplano period site with a scatter of pottery on slightly elevated ground with some very low artificial terraces. The site also has a modern apacheta that is used for contemporary pagos.

Hu-525.

This is a single chulpa, 1.40 m in diameter, on the side of a hill. There are a few Altiplano period sherds associated with the looted tomb.

Hu-526. (Figs. 3.36, 3.108)

This area has six tombs, two chulpas and four slab cist tombs. One chulpa is large, with a 3.50 m diameter. The second chulpa is smaller and very poorly preserved. It was probably less than 2.0 m in diameter originally. The four slab cists are approximately 0.80 m in diameter. Human bones are found on the surface of many of these tombs.

Hu-527. (Fig. 3.36)

This is a cemetery area spread over about 2 ha. There is one chulpa with a diameter of 1.50 m and two others with diameters of 1.20 m. There are several slab cists with diameters of about 0.80–1.00 m as well. The pottery is all Altiplano period in date.

Hu-528.

This is a single chulpa with a 1.50 m diameter.

Hu-529.

This is a pukara with large circular structures 6.0 m in diameter. There are also a number of cist tombs on terraces. This is a minor pukara, one not used as a permanent habitation but rather as a refuge site.

Hu-530.

This site is 1.50 ha in size and on a hill. The pottery is Altiplano period in date. There are a number of circular structures from 4.0 to 6.0 m in diameter. There are also chulpas from 1.20 to 1.40 m in diameter.

Hu-531. (Fig. 3.109)

This is a 1.5 ha habitation and cemetery site with a light scatter of Altiplano period and Formative I pottery. A number of circular structures are found on the surface of this hilltop site. The diameters of these structures range from 4.0 to 6.0 m. There are also some smaller structures with 1.2 m diameters. These latter structures are possible chulpa bases. However, the construction is more similar to domestic structures and it is possible that these were storage features of some sort. Chulpas on the site include some with 3.5 m diameters. There are some human bones on the surface.

Hu-532. (Figs. 3.36, 3.110–3.113)

This Formative and Altiplano period site is located on the top of a low hill. The site is approximately 1.50 ha in size. There are a large number of tombs on the south side that are next to, and inside of, a sunken court. The court measures approximately 20 m on a side, with a possible monolith. It is about 25 degrees east of north. The chulpa diameters range between 1.5 and 3.0 m.

Hu-533. (Fig. 3.36)

This is a Late Horizon cemetery with a number of slab cist and chulpa tombs. The site is located on the side of a hill.

Figure 3.100. Chulpa on Hu-508.

Hu-534.
This is an Altiplano period cemetery site with three slab cist tombs on a low promontory. Human bones and Altiplano period pottery fragments are associated with these tombs.

Hu-535.
This is an Altiplano period cemetery site with at least six slab cist tombs with diameters of about 0.80 m. Human bones are associated with these tombs.

Hu-536. (Fig. 3.114)
This Formative, Huaña, and Altiplano period site is located on the tops of two low hills that are adjacent to a much larger hill to the east of the community of Sunuoco. One of the hills holds a platform at the top, cardinally oriented, that measures about 6.0 × 12.0 m. To the south side of the site are a number of tombs, approximately sixteen in number, that are small slab cists. There are abundant agricultural implements as well as obsidian, quartz, and quartzite on the surface. This site is most likely part of the settlement that includes Hu-512.

Hu-537.
This site is located on the pampa adjacent to the Huancané River. The modern road cuts through this site and one can see stratified midden and/or construction sequences for about 2.0 m. Huge quantities of midden are eroding out of these artificial cuts and natural cuts from the river. The surface contains Qaluyu and Pucara pottery. There are Huaña I and Tiwanaku I diagnostics as well, with no evident later occupations. The river cut indicates that there are burials. There is abundant lithic debris including agricultural implements, obsidian, chert, quartz, and quartzite. There is an Archaic scatter as well. We also found bone artifacts, specifically needles.

Hu-538.
This is a small rise in the pampa with a few slab cist tombs. The associated pottery is Altiplano period and Late Horizon. There are no bones or other artifacts associated with these tombs.

Figure 3.101.
View of sites Hu-514 and Hu-515.

Figure 3.102.
Tomb on Hu-514.

Figure 3.103.
View of sites Hu-515, Hu-516, Hu-520, and Hu-521.

Figure 3.104.
View of site Hu-517.

Figure 3.105.
View of site Hu-518.

Figure 3.106.
Limestone monolith on Hu-521.

Figure 3.107.
Chulpa on Hu-522.

Figure 3.108.
Chulpa on Hu-526.

Figure 3.109.
Chulpa on Hu-531.

Figure 3.110. Topographical location of Hu-532.

Figure 3.111. Close-up of sunken court area in Hu-532.

Figure 3.112. Chulpa on Hu-532.

Figure 3.113. Chulpa on Hu-532.

Figure 3.114. Site area of Hu-536.

4 | Huancané-Putina Settlement Patterns: Interpretations and Discussion

Thanks to the fine-grained ceramic typology developed by C. Chávez (Chapter 2 of this volume), we are now able to detect some broad patterns of settlement shifts over time. The following analysis of the settlement pattern data relies solely on sites with a domestic component (Table 3.1). Sites with cemeteries are found in Table 3.2. Habitation sites usually contain tombs and some included ritual components, and these of course are included in Table 3.1 and are represented in the analyses of the settlement patterns.

While we wish to avoid going beyond the Huancané-Putina data until we have fully analyzed the other 700+ sites from the Arapa and Taraco areas, we are able to draw some conclusions from this sector of the survey.

Almost 500 sites were documented in the survey areas of Huancané-Putina (Fig. 4.1; Tables 3.1–3.3), with all ecological zones utilized. Site functions include habitation, burial, defense, agriculture, ritual, and special purpose. Raised field remnants were found far up the valley into the Putina sector, and agricultural terracing is virtually ubiquitous in the area. It is curious that the area north of Huatasani and south of Putina was not as extensively utilized in virtually all time periods, indicating that there must be some environmental constraints for intensive human land use in the region or that the area was a buffer zone between ethnic or sociopolitical groups.

In contrast, the lakeshore, which probably took its present form about 2000 years ago, was extensively utilized since the Early Formative. And, interestingly enough, during this time span, there was at least a five-meter variation in lake levels that would have resulted in shifting shorelines through time.

The Archaic Period

We recorded almost 100 Archaic period sites in the Huancané-Putina survey area (Table 3.3). These sites contained a number of identifiable occupations from the Early Archaic through the Terminal Archaic. Along with the diagnostic assemblages, there were 57 nondiagnostic Archaic components plus sites with possible Terminal Archaic occupations. We identified the components using the previous lab work on these materials and/or the use of published material by Mark Aldenderfer and Luis Flores Blanco (2011), Cynthia Klink, Nathan Craig (2005), Craig et al. (2010), and Lisa Cipolla (2005).

All Archaic sites were found along the river or in the lowland areas on low terraces near good water sources (Cipolla 2005: Figs. 4.3–4.6). As seen in Figure 4.2, groundwater rises to the surface and creates rich micro-zones of plant life that attracts animals. Archaic sites are located in the background on the higher

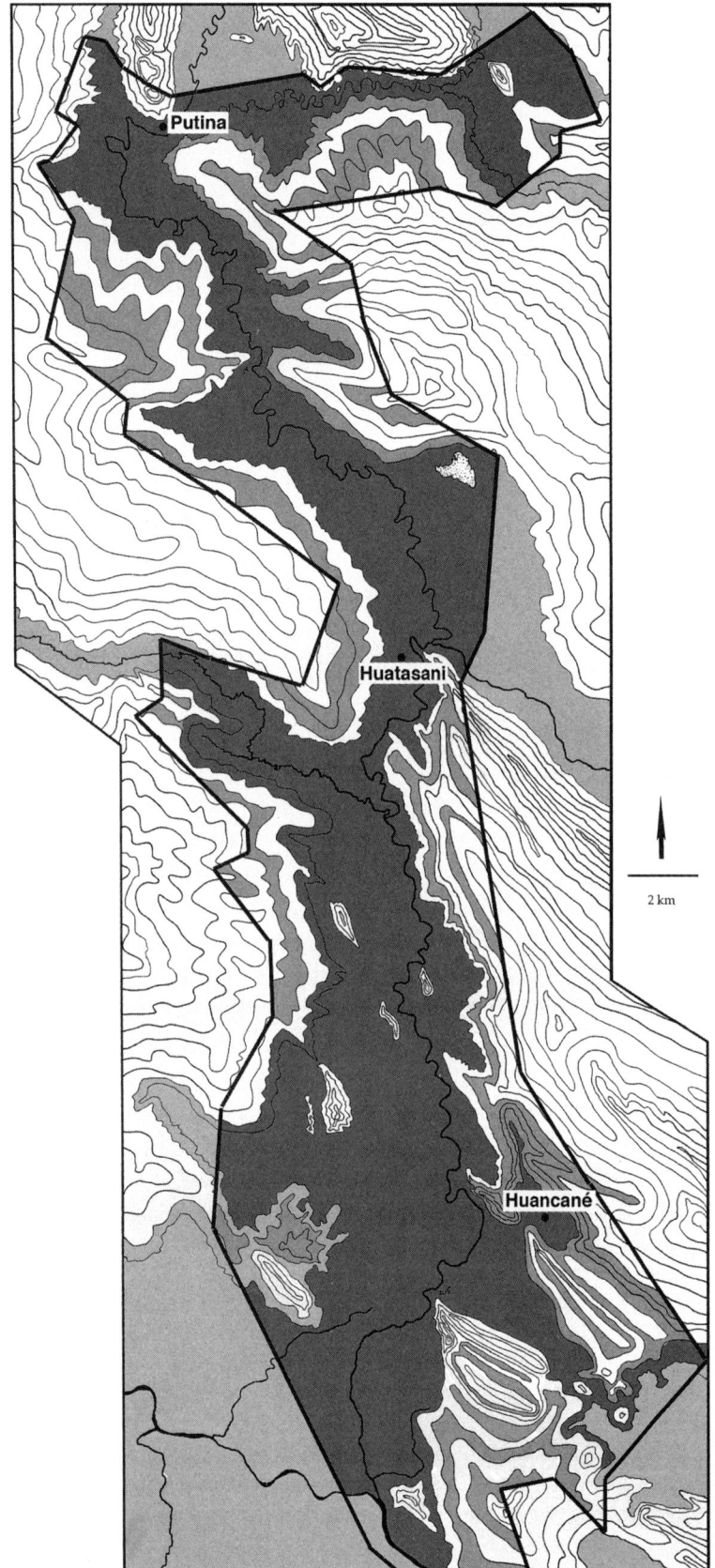

Figure 4.1. The Huancané-Putina survey area.

hill area overlooking the bofedal in the foreground below the grazing animals. Figure 4.3 illustrates how these bofedal areas can swell with heavy rains and be used as cochas or small artificial lakes. The Archaic period peoples in the survey area were almost exclusively focused on these low and wet areas throughout their millennia of occupation.

The Early Archaic is represented by 6 sites, possibly 8 (see Cipolla 2005: Fig. 4.3).[1] The Early Archaic, according to Klink and Aldenderfer (2005) and Cipolla (2005), dates to approximately 10,000–8000 BP. All the sites, except one, cluster in the Cala Cala area above the river in a well-watered and rich ecozone. The one site with the Early Archaic component to the south, Hu-406, is on a natural hill above the river.

The Middle Archaic is represented by 14 sites (Cipolla 2005: Fig. 4.4). The Middle Archaic, according to Klink and Aldenderfer (2005) and Cipolla (2005), dates to approximately 8000–6000 BP. The Cala Cala area continues to be a major focus of activity from the Early Archaic, but there is an expansion throughout the entire survey area where bofedales and springs are found today. The only area with no Middle Archaic use recorded is the middle of the survey area, from Huatasani into the Putina Valley above Cachichupa. This is a generally rich area of cocha today but we do not know what the landscape was in the Middle Archaic. There is only one site with a Middle Archaic component near the lake (Hu-522). This site is located on the side of a hill and not in pampa. The absence of a Middle Archaic presence could be a result of the geomorphological characteristics; for example, the sites may be buried under alluvium. It is also possible that the subterranean waters did not reach the surface in this period, or that there was simply little interest in this otherwise potentially resource-rich region. It is also possible that the sites were so short-term or ephemeral that no artifacts remained.

The Late Archaic is represented by 27 sites (Cipolla 2005: Fig. 4.5). This period, according to Klink and Aldenderfer (2005) and Cipolla (2005), dates to approximately 6000–4400 BP. The Late Archaic is an amplification of the Middle Archaic pattern with the addition of land use in the present-day lake edge. It is possible that the lake had expanded to its current level by the end of this period, though this would be somewhat inconsistent with paleoclimate interpretations that show the lake reaching its current levels by around 2000 years ago.

The Terminal Archaic is represented by 7 securely dated sites and several others that most likely date

---

1. Since Cipolla's (2005) initial analysis, we have resurveyed some areas. As a result, the numbers in this manuscript are slightly revised.

Figure 4.2. A bofedal or low, swampy area in the Putina area. Bofedales were exploited extensively by Archaic peoples.

Figure 4.3. A very large cocha created by a natural bofedal near the village of Kakachi in the southern part of the survey area. The photograph was taken in the wet season. Note the stands of reeds that are cultivated today. In the past, areas like this were prime zones for Archaic exploitation.

to this period (Cipolla 2005: Fig. 4.6). The Terminal Archaic, according to Klink and Aldenderfer (2005) and Cipolla (2005), dates to approximately 4400–3600 BP. There are an additional 33 sites with materials that could range from Terminal Archaic to the Late Horizon. There is a high density of Terminal Archaic sites in the Cala Cala region and Huatasani areas (Figs. 4.4, 4.5). The total number of Terminal Archaic sites is most likely similar to the Late Archaic given the uncertainty of the diagnostic material. The one possible difference is the absence of diagnostic sites from the lakeshore area. Again, the large number of possible Terminal Archaic sites makes any interpretations of this period a bit difficult at the present time. Much more research is necessary for this fascinating time period.

Formative I

We discovered 61 habitation sites with Formative I diagnostics in the study area (Fig. 4.6). As described in Chapter 2, the Formative I ceramic categories correlate to the Qaluyu period and are dated by Chávez (Chapter 2, this volume) to around 1300–750 BCE. Formative I ware is associated exclusively with Qaluyu, and would be considered equivalent to Early Qaluyu in other chronologies. Sites with Formative I are distributed up and down the Putina River, but there is no extension of sites into the eastern section of the survey region. The northernmost Formative I sites cluster around Putina.

One of the most significant results of this survey is the discovery that Formative I materials are unequivocally found on defensible sites. The settlement pattern of the pukaras of this time period generally matches the distribution of the large habitation sites as well, a pattern that continues into the Altiplano period. That is, we learned from research in the Juli-Pomata region (Stanish et al. 1997) that the Late Intermediate period habitation areas were not exclusively inside the fortified walls themselves (see Arkush 2005a, 2011). Rather, the pukaras were built as temporary refuges for scattered settlements around the landscape. The same appears to be true for the Formative I occupations. Unlike the Juli-Pomata area (or the southern Titicaca region where other surveys have been conducted), raiding and conflict developed at a much earlier date in the northern region.

We have no excavation data from these pukaras except for those from one pukara excavated by Cipolla at the site of Hu-81. The date that she recovered lies in the Formative III period (see below). However, there is little doubt that people were using and possibly living on these defensible locations in the earliest Formative periods.

The site of Hu-068 is typical of fortified sites with a Formative I occupation (Figs. 3.23, 3.24). The site has the classic form of a pukara, but the hill itself is lower than the ones found in the Altiplano period and the walls are considerably smaller. However, the site has three walls and throwing stones. The major occupations are Formative I–III, and while some Late Intermediate period pottery was on the surface, the bulk of the recovered fragments were Formative in date. We have to conclude, as with Hu-079 and Hu-081, that there were pukaras in the earliest Formative periods.

Working in the Pukara Valley, Amanda Cohen (2010) discovered some of the earliest sunken courts in the region. The site of Huatacoa has a sunken court with the earliest dates coming in at circa 1450–1300 BCE (Cohen 2010: Chap. 4). This would of course be in the earliest periods of the Formative I ceramic group affiliated with Qaluyu. The distribution of sunken court sites in the Huancané-Putina survey correlates well with the distribution of habitation settlements in general, supporting models of numerous competing elite political formations in this early period (Stanish 2003; Griffin and Stanish 2007; Stanish and Levine 2011).

Formative II

We discovered 82 habitation sites with Formative II diagnostics in the study area (Fig. 4.7). As described in Chapter 2, the Formative II ceramic categories correlate to a transitional period between and *within* Qaluyu and Pucara. This period is dated by Chávez (Chapter 2) to around 750–200 BCE. This would correspond to a Late Qaluyu/Early Pucara date in other chronologies. This date does not fit the traditional chronologies where relatively abrupt breaks between Qaluyu and Pucara styles are assumed. Our data from excavations in Taraco (Levine 2012; Stanish and Levine 2011) indicate a fairly long transitional period, represented by the Formative II, of at least 300 years during which both Qaluyu and Pucara styles were being manufactured. Thus, they overlap and co-occur for at least three centuries.

As with the Formative I settlement pattern, sites are distributed up and down the rivers, with the northernmost Formative II sites clustering around Putina. As with Formative I, there is no extension of settlement to the east. The total number of habitation sites increased by about 30% from the Formative I period (from 90 to 106 sites). Both periods are the same length in estimated years so there is some commensurability in the comparison. The number of large sites remains effectively the same, so most population increases appear to have occurred in the smaller sites surrounding the larger ones.

The total number of defensible sites remains roughly the same with 2 new ones built (Hu-172 and Hu-241). The establishment of Hu-172 in the Huatasani area effectively bridges the two areas and provides a refuge for the expanding populations in the center of the survey area. Three carbon dates for pukaras excavated by Arkush (2005: Table D1) in the nearby northern Titicaca region of Asillo fall into this period. These dates are 914–375 calBC (95.4%), 793–540 calBC (95.4%), and 518–210 calBC (95.4%).[2] These data, along with those from the Formative I distribution, strongly suggest that pukaras developed quite early in the northern Titicaca Basin.

---

2. The sample numbers are: AA12871, AA56161, and AA54250; calibrations with OxCal 4.1, IntCal 09 curve.

Figure 4.4. The Cala Cala region looking west from the river. This was an area of high Archaic site densities.

Figure 4.5. The Huatasani area with the town in the center of the photograph.

266 — *The Northern Titicaca Basin Survey*

Figure 4.6. The Formative I ware distribution (habitation sites only).

Figure 4.7. The Formative II ware distribution (habitation sites only).

Formative III

We discovered 65 sites with Formative III diagnostics in the study area (Fig. 4.8). As described in Chapter 2, the Formative III ceramic categories correlate to Initial Pucara. This time period is dated by Chávez (Table 2.8) to around 200 BCE–AD 300. As with the Formative II settlement pattern, sites are distributed up and down the river valley. Likewise, the northernmost Formative III sites cluster around Putina with no extension to the east. The total number of large sites remains the same, so the decrease in the number of total sites comes at the expense of the smaller ones.

There are 8 defensive sites or pukaras in the Formative III, 1 less than the Formative II. Significantly, there is a large gap in the middle of the survey area in the distribution of the large sites. The distribution of sunken courts also follows this pattern, with two distinct areas. For the first time in the history of the valley, there appear to be two distinct polities forming in the north and south of the Huancané-Putina river valley.

One carbon date excavated by Cipolla and described in Chapter 3 (footnote 1) for the defensive site Hu-081 came in at 108 calBC (94.2%) 87 calAD. The earlier date range could possibly include Qaluyu materials. However, this date is most likely typical of Formative III.

Huaña I

We discovered 32 sites with Huaña I diagnostics in the study area (Fig. 4.9). As described in Chapter 2, the Huaña I ceramic types correlate stylistically to Late Pucara but also include the emergence of a local tradition diverging out of Pucara. We refer to this tradition as Huaña. Chávez dates this period (Chapter 2) to around AD 300–500. Classic Pucara pottery styles most likely cease around AD 300 but the red slip and paste characteristics of Pucara comprise the Huaña tradition.

The general settlement pattern is similar to Formative III though much less dense, suggesting, perhaps, a collapse in the regional political system. Sites are distributed up and down the rivers. Likewise, the northernmost Formative III sites cluster around Putina with no extension to the east. One big shift was the dramatic drop in pukaras during the Huaña I period. There were only 2 defensive sites with Huaña I materials. In effect, defensive sites largely disappear in the north and there are just a few in the central and southern area of the survey zone.[3]

Huaña II and Tiwanaku I

We discovered 11 sites with Huaña II diagnostics in the study area. As described in Chapter 2, the Huaña II ceramic types cor-

---

3. Arkush (2008: Table 2) reports one date from a pukara in her survey area that dates to 435–887 calAD (95.3%). The carbon age is 1370 +/- 100. Sample number AA54218.

relate to a period of Tiwanaku influence on the Pucara-derived local tradition from the previous centuries (Fig. 4.9). It is likely that Tiwanaku I materials coexisted with Huaña II, making this a difficult period to interpret. One hypothesis is that Huaña II and Tiwanaku I (Figs. 4.10, 4.11) effectively overlap between approximately AD 750 and 850, with the former representing local populations and the second representing either Tiwanaku colonies or affiliated settlements that were part of a Tiwanaku political system.

We do not have sufficient data at this time to propose a model of the nature of this Tiwanaku-local interaction. What we can say is that the pattern here is strikingly different from that seen in the western and southern sides of the Titicaca Basin. In this initial century of Tiwanaku influence in the Huancané-Putina areas, we see at the very least the coexistence of several sites with no Tiwanaku materials.

The Tiwanaku-affiliated settlements cluster near the lake up to 17 km or so from the shore. Only 5 sites with Tiwanaku materials have Huaña II, a surprisingly stark pattern. This indicates that there were Tiwanaku-affiliated sites that existed simultaneously with others that were not interacting with this expanding state. Interestingly, the Huaña II materials are concentrated on large (> 2 ha) habitation sites. All the Huaña II sites are located along the road up the river valley. Tiwanaku I-affiliated sites, in contrast, are dispersed along the landscape.

Only one pukara has any Huaña II or Tiwanaku I diagnostics, and even the presence of a few sherds may be incidental or indicative of gift-giving or an occasional trade item. A similar pattern was noted by Arkush (2005a). In short, the previous ritual and defensive patterns of earlier periods effectively end at this time. It would also appear, somewhat counterintuitively, that the level of conflict subsided with the onset of Tiwanaku influence, suggesting that the expanding state suppressed conflict. It is also possible that there was a regional shift that will be detected in the other survey data as yet unanalyzed.

Tiwanaku II

The Tiwanaku II ceramic types as defined by Chávez in Chapter 2, date, we propose, to approximately AD 850–1000. We find 20 sites in the survey area with Tiwanaku II diagnostics (Fig. 4.12). The Tiwanaku II style is correlated to the very strong presence of this foreign polity in the region. It most likely represents actual geopolitical control by groups incorporated into the Tiwanaku orbit.

Tiwanaku sites cluster within 15 km of the lake shore. There are 4 large (more than 2 ha) sites in the cluster in the southern side of the survey near the lake. Three sites are found along the road leading into the higher reaches of the study area. The 3 sites—Hu-506, Hu-126, and Hu-042—comprise a pattern similar to that found in the Juli-Pomata area and the Mazo Cruz region. This pattern is interpreted as one reflecting a focus on trade into the forested region, with Tiwanaku-affiliated sites along the entire roadway and with access to the eastern slopes.

Huancané-Putina Settlement Patterns 269

Figure 4.8. The Formative III ware distribution (habitation sites only).

270 | *The Northern Titicaca Basin Survey*

Figure 4.9. The Huaña I ware distribution (habitation sites only).

Figure 4.10. The Huaña II ware distribution (habitation sites only).

Figure 4.11. The Tiwanaku I ware distribution (habitation sites only).

Figure 4.12. The Tiwanaku II ware distribution (habitation sites only).

The Tiwanaku settlement pattern is typical of the Juli-Pomata and Puno region. Each of these areas sees a decrease in the number of sites with what appears to be a similar or even slightly higher population based upon total site size. In other words, we see a substantial aggregation of population into fewer but larger sites. Only 3 sites, all near the lake edge, have sunken courts and Tiwanaku II styles. It is likely that these earlier courts were used during the Tiwanaku occupation. This observation requires further testing with the data from the Arapa-Taraco regional data.

Altiplano I

The Altiplano I diagnostic styles date to around AD 1000–1275. The date of 1275 is based upon the work of Arkush (2008, 2011) in adjacent areas where she found a relatively late construction episode of pukaras at this time. Her "Phase I" (2008:14) is identical in age range to our Altiplano I. This likely rapid increase in pukara construction begins in the Altiplano II period. Altiplano I still has eleven pukaras, though this represents only about half of the pukaras in the Altiplano II period. Arkush's (2008: Table 2) research discovered only two pukaras with probable use dates between AD 1000 and 1300.[4] The pattern in which defensive posturing decreases in the Huaña II/Tiwanaku I and Tiwanaku II times ceases in the Altiplano I period. Altiplano I represents the development of a local agropastoral lifeway with the collapse of the Tiwanaku state influence in the region and a small but rising increase in conflict.

We found 140 habitation sites that have these Altiplano I materials (Fig. 4.13; Table 3.1). Sites are found throughout the survey region with a large number of pukaras. This pattern is very similar to other post-Tiwanaku settlement patterns in the region with a collapse of regional centers and a dispersal of the population throughout the region. Sites are small and transient. Above-ground burials become the norm as populations constantly move about the landscape but seek to mark ancestral territories.

All previous research in the Titicaca Basin has failed to discover any use of the sunken courts in the post-Tiwanaku periods. We found a fair quantity of Altiplano-style pottery on the surface of some sunken court sites. However, we do not believe that these were functioning at this time or later. Rather, post-Tiwanaku peoples used the sites in the same way that virtually all the hills in the study area were used—permanent or semi-permanent habitation, defensive sites, and possibly burial and ritual locations.

Altiplano II

Altiplano II is dated from approximately AD 1275 to around 1400. This corresponds in part to Arkush's Phase II at AD 1275–1450+ (2008:15). The Altiplano II would be the classic Late Intermediate period lifeway of large pukaras surrounded by scores of small villages and hamlets.

We found 266 Altiplano II habitation sites spread throughout the survey zone (Fig. 4.14). Again, this pattern is consistent with other surveys in the region including the Juli-Pomata and Mazo Cruz areas where there is a substantial dispersal of small permanent and semi-permanent sites. The distribution of above-ground tombs parallels the distribution of habitation sites in the study area.

We found twenty-four pukaras including substantial use of all the large and imposing ones such as Hu-008. The vast numbers of pukaras excavated by Arkush in neighboring areas were first occupied and utilized between AD 1275 and 1400. That pattern seems to be confirmed in the Huancané-Putina study area as well. This period represents the maximum extent of pukara use in the study area.

Altiplano III

Altiplano III is dated from approximately AD 1400 to the first Inca settlements circa AD 1450/1475. It may overlap somewhat with Inca I in its later phase. Altiplano III represents the apogee of the Aymara señoríos of the ethnohistoric texts.

We found 183 sites that have Altiplano III materials (Fig. 4.15). There are eighteen pukaras utilized in this period as well, including many of the very large ones. Two large pukaras in the northern survey region were not utilized in this period, as were some smaller pukaras in the south. These data support the conclusions of Arkush who sees continued use of the pukaras into the latter part of the fifteenth century in the region. She notes that "in the first half of the fifteenth century, the threat of attack on pukara populations had not lessened" (Arkush 2008:356). We see this pattern in our survey area as well.

Habitation settlement expands throughout the study area as is typical for Late Intermediate period settlements in the Titicaca region. All areas were occupied and utilized by these agropastoral peoples.

Inca I

The pottery analysis is sufficiently sensitive to pick up the initial contact of the Aymara señoríos with the expanding Inca state. This Inca I period dates to the brief time from AD 1450 prior to the actual geopolitical control of the region by the Inca state circa AD 1475/1500. It is associated with the styles Inca Collao and Inca Huatasani or Inca I. It is possible that there was overlap with Inca I and Altiplano III for some of the time. The 1450 date is taken to be the approximate period when influence, though not control, from the Cuzco region is first seen in the region. This relationship between the expanding Inca state and local polities is similar to that discovered by Stanish (1985) in

---

4. The two dates come from sites in the Azángaro area and are calibrated 2-sigma between AD 1000 and 1300 (sample numbers AA54220 and AA54233 in Table 2).

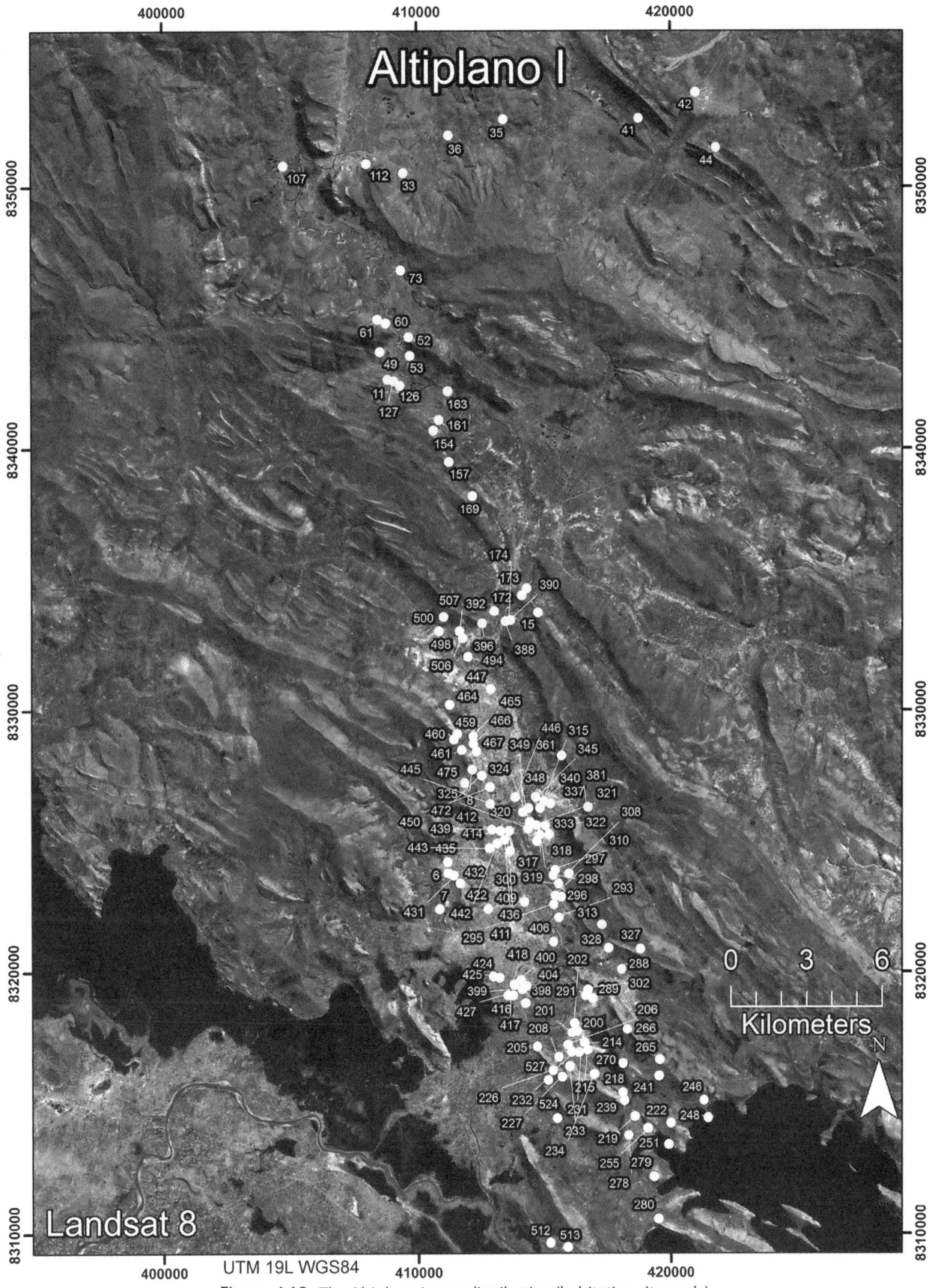

Figure 4.13. The Altiplano I ware distribution (habitation sites only).

Figure 4.14. The Altiplano II ware distribution (habitation sites only).

Figure 4.15. The Altiplano III ware distribution (habitation sites only).

the Moquegua region. The Estuquiña-Inca period was defined as the time in which Inca trade goods filtered into the valley, but prior to actual Inca geopolitical control. Well-made Cuzco Inca pottery was found in unequivocal Late Intermediate period contexts. Once the Inca controlled the region, sites moved down valley and the Late Horizon pottery styles shifted. We see a similar pattern here with the Inca I and Inca II periods.

The survey located 157 habitation sites with Inca I materials (Fig. 4.16). The settlement pattern is similar to that of Altiplano III with sites throughout the survey area. Inca I materials were found on more than a dozen pukaras, though many of these were associated with chulpa burials or ritual sites.

Inca II

The Inca established their political domination over the region during the last three decades of the fifteenth century, a control that extended up to AD 1532. The presence of the Inca Empire is associated with local styles and imitation Inca (Inca II) that began around 1475–1500 and continued to the Spanish Conquest a generation later in 1532. There are virtually no sherds in the survey area that were imported from the Inca capital Cuzco. Virtually all pottery was locally manufactured.

There are 78 sites with Inca II pottery styles (Fig. 4.17). The number of sites decreases but the average size increases. Curiously, the number of pukaras with Inca II materials drops in half from Inca I. Even if these were used for ritual, the data indicate a sharp drop in the use of pukaras or defended hills during this period.

The data suggest that there is a slight decrease in the population during Inca control. This contrasts sharply with the data from the Juli-Pomata area where the Inca period populations were the highest of the occupational sequence. What we see here is a movement away from the northern part of the survey area and a move even closer to the roads. With the exception of Huancané and Milliraya, we also see a shift out of the Huancané-Putina area to perhaps the Arapa region to the west.

Inca III

Inca III pottery styles represent the very early Colonial period in the region. The number of sites remained relatively constant from the preceding Inca II at 82 total habitation occupations (Fig. 4.18). Only four pukaras have Inca III pottery, suggesting an abandonment of the hilltops for defense or ritual, with just a handful of exceptions. The settlement pattern is very similar to the Inca II period, indicating not much change under early Spanish rule, at least vis á vis settlement location. With the exception of Huancané, Spanish Colonial state interest shifted to the Arapa area in the north.

Discussion

The approximately 450 sites in the Huancané-Putina survey zone contain approximately 1800 distinct occupations in both cemetery and habitation sites. This is a large data base, but it is a fraction of the number of sites and occupations in the entire northern Titicaca survey area. In the Arapa-Taraco region, we have at least 800 additional sites with more than 2800 occupations that will be published in the future. These data, along with continuing excavation research (e.g., Levine et al. 2013; Stanish and Levine 2011), provide us with a very solid foundation to understand the evolutionary dynamics of the region.

As mentioned above, we do not want to over-interpret in the absence of a full analysis of the Arapa-Taraco data. However, we can point out a few significant features of the Huancané-Putina data, including several of the Formative period. The ceramic analysis by Chávez in Chapter 2 shows us that the widespread notion of a smooth transition from Qaluyu to Pukara is not correct. Rather, there is substantial overlap in these styles that is fortunately reflected in the Formative II group. Excavations at Taraco confirm this overlap where both styles were found in good stratigraphic contexts (Levine 2012). This overlap in time is quite substantial, and one not predicted by the Horizon framework as commonly used in the central Andes (see Moseley 2013).

Rather, what we see in the northern Titicaca region is the emergence of a widespread Qaluyu style early on, with the development of the Pukara style in the late first millennium BCE. We hypothesize that these two styles were associated with the Taraco and Pukara sites respectively, up to around AD 100 or so when the site of Taraco was raided and burned (Stanish and Levine 2011). At this point, the Qaluyu style ended coincident with the fall of Taraco as a political center in the region. The Formative III group represents this time when the Pukara style and the site dominated the region.

We also find Formative pottery groups on fortified, or at least defensible, locations in the northern Titicaca Basin. This pattern is not seen in the south or southwest (Stanish et al. 1997; Albarracin-Jordan and Mathews 1990). The southernmost defensible Formative site that we know of is Incatunuhuiri, a few kilometers west of modern Chucuito (Kidder 1943). There are, however, some Formative sites in the Juli-Pomata region that are located on hilltops surrounded by terraces. This is a defensible location but not to the degree that we see in the north.

What these settlement data strongly suggest is that conflict was part of the political landscape much earlier in the northern Titicaca Basin than in the south. Moreover, it appears that there was a different dynamic in the processes of state formation in the two areas. In the north, conflict between complex polities emerged early, a process of cycling between periods of political "consolidation and dissolution" (Marcus 2008:257). In the south, in contrast, conflict emerged later in time though there is some evidence of competition in the formation of the state in this region as well.

Figure 4.16. The Inca I ware distribution (habitation sites only).

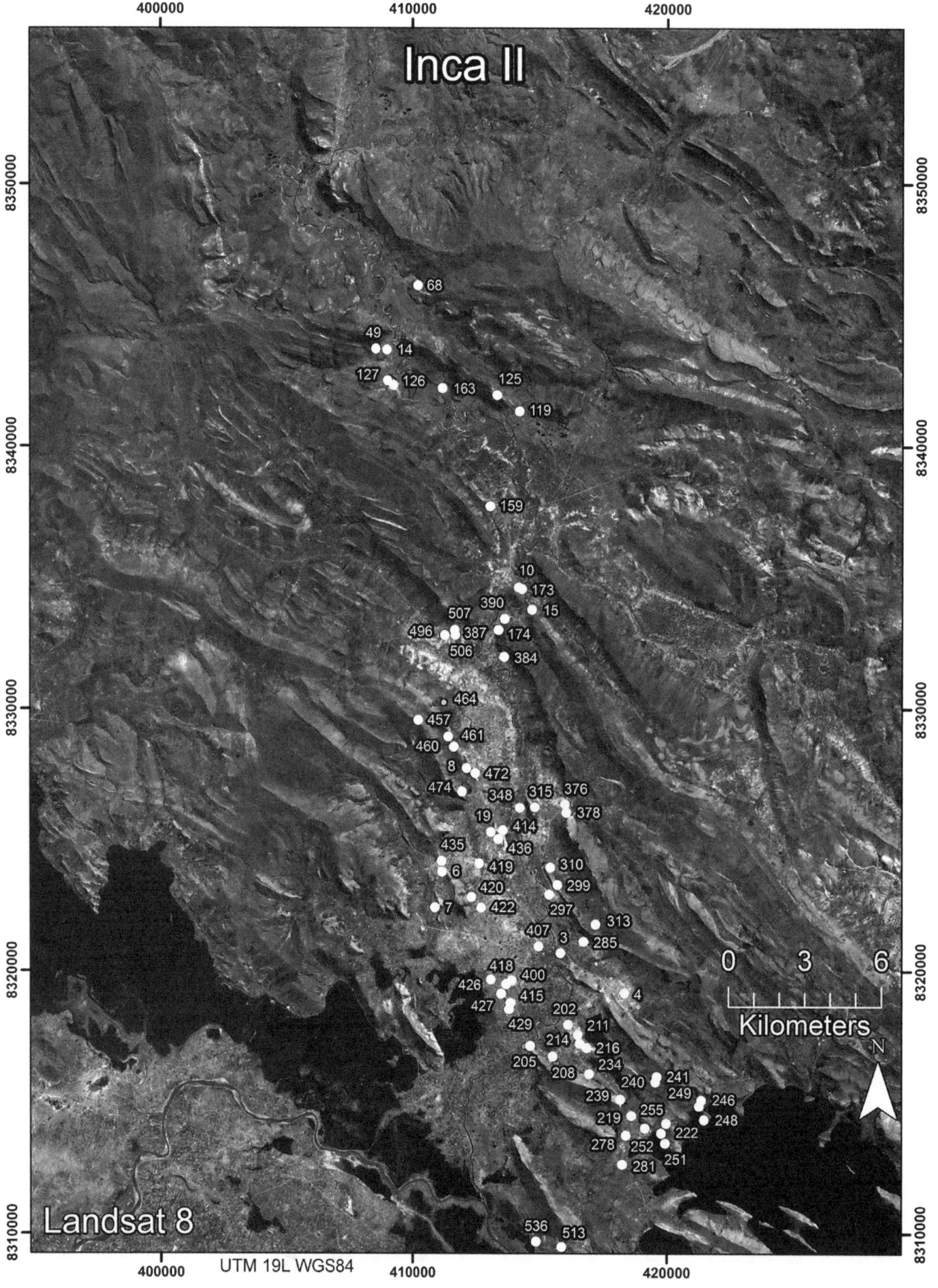

Figure 4.17. The Inca II ware distribution (habitation sites only).

Figure 4.18. The Inca III ware distribution (habitation sites only).

The post-Formative periods in the northern Titicaca Basin are substantially different from those in the south. In the Tiwanaku or Pacajes region, there is a fairly smooth transition from the Upper Formative into the Tiwanaku period. Tiwanaku occupations were established in a wide area in the south, southwest, and southeast Titicaca region. Work in the Juli-Pomata region (Stanish et al. 1997), the Tiwanaku Valley (Albarracin-Jordan and Mathews 1990), the Island of the Sun (Bauer and Stanish 2001), and other areas indicates a process of fairly slow but steady Tiwanaku state incorporation in the Pacajes region. The appearance of Tiwanaku pottery styles in any region in the south generally coincides with the disappearance of existing ones. This is most profitably interpreted as the consolidation of power by the Tiwanaku state, reflected in shifting types of politically- and ritually-charged art styles. A good example of this is seen at the site of Tumantumani near Juli, where the earlier Sillumocco styles (local Upper Formative) were replaced by Tiwanaku canons (Stanish, Steadman, and Seddon 1988).

In the north, earlier art styles (collectively called Huaña) were not replaced with Tiwanaku ones. Rather, there is a fairly long period in which Tiwanaku pottery was imported into the region, coexisting with the local Huaña styles. This ultimately gave way to the establishment of Tiwanaku colonies. However, the local traditions persisted while these enclaves were established, continuing on into post-Tiwanaku times.

The post-Tiwanaku Altiplano periods in the north are similar to the south in terms of settlement patterns, evidence of intense conflict, the use of pukaras, the dispersal of populations from political centers, and a greater emphasis on pastoralism in the economy. Like in the south, the sunken court and monolith traditions end. There is a proliferation of sites throughout the study area.

The pottery analysis of Chávez likewise picks up the first evidence of Inca contact in the region, in a manner similar to what Julien (1983) found at Hatuncolla. That is, initial Inca contact with the Colla peoples was indirect, first detected as some subtle changes in pottery styles that show clear influence from Cuzco. Once the Inca conquered the region, the pottery styles substantially shifted to Cuzco canons, but with the use of local pastes.

In short, the regional research in the Huancané-Putina has provided a broad overview of the evolutionary dynamics in this region of first-generation state development. Future research, particularly intensive excavations in key sites, will allow us to refine this work and pick up even more subtle details of this incredible region of indigenous social complexity.

Appendix A
Ceramic Materials from the Huancané-Putina Survey

Appendix A contains a sample of the pottery styles not contained in Chapter 2. These fragments complement those used in the construction of the typology in Chapter 2 with some of the more prominent and highly diagnostic pieces found on the survey. The attributes for the figures in Appendix A are found in Table A1 immediately following the figures. This table does not contain the attributes for those ceramic objects used in Chapter 2 because this would be redundant. All the attribute information for the pieces illustrated in Chapter 2 is found in that chapter.

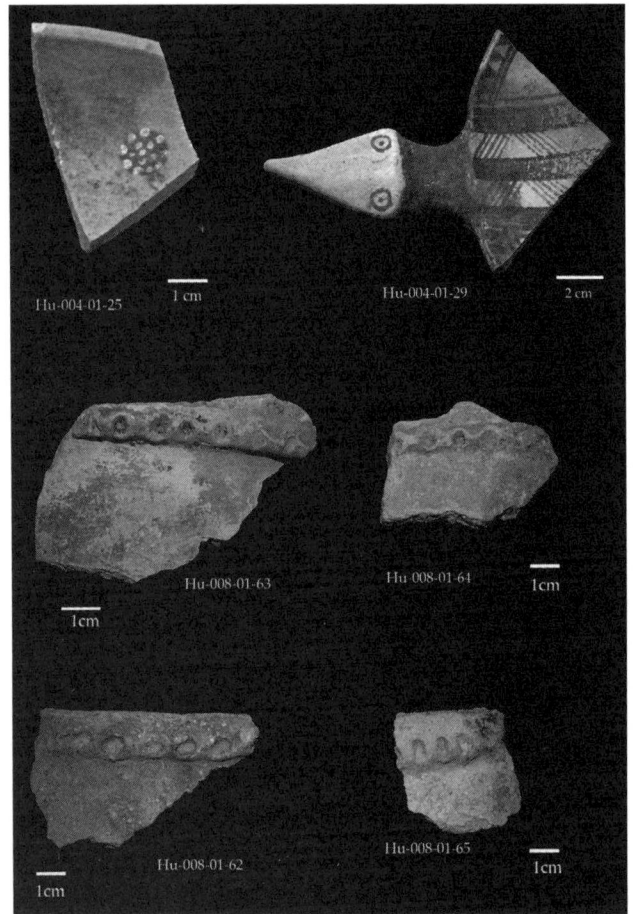

Figure A1. Ceramic fragments from Hu-004 and Hu-008.

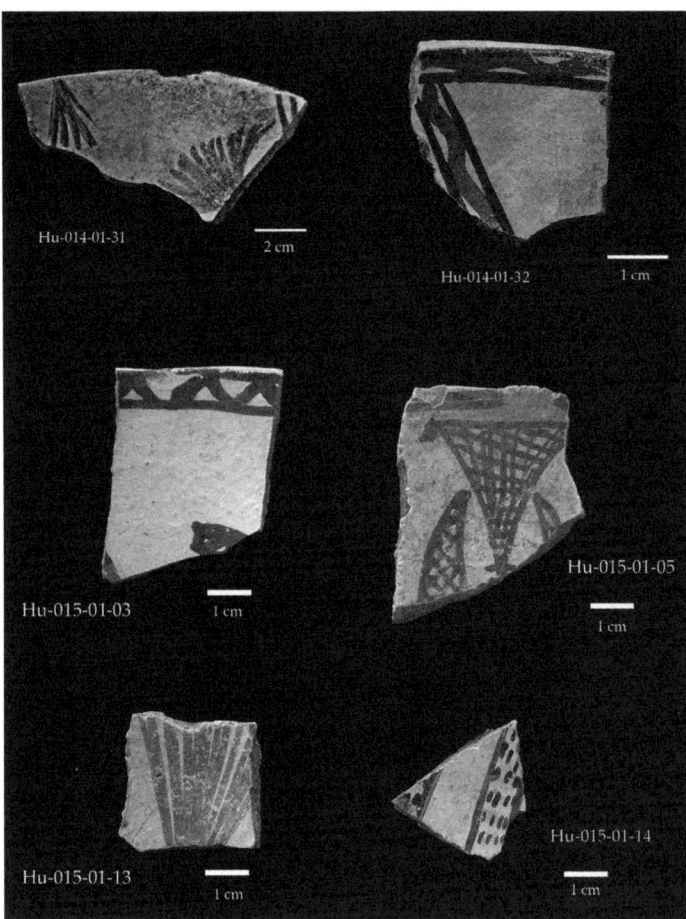

Figure A2. Ceramic fragments from Hu-014 and Hu-015.

Appendix A 285

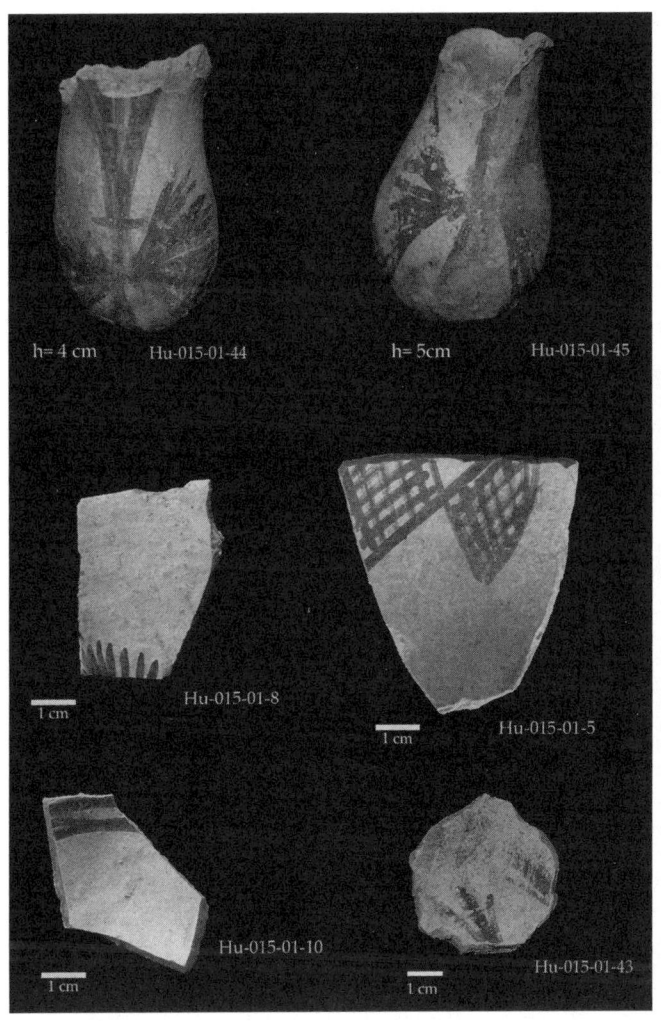

Figure A3. Ceramic fragments from Hu-015.

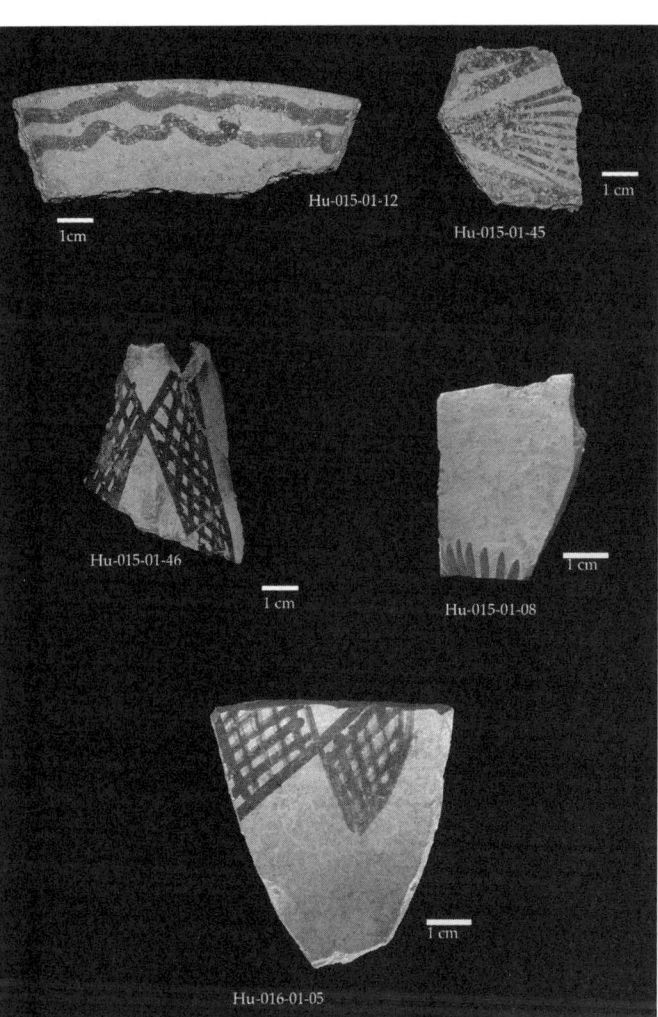

Figure A4. Ceramic fragments from Hu-015 and Hu-016.

Figure A5. Ceramic fragments from Hu-015.

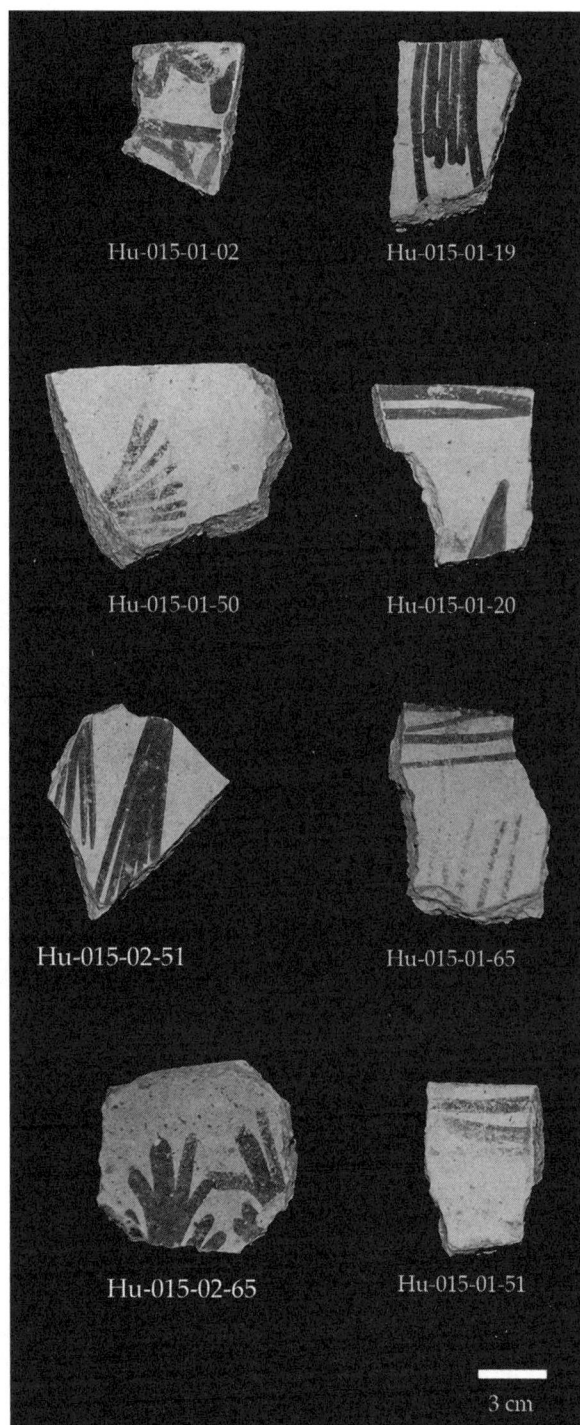

Figure A6. Ceramic fragments from Hu-015.

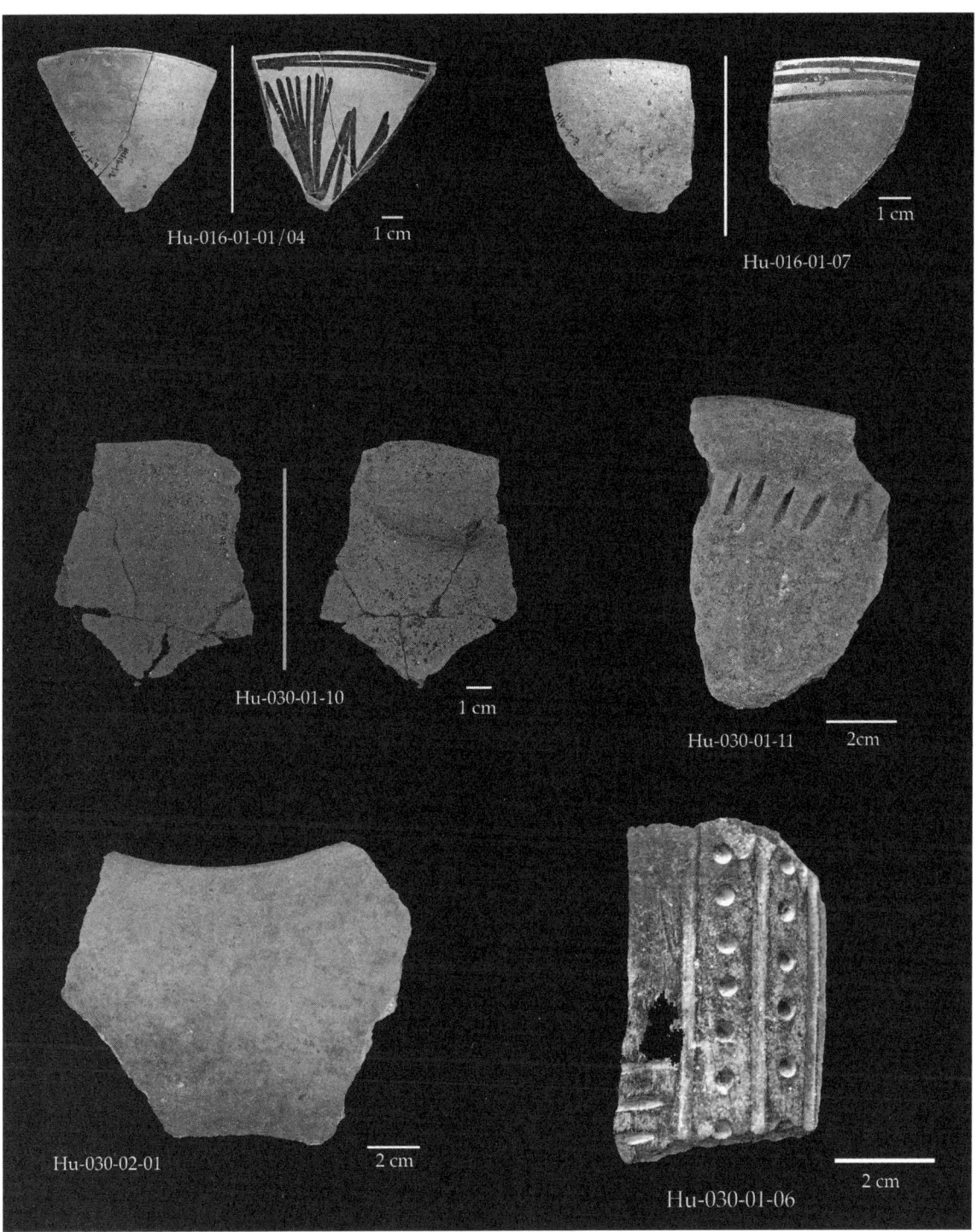

Figure A7. Ceramic fragments from Hu-016 and Hu-030.

288 The Northern Titicaca Basin Survey

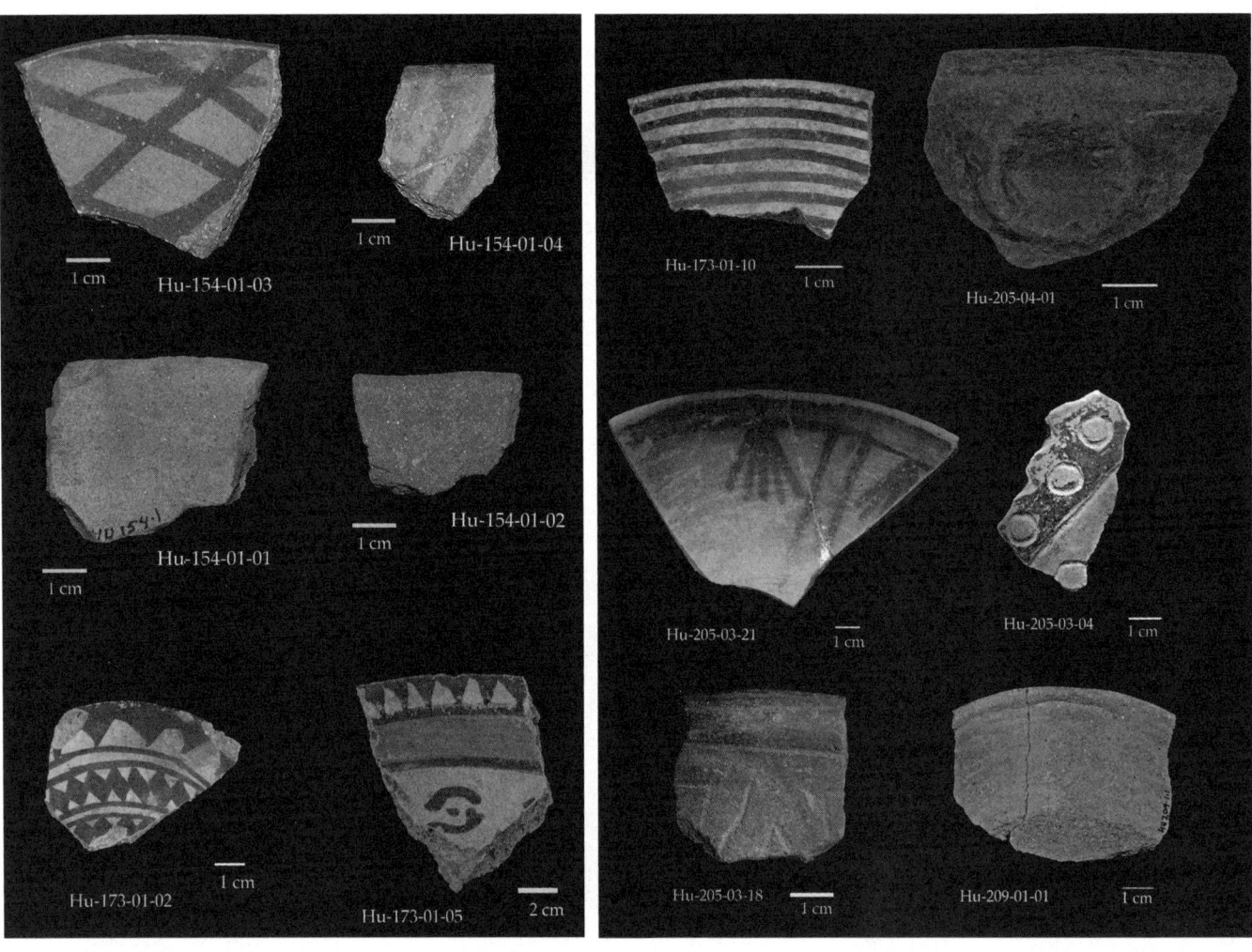

Figure A8. Ceramic fragments from Hu-154 and Hu-173.

Figure A9. Ceramic fragments from Hu-173, Hu-205, and Hu-209.

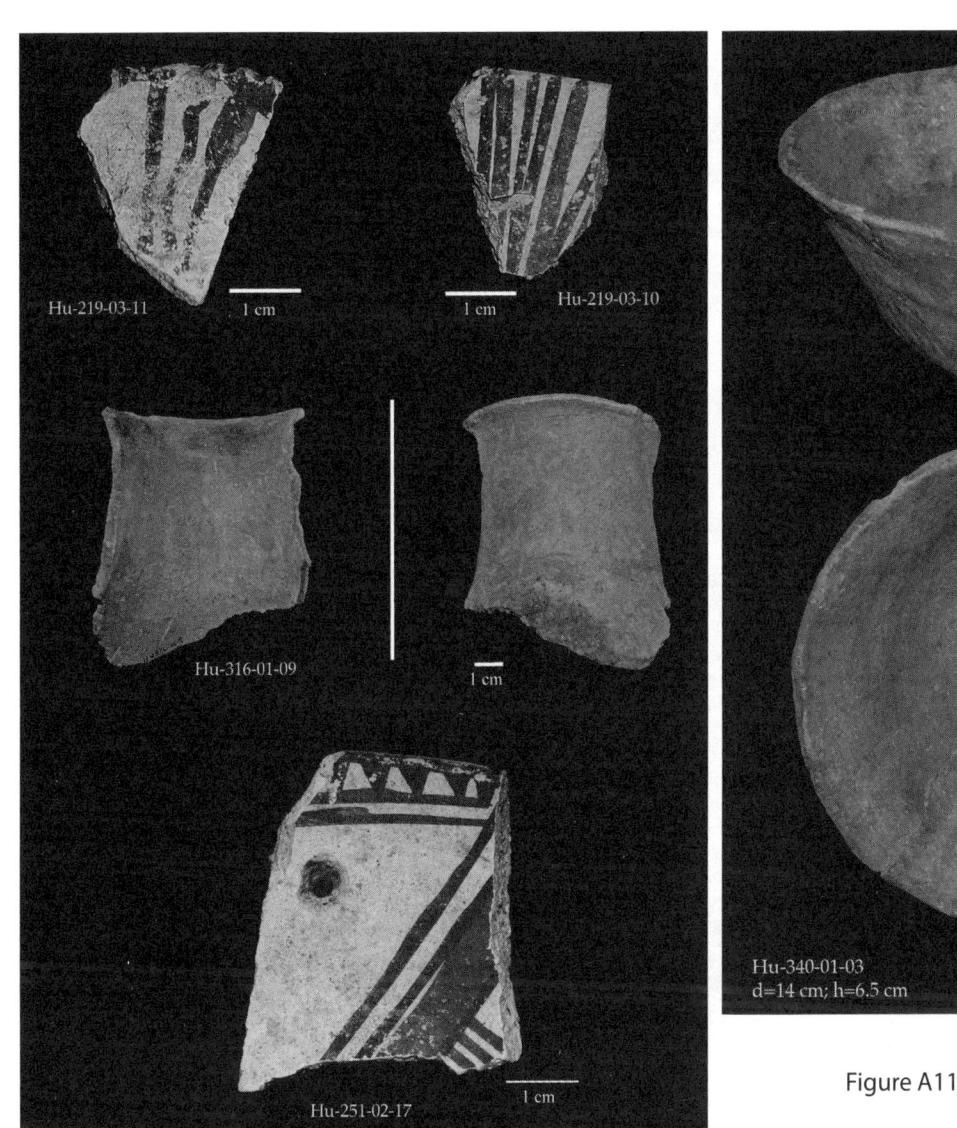

Figure A10. Ceramic fragments from Hu-219, Hu-251, and Hu-316.

Figure A11. Whole vessel from Hu-340.

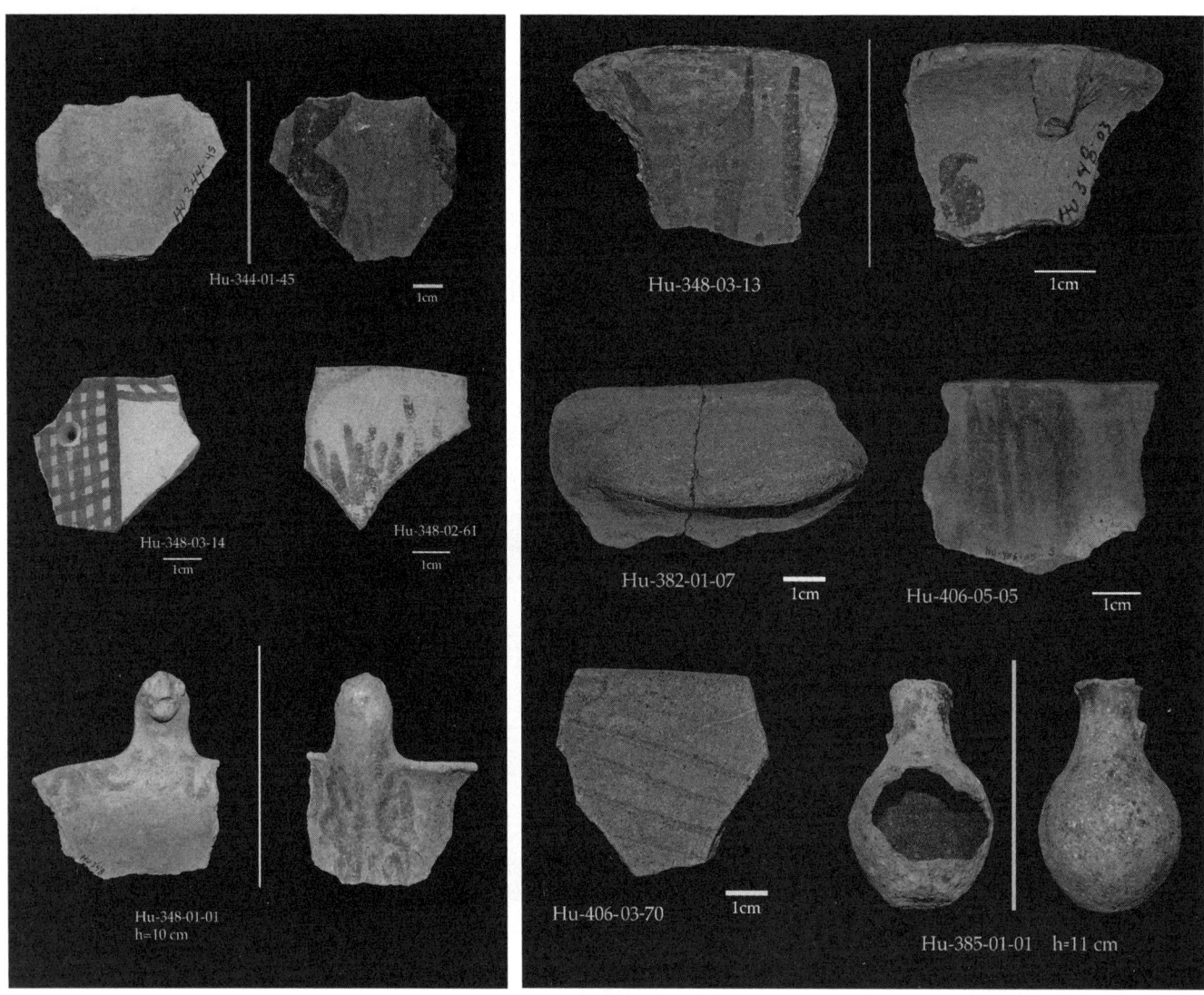

Figure A12. Ceramic fragments from Hu-344 and Hu-348.

Figure A13. Ceramic fragments from Hu-348, Hu-382, Hu-385, and Hu-406.

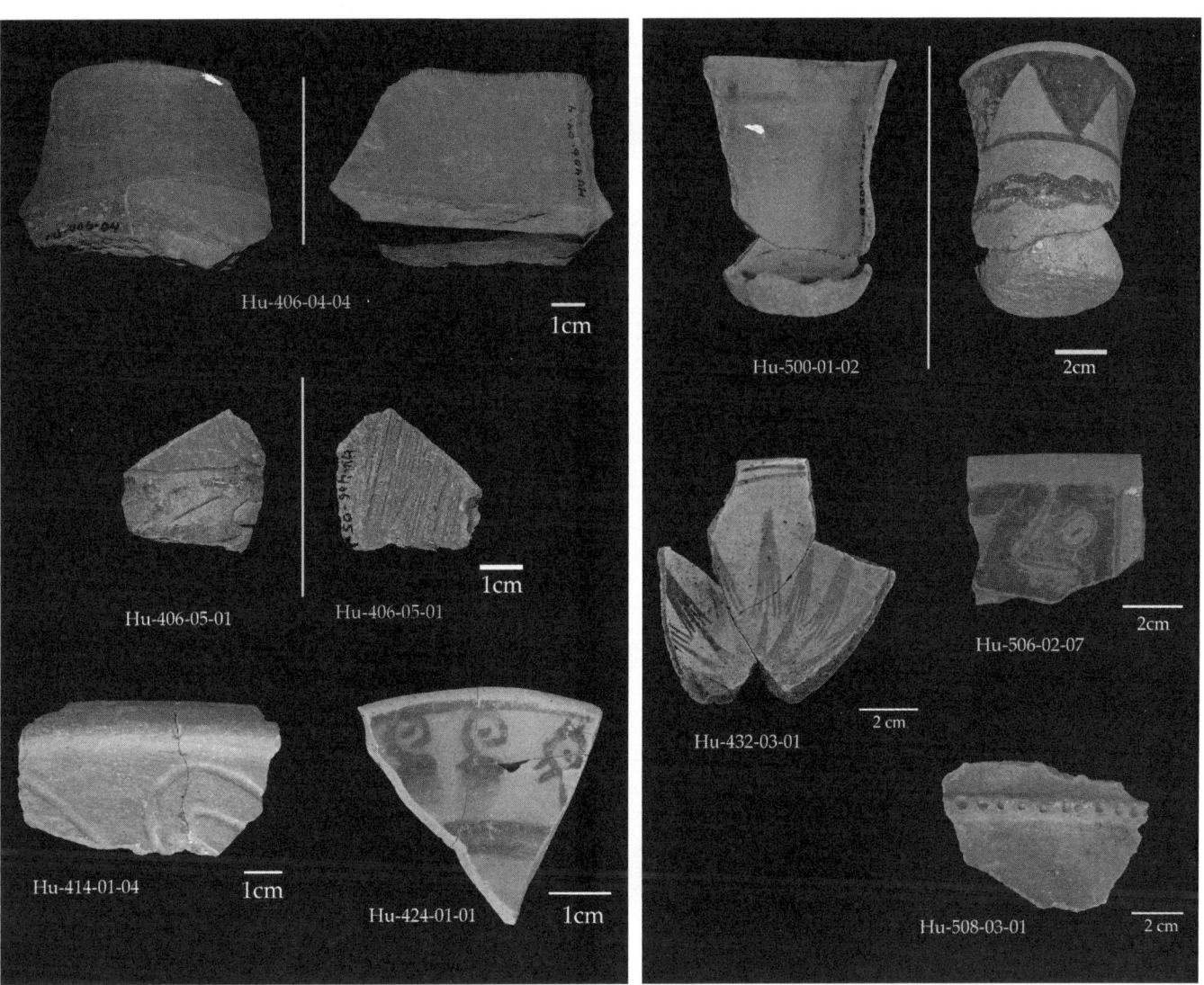

Figure A14. Ceramic fragments from Hu-406, Hu-414, and Hu-424.

Figure A15. Ceramic fragments from Hu-432, Hu-500, Hu-506, and Hu-508.

292 · The Northern Titicaca Basin Survey

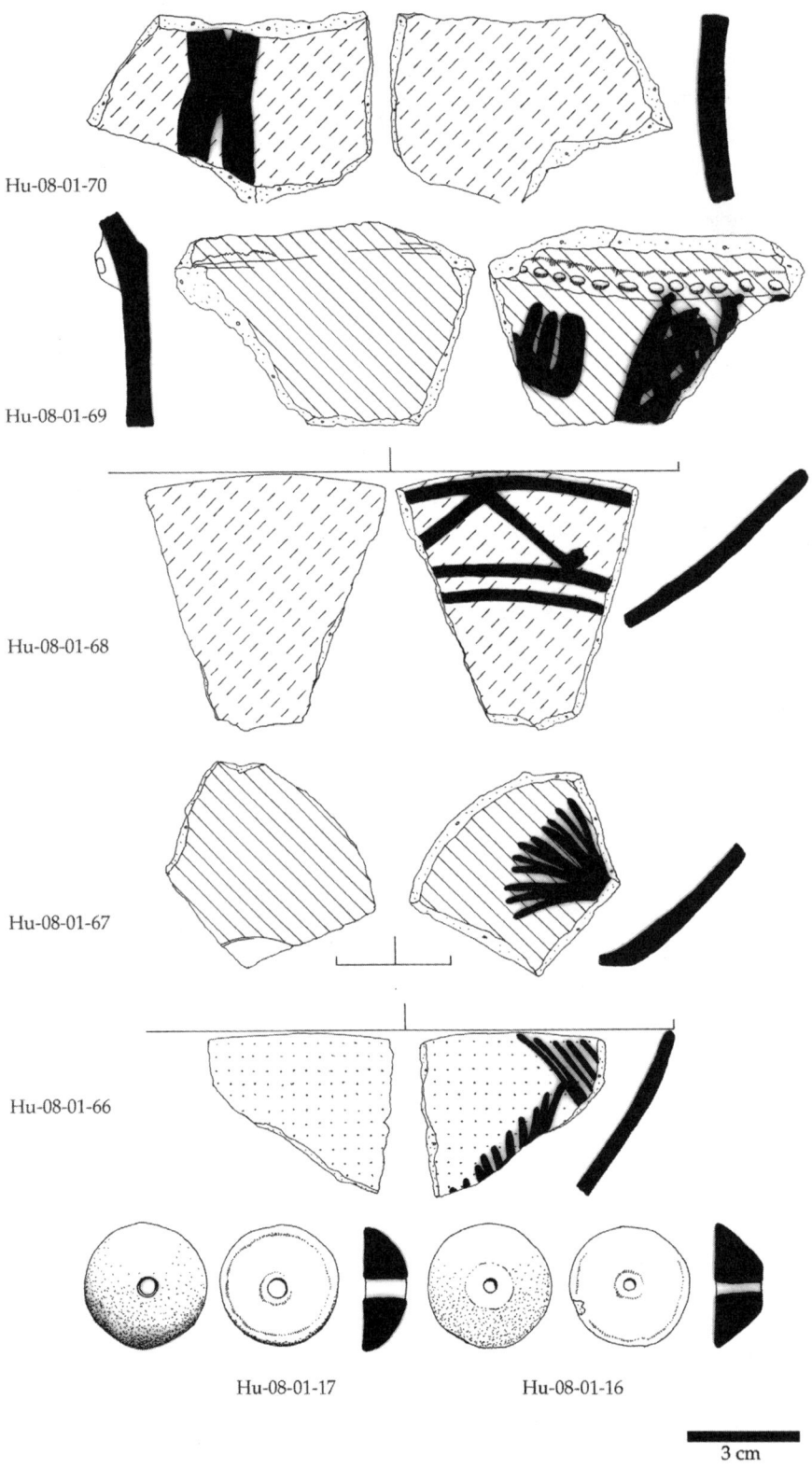

Figure A16. Ceramic fragment drawings from Hu-008.

Appendix A 293

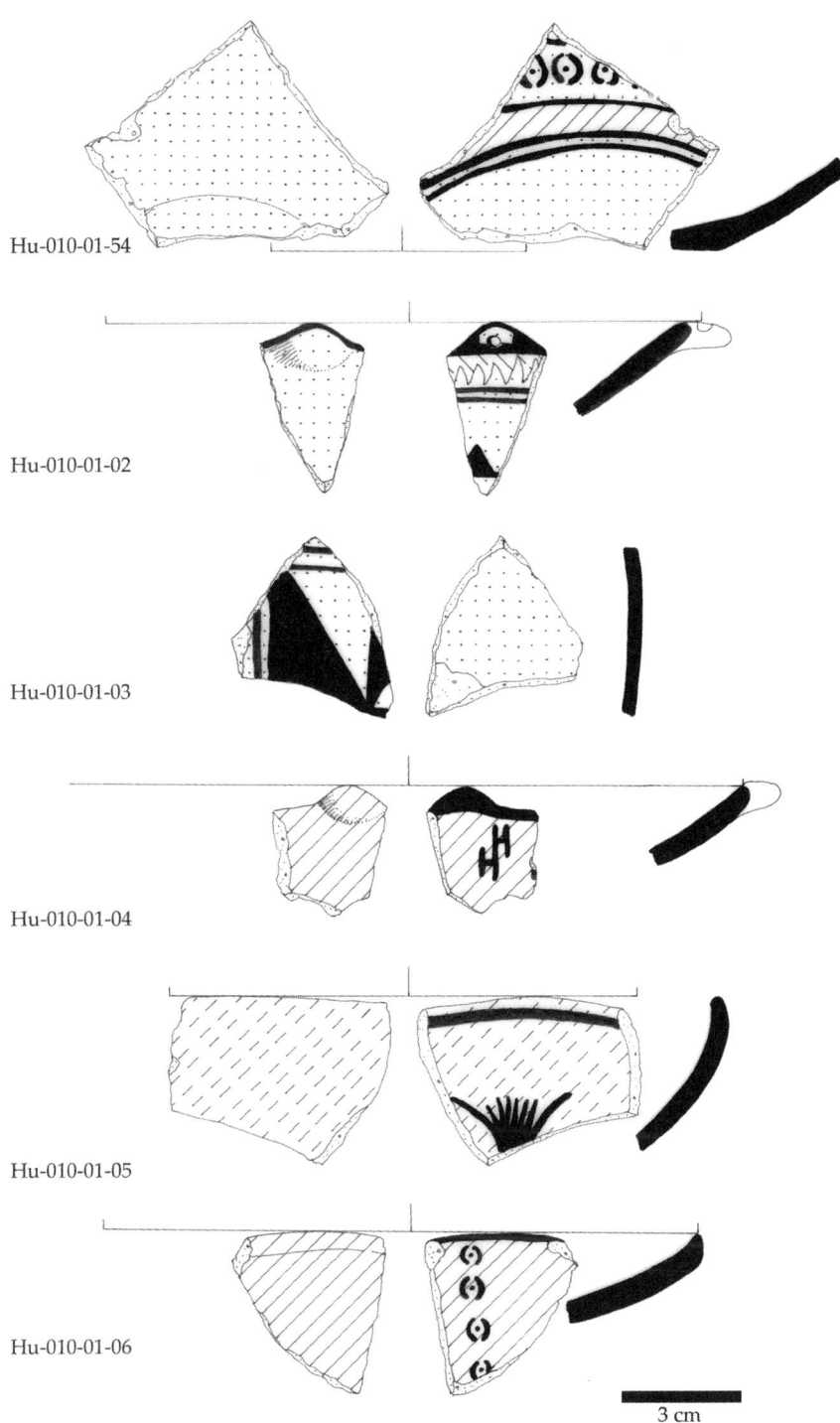

Figure A17. Ceramic fragment drawings from Hu-010.

294 The Northern Titicaca Basin Survey

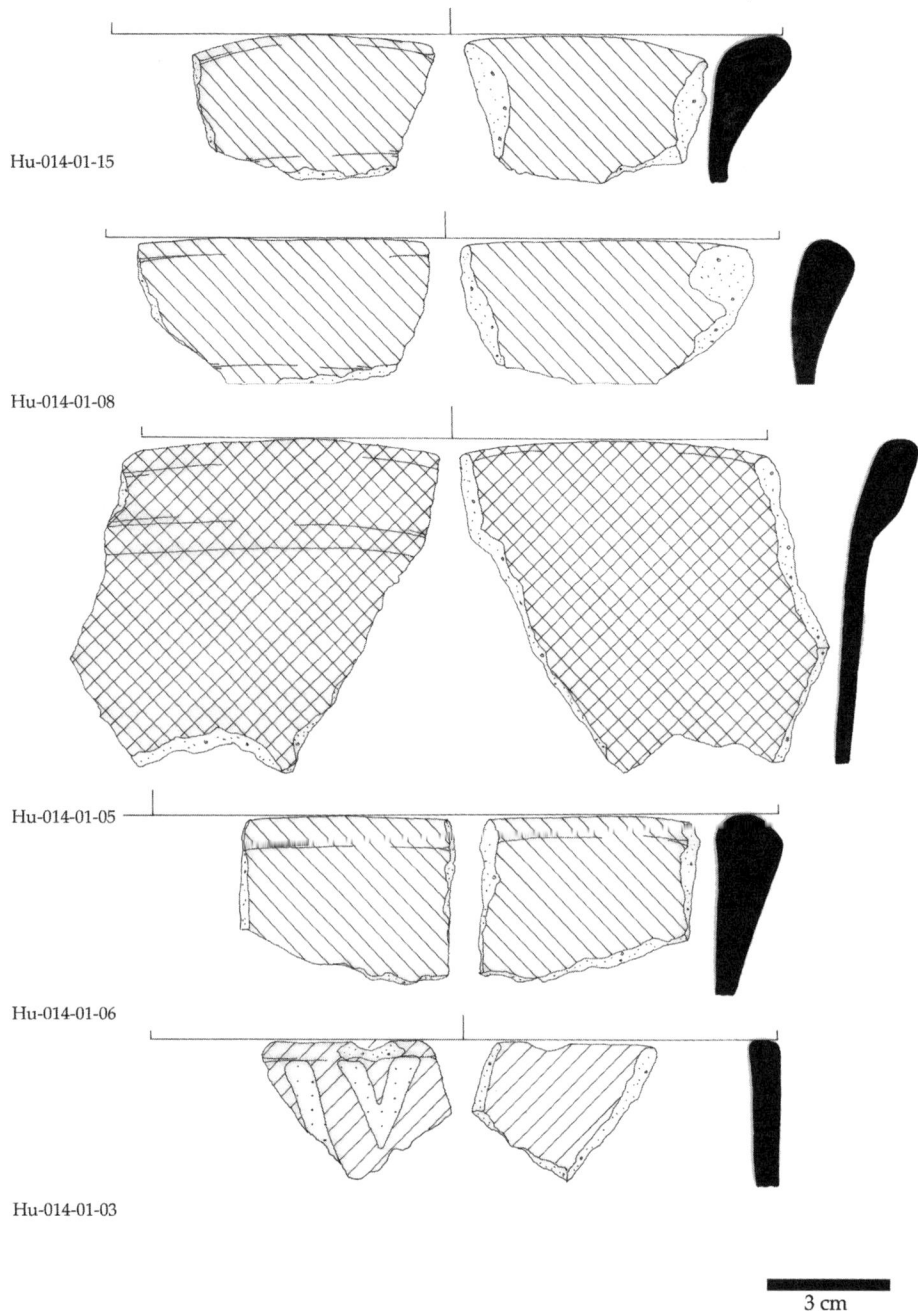

Figure A18. Ceramic fragment drawings from Hu-014.

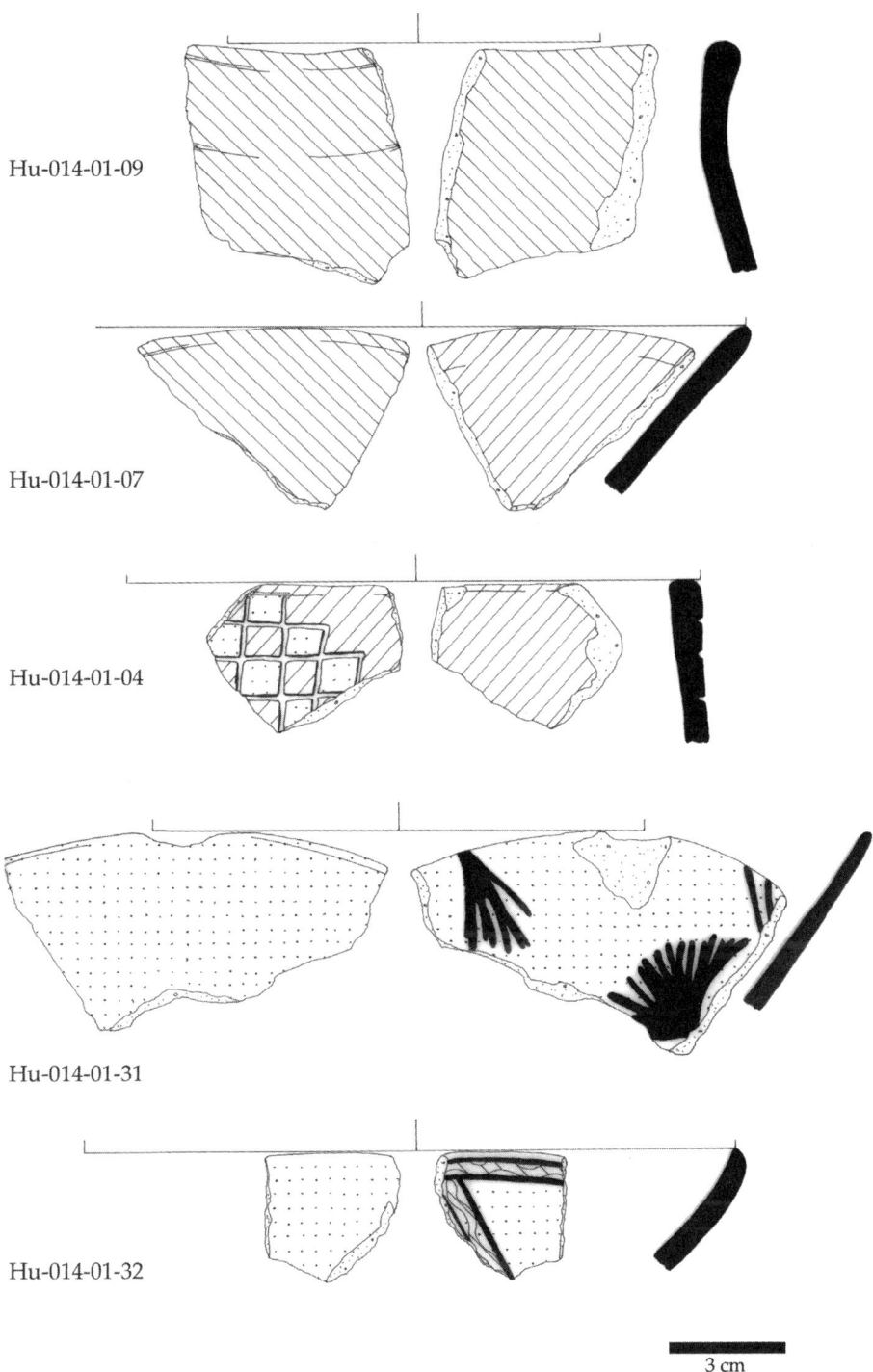

Figure A19. Ceramic fragment drawings from Hu-014.

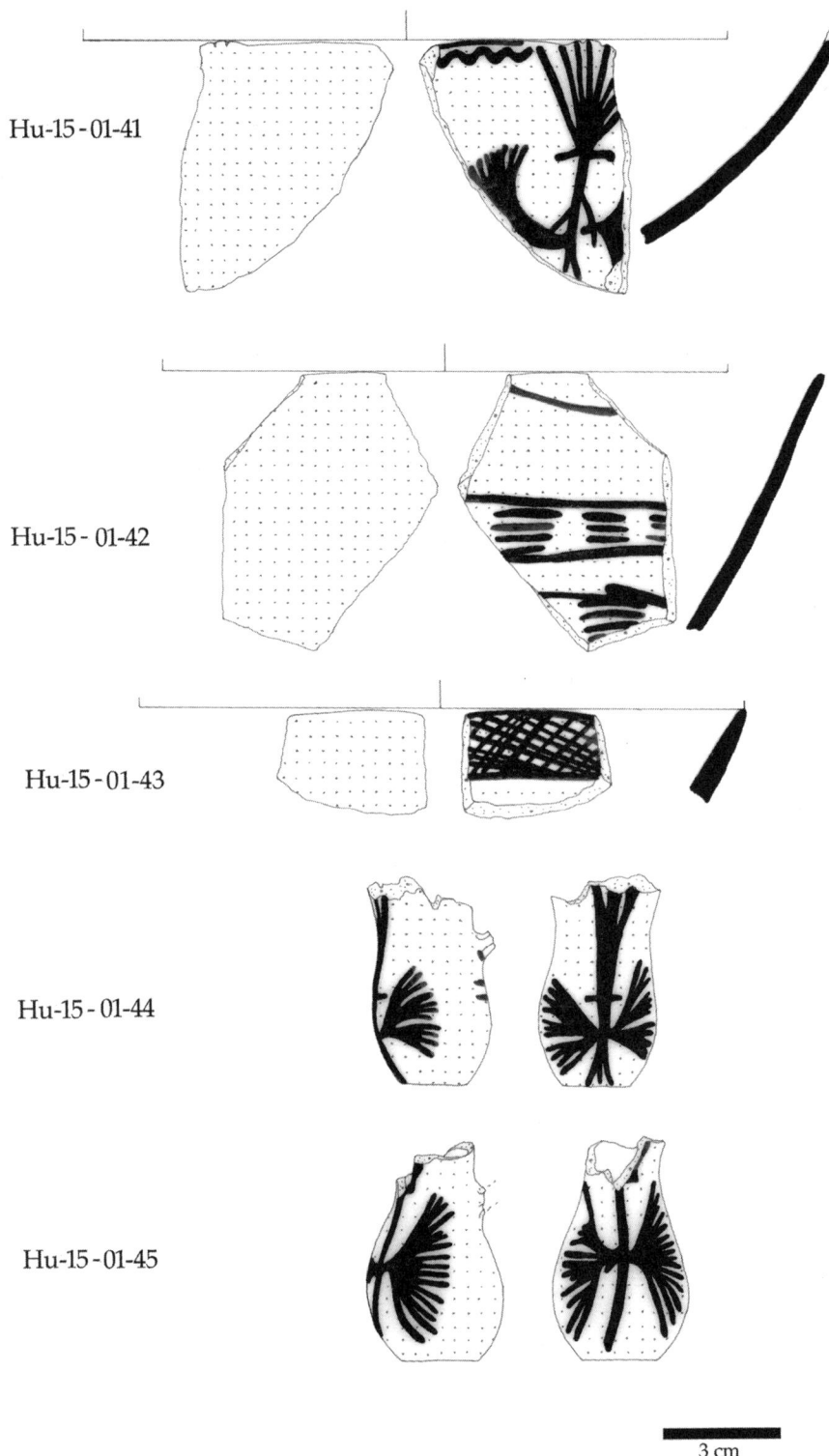

Figure A20. Ceramic fragment drawings from Hu-015.

Appendix A

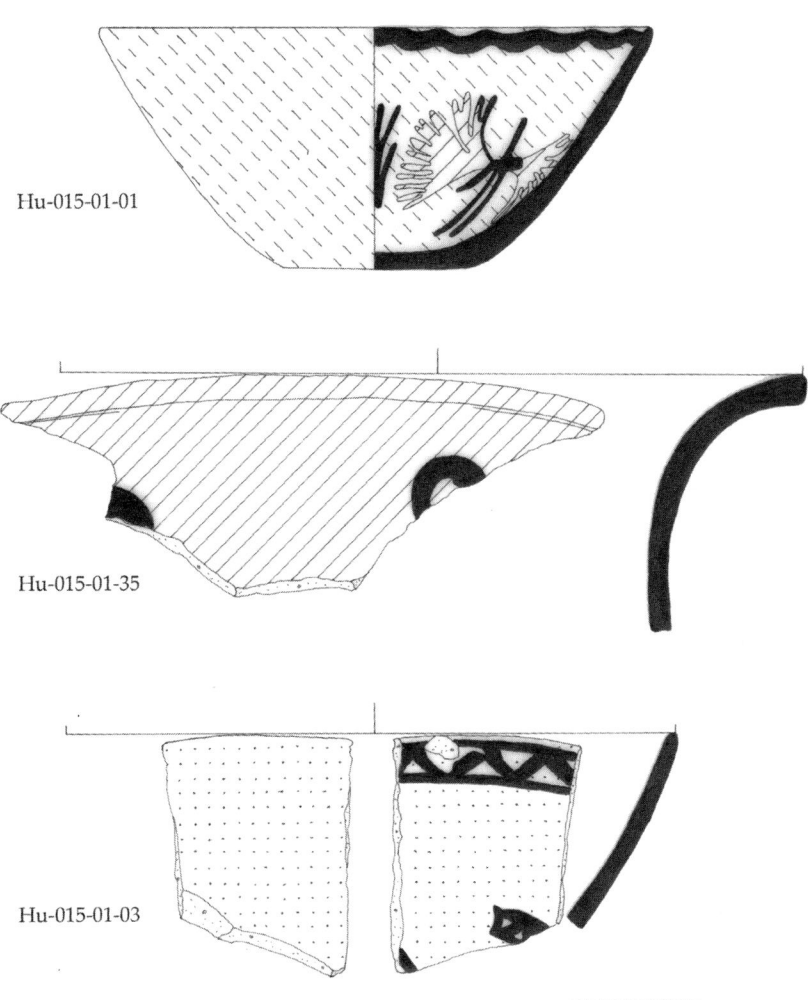

Figure A21. Ceramic fragment drawings from Hu-015.

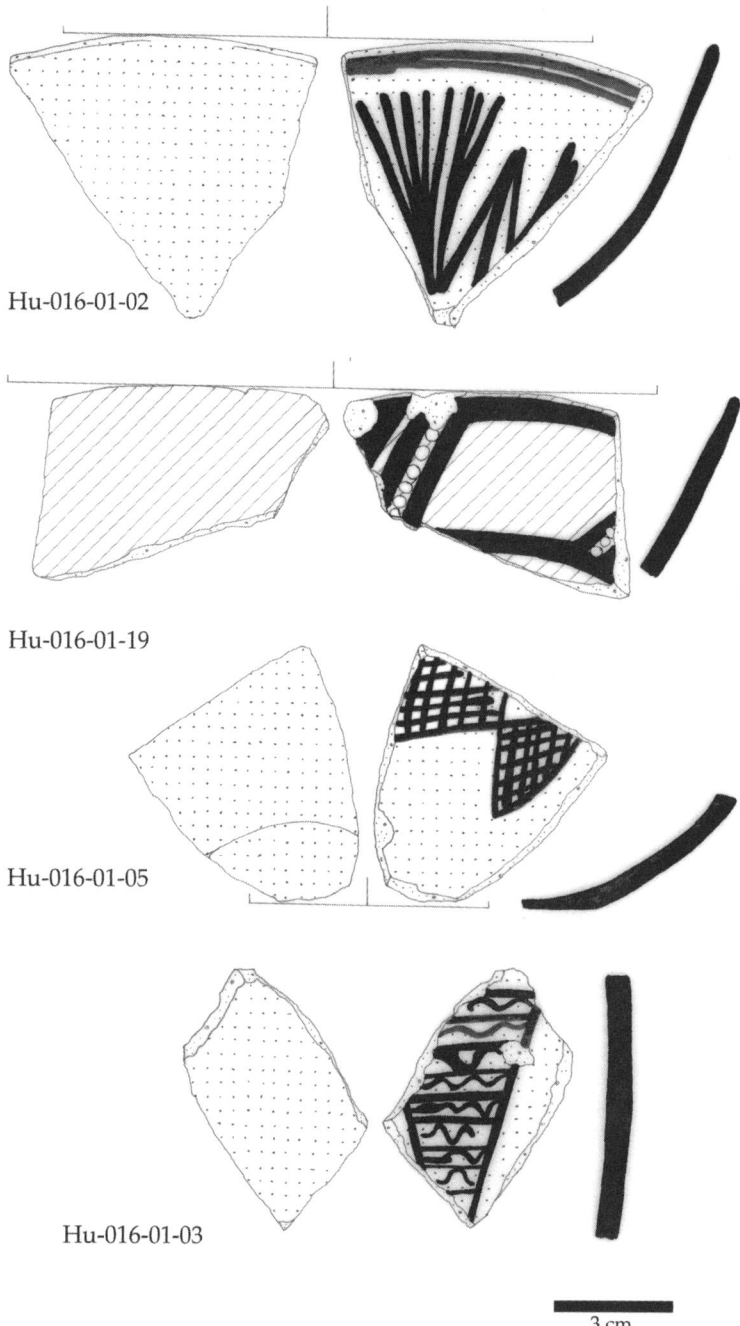

Figure A22. Ceramic fragment drawings from Hu-016.

Appendix A 299

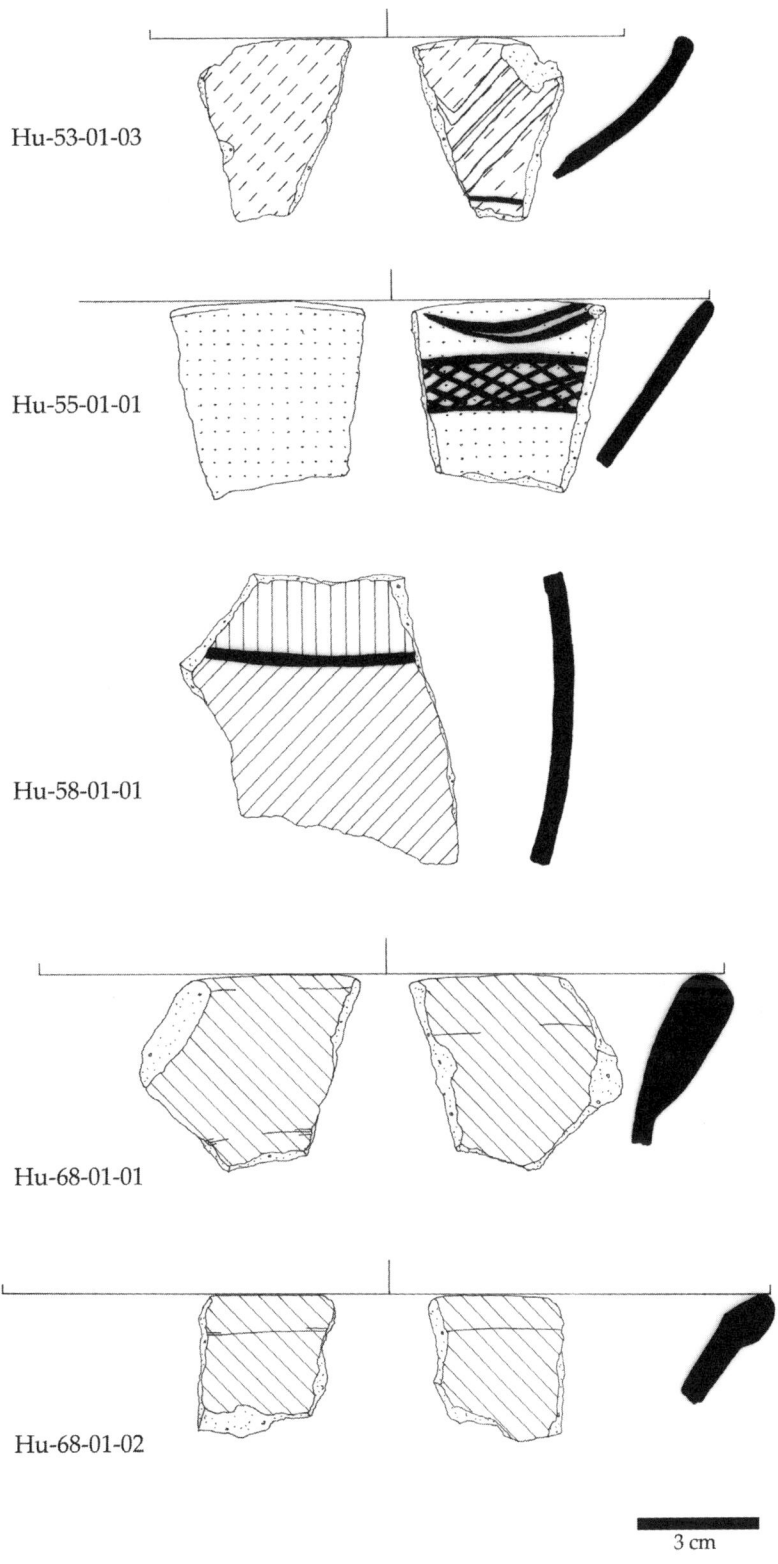

Figure A23. Ceramic fragment drawings from Hu-053, Hu-055, Hu-058, and Hu-068.

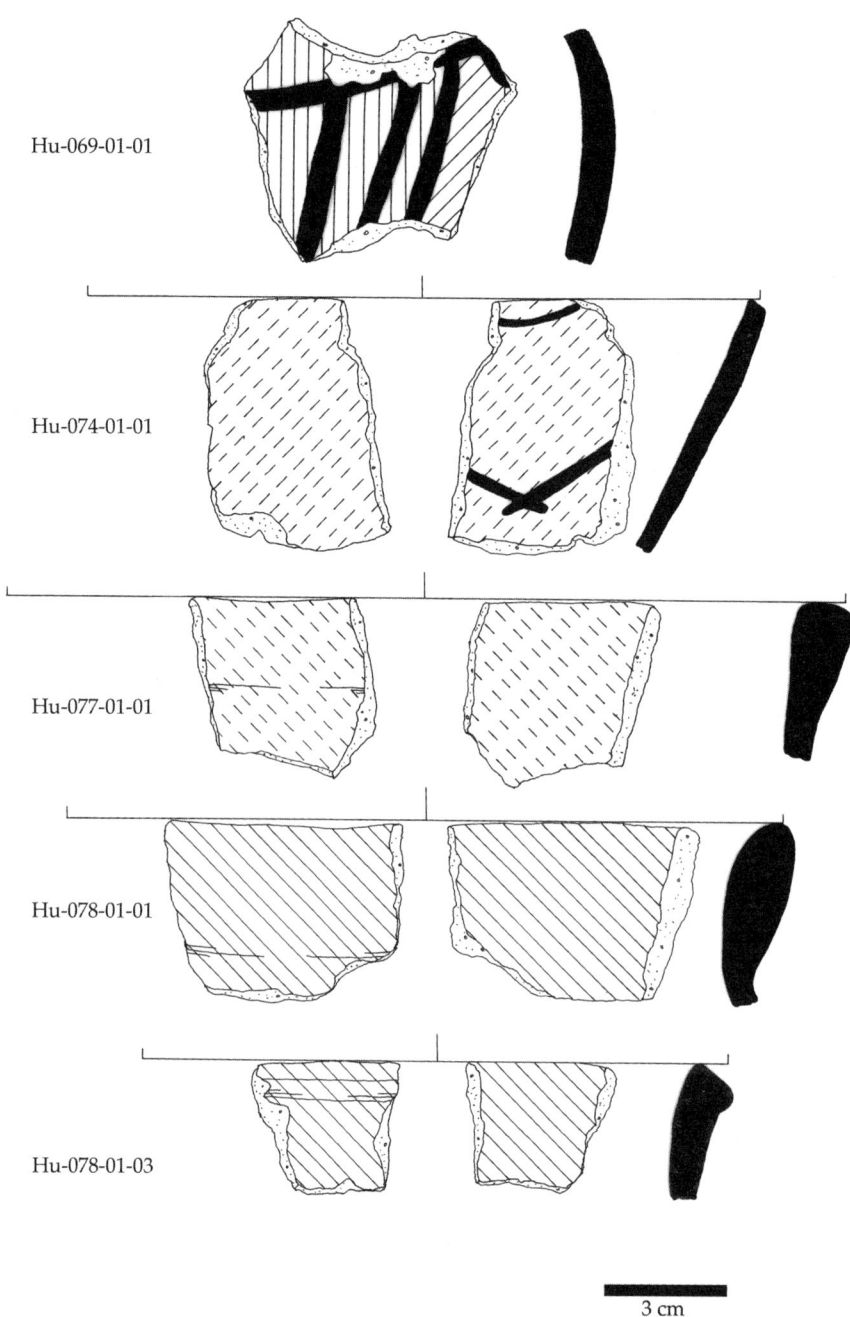

Figure A24. Ceramic fragment drawings from Hu-069, Hu-074, Hu-077, and Hu-078.

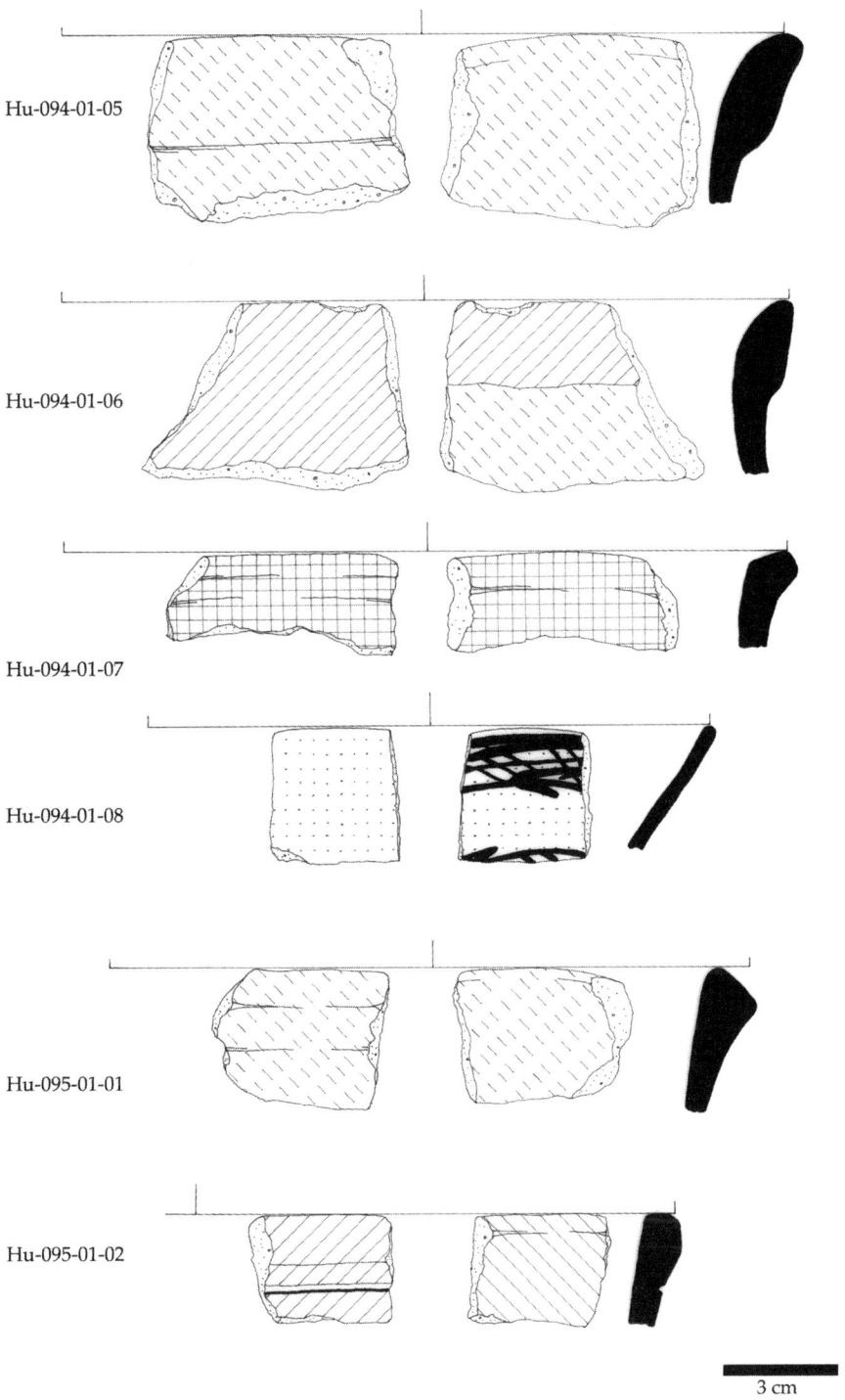

Figure A25. Ceramic fragment drawings from Hu-094 and Hu-095.

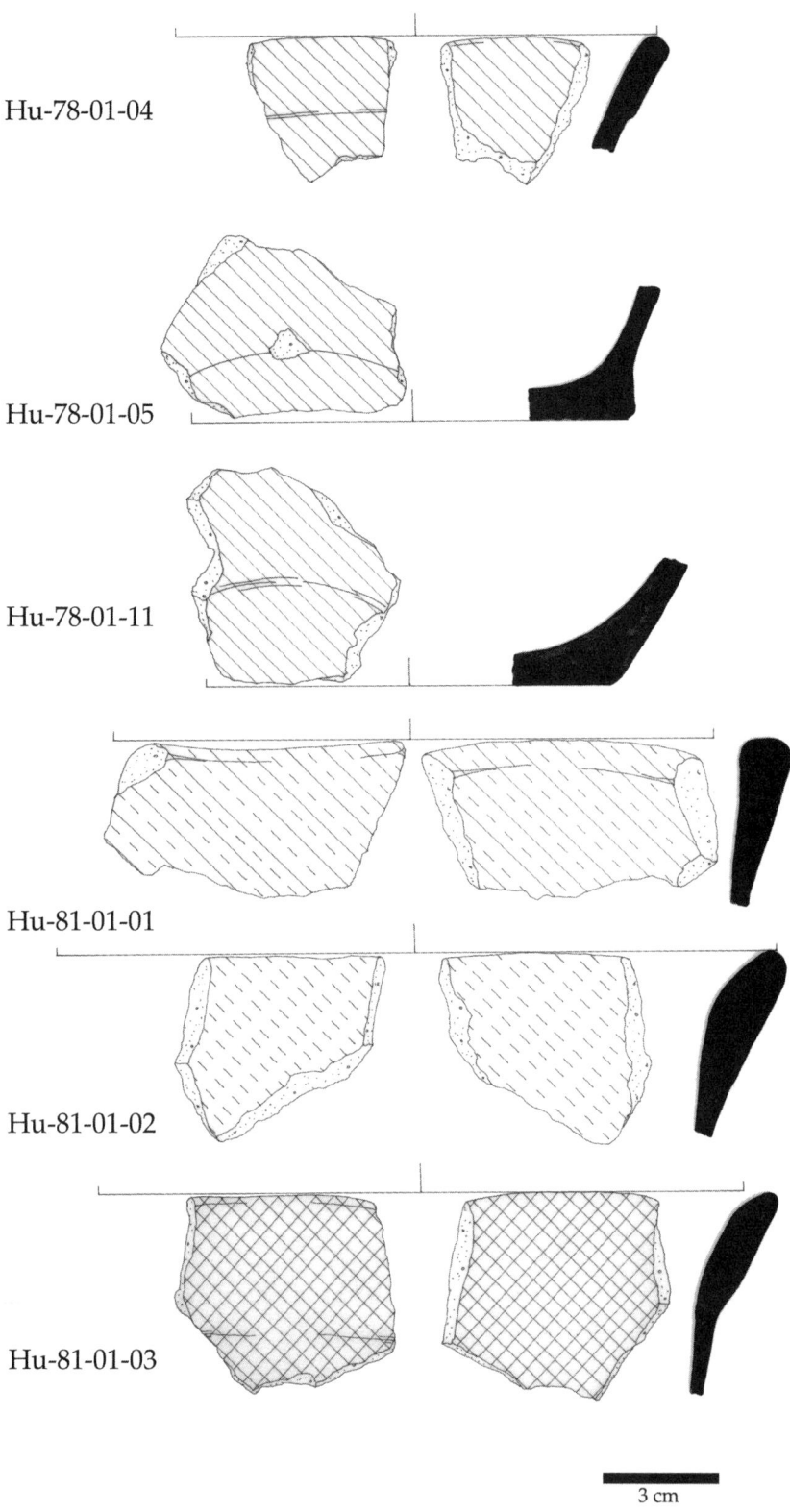

Figure A26. Ceramic fragment drawings from Hu-078 and Hu-081.

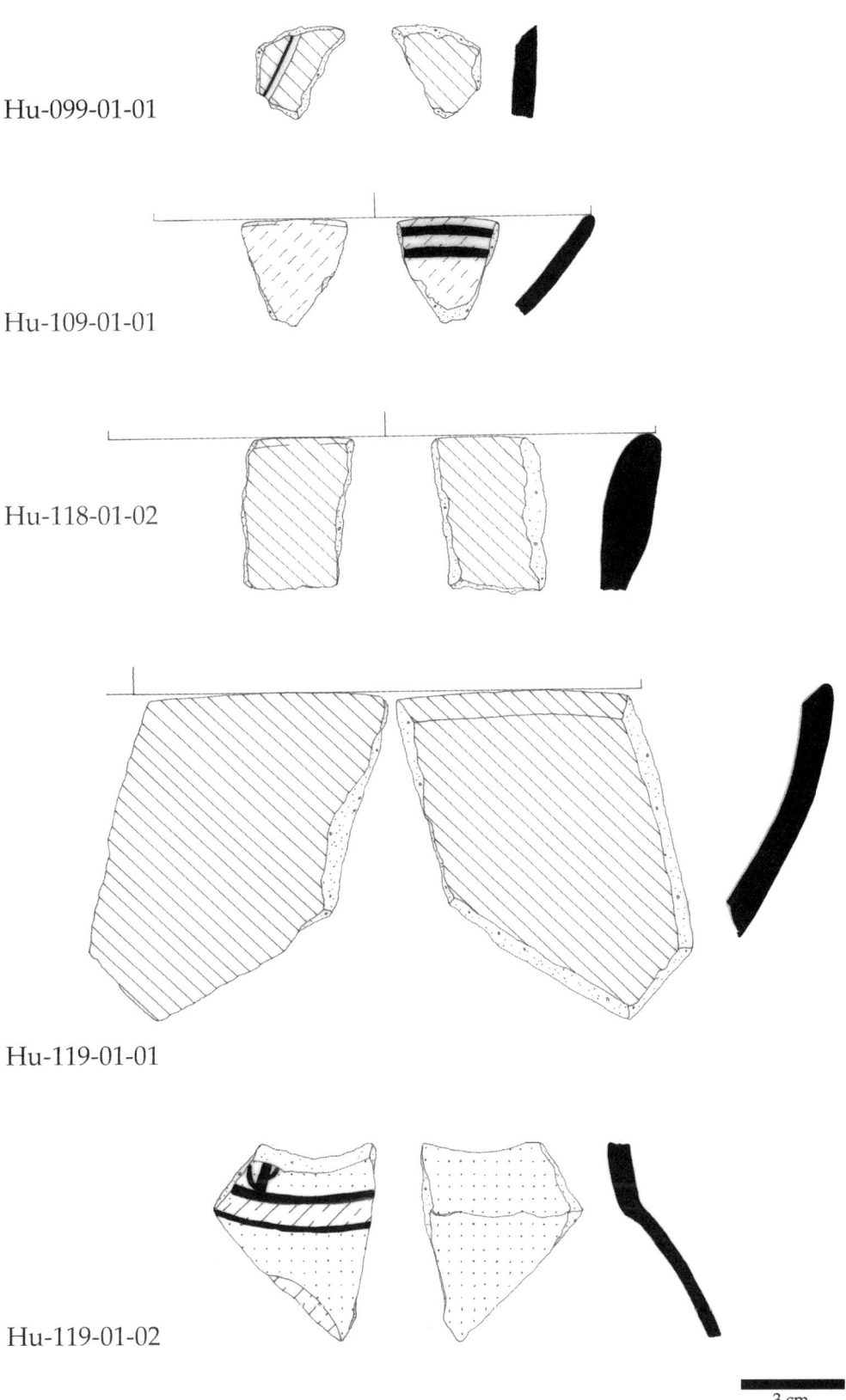

Figure A27. Ceramic fragment drawings from Hu-099, Hu-109, Hu-118, and Hu-119.

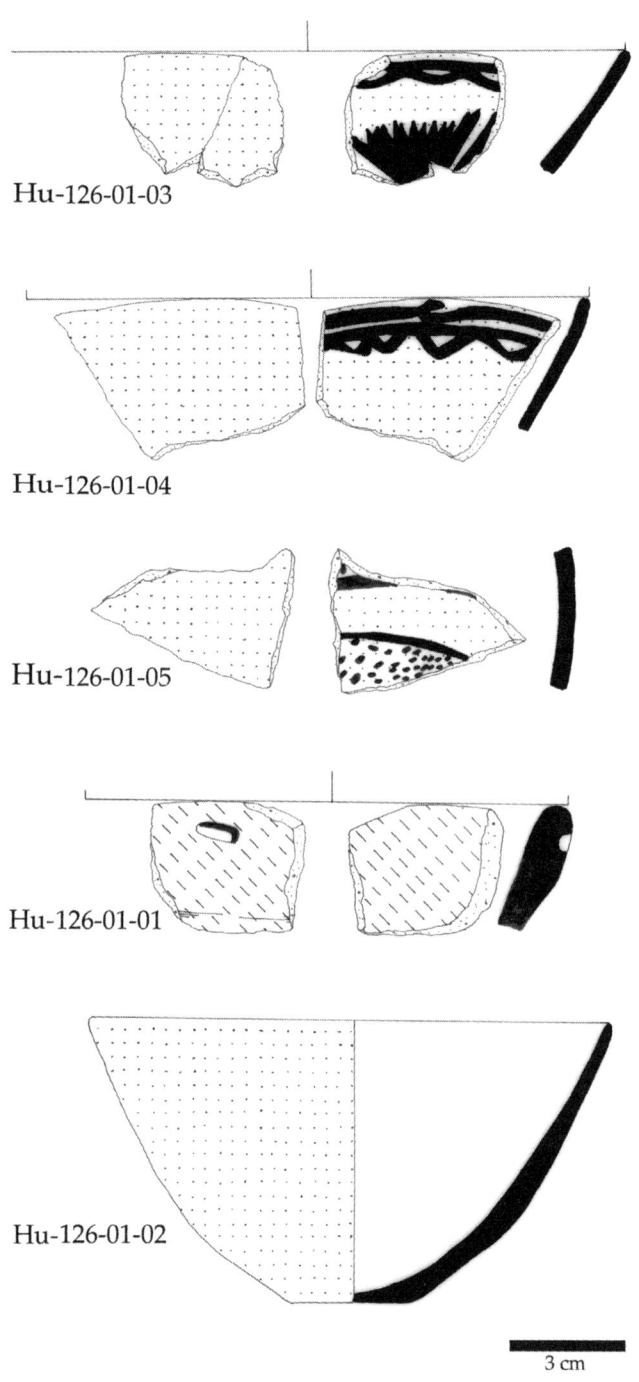

Figure A28. Ceramic fragment drawings from Hu-126.

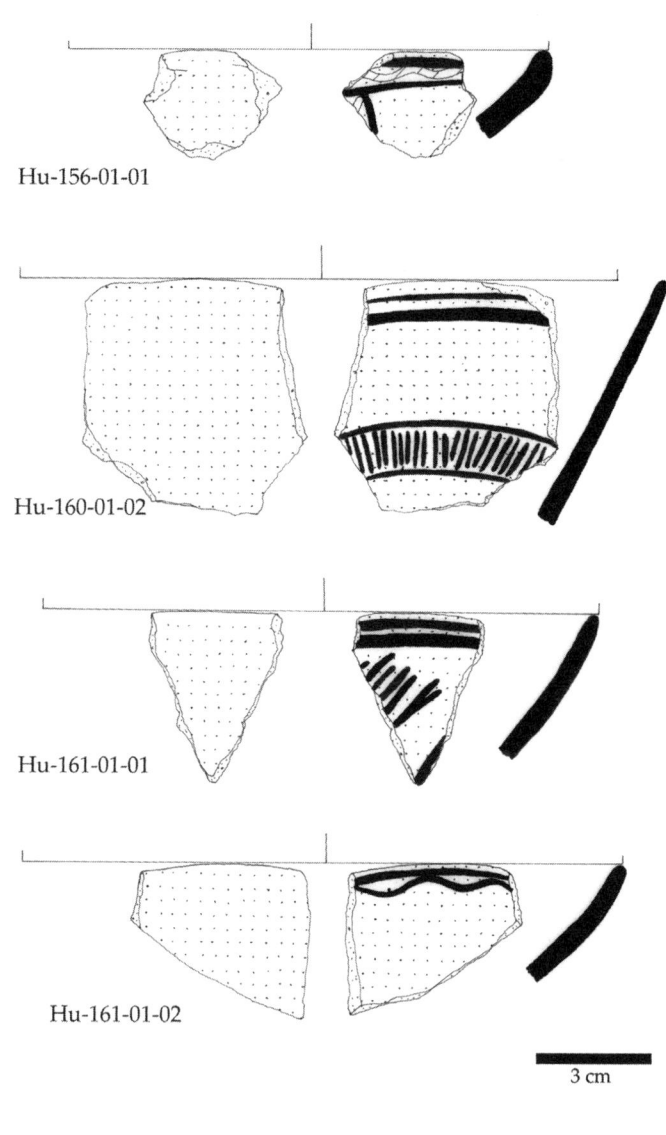

Figure A29. Ceramic fragment drawings from Hu-156, Hu-160, and Hu-161.

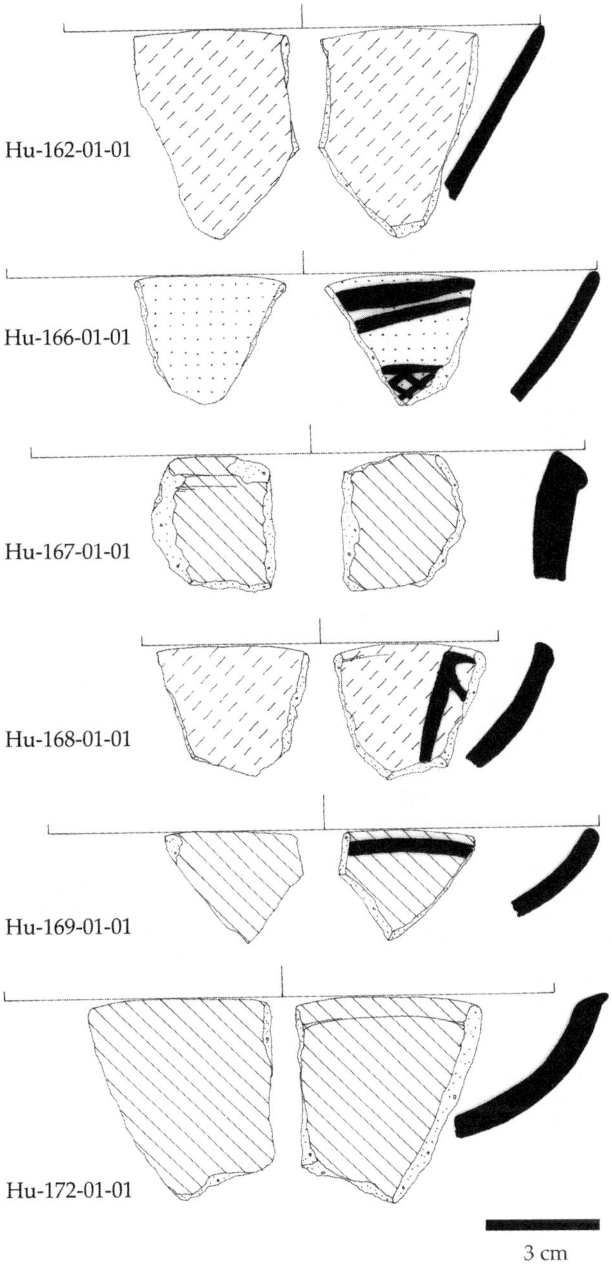

Appendix A

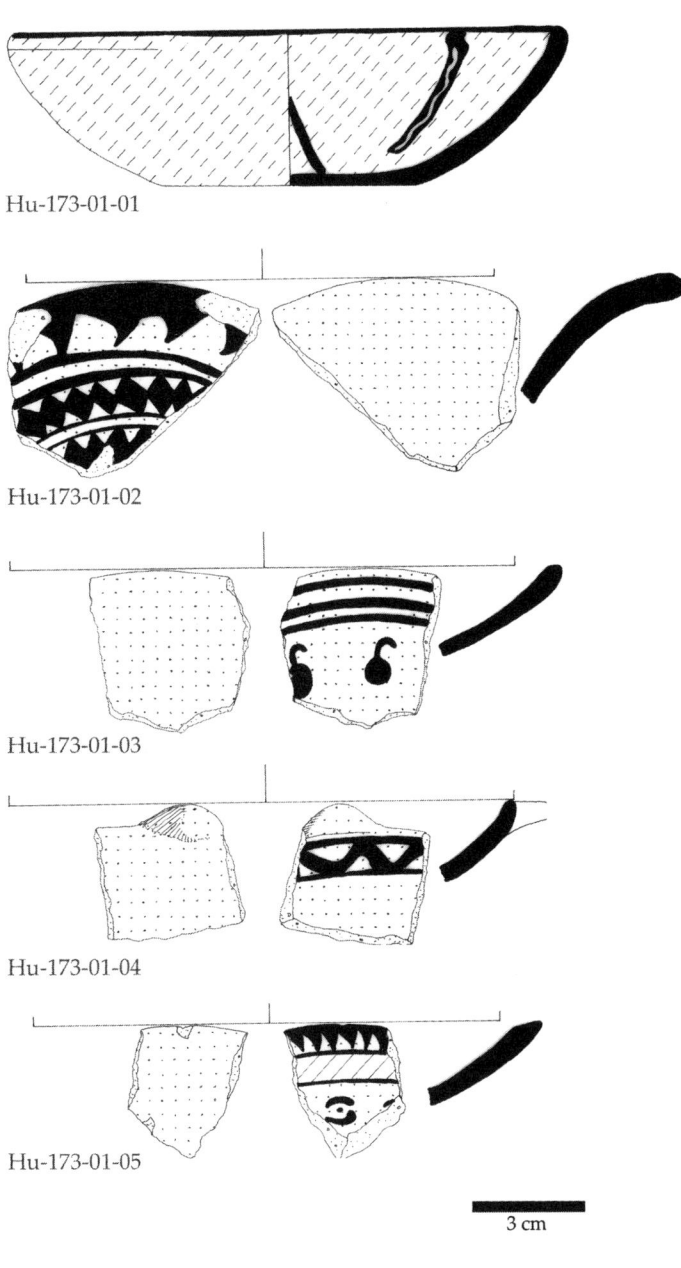

Hu-162-01-01

Hu-166-01-01

Hu-167-01-01

Hu-168-01-01

Hu-169-01-01

Hu-172-01-01

3 cm

Hu-173-01-01

Hu-173-01-02

Hu-173-01-03

Hu-173-01-04

Hu-173-01-05

3 cm

Figure A30. Ceramic fragment drawings from Hu-162, Hu-166, Hu-167, Hu-168, Hu-169, and Hu-172.

Figure A31. Ceramic fragment drawings from Hu-173.

306

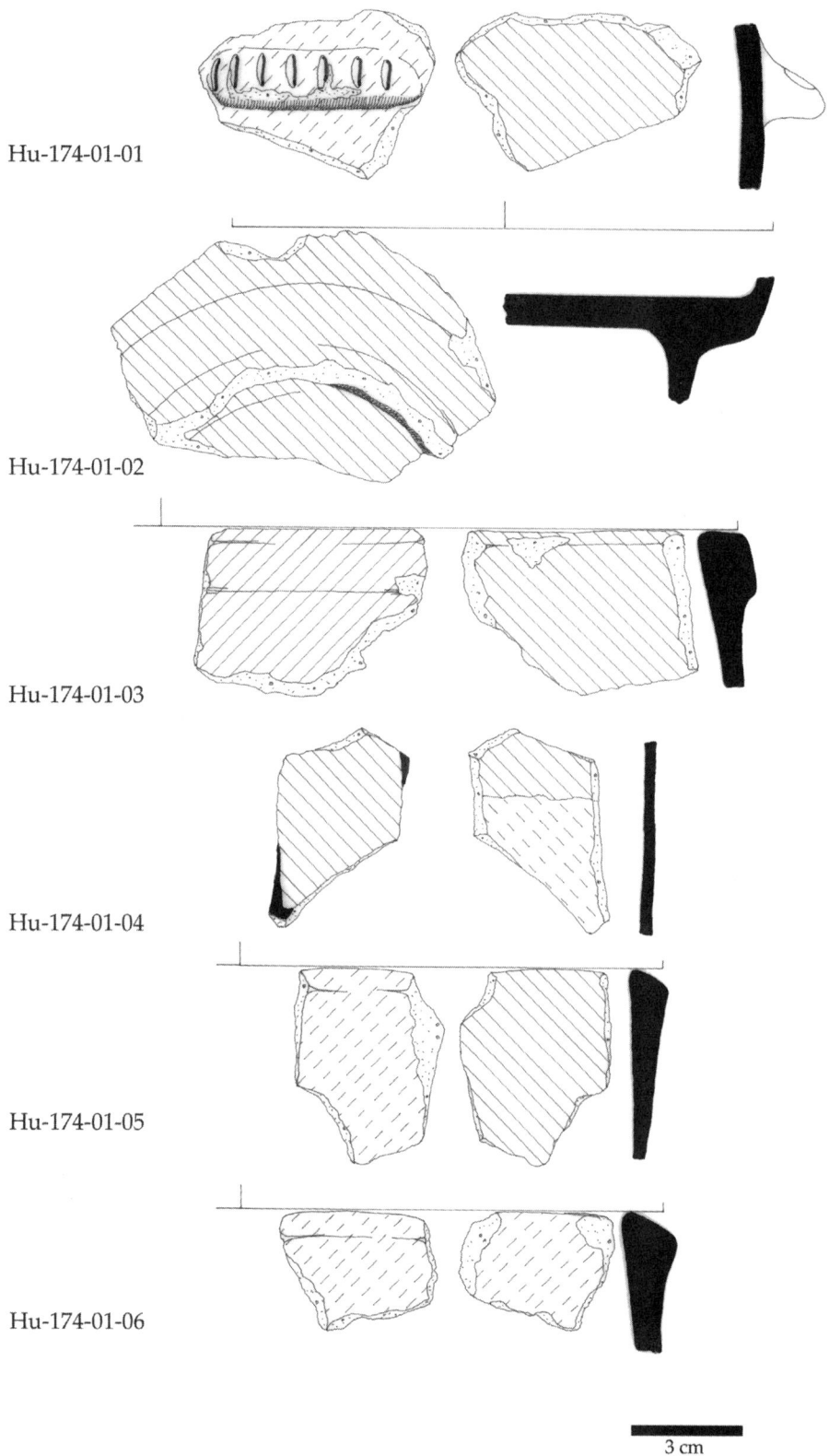

Hu-174-01-01

Hu-174-01-02

Hu-174-01-03

Hu-174-01-04

Hu-174-01-05

Hu-174-01-06

3 cm

Figure A32. Ceramic fragment drawings from Hu-174.

Appendix A

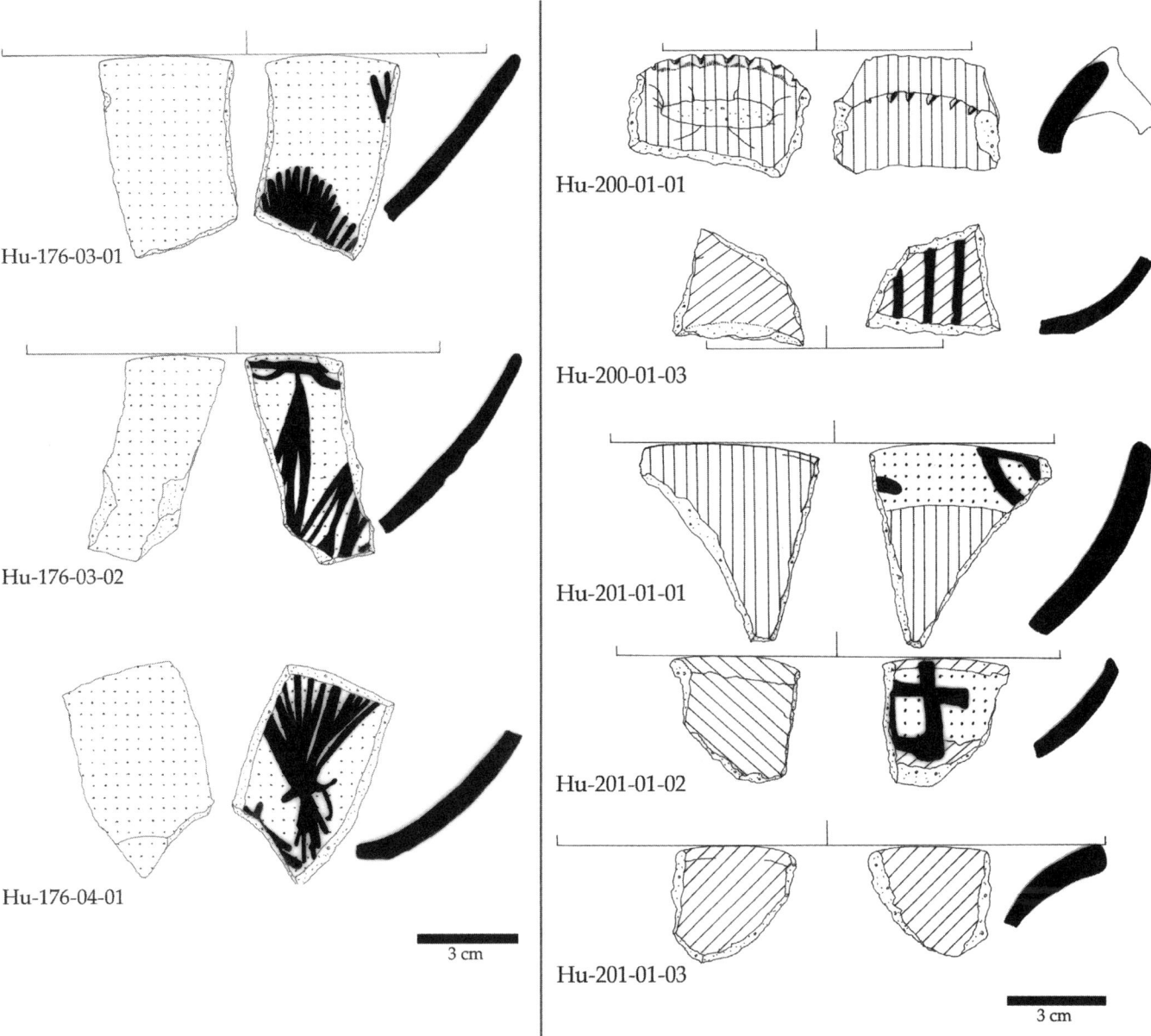

Figure A33. Ceramic fragment drawings from Hu-176.

Figure A34. Ceramic fragment drawings from Hu-200 and Hu-201.

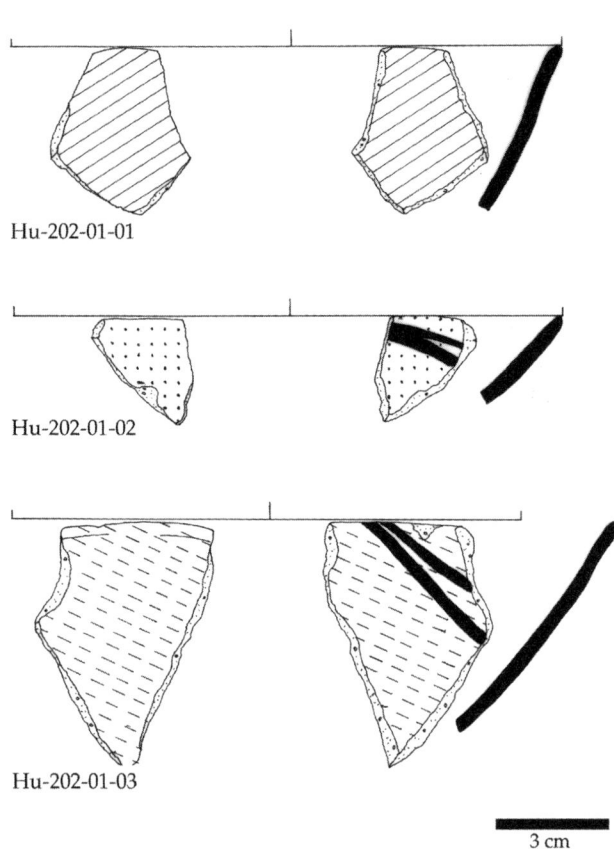

Figure A35. Ceramic fragment drawings from Hu-202.

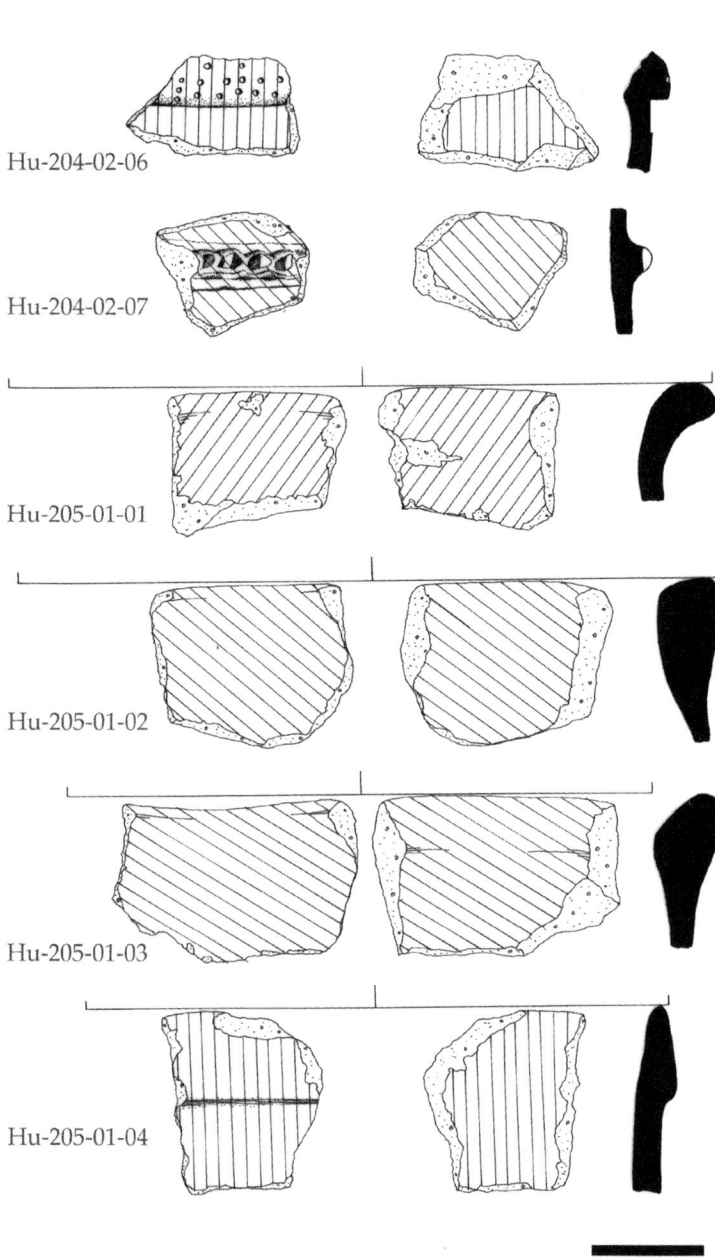

Figure A36. Ceramic fragment drawings from Hu-204 and Hu-205.

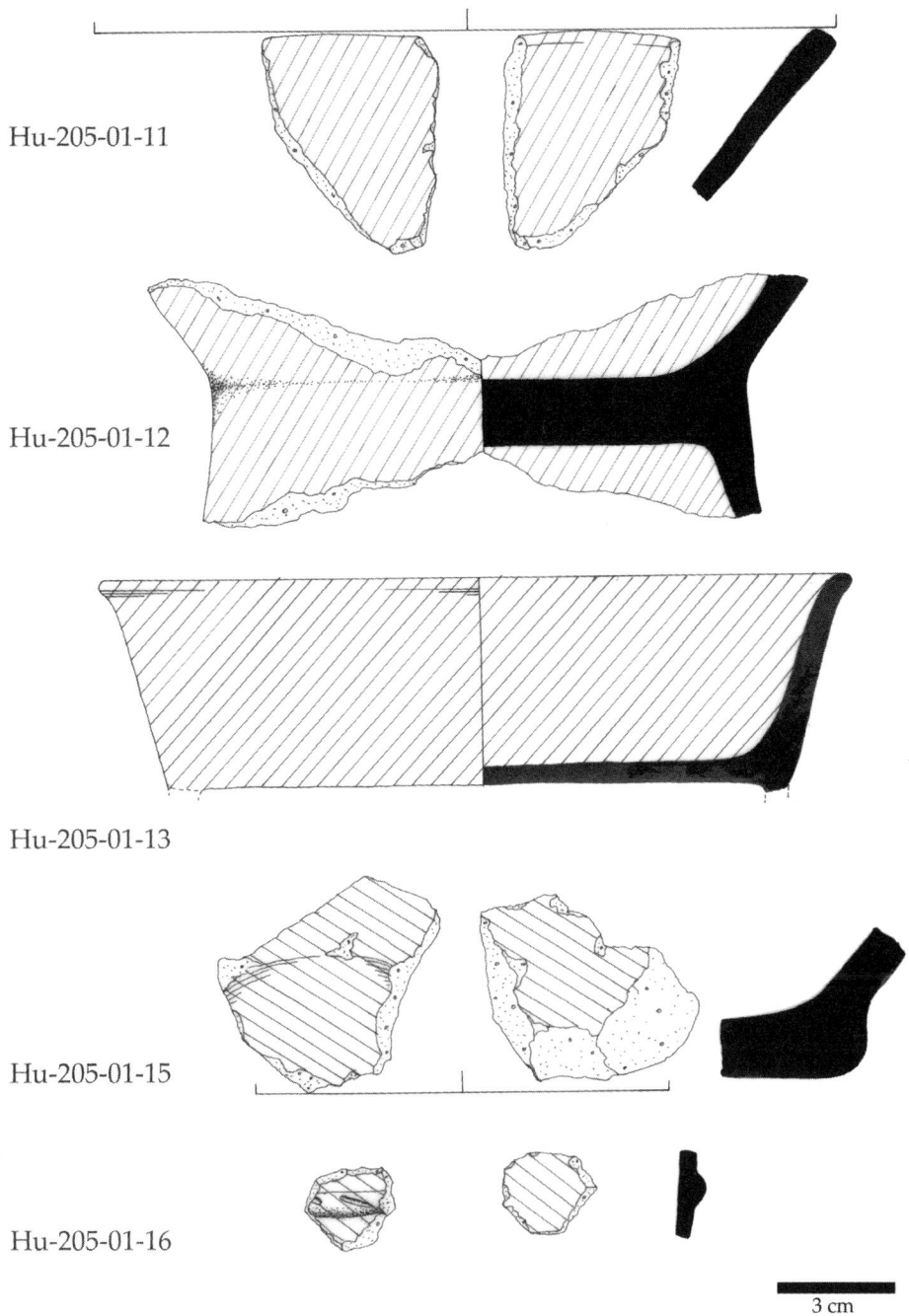

Figure A37. Ceramic fragment drawings from Hu-205.

310   The Northern Titicaca Basin Survey

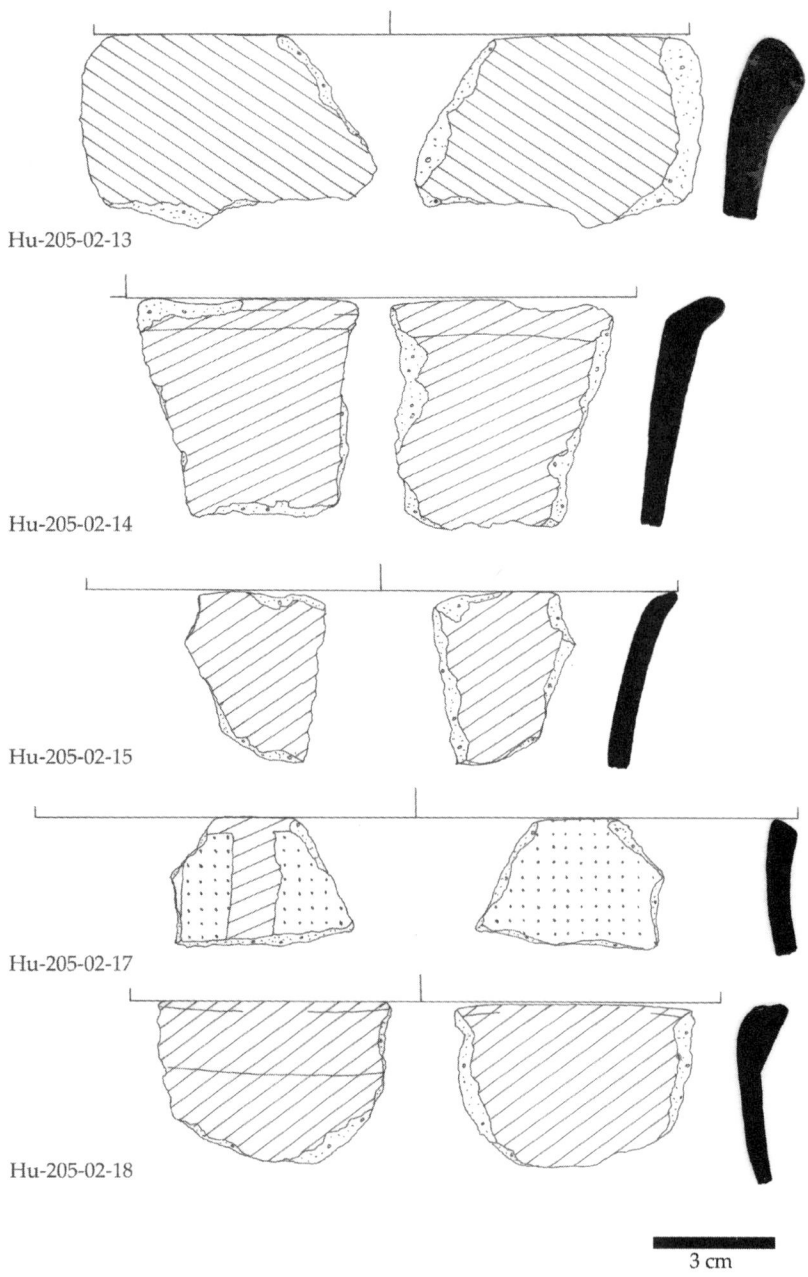

Figure A38. Ceramic fragment drawings from Hu-205.

Appendix A   311

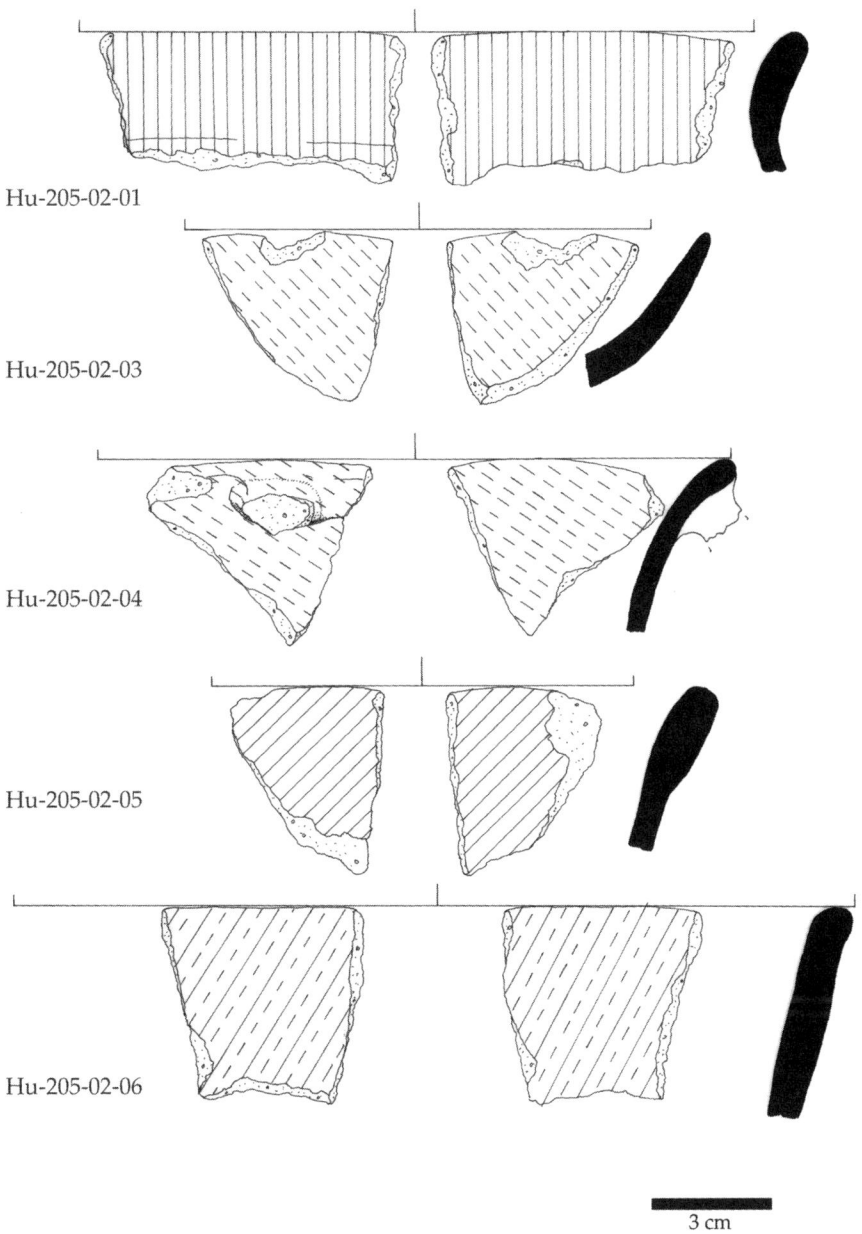

Figure A39. Ceramic fragment drawings from Hu-205.

312　　*The Northern Titicaca Basin Survey*

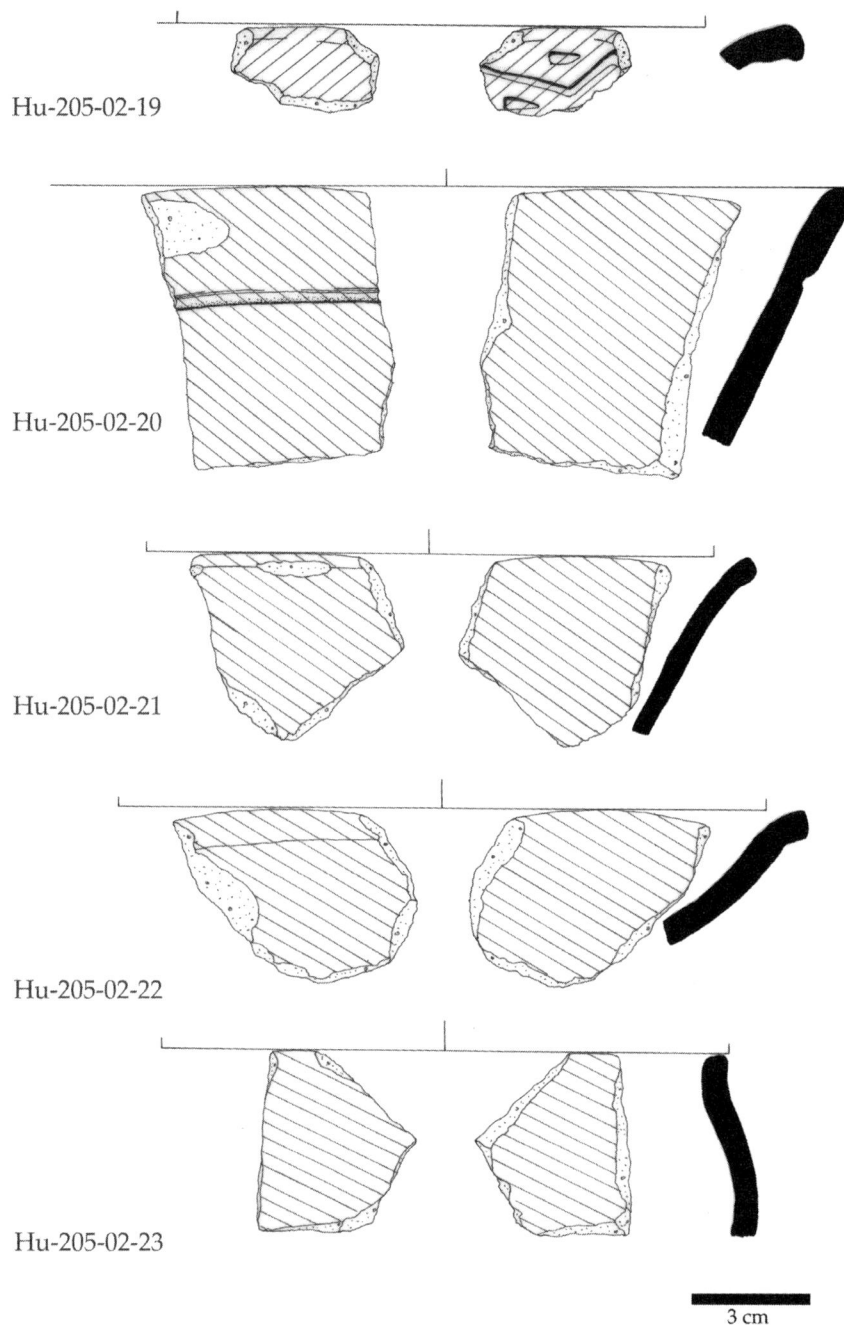

Figure A40. Ceramic fragment drawings from Hu-205.

Appendix A 313

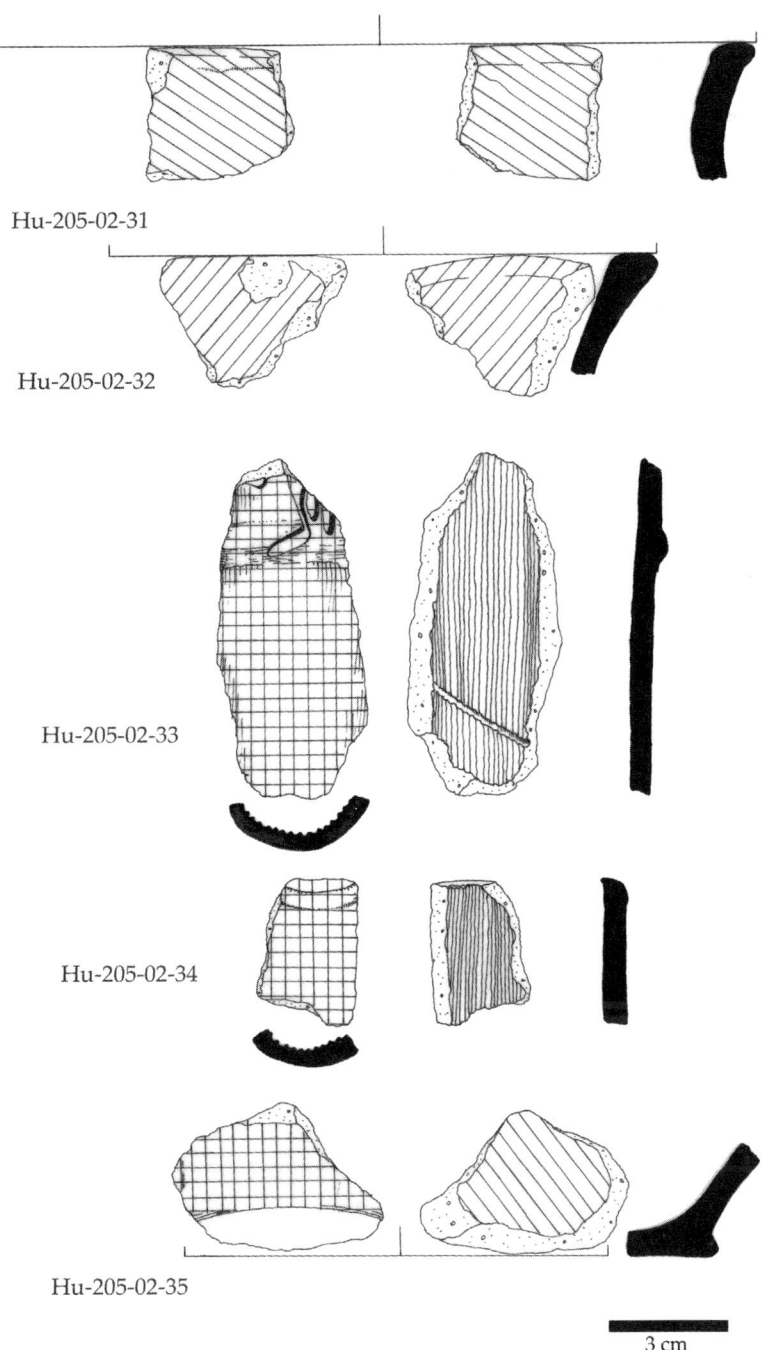

Figure A41. Ceramic fragment drawings from Hu-205.

314　　　　　　　　　　　　*The Northern Titicaca Basin Survey*

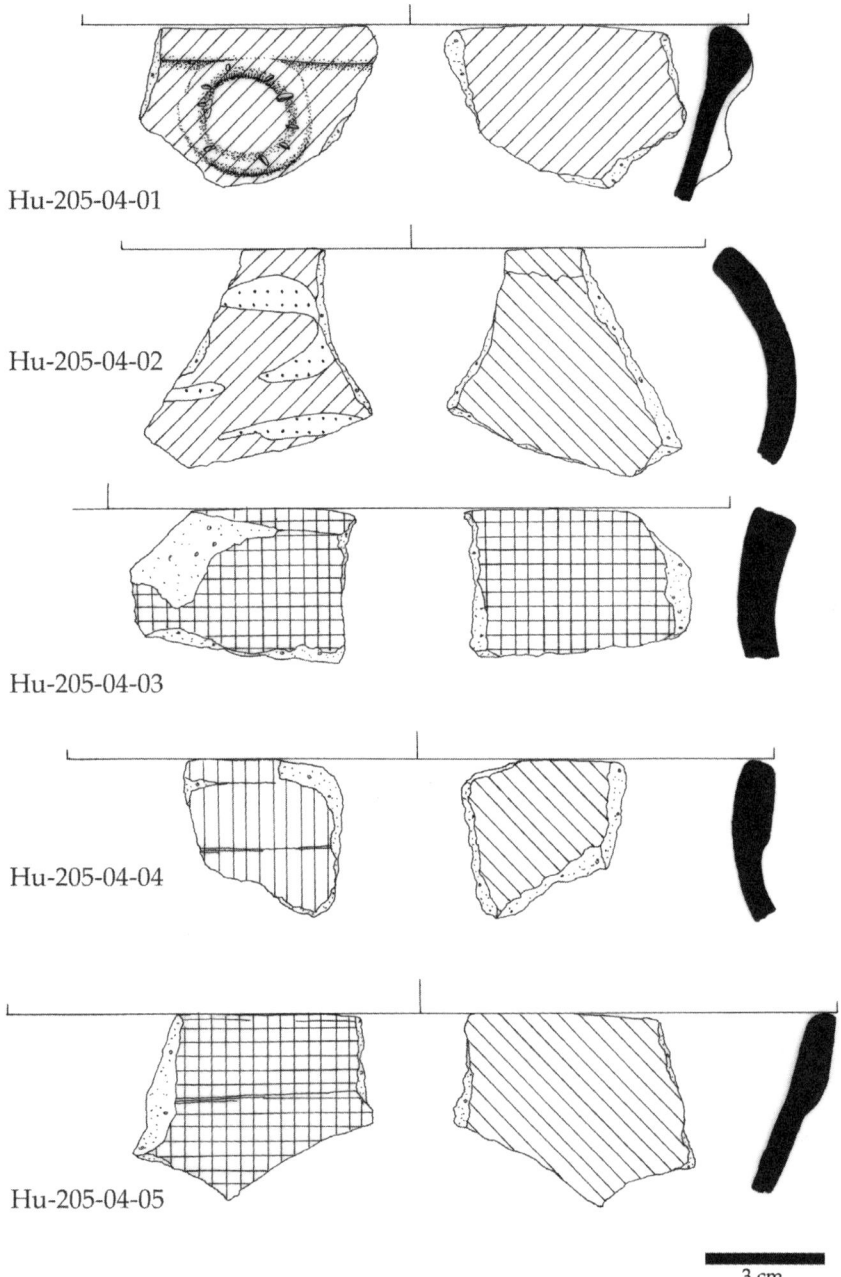

Figure A42. Ceramic fragment drawings from Hu-205.

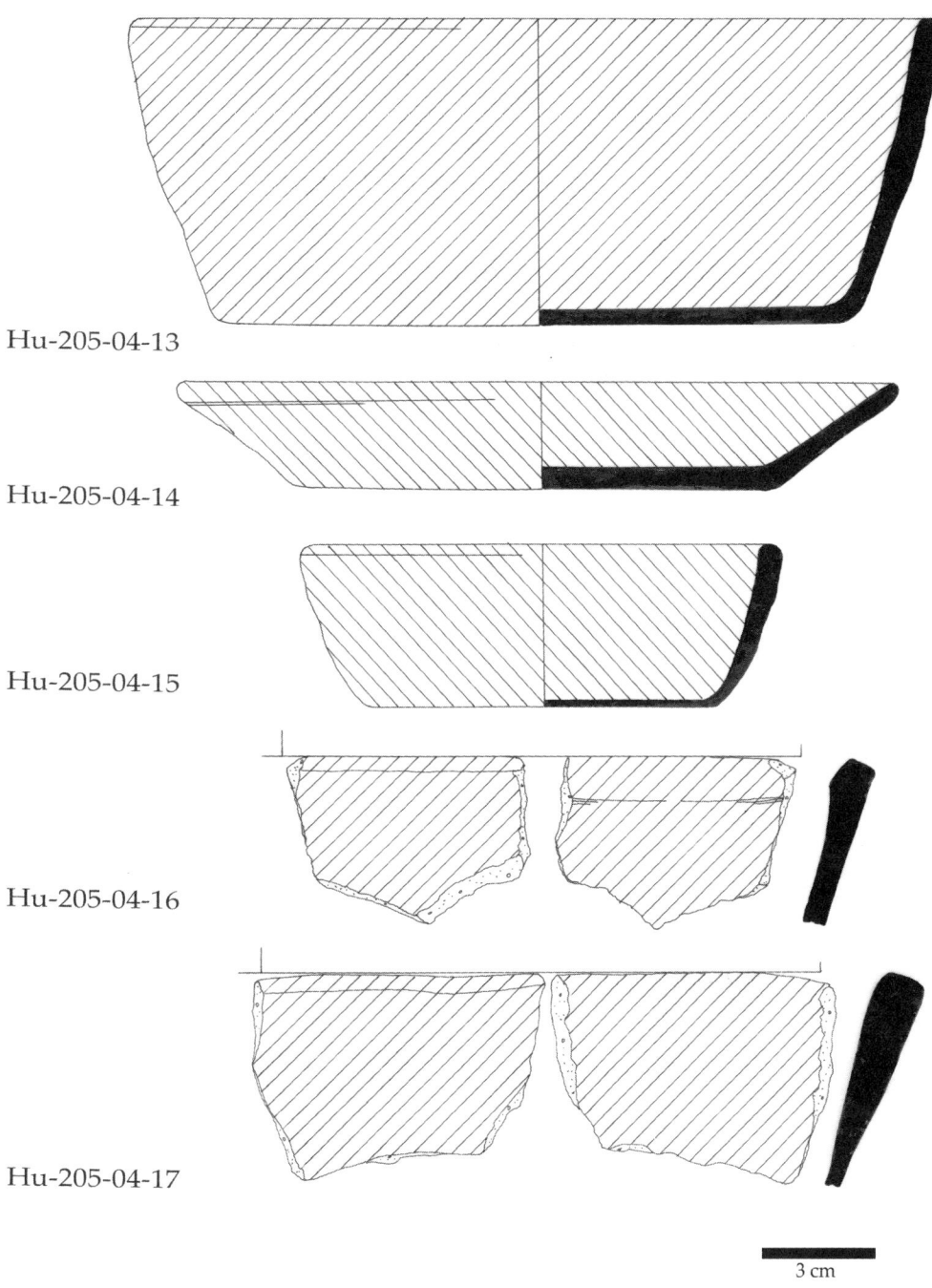

Figure A43. Ceramic fragment drawings from Hu-205.

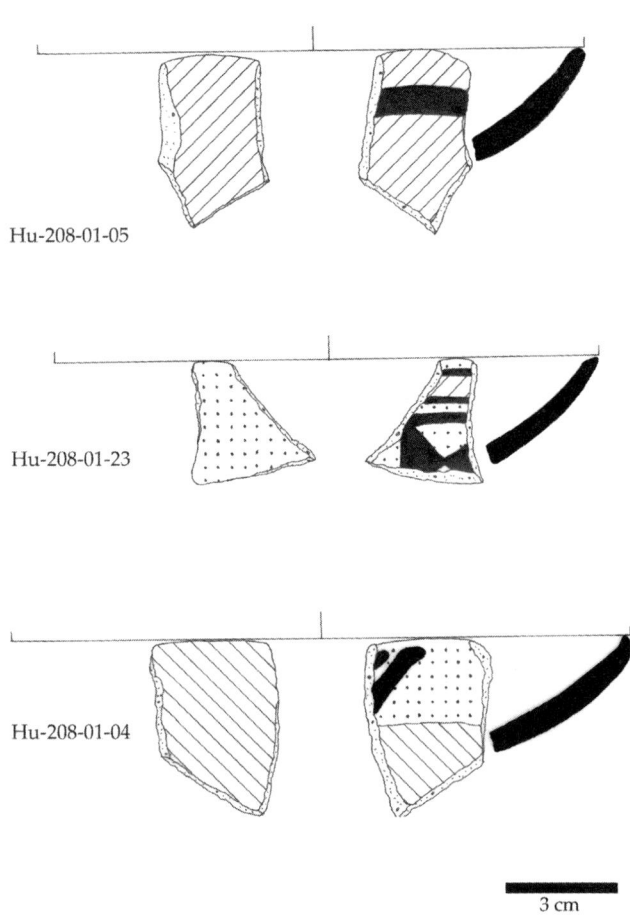

Figure A44. Ceramic fragment drawings from Hu-208.

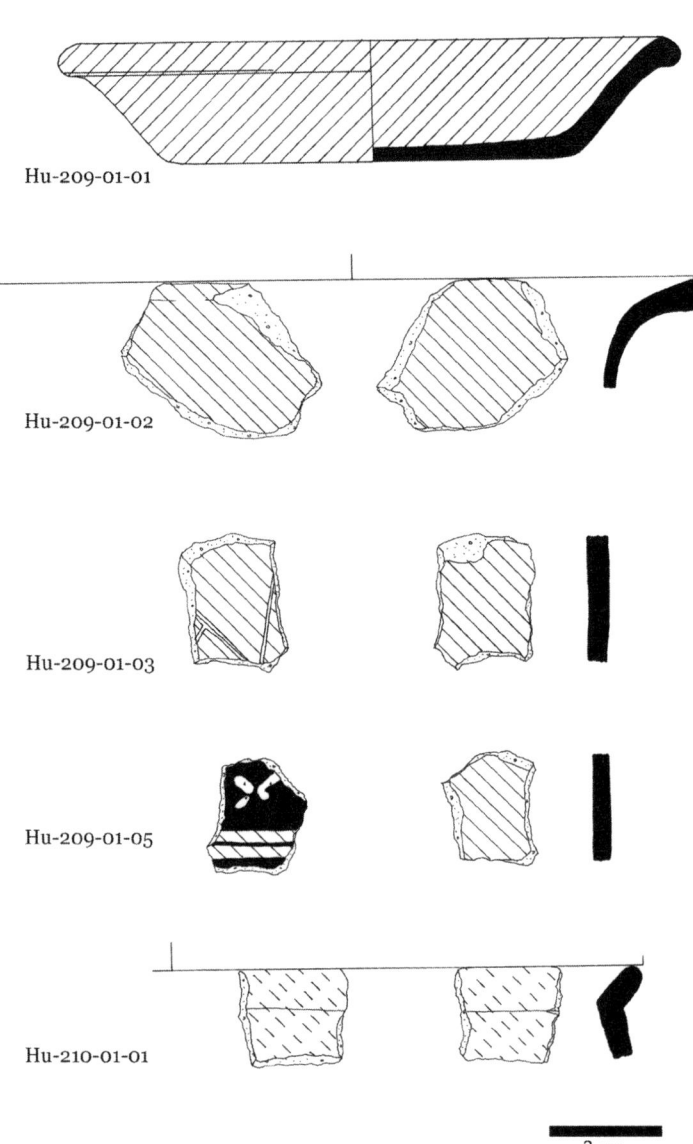

Figure A45. Ceramic fragment drawings from Hu-209 and Hu-210.

Appendix A

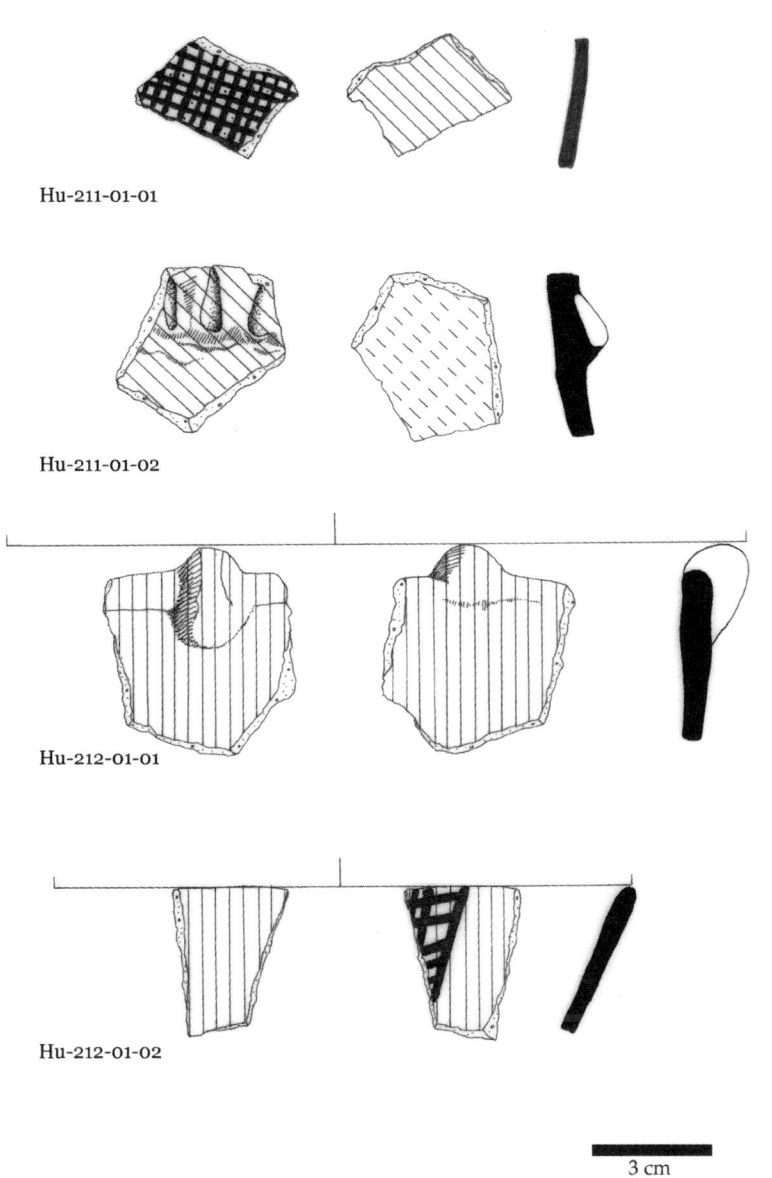

Figure A46. Ceramic fragment drawings from Hu-211 and Hu-212.

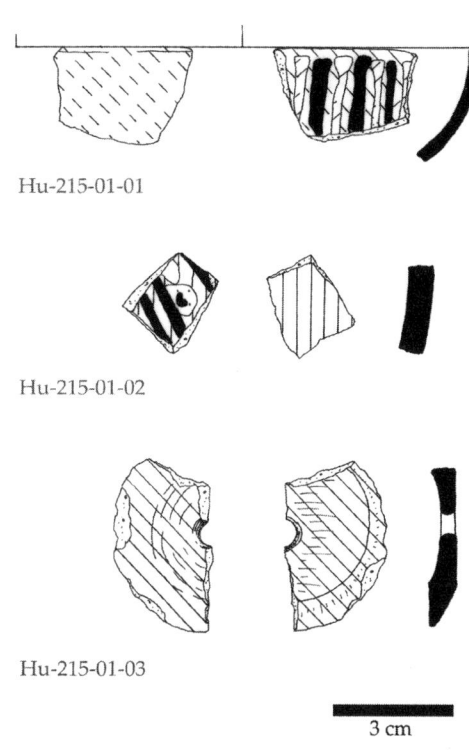

Figure A47. Ceramic fragment drawings from Hu-215.

318 *The Northern Titicaca Basin Survey*

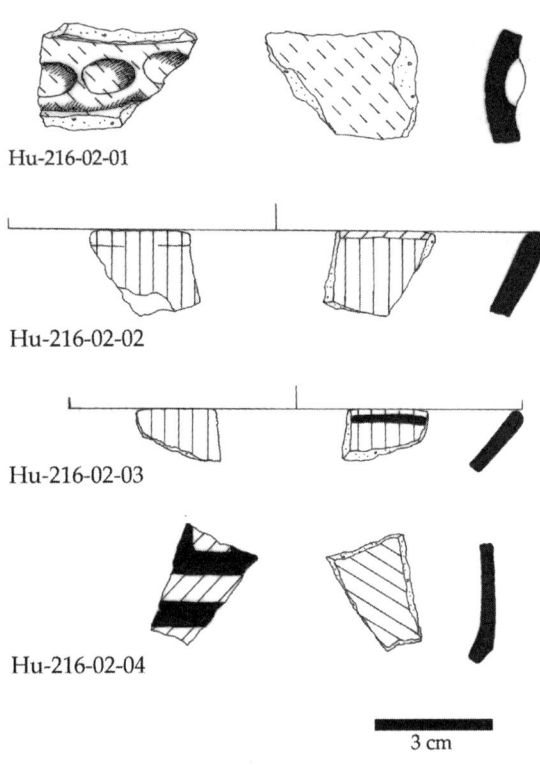

Figure A48. Ceramic fragment drawings from Hu-216.

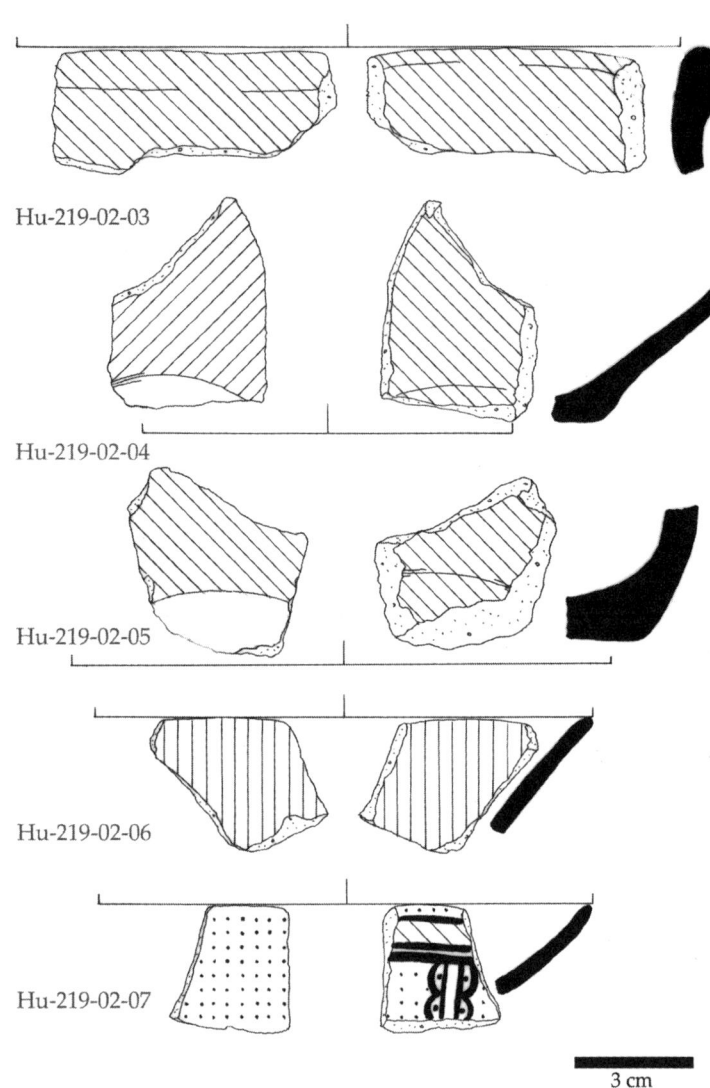

Figure A49. Ceramic fragment drawings from Hu-219.

Appendix A   *319*

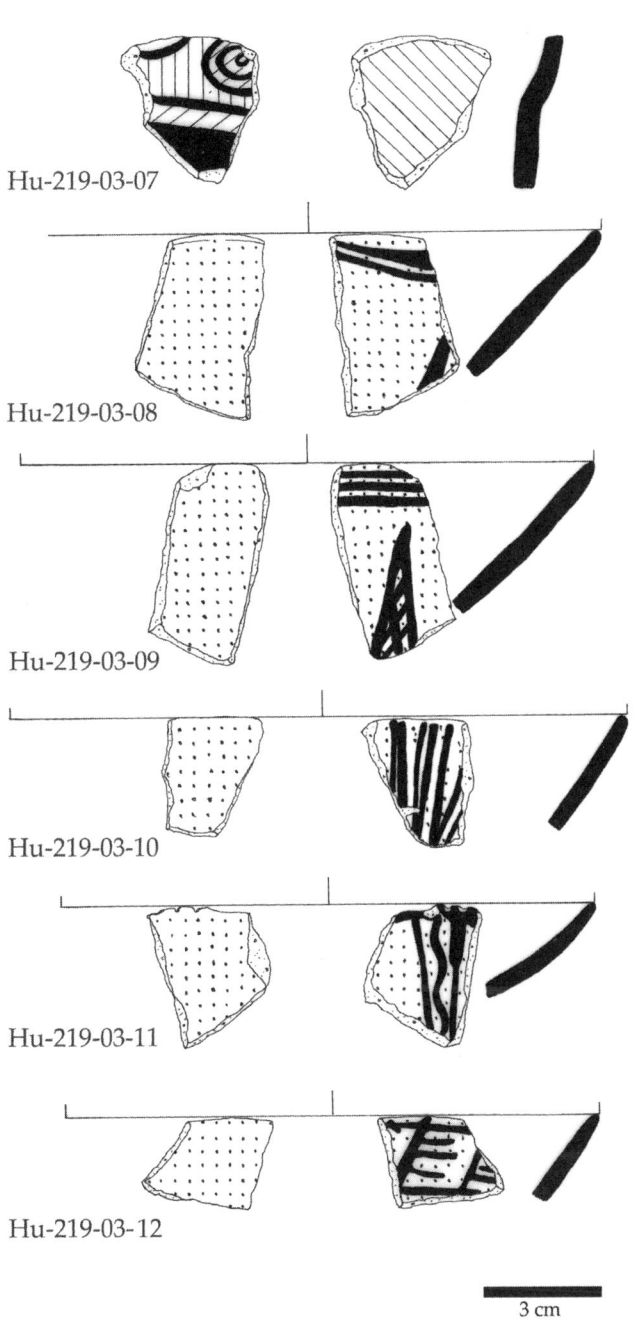

Figure A50. Ceramic fragment drawings from Hu-219.

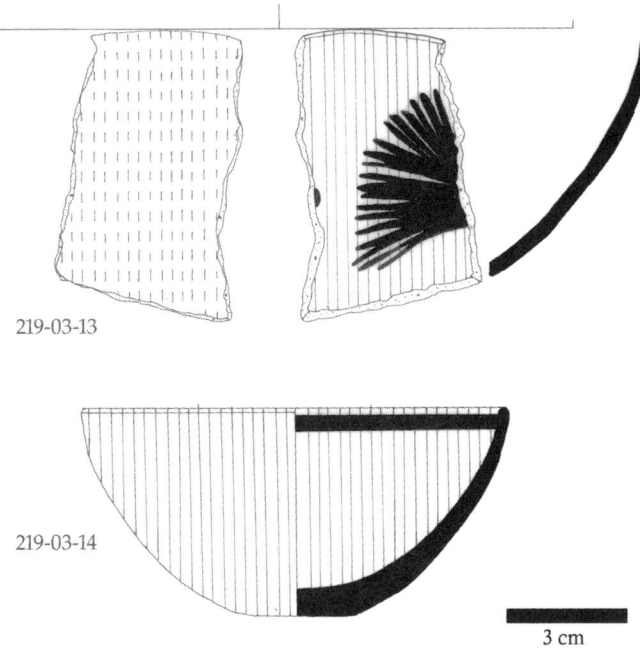

Figure A51. Ceramic fragment drawings from Hu-219.

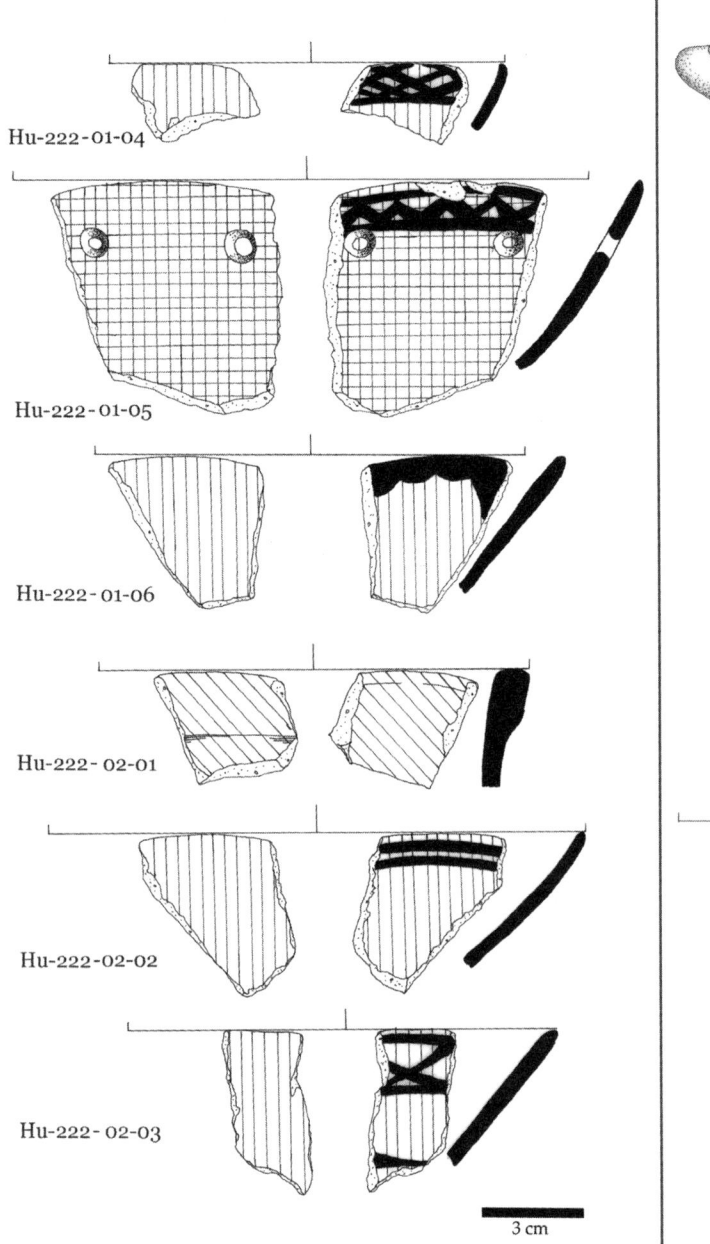

Figure A52. Ceramic fragment drawings from Hu-222.

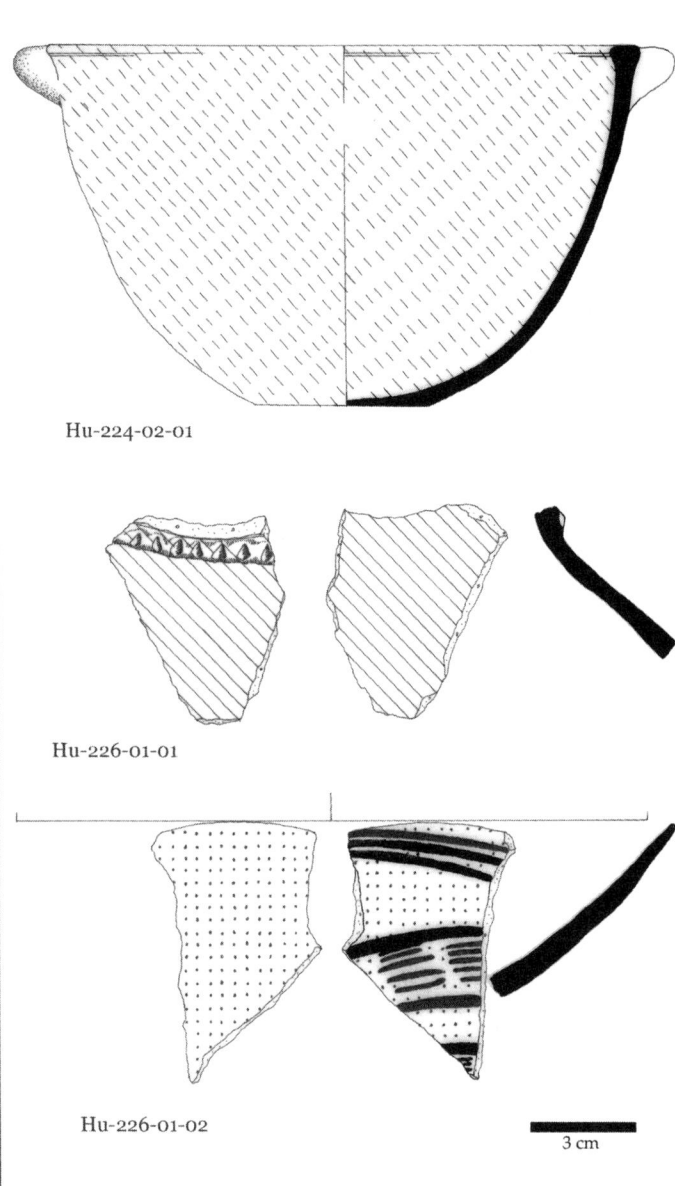

Figure A53. Ceramic fragment drawings from Hu-224 and Hu-226.

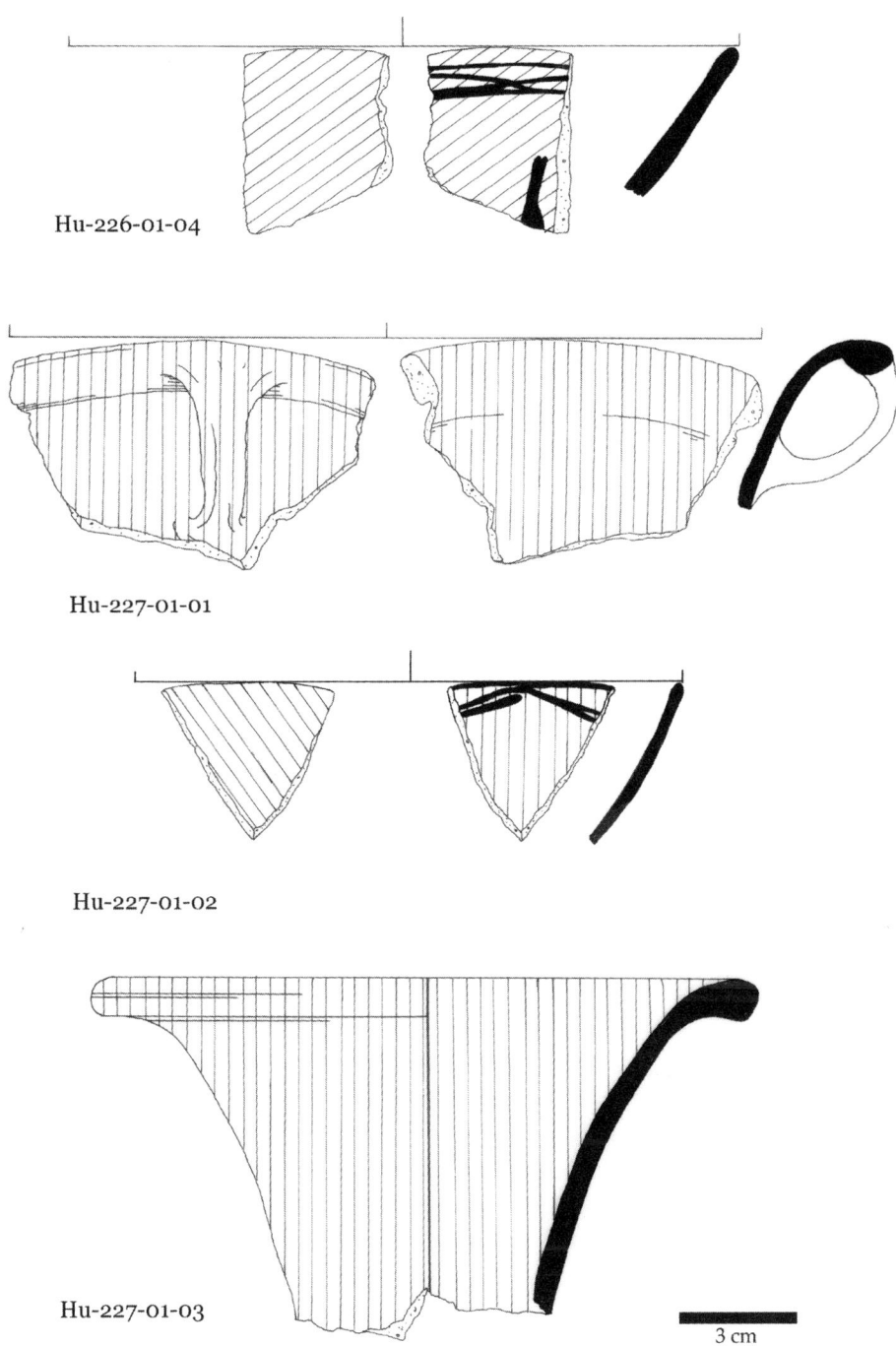

Figure A54. Ceramic fragment drawings from Hu-226 and Hu-227.

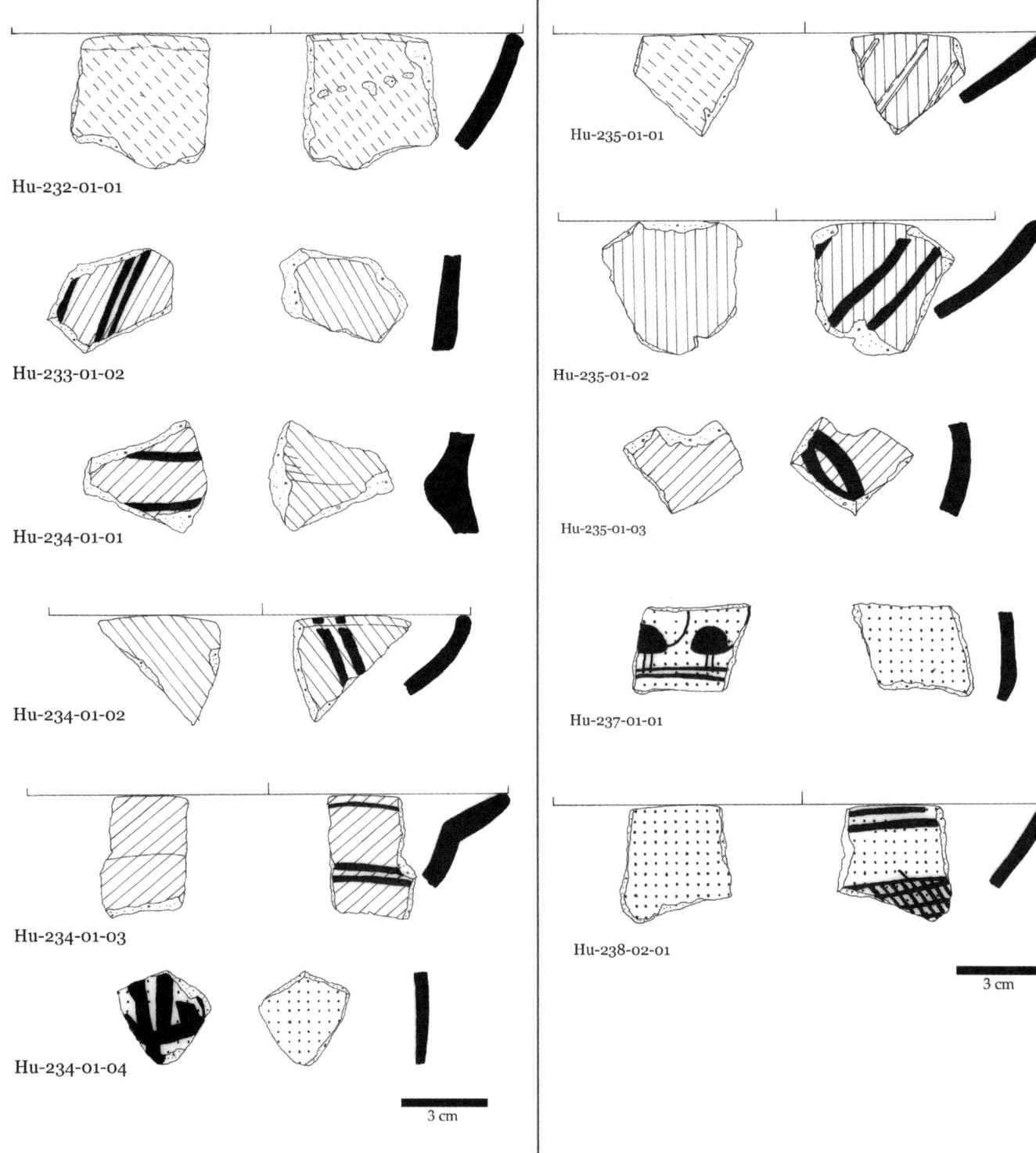

Figure A55. Ceramic fragment drawings from Hu-232, Hu-233, and Hu-234.

Figure A56. Ceramic fragment drawings from Hu-235, Hu-237, and Hu-238.

Appendix A 323

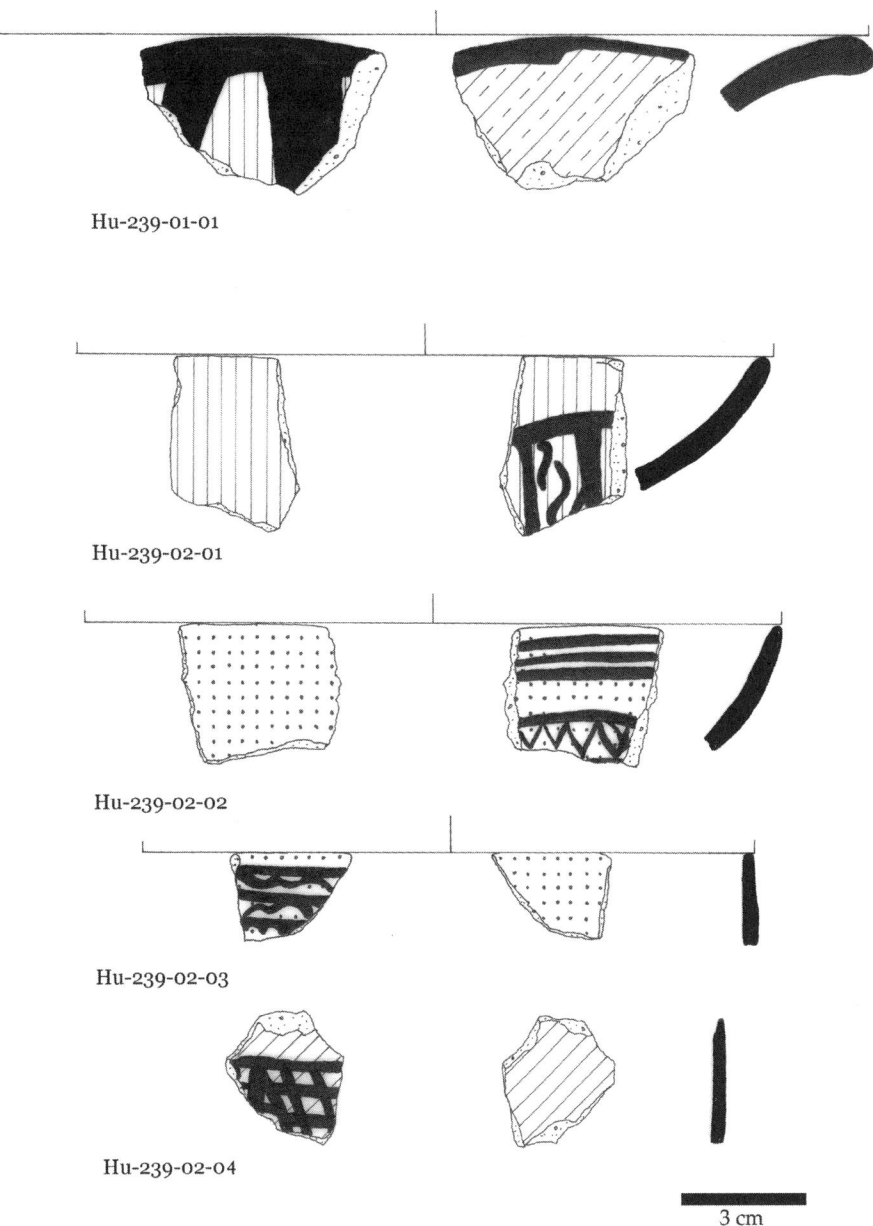

Figure A57. Ceramic fragment drawings from Hu-239.

324 *The Northern Titicaca Basin Survey*

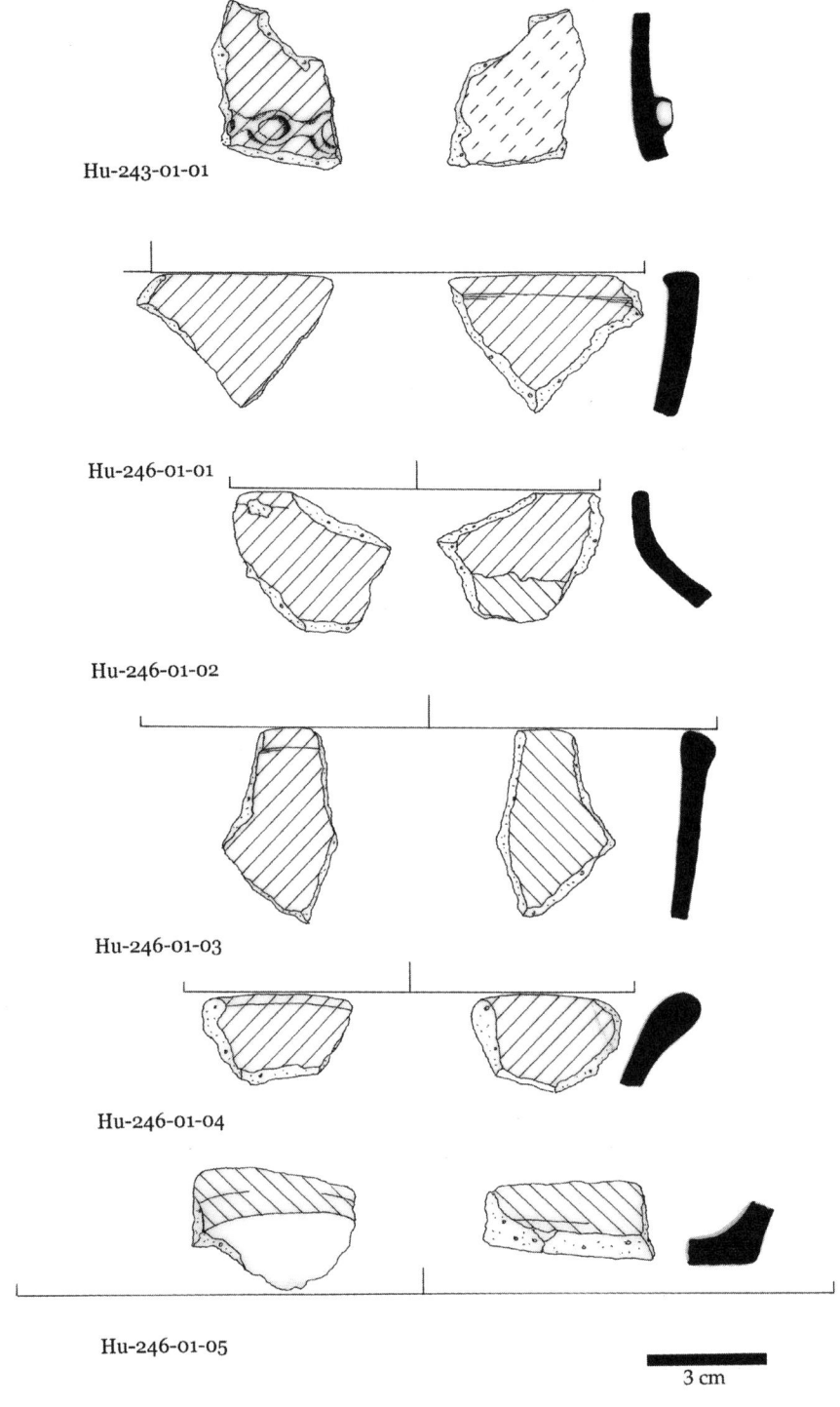

Figure A58. Ceramic fragment drawings from Hu-243 and Hu-246.

Appendix A 325

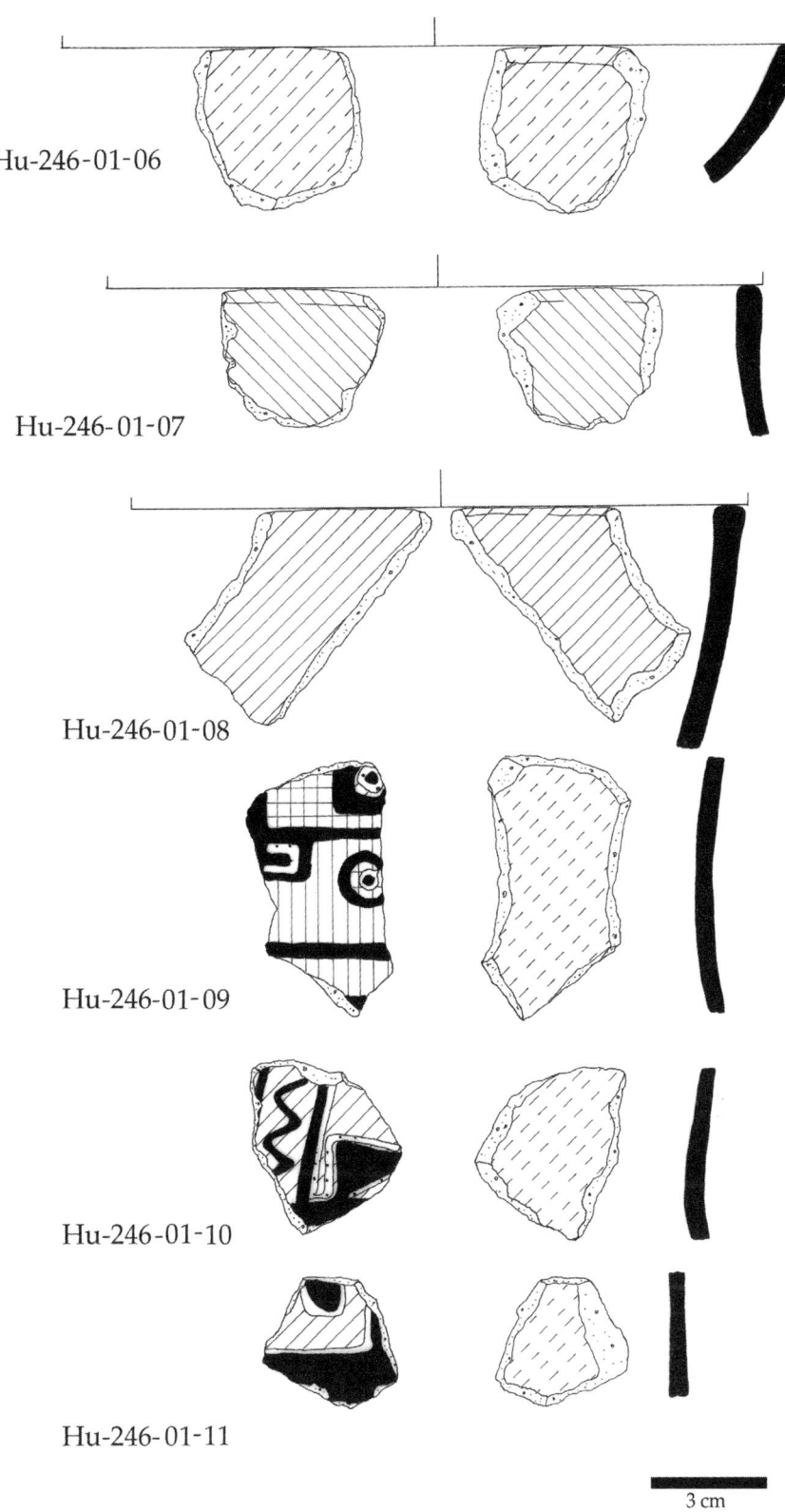

Figure A59. Ceramic fragment drawings from Hu-246.

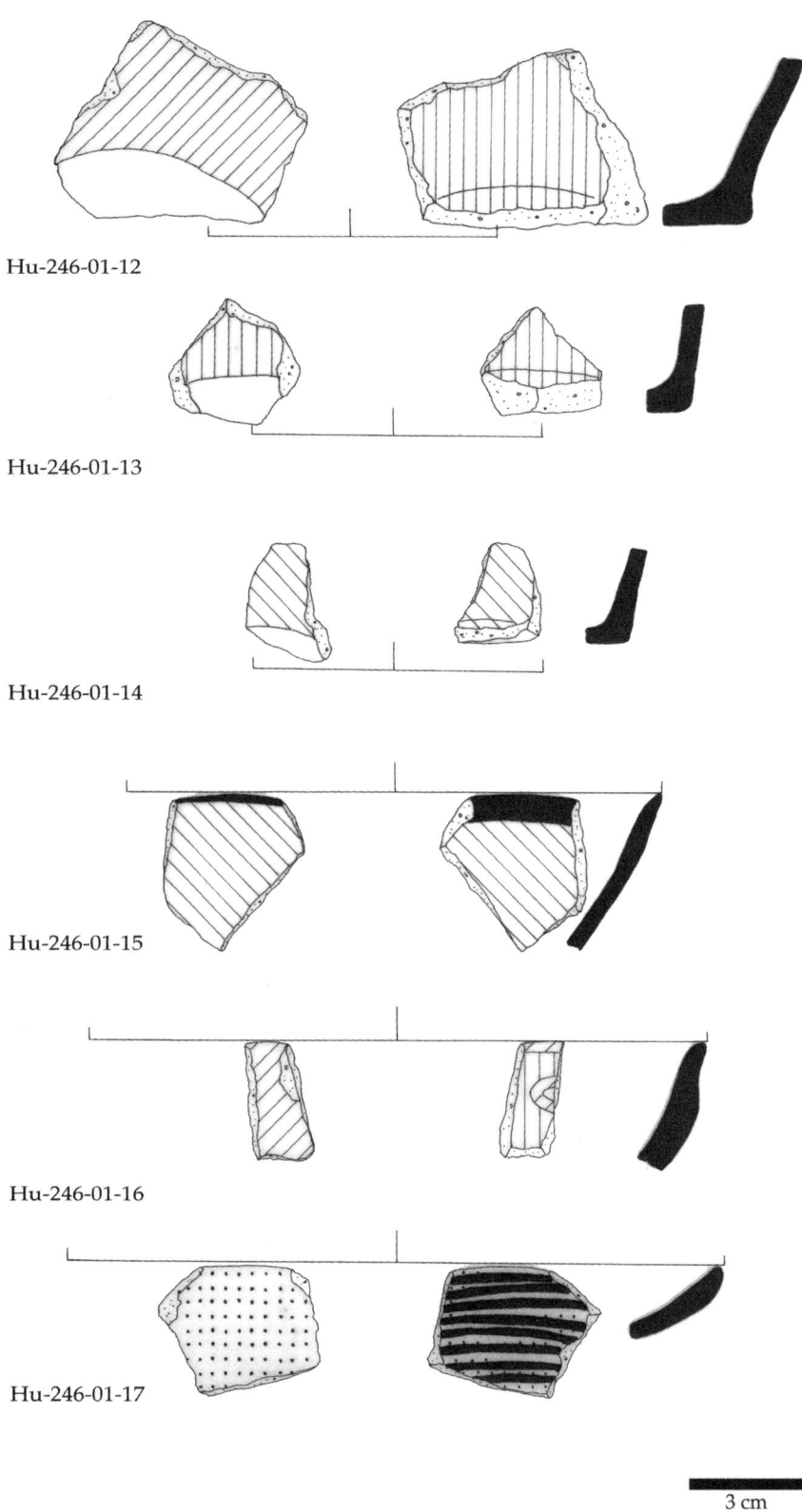

Figure A60. Ceramic fragment drawings from Hu-246.

Appendix A

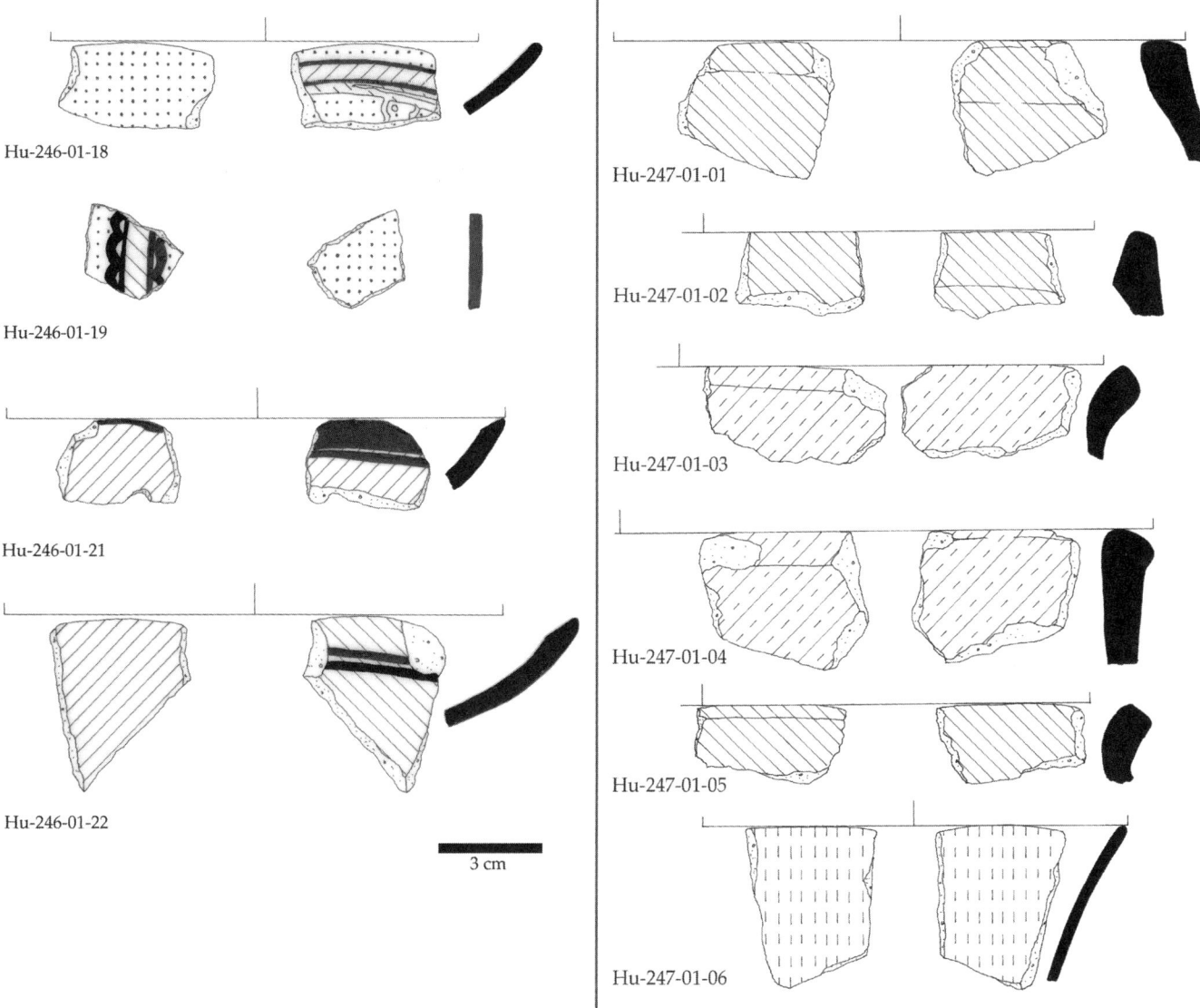

Figure A61. Ceramic fragment drawings from Hu-246.

Figure A62. Ceramic fragment drawings from Hu-247.

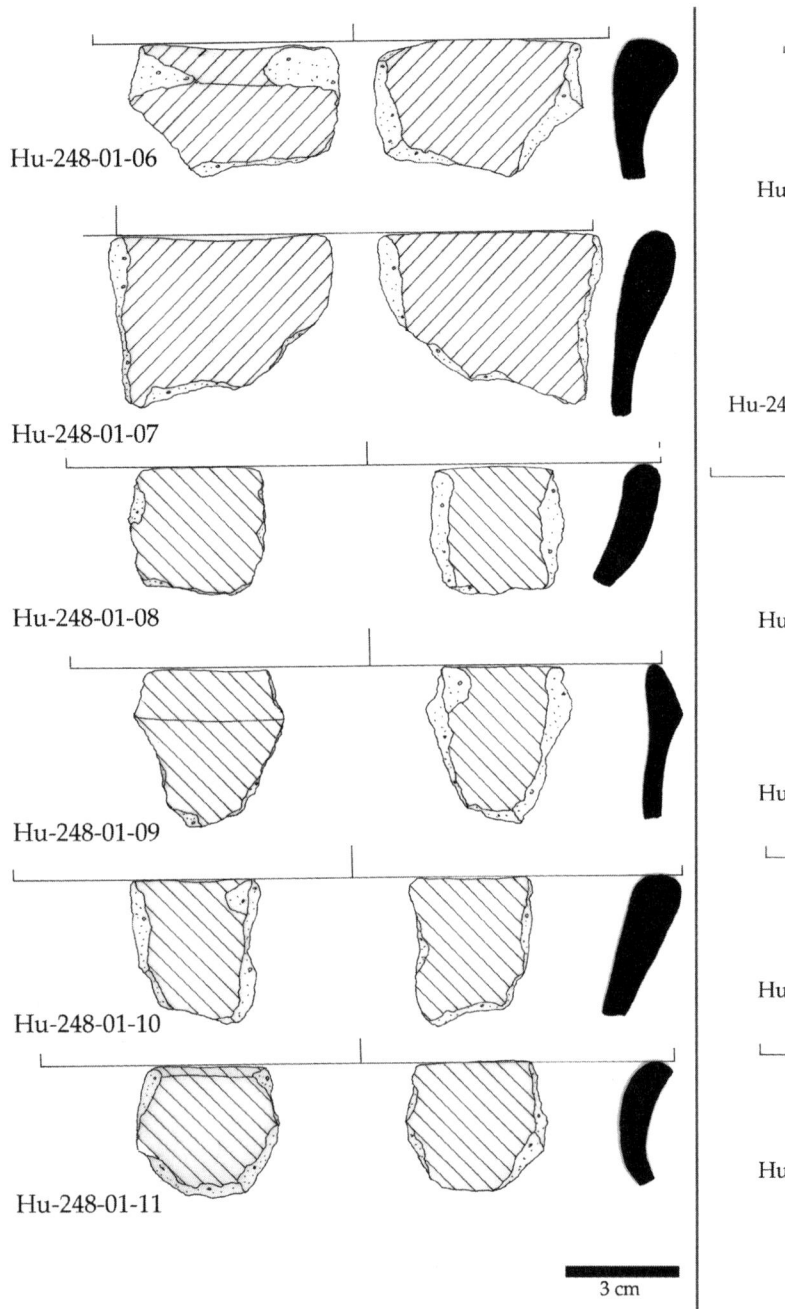

Figure A63. Ceramic fragment drawings from Hu-248.

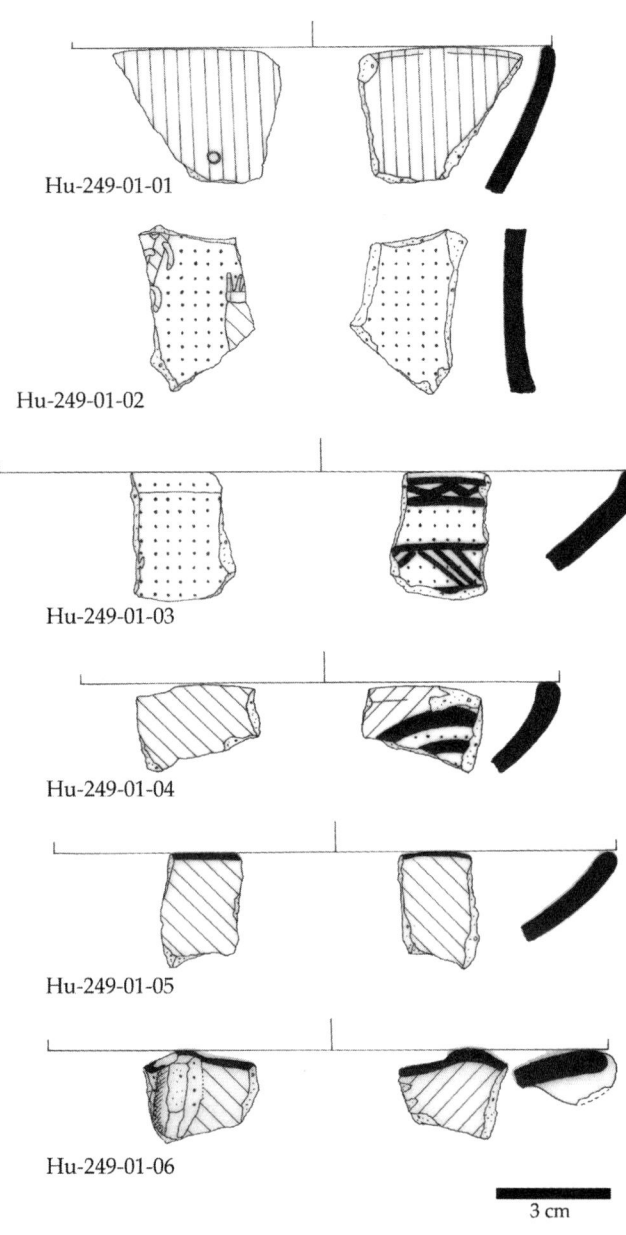

Figure A64. Ceramic fragment drawings from Hu-249.

Appendix A

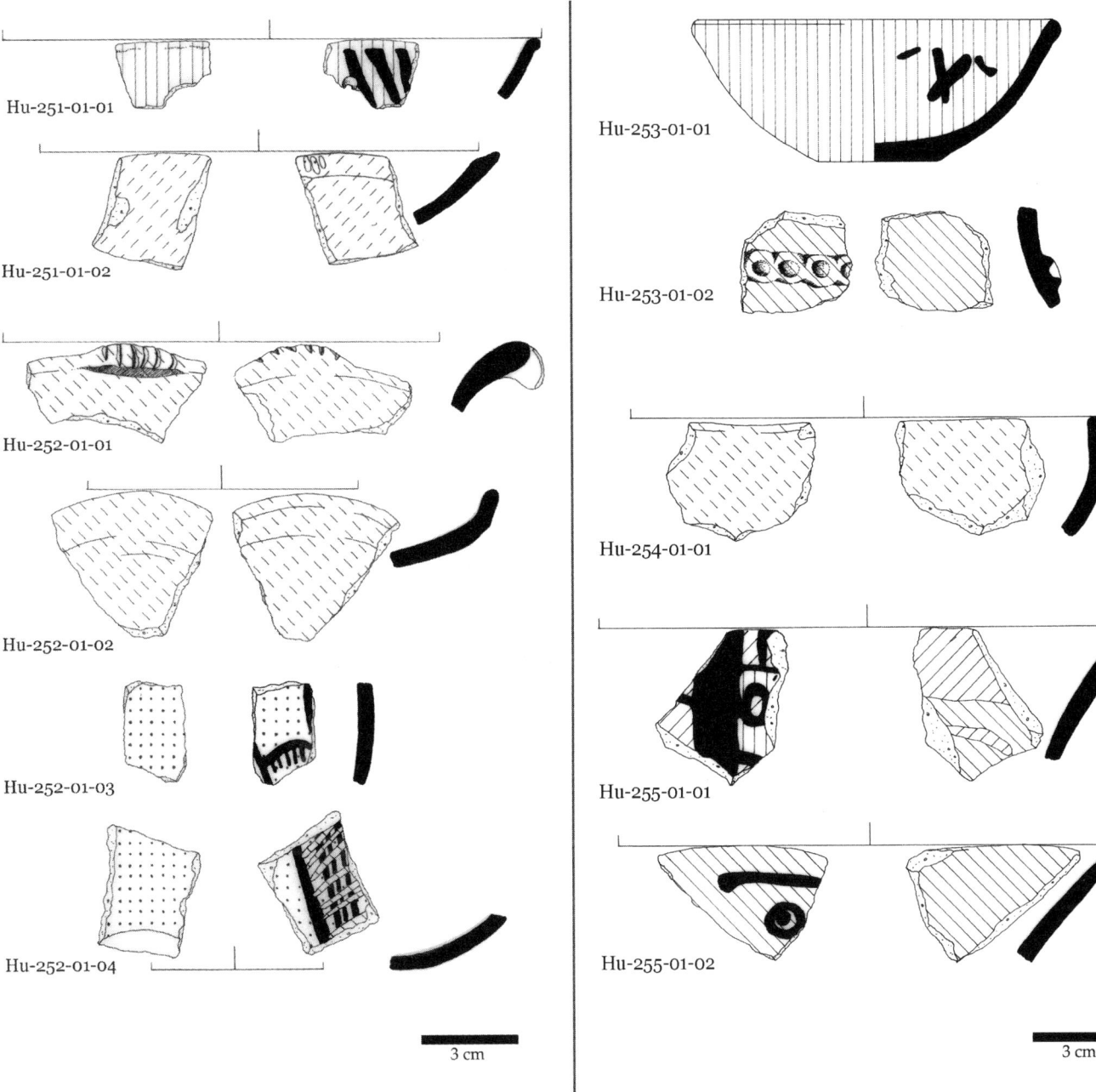

Figure A65. Ceramic fragment drawings from Hu-251 and Hu-252.

Figure A66. Ceramic fragment drawings from Hu-253, Hu-254, and Hu-255.

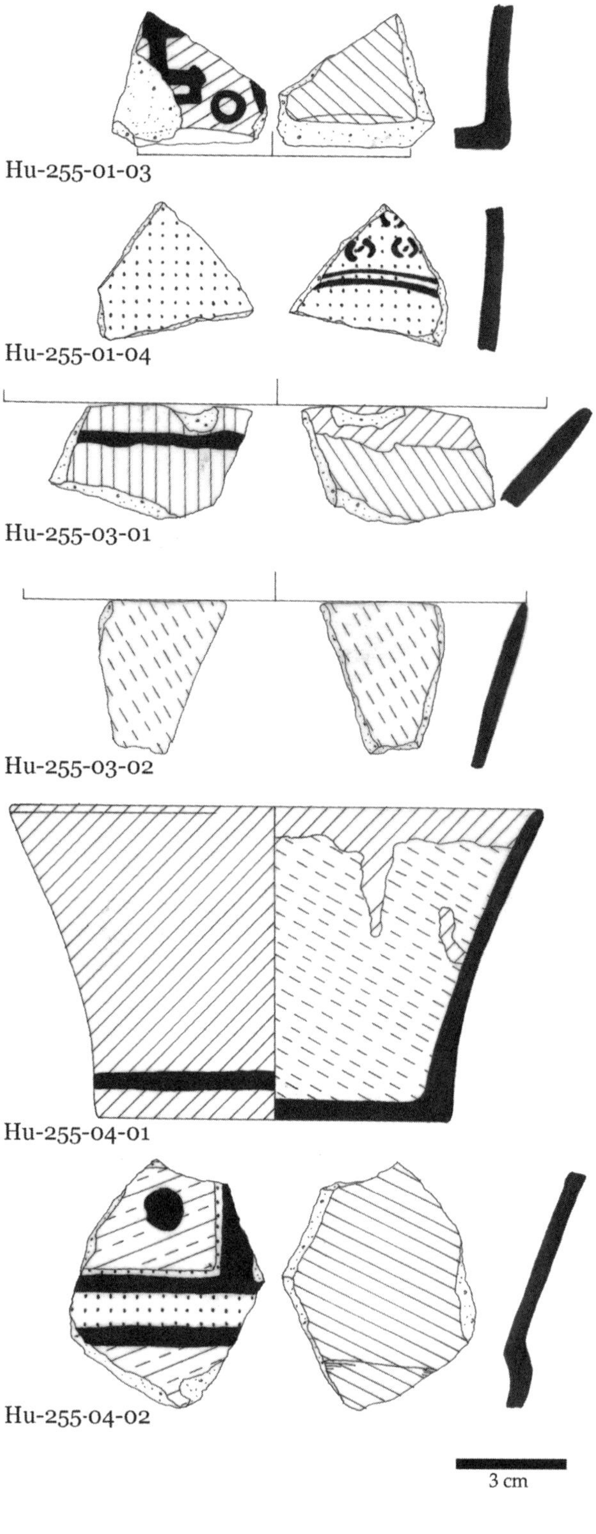

330   *The Northern Titicaca Basin Survey*

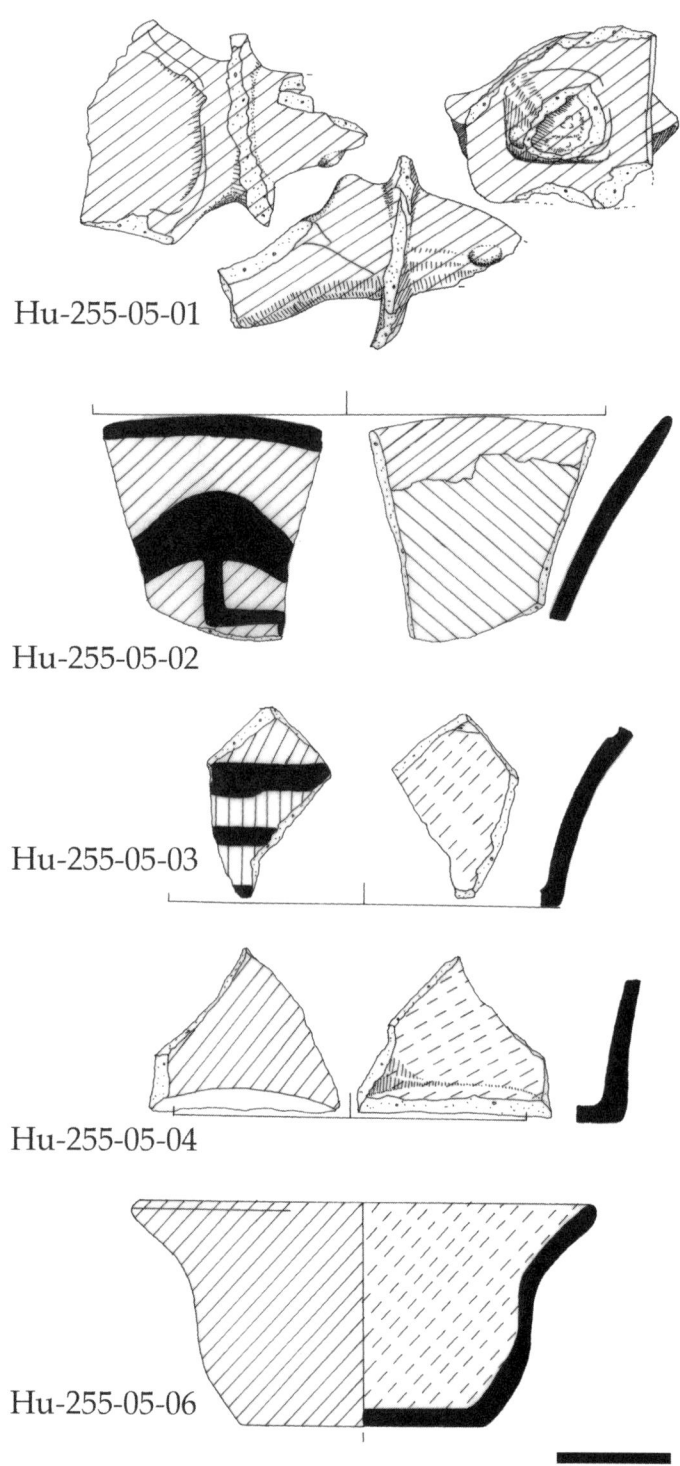

Figure A67. Ceramic fragment drawings from Hu-255.

Figure A68. Ceramic fragment drawings from Hu-255.

Appendix A

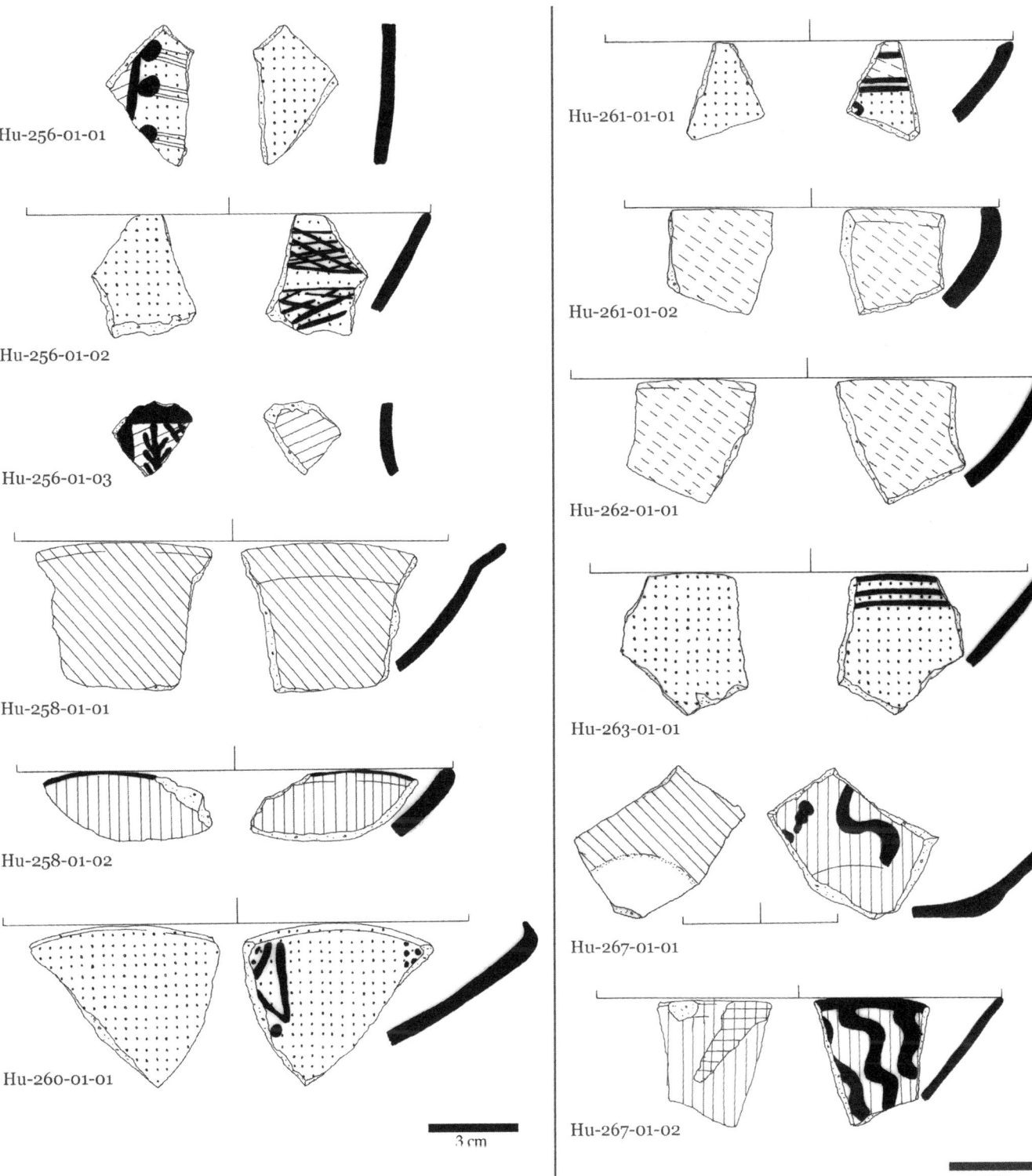

Figure A69. Ceramic fragment drawings from Hu-256, Hu-258, and Hu-260.

Figure A70. Ceramic fragment drawings from Hu-261, Hu-262, Hu-263, and Hu-267.

332   The Northern Titicaca Basin Survey

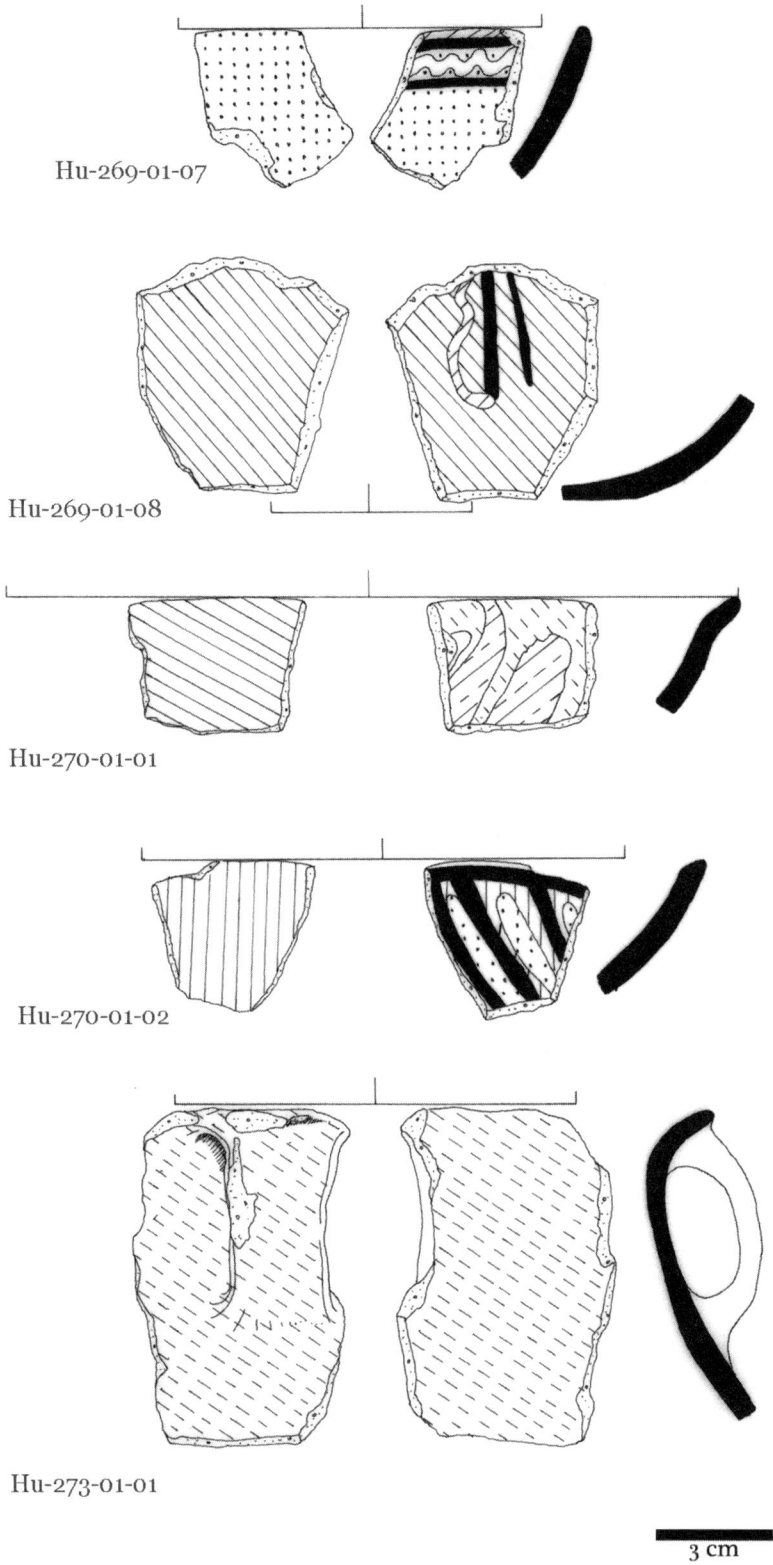

Figure A71. Ceramic fragment drawings from Hu-269, Hu-270, and Hu-273.

Appendix A

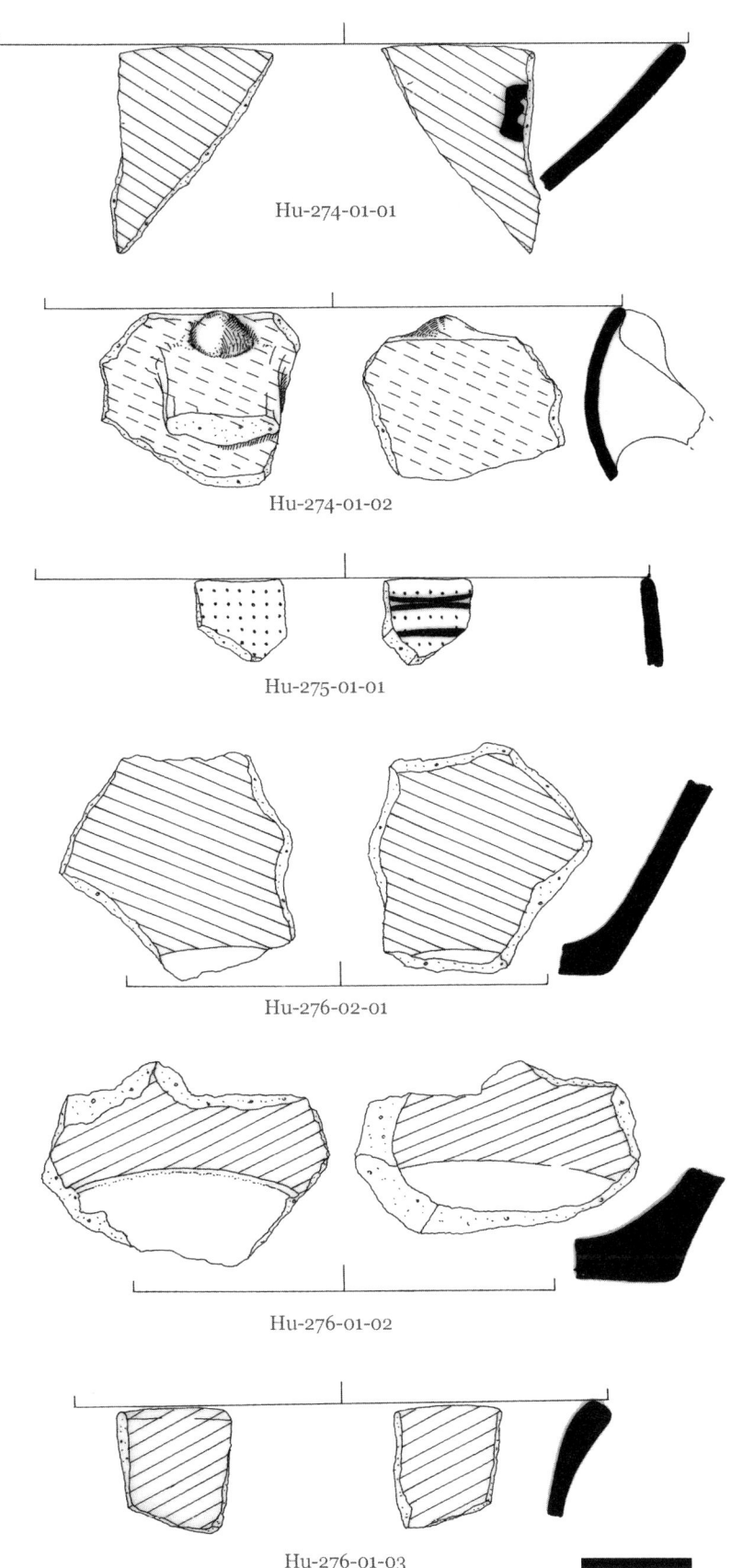

Figure A72.
Ceramic fragment drawings from
Hu-274, Hu-275, and Hu-276.

334 · The Northern Titicaca Basin Survey

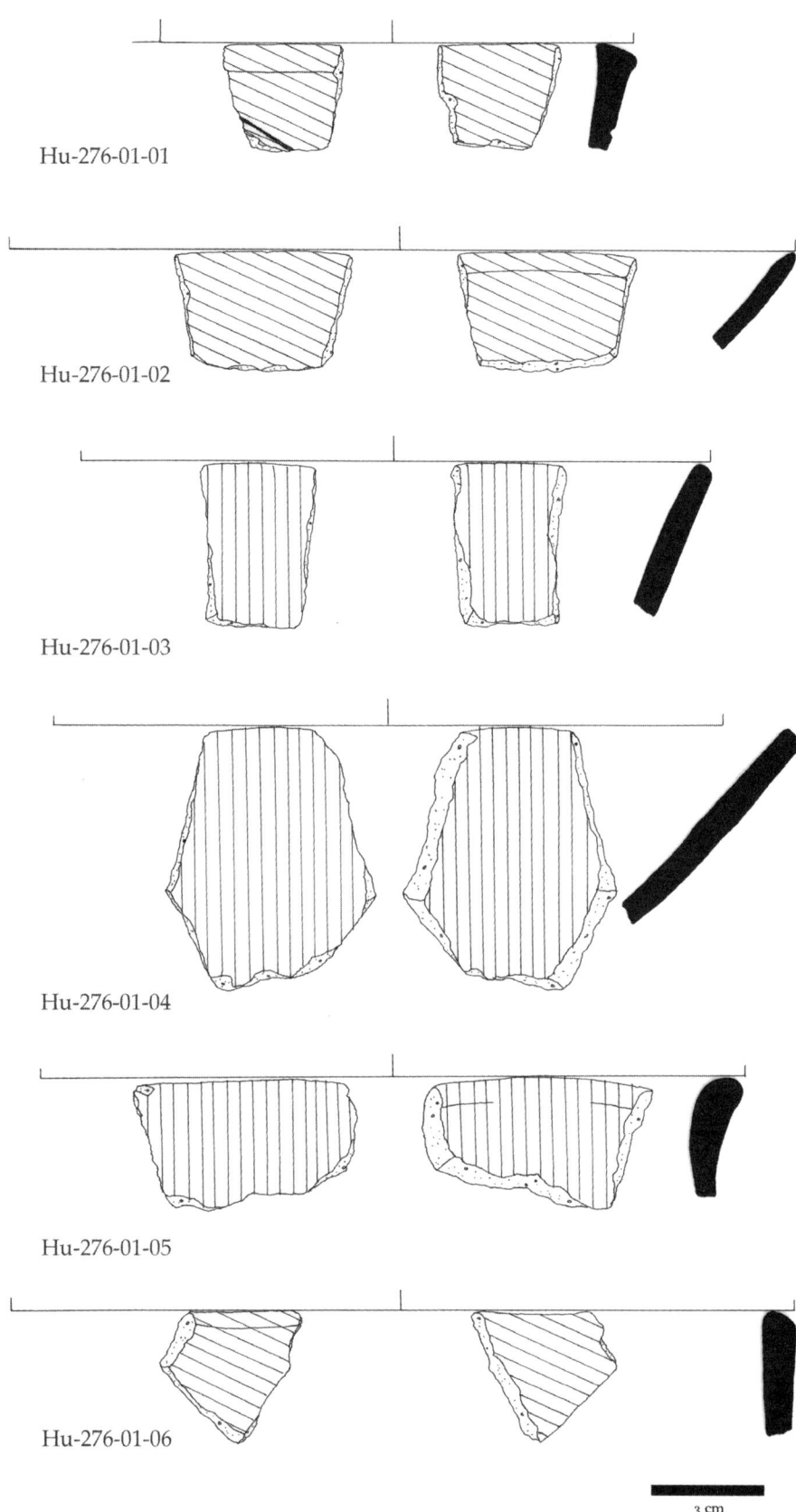

Figure A73. Ceramic fragment drawings from Hu-276.

Appendix A

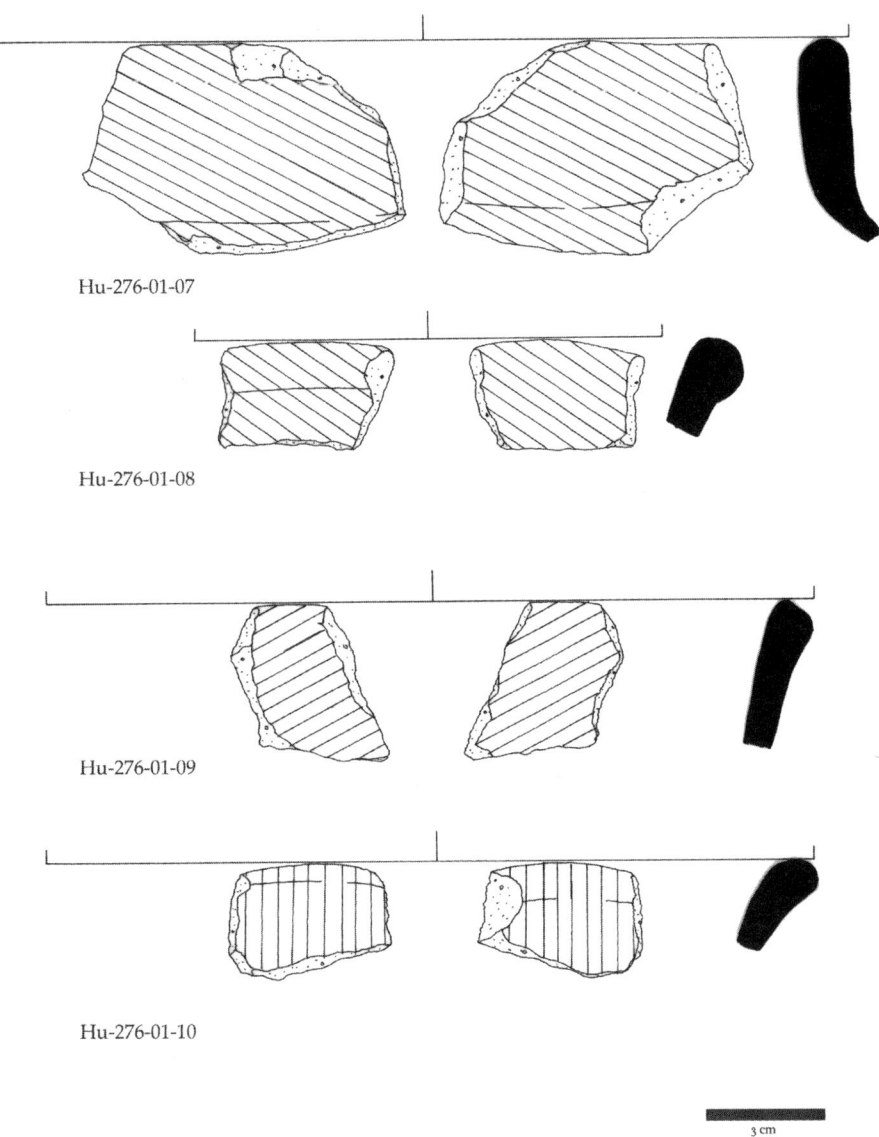

Figure A74. Ceramic fragment drawings from Hu-276.

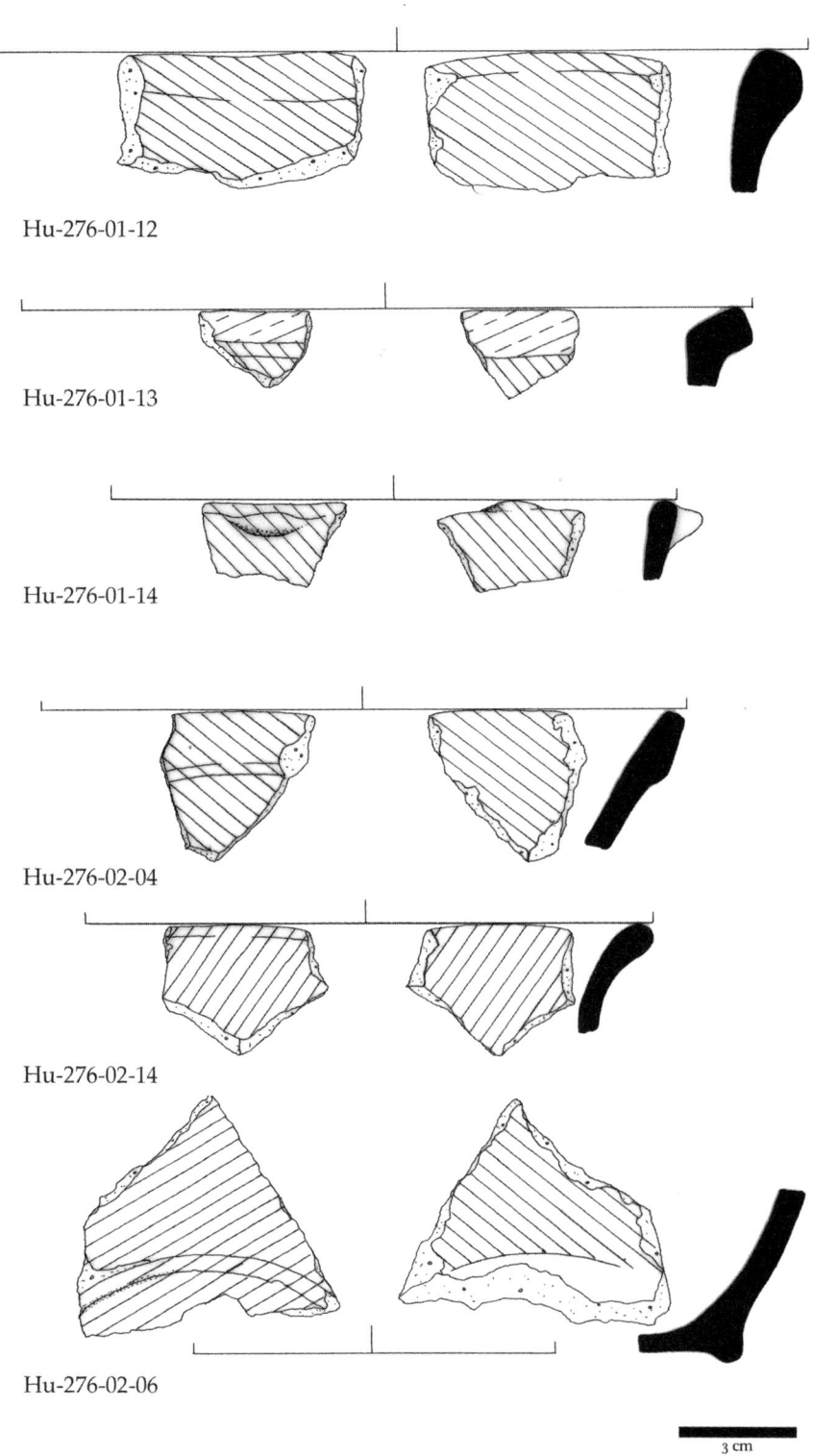

Figure A75. Ceramic fragment drawings from Hu-276.

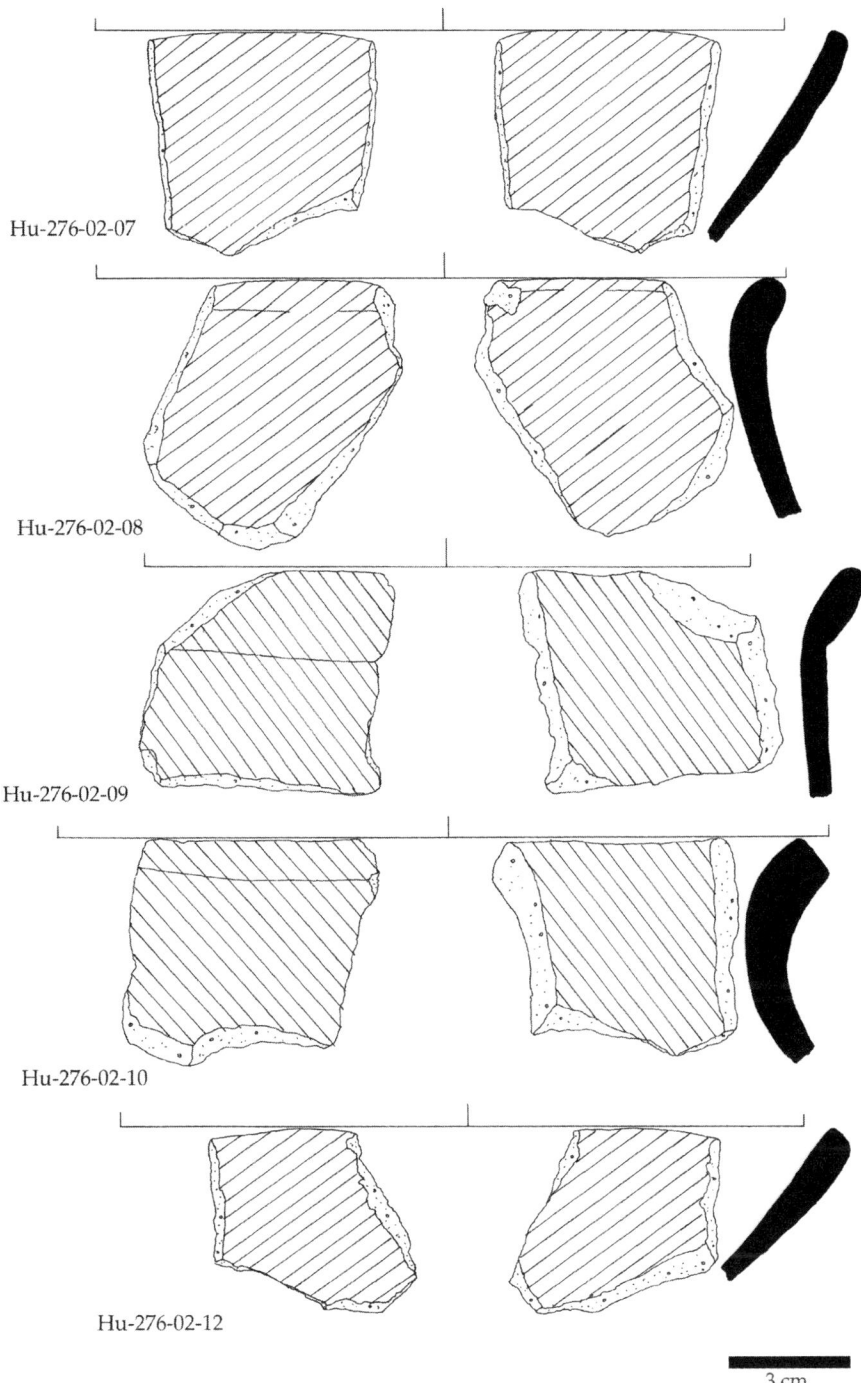

Figure A76. Ceramic fragment drawings from Hu-276.

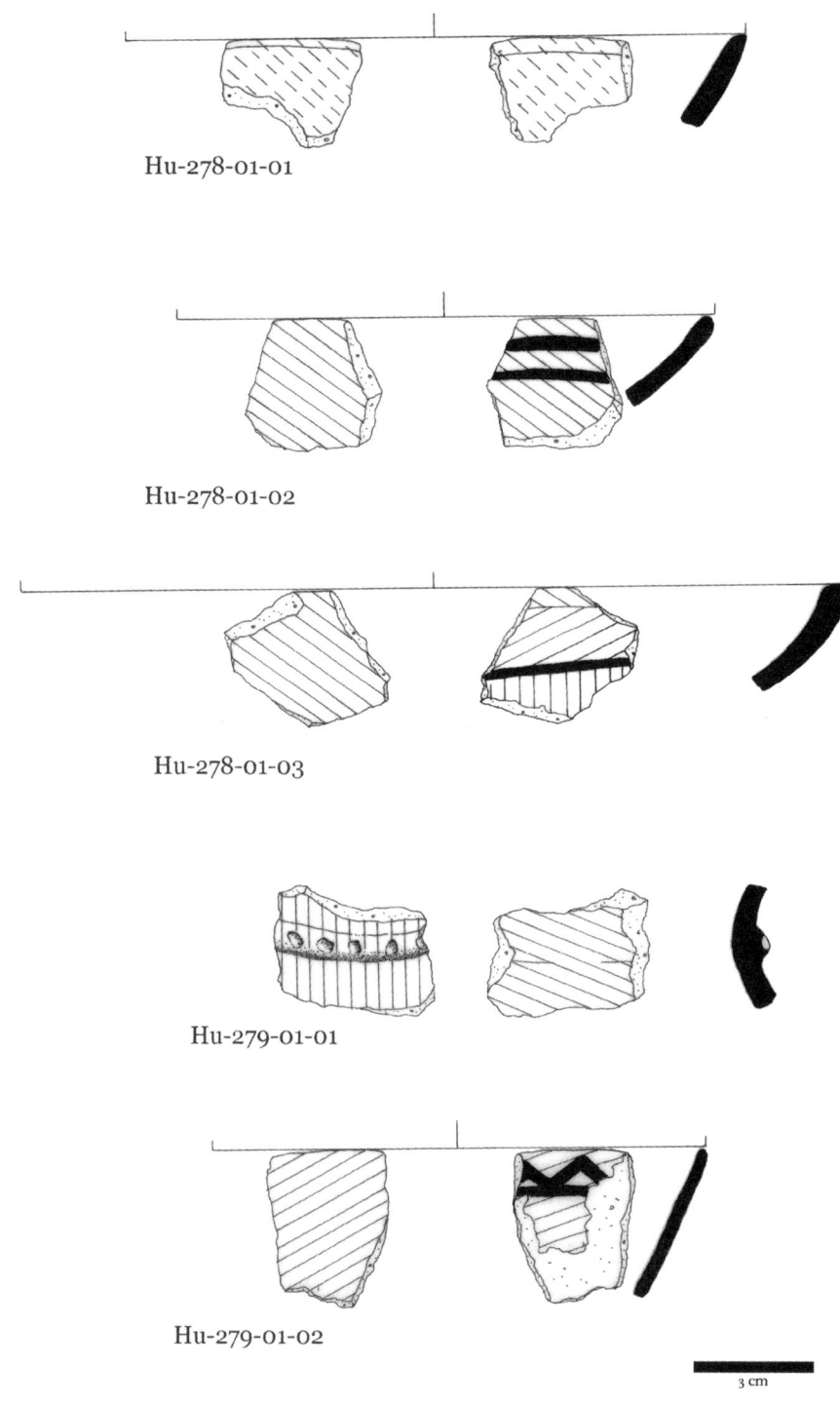

Figure A77. Ceramic fragment drawings from Hu-278 and Hu-279.

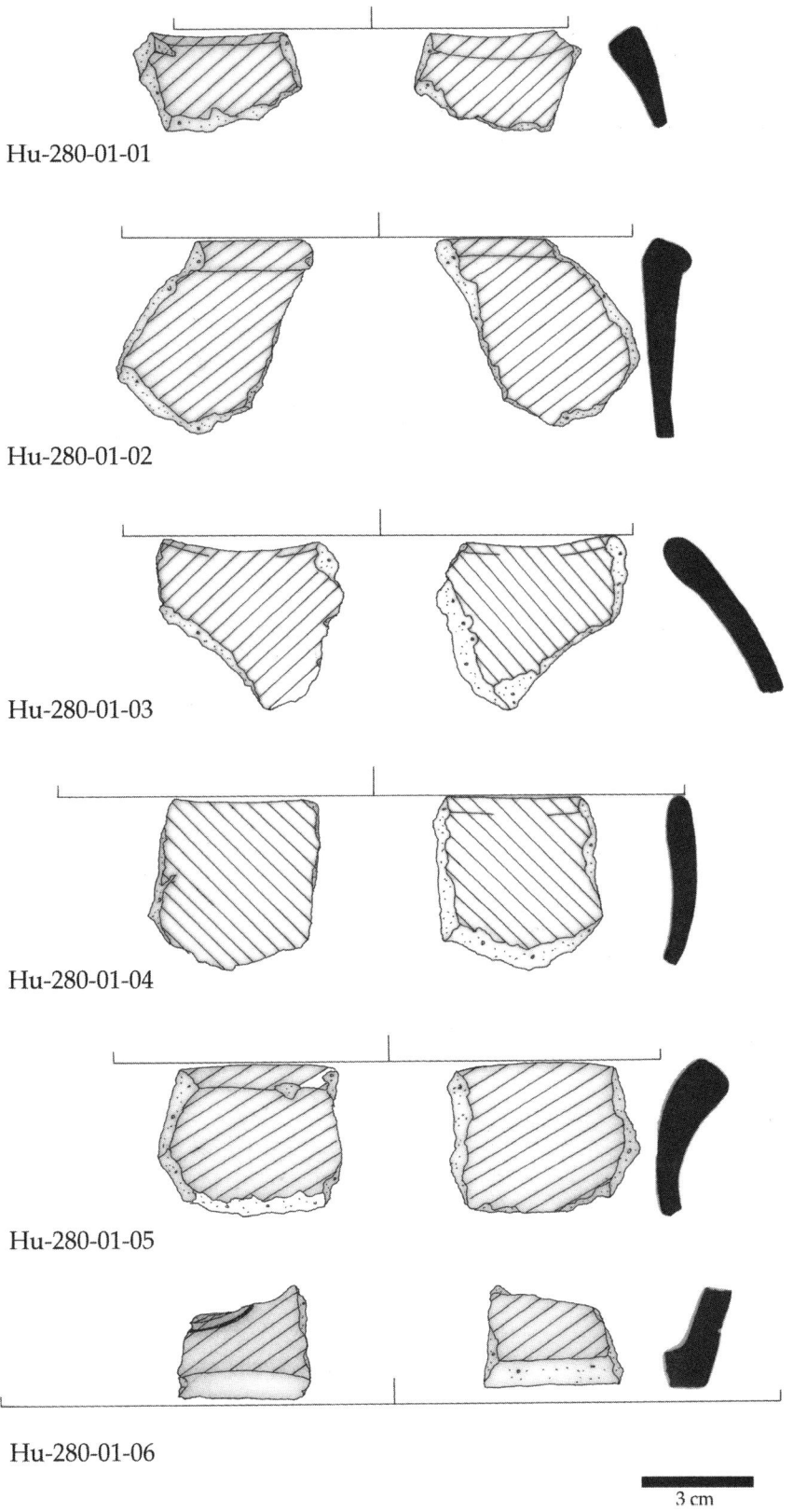

Figure A78. Ceramic fragment drawings from Hu-280.

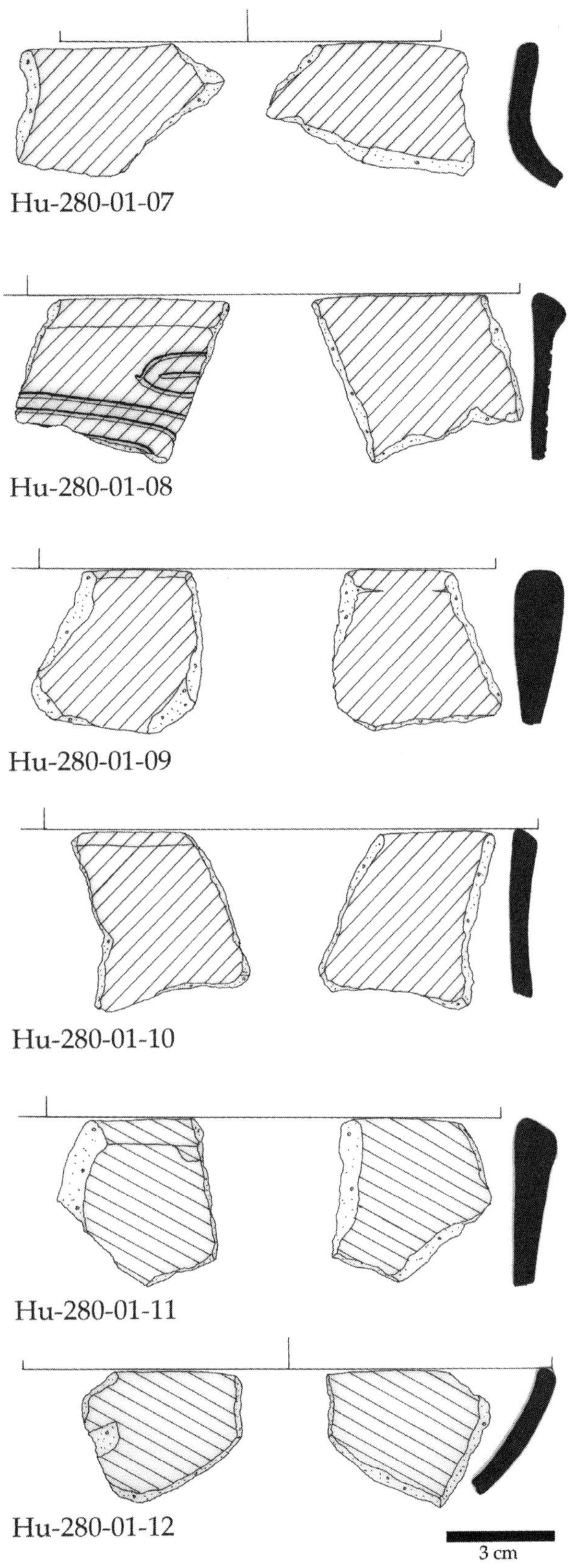

340   *The Northern Titicaca Basin Survey*

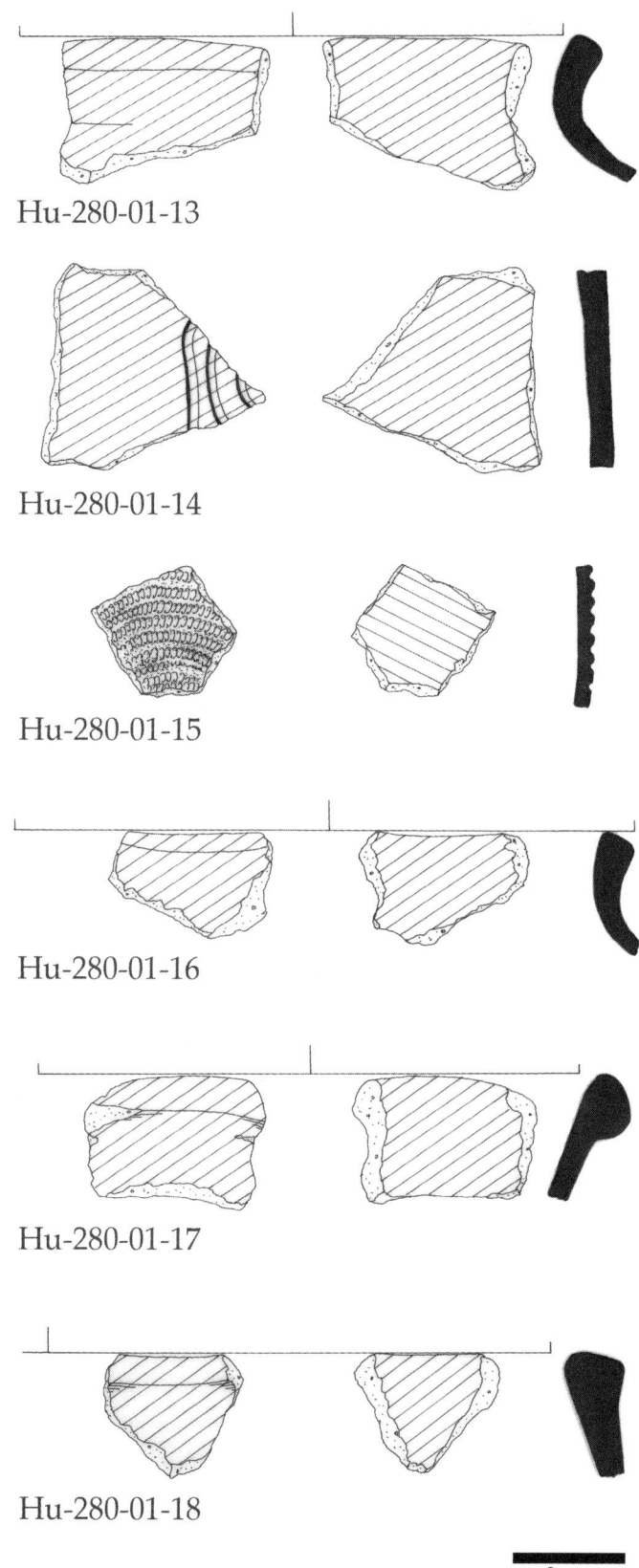

Hu-280-01-07

Hu-280-01-08

Hu-280-01-09

Hu-280-01-10

Hu-280-01-11

Hu-280-01-12

Hu-280-01-13

Hu-280-01-14

Hu-280-01-15

Hu-280-01-16

Hu-280-01-17

Hu-280-01-18

Figure A79. Ceramic fragment drawings from Hu-280.

Figure A80. Ceramic fragment drawings from Hu-280.

Appendix A 341

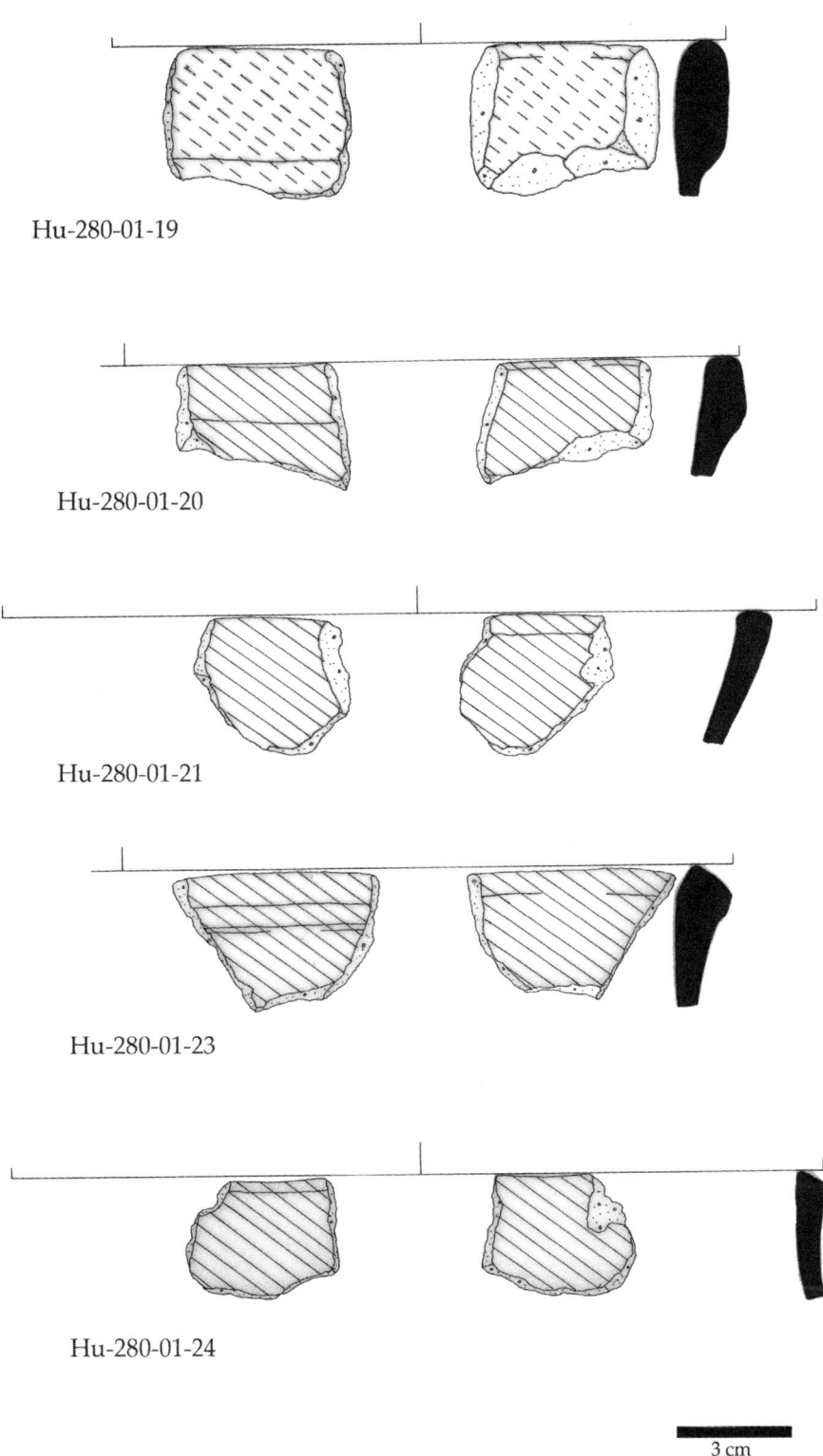

Hu-280-01-19

Hu-280-01-20

Hu-280-01-21

Hu-280-01-23

Hu-280-01-24

3 cm

Figure A81. Ceramic fragment drawings from Hu-280.

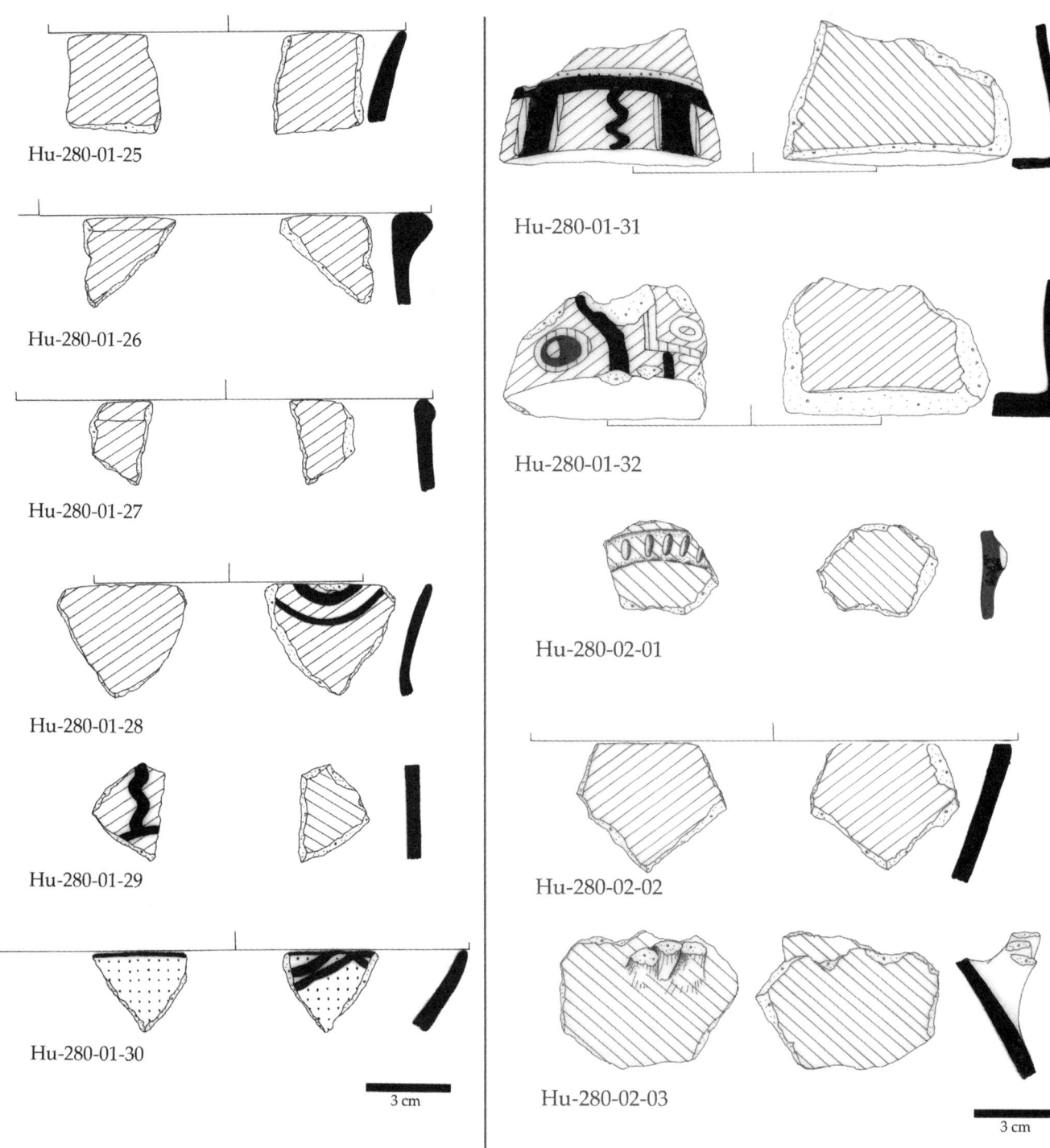

Figure A82. Ceramic fragment drawings from Hu-280.

Figure A83. Ceramic fragment drawings from Hu-280.

Appendix A 343

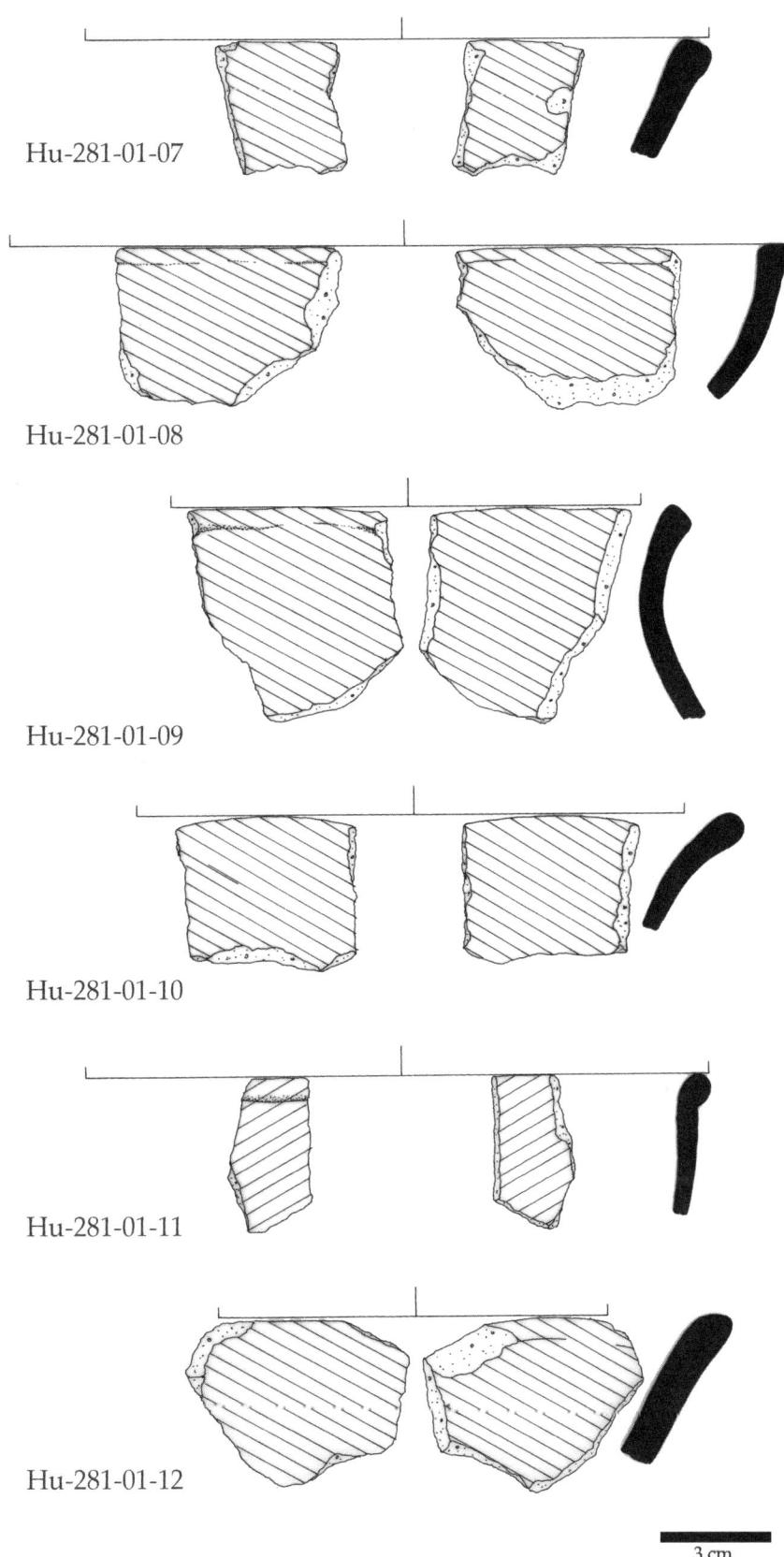

Figure A84. Ceramic fragment drawings from Hu-281.

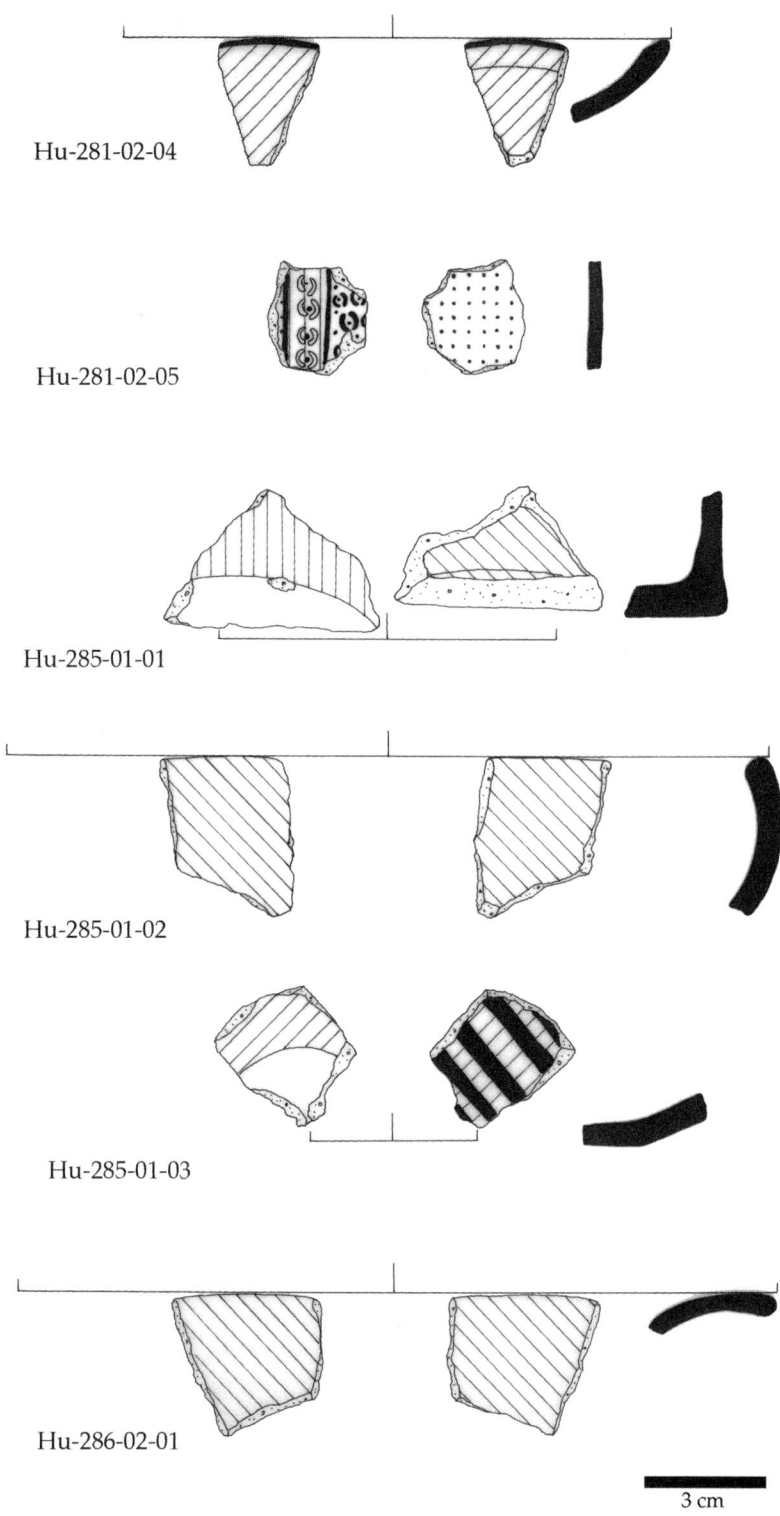

Figure A85. Ceramic fragment drawings from Hu-281, Hu-285, and Hu-286.

Appendix A   *345*

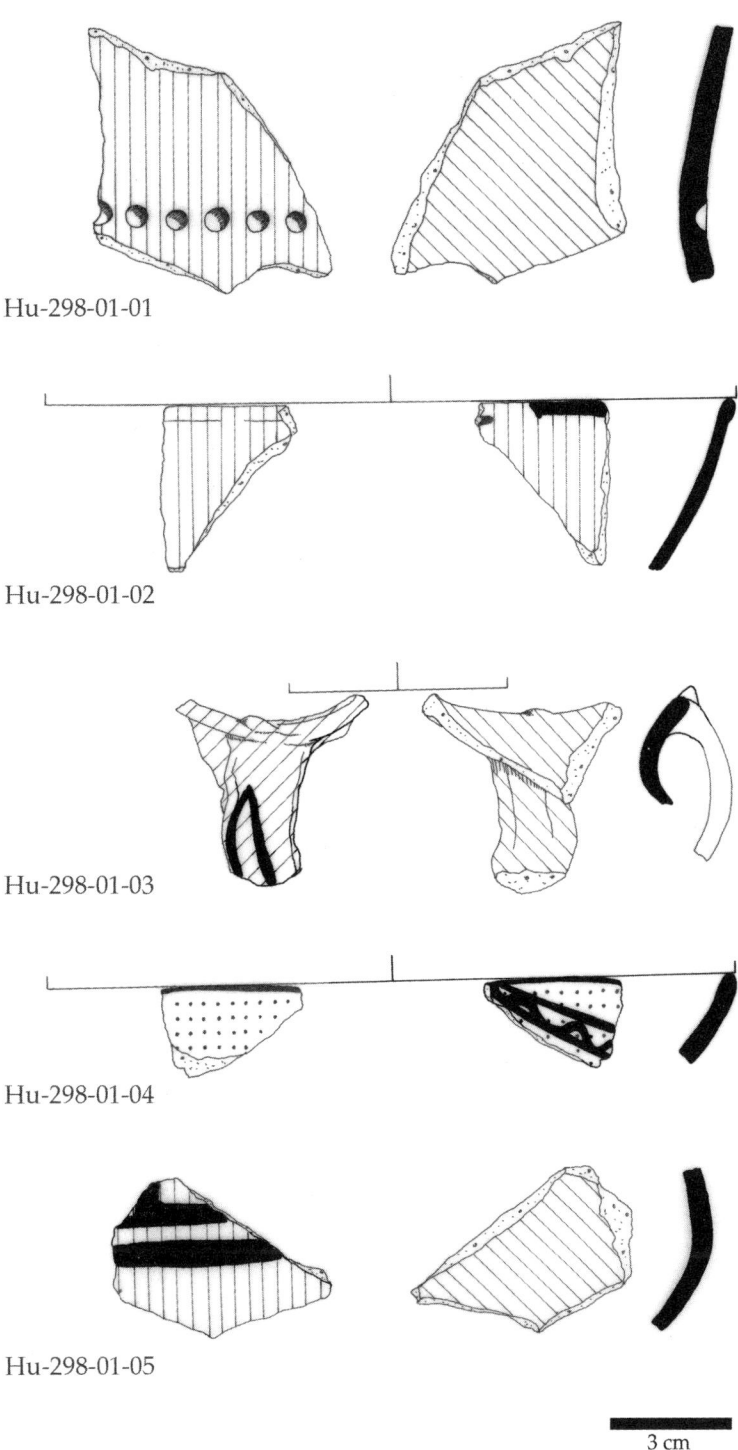

Hu-298-01-01

Hu-298-01-02

Hu-298-01-03

Hu-298-01-04

Hu-298-01-05

3 cm

Figure A86. Ceramic fragment drawings from Hu-298.

346 The Northern Titicaca Basin Survey

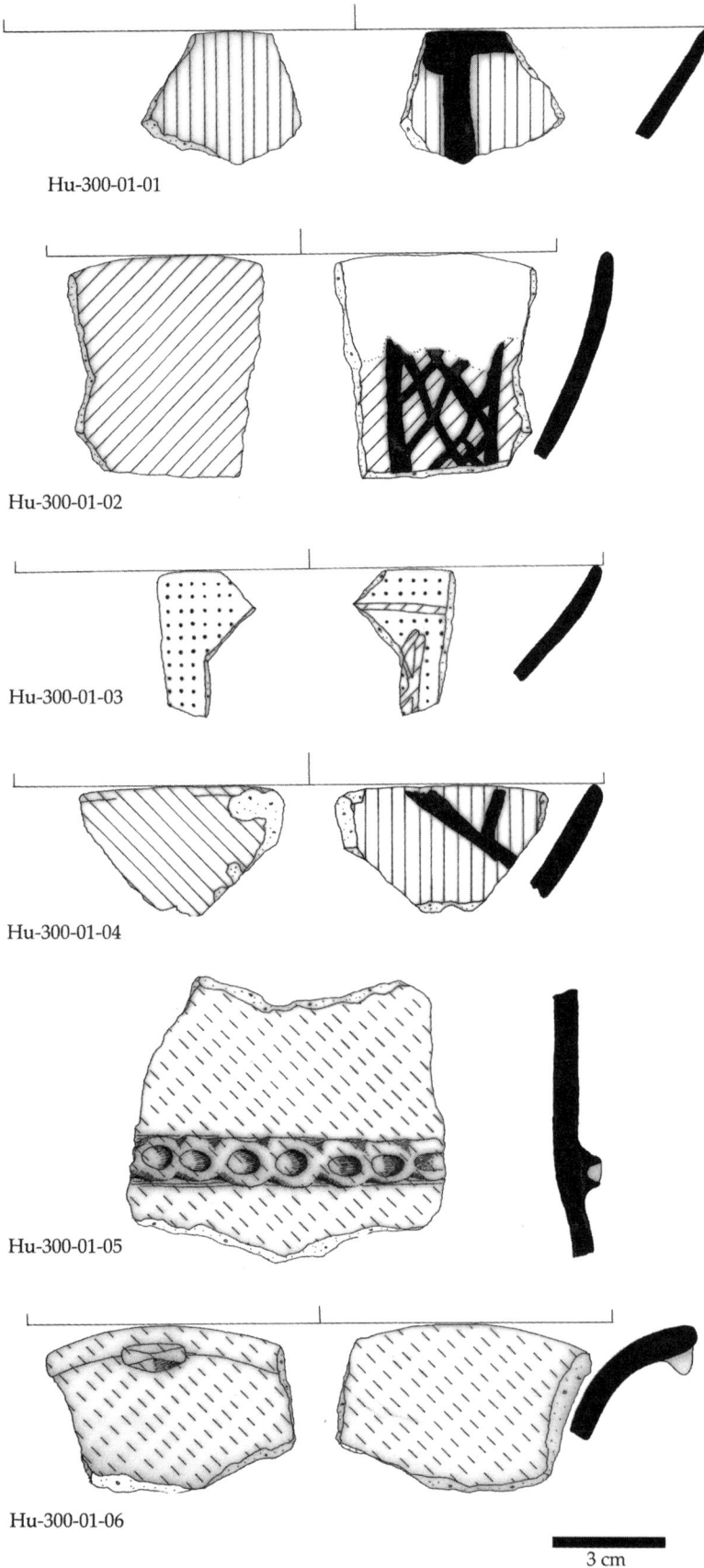

Figure A87. Ceramic fragment drawings from Hu-300.

Appendix A

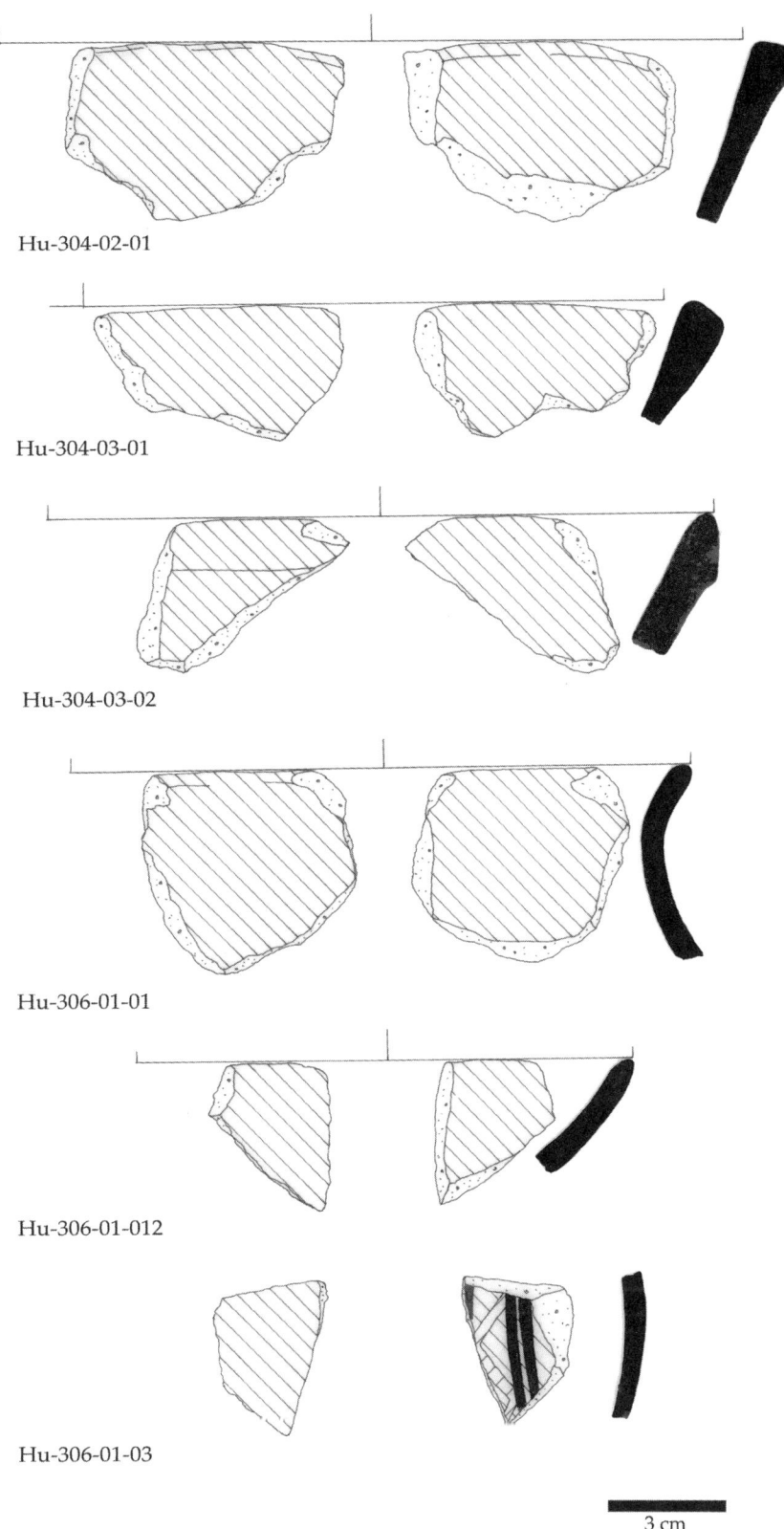

Figure A88. Ceramic fragment drawings from Hu-304 and Hu-306.

348 *The Northern Titicaca Basin Survey*

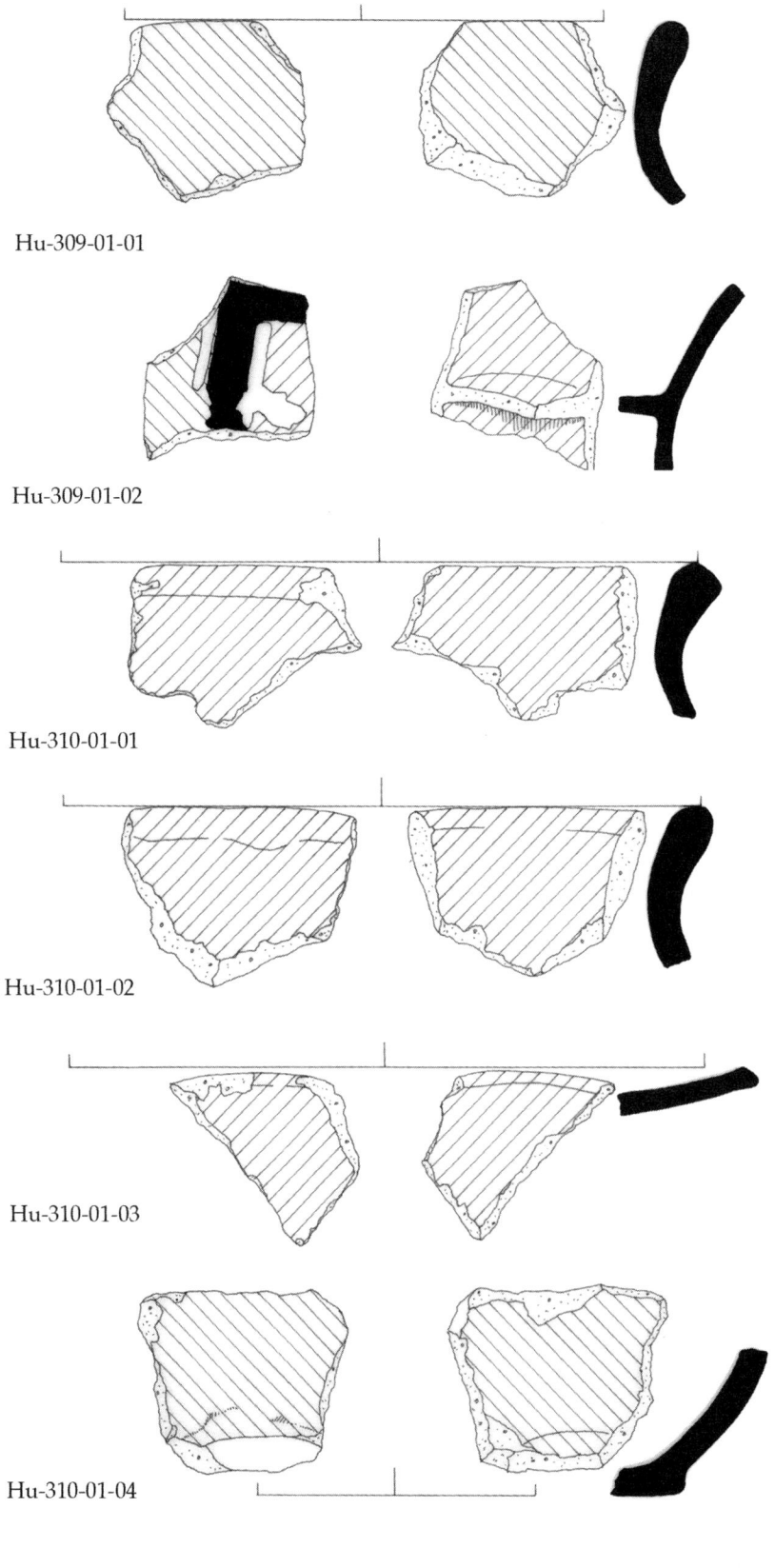

Figure A89. Ceramic fragment drawings from Hu-309 and Hu-310.

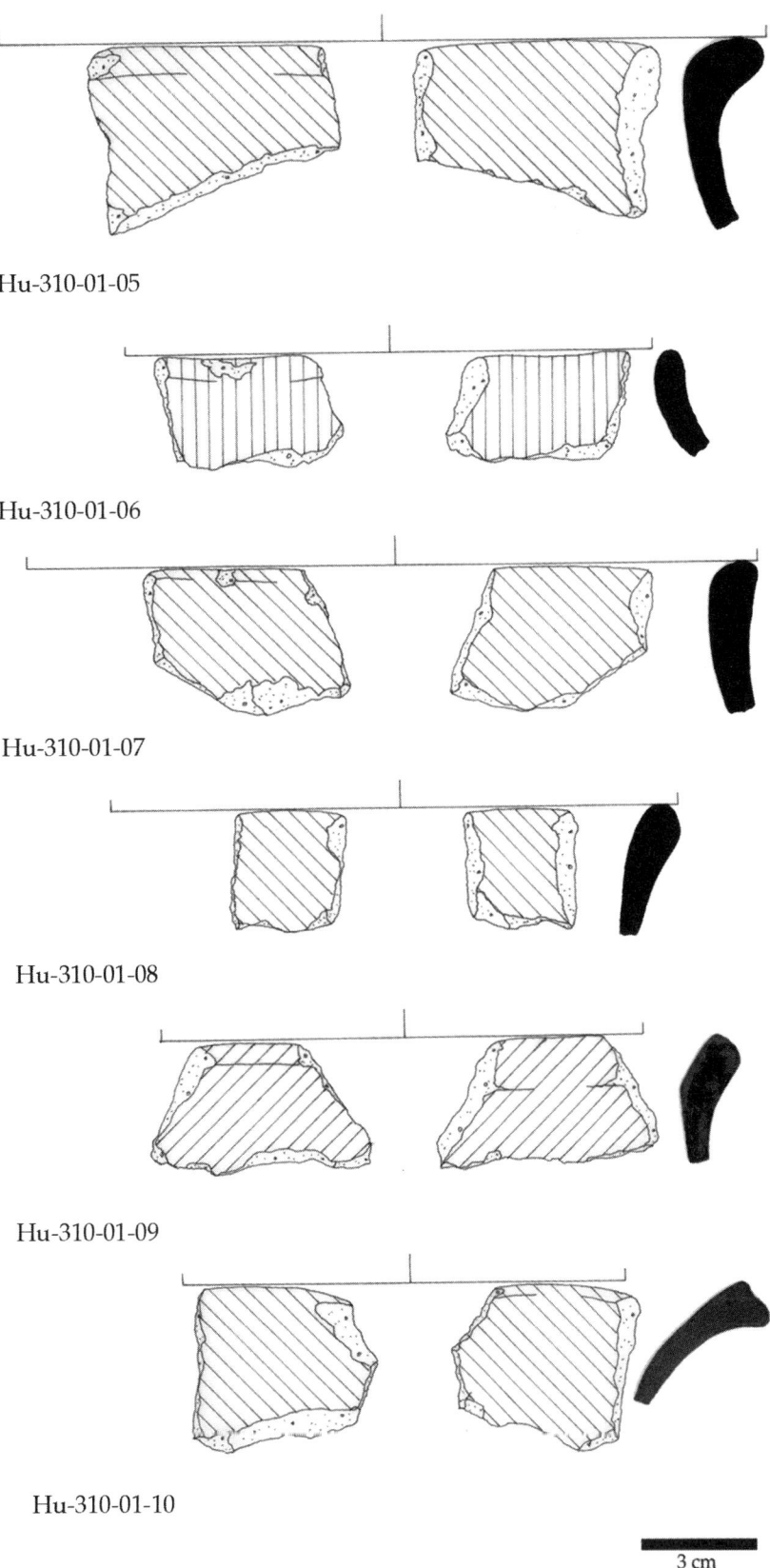

Figure A90. Ceramic fragment drawings from Hu-310.

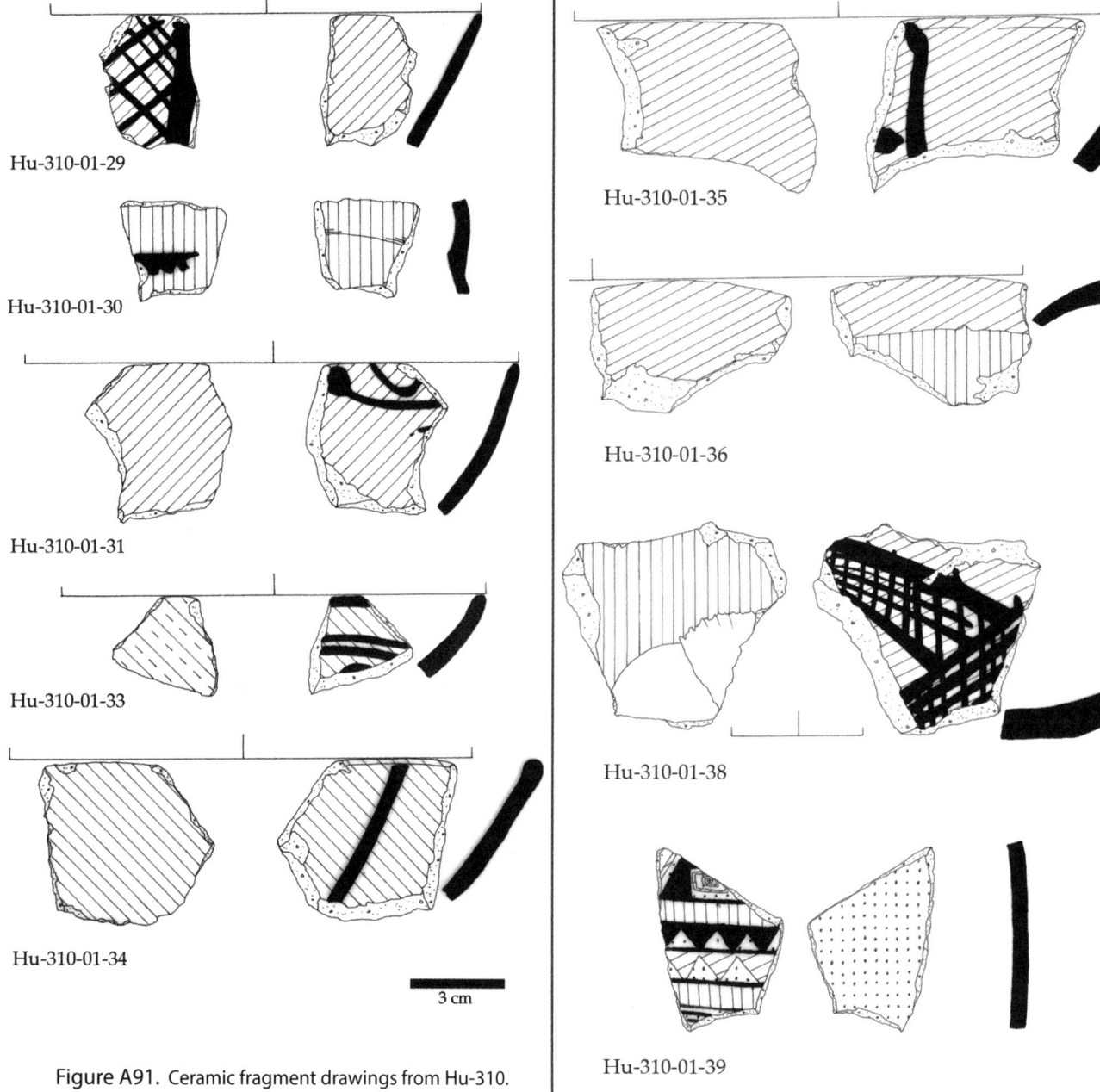

Figure A91. Ceramic fragment drawings from Hu-310.

Figure A92. Ceramic fragment drawings from Hu-310.

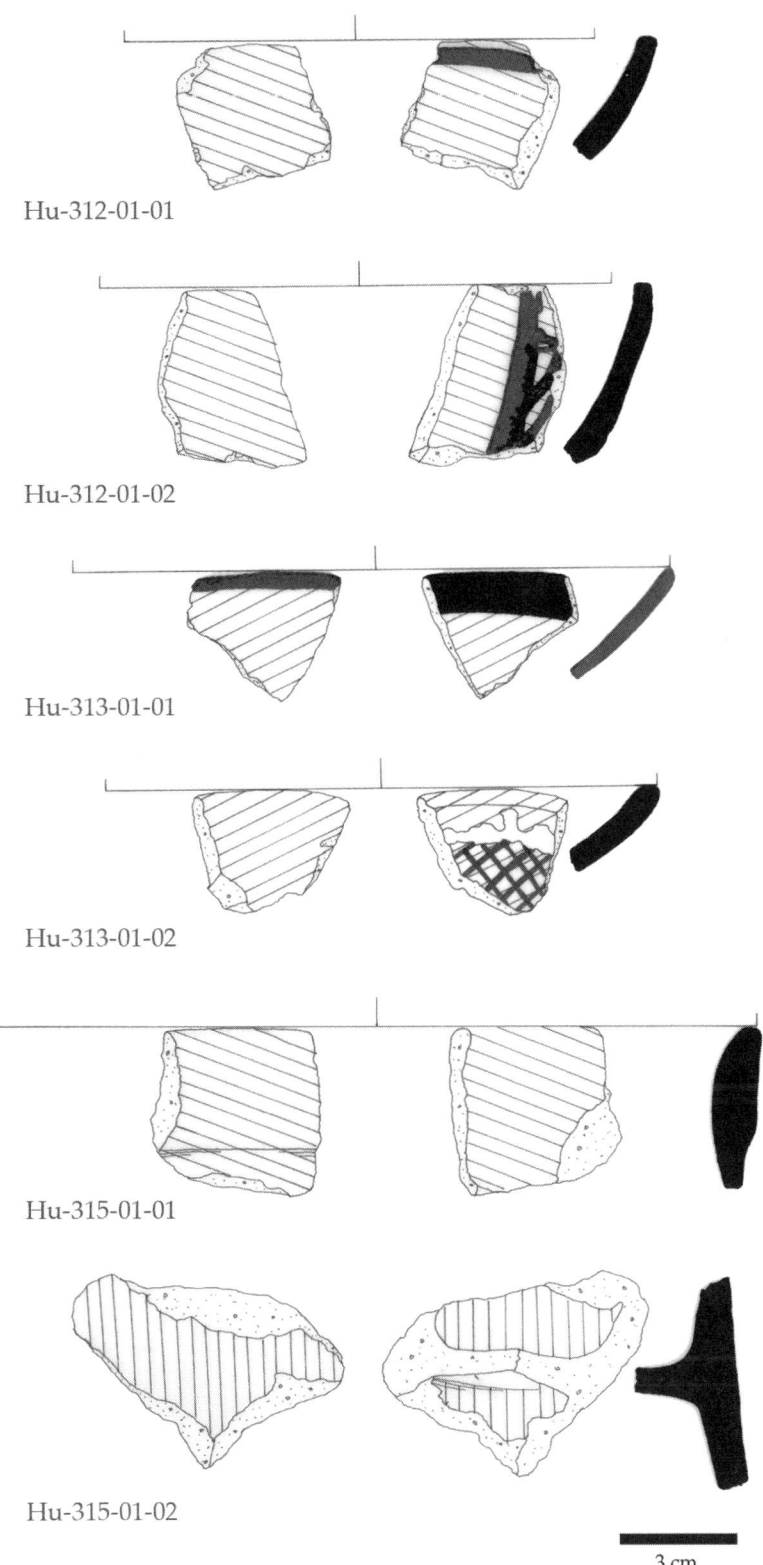

Figure A93. Ceramic fragment drawings from Hu-312, Hu-313, and Hu-315.

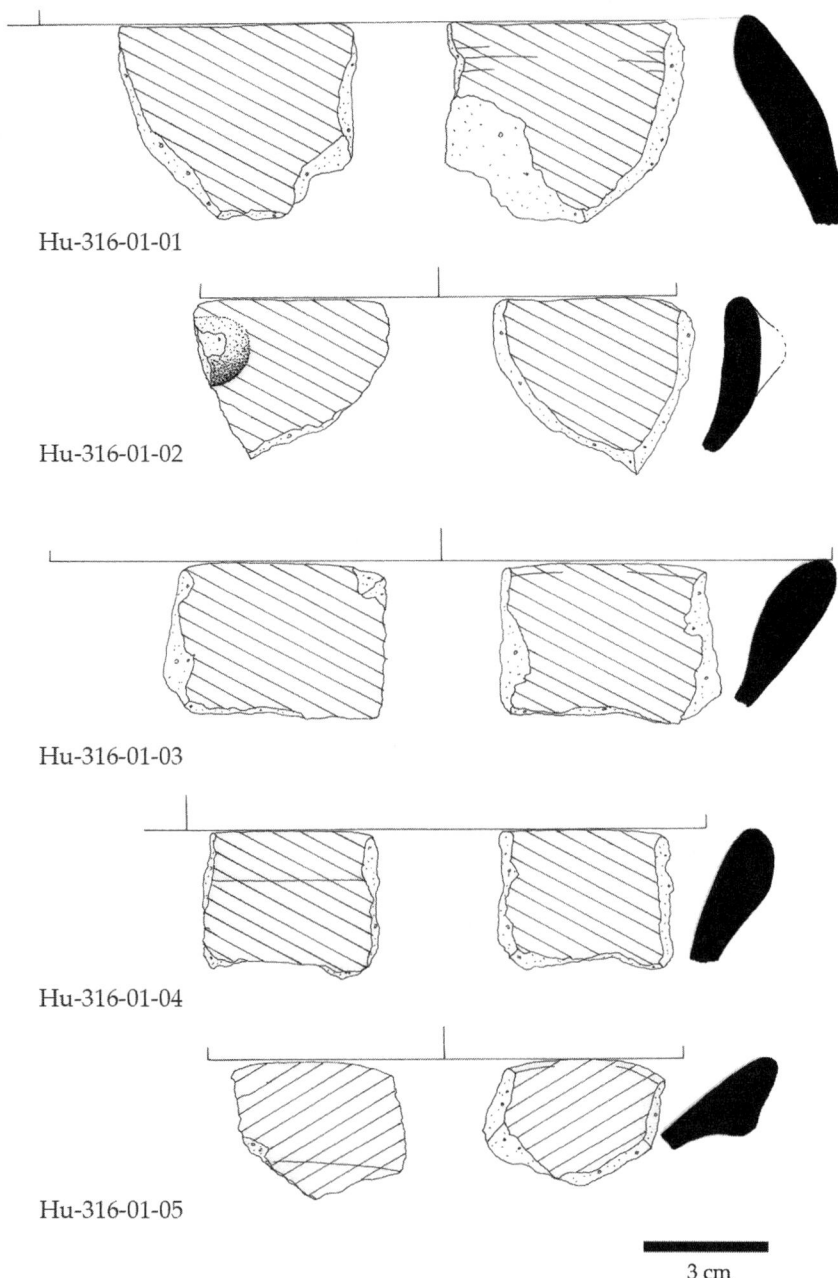

Figure A94. Ceramic fragment drawings from Hu-316.

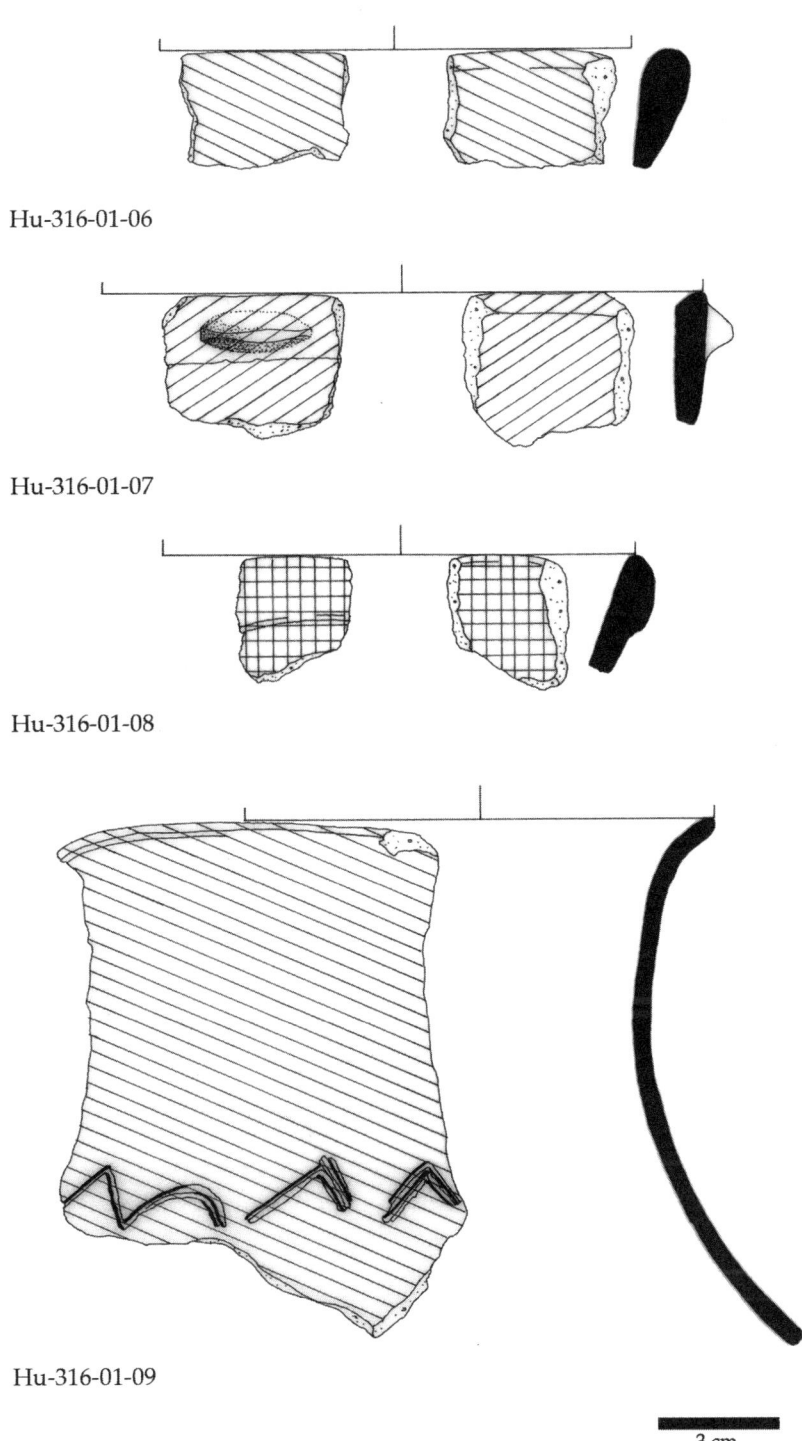

Hu-316-01-06

Hu-316-01-07

Hu-316-01-08

Hu-316-01-09

Figure A95. Ceramic fragment drawings from Hu-316.

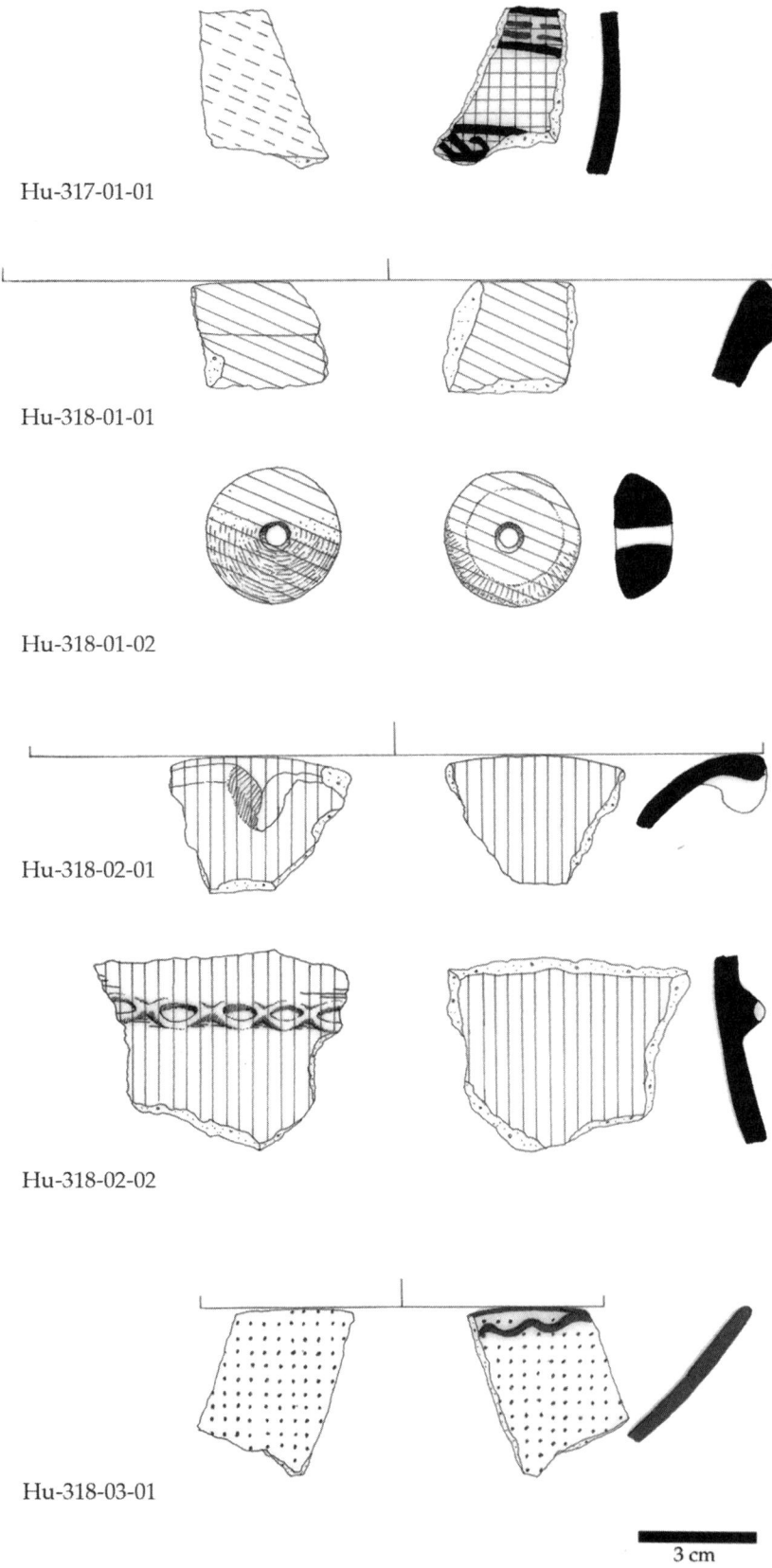

Figure A96. Ceramic fragment drawings from Hu-317 and Hu-318.

Appendix A 355

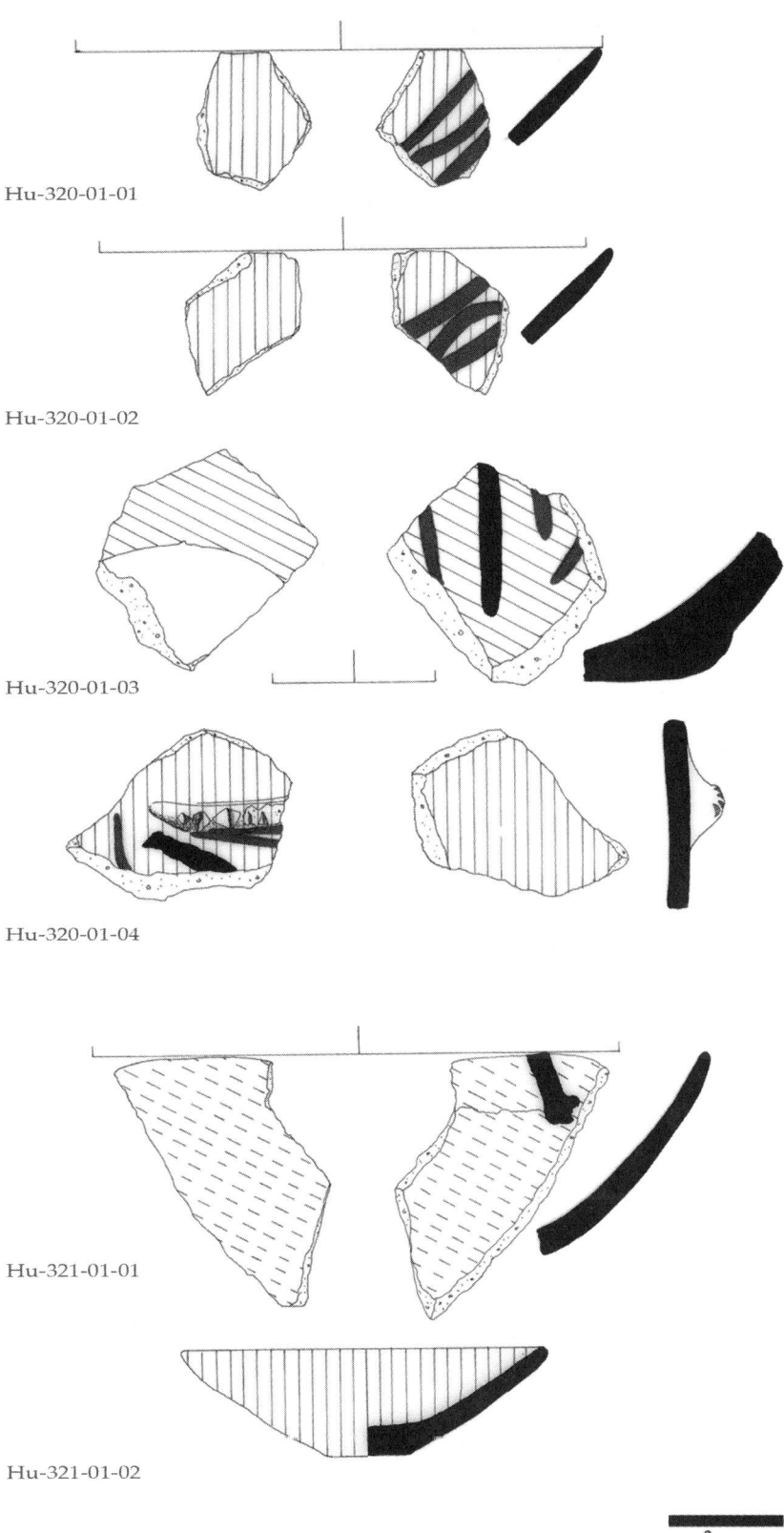

Figure A97. Ceramic fragment drawings from Hu-320 and Hu-321.

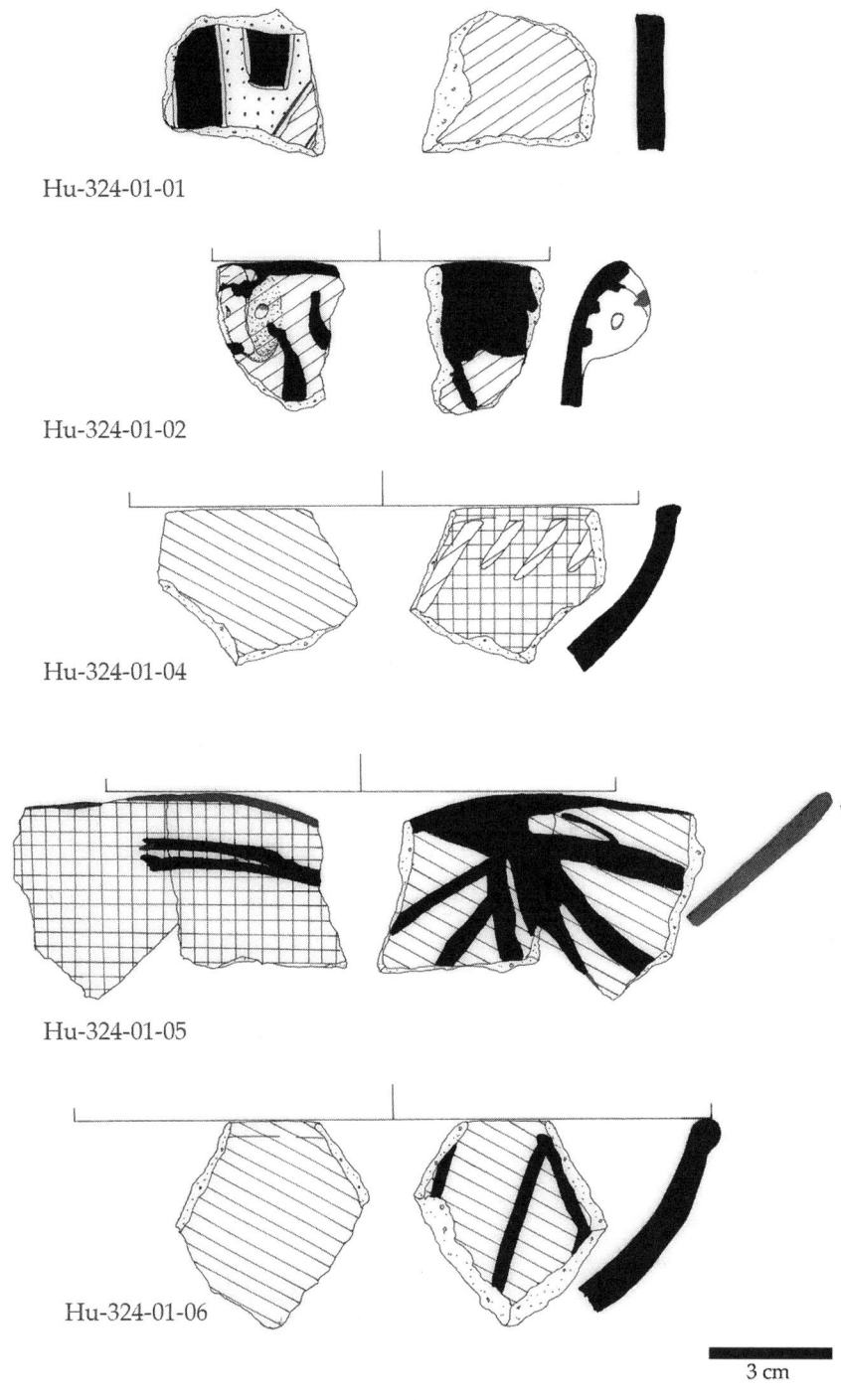

Figure A98. Ceramic fragment drawings from Hu-324.

Appendix A *357*

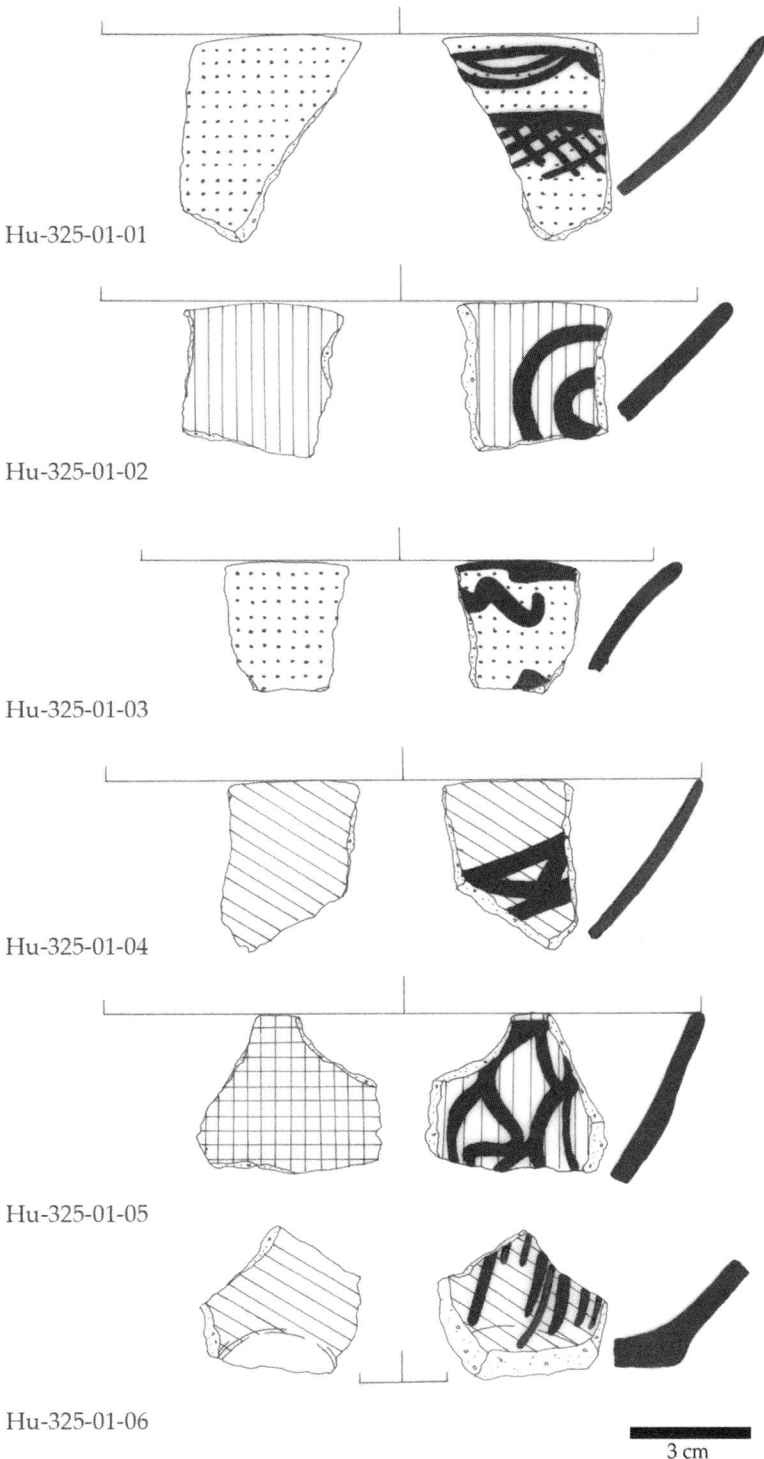

Figure A99. Ceramic fragment drawings from Hu-325.

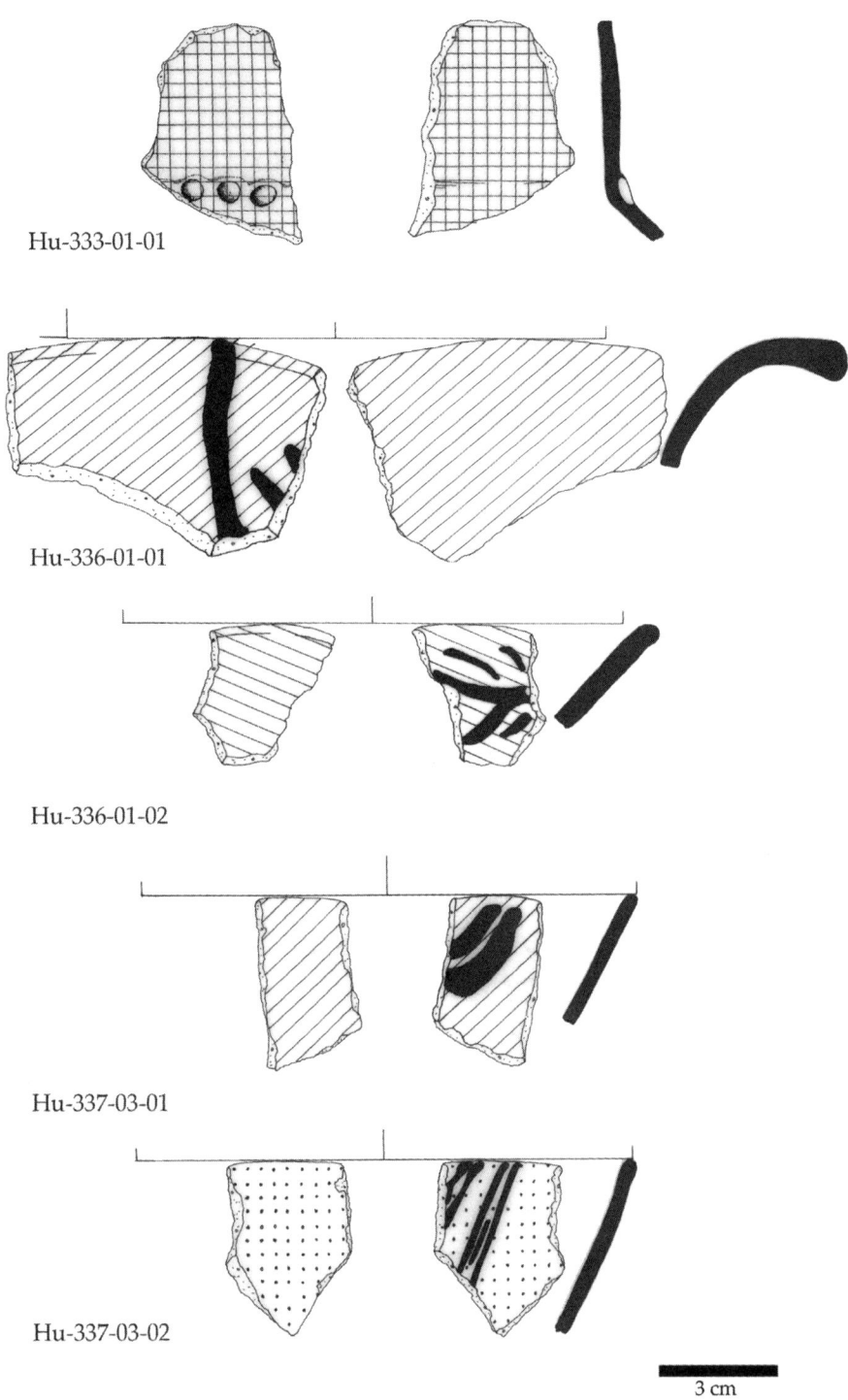

Figure A100. Ceramic fragment drawings from Hu-333, Hu-336, and Hu-337.

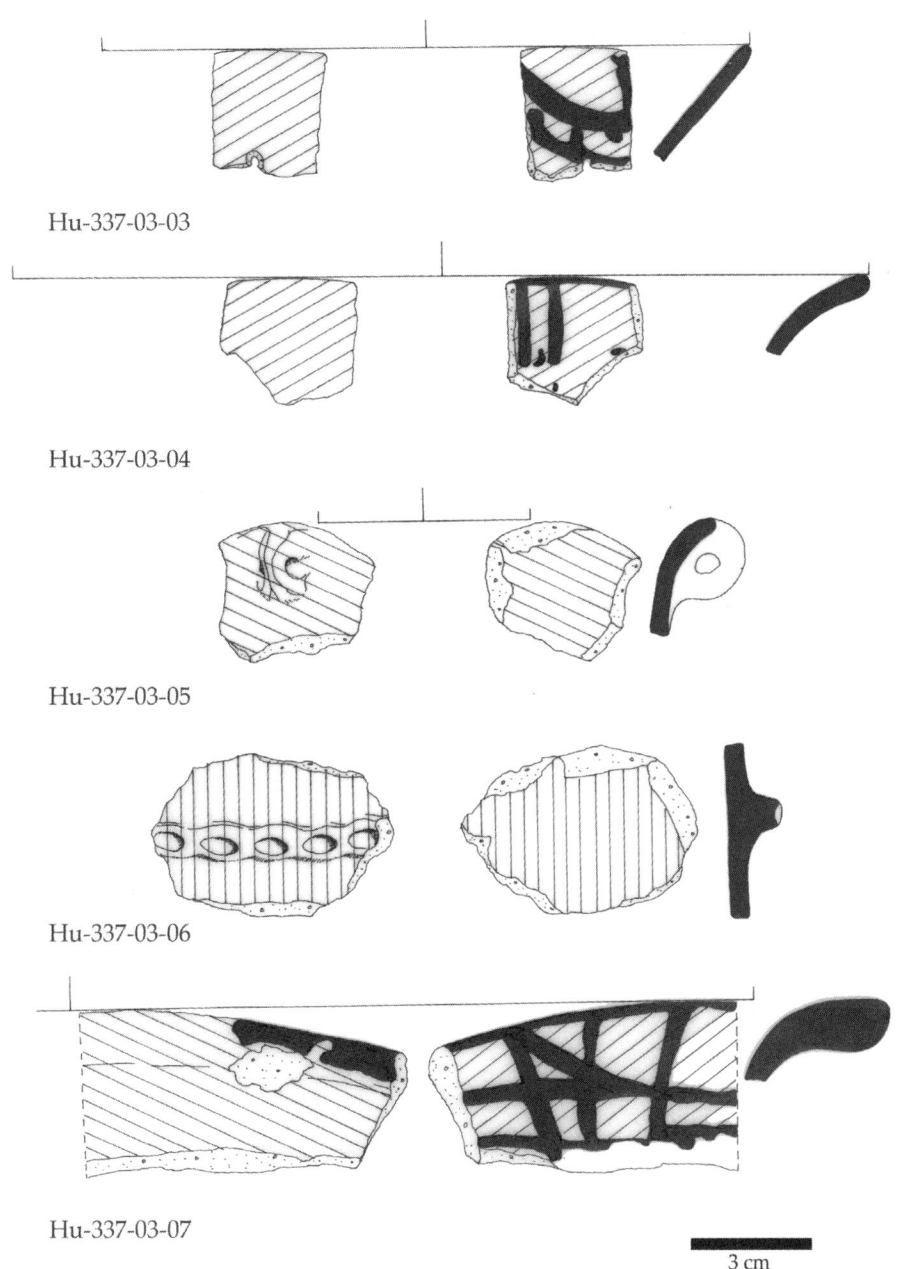

Figure A101. Ceramic fragment drawings from Hu-337.

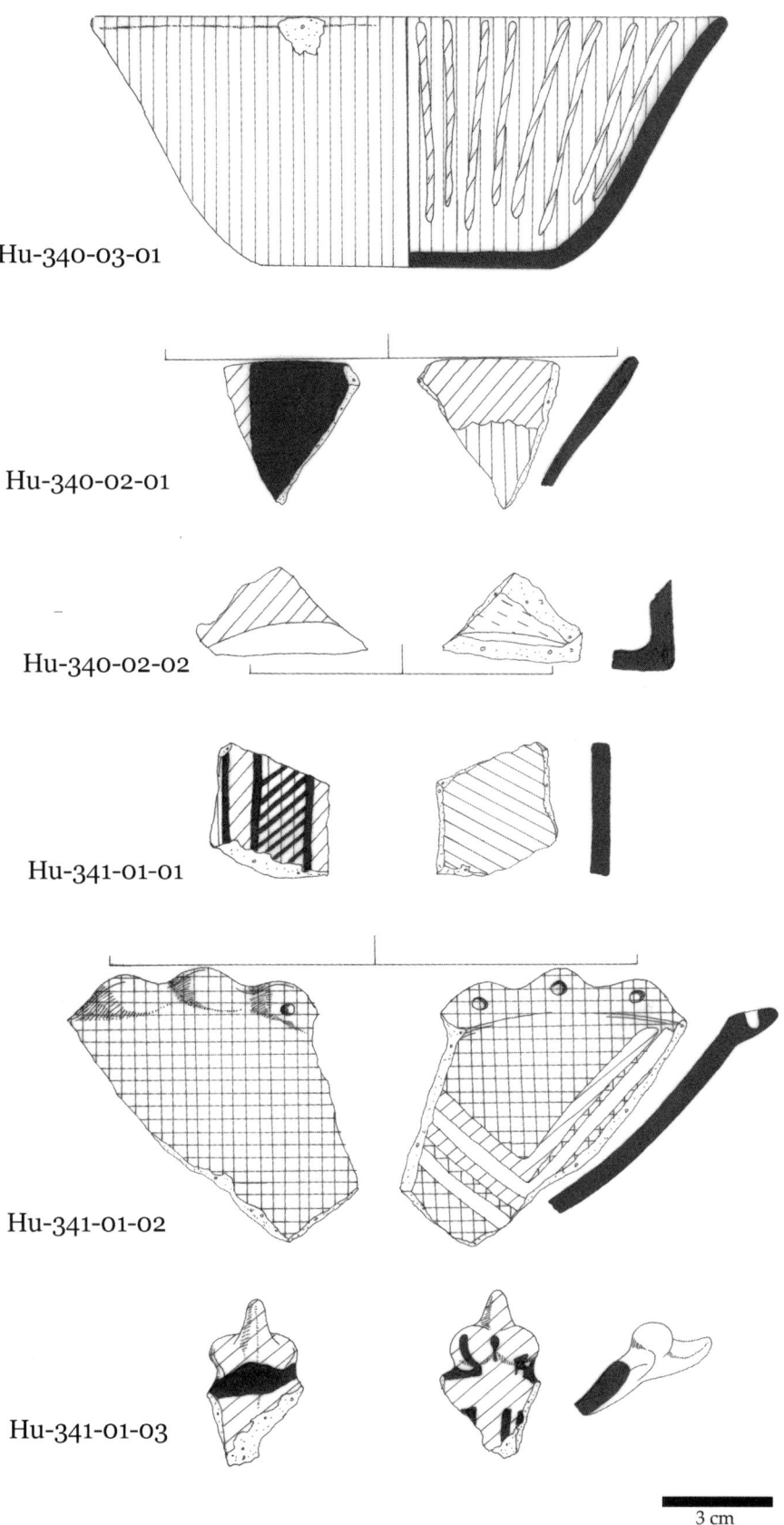

Figure A102. Ceramic fragment drawings from Hu-340 and Hu-341.

Appendix A

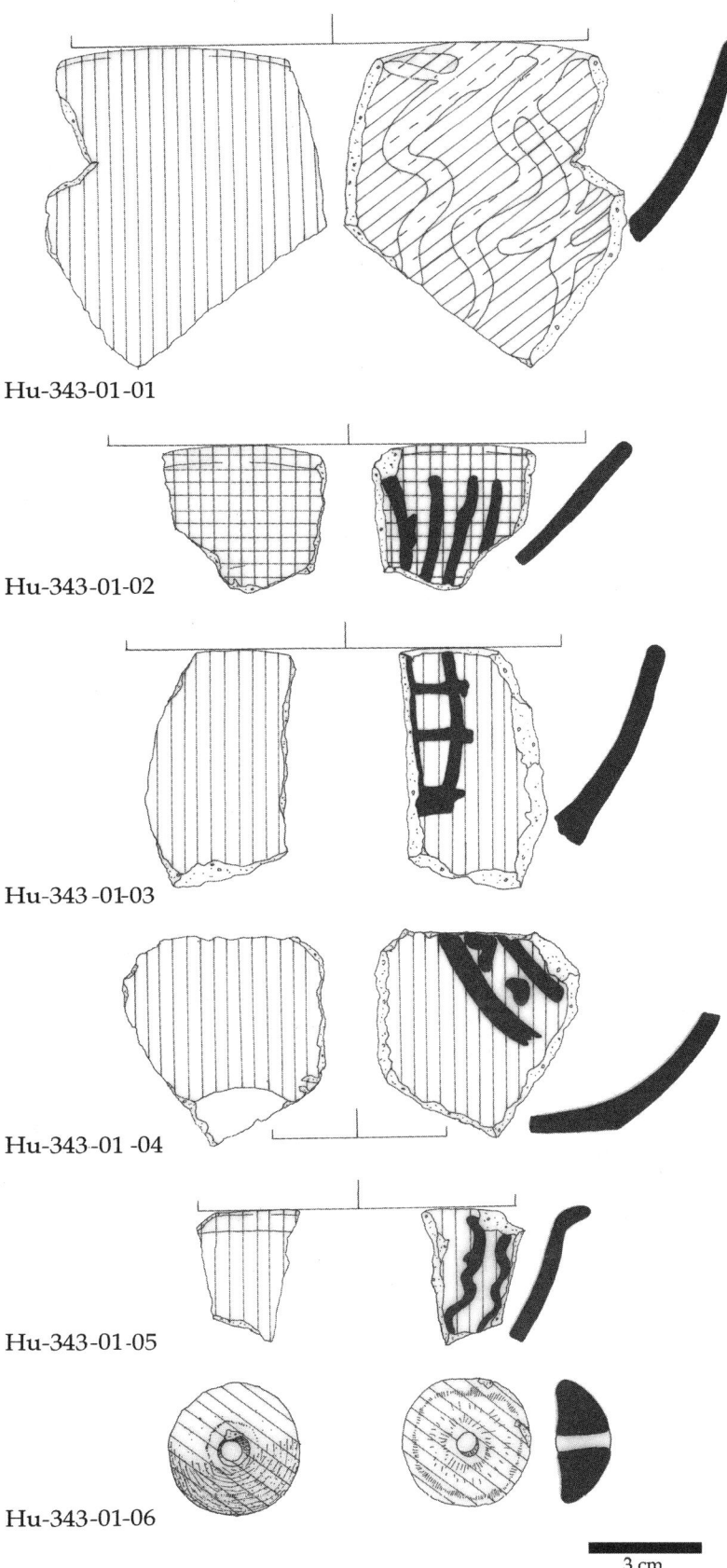

Figure A103. Ceramic fragment drawings from Hu-343.

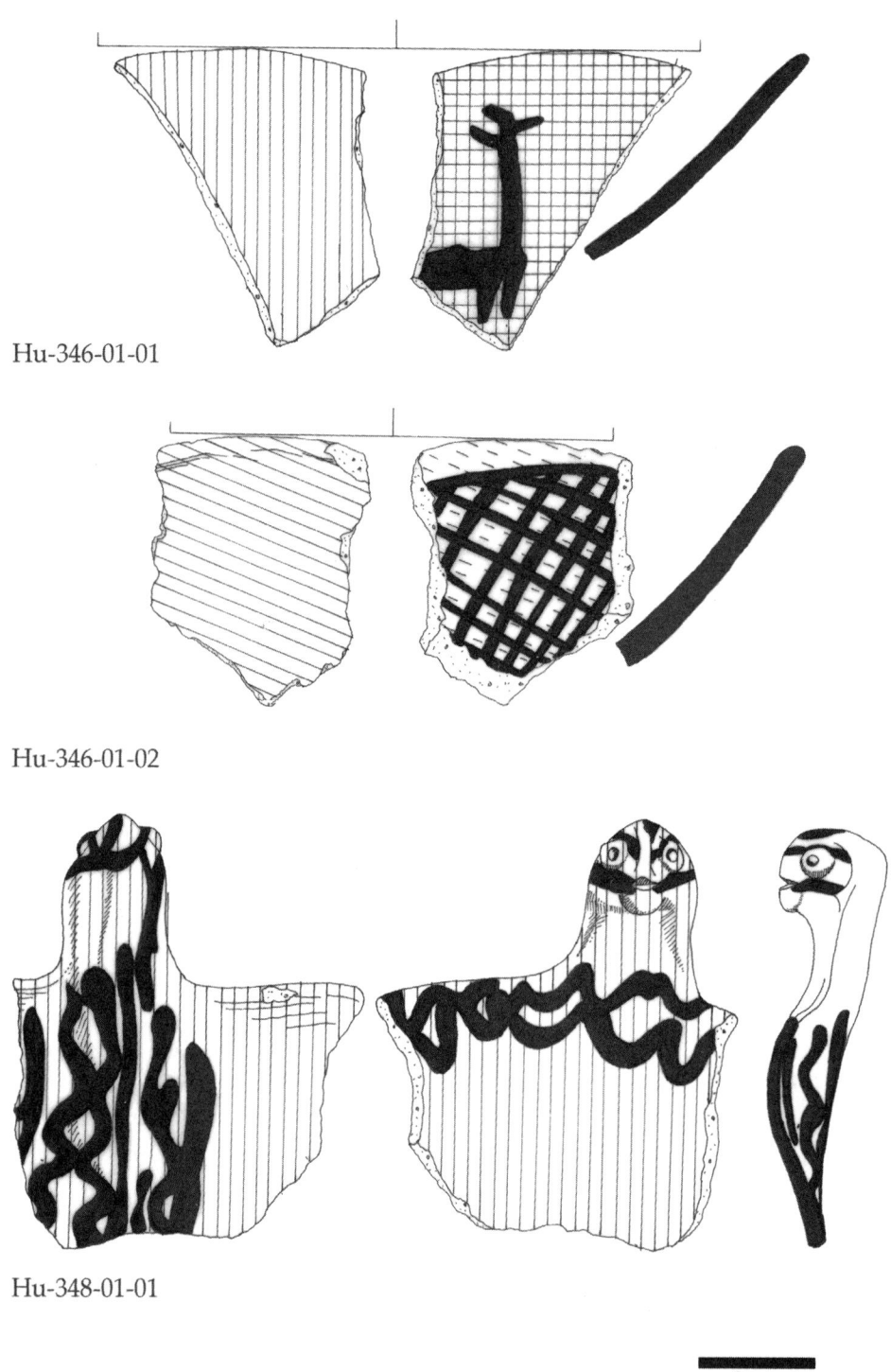

Figure A104. Ceramic fragment drawings from Hu-346 and Hu-348.

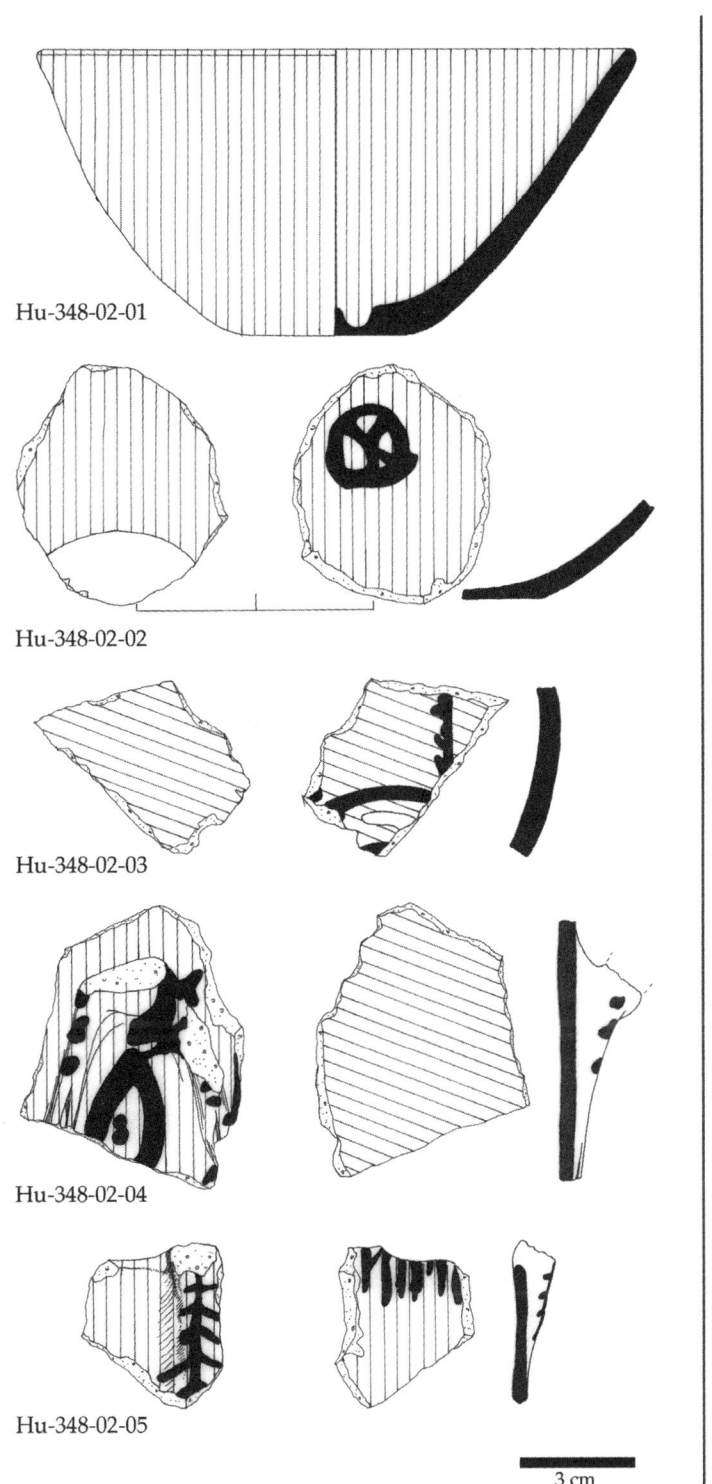

Figure A105. Ceramic fragment drawings from Hu-348.

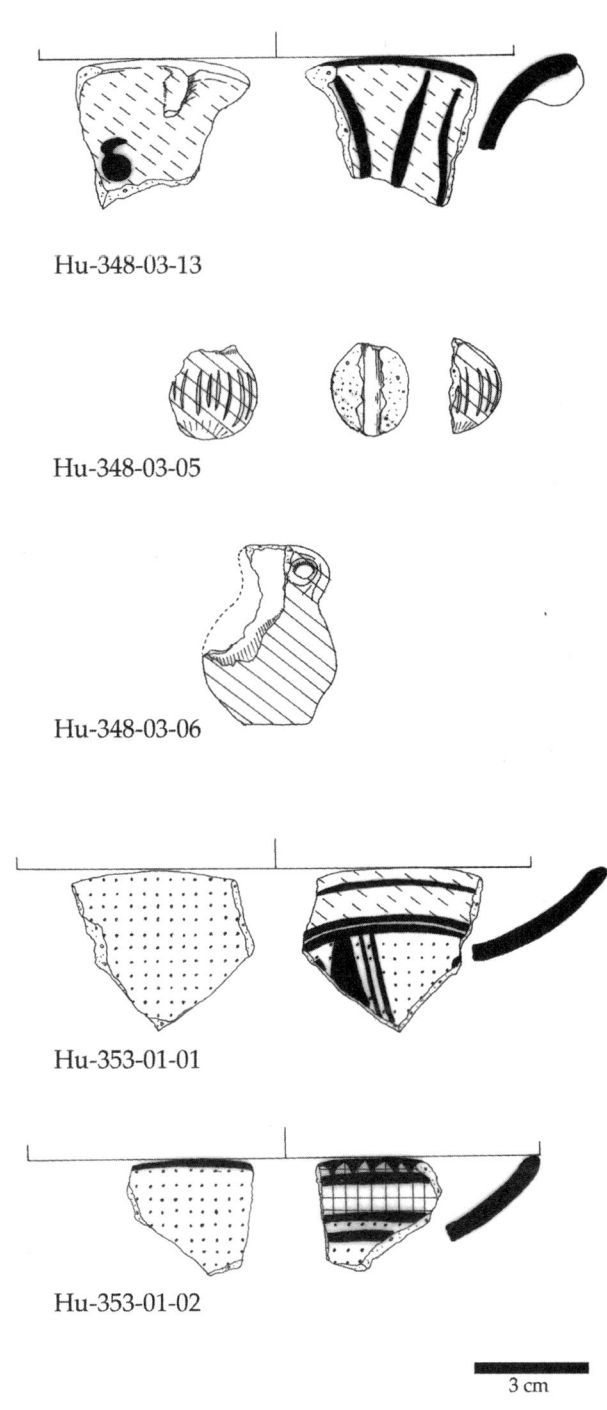

Figure A106. Ceramic fragment drawings from Hu-348 and Hu-353.

364   *The Northern Titicaca Basin Survey*

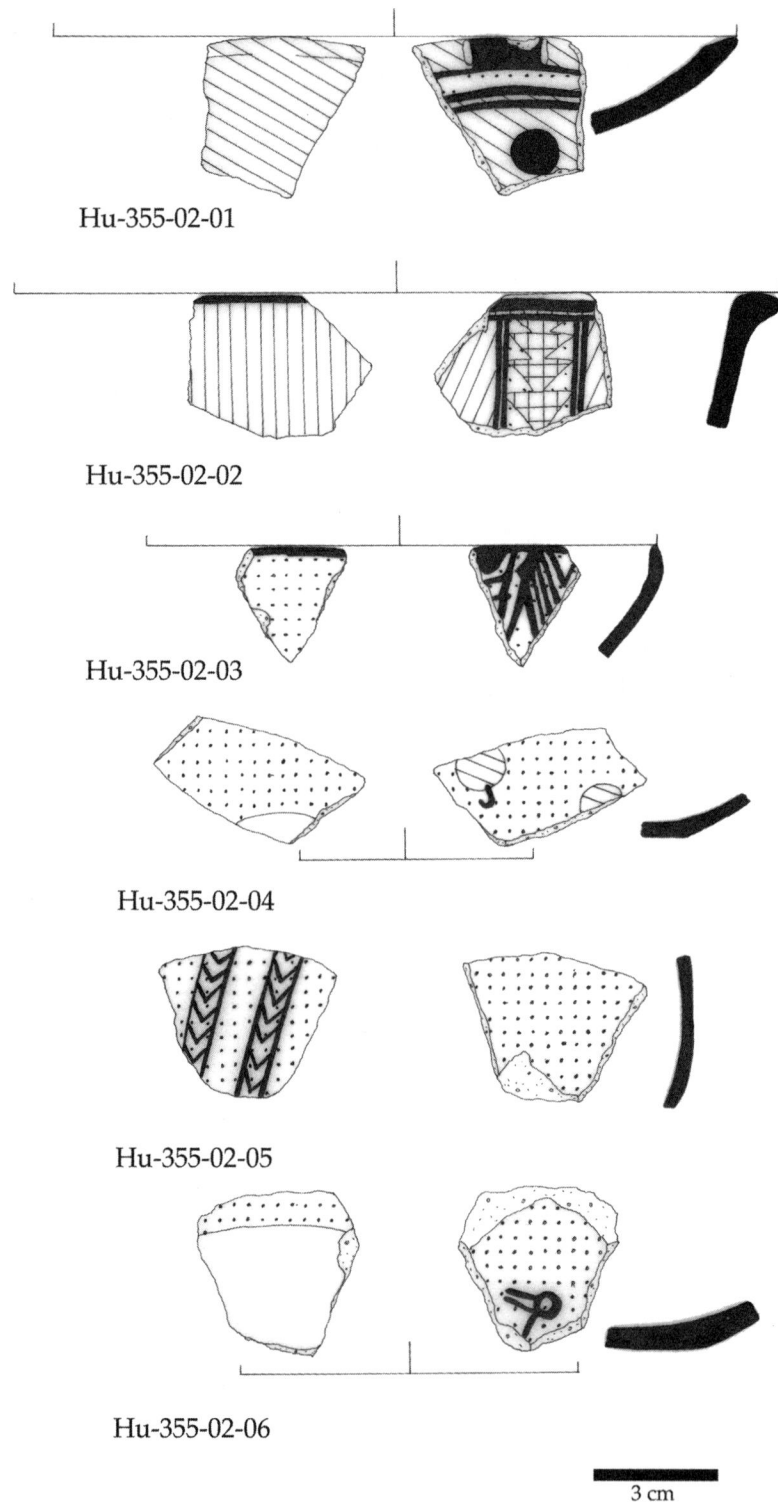

Figure A107. Ceramic fragment drawings from Hu-355.

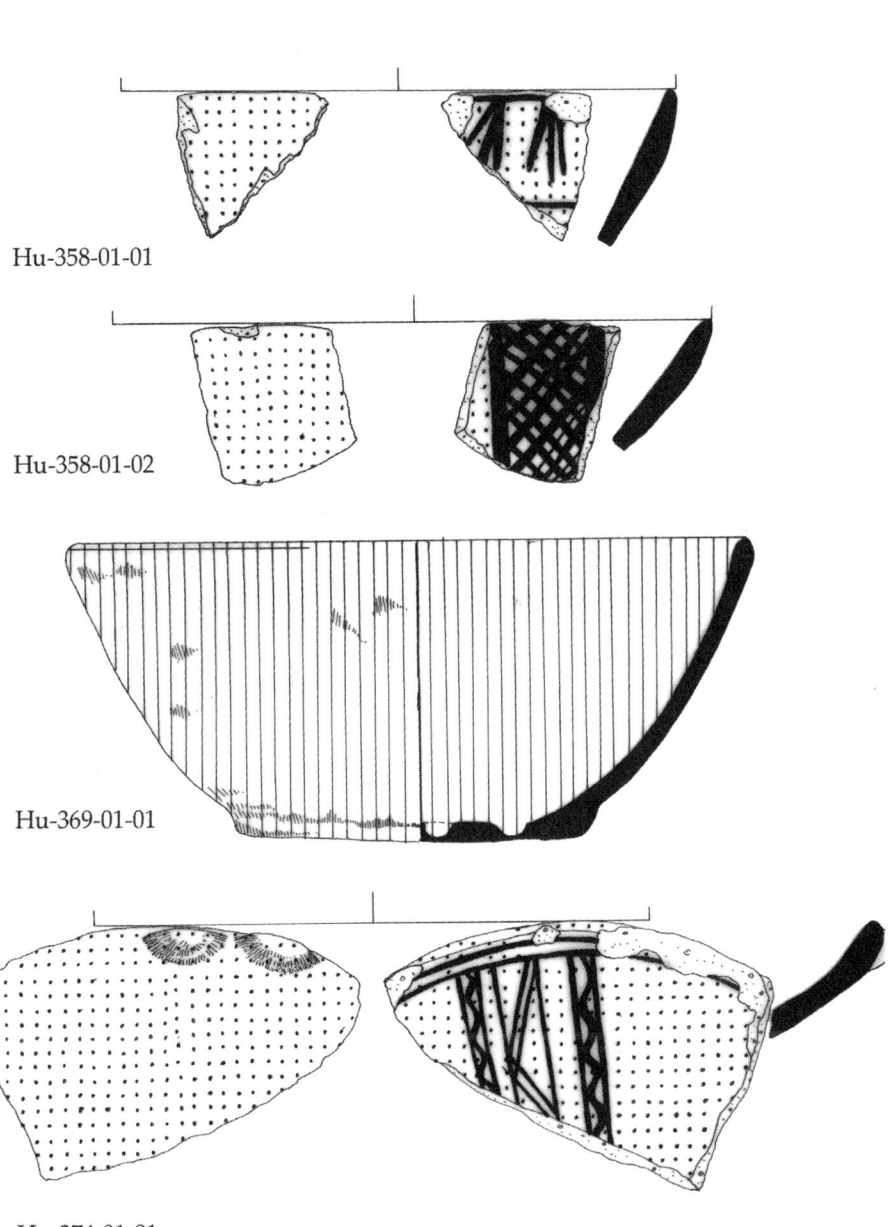

Figure A108. Ceramic fragment drawings from Hu-358, Hu-369, and Hu-374.

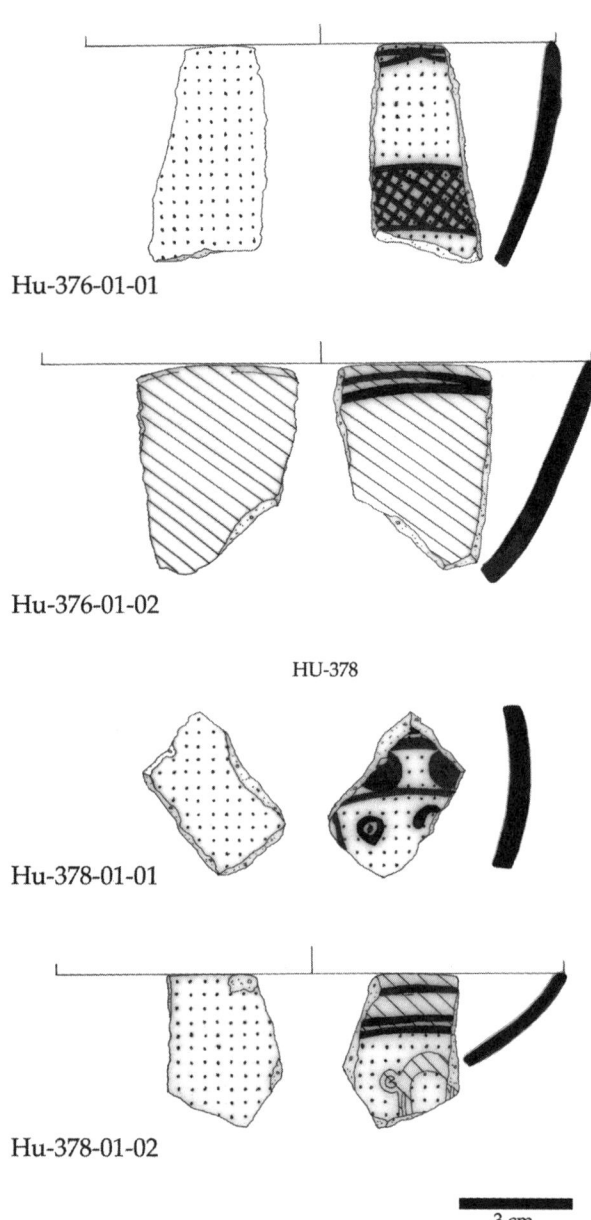

Hu-376-01-01

Hu-376-01-02

HU-378

Hu-378-01-01

Hu-378-01-02

3 cm

Figure A109. Ceramic fragment drawings from Hu-376 and Hu-378.

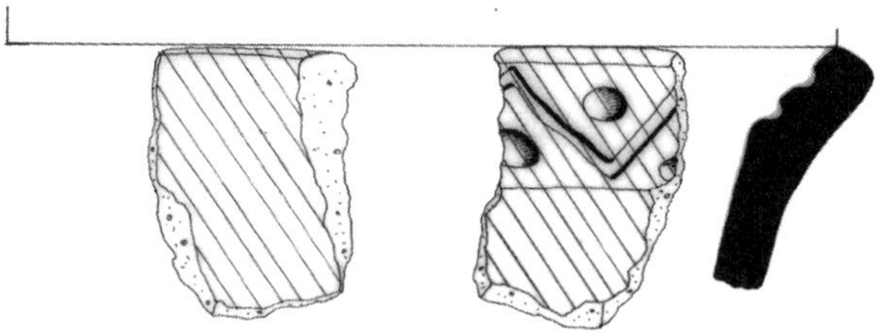

Hu-382-01-01

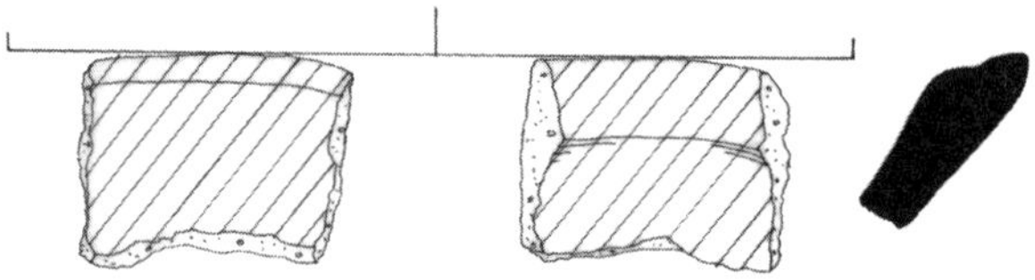

Hu-382-01-02

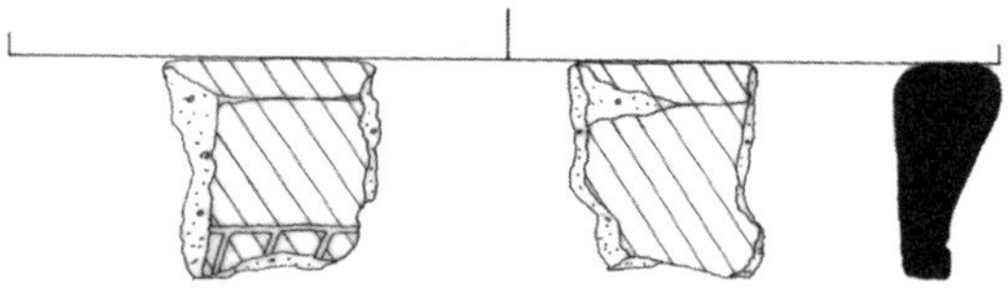

Hu-382-01-03

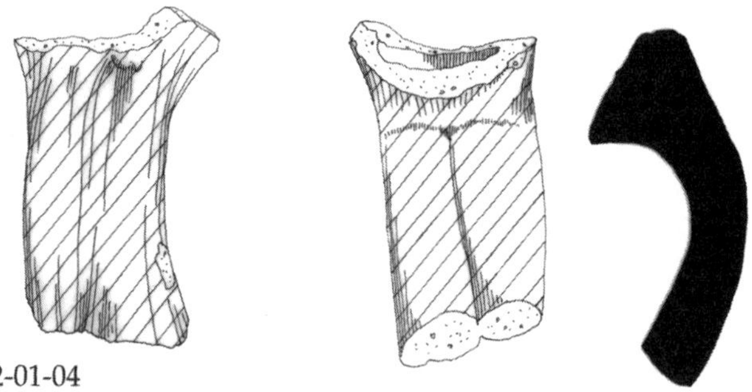

Hu-382-01-04

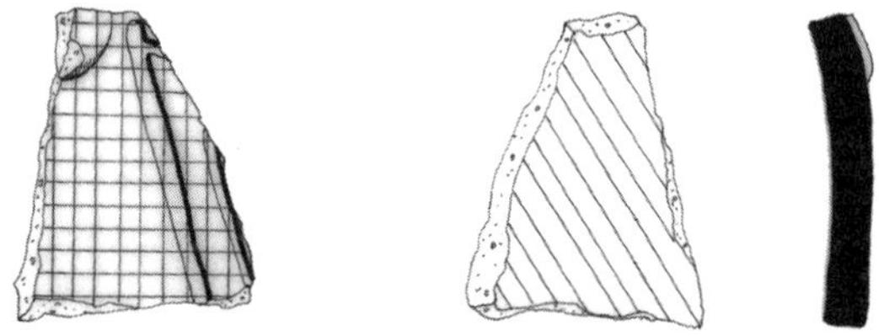

Hu-382-01-05

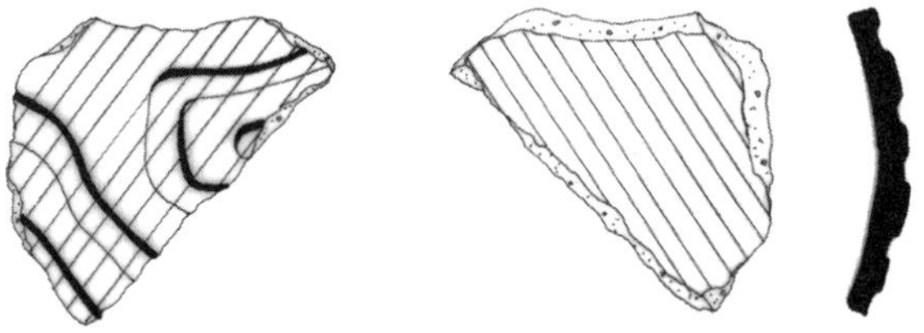

Hu-382-01-06

3 cm

Figure A110. Ceramic fragment drawings from Hu-382.

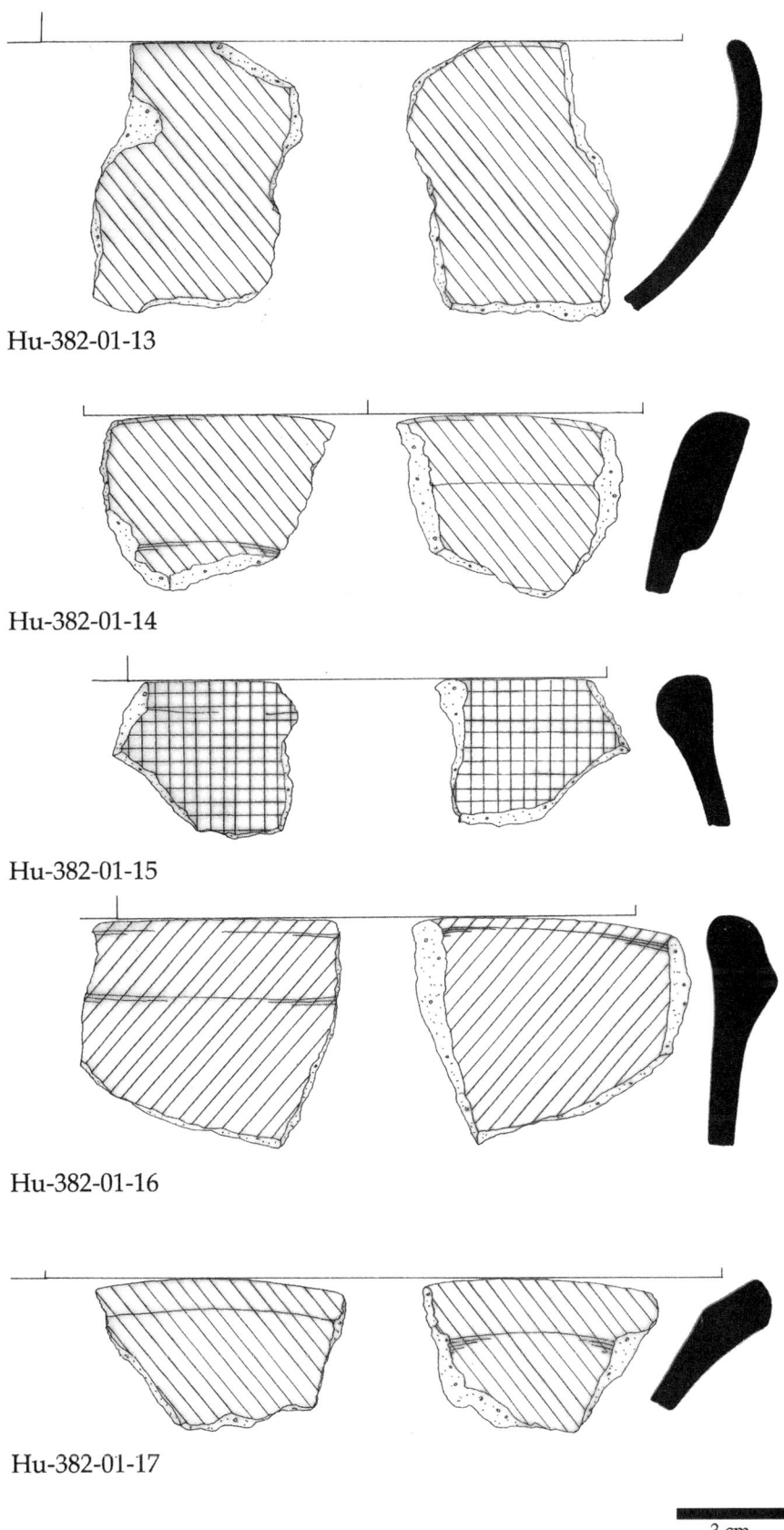

Figure A111. Ceramic fragment drawings from Hu-382.

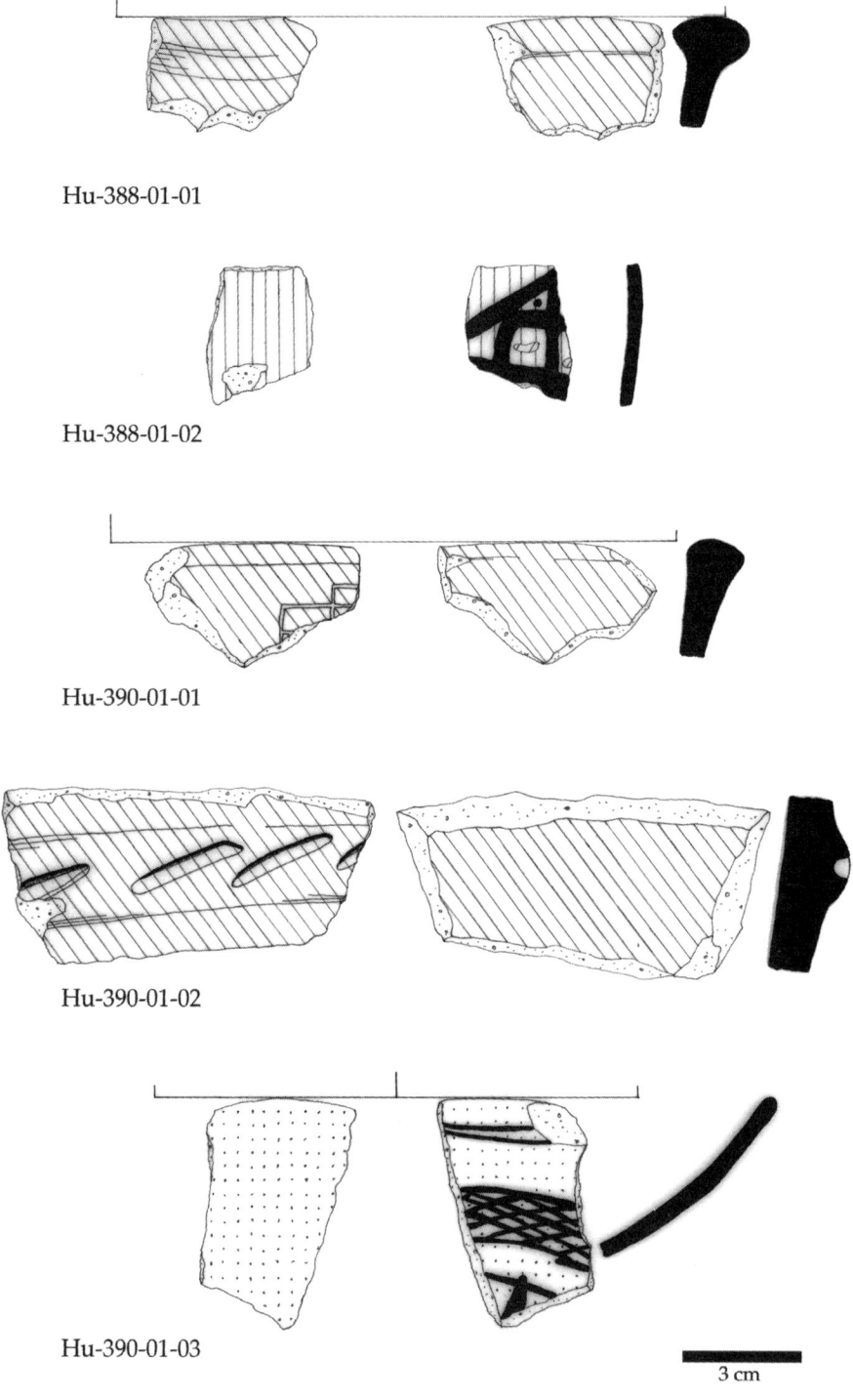

Figure A112. Ceramic fragment drawings from Hu-388 and Hu-390.

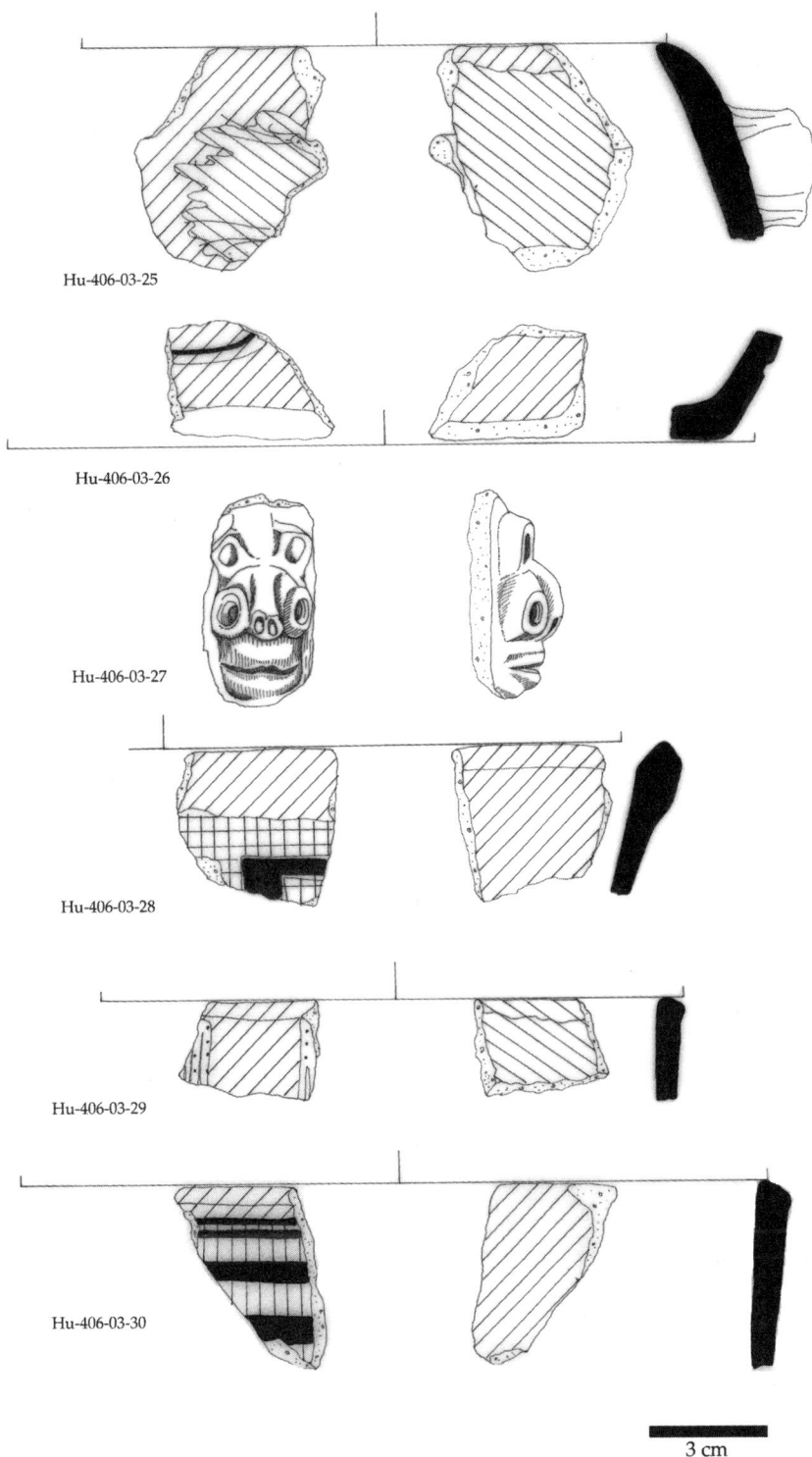

Figure A113. Ceramic fragment drawings from Hu-406.

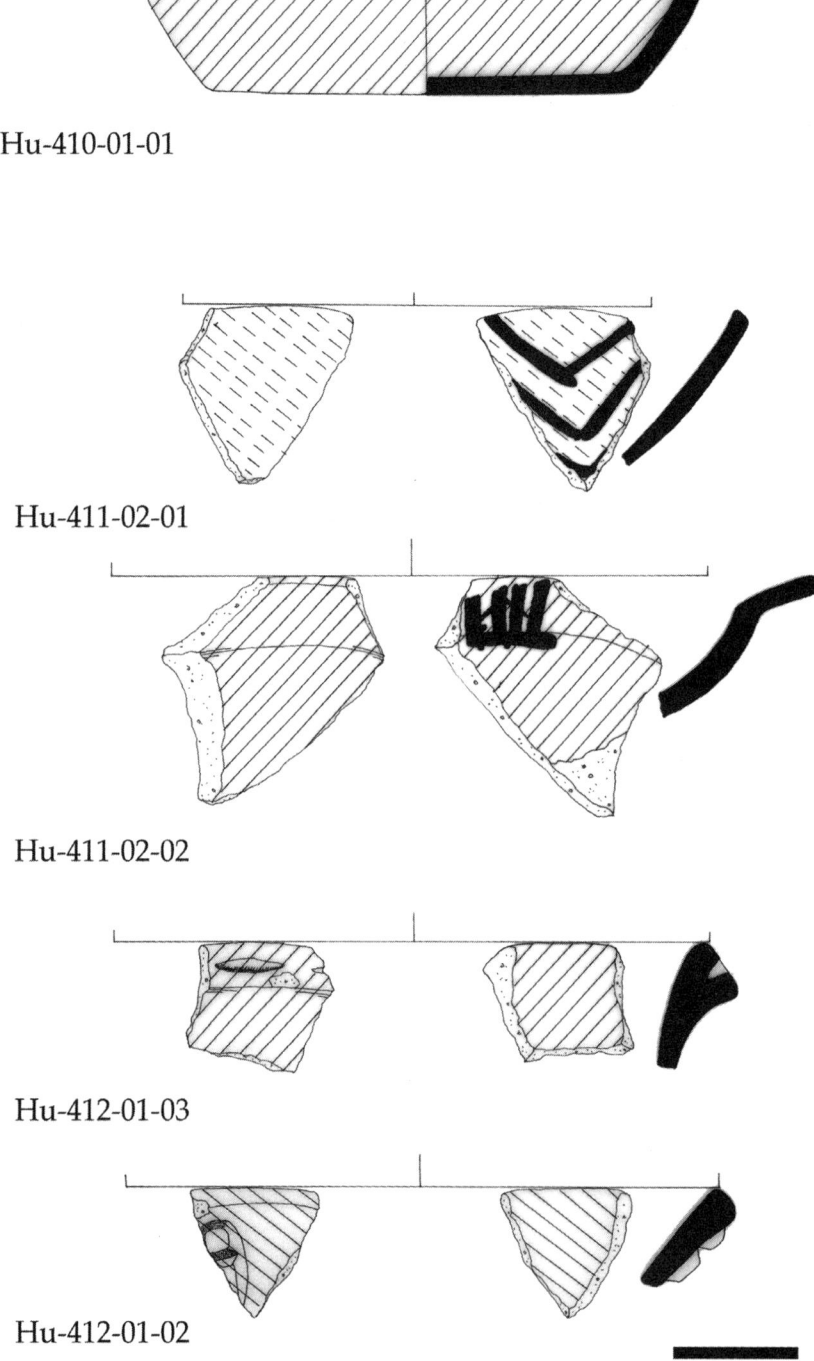

Figure A114. Ceramic fragment drawings from Hu-410, Hu-411, and Hu-412.

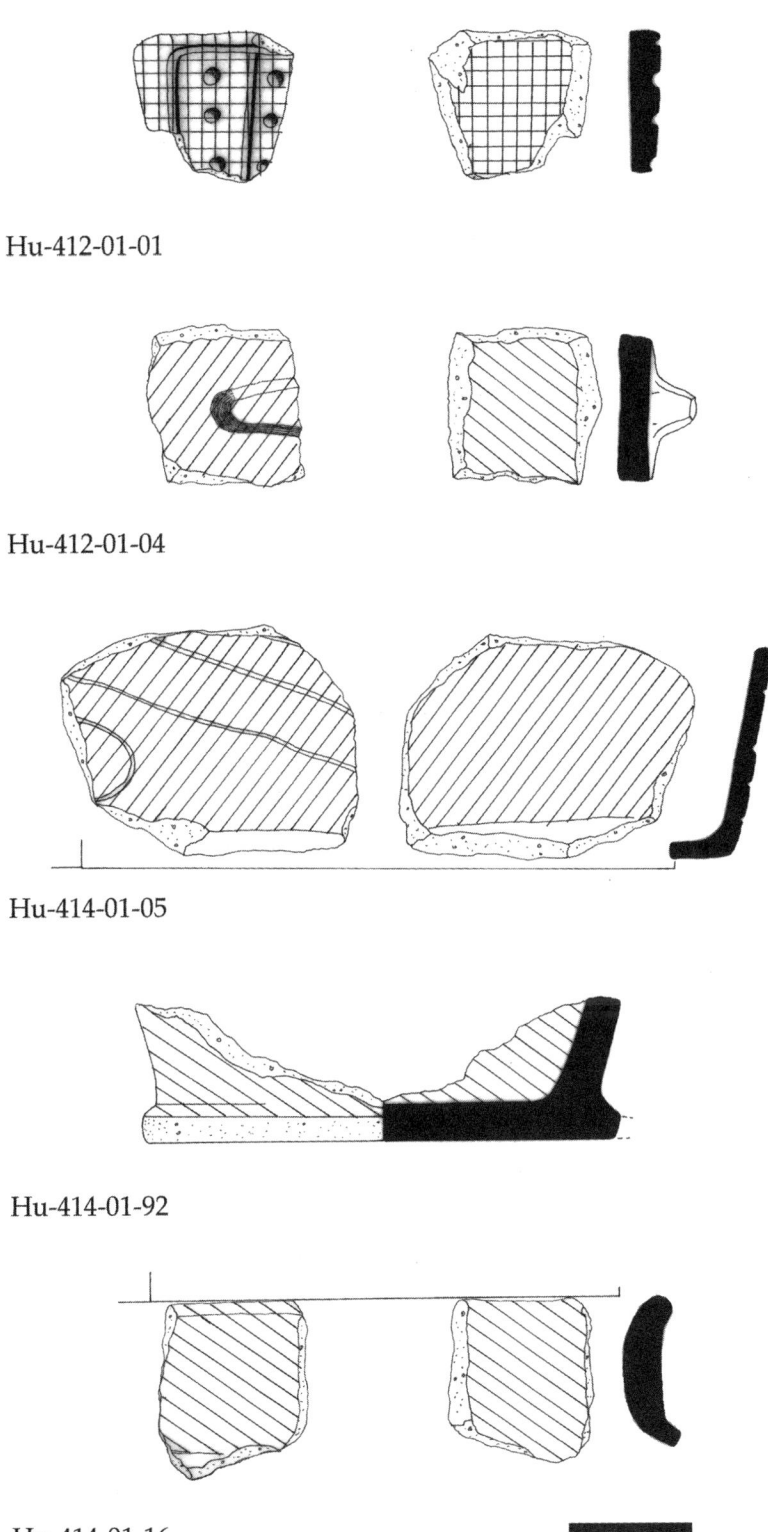

Figure A115. Ceramic fragment drawings from Hu-412 and Hu-414.

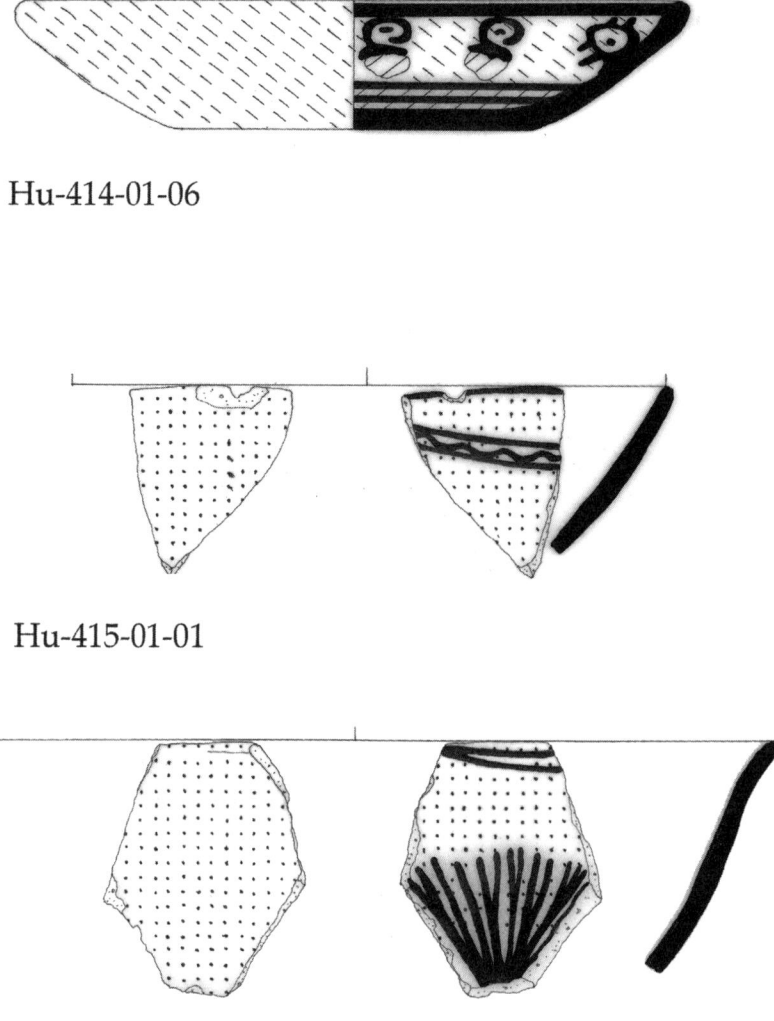

Figure A116. Ceramic fragment drawings from Hu-414, Hu-415, and Hu-416.

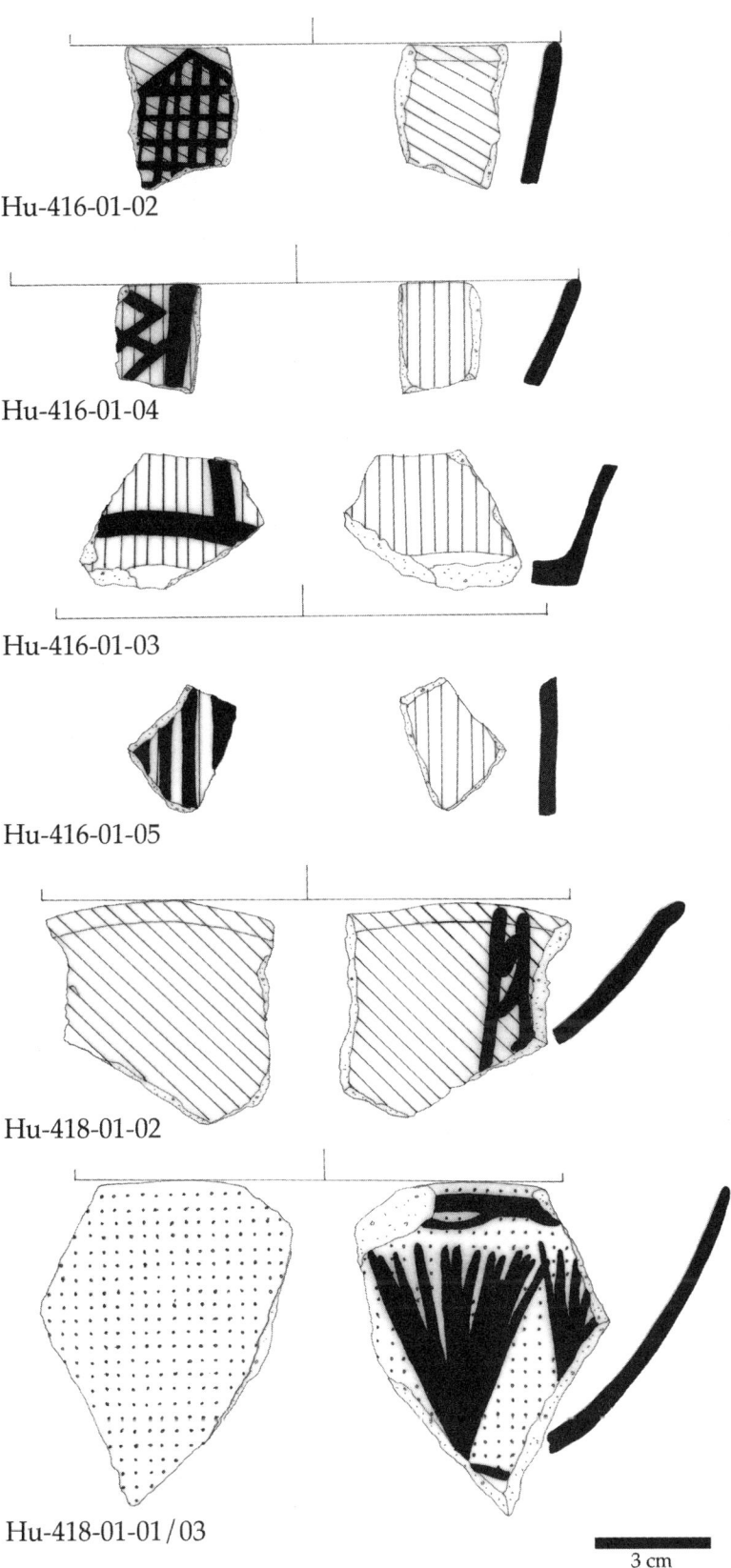

Figure A117. Ceramic fragment drawings from Hu-416 and Hu-418.

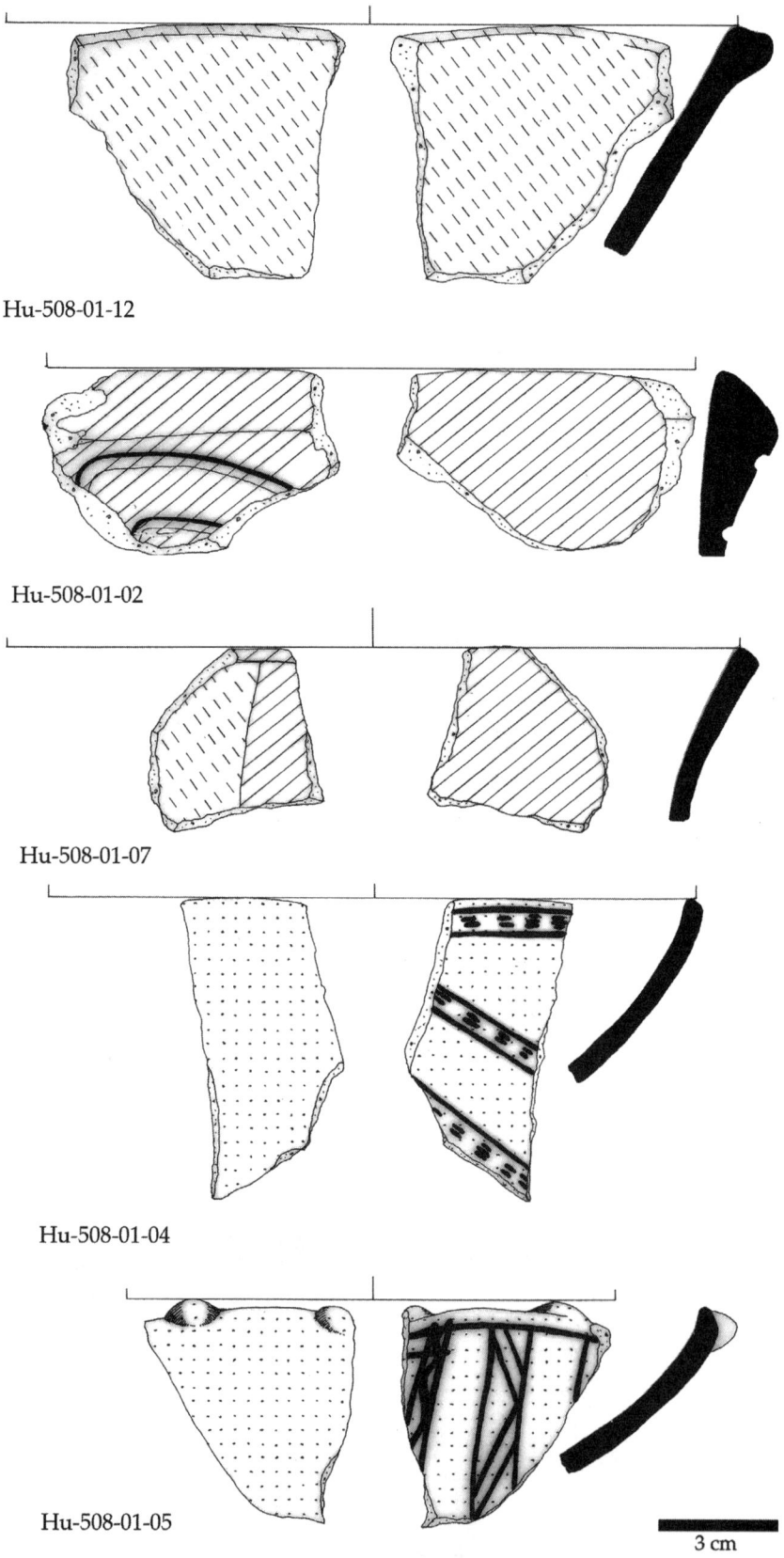

Figure A118. Ceramic fragment drawings from Hu-508.

Appendix A

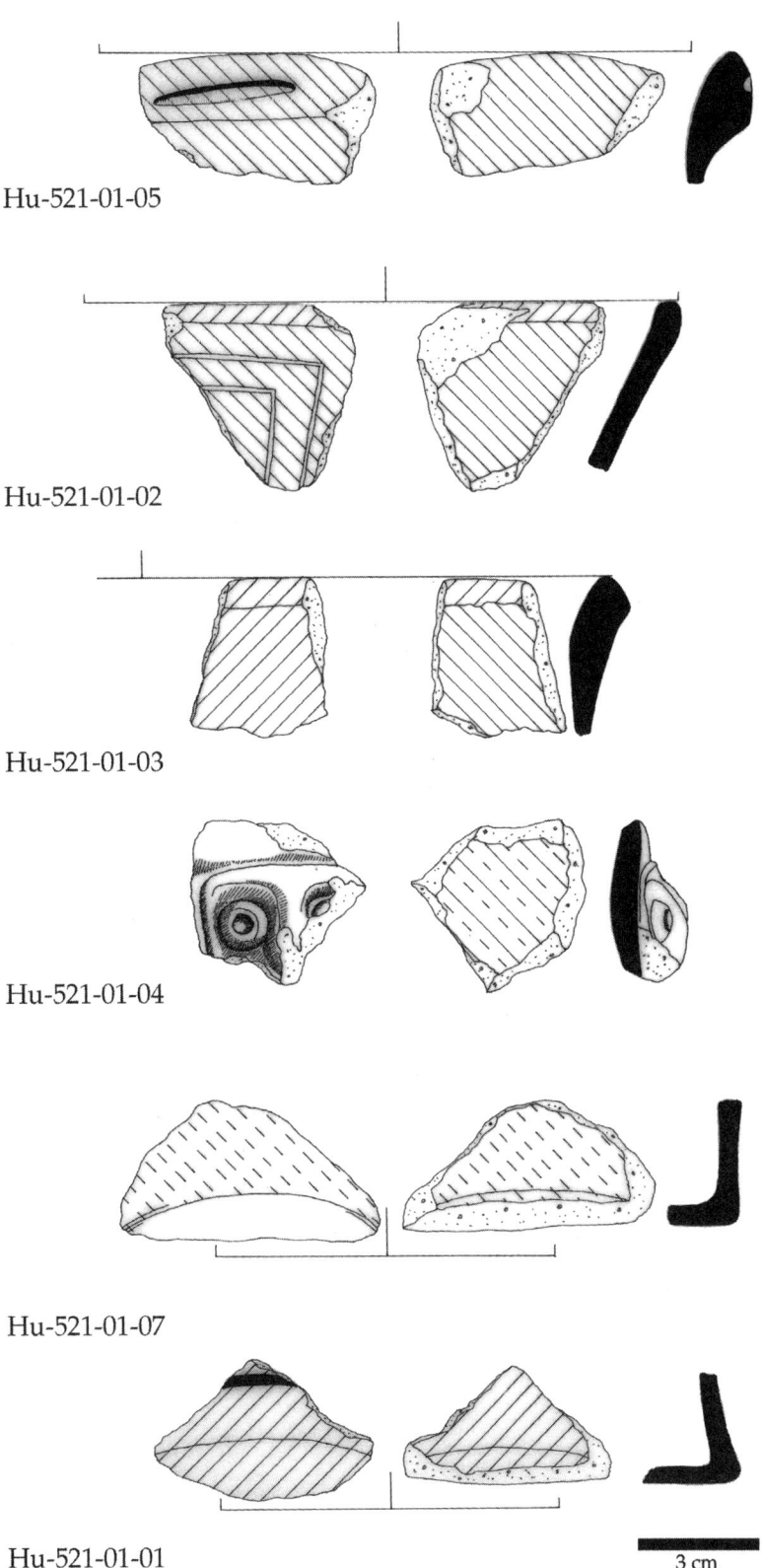

Hu-521-01-05

Hu-521-01-02

Hu-521-01-03

Hu-521-01-04

Hu-521-01-07

Hu-521-01-01

Figure A119. Ceramic fragment drawings from Hu-521.

376 *The Northern Titicaca Basin Survey*

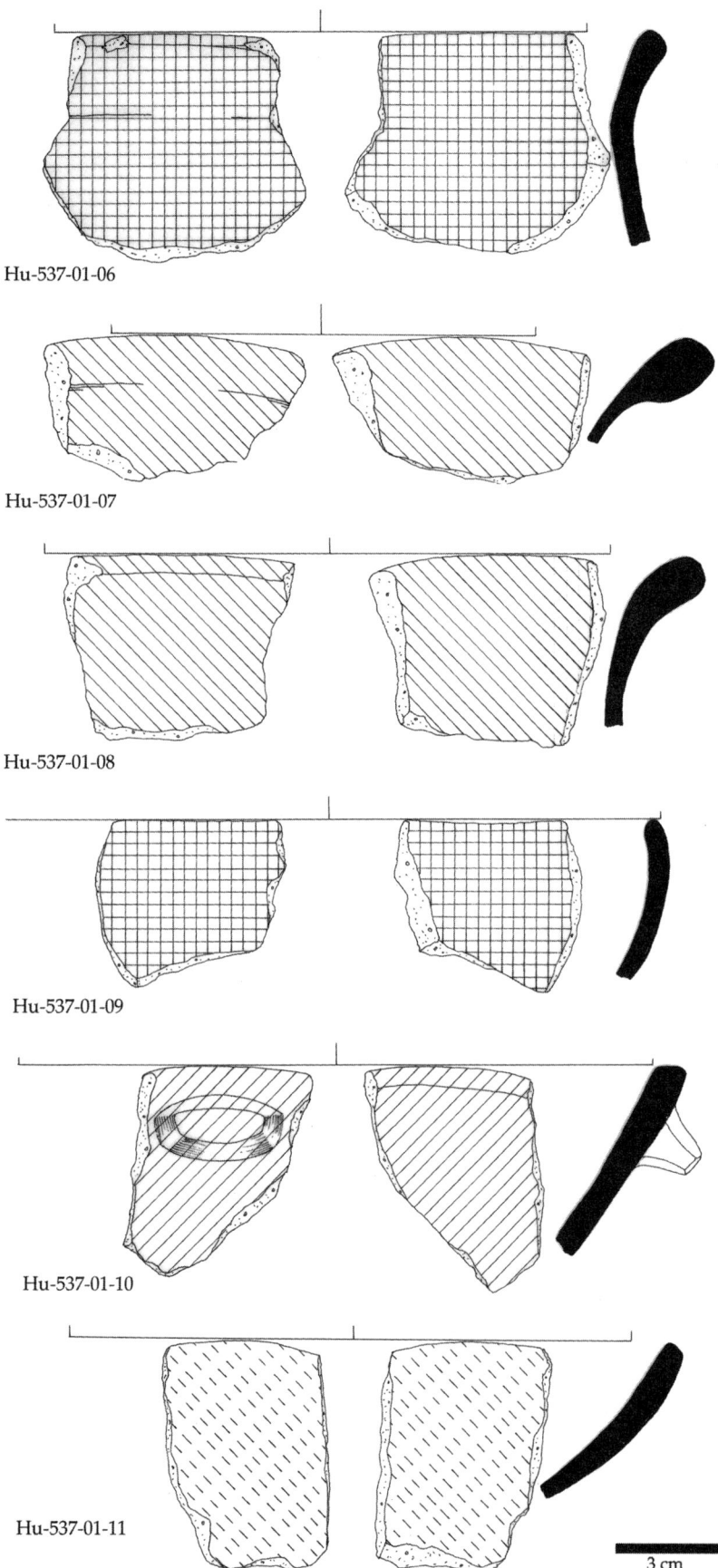

Hu-537-01-06

Hu-537-01-07

Hu-537-01-08

Hu-537-01-09

Hu-537-01-10

Hu-537-01-11

Figure A120.
Ceramic fragment drawings from Hu-537.

3 cm

Appendix A

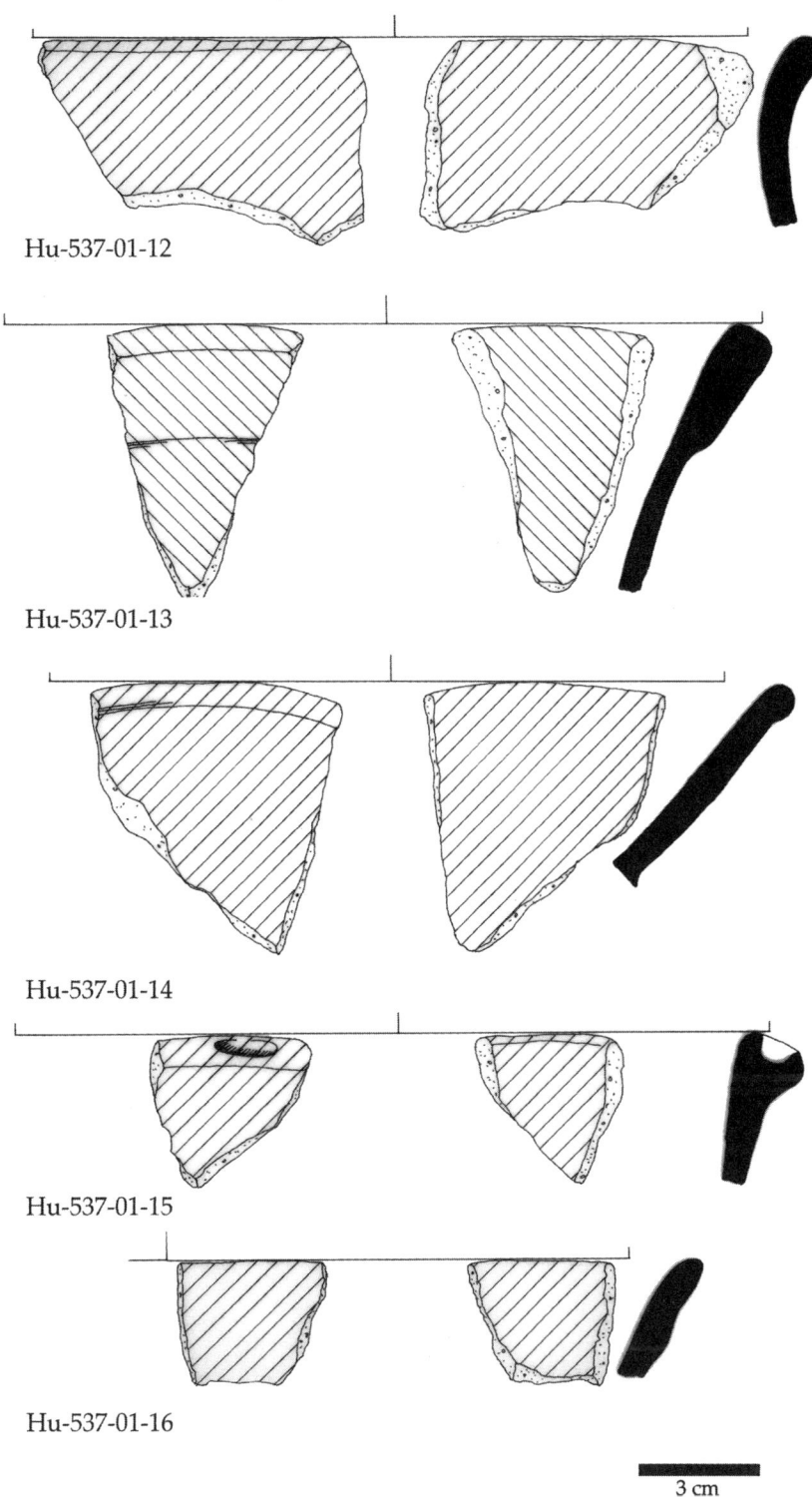

Figure A121. Ceramic fragment drawings from Hu-537.

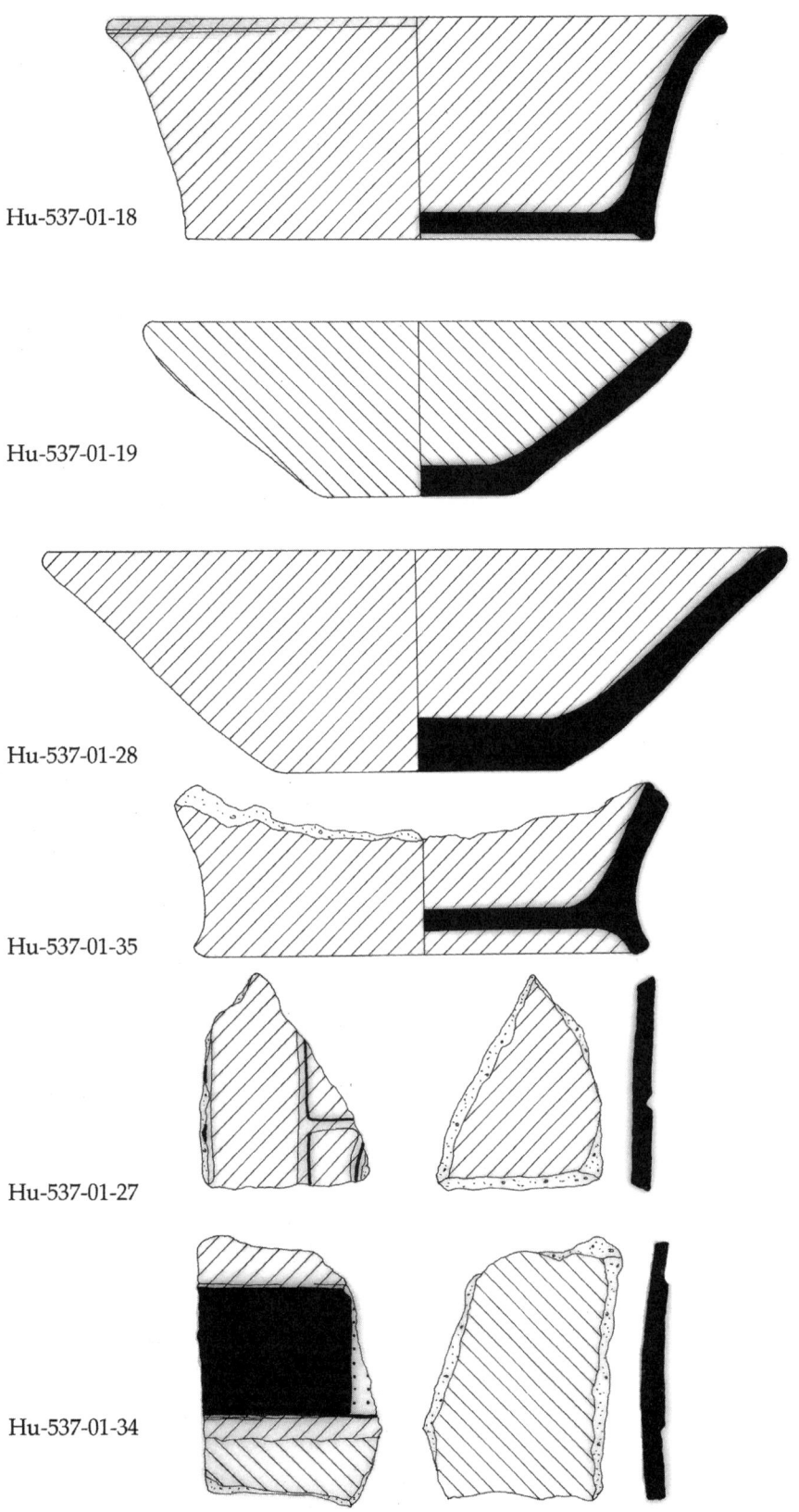

Figure A122.
Ceramic fragment drawings from Hu-537.

Appendix A

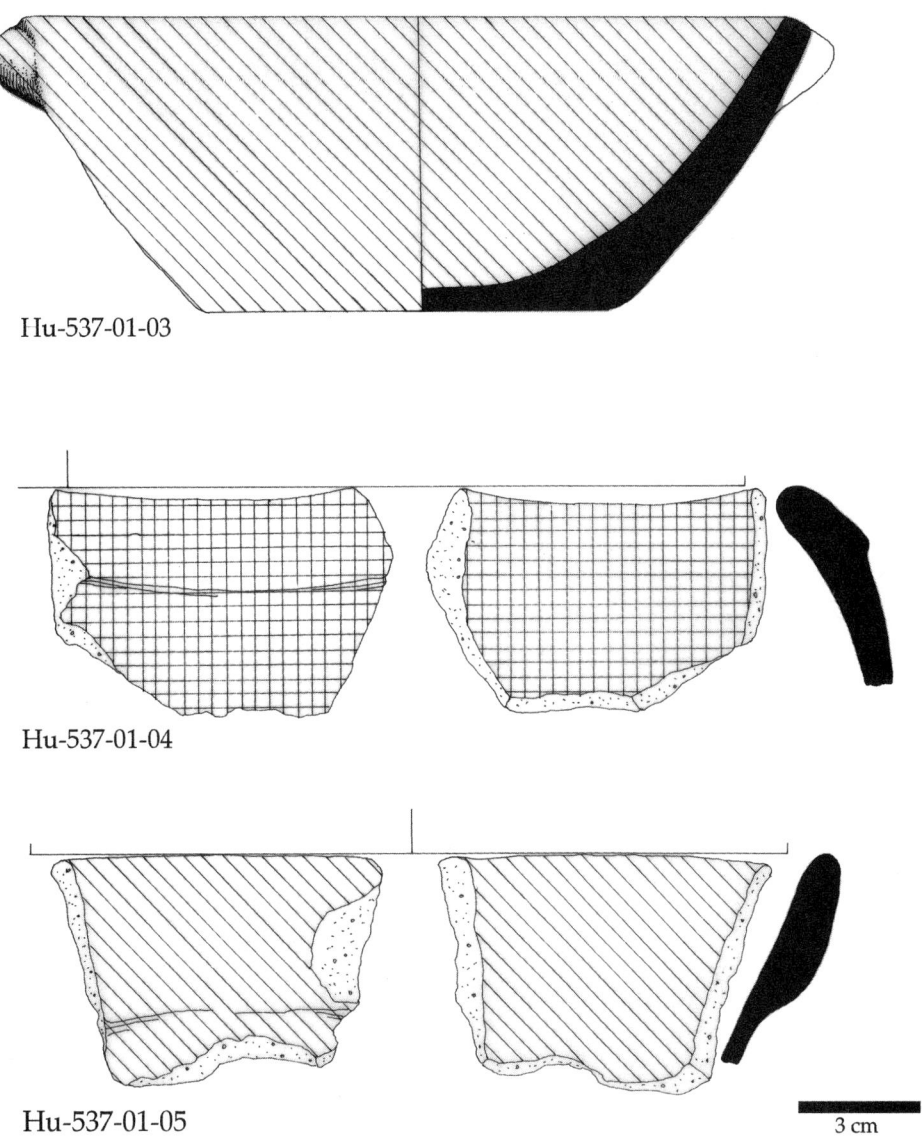

Figure A123. Ceramic fragment drawings from Hu-537.

Table A1. Metrics of illustrated ceramic data.

Specimen No.	Period	Ware Group[a]	Paste[a]	Form	Type[b]	Diameter[c] (cm)	Exterior Finish[d]	Interior Finish[d]	Firing[e]
Hu-004-01-25	Inca I	II-5	7	bowl	C2	12	A8	A2	A X
Hu-004-01-29	Inca I	III-8	4	bowl	A5	15	B2	A8	A II
Hu-008-01-16	Alt III	III	20	whorl	–	–	P1	E	A II
Hu-008-01-17	Alt III	III	20	whorl	–	–	P1	E	A IX
Hu-008-01-62	Alt II	I-2	7	closed vessel	–	–	E	D	H VIII
Hu-008-01-63	Alt I	I-3	10	closed vessel	–	–	A2	A2 + D	D VI
Hu-008-01-64	Alt II	I-2	5	closed vessel	–	–	B1	A2	A II
Hu-008-01-65	Alt II	I-2	5	closed vessel	–	–	A2	A6	A II
Hu-008-01-66	Inca I	III-7	3	bowl	A1	14	A2	A2	A XI
Hu-008-01-67	Alt I	I-3	10	bowl	–	3b	A2	A6	A II
Hu-008-01-68	Alt III	I-4	25	bowl	B1	15	A6	A2	A X
Hu-008-01-69	Alt III	III	22	closed vessel	–	–	B4	B4	K I
Hu-008-01-70	Inca I	I-4	27	closed vessel	–	–	B4	A1	A V
Hu-010-01-01	Inca I	III-8	4	bowl	A5	16	A2	A2	A XI
Hu-010-01-02	Inca I	III-8	4	open vessel	–	7b	A2	A2	A XI
Hu-010-01-03	Inca I	III-8	4	open vessel	–	6b	A2	A2	A XI
Hu-010-01-04	Inca II	III-9	16	plate	C	20	A2	A2	A XIV
Hu-010-01-05	Inca I	III-8	4	open vessel	–	–	A2	A2	A XI
Hu-010-01-06	Inca I	III-8	4	open vessel	–	–	A2	A2	A XI
Hu-010-01-54	Inca II	III-9	16	open vessel	–	6b	A2	A2	A XI
Hu-014-01-03	Form III	I-3	15	tazón	B5	15	B2	B2	I VI
Hu-014-01-04	Form II	II-5	41	tazón	A5	14	B2	B2	A II
Hu-014-01-05	Form III	I-3	14	jar	A	15	A2	A2	A VI
Hu-014-01-06	Form III	I-3	12	tazón	B5	30	A8	A8	D II
Hu-014-01-07	Form III	I-3	14	bowl	A1	16	B9	A8	C II
Hu-014-01-08	Form III	I-3	15	jar	B2	16	A2	A2	E VI
Hu-014-01-09	Form III	I-3	14	jar	A	9	A2	A6	A VI
Hu-014-01-15	Form I	I-1	1	jar	A	10	A2	A6	K I
Hu-014-01-31	Inca I	III-7	3	tazón	A1	14	A8	A8	A XI
Hu-014-01-32	Inca I	III-7	3	bowl	C1	16	A6	A8	A II
Hu-015-01-01	Alt III	III	18	bowl	A2	13	A8	A7	A VII
Hu-015-01-02	Alt III	III	18	bowl	A2	13	A8	A7	A VII
Hu-015-01-03	Inca I	III-8	4	bowl	B1	14	D	A8	A XI
Hu-015-01-05	Inca I	III-7	3	bowl	A2	15	T	A8	A VIII
Hu-015-01-08	Inca I	III-8	4	tazón	A2	14	A2	A8	A II
Hu-015-01-10	Inca I	III-8	4	bowl	–	5b	A8	A8	A IX
Hu-015-01-12	Inca I	III-7	3	open vessel			A8	A8	C XI
Hu-015-01-13	Inca I	III-7	3	open vessel	–	–	A2	A8	A XI
Hu-015-01-14	Inca I	III-7	3	open vessel	–	–	A8	A8	B XI
Hu-015-01-19	Inca II	III-9	5	open vessel	A2	–	–	–	A XIV
Hu-015-01-20	Inca II	III-9	5	open vessel	A2	–	–	–	A XIV
Hu-015-01-35	Alt II	I-1	3	jar	B1	16	A2	A2	A V
Hu-015-01-41	Inca I	III-7	3	bowl	A1	16	A2	A2	A IX
Hu-015-01-42	Inca I	III-8	4	tazón	A1	14	A2	A2	C XI
Hu-015-01-43	Inca I	III-7	3	bowl	A2	15	A2	A2	A IX
Hu-015-01-44	Inca I	III-7	3	jar	MINI	2b	A8	A2	A XI
Hu-015-01-45	Inca I	III-7	3	jar	MINI	2b	A8	A2	A XI
Hu-015-01-47	Alt III	III	18	tazón	A2	10	A2	A2	G VII
Hu-015-01-49	Inca I	I-4	27	tazón	A1	14	E	E	A VIII
Hu-015-01-50	Inca I	I-4	27	pitcher	B1	21	T	A2	I V
Hu-015-01-51	Inca I	III-7	3	bowl	–	4b	A8	A8	A XI
Hu-015-02-12	Inca I	III-7	3	bowl	B1	13	A2	A2	A IX
Hu-015-02-51	Inca I	III-7	3	open vessel	–	–	A8	A8	A XI
Hu-015-02-56	Inca I	III-7	1	open vessel	–	–	A8	A8	V IX
Hu-016-01-02	Inca I	III-8	4	bowl	B1	13	A2	A2	A IX
Hu-016-01-03	Inca I	III-7	3	open vessel	–	–	A2	A2	A XI
Hu-016-01-05	Inca I	III-7	3	bowl	–	5b	A2	A2	B XI
Hu-016-01-07	Inca I	III-7	3	bowl	B1	13	A2	A8	B XI
Hu-016-01-19	Inca III	II-5	7	tazón	A1	16	A2	B1	A X
Hu-030-01-06	Form III	I-3	12	trumpet	–	–	Q	Q	
Hu-030-01-10	Form II	II-5	41	tazón	A1	27	B2	B2	M III
Hu-030-01-13	Form I	I-6	25	olla	D4	22	B2	B2	A VII
Hu-030-02-01	Form III	I-3	14	olla	D4	19	A3	T	V IV
Hu-053-01-03	Alt III	III	20	bowl	B1	11	A8	A8	B VII
Hu-053-01-04	Alt II	I-2	7	bowl	A5	16	E	E	A I
Hu-055-01-01	Inca I	III-7	3	tazón	A1	15	A2	A8	A XII
Hu-058-01-01	Inca II	I-1	6	closed vessel	–	–	B4	A6	A V
Hu-068-01-01	Form I	II-1	28	jar	B2	16	A8	A8	A II
Hu-068-01-02	Form III	I-3	14	tazón	B8	18	A8	B2	A VI
Hu-069-01-01	Alt II	I-1	2	closed vessel	–	–	A8	A8	T V
Hu-074-01-01	Alt II	I-1	3	tazón	A2	16	T	A8	A V
Hu-077-01-01	Form III	I-3	15	tazón	A3	20	E	A2	A II
Hu-078-01-01	Form II	II-6	43	olla	B2	17	A2	A2	A II

Table A1 cont.

Specimen No.	Period	Ware Group[a]	Paste[a]	Form	Type[b]	Diameter[c] (cm)	Exterior Finish[d]	Interior Finish[d]	Firing[e]
Hu-078-01-03	Form II	II-7	46	jar	C3	17	A8	A8	F VIII
Hu-078-01-04	Form III	I-3	15	tazón	A1	15	A8	A8	G I
Hu-078-01-05	Form III	I-3	13	closed vessel	–	11b	B2	A2	E VI
Hu-078-01-11	Form II	II-7	46	closed vessel	–	9b	A8	E	C I
Hu-081-01-01	Form II	II-6	43	tazón	A3	15	E	A2	A VII
Hu-081-01-02	Form III	II-3	33	jar	A1	18	E	E	A II
Hu-081-01-03	Form III	I-3	14	jar	B2	16	E	E	A VIII
Hu-094-01-05	Form III	I-3	13	pitcher	A2	18	E	E	L V
Hu-094-01-06	Form III	I-3	12	jar	B2	18	B2	B2 + A8	A VI
Hu-094-01-07	Form III	I-3	14	tazón	D3	18	E	E	A VIII
Hu-094-01-08	Inca I	III-7	4	tazón	A1	14	E	A8	A IX
Hu-095-01-01	Form III	I-2	11	tazón	B2	16	E	E	O VI
Hu-095-01-02	Form III	I-3	12	tazón	B3	24	E	E	D VI
Hu-096-01-01	Inca II	I-3	8	jar	B1	13	B2	B2	A II
Hu-099-01-01	Form II	I-4	38	open vessel	–	–	E	E	D II
Hu-109-01-01	Inca III	II-6	18	bowl	A1	12	B2	B2	A X
Hu-118-01-02	Form I	I-1	1	olla	A1	20	A8	A8	A II
Hu-119-01-01	Form I	I-1	6	bowl	A3	25	B2	B2	A VII
Hu-119-01-02	Inca I	III-8	4	closed vessel	–	–	B2	A8 + T	A XIII
Hu-126-01-01	Form III	I-3	14	jar	B2	12	E	E	A VI
Hu-126-01-02	Inca I	III-7	3	bowl	A2	13	E	E	A II
Hu-126-01-03	Inca I	III-7	3	tazón	A1	16	A8	A8	B XI
Hu-126-01-04	Inca I	III-7	3	bowl	A1	14	A8	A8	A IX
Hu-126-01-05	Inca I	III-7	3	open vessel	–	–	A8	A8	A II
Hu-154-01-01	Form III	I-3	3	olla	A1	22	A8	A8	F VI
Hu-154-01-02	Form I	I-1	6	olla	A1	32	E	E	B VII
Hu-154-01-03	Alt III	I-4	26	bowl	A4	14	E	A2	U IX
Hu-154-01-04	Alt III	I-4	28	bowl	A3	14	B2	B2	A X
Hu-156-01-01	Inca I	III-7	3	bowl	D1	12	A8	A8	V IX
Hu-160-01-02	Inca I	III-7	3	bowl	A1	13	A8	A8	V IX
Hu-161-01-01	Inca I	III-7	3	bowl	A1	14	A8	A8	A IX
Hu-161-01-02	Inca I	III-7	3	bowl	A1	15	A2	A8	A XI
Hu-162-01-01	Inca I	I-4	27	tazón	A1	12	A8	A8	T V
Hu-166-01-01	Inca I	III-7	3	bowl	B5	15	B2	B2	A XI
Hu-167-01-01	Huaña I	II-1	20	jar	B2	14	A8	A2	A II
Hu-168-01-01	Alt II	I-1	3	bowl	C1	9	B2	B2	A V
Hu-169-01-01	Inca III	II-5	7	bowl	A1	14	A8	A8	A V
Hu-172-01-01	Alt III	III	22	bowl	D2	14	B2	B2	E I
Hu-173-01-01	Inca II	I-3	8	bowl	A5	14	B2	B2	A V
Hu-173-01-02	Inca I	III-8	4	jar	B1	12	B2	B2	A IX
Hu-173-01-03	Inca I	III-8	4	bowl	A1	13	A8	A8	A IX
Hu-173-01-04	Inca I	III-8	4	bowl	A1	13	A8	A8	A IX
Hu-173-01-05	Inca I	III-8	4	bowl	A3	12	A8	A8	A XI
Hu-173-01-10	Inca II	I-3	8	bowl	A5	14	B2	B2	A XI
Hu-174-01-01	Form III	I-5	21	closed vessel	–	–	B4	B4	Z VI
Hu-174-01-02	Form III	I-3	12	incense burner	–	30	A8	E	J VI
Hu-174-01-03	Form III	I-3	12	incense burner	–	30	A8	E	J VI
Hu-174-01-04	Tiw I	III	10	closed vessel	–	–	B2	A8	D II
Hu-174-01-05	Huaña I	II-2	29	tazón	A4	22	E	A8	D IX
Hu-174-01-06	Form III	I-5	19	tazón	A4	22	E	E	A X
Hu-176-01-01	Alt II	I-1	3	bowl	B1	15	D	A8	A V
Hu-176-01-02	Alt II	II	16	bowl	A2	16	A8	A8	A XI
Hu-176-03-01	Alt II	II	16	bowl	A1	14	A8	A8	A XI
Hu-176-03-02	Alt II	II	16	bowl	A1	12	A8	A8	A XI
Hu-176-03-03	Alt III	III	19	pitcher	B2	19	A8	A5	A VII
Hu-176-04-01	Alt II	II	17	bowl	–	4b	A8	A8	A IX
Hu-200-01-01	Alt II	I-1	1	jar	B2	9b	A8	A8	T V
Hu-200-01-02	Alt I	I-3	10	bowl	A1	10	A2	A8	A VI
Hu-200-01-03	Inca III	II-5	7	bowl	–	6b	B2	A8	A X
Hu-201-01-01	Form III	III	52	bowl	B1	13	A8	R	B VII
Hu-201-01-02	Alt II	I-1	1	bowl	C2	13	A8	A8	T V
Hu-201-01-03	Alt I	I-3	9	jar	B2	16	A8	A8	D VI
Hu-202-01-01	Alt III	III	20	bowl	B1	14	A8	A8	A VII
Hu-202-01-02	Inca I	III-7	3	bowl	B1	14	A2	A2	A XI
Hu-202-01-03	Alt I	I-3	13	jar	B1	12	A8	QUEM	A IX
Hu-204-01-02	Form I	I-1	2	bowl	A1	16	A8	A8	A VI
Hu-204-01-03	Form III	III	52	jar	B2	13	A8	T	F I
Hu-204-01-04	Form II	II-6	43	tapa	–	11	A8	A8	A VII
Hu-204-01-05	Form II	II-6	45	jar	B1	11	A1	A1	B VII
Hu-204-01-06	Form II	II-6	45	closed vessel	–	10b	A8	A8	A I
Hu-204-02-06	Form I	I-1	2	closed vessel	–	–	A2	A2	A VI
Hu-204-02-07	Alt II	I-2	6	closed vessel	–	–	T	A8	A IX
Hu-205-01-01	Form III	II-3	33	pitcher	B2	18	A8	A8	A IX
Hu-205-01-02	Form II	II-7	47	olla	A3	18	B2	A8	A II
Hu-205-01-03	Form II	II-7	48	olla	C1	15	A8	A1	A I

Table A1 cont.

Specimen No.	Period	Ware Group[a]	Paste[a]	Form	Type[b]	Diameter[c] (cm)	Exterior Finish[d]	Interior Finish[d]	Firing[e]
Hu-205-01-04	Form III	I-3	13	jar	A	15	A8	A8	A VI
Hu-205-01-11	Form I	I-6	25	bowl	B1	18	B2	B2	A VII
Hu-205-01-12	Form III	III	52	incense burner	–	–	B1	B1	A VI
Hu-205-01-12	Tiw II	II	5	kero	A1	10	B2	B2	A IX
Hu-205-01-13	Form I	I-6	25	bowl	B5	18	B2	B2	A VII
Hu-205-01-15	Form II	II-6	45	closed vessel	–	10b	T	A8	A III
Hu-205-01-16	Form II	II-7	50	closed vessel	–	–	T	A8	A VIII
Hu-205-02-01	Form III	III	52	jar	A	16	A2	A2	A VI
Hu-205-02-03	Form I	I-1	4	bowl	A2	11	A8	A8	A II
Hu-205-02-04	Form III	II-7	47	jar	B2	15	A5	T	A II
Hu-205-02-05	Form III	III	52	jar	A	10	A8	A8	A VI
Hu-205-02-06	Form I	I-6	24	pitcher	A1	20	B13	B13	G VII
Hu-205-02-13	Huaña I	II-2	30	jar	C1	14	A8	A8	A VI
Hu-205-02-14	Form III	I-3	12	tazón	B8	24	A8	A8	A VIII
Hu-205-02-15	Form I	I-6	23	jar	A	14	B13	B13	A III
Hu-205-02-17	Form I	I-1	2	tazón	B5	18	B2	B2	I VI
Hu-205-02-18	Form I	I-6	25	jar	B2	14	A8	A8	A VII
Hu-205-02-19	Form I	I-1	2	tazón	D3	26	B2	B2	C VI
Hu-205-02-20	Form I	I-6	23	tazón	B4	20	B13	B13	A III
Hu-205-02-21	Form III	I-3	12	jar	B4	14	B13	B13	A VI
Hu-205-02-22	Form I	I-6	23	bowl	B2	16	A8	A8	A VII
Hu-205-02-23	Form I	I-6	25	olla	E1	14	A8	A8	A VII
Hu-205-02-31	Form I	I-1	6	pitcher	A3	18	A8	A8	A III
Hu-205-02-32	Form III	I-3	12	jar	A	13	B13	B13	A VI
Hu-205-02-33	Form III	I-5	20	trumpet	–	–	B9		A X
Hu-205-02-34	Form III	II-3	34	trumpet	–	–	B9	A8	A VIII
Hu-205-02-35	Form III	I-3	12	closed vessel	–	10b	A8	A8	A VIII
Hu-205-03-04	Form II	I-2	11	open vessel	–	–	B2	C2	I K
Hu-205-03-18	Form I	I-1	4	tazón	A5	29	B2	B2	E II
Hu-205-03-21	Inca III	II-5	7	bowl	C2	15	A8	A2	A X
Hu-205-04-01	Form I	I-1	5	bowl	B3	16	B4	B4	A II
Hu-205-04-02	Form I	I-1	5	bowl	E1	14	B4	B4	Q II
Hu-205-04-03	Form I	I-1	6	olla	B2	30	B2	B2	A VII
Hu-205-04-04	Huaña I	II-2	31	jar	A	17	A8	A5	A II
Hu-205-04-05	Form I	II-1	28	tazón	B1	20	B5	B5	A IX
Hu-205-04-13	Form III	I-3	12	tazón	A1	20	B13	B13	I VI
Hu-205-04-14	Form II	II-6	45	open vessel	A1	18	B2	B2	A III
Hu-205-04-15	Form III	I-3	12	bowl	B1	8b	B13	B13	A VIII
Hu-205-04-16	Form III	III	51	tazón	A3	26	B13	B13	A VII
Hu-205-04-17	Form III	I-2	11	tazón	A4	28	T	B4	I VI
Hu-208-01-04	Alt III	III	18	bowl	C1	14	A8	A8	A IX
Hu-208-01-05	Inca III	II-6	18	bowl	–	10	A2	A2	A X
Hu-208-01-23	Inca I	III-8	4	bowl	A1	14	A8	A8	A II
Hu-209-01-05	Inca III	II-6	18	bowl	–	10	A2	B2	A X
Hu-209-01-01	Huaña II	I-1	14	bowl	B5	16	B2	B2	A VI
Hu-209-01-02	Alt II	I-1	1	pitcher	B1	18	A8	A1	A1 V
Hu-209-01-03	Form I	I-6	25	open vessel	–	–	A8	A1	A III
Hu-209-01-04	Form III	II-5	41	open vessel	–	–	B8	A8	A II
Hu-209-01-05	Tiw II	II	5	closed vessel	–	–	A8	A8	A IX
Hu-210-01-01	Form II	I-4	38	olla	E3	24	A8	A8	A II
Hu-211-01-01	Alt III	III	19	closed vessel	–	–	P1	A8	A III
Hu-211-01-02	Alt II	I-1	2	closed vessel	–	–	A8	A8	F V
Hu-212-01-01	Alt II	I-2	5	bowl	B1	20	A2	A2	S VIII
Hu-212-01-02	Alt II	I-2	6	tazón	A1	16	B2	B2	T V
Hu-215-01-01	Alt III	III	20	bowl	E1	11	A8	A8	B VII
Hu-215-01-02	Alt III	III	21	open vessel	–	–	B9	B9	L VII
Hu-215-01-03	Alt I	I-3	11	whorl	–	–	A5	A5	A IX
Hu-216-02-01	Alt I	I-3	9	closed vessel	–	–	A1	A8	D VI
Hu-216-02-02	Inca III	II-6	18	bowl	A1	13	B2	B2	A X
Hu-216-02-03	Inca III	II-6	18	bowl	A1	11	B2	B2	A X
Hu-216-02-04	Tiw II	II	5	closed vessel	–	–	B2	A1	O VI
Hu-219-01-01	Form III	II-3	35	open vessel	–	8b	A8	A8	D VI
Hu-219-01-02	Tiw II	I-1		closed vessel			B10	B10	A VI
Hu-219-02-03	Form II	I-4	40	jar	B2	16	A1	A1	A II
Hu-219-02-04	Form III	III	52	closed vessel	–	9b	A1	A1	A VI
Hu-219-02-05	Form II	II-7	48	closed vessel	–	10b	A9	A9	A III
Hu-219-02-06	Tiw II	III	10	kero	A1	12	A8	A8	F X
Hu-219-02-07	Inca II	III-9	16	bowl	B1	12	A8	B2	A XIV
Hu-219-03-01	Form III	I-3	12	tazón	B2	26	E	E	Q II
Hu-219-03-02	Form II	II-7	47	olla	E2	26	A8	A8	D II
Hu-219-03-03	Alt II	I-2	5	jar	B1	16	A8	A8	F V
Hu-219-03-04	Form I	I-1	3	tazón	B2	20	A2	E	A VI
Hu-219-03-05	Form I	I-1	4	tazón	B2	16	E	A8	A II
Hu-219-03-07	Tiw II	I	2	closed vessel	–	–	B2	A8	D VI
Hu-219-03-08	Inca I	III-7	3	bowl	B1	14	A2	A2	A IX

Table A1 cont.

Specimen No.	Period	Ware Group[a]	Paste[a]	Form	Type[b]	Diameter[c] (cm)	Exterior Finish[d]	Interior Finish[d]	Firing[e]
Hu-219-03-09	Inca I	III-7	3	bowl	A2	14	A2	A8	C XI
Hu-219-03-10	Inca I	III-7	3	bowl	A1	15	A8	A8	A XI
Hu-219-03-11	Inca I	III-7	3	bowl	A2	13	A8	A8	A IX
Hu-219-03-12	Inca I	III-8	4	bowl	A1	13	A2	A2	A XI
Hu-219-03-13	Alt II	II	14	bowl	B1	16	A2	A2 + D	I IX
Hu-219-03-14	Huaña I	II-1	4	bowl	B1	13	A8	A1	A V
Hu-222-01-01	Alt III	I-4	26	bowl	B1	15	A8	A8	A IX
Hu-222-01-02	Inca I	III-7	3	bowl	A1	12	A2	A8	A XI
Hu-222-01-03	Inca I	III-7	3	tazón	A2	13	A2	A8	A IX
Hu-222-01-04	Inca I	III-7	3	bowl	B1	11	A8	A8	A XI
Hu-222-01-05	Alt II	I-2	5	bowl	B2	16	A9	P1	A V
Hu-222-01-06	Alt II	I-1	2	tazón	A1	12	A1	A1	F V
Hu-222-02-01	Form II	II-7	47	jar	A	12	A8	A8	A I
Hu-222-02-02	Inca I	I-4	29	bowl	B1	15	A8	B10	C X
Hu-222-02-03	Inca I	I-4	27	tazón	A1	14	B2	B2	T V
Hu-224-02-01	Alt II	I-2	8	bowl	A6	18	T	E	C II
Hu-226-01-01	Alt II	I-2	8	closed vessel	–	–	T	T	A IX
Hu-226-01-02	Inca I	III-7	3	bowl	B1	17	A2	A2	V XI
Hu-226-01-04	Inca I	III-7	3	bowl	A1	14	A2	A2	C XI
Hu-227-01-01	Alt III	III	20	pitcher	B1	18	A8	A8	L VII
Hu-227-01-02	Inca I	I-4	29	bowl	B1	15	A2	A2	A V
Hu-227-01-03	Alt III	I-3	11	jar	B2	18	T	A8	D VI
Hu-232-01-01	Alt I	I-3	11	tazón	B1	15	T	A5	A IX
Hu-233-01-02	Inca II	I-1	9	closed vessel	–	–	B2	A2	T V
Hu-234-01-01	Alt II	I-2	5	closed vessel	–	–	B10	T	A V
Hu-234-01-02	Alt III	III	18	bowl	A3	14	A8	A8	A III
Hu-234-01-03	Inca III	II-5	7	bowl	D2	16	B2	B2	D II
Hu-234-01-04	Inca II	I-2	14	closed vessel	–	–	A8	A8	A V
Hu-235-01-01	Alt II	I-1	3	bowl	A1	16	A2	A2	T V
Hu-235-01-02	Alt II	I-1	3	bowl	D2	14	D	A2	T V
Hu-235-01-03	Inca III	II-5	7	open vessel	–	–	A8	B2	A X
Hu-237-01-01	Inca I	III-7	3	closed vessel	–	–	A8	A2	A XI
Hu-238-02-01	Alt II	II	16	bowl	A1	16	A2	A8	A XI
Hu-238-02-02	Alt II	II	16	bowl	A1	16	A2	A8	A IX
Hu-239-01-01	Inca III	II-5	12	pitcher	B1	20	B2	B2	I X
Hu-239-02-01	Inca III	II-5	12	bowl	A1	16	A8	A8	B X
Hu-239-02-02	Inca I	III-8	4	bowl	A2	16	E	A8	A II
Hu-239-02-03	Inca I	III-7	3	tazón	B1	14	A8	A2	A XI
Hu-239-02-04	Alt II	I-1	3	open vessel	–	–	A1	A8	T V
Hu-243-01-01	Alt II	I-2	5	closed vessel	–	–	A1	A5	T V
Hu-246-01-01	Form II	I-4	39	olla	D2	24	B1	B1	A II
Hu-246-01-02	Form I	I-6	23	olla	A3	9	B2	B2	A VII
Hu-246-01-03	Form III	II-3	37	tazón	B2	21	A2	A2	A II
Hu-246-01-04	Form I	I-6	23	jar	B2	11	B2	B2	A VII
Hu-246-01-05	Form III	I-3	13	tazón	–	20b	A8	B2	A VI
Hu-246-01-06	Huaña I	II-1	20	bowl	A4	18	B2	B2	A VI
Hu-246-01-07	Form I	I-1	6	olla	A3	16	A1	A1	A II
Hu-246-01-08	Form I	I-1	7	bowl	B4	30	B4	B4	A I
Hu-246-01-09	Tiw II	II	1	tazón	A2	13	A8	A8	A VI
Hu-246-01-10	Tiw II	I	3	closed vessel	–	–	B2	A2	C VI
Hu-246-01-11	Tiw II	II	5	closed vessel	–	–	B5	A8	A IX
Hu-246-01-12	Form I	I-1	2	open vessel	–	7b	A8	A8	A IX
Hu-246-01-13	Tiw II	I	1	tazón	–	7b	B13	A2	A VI
Hu-246-01-14	Tiw II	I	1	tazón	–	7b	A8	A8	A VI
Hu-246-01-15	Alt II	I-1	3	bowl	B1	13	A1	A1	A II
Hu-246-01-16	Alt III	III	21	bowl	B4	15	T	A8	B VII
Hu-246-01-17	Inca I	III-8	4	bowl	A1	16	A2	A2	A XI
Hu-246-01-18	Inca II	III-9	5	bowl	A5	12	A8	A8	A XIV
Hu-246-01-19	Inca I	III-7	3	closed vessel	–	–	A8	A2	B XI
Hu-246-01-20	Alt III	I-4	26	open vessel	–	–	A8	A8	A X
Hu-246-01-21	Inca I	I-2	14	bowl	A3	14	B2	B2	A V
Hu-246-01-22	Inca II	I-3	8	bowl	A3	14	B2	B2	A V
Hu-247-01-01	Form II	II-6	45	olla	D4	16	A8	A1	A VIII
Hu-247-01-02	Form II	II-6	45	olla	E1	22	A8	A8	A IX
Hu-247-01-03	Form II	II-7	48	tazón	B8	24	B2	B2	A I
Hu-247-01-04	Form I	I-1	1	tazón	B2	30	B2	B2	H VIII
Hu-247-01-05	Form II	II-6	45	olla	B2	19	A5	A8 + Q	F VIII
Hu-247-01-06	Tiw I	III	11	tazón	A1	12	A8	A8	B I
Hu-247-01-07	Form I	I-1	1	olla	A1	24	B2	B2	A II
Hu-248-01-06	Form II	II-7	46	jar	C1	13	B13	B13	A II
Hu-248-01-07	Form I	I-1	1	olla	A1	24	B2	B2	A II
Hu-248-01-08	Form I	I-1	1	bowl	A1	15	A1	A1	A II
Hu-248-01-09	Form II	II-4	39	olla	D3	15	A1	T	A IX
Hu-248-01-10	Form I	I-1	1	jar	A	17	B2	B2	A II
Hu-248-01-11	Form I	I-1	1	olla	B2	16	B2	B2	A II
Hu-249-01-01	Alt I	I-3	9	bowl	A4	12	A1	A1	D VI

Table A1 cont.

Specimen No.	Period	Ware Group[a]	Paste[a]	Form	Type[b]	Diameter[c] (cm)	Exterior Finish[d]	Interior Finish[d]	Firing[e]
Hu-249-01-02	Inca II	III-9	16	closed vessel	–	–	A8	T	A XIV
Hu-249-01-03	Inca I	III-7	3	bowl	C1	16	A2	A8	A III
Hu-249-01-04	Inca I	I-4	29	bowl	A4	12	B2	B2	A V
Hu-249-01-05	Inca II	I-3	8	bowl	A4	14	B2	B2	A II
Hu-249-01-06	Inca II	I-2	14	jar	B1	14	A8	B2	A V
Hu-249-01-09	Tiw II	I	2	tazón	–	–	A1	AI	F V
Hu-251-01-01	Alt III	III	20	bowl	B3	16	A1	A1	B VII
Hu-251-01-02	Alt III	III	20	bowl	A3	13	A2	A2	A IX
Hu-251-02-17	Inca I	III-7	3	bowl	B1	16	A2	A2	A XI
Hu-252-01-01	Alt II	I-2	6	jar	B1	15	A2	A2	T V
Hu-252-01-02	Inca I	I-4	27	bowl	A4	8	A8	A8	G V
Hu-252-01-03	Inca I	III-7	3	open vessel	–	–	A2	A2	A XI
Hu-252-01-04	Inca I	III-7	3	open vessel	–	5b	A2	A2	A II
Hu-253-01-01	Alt II	I-1	3	bowl	B6	11	A8	A8	A V
Hu-253-01-02	Alt II	I-2	5	closed vessel	–	–	A8	A1	T V
Hu-254-01-01	Inca III	II-5	12	bowl	E2	14	B2	E	A X
Hu-255-01-01	Tiw II	I	2	tazón	A1	16	B2	B2 + A2	T V
Hu-255-01-02	Tiw I	III	11	tazón	A2	15	B2	B2	F X
Hu-255-01-03	Tiw I	III	9	open vessel		7b	B4	A2	A X
Hu-255-01-04	Inca I	III-7	3	open vessel			A8	A8	A XI
Hu-255-03-01	Tiw I	III	9	kero	A1	14	B2	A8	A X
Hu-255-03-02	Tiw I	III	11	tazón	A2	13	D	B2	K X
Hu-255-04-01	Tiw I	III	9	tazón	A1	16	B2	B2 + A2	A VIII
Hu-255-04-02	Tiw I	III	11	closed vessel	–	–	B2	A6	H X
Hu-255-05-01	Tiw I	III	9	incense burner	–	–	A8	T	C X
Hu-255-05-02	Tiw I	III	9	tazón	A2	13	B2	B2 + A2	G X
Hu-255-05-03	Tiw I	III	9	tazón	A2	7b	B2	A8	G X
Hu-255-05-04	Tiw I	III	9	tazón	–	9b	B2	A8	B IX
Hu-255-05-05	Inca III	II-5	7	bowl	D1	12	B2	T	C IX
Hu-255-05-06	Tiw II	II	6	kero	A1	10	B2	A2	A IX
Hu-256-01-01	Inca I	III-8	4	closed vessel	–	–	A8	A2	A XI
Hu-256-01-02	Inca I	III-7	3	tazón	A1	13	A2	A8	A IX
Hu-256-01-03	Tiw I	III	9	closed vessel	–	–	B4	B6	B X
Hu-258-01-01	Alt I	I-3	12	bowl	D2	15	A8	E	D II
Hu-258-01-02	Inca II	I-3	8	bowl	A4	14	B2	B2	A V
Hu-260-01-01	Inca I	III-8	4	bowl	C2	14	A8	A8	A III
Hu-261-01-01	Alt III	III	21	jar	B1	12	A8	T	A IX
Hu-261-01-02	Inca I	III-7	3	bowl	A3	13	A8	A8	A XI
Hu-261-02-01	Alt I	I-3	9	bowl	E3	12	A1	A1	D VI
Hu-262-01-01	Inca I	III-7	3	tazón	A2	15	A8	E	A II
Hu-263-01-01	Inca I	III-7	3	tazón	A1	15	A8	A8	A XI
Hu-267-01-01	Alt III	III	20	closed vessel	–	5b	T	A8	S VII
Hu-267-01-02	Alt II	I-2	6	bowl	B1	18	A6	A2	T V
Hu-269-01-01	Form I	I-1	3	olla	B2	19	E	E	A VI
Hu-269-01-02	Form II	II-7	47	jar	A	17	A2	A2	A I
Hu-269-01-03	Form III	I-3	13	olla	E2	18	A8	D	I VI
Hu-269-01-04	Form II	II-6	43	olla	E2	23	E	E	A VIII
Hu-269-01-05	Form II	II-7	47	olla	E2	20	B2	B2	A VIII
Hu-269-01-06	Inca I	III-7	3	bowl	C2	16	A2	A2	A XI
Hu-269-01-07	Inca I	III-7	3	bowl	A1	10	A2	A2	A II
Hu-269-01-08	Alt III	I-4	26	open vessel	–	5b	A1	A1	T V
Hu-270-01-01	Alt I	IV	24	bowl	D2	18	A5	A5	D VI
Hu-270-01-02	Alt II	I-1	3	bowl	A3	10	T	A5	A V
Hu-273-01-01	Alt III	III	21	jar	B1	10	T	A1	A VIII
Hu-274-01-01	Inca I	I-4	29	bowl	A1	18	A8	A8	A IX
Hu-274-01-02	Alt II	I-1	1	jar	B2	15	A1	A1	A V
Hu-274-01-03	Alt III	III	21	jar	B2	16	T	A8	A IX
Hu-275-01-01	Inca I	III-7	3	bowl	A1	16	A2	A8	A XI
Hu-276-01-01	Form III	I-3	12	tazón	B2	24	A8	A8	K I
Hu-276-01-02	Alt III	I-4	26	bowl	A2	20	A2	A2	A X
Hu-276-01-03	Form I	I-6	23	tazón	A1	17	A8	B2	A VII
Hu-276-01-04	Huaña I	II-1	17	tazón	B1	17	B2	B2	A V
Hu-276-01-05	Form III	I-3	15	olla	B2	21	A8	A8	A VI
Hu-276-01-06	Huaña I	II-2	29	olla	A2	20	E	E	A VIII
Hu-276-01-07	Form I	I-1	2	olla	A2	20	A8	A8	O II
Hu-276-01-08	Form I	I-1	2	jar	C2	11	A8	A8	A VI
Hu-276-01-09	Form III	I-5	19	olla	E2	20	B2	B2	A X
Hu-276-01-10	Form II	II-7	46	olla	B2	21	A2	A2	A I
Hu-276-01-12	Huaña I	II-2	31	olla	B2	22	A2	A2	A I

Table A1 cont.

Specimen No.	Period	Ware Group[a]	Paste[a]	Form	Type[b]	Diameter[c] (cm)	Exterior Finish[d]	Interior Finish[d]	Firing[e]
Hu-276-01-13	Form II	II-6	44	tazón	B8	19	B13	B13	A III
Hu-276-01-14	Form III	II-3	33	tazón	A1	14	E	E	M II
Hu-276-02-01	Form II	II-7	47	open vessel	–	11b	B4	B4	C III
Hu-276-02-02	Form III	I-3	15	open vessel	–	11b	A8	A8	C II
Hu-276-02-03	Form I	I-1	2	pitcher	B2	18	B2	B2	A VI
Hu-276-02-04	Form I	I-1	2	tazón	B6	22	A8	A8	A I
Hu-276-02-05	Form III	I-3	15	olla	B2	18	A8	A2	G VII
Hu-276-02-06	Form III	I-3	12	closed vessel	–	9b	B4	A8	E VII
Hu-276-02-07	Form II	II-7	48	tazón	A1	21	B2	B2	A III
Hu-276-02-08	Form III	I-3	13	olla	A1	22	B2	B2	A II
Hu-276-02-09	Form I	I-1	2	jar	B2	15	A8	A2 + E	A VI
Hu-276-02-10	Huaña I	II-2	29	olla	B2	20	E	E	D II
Hu-276-02-12	Form II	II-7	46	bowl	B3	20	B4	B4	A I
Hu-276-02-14	Huaña I	II-2	30	olla	B2	20	B4	B4	A VI
Hu-278-01-01	Inca III	IV-10	10	tazón	A1	15	A8	A8	B IX
Hu-278-01-02	Inca III	IV-10	10	bowl	A1	13	A8	A8	A II
Hu-278-01-03	Inca III	II-6	18	plate	A1	20	B2	B2	A X
Hu-279-01-01	Alt III	III	21	closed vessel	–	–	A1	A8	L VII
Hu-279-01-02	Alt II	I-1	3	tazón	B1	12	A1	A8	A V
Hu-279-01-03	Inca I	I-4	27	closed vessel	–	–	A8	A1	A V
Hu-279-01-04	Alt II	I-1	1	pitcher	B2	21	A8	A8	A V
Hu-280-01-01	Form I	I-1	6	olla	D2	15	B2	B2	A VII
Hu-280-01-02	Form III	I-3	12	olla	E2	25	B2	B2	F VII
Hu-280-01-03	Form I	I-1	6	olla	D1	23	A8	A2	L VII
Hu-280-01-04	Form III	I-3	12	olla	D1	20	A8	A8	K I
Hu-280-01-05	Form I	I-6	24	olla	B2	23	A6	A6	A VII
Hu-280-01-06	Form III	I-3	12	tazón	–	20b	B2	B2	I VI
Hu-280-01-07	Form I	I-1	2	olla	B2	12	A8	A8	A VI
Hu-280-01-08	Form III	I-3	15	tazón	B5	21	B2	B2	A VI
Hu-280-01-09	Form III	I-3	12	olla	A3	24	B2	B2	I VI
Hu-280-01-10	Form I	I-1	2	tazón	B5	26	B2	B2	A VII
Hu-280-01-11	Form III	I-2	9	tazón	B2	24	A2	A8	H VIII
Hu-280-01-12	Form II	II-6	44	bowl	A5	14	A2	A2	A VIII
Hu-280-01-13	Form III	I-3	15	olla	B2	20	A2	A2	C VI
Hu-280-01-14	Form III	I-3	12	open vessel	–	–	B2	B2	K I
Hu-280-01-15	Form II	II-7	47	closed vessel	–	–	E	A8	F VIII
Hu-280-01-16	Form II	II-6	45	olla	B2	16	A8	A8	A VII
Hu-280-01-17	Form I	I-1	3	jar	C3	15	A8	A8	A I
Hu-280-01-18	Form I	I-1	3	olla	D4	26	B2	B2	J I
Hu-280-01-19	Form II	II-7	47	jar	A	15	A6	A2	A I
Hu-280-01-20	Form II	II-5	41	olla	E2	25	A8	A8	A VIII
Hu-280-01-21	Form II	II-6	43	bowl	A4	20	A8	A2	B VII
Hu-280-01-23	Form III	I-3	12	tazón	B2	30	B2	B2	A I
Hu-280-01-24	Form II	II-4	40	tazón	B5	20	A8	A8	I II
Hu-280-01-25	Tiw II	II	6	kero	A2	12	B2	B2	A IX
Hu-280-01-26	Form II	II-6	45	olla	A2	26	A1	A1	A III
Hu-280-01-27	Form II	II-7	49	olla	C	14	B13	B13	D VI
Hu-280-01-28	Tiw I	III	11	kero	A1	9	B2	B2	F X
Hu-280-01-29	Tiw I	III	12	closed vessel	–	–	B2	A8	B X
Hu-280-01-30	Inca I	III-7	3	bowl	B1	16	A8	A8	C XI
Hu-280-01-31	Tiw I	III	12	kero	–	8b	B4	A8	J VIII
Hu-280-01-32	Tiw I	III	12	kero	–	9b	B2	A8	B X
Hu-280-02-01	Form I	I-1	1	closed vessel	–	–	A8	A8	A II
Hu-280-02-02	Form III	II-3	33	tazón	A1	16	B2	B4	P II
Hu-280-02-03	Form II	II-6	45	closed vessel	–	–	A8	A1	A III
Hu-281-01-06	Form III	I-2	9	tazón	B5	20	A2	A2	C I
Hu-281-01-07	Form I	I-1	6	jar	B2	16	A5	A5	A VII
Hu-281-01-08	Form III	I-2	9	bowl	B4	20	D	A2	M II
Hu-281-01-09	Form I	I-6	23	olla	B2	14	A6	A6	A VII
Hu-281-01-10	Form I	I-1	2	pitcher	B2	18	A2	A2	A VIII
Hu-281-01-11	Form II	II-7	49	olla	E2	16	B13	B13	A III
Hu-281-01-12	Form II	II-6	45	tazón	A5	12	E	E	A VII
Hu-281-02-04	Inca II	I-1	9	bowl	A3	13	B2	B2	A V
Hu-281-02-05	Inca I	III-7	3	closed vessel	–	–	A8	A2	A XI
Hu-285-01-01	Tiw I	III	11	kero	–	8b	A8	A8	O X
Hu-285-01-02	Inca III	I-4	29	bowl	E1	18	A1	A8	A IX
Hu-285-01-03	Inca III	II-5	7	open vessel	–	4b	B2	B2	A X
Hu-286-02-01	Alt I	I-3	11	jar	B1	11	A8	A8	A IX

Table A1 cont.

Specimen No.	Period	Ware Group[a]	Paste[a]	Form	Type[b]	Diameter[c] (cm)	Exterior Finish[d]	Interior Finish[d]	Firing[e]
Hu-298-01-01	Alt III	III	20	closed vessel	–	–	A2	A1	L VII
Hu-298-01-02	Alt II	I-2	5	bowl	B6	16	A1	A1	A V
Hu-298-01-03	Alt III	I-4	26	jar	B2	5	T + D	A1	A V
Hu-298-01-04	Inca I	III-7	3	bowl	A4	16	A8	A8	A II
Hu-298-01-05	Tiw II	I	4	closed vessel	–	–	A8	A1	A VI
Hu-298-01-06	Alt I	I-3	10	jar	B2	11	A8	A8	A VI
Hu-300-01-01	Inca I	I-4	27	bowl	A7	18	A1	A1	A V
Hu-300-01-02	Alt I	I-3	11	bowl	B1	13	A3	A3	A IX
Hu-300-01-03	Alt II	II	16	bowl	A1	15	A8	A8	A XI
Hu-300-01-04	Alt II	I-1	2	bowl	A1	15	T	A8	D IX
Hu-300-01-05	Alt I	I-3	10	closed vessel	–	–	B2	E	A VI
Hu-300-01-06	Alt I	I-3	12	jar	B1	15	A1	A1	D VI
Hu-304-02-01	Form II	I-4	39	tazón	B4	18	A1	T	C III
Hu-304-03-01	Form III	III	52	olla	A3	18	A1	A8 + R	F VI
Hu-304-03-02	Huaña I	II-2	29	jar	B2	16	A1 + R	A1	A VI
Hu-306-01-01	Form I	I-1	2	olla	A3	20	A2	A2	A VI
Hu-306-01-02	Inca II	I-3	8	bowl	A3	12	A2	E	A VII
Hu-306-01-03	Inca III	II-5	7	open vessel	–	–	A2	A2	A X
Hu-309-01-01	Form II	II-6	45	jar	A1	12	A1	A8	A III
Hu-309-01-02	Tiw I	III	12	kero	–	–	A3	A3	R X
Hu-310-01-01	Form I	I-6	24	olla	B2	21	A2	B2	A II
Hu-310-01-02	Huaña I	II-2	29	olla	B2	21	A2	B2	A II
Hu-310-01-03	Form I	I-6	25	open vessel	–	14b	B2	B2	A VII
Hu-310-01-04	Form II	II-7	49	closed vessel	–	7b	A9	A9	C VI
Hu-310-01-05	Huaña I	II-2	31	olla	B2	18	A2	A2	J III
Hu-310-01-06	Huaña I	II-2	31	olla	E2	13	A1	A1	A II
Hu-310-01-07	Form III	I-3	12	olla	A3	20	E	E	K I
Hu-310-01-08	Form II	II-6	43	jar	A	14	A1	A1	A VII
Hu-310-01-09	Form II	II-7	46	tazón	B8	24	B1	B13	A III
Hu-310-01-10	Form II	I-3	12	jar	C2	17	A2	B4	G II
Hu-310-01-11	Huaña I	II-2	31	closed vessel	–	9b	T	A8	I II
Hu-310-01-12	Form I	I-1	2	pitcher	B2	21	B2	B2	A II
Hu-310-01-13	Form I	I-1	2	olla	B2	18	A2	A2	A VII
Hu-310-01-14	Form I	I-1	2	olla	D4	20	A2	A2	A II
Hu-310-01-15	Inca II	I-1	9	tazón	B3	13	B2	B2	A V
Hu-310-01-17	Huaña II	I-1	14	closed vessel	–	–	B2	A8	A VII
Hu-310-01-18	Tiw II	I	3	closed vessel	–	–	B9	A2	C II
Hu-310-01-20	Tiw I	III	10	closed vessel	–	–	B9	A2	B VI
Hu-310-01-21	Tiw II	I	2	closed vessel	–	–	B2	A8	C VI
Hu-310-01-24	Tiw II	II	6	closed vessel	–	–	A8	A8	D VIII
Hu-310-01-25	Tiw I	III	10	closed vessel	–	–	B9	A2	A X
Hu-310-01-27	Tiw I	III	10	kero	–	–	B9	D	S X
Hu-310-01-28	Tiw I	III	10	kero	A1	12	B4	A2	F II
Hu-310-01-29	Tiw I	III	9	tazón	A1	13	B2	A2	J X
Hu-310-01-30	Tiw I	III	10	closed vessel	–	–	A8	A1	D X
Hu-310-01-31	Inca III	II-5	7	bowl	A2	15	B2	A1	E V
Hu-310-01-33	Inca III	II-5	7	bowl	A3	13	B2	B2	O I
Hu-310-01-34	Alt III	III	21	tazón	B1	14	A5 + D	A1	A IX
Hu-310-01-35	Inca III	II-5	7	bowl	E7	16	B2	B2	A V
Hu-310-01-36	Inca II	I-3	8	pitcher	B1	26	B2	B2	A V
Hu-310-01-38	Inca III	II-5	7	open vessel	–	4d	A8	B2	A X
Hu-310-01-39	Inca I	III-7	3	closed vessel	–	–	B2	A2	A XI
Hu-312-01-01	Alt III	III	18	bowl	A4	11	A1	A1	B VII
Hu-312-01-02	Inca II	II-5	7	bowl	B4	12	A2	A2	A X
Hu-313-01-01	Alt III	I-4	26	bowl	A2	14	A1	A1	A X
Hu-313-01-02	Alt III	III	20	bowl	A1	13	A1	A8	B VII
Hu-315-01-01	Form II	II-4	39	olla	A2	18	A1	A1	A IX
Hu-315-01-02	Form I	I-6	23	incense burner	—	–	A8	A8	P VII
Hu-316-01-01	Form III	I-3	12	olla	D3	28	A2	A2	G I
Hu-316-01-02	Form II	II-7	46	bowl	A1	11	A3	A8	D V
Hu-316-01-03	Form I	I-1	3	olla	A3	18	A5	A5	I VI
Hu-316-01-04	Form I	I-1	1	jar	A	15	A6	A6	A II
Hu-316-01-05	Form I	I-1	1	jar	A	11	A1	A1	E II
Hu-316-01-06	Form I	I-1	2	olla	B2	24	B2 + E	A8	A VII
Hu-316-01-07	Form III	I-2	9	bowl	A3	14	B2	B2	E II
Hu-316-01-08	Form I	I-1	2	olla	D3	11	B2	B2	A II
Hu-316-01-09	Alt III	III	21	jar	B2	11	A2	A2	E II
Hu-317-01-01	Inca I	III-7	3	closed vessel			A2	A8	A XI

Table A1 cont.

Specimen No.	Period	Ware Group[a]	Paste[a]	Form	Type[b]	Diameter[c] (cm)	Exterior Finish[d]	Interior Finish[d]	Firing[e]
Hu-317-01-04	Alt III	III	21	jar	A	10	A8	A8	B VII
Hu-318-01-01	Form III	II-3	33	bowl	B1	19	A8	A8	H II
Hu-318-01-02	Alt I	I-3	13	whorl	–	–	A8	A8	A IX
Hu-318-02-01	Alt II	I-1	2	pitcher	B1	18	A2	A2	F V
Hu-318-02-02	Alt II	I-2	8	closed vessel	–	–	E	A2	A I
Hu-318-03-01	Inca I	III-7	3	tazón	B1	10	A8	A8	C VIII
Hu-320-01-01	Alt III	I-4	25	bowl	B1	13	A1	A1	A X
Hu-320-01-02	Alt III	III	19	bowl	A2	12	A8	A8	X VIII
Hu-320-01-03	Alt II	I-2	7	open vessel	–	6b	T	A8	A VIII
Hu-320-01-04	Alt II	I-1	1	closed vessel	–	–	A1 + R	A1	T V
Hu-321-01-01	Alt I	I-3	13	bowl	B3	17	A1	A1	A IX
Hu-321-01-02	Alt II	I-1	4	pitcher	B1	22	A1	A1	A V
Hu-324-01-01	Form II	II-7	48	open vessel	–	–	B2	A8	A I
Hu-324-01-02	Alt III	III	21	jar	B2	8	A1 + T	A1 + T	B VII
Hu-324-01-3+5	Alt III	III	21	bowl	A1	13	T	T	A VIII
Hu-324-01-04	Alt I	I-3	11	bowl	B4	12	A1	A1	L IV
Hu-324-01-06	Alt I	I-3	12	bowl	B6	15	A1	A1	A III
Hu-325-01-01	Inca I	III-8	4	tazón	B1	14	A8	E	A XI
Hu-325-01-02	Inca I	I-4	27	tazón	B1	14	A8	A8	A V
Hu-325-01-03	Inca I	III-8	4	jar	B1	12	A8	A8	A XI
Hu-325-01-04	Alt III	III	20	tazón	A1	14	A1	A1	B VII
Hu-325-01-05	Alt I	IV	24	bowl	B1	14	T	A1	A VI
Hu-325-01-06	Inca I	I-4	29	bowl	–	3b	T	T	A IX
Hu-333-01-01	Alt I	I-3	11	closed vessel	–	–	T	A1 + T	A IX
Hu-336-01-01	Alt II	I-1	1	pitcher	B1	27	A1	A1	E V
Hu-336-01-02	Alt I	I-3	12	tazón	B1	12	T	A8	D VI
Hu-337-03-01	Inca I	I-4	27	tazón	B1	12	A8	A8	A V
Hu-337-03-02	Inca I	III-8	4	tazón	B1	12	A8	A8	A XI
Hu-337-03-03	Alt III	I-4	26	bowl	B1	15	A8	A8	A X
Hu-337-03-04	Alt II	I-1	4	pitcher	B2	20	A8	A8	A V
Hu-337-03-05	Alt II	I-2	5	jar	B2	5	T	A8	A V
Hu-337-03-06	Alt II	I-1	1	closed vessel	–	–	A8	A8	T V
Hu-337-03-07	Alt II	I-1	1	pitcher	B1	32	A1	A1	T V
Hu-337-03-09	Inca II	I-1	6	closed vessel	–	–	B9	A2	A V
Hu-340-01-03	Alt I	I-3	12	jar	B2	14	A1	A8	A I
Hu-340-02-01	Tiw I	III	9	kero	A1	12	A8	A8	A X
Hu-340-02-02	Tiw I	III	10	kero	–	8b	B2	B2	C X
Hu-340-03-01	Alt I	I-3	11	jar	B1	14	A5	A8	D VI
Hu-341-01-01	Inca II	I-3	8	closed vessel	–	–	B2	A2	A V
Hu-341-01-02	Alt II	I-2	5	bowl	B2	14	A1	A1	A V
Hu-341-01-03	Inca I	I-4	29	closed vessel	–	–	A8	A8	A V
Hu-343-01-01	Alt I	IV	24	bowl	B1	13	T	A8	F VI
Hu-343-01-02	Alt I	I-3	11	tazón	A1	12	D	D	A IX
Hu-343-01-03	Alt II	I-1	1	bowl	B1	11	T	A8	T V
Hu-343-01-04	Alt II	I-2	5	bowl	–	4b	T	A8	K V
Hu-343-01-05	Alt II	I-1	4	bowl	D2	8	A8	A8	A V
Hu-343-01-06	Alt I	I-3	13	whorl			A8	A8	A VIII
Hu-344-01-45	Inca I	I-4	27	closed vessel	–	–	B9	A2	A V
Hu-346-01-01	Alt III	I-4	26	bowl	B1	15	A1	A8	A X
Hu-346-01-02	Alt III	III	22	bowl	B2	11	T	A1	L VII
Hu-348-01-01	Inca I	I-4	27	kero	A1	15	B9	B9	A V
Hu-348-02-01	Alt II	I-1	12	tazón	A1	–	T	A1	A X
Hu-348-02-02	Inca I	I-4	27	bowl	–	6b	B2	B2	A V
Hu-348-02-03	Alt III	I-4	26	bowl	–	–	B2	B2	E VII
Hu-348-02-04	Alt III	III	20	closed vessel	–	–	B9	A2	B VII
Hu-348-02-05	Alt III	III	21	closed vessel			B2	B2	T V
Hu-348-02-61	Inca II	III-9	5	bowl	B1	17	A2	A2	A XIV
Hu-348-03-05	Alt I	II	17	adorno			A8	T	A VIII
Hu-348-03-06	Alt II	I-2	7	jar	MINI	1.6	A8	T	A IX
Hu-348-03-13	Inca I	III-7	3	jar	B2	14	A2	A2	A IX
Hu-348-03-14	Inca II	III-9	5	tazón	B1	17	A2	A2	A XIV
Hu-353-01-01	Inca I	III-8	4	bowl	A1	15	A8	A8	A XI
Hu-353-01-02	Inca I	III-7	3	bowl	A4	17	A8	A8	A XI
Hu-355-02-01	Inca II	I-3	8	bowl	A3	16	B2	B2	O II
Hu-355-02-02	Inca II	I-1	20	tazón	D2	18	B2	B2	A V
Hu-355-02-03	Inca II	I-3	8	bowl	A3	15	B2	B2	A V
Hu-355-02-04	Inca I	III-7	3	bowl	–	5b	A2	A2	A XI

Table A1 cont.

Specimen No.	Period	Ware Group[a]	Paste[a]	Form	Type[b]	Diameter[c] (cm)	Exterior Finish[d]	Interior Finish[d]	Firing[e]
Hu-355-02-05	Inca I	III-8	4	closed vessel	–	–	A8	A2	A XIII
Hu-355-02-06	Inca I	III-7	3	open vessel	–	8b	A2	A8	A XI
Hu-355-02-07	Inca I	III-8	4	bowl	A2	12	A2	A2	A XI
Hu-355-02-08	Inca II	I-1	20	bowl	B5	13	B2	B2	A V
Hu-355-02-09	Inca I	III-8	4	bowl	C1	17	A8	A8	A XI
Hu-358-01-01	Inca I	III-7	3	bowl	B6	17	A6	A2	A XI
Hu-358-01-02	Inca I	III-7	3	bowl	B4	15	A2	A2	J XI
Hu-369-01-01	Alt II	I-1	2	bowl	B1	16	T	A8	Q II
Hu-374-01-01/2	Inca I	III-7	3	bowl	A5	13	A8	A8	A XIII
Hu-376-01-01	Alt II	II	14	tazón	A1	18	A7	A2	A II
Hu-376-01-02	Alt II	II	15	bowl	A1	15	A2	A2	A XIV
Hu-376-01-03	Alt II	II	16	closed vessel	–	5b	A7	A2	A XI
Hu-378-01-01	Inca I	III-8	4	bowl	B4	15	A2	A2	A XI
Hu-378-01-02	Inca II	III-9	5	open vessel	–	–	A8	A8	I XIV
Hu-379-01-01	Inca I	III-7	3	closed vessel	–	–	B2	A8	A XI
Hu-382-01-01	Form III	I-3	12	pitcher	A3	28	B2	B2	E I
Hu-382-01-02	Form I	I-6	24	tazón	A3	12	B13	B13	A VII
Hu-382-01-03	Form I	I-1	7	tazón	B7	16	A1	A1	A VI
Hu-382-01-04	Form III	I-3	12	closed vessel	–	–	B13	B13	O VI
Hu-382-01-05	Form III	I-3	12	open vessel	–	–	B9	T	A VIII
Hu-382-01-06	Form III	I-1	3	open vessel	–	–	B2	E	A VI
Hu-382-01-07	Form II	II-6	43	bowl	E3	28	A8	B2	S VII
Hu-382-01-13	Form III	I-3	12	bowl	E3	16	B13	B13	I VI
Hu-382-01-14	Form II	II-7	47	jar	A	14	A1	A1	M II
Hu-382-01-15	Form II	II-7	47	olla	D2	27	B2	B2	A I
Hu-382-01-16	Form II	I-1	5	tazón	B2	26	B13	B13	E II
Hu-382-01-17	Form III	I-2	11	tazón	B8	34	B2	B2	D VI
Hu-382-01-18	Form I	I-1	1	closed vessel	–	–	A8	A8	A III
Hu-385-01-01	Alt II	I-1	2	jar	Miniature	3.5	T	T	S II
Hu-388-01-01	Form I	I-1	2	tazón	B7	30	A8	A8	C I
Hu-388-01-02	Alt III	III	20	open vessel	–	–	A2	A8	F VII
Hu-390-01-01	Form III	I-3	12	tazón	B7	28	A8	A1	I VI
Hu-390-01-02	Form III	I-3	12	closed vessel	–	–	A8	A8	Q II
Hu-390-01-03	Inca I	I-1	1	bowl	A1	–	B2	B2	A V
Hu-406-03-03	Form III	I-3	12	tazón	B5	26	B2	B2	D VI
Hu-406-03-24	Form III	I-3	12	tazón	–	–	A8	A8	O VI
Hu-406-03-25	Form I	I-1	1	olla	D1	14	B2	B2	A II
Hu-406-03-26	Form I	I-1	7	tazón	–	18b	B13	B13	A VI
Hu-406-03-27	Form III	II-3	35	trumpet	–	–	A8	D	E II
Hu-406-03-28	Form III	I-3	12	tazón	B6	22	B2	B2	H VIII
Hu-406-03-29	Form I	I-1	7	tazón	B5	14	B13	B13	A VI
Hu-406-03-30	Huaña I	II-1	17	tazón	B5	18	B13	B13	A IV
Hu-406-04-04	Form I	I-1	2	incense burner	–	12	B2	A2	C VI
Hu-406-05-01	Form I	I-1	6	trumpet	–	–	B2	A8	E VII
Hu-406-05-05	Huaña I	II-2	32	pitcher	A3	20	B2	B2	X II
Hu-410-01-01	Alt I	I-3	10	bowl	A2	14	A2	A2	D VI
Hu-410-01-02	Alt II	I-1	2	bowl	A1	14	B2	A2	A V
Hu-411-02-01	Alt II	I-1	3	bowl	A5	11	A8	A8	A V
Hu-411-02-02	Inca III	II-5	7	bowl	D1	14	B2	B2	A X
Hu-412-01-01	Form III	II-3	34	trumpet	–	–	A8	A8	D IX
Hu-412-01-02	Form II	II-6	43	jar	B2	14	A8	A8	A I
Hu-412-01-03	Form I	I-1	7	jar	C3	14	A1	A1	A III
Hu-412-01-04	Form I	I-6	23	closed vessel	–	–	B2	B2	A VII
Hu-414-01-05	Form III	I-3	12	tazón	–	28b	A8	B2	I VI
Hu-414-01-06	Inca III	II-5	7	bowl	A1	16	A8	A8	A X
Hu-414-01-04	Form III	III	51	tazón	B5	19	B2	B2	K I
Hu-414-01-05	Form III	I-3	12	tazón	–	28b	A8	B2	I VI
Hu-414-01-06	Inca III	II-5	7	bowl	A1	16	A8	A8	A X
Hu-414-01-16	Form III	II-3	33	olla	A2	22	B13	B13	A II
Hu-414-01-92	Form III	I-3	12	open vessel	–	–	B2	B2	I VI
Hu-415-01-01	Alt II	II	16	bowl	A1	15	A8	A8	A XI
Hu-416-01-01	Alt II	II	14	bowl	B2	20	A8	A8	A I
Hu-416-01-02	Tiw II	I	4	kero	A1	12	A8	A1	A VI
Hu-416-01-03	Tiw II	I	2	tazón	–	12b	A8	A2	H IX
Hu-416-01-04	Tiw II	I	3	tazón	A1	14	A8	A1	A I
Hu-416-01-05	Tiw II	I	1	closed vessel	–	–	A8	A1	A VI
Hu-418-01+03	Inca I	III-7	3	bowl	A2	12	A2	A2	V IX

Table A1 cont.

Specimen No.	Period	Ware Group[a]	Paste[a]	Form	Type[b]	Diameter[c] (cm)	Exterior Finish[d]	Interior Finish[d]	Firing[e]
Hu-418-01-02	Alt III	III	21	bowl	B2	13	A2	A8	A VIII
Hu-422-01-01	Alt II	I-1	2	spoon	–	–	A2	A2	A IX
Hu-422-01-02	Alt II	I-2	7	bowl	B1	6	T	A8	A IX
Hu-424-01-01	Inca II	I-1	3	bowl	C2	15	T	A2	A V
Hu-425-01-02	Alt II	II	15	tazón	A1	12	A2	A8	A XIV
Hu-425-01-03	Alt II	II	17	bowl	A1	12	A2	A2	A XIV
Hu-425-01-04	Alt II	I-1	2	bowl	B1	13	T	A2	T V
Hu-427-01-01	Inca III	IV-11	21	bowl	B2	12	B2	B2	A II
Hu-432-03-01	Inca I	III-7	3	tazón	A2	15	A2	A8	C XI
Hu-500-01-02	Alt II	II	14	open vessel	A1	7.5	A8	A2	A XIV
Hu-506-02-07	Form III	I-3	12	tazón	B9	29	B2	B2	V I
Hu-508-01-02	Form III	I-3	12	tazón	B2	32	B2	B2	Q II
Hu-508-01-04	Inca I	III-7	3	bowl	A5	16	A2	A2	I XI
Hu-508-01-05	Inca I	III-7	3	bowl	C1	12	A2	A2	B IX
Hu-508-01-07	Form II	II-7	46	tazón	B5	18	B2	B2	F VIII
Hu-508-01-12	Form III	I-3	14	tazón		26b	A8	B2	A VIII
Hu-508-03-01	Alt III	III	20	closed vessel	–	–	A8	T	R IX
Hu-521-01-01	Tiw I	III	12	kero		8b	B2	A8	F X
Hu-521-01-02	Form III	I-3	14	tazón	B4	14	A8	E	A VI
Hu-521-01-03	Form I	I-1	7	jar	B2	11	B2	A1	A VI
Hu-521-01-04	Form II	II-7	46	closed vessel	–	–	B2	A8	A III
Hu-521-01-05	Form II	II-7	47	jar	A	14	T	T	G I
Hu-521-01-06	Huaña II	I-1	11	closed vessel	–	–	T	T	D VI
Hu-521-01-07	Tiw II	II	4	open vessel		8b	T	T	A VI
Hu-537-01-03	Form I	I-1	3	bowl	A7	25	T	A2	D VI
Hu-537-01-04	Form II	I-2	11	olla	D3	36	B2	B2	A VIII
Hu-537-01-05	Form I	I-1	6	pitcher	A3	21	A2	A2	A VI
Hu-537-01-06	Huaña I	II-1	17	jar	B2	15	B2	B2	A IV
Hu-537-01-07	Form I	I-1	4	pitcher	B2	24	A1	A1	A II
Hu-537-01-08	Huaña I	II-2	32	jar	B2	16	A1	A1	A II
Hu-537-01-09	Form III	I-3	12	bowl	E3	19	B2	B2	O VI
Hu-537-01-10	Form II	II-7	47	bowl	A4	18	B13	B13	B III
Hu-537-01-11	Form I	I-2	11	bowl	A5	16	B2	B2	O VI
Hu-537-01-12	Form III	I-5	19	jar	B2	17	B2	B2	A X
Hu-537-01-13	Form I	I-1	7	pitcher	A1	18	T	T	A VI
Hu-537-01-14	Form I	I-6	23	tazón	B6	16	B2	B2	A VII
Hu-537-01-15	Form II	II-7	47	tazón	B2	18	A8	A8	E III
Hu-537-01-16	Form I	I-1	2	pitcher	B2	22	B13	B13	A VI
Hu-537-01-17	Form III	I-2	9	olla	B2	14	A2	A2	A VIII
Hu-537-01-18	Form I	I-6	25	tazón	B4	16	B13	B13	A VII
Hu-537-01-19	Huaña I	II-1	17	bowl	A5	14	B13	B13	A IV
Hu-537-01-27	Form III	I-3	12	open vessel	–	–	B13	B13	I VI
Hu-537-01-28	Huaña I	II-1	17	bowl	A1	20	B2	B2	A IV
Hu-537-01-34	Form I	I-1	7	open vessel			B13	B13	A VI
Hu-537-01-35	Form I	I-6	23	open vessel	–	–	B2	B2	A VII

[a]See descriptions in Chapter 2.
[b]See Figures 2.5–2.10.
[c]A "b" means that the base of the vessel was measured.
[d]See Figure 2.3.
[e]See Figure 2.2.

Appendix B
Lithic Materials from the Huancané-Putina Survey

Table B1. Metrics of illustrated lithic data.

Number		Height (mm)	Material	Color
Hu-	06-001	21	andesite	black
Hu-	099-01	27	quartz	10 R 2.5/2
Hu-	113-1	31	chert	10 YR 4/1
Hu-	113-2	25	quartz	white
Hu-	113-4	24	chert	10 YR 6/3
Hu-	113-5	46	basalt	7.5 YR 3/1
Hu-	113-6	30	quartz	10 R 3/3 white
Hu-	113-7	36	quartz	white
Hu-	113-9	33	slate	black
Hu-	113-11	14	quartz	white
Hu-	113-50	23	slate	black
Hu-	128-1	32	andesite	10 R 3/2
Hu-	219-03-1	25	chert	white
Hu-	246-1	18	quartz	white
Hu-	247-1	42	basalt	black
Hu-	247-2	33	quartz	white
Hu-	247-50	34	quartz	white
Hu-	247-51	40	quartz	white
Hu-	247-52	40	quartz	white
Hu-	276-1	30	andesite	gley 1 4/
Hu-	276-2	40	chert	gley 1 4/
Hu-	276-50	24	quartz	white
Hu-	276-51	37	quartz	white
Hu-	280-26	45	quartz	white
Hu-	280-50	44	basalt	black
Hu-	280-51	37	slate	black
Hu-	280-52	51	slate	black
Hu-	326-01-1	24	obsidian	black
Hu-	326-24	17	obsidian	black
Hu-	359-1	33	basalt	black
Hu-	359-2	33	quartz	7.5 YR 7/3
Hu-	368-1	29	quartz/chert	10 R 6/1
Hu-	368-2	22	quartz	white
Hu-	373-1	21	obsidian	black
Hu-	380-1	22	andesite	5 YR 5/1
Hu-	380-2	23	quartz	white
Hu-	381-1	22	quartz	white
Hu-	381-2	20	obsidian	black
Hu-	382-1	18	obsidian	black
Hu-	382-2	23	quartz	7.5 YR 8/1
Hu-	382-50	26	quartz	white
Hu-	382-51	31	quartz	7.5 YR 7/3
Hu-	382-52	19	quartz	white
Hu-	382-53	24	quartz	white
Hu-	382-54	20	obsidian	black
Hu-	382-55	18	obsidian	black
Hu-	391-1	32	basalt	gley 1 4/
Hu-	406-01	16	obsidian	black
Hu-	406-01-1	24	obsidian	black
Hu-	406-01-2	15	obsidian	black
Hu-	406-01-4	26	obsidian	black
Hu-	406-01-8	13	obsidian	black
Hu-	406-01-9	14	obsidian	clear
Hu-	406-01-10	16	obsidian	clear
Hu-	406-01-11	17	obsidian	black
Hu-	406-01-12	14	obsidian	black
Hu-	406-01-13	20	obsidian	black
Hu-	406-01-14	21	obsidian	black
Hu-	406-01-15	19	obsidian	black
Hu-	406-01-19	20	obsidian	black

Table B1 cont.

Number		Height (mm)	Material	Color
Hu-	406-01-20	17	obsidian	black
Hu-	406-02-1	22	obsidian	clear
Hu-	406-02-2	25	quartz	white
Hu-	406-02-3	49	slate	black
Hu-	406-02-4	14	obsidian	black
Hu-	406-03-2	17	obsidian	black
Hu-	406-05-1	46	quartz	10 YR 6/1
Hu-	412-1	34	chert	10 R 5/4
Hu-	412-2	15	obsidian	clear
Hu-	412-50	31	quartz	7.5 YR 6/1
Hu-	412-51	35	quartz	white
Hu-	417-1	17	quartz	5 Y 8/1
Hu-	422-1	28	andesite	10 YR 5/1
Hu-	448-1	19	quartz	2.5 YR 8/3
Hu-	448-2	24	quartz	10 R 4/6
Hu-	448-3	29	quartz	7.5 YR 8/2
Hu-	448-4	27	andesite	2.5 Y 6/1
Hu-	452-01	43	andesite	black
Hu-	459-1	21	chert	white
Hu-	463-2	39	quartz	white
Hu-	480-8	32	andesite	black
Hu-	482-1	37	chert	5 YR 7/4
Hu-	482-2	31	quartz	white
Hu-	482-3	32	chert	white
Hu-	482-4	29	quartz	white
Hu-	482-5	27	quartz	7.5 YR 7/6
Hu-	482-6	26	andesite	black
Hu-	482-7	31	chert	white
Hu-	484-1	29	chert	5 YR 7/6
Hu-	484-2	32	chert	5 YR 7/6
Hu-	484-3	34	quartz	5 YR 7/3
Hu-	484-4	37	quartz	5 YR 8/2
Hu-	484-5	34	quartz	7.5 YR 7/1
Hu-	484-7	33	quartz	5 YR 7/4
Hu-	484-8	32	quartz	2.5 YR 8/2
Hu-	484-9	23	basalt	5 YR 4/1
Hu-	484-10	23	basalt	black
Hu-	485-1	27	quartz	10 YR 6/1
Hu-	485-2	24	chert	10 YR 6/1
Hu-	485-3	18	basalt	black
Hu-	485-4	21	quartz	7.5 YR 7/1
Hu-	485-5	24	chert	7.5 YR 5/1
Hu-	485-6	31	chert	5 YR 8/1
Hu-	485-7	20	obsidian	black
Hu-	486-1	20	basalt	black
Hu-	486-2	37	quartz	2.5 Y 7/1
Hu-	486-3	31	andesite	2.5 Y 1
Hu-	486-4	21	quartz	white
Hu-	486-5	15	obsidian	clear
Hu-	486-6	12	obsidian	black
Hu-	486-7	8	obsidian	black
Hu-	487-1	16	basalt	black
Hu-	488-1	17	obsidian	black
Hu-	488-2	25	quartz	2.5 YR 8/3
Hu-	488-3	24	basalt	black
Hu-	489-2	21	quartz	10 YR 7/1
Hu-	489-3	31	quartz	7.5 YR 8/1
Hu-	489-4	30	chert	2.5 YR 8/3
Hu-	489-5	31	quartz	5 R 6/4
Hu-	489-6	33	basalt	black

Table B1 cont.

	Number	Height (mm)	Material	Color
Hu-	489-7	41	quartz	7.5 YR 8/1
Hu-	489-8	31	quartz	white
Hu-	489-9	15	basalt	5 Y 4/1
Hu-	490-1	25	basalt	black
Hu-	490-2	32	andesite	7.5 YR 4/1
Hu-	491-1	28	quartz	white
Hu-	492-1	20	basalt	black
Hu-	491-2	17	andesite	10 YR 4/1
Hu-	493-1	31	quartz	white
Hu-	502-02-1	25	andesite	7.5 YR 4/1
Hu-	506-02-1	23	obsidian	black
Hu-	506-02-99	52	quartz	white
Hu-	506-05-1	15	obsidian	black
Hu-	506-05-2	17	obsidian	black
Hu-	506-04-1	34	quartz	2.5 YR 7/3
Hu-	506-04-2	29	andesite	gley 1 4/
Hu-	506-04-3	16	obsidian	black
Hu-	506-04-4	23	quartz	5 YR 8/2
Hu-	506-05-3	18	obsidian	black
Hu-	506-05-4	14	obsidian	black
Hu-	506-05-5	12	obsidian	black
Hu-	506-05-6	11	obsidian	black
Hu-	506-06-1	12	obsidian	black
Hu-	506-06-2	15	obsidian	black
Hu-	506-06-3	12	obsidian	black
Hu-	506-06-4	10	obsidian	black
Hu-	506-06-5	9	obsidian	black
Hu-	506-06-6	22	obsidian	black
Hu-	506-06-7	23	basalt	black
Hu-	506-06-8	37	quartz	5 YR 8/3
Hu-	507-01-1	36	quartz	2.5 YR 7/3
Hu-	507-01-2	13	quartz	black
Hu-	508-1	16	obsidian	black
Hu-	508-2	18	obsidian	black
Hu-	508-3	17	obsidian	black
Hu-	508-4	19	obsidian	black
Hu-	508-5	18	obsidian	black
Hu-	508-6	16	obsidian	black
Hu-	508-7	12	obsidian	black
Hu-	508-9	14	obsidian	black
Hu-	521-1	26	quartz	white
Hu-	521-2	27	quartz	white
Hu-	521-3	19	quartz	white
Hu-	522-1	29	chert	white
Hu-	522-2	28	quartz	2.5 YR 7/3
Hu-	522-3	37	quartz	10 R 6/3
Hu-	537-2	35	quartz	white

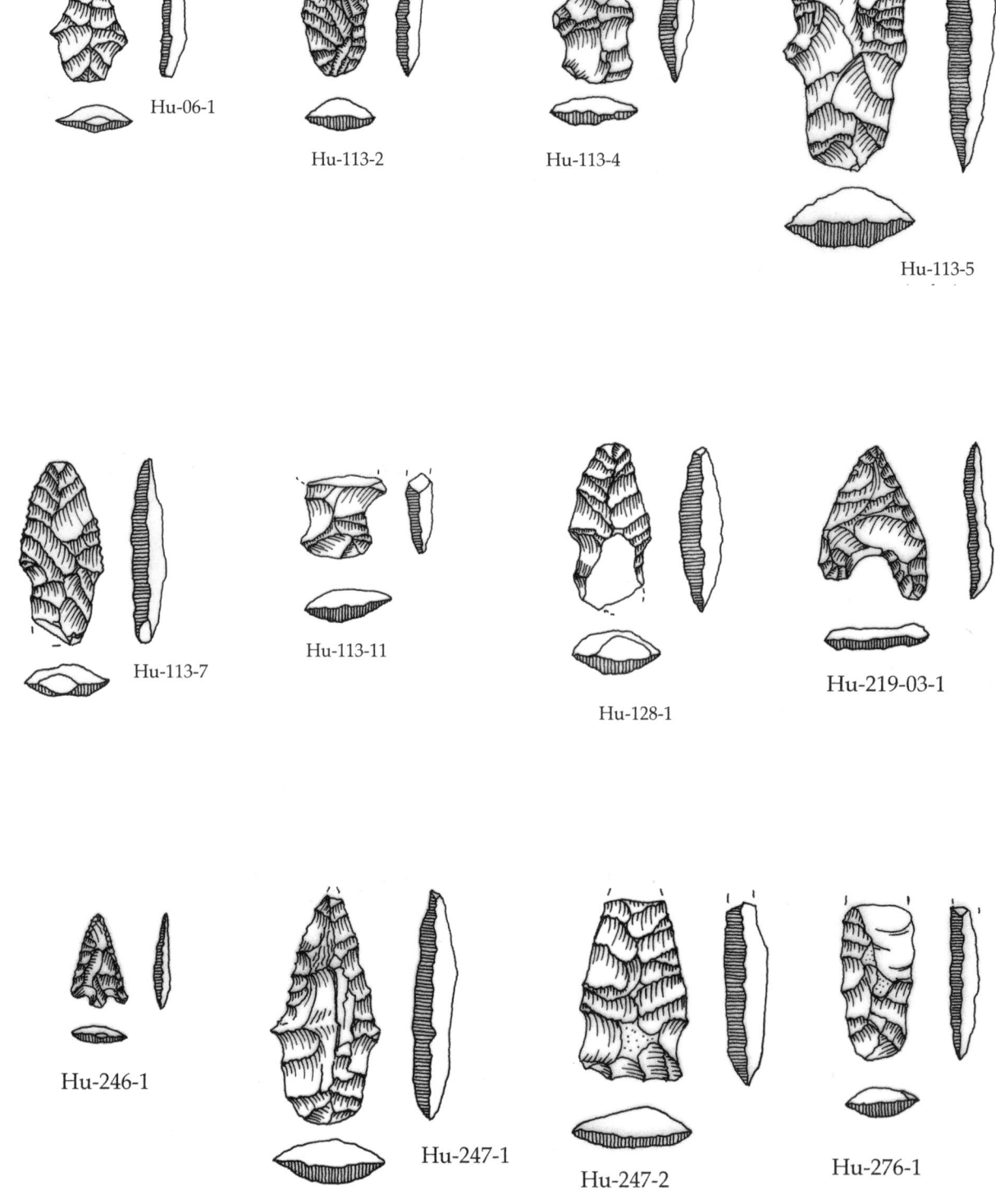

Figure B1. Bifaces from various sites in the survey area. See Table B1 for metrics.

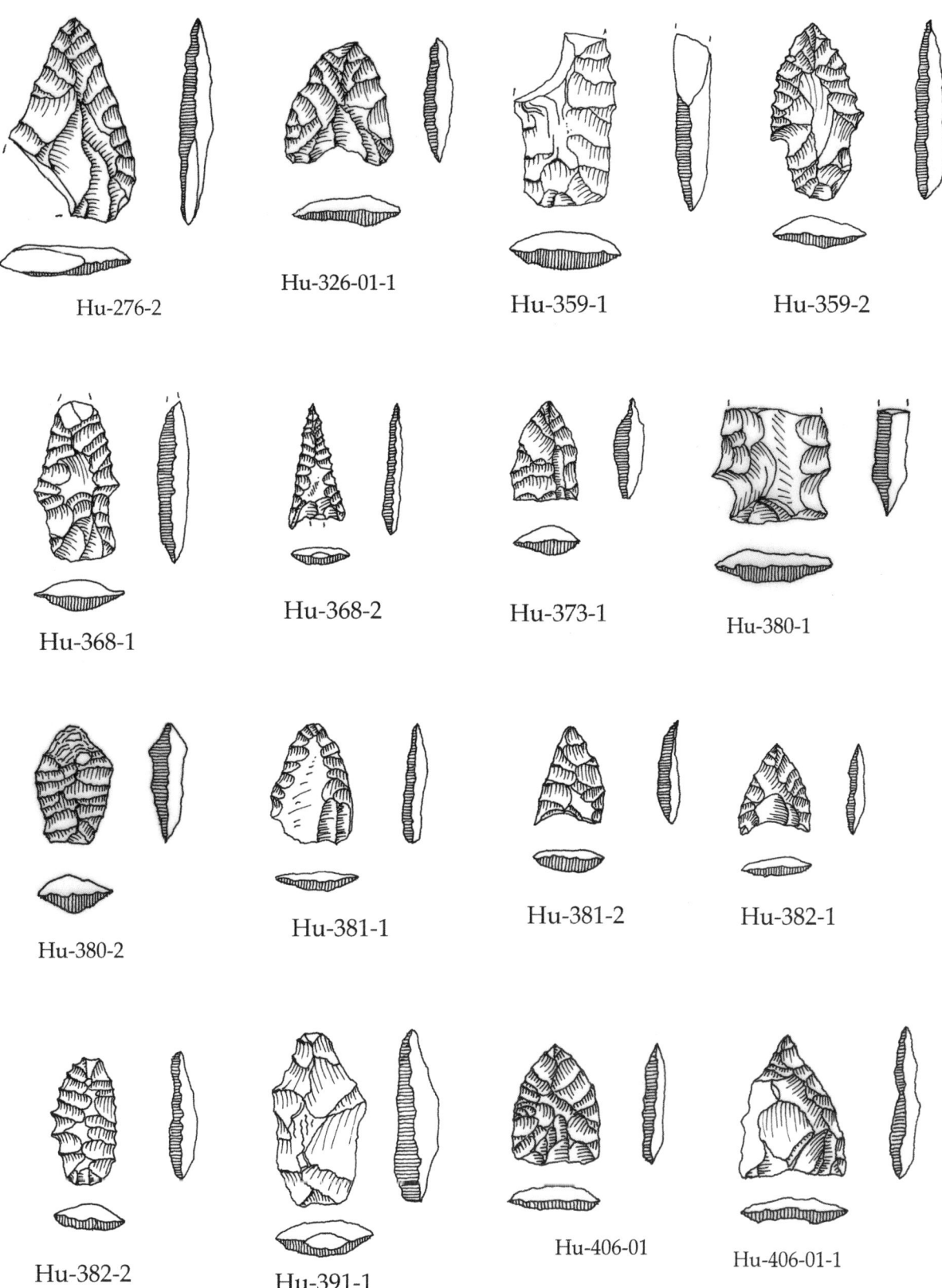

Figure B2. Bifaces from various sites in the survey area. See Table B1 for metrics.

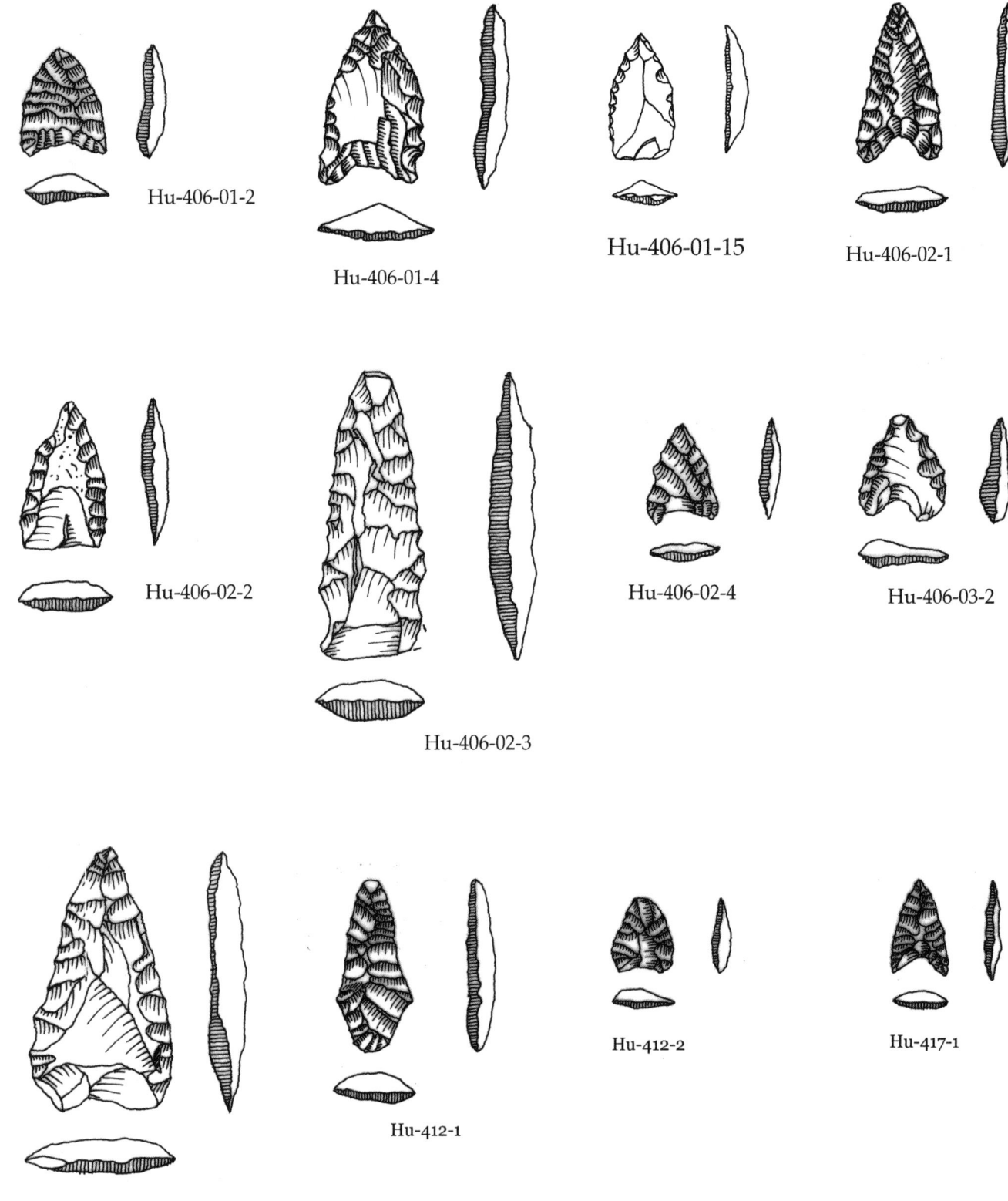

Figure B3. Bifaces from various sites in the survey area. See Table B1 for metrics.

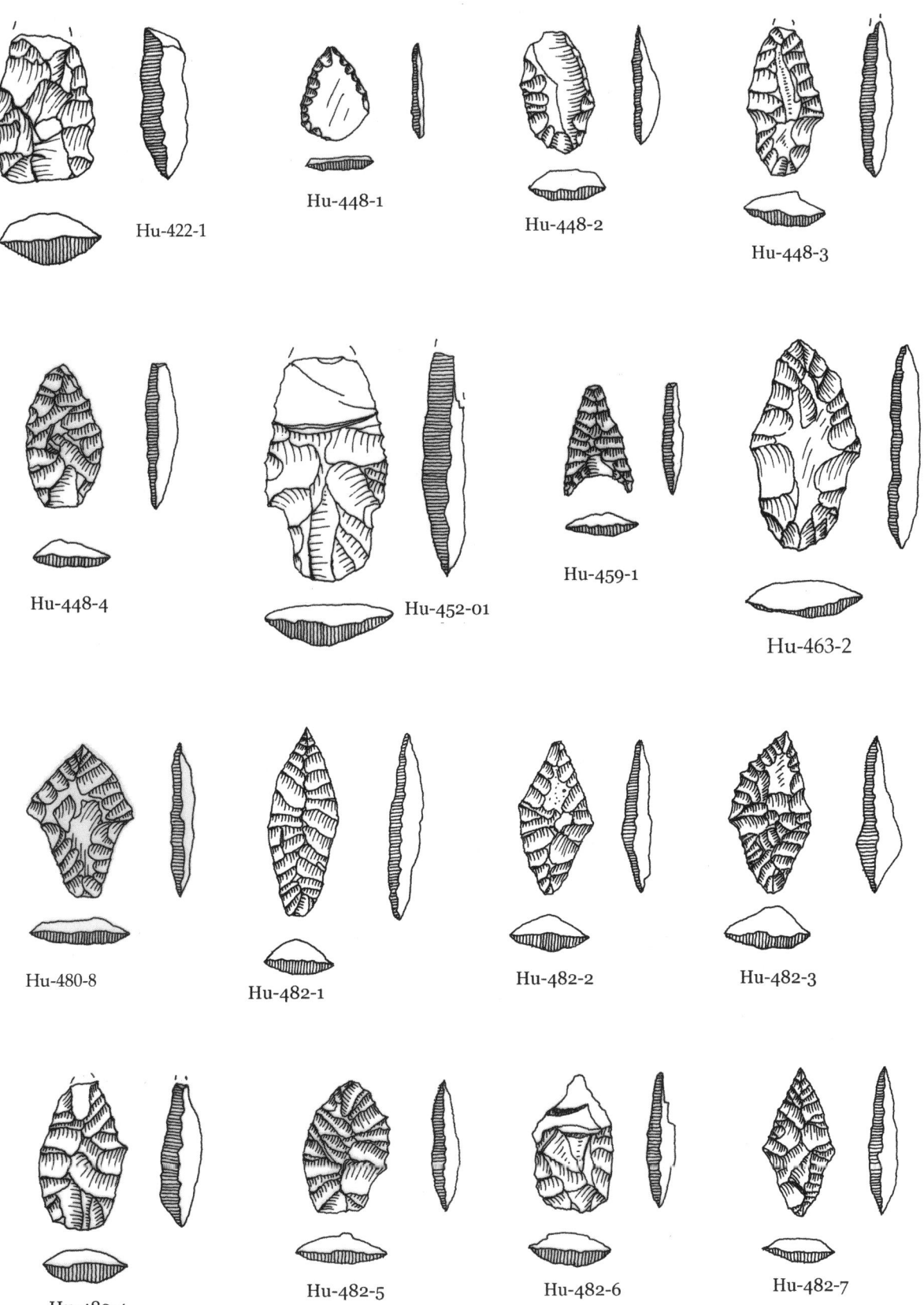

Figure B4. Bifaces from various sites in the survey area. See Table B1 for metrics.

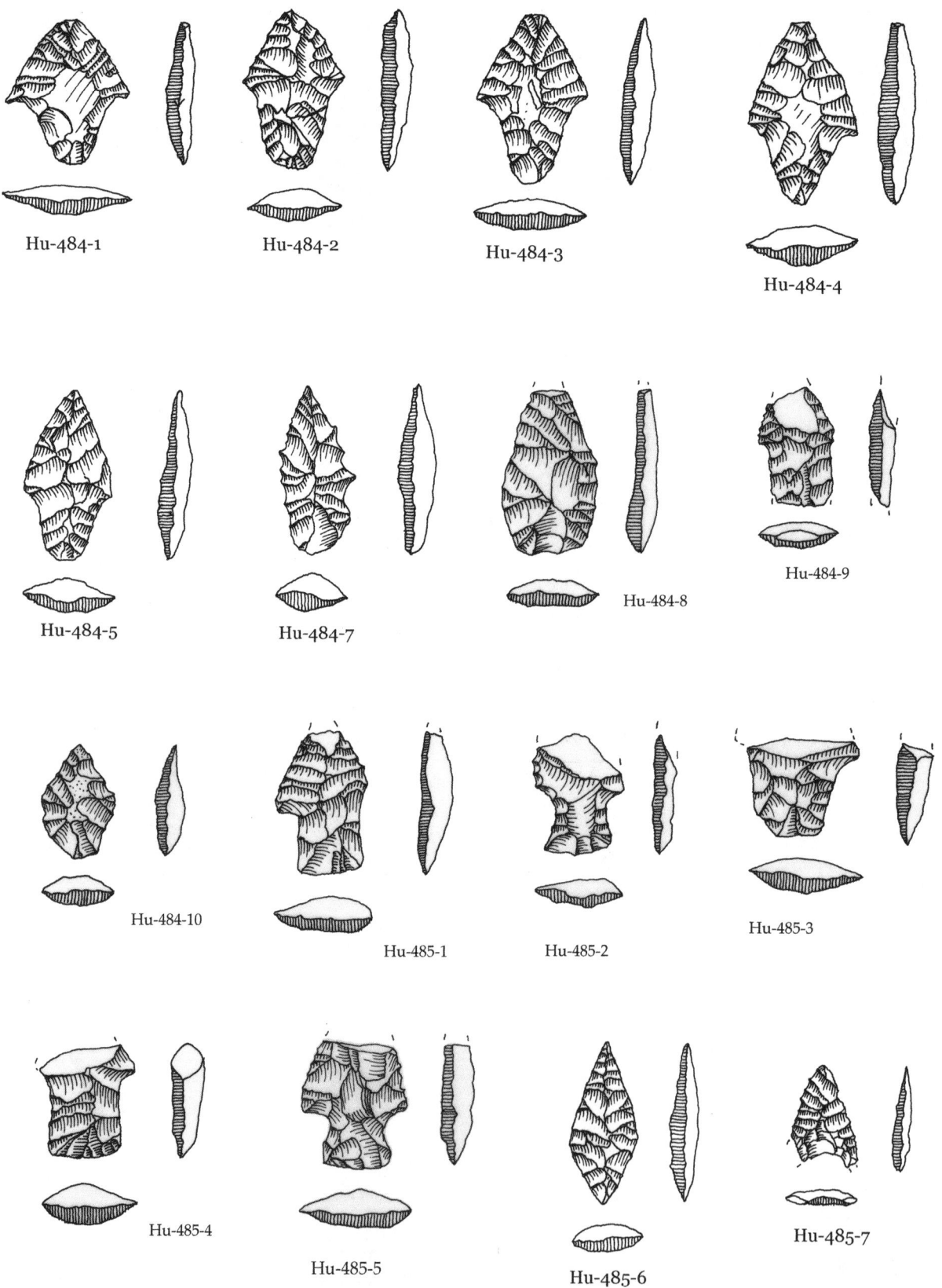

Figure B5. Bifaces from various sites in the survey area. See Table B1 for metrics.

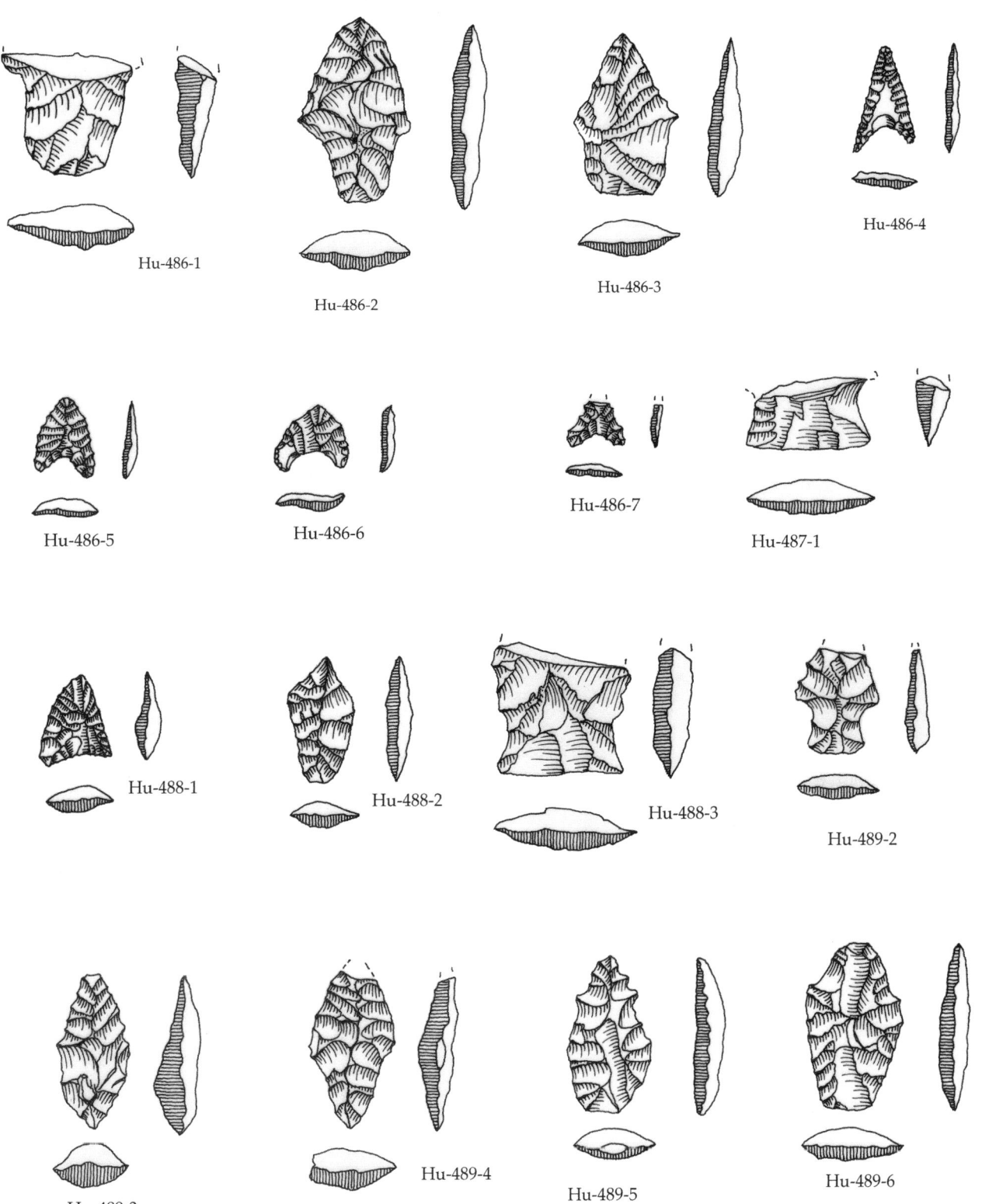

Figure B6. Bifaces from various sites in the survey area. See Table B1 for metrics.

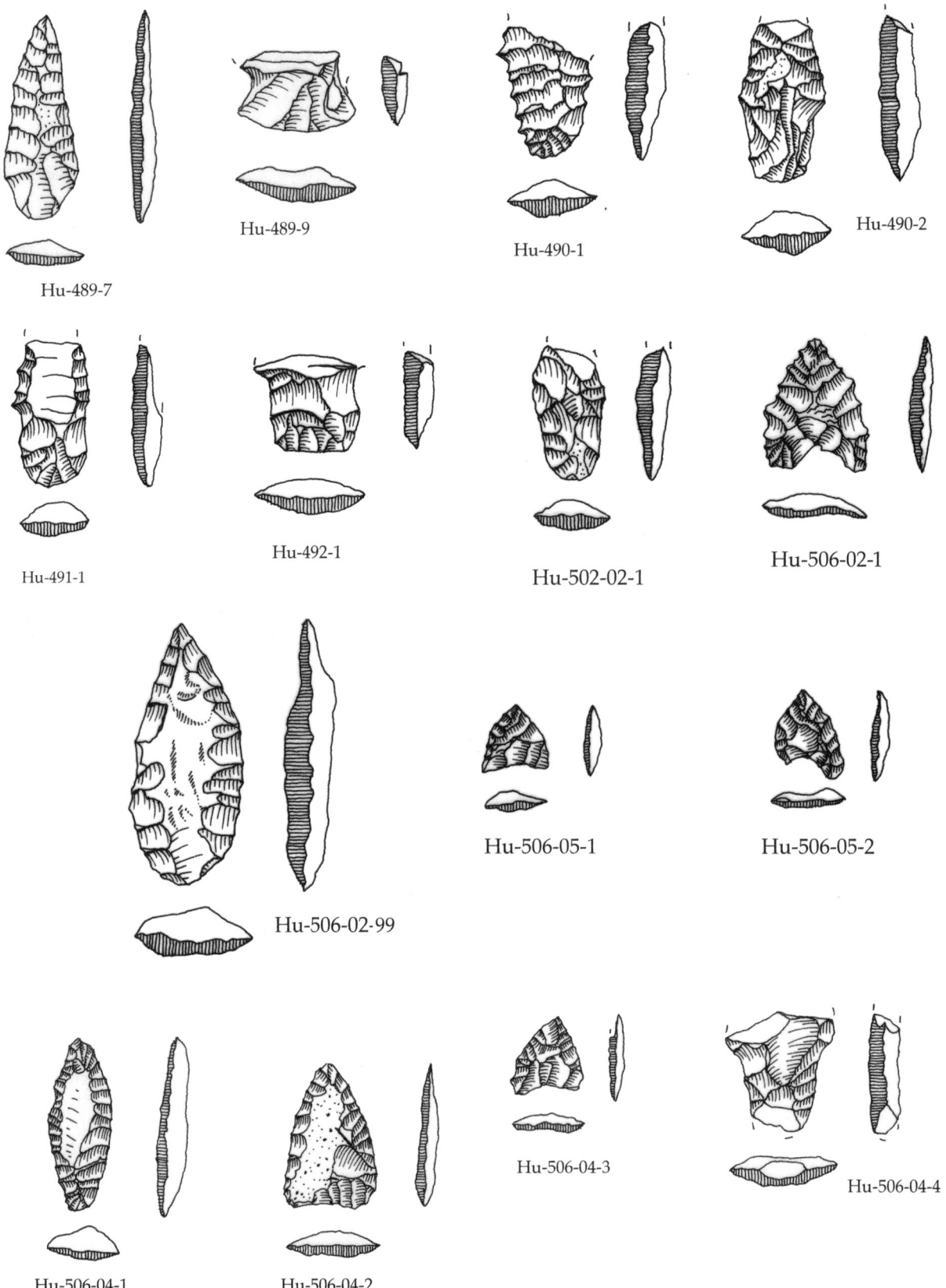

Figure B7. Bifaces from various sites in the survey area. See Table B1 for metrics.

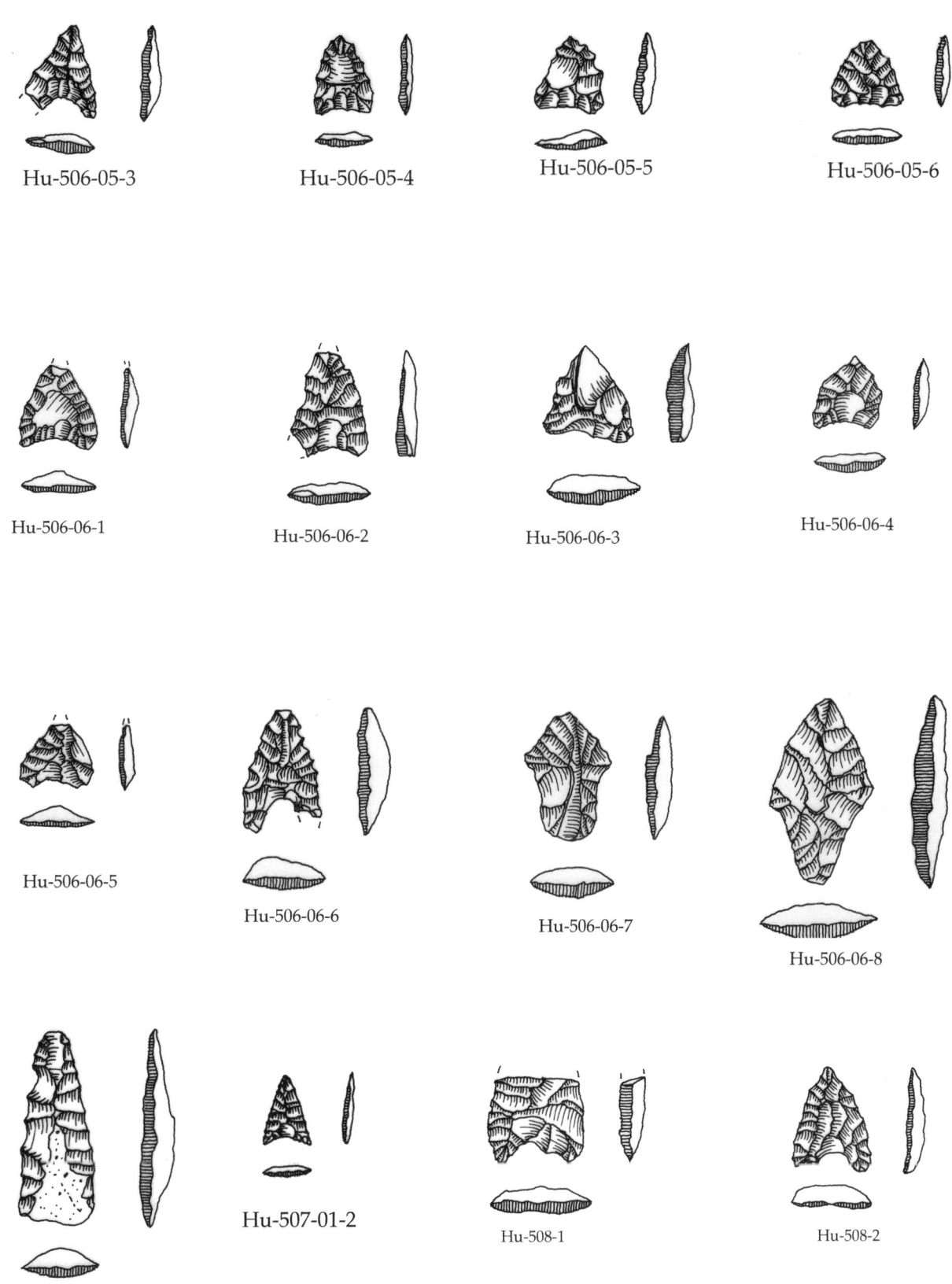

Figure B8. Bifaces from various sites in the survey area. See Table B1 for metrics.

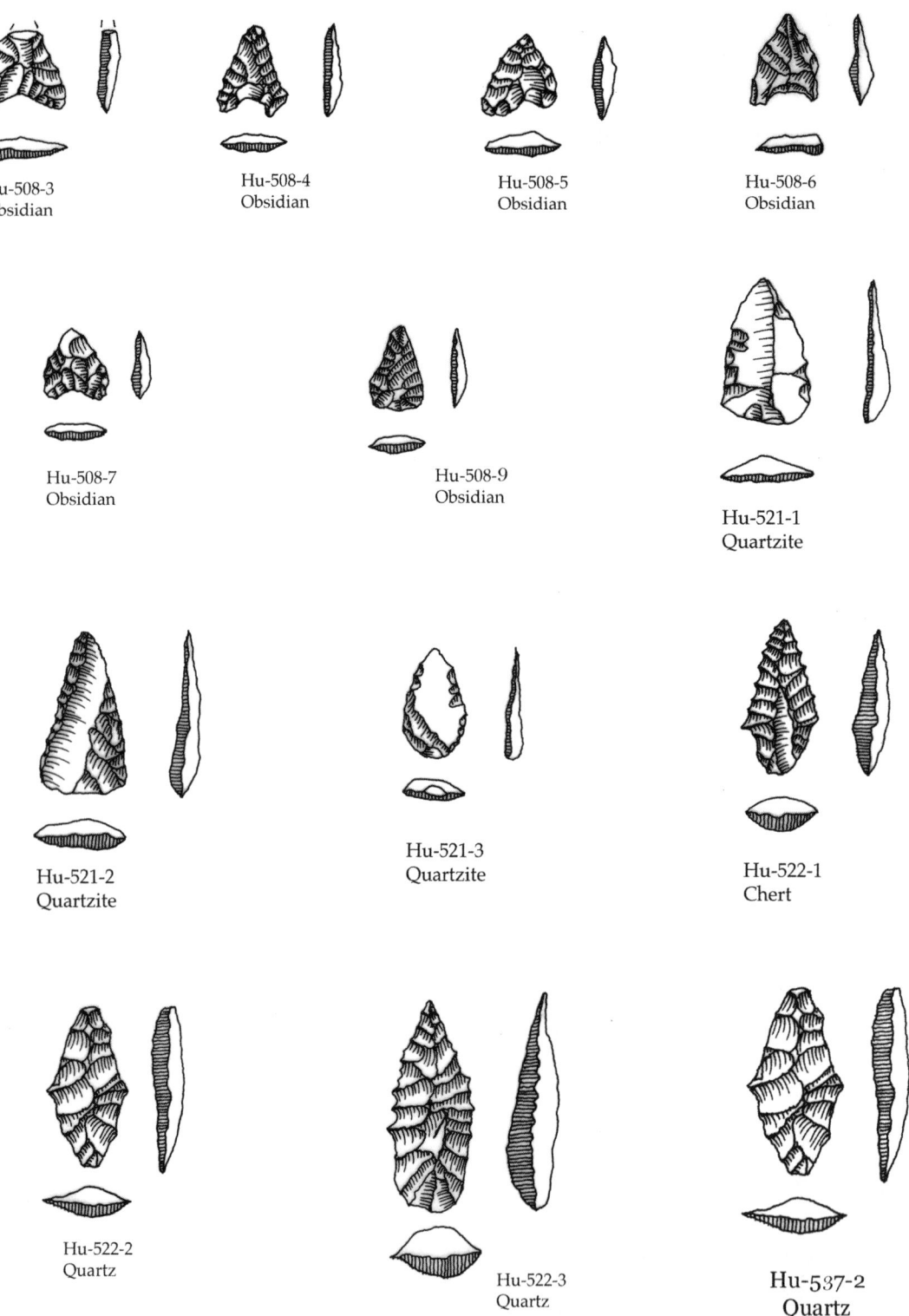

Figure B9. Bifaces from various sites in the survey area. See Table B1 for metrics.

References Cited

Abbott, Mark B., Michael W. Binford, Mark Brenner, and Kerry R. Kelts
1997 A 3500 ^{14}C yr high-resolution record of water-level changes in Lake Titicaca, Bolivia/Peru. *Quaternary Research* 47:169–80.

Abbott, Mark B., Brent B. Wolfe, Alexander P. Wolfe, Geoffrey O. Seltzer, Ramón Aravena, Brian G. Mark, Pratigya J. Polissar, Donald T. Rodbell, Harry D. Rowe, and Mathias Vuille
2003 Holocene paleohydrology and glacial history of the central Andes using multiproxy lake sediment studies. *Palaeogeography, Palaeoclimatology, Palaeoecology* 194:123–38.

Albarracin-Jordan, Juan, and James Edward Mathews
1990 *Asentamientos prehispánicos del Valle de Tiwanaku*, vol. 1. Producciones CIMA, La Paz.

Alconini, Sonia
1995 *Rito, símbolo e historia en la Pirámide de Akapana, Tiwanaku: Un análisis de cerámica ceremonial prehispánica*. Editorial Acción, La Paz.

Aldenderfer, Mark S.
1989 The Archaic period in the south-central Andes. *Journal of World Prehistory* 3(2):117–58.

Aldenderfer, Mark S., and Luis Flores Blanco
2011 Reflexiones para avanzar en los estudios del período arcaico en los Andes centro–sur. *Chungará* 43 (número especial 1):531–50.

Amat Olazabal, Hernán
1977 Los reinos altiplánicos del Titicaca. *Rumi* 8:1–8.

Arkush, Elizabeth
2005a Colla Fortified Sites: Warfare and Regional Power in the Late Prehispanic Titicaca Basin, Peru. PhD dissertation, Department of Anthropology, University of California, Los Angeles.
2005b Inka ceremonial sites in the southwest Titicaca Basin. In *Advances in Titicaca Basin Archaeology–I*, edited by Charles Stanish, Amanda Cohen, and Mark Aldenderfer, pp. 209–42. Cotsen Institute of Archaeology, University of California, Los Angeles.
2008 War, chronology, and causality in the Titicaca Basin. *Latin American Antiquity* 19(4):339–73.
2011 *Hillforts of the Ancient Andes: Colla Warfare, Society, and Landscape*. University Press of Florida, Gainesville.

Augustyniak, Szymon
2004 Análisis cronológico del estado Tiwanaku. *Chungará* (Arica) 36(1):19–35 (online). Accessed December 20, 2010.

Baker, Paul A., Sherilyn C. Fritz, Stephen J. Burns, Erik Ekdahl, and Catherine A. Rigsby
2009 The nature and origin of decadal to millennial scale climate variability in the southern tropics of South America: The Holocene record of Lago Umayo, Peru. In *Past Climate Variability in South America and Surrounding Regions: From the Last Glacial Maximum to the Holocene*, pp. 301–22. Developments in Paleoenvironmental Research, vol. 14. Springer, New York.

Bauer, Brian, and Charles Stanish
2001 *Ritual and Pilgrimage in the Ancient Andes: The Islands of the Sun and the Moon.* University of Texas Press, Austin.

Bennett, Wendell C. (editor)
1948 *A Reappraisal of Peruvian Archaeology.* Memoirs of the Society for American Archaeology, no. 4. Society for American Archaeology; Institute of Andean Research, Menasha, Wisconsin.

Bermann, Marc
1994 *Lukurmata: Household Archaeology in Prehispanic Bolivia.* Princeton University Press, Princeton.

Bertonio, Ludovico
1956 [1612] *Vocabulario de la lengua Aymara.* CERES, La Paz.

Betanzos, Juan de
1996 [1551–1557] *Narrative of the Incas*, translated and edited by D. Buchanan and R. Hamilton. University of Texas Press, Austin.

Binford, Michael, and Alan Kolata
1996 The natural and human setting. In *Tiwanaku and Its Hinterland. Archaeology and Paleoecology of an Andean Civilization*, edited by Alan Kolata, pp. 23–56. Smithsonian Institution, Washington, D.C.

Boulange, Bruno, and Jaen E. Aquize
1981 Morphologie, hydrographie et climatologie du lac Titicaca et de son bassin versant. *Revue d'Hydrobiologie Tropicale* 14(4):269–87.

Burger, Richard L., Karen L. Mohr Chávez, and Sergio Chávez
2000 Through the glass darkly: Prehispanic obsidian procurement and exchange in southern Peru and northern Bolivia. *Journal of World Prehistory* 14(3):267–362.

Cabello de Balboa, Miguel
1602–1603 Orden y traza para descubrir y poblar la tierra de los Chunchos y otras provincias. In *Relaciones geográficas de Indias*, *Perú*, vol. 2. Biblioteca de Autores Españoles, Madrid.

Chávez, Cecilia
2008 Analysis of Ceramic Materials from the Middle and Lower Río Huancané Subdrainage, Department of Puno, Peru. Accessed January 11, 2011. http://www.sscnet.ucla.edu/ioa/collasuyu.

Chávez, Sergio
1975 The Arapa and thunderbolt stelae: A case of stylistic identity with implications for Pucara influences in the area of Tiahuanaco. *Ñawpa Pacha* 13:3–26.
1981 Notes on some stone sculpture from the northern Lake Titicaca Basin. *Ñawpa Pacha* 19:79–91.
1984 La piedra del rayo y la estela de Arapa: Un caso de identidad estilística, Pucara-Tiahuanaco. *Arte y Arqueología* 8–9:1–27.
1988 Archaeological reconnaissance in the province of Chumbivilcas, south highland Peru. *Expedition* 30(3):27–38.

Chávez, Sergio J., and Karen L. Mohr Chávez
1970 Newly discovered monoliths from the highlands of Puno, Peru. *Expedition* 12(4):25–39.
1975 A carved stela from Taraco, Puno, Peru and the definition of an early style of stone sculpture from the altiplano of Peru and Bolivia. *Ñawpa Pacha* 13:45–83.

Cieza de León, Pedro de
1553 La Crónica del Perú. In *Crónica de la Conquista del Perú*. Editorial Nueva España, S.A., México D.F.

Cipolla, Lisa M.
2005 Preceramic period settlement patterns in the Huancané-Putina river valley, northern Titicaca Basin, Peru. In *Advances in Titicaca Basin Archaeology–I*, edited by Charles Stanish, Amanda Cohen, and Mark Aldenderfer, pp. 55–63. Cotsen Institute of Archaeology, University of California, Los Angeles.

Cobo, Bernabé
1956 [1653] *Historia de Nuevo Mundo*, edited by F. Mateos. Biblioteca de Autores Españoles. Ediciones Atlas, Madrid.

Cohen, Amanda
2010 Ritual and Architecture in the Titicaca Basin: The Development of the Sunken Court Complex in the Formative Period. PhD dissertation, Department of Anthropology, University of California, Los Angeles.

Cook, David N. (compiler)
1975 *Tasa de la Visita General de Francisco de Toledo.* Universidad Nacional Mayor de San Marcos, Lima.

Craig, Nathan M.
2005 The Formation of Early Settled Villages and the Emergence of Leadership: A Test of Three Theoretical Models in the Rio Ilave, Lake Titicaca Basin, Southern Peru. PhD dissertation, Department of Anthropology, University of California, Santa Barbara.

Craig, Nathan, Mark Aldenderfer, Paul Baker, and Catherine Rigsby
2010 Terminal Archaic settlement pattern and land cover change in the Rio Ilave, southwestern Lake Titicaca Basin, Peru. *The Archaeology of Anthropogenic Environments*, edited by Rebecca Dean, pp. 35–53. Southern Illinois University, Carbondale.

Craig, Nathan, Mark S. Aldenderfer, Catherine A. Rigsby, Paul A. Baker, and Luis Flores Blanco
2011 Geologic constraints on rain-fed qocha reservoir agricultural infrastructure, northern Lake Titicaca Basin, Peru. *Journal of Archaeological Science* 38(11):2897–907.

D'Altroy, Terence N.
2002 *The Incas.* Blackwell Publishing, Oxford.

Dejoux, Claude, and Andre Iltis
1991 Introduction. In *El Lago Titicaca*, edited by C. Dejoux and A. Iltis, pp. 11–16. ORSTOM/HISBOL, La Paz.

Erickson, Clark L.
1987 The dating of raised field agriculture in the Lake Titicaca Basin, Peru. In *Pre-Hispanic Agricultural Fields in the Andean Region*, edited by W. M. Denevan, K. Mathewson, and K. Knall, pp. 373–84. BAR International Series, vol. 359. Oxford.
1988a An Archaeological Investigation of Raised Field Agriculture in the Lake Titicaca Basin of Peru. PhD dissertation, Department of Anthropology, University of Illinois, Champaign-Urbana. University Microfilms #8908674, Ann Arbor.
1988b Raised field agriculture in the Lake Titicaca Basin. *Expedition* 30(3):8–16.
1992 Prehistoric landscape management in the Andean highlands: Raised field agriculture and its environmental impact. *Population and Environment* 13(4):285–300.
2000 The Lake Titicaca Basin. A pre-Columbian built landscape. In *Imperfect Balance: Landscape Transformations in the Precolumbian Americas*, edited by David L. Lentz, pp. 211–356. Columbia University Press, New York.

Flores Ochoa, Jorge A., and Magno Percy Paz Flores
1983 La agricultura en lagunas del altiplano. *Ñawpa Pacha* 21:127–52.

Griffin, Arthur F., and Charles Stanish
2007 An agent-based model of prehistoric settlement patterns and political consolidation in the Lake Titicaca Basin of Peru and Bolivia. *Structure and Dynamics* 2.2 (online). https://escholarship.org/uc/item/2zd1t887.

Henderson, D. Michael
2012 The ancient raised fields of the Taraco region of northern Lake Titicaca. In *Advances in Titicaca Basin Archaeology–III*, edited by A. Vranich, E. Klarich, and C. Stanish, pp. 221–64. Memoirs, no. 51. Museum of Anthropology, University of Michigan, Ann Arbor.

Janusek, John W.
1994 Tiwanaku and its precursors: Recent research and emerging perspectives. *Journal of Archaeological Research* 12(2):121–83.
2003 Vessels, time, and society: Toward a chronology of ceramic style in the Tiwanaku heartland. In *Tiwanaku and Its Hinterland: Archaeology and Paleoecology of an Andean Civilization, Vol. 2*, edited by Alan Kolata, pp. 30–92. Smithsonian Institution Press, Washington, D.C.
2004 *Identity and Power in the Ancient Andes: Tiwanaku Cities through Time*. Routledge, New York.

Julien, Catherine
1983 *Hatunqolla: A View of Inca Rule from the Lake Titicaca Region*. Publications in Anthropology, vol. 15. University of California Press, Berkeley.

Kidder II, Alfred
1943 *Some Early Sites in the Northern Lake Titicaca Basin*. Papers of the Peabody Museum, vol. 27, nos. 1–4. The Museum, Cambridge, Massachusetts.

Klink, Cynthia, and Mark Aldenderfer
2005 A projectile point chronology for the south-central Andean highlands. In *Advances in Titicaca Basin Archaeology–I*, edited by Charles Stanish, Amanda Cohen, and Mark Aldenderfer, pp. 25–54. Cotsen Institute of Archaeology, University of California, Los Angeles.

Klarich, Elizabeth
2004 ¿Quienes eran los invitados? Cambios temporales y funcionales de los espacios públicos de Pukara como reflejo del cambio de las estrategias de liderazgo durante el periodo formativo tardío. *Boletín de Arqueología PUCP* 9:185–206.
2005 From the Monumental to the Mundane: Defining Early Leadership Strategies at Late Formative Pukara, Peru. PhD dissertation, Department of Anthropology, University of California, Santa Barbara.

Las Casas, Bartolomé de
1939 [ca. 1550] *Las antiguas gentes del Perú. Colección de libros y documentos referentes a la historia del Perú*, serie 2, tomo 11, capítulos 56–261. Imprenta y Librería Sanmarti y Cs. de Apologetica historia sumaria, Lima.

Levine, Abigail
2012 Competition, Cooperation, and the Emergence of Regional Centers in the Northern Lake Titicaca Basin, Peru. PhD dissertation, Department of Anthropology, University of California, Los Angeles.

Levine, Abigail, Charles Stanish, P. Ryan Williams, Cecilia Chávez, and Mark Golitko
2013 Trade and early state formation in the northern Titicaca Basin, Peru. *Latin American Antiquity* 24(3):289–308.

Lizarraga, Reginaldo de
1968 [1605] *Descripción breve de toda la tierra del Perú, Tucuman, Río de La Plata y Chile*, pp. 1–213. Biblioteca de Autores Españoles, tomo 216. Ediciones Atlas, Madrid.

Lumbreras, Luis Guillermo
1974 Los reinos post-Tiwanaku en el área altiplánica. *Revista del Museo Nacional* 40:55–85.

Lumbreras, Luis, and Hernán Amat
1968 Secuencia arqueológica del altiplano occidental del Titicaca. *37th International Congress of Americanists, Actas y Memorias* 2:75–106. Buenos Aires.

Lynch, Thomas
1981 Current research: Andean South America. *American Antiquity* 46(1):201–4.

Mannheim, Bruce
1991 *The Language of the Inka since the European Invasion*. University of Texas Press, Austin.

Marcus, Joyce
2008 The archaeological evidence for social evolution. *Annual Review of Anthropology* 37:251–66.

Mohr, Karen
1966 An Analysis of the Pottery of Chiripa, Bolivia: A Problem in Archaeological Classification and Inference. Master's thesis, Department of Anthropology, Graduate School of Arts and Sciences, University of Pennsylvania.

Mohr Chávez, Karen L.
1988 The significance of Chiripa in Lake Titicaca Basin developments. *Expedition* 30(3):17–26.
1992 The organization of production and distribution of traditional pottery in south highland Peru. In *Ceramic Production and Distribution: An Integrated Approach*, edited by George Bey and Christopher Pool, pp. 49–92. Westview Press, Boulder, Colorado.

Moseley, Michael E.
2013 Stylistic variation and seriation. In *Visions of Tiwanaku*, edited by A. Vranich and C. Stanish, pp. 11–25. Cotsen Institute of Archaeology, University of California, Los Angeles.

Mujica, Elias
1978 Nueva hipótesis sobre el desarrollo temprano del altiplano del Titicaca y de sus áreas de interacción. *Arte y Arqueología* (La Paz, 1978)5–6:285–308.
1985 Altiplano-coast relationships in the south-central Andes: From indirect to direct complementarity. In *Andean Ecology and Civilization*, edited by Shozo Masuda, Izumi Shimada, and Craig Morris, pp. 103–40. University of Tokyo Press, Tokyo.
1987 Cusipata: Una fase pre-Pucara en la cuenca norte del Titicaca. *Gaceta Arqueológica Andina* 13:22–28.
1990 Pukara: Une société complexe ancienne du bassin septentrional du Titicaca. In *3000 ans d'histoire Inca-Peru*, edited by S. Purin, pp. 156–77. Musées Royaux d'Arte et d'Histoire, Brussels.

Murra, John V.
1968 An Aymara kingdom in 1567. *Ethnohistory* 15:115–51.

Murra, John V., and Craig Morris
1976 Dynastic oral tradition, administrative records, and archaeology in the Andes. *World Archaeology* 7(3):269–79.

Murra, John V., Nathan Wachtel, and Jacques Ravel (editors)
1986 *Anthropological History of Andean Polities*. Cambridge University Press, Cambridge.

Myres, Joel, and Rolando Paredes
2005 Pukara influence on Isla Soto, Lake Titicaca, Peru. In *Advances in Titicaca Basin Archaeology–I*, edited by Charles Stanish, Amanda B. Cohen, and Mark S. Aldenderfer, pp. 95–102. Cotsen Institute of Archaeology, University of California, Los Angeles.

Neira Avendaño, Máximo
1967 Informe preliminar de las investigaciones arqueológicas en el Departamento de Puno. Paper presented at the Anales del Instituto de Estudios Socio-Económicos, Universidad Nacional Técnica del Altiplano, Puno.

Niles, Susan
1987 The temples of Amantaní. *Archaeology* 40(6):30–37.

Núñez del Prado, Juan V.
1972 Dos nuevas estatuas del estilo Pucara en Chumbivilcas, Perú. *Ñawpa Pacha* 9:23–32.

Núñez Mendiguri, M., and Rolando Paredes
1978 Estévez: Un sitio de ocupación Tiwanaku. In *III Congreso Peruano del Hombre y la Cultura Andina*, vol. 2, edited by Ramiro Matos Mendieta, pp. 757–64. Lima.

Plourde, Aimée M.
2006 Prestige Goods and Their Role in the Evolution of Social Ranking: A Costly Signaling Model with Data from the Formative Period of the Northern Lake Titicaca Basin, Peru. PhD dissertation, Department of Anthropology, University of California, Los Angeles.

Pulgar Vidal, J.
1946 *Historia y geografía del Perú*. Universidad Nacional Mayor de San Marcos, Lima.

Roche, M. A., J. Bourges, J. Cortes, and R. Mattos
1992 Climatology and hydrology of the Lake Titicaca Basin. In *Lake Titicaca: A Synthesis of Limnological Knowledge*, edited by C. DeJoux and A. Iltis, pp. 63–88. Monographiae Biologicae, vol. 68. Kluwer Academic Publishers, Dordrecht.

Rowe, John H.
1944 *An Introduction to the Archaeology of Cuzco*. Papers of the Peabody Museum of American Archaeology and Ethnology, vol. 27, no. 2. The Museum, Cambridge, Massachusetts.

Rowe, John H., and Catherine Brandel
1971 Pucara style pottery designs. *Ñawpa Pacha* 7–8(1969–70):1–16.

Sarmiento de Gamboa, Pedro
1572 *Historia de los Incas*, pp. 193–279. Biblioteca de Autores Españoles, vol. 135. Ediciones Atlas, Madrid.

Schultze, Carol
2008 The Role of Silver Ore Reduction in Tiwanaku State Expansion into Puno Bay, Peru. PhD dissertation, Department of Anthropology, University of California, Los Angeles.

Schultze Carol A., Charles Stanish, David A. Scott, Theo Rehren, Scott Kuehner, and James K. Feathers
2009 Direct evidence of 1,900 years of indigenous silver production in the Lake Titicaca Basin of southern Peru. *Proceedings of the National Academy of Sciences* 106(41):17280–83.

Sever, Jacques
1921 Chullpas des environs de Pucará (Bolivie). *Société des Américanistes* 13:55–58. Paris.

Spurling, Geoffrey
1992 The Organization of Craft Production in the Inka State: The Potters and Weavers of Milliraya. PhD dissertation, Department of Anthropology, Cornell University, Ithaca.

Stanish, Charles
1985 Post Tiwanaku Regional Economies in the Otora Valley, Southern Peru. PhD dissertation, Department of Anthropology, University of Chicago, Illinois.

2003 *Ancient Titicaca. The Evolution of Complex Society in Southern Peru and Northern Bolivia.* University of California Press, Berkeley.
2009 The Tiwanaku occupation of the northern Titicaca Basin. In *Andean Civilization: A Tribute to Michael E. Moseley*, edited by Joyce Marcus and Patrick Ryan Williams. Cotsen Institute of Archaeology, University of California, Los Angeles.
2011 *Lake Titicaca. Legend, Myth and Science.* Cotsen Institute of Archaeology, University of California, Los Angeles.
2012a Above-ground tombs in the circum-Titicaca Basin. In *Advances in Titicaca Basin Archaeology–III*, edited by A. Vranich, E. A. Klarich, and C. Stanish, pp. 203–20. Memoirs, no. 51. Museum of Anthropology, University of Michigan, Ann Arbor.
2012b Prehispanic carved stones in the northern Titicaca Basin. In *Advances in Titicaca Basin Archaeology–III*, edited by A. Vranich, E. A. Klarich, and C. Stanish, pp. 121–40. Memoirs, no. 51. Museum of Anthropology, University of Michigan, Ann Arbor.
2012c The revaluation of landscapes in the Inca empire as Peircean replication. In *The Construction of Value in the Ancient World*, edited by J. Papadopoulos and G. Urton, pp. 80–88. Cotsen Institute of Archaeology Advanced Seminar, Los Angeles.

Stanish, Charles, and Cecilia Chávez
2012 Ritual use of Isla Tikonata in northern Lake Titicaca. In *Advances in Titicaca Basin Archaeology–III*, edited by A. Vranich, E. A. Klarich, and C. Stanish, pp. 183–92. Memoirs, no. 51. Museum of Anthropology, University of Michigan, Ann Arbor.

Stanish, Charles, Amanda B. Cohen, and Mark S. Aldenderfer (editors)
2005 *Advances Titicaca Basin Archaeology–I.* Cotsen Institute of Archaeology, University of California, Los Angeles.

Stanish, Charles, Edmundo de la Vega, Lee Hyde Steadman, Kirk Lawrence Frye, Cecilia Chávez J., Luperio Onofre, and Matthew Seddon
1997 *Archaeological Survey in the Juli-Desaguadero Area, Lake Titicaca Basin, Peru.* Fieldiana Anthropology, no. 29. Field Museum of Natural History, Chicago.

Stanish, Charles, and Abigail Levine
2011 War and early state formation in the northern Titicaca Basin, Peru. *Proceedings of the National Academy of Science* 108(34):13901–6.

Stanish, Charles, Lee Hyde Steadman, and Matthew T. Seddon
1994 *Archaeological Research at Tumatumani, Juli, Peru.* Fieldiana Anthropology, no. 23. Field Museum of Natural History, Chicago.

Steadman, Lee Hyde
1995 Excavations at Camata: An Early Ceramic Chronology for the Western Titicaca Basin, Peru. PhD dissertation, Department of Anthropology, University of California, Berkeley.

Tantaleán, Henry
2005 *Arqueología de la formación del Estado. El caso de la cuenca norte del Titicaca.* IEP, Lima.
2006 Regresar para construir: Prácticas funerarias c ideología(s) durante la ocupación Inka en Cutimbo, Puno-Perú. *Chungará* 38:129–43.
2012 Archaeological excavation at Balsapata, Ayaviri. In *Advances in Titicaca Basin Archaeology III*, edited by A. Vranich, E. A. Klarich, and C. Stanish, pp. 49–75. Memoirs, no. 51. Museum of Anthropology, University of Michigan, Ann Arbor.

Tantaleán, Henry, and C. Pérez Maestro
2000 Muerte en el altiplano andino: Investigaciones en la necrópolis Inka de Cutimbo (Puno, Perú). *Revista de Arqueología* 228:26–37.

Tapia Pineda, Felix B.
1975 Cerámica Tiwanakota en Puno. *Jornadas Peruano-Bolivianas de Estudio Científico del Altiplano Boliviano y del Sur del Perú* 2:339–60.
1978 *Contribuciones al estudio de la cultura precolombina en el Altiplano Peruano.* Publication no. 16. Instituto Nacional de Arqueología (Bolivia), La Paz.

Thompson, Lonnie, and E. Mosely-Thompson
1987 Evidence of abrupt climatic change during the last 1500 years recorded in ice cores from the tropical Quelccaya ice cap. In *Abrupt Climate Change: Evidence and Implications,* edited by W. Bergen and L. Labeyrie, pp. 99–110. D. Reidel, New York.

Thompson, Lonnie, E. Mosely-Thompson, M. E. Davis, and K.-B. Liu
1988 Pre-Incan agricultural activity recorded in dust layers in two tropical ice cores. *Nature* 336:763–65.

Tschopik, Marion
1946 *Some Notes of the Archaeology of the Department of Puno.* Papers of the Peabody Museum, vol. 27, no. 3. The Museum, Cambridge, Massachusetts.

Valcárcel, Luis Eduardo
1925 Informe sobre las exploraciones arqueológicas en Pukara. *Revista Universitaria del Cuzco* Año XV(48):14–21.
1932 El personaje mítico de Pukara. *Revista del Museo Nacional* 1(1):18–30, 122–23.
1935 Litoesculturas y cerámica de Pukara. *Revista del Museo Nacional* 4(1):25–28.
1938 Los estudios peruanistas en 1937. *Revista del Museo Nacional* 7(1):6–20.

Vásquez, Emilio
1937 Sillustani: Una metrópoli pre-Incásica. *Revista del Museo Nacional* 6(2):278–90. Lima.

von Hagen, Victor (editor)
1959 Introduction. In *The Incas of Pedro Cieza de León.* University of Oklahoma Press, Norman.

Wirrmann, Denis, Philippe Mourguiart, and Luis Fernando de Oliveira Almeida
1990 Holocene sedimentology and ostracods distribution in Lake Titicaca–Paleohydrological interpretations. In *Quaternary of South America and Antarctic Peninsula*, edited by Jorge Rabassa, pp. 89–128. Balkema, Rotterdam.

Wirrmann, Denis, Jean-Pierre Ybert, and Philippe Mourguiart
1991 Una evaluación paleohidrológica de 20.000 años. In *El Lago Titicaca.* HISBOL, La Paz.